S0-CDP-839

The
Democratic
Imagination

Pryde Brown / Helen Coffee

The
Democratic
Imagination

Dialogues
on
the
Work
of
Irving
Louis
Horowitz

Edited by

Ray C. Rist

Transaction Publishers
New Brunswick (U.S.A.) and London (U.K.)

Copyright © 1994 by Transaction Publishers, New Brunswick, New Jersey 08903.

All rights reserved under International and Pan-American Copyright Conventions. No part of this book may be reproduced or transmitted in any form or by any means, electronic or mechanical, including photocopy, recording, or any information storage and retrieval system, without prior permission in writing from the publisher. All inquiries should be addressed to Transaction Publishers, Rutgers—The State University, New Brunswick, New Jersey 08903.

Library of Congress Catalog Number: 94-4770
ISBN: 1-56000-174-7
Printed in the United States of America

Library of Congress Cataloging-in-Publication Data

The democratic imagination : dialogues on the work of Irving Louis
  Horowitz / edited by Ray C. Rist.
    p. cm.
  Includes bibliographical references and index.
  ISBN 1-56000-174-7
  1. Horowitz, Irving Louis. 2. Sociology. I. Rist, Ray C.
HM22.U6H674 1994
301'.902—dc20   94-4770
[B]   CIP

Contents

Section Seven: Publishing and the Craft of Writing

Section Eight: Closing Remarks

Introduction

Dear Irving:

While the format for this Introduction may be somewhat unorthodox, I have taken on the prerogative as editor to frame these opening remarks in a way different from those of the twenty-seven papers to follow. The greeting is personal. It is meant to be. I have chosen this means of introducing the book for the reason that this book is for you as much as it is about you.

In preparing this *festschrift,* all of us involved have sought formally to recognize your many academic and literary accomplishments. But these efforts are no less to acknowledge the influence you have had on us as individuals. The papers to follow rightly analyze and summarize the intellectual contributions you have made over the past forty years. That your contributions are profound and far-reaching are attested to time and again in the pages to follow by authors from five continents. This is as it should be, for your views are global and your discourse has never been restricted to national boundaries. That you are one of the giants of modern-day social science is readily and willingly granted by each of us. We know intellectually the size of your shadow and your shoulders.

But it is important also to stress that the creation of this volume has happened because each of us also knows you in other roles—most notably as friend, colleague, former professor, publisher and editor, and adversary on the basketball court—and, in one instance, as your spouse. This book represents a personal as well as an intellectual statement. It comes from our hearts as well as our heads. We have come together to acknowledge the impacts you have made on our lives no less than those you have made on our thinking. And it does not take an overly careful reading between the lines of the papers to see that your influence has been real, sustained, and enduring. Our contributions are the statements of those who believe themselves to be a part of a very special community.

This *festschrift* has been written because it seeks to honor you. It is at times critical and, in other instances, laudatory. It is not bland. It is affirmative without being disingenuous. It takes you and your work seriously. It is dedicated to an examination of your ideas, your actions, and your impacts.

I would hasten to add that although the tradition of the *festschrift* is to honor a person near to or at the end of his or her career, it is not the intent here to convey such a message to either you or the reader. This book is an effort to celebrate and recognize your achievements to date, period. None of us thinks of you as ready to go off into the sunset. Your productivity and creativity continue unabated. What we offer here is a synthesis of and reflection on key aspects of your work thus far.

It is clear to us that your contributions are far from over. The life span of your ideas stretches to the horizon. We have only to witness your continued analysis of the situation in Cuba, the disarray in American sociology, the impacts of technology on the publishing industry, and policy-making in the post-cold war era to be aware that you are still firmly in the middle of the fray. There is no evidence that you are moving to the sidelines.

In a description that you once penned about the *festschrift* as a literary genre, you wrote, "... a *festschrift* is an effort to repudiate the forces of death and mortality, to cheat the devil of any victory by reasserting the immortality of the Word." I dare say that, while granting such an assertion has both a biological and theological aura to it, the present volume has been constructed with neither aim in mind—neither repudiating the forces of death nor cheating the devil.

I think we are all acutely aware of our mortality, and yours. In the time since this book was begun, you have suffered a serious heart attack. That you have come back so strong is a testament to your will, your physical strength, and the loving care of your wife. We were all frightened and saw in your struggle to recuperate the reality of our own frailty. In the same period, we have witnessed the death of Aaron Wildavsky, one of the contributors. His paper arrived only a short time before he died. It was written for you at a time in his life when I am sure he knew his own days were numbered.

This volume is not a statement about cheating death. It is about celebrating your life and the creative genius with which you have been blessed. One clear testament to the belief that you are still intellectually very much with us and that we continue to expect incisive analysis from you is that many of the authors in the pages to follow call on you to elaborate further on one issue or another that you have previously addressed. In some instances, the challenge is for continued development of your own intellectual position. It is a call for still more work and effort on your part. In this sense, the perspective embedded in the papers to follow is not simply retrospective but profoundly prospective as well. The intellectual engagement continues—both for you and for us.

This *festschrift* can be distinguished from many others by the fact that each of the papers directly addresses some aspect of your work. We have pushed hard to address key domains of your intellectual and professional career. We do not do you honor with a random collection of papers that may or may not be remotely tied to your efforts. These are not twenty-seven bottom-of-the-drawer papers in search of someone to honor so as to find their way into publication. Quite the contrary. In that we have specifically chosen to address your work, your ideas, and your influence, we can only hope that you will accept this volume as the honor it is meant to be. If there is discomfort for you in such scrutiny and critique (which I truly doubt, given the joy with which I know you experience vigorous intellectual combat), please know that by taking you seriously we wish to affirm your work.

It is, in fact, because we know your love of generating and discussing ideas that we have given you the last word. After we have had our say, the floor is yours. The discourse with you continues here as it has for many of us over the years. None of us ever wants this *festschrift* to be seen as an example of "hit and run" social science. We have cherished the engagement. I personally have been the recipient of more than one of your caring, though no less than razor-sharp, critiques. Why stop now? Your involvement in the creation of this book and your efforts to craft a response to that which has been written about you and your work does all of us honor.

It is important to stress that the material covered here is selective. We have tried to cover key substantive areas, but we cannot say, nor would we presume to claim, all there is to be said on your work. The prodigious level of writing you have sustained throughout your career is simply off the scale. I count 600 books, articles, reviews, and occasional pieces. This makes for roughly one publication every three weeks for the past forty years. Such a level of sustained writing and analysis is witness to the intensive effort and amazing creativity you possess—and it leaves the rest of us humble in our ability to grasp the breadth and depth of your contributions. But rest assured, while we may be awed, we will analyze and argue as we can. Otherwise, this book could simply be a collection of twenty-seven of your own best chapters, articles, and reviews.

There is another domain in which we have been selective with our writing. This book has had as its clear intent the analysis and distillation of your ideas. Less addressed here are other dimensions of your career and life that also have made you who you are to all of us. You have been highly productive in the intellectual arena, and this book reflects some portions of that productivity. But you also have been highly engaged in the public affairs of our time. I suspect no one but yourself knows the full extent of all that engages your time and effort. References to your involvement in different contexts occur throughout the book. Some make reference to your relation to Robert Kennedy; others know of your work with Radio Martí; still others (and I personally) know of your advice and counsel over these past ten years to the United States General Accounting Office, your support of dissidents on many continents, and your efforts on behalf of the freedom of the press. We will have to await your autobiography that covers these past four decades to learn the full picture.

Perhaps least discussed here are the aspects of your career that are most personal and, thus, most profound. You have been a friend, confidant, mentor, and supporter. You are unfailing in your friendship, encouragement, and willingness to push all of us to excel—traits that speak of your humanity and your generosity. That you have taken us seriously is the deepest compliment of all.

In 1967, when I was in my first semester of graduate school at Washington University in St. Louis, I took your course in political sociology. Being ill-equipped for the pace of your lectures and demands, you made me run hard so as not to be left too far behind. But amid my panic, I heard you say that the major task of the social sciences was to make some sense out of the madness. You have been true to your own admonition. Your own life and work have, indeed, pierced the darkness of modern society.

The title of this book, *The Democratic Imagination,* reflects the way in which you have illuminated the darkness. The gift you have given to all who read your work is an honest and forthright assessment of whatever issue you address. You trust that people will do better with than without the truth. You write without rancor. Your values and perspectives reflect how deeply you care for and respect the worth of the individual. They also address the kind of society needed if authentic democratic space is to flourish, space where ideas can be discussed and debated on their merits. You contribute to the continual building and rebuilding of democratic values by placing honesty ahead of ideology, candor ahead of correctness, and sensibility ahead of sentimentality. You have pushed back the madness. You are a true democrat.

Thank you.

With my kind regards,
RAY C. RIST
The George Washington University
Office of the Dean
School of Education and Human Development

Section One

The Theory of Social Practice

1

Values, Technology, and Administration: The Weberian Inheritance

James E. Katz

When confronting Irving Louis Horowitz's writing, especially on policy, one is struck by its sheer volume. Commanding our attention is the prodigious outpouring of scholarship from this man. Rarely have so few written so much for so many. As recognized by Howard Becker,[1] among others, even enumerating his writings could occupy an entire treatise of its own. Indeed nothing but the simple listing of his publications has received book-length treatment; now even this compilation itself requires a bulky supplement.[2] Yet this man must be measured by more than what verbiage issues from his hand. He must also be measured by whether what is in his head gets into the heads of others. Here a rudimentary quantitative measure may suffice: in the past two decades, he has been cited in scholarly articles of others no fewer than 600 times.[3] Moreover, this figure excludes the manifold citations in books, chapters, reviews, and conference papers: it includes only academic journal articles. The span of topics, as reflected in these festschrift papers, includes a wide range from Cuban politics to the publishing industry. This is a man of very large intellectual proportions indeed.

Given the magnitude of his work, even within policy studies, I have little choice but to select a few themes for discussion. I will focus on his: intellectual linkages to Max Weber; insights about the intersection of values, social science, and political action; and stress on technology's impact on administrative power and paths of policy analysis as yet untaken.

Shared and Conflicting Perspectives with Weber

Horowitz places himself firmly in the tradition of Max Weber. Perhaps it is not out of place in this honorary essay to recall Horowitz's own words on the occasion of a seminar recognizing Weber's 100th birthday: "If there is one figure in the sociological firmament who needs no special Festschrift one hundred years after his birth, it is Max Weber. Why? Simply because we celebrate him every working day in every scholarly way."[4]

Like Weber, Horowitz has sought as his central line of effort to summarize vast sweeps of political, economic, and intellectual history and distill them into multisided explanations of seemingly unrelated phenomena. Both have been intrigued by religion, the social order, and leadership forms. Both delight in theories that weave together politics and power, economics and phenomenology. There are also some remarkable similarities between the two men's styles: both are discursive and sometimes nebulous in their explanations. Both like generalizing from historical particulars to transcendental generalities. Both eschew the terse, narrow style of those who would ape the laboratory reports of physical scientists. As was true of Weber, Horowitz has attracted the interest of disparate groups and ideologues from all points along the political spectrum: conservative, liberal, and radical. (Or perhaps a better word choice than "spectrum" would be "circle," for Horowitz makes the point that there is an odd melding of extreme "left" and "right" where the terms become blurred and overlap one another.)[5] Of course this "interest" means not only cited as evidence in support or refutation of intellectual arguments, but also chastised for their deviation from a temporarily immutable party line.

Another parallel is that each cofounded and edited influential social scientific journals.[6] So while both have been prodigious workers in their own right, they also have served as catalysts, gatekeepers, and intellectual brokers for the scholarly community. Weber and Horowitz have been fully engaged in the intellectual and political debates of their day and relished mixing social science with policy analysis.[7] Yet neither has a straightforward ideological identity. Weber was a founding member of the *Evangelisch-Soziale Verein,* which was a relatively liberal group, yet endorsed Bismarck's antisocialist laws. Horowitz was involved with Robert F. Kennedy's 1968 presidential bid and also the Council on Foreign Relations' efforts to counter international terrorism.

An underlying theme to all their political efforts, though, is revulsion to the fearsome terror resulting from irrational group and mass violence. This theme has been matched with a concomitant attachment to the idea that, if only enough good people were to help, logic and morality can prevail. So in their oscillation between scholar and policy participant, they remain steadfast in their desire to make the world a better place for democracy and enlightenment. What Dennis Wrong said of Weber—"all his work expresses his intense concern over the fate of Western civilization"—could also be said of Horowitz.[8]

Still, despite these connecting themes, neither individual has been committed to a coherent set of beliefs that could be translated into a consistent *Weltanschauung* or political road map. Certainly both have advocated specific national policies: Weber encouraged German imperialism (in the 1890s) but opposed annexation of conquered European territory (during World War I). Horowitz encouraged formation of a White House Council of Social Advisors (in the 1960s), but opposed a nonindustrial based ecology movement (in the 1970s). But much more so than Weber, Horowitz is ever the public critic. For instance, during the Vietnam War, he remonstrated the military without venerating the militants. When discussing the purported role of entertainers in the power elite, he debunks the celebrity and athlete without celebrating the aesthete.[9] In fact his position often seems to roughly approximate the adage, "a pox on both your houses."

Yet his disinclination to exalt the obverse of the object of his criticism is one reason Horowitz is not more popular among contemporary academic audiences. He confuses conventional expectations. Thus, he can be described as "a man of the left" by Walter Dean Burnham,[10] but offers a home to the "library of conservative thought" at his publishing house. His position eludes those who like pigeonholing thinkers. The difficulty, in a sense, is that Horowitz does not always fit comfortably into the stark ideological categories we traditionally use. Along this vein, the thinking of Murray Davis is relevant. Davis argues, in a broader context, that scholars have certain "audience expectations" that theories need to conform with in order for them to become "classic" or even "interesting."[11] I will return to this subject in the next section , but suffice it here to say that while Horowitz's theories are universally relevant, his lack of precise harmonization with "audience expectations" hinders their wider adoption. This affects not one iota the theories' quality, but rather their reception.[12]

Not surprisingly, stylistic and substantive differences exist between Weber and Horowitz. One example is that they seem to disagree on the deeper role of morality and "political interests" of administrators in the policy-making process. To illustrate, Weber says "the genuine official... will not engage in politics. Rather he should engage in impartial 'administration.' This also holds for the so-called 'political' administrator... Hence he shall not do precisely what the politician, the leader as well as his following, must always and necessarily do, namely, *fight*."[13] (Weber's strong belief about this point appears in several other places in his works.)[14] Yet bureaucratic fighting, the struggle both within the administrative class, and between it and other classes, appears central to Horowitz's theorizing on the subject.

There also appears to be disjunction in terms of the role values play in policy. "Policy making is not a moral trade, nor can it ever be," said Weber in a letter.[15] I think Horowitz would disagree. It is fundamental to his approach that policy-making be a moral trade, and that those who violate morality be called to account. That is the impetus of his work on genocide, on "winners and losers," and on civilian militarists. For he sees policy-making not only as an activity that is guided and predicated on values (not always savory ones) but as one that creates them as well. So it is not just sociology *for whom* but also sociology *for what*. Thus, values and the "moral trade" are at the foundation of his analytical approach.

By no means was Weber insensitive to the question of values; indeed, among other places, it was lengthily explored in his treatises on methodology. Moreover, Weber's crucial distinction between goal-oriented rationality and process rationality appears muted if not absent in Horowitz's writings. (Horowitz's arguments about the evolving power of the bureaucratic classes, with their use of expertise and hard data, would benefit by the explicit addition of this distinction.) Albeit, Weber's "ideal type" bureaucrat seemingly transcends more socially anchored values, while Horowitz's never does. Horowitz, always the realist, stresses that policy requires pulling strings—from purse strings to heart strings—as well as pulling triggers.

Weber and Horowitz do share an interest in the tension between experts and politicians as well as the competition between specialized knowledge and legally constrained power. As will be seen next, their relative emphases on "ideal types" versus savvy realism leads to different perspectives on these tensions. This will be explored in the balance of this section beginning with a discussion of Weber's twin essays on science and politics as vocations.

Science, Politics, and Morality

Weber often builds arguments by marshaling evidence from an astonishing array of sources, building architectonically an edifice that can be defended. His style is both discursive and wide-ranging, as seen with his work on religion and the economy.[16] Yet when he discusses the vocations of science and politics,[17] he relies more heavily on his own experience and authority to make judgments about these two professions. His use of *ex cathedra* assertions comes across plausibly and has face validity, but does not appear to draw on the work of others in its formulation.

By comparison, Horowitz favors an analytical technique of posing antipodes, then examining where the weaknesses and foibles of each extreme are. His next step is to demonstrate why, paraphrasing Yates, "the center does not hold." Once this demolishing of both ends and the middle is completed, he takes his third and most important step. He reframes the arguments on a higher level of discourse for his audience. This reframing generally includes three elements: (1) a challenge to his audience's comforting but unexamined assumptions; (2) an appeal that they consider important groups neglected in prior discussion; and (3) a call for an accounting of the moral and value dimensions that are implied by the conclusions.

This is in marked contrast to Weber's symmetrical discourses on topics such as the emergence of rational bureaucrat and expositions on the vocations of science and politics. In Weber's seminal explorations of these topics, it is clear who the good and bad guys are: administrators drive out the irrational forces of charisma and tribalism, dispassionately dispensing collective goods and services. Objective, skeptical, selfless scientists push back the forces of darkness to discover eternal Truth.

Weber was reserved about the ultimate teleology of bureaucracy, and ruminated on the potential paralysis from overexpansion of administrative prerequisites. Yet this moralism of Weber is a personal moralism carefully in keeping with stereotypes of Anglo-Germanic culture, or, if you rather, ideal types. Further, this moralism is a carefully circumscribed set of beliefs. As Horowitz himself observed, "Weber uttered no cry for social change, for just laws, or for extending human rights."[18] None of this suggests he was an unkind, immoral, or insensitive person; indeed he appears not to have been. Rather in his writing and public utterances, one detects no moral outrage, no call to arms, no demands for justice. Science and social logic were his transcendental ideals. The unpleasantness of ascriptive discrimination, while regrettable, was simply something with which a civilized person must cope. Thus, in his lecture about science as a vocation, Weber tells of his response to young scholars seeking advice about pursuing habilitation. "If he is a Jew, *naturally* one says *lasciate ogni speranza*" (my emphasis).[19] There is no indignation, no elliptical comment about the waste of resources and the misfortune of people who are arbitrarily forbidden entrance to the purest calling, that of creating scientific knowledge. And his invocation of Dante's vision of abandoning all hope before entering a fiery inferno was eerily ominous of the fate Jewry suffered at Nazi hands.

It is also worth noting the words that Weber chose when he continued to elaborate his advice to young scholars since it ties into a point made earlier about the role of the truly rational thinker as Apollonian demigod: "But the others, too, must be asked with the utmost seriousness: Do you think that, year after year, you will be able to stand seeing one mediocrity after another promoted over you, and still not become embittered and dejected?"[20]

Weber notes that few indeed can withstand this situation. Though he is well aware of the human and petty side of the scientific profession, he can only acknowledge it obliquely. In a sense, their ability to withstand such outrageous fortune yet further proves what supermen fine scientists must be. But perhaps this is too indirect. Let Weber speak forthrightly in his own words about the role of a scientist: "In the field of science only he who is devoted *solely* to the work at hand has 'personality.' And this holds not only of the field of science; we know of no great artist who has ever done anything but serve the work and only his work."[21] As we shall see, this vision stands in stark contrast to Horowitz's image of scientist, not only interested in research but also, with hand outstretched, palm upward, concerned about social standing, professional status, and self-advancement.

Weber never departs from a view of science as the highest form of endeavor, one that is "autonomous and of a Promethean character."[22] Weber understands the self-seeking, position-enhancing behavior of all social groups in society save the scientists. This group alone does he characterize as passionately committed to the dispassionate pursuit of truth. Religious, business, trade, and political leaders are all bound by the need for creating legitimacy, enforcing authority, and generating boundaries to establish and perpetuate privilege. Only true scientists are exempt from this and, by contrast, Weber holds in especially icy disdain those homes of the scientists, the universities, that "are engaged in a most ridiculous competition for enrollments."[23]

Moving from Weber's to Horowitz's view of the scientist is dramatic. The focus shifts from the Promethean god's heavenly gaze to his feet of clay.

Social Scientists, Experts, and Politicians:
Knowledge and Administration for Whom?

Policy analysis as a form and value explication as a function come together nicely in Horowitz's work on the role conflicts between social scientists and administrators. His essay and book chapters on this subject show some interesting parallels and departures relative to Weber. They also show his unwillingness to romanticize what people do. One sharply focused discussion of this topic is contained in an essay entitled "The Academy and the Polity: Interaction between Social Scientists and Federal Administrators.[24]" An ethnography, it traces some conflicting points between academics and politicians, and shows how reciprocal role misperceptions become a major source of strain.

From the academic perspective, conflict centers primarily around money. Other major conflicts focus on secrecy, loyalty, ideology, and rewards. From the governmental perspective, the criticisms are waste, inutility, access, and marginality.

In terms of the bureaucratic politics perspective on this problem, Horowitz's thinking extends some of Weber's, especially on the secrecy issue. Weber notes: "Every bureaucracy seeks to increase the superiority of the professionally informed by keeping their knowledge and intentions secret...in so far as it can, it hides its knowledge and action from criticism."[25] And, moreover, even the drawing upon advisory groups—like social scientists—as a social process worthy of attention was underscored by Weber: he made much of the fact that the bureaucratic structure was "strengthened by the calling in of interest groups as advisory bodies recruited from among the economically and socially most influential strata. This practice...is increasingly frequent.[26]" Once again, then, Weber and Horowitz are on the same intellectual track.

Horowitz highlights the conflict inherent in the Weberian advisory process, particularly at the methodological level. Social scientists, he says,

> provide information which cannot be derived from sheer public opinion. In some degree social scientists consider that they are hired or utilized by government agencies because they will say things that may be unpopular but nonetheless significant. Thus the very agencies which contract out their "need to know" impose a norm of secrecy which strains the premises upon which most social scientists seek to work.[27]

As Horowitz delineates this and other conflict points, he makes no pretense of being exhaustive in his characterization. Even so, his analysis focuses on the sociological dimension rather than institutional, political, or psychological. Of course all these aspects play upon the sociological, but his focus is notably on inherent characteristics of roles, socialization experiences, and normative conflicts based upon separate, competing constructions of reality.

It is in this area that he makes an interesting contribution through a system of contrasting "ideal types" to demonstrate how these policy elites must inherently conflict due to the structures of their social roles and the bases of their legitimacy. Horowitz figuratively "takes off the gloves" to show how social scientists (although we could extend the analysis to scientists in general) need to protect their privileges and serve their reference groups, often to the dismay and displeasure of their nominal clients, the government administrators. Moreover, he used that crassest of words when talking about science: money. And not just in the context of using money to accomplish worthy ends. No, money is something that social scientists unabashedly want more of for ends that fit with their personal view of the world.

He sees the self-interest of scientists as a natural condition of their role and status. He of course was not the first to see this; likely, politicians recognized the "normalcy" of scientists *qua* a constituency, needing palm greasing and aggressively pursuing self-seeking benefits, long before there even was any such a thing as a social scientist.[28]

Horowitz also confronts the other side of the coin: the value lading and social ramifications of bureaucracies that use expertise. He demands that public bureaucracies be held accountable to both the public and politicians whom they serve. So the at once immensely powerful instrument of bureaucracy must also be brought to heel by those who can call upon and apply the democratic standard. In one of his ruminations on bureaucratic and state power, he surmises, "major movements of our time revolve around the size and strength of the administrative bureaucracy. It becomes necessary to make it responsible, increase its efficiency, and decrease its power." [29]

On this point Horowitz departs from Weber. Weber saw that "the fate of our times [must be] mechanical petrifaction" because of bureaucracy's dehumanizing drive.[30] He saw the bureaucratic form of administration as permanent and preferable to any future social order that could only be more oppressive.[31] In contrast, Horowitz is an optimist who believes that bureaucracy can be tamed and reformed. He anticipates that we not only can have "bureaucracy with a human face" but that there is potential for enlightened administration to become a servant of democratic liberation rather than a form of class oppression and social entropy.

It is pertinent to note that even though Horowitz's exhortation about bureaucracy being made smaller but better was penned in the 1970s, it sounds like a quote from the 1992 best-seller, *Reinventing Government*.[32] This book, written by two influential Clinton advisers, has become one of the ideological pillars of the Clinton presidency. So Horowitz's thinking is clearly in the vanguard of the intellectual community, and he can be involved in thinking about issues years before they catch Washington's attention. Hence, Horowitz anticipates intellectual fashion as much as he help fashions the intellect.

The Intersection of Values, Social Sciences, and Political Action: Social Science Legitimates Policy

Nearly every aspect of policy as an object of social scientific analysis has been commented upon by Horowitz. While it is true that other scholars have covered any given aspect in greater depth, it is likewise the case that none has covered as many as Horowitz. But from my perspective, his contribution is particularly important because he has put the issue of values at the center of his analytical universe. His policy discussion nearly always delineates the values of actors and institutions. He usually also considers the question of how competing and supporting values play upon the policy process and how they affect the acceptability of outcomes. Yet unlike many who use values to castigate those in power and second-guess decisions, he employs them as a tool for understanding and clarifying what has and might happen.

But social science not only analyzes policy but itself is grist for policy mills. Horowitz believes that social science is vital to the policy process, not simply a handmaiden, as for example Ithiel de sola Pool suggested.[33] Horowitz says, "social science may in part—a large part—serve as a legitimating mechanism for enacting or originating policy at least as often as it serves empirically to explain the world."[34] So Horowitz conceives of social science as more than informing the rational merits of the various sides in a policy debate. Increasingly it is part of the "grammar" of the debates themselves. Like others, such as Judith Eleanor Innes,[35] he holds that social science influences policy since it is incorporated into the myths affecting public discourse; it differentially advantages some policy actors, sets agendas, brackets discussion, and provides terms of negotiation. Hence, he sees that such sociological concepts as "victimization" have become the basis for political claims from all sectors of the social structure. And he has observed that these claims are not simply attempts to get the political system to reallocate economic resources. They are also claims that each individual in the "victimized" group has a legitimate demand for the attention, commiseration, and succor of mainstream society. Moreover, he has noted with irony that all individuals in society can make a plausible claim that they are a victim, and therefore worthy of special consideration. But victimization, just like crime, is a socially constructed, value-laden term that can expand or contract as a result of various sociological phenomena.[36] These are the sort of wry, acute insights about the relationship between values and policy that make the work of Horowitz both provocative and rewarding reading.

Yet his insight goes deeper than the ironies of regulation and reform, and beyond the processes of canonizing culture and saints. He goes to the very heart of the matter to maintain that policy is fundamentally an expression of not only reigning ideologies or empirical rationalities but ultimately values. Clearly ideologies and rationality are part of the policy foundation. But the choice of them, as well as every other aspect of the policy process is a value expression, and the results of all policies in a sense both create and modify values. Moreover, Horowitz recognizes that rationality itself is a value. Hard, carefully created and tested numbers that constitute "proof" for technocratic experts are nothing but "damn lies" for others who see a truth beyond any number or mathematical equation. Consistency, which is part of the taken-for-granted reality in individual policy pronouncements (although certainly not at all taken-for-granted between sets of policies), is also a value. None of these values can be prejudged as being the most important in the policy process, but they can all play a role.

This Horowitzian line of argument poses great difficulty for those who propound public choice theories of policy-making, and it has bedeviled those who look to technocratic, liberal interest group, and even power elite models of decision-making. So regardless of the model one holds of the policy process—whether it be the lens of Mills or Dahl, Marx or Giddens—the value dimension must be included.

The Value of Values in Policy

His insight into the "value of values" is made palpable in his critique of J. A. Barnes's book, *Who Should Know What*. He agrees with Barnes when the latter says that we need "not only empirical social science but also an awareness of the ethical issues that form an intrinsic part of its praxis."[37] But Horowitz argues that it is yet more vital to "move ahead with the task of showing how ethical issues are themselves subject to social scientific analysis, that is, to move beyond a sociology of knowledge into a sociology of values."[38]

In an important sense, Horowitz rejects the positivist optimism so frequently heard from American policy analysts that efficient administration can replace politics. Like latter-day Saint-Simons,[39] we hear often from many academic experts about the need of fulfilling the prophetic vision of a mandarin-run superstate. Such a vision, though, as a desirable state of affairs, is one that Horowitz sees as misleading and ultimately chilling.

These contrasting perspectives might well be seen yet more clearly if we juxtapose Horowitz's approach to policy and administration as a value-fulfilling (and value-making) activity, with those who have a more traditional academic thinking. Hence, it might be worthwhile to examine a recent article in a leading publication for scholars and intellectually oriented practitioners of administration, *Public Administration Review*. In this analysis, which seems to typify most ruminations on the subject of values and policy from a public administration viewpoint,

Francis E. Rourke, the Benjamin H. Griswold III professor of public policy studies at Johns Hopkins University, juxtaposes the political appointee with the neutral competent administrator *a la* Weber. He asserts that both are important but clearly shows which to his taste is preferable. "Politics," he says, "only gives government its direction in a democratic order. It is commonly left to highly trained officials within the bureaucracy to provide the knowledge and skill that will enable government policy to arrive safely at its destination."[40]

Rourke points out, as has Horowitz, how presidential staff and their appointive administrative officers have increasingly enforced rough justice on recalcitrant public administrators who were seemingly loyal to their profession and own reading of the laws rather than White House instructions. That is, the administrators were dedicated to the dispassionate execution of their responsibilities, as they saw them, rather than the directives emanating from the executive office of the president and its surrogate appointees in the bureaucracy, which were instructing them to follow a particular ideological path. Rourke interprets this as a deviation from the march to Saint-Simon's techno-bureaucratic ideal, as presumably would Weber. However, rather than a deviation, this injection of political directives into administrative processes is more plausibly an exigency stemming from the exercise of power, which is part of the governing (and, ultimately, the domination) process. Such an interpretation would fit better Horowitz's view of administration as essentially a political process.

Moreover, Rourke's conventional juxtaposition of politics intruding on reason could be reversed, a possibility to which he admits. This reversal has already been sketched out by Horowitz.[41] In this scenario, bureaucrats, interested in preserving their status and following their ideological inclinations, are enforcing their will on a grudging public. To continue the reversed story, only a mobilized electorate can legitimize a political leader who can then save the people. But it appears to me that Rourke does not fully grapple with the implications of this possible reversal in position. He celebrates the virtue and value of the dedicated professional and denigrates the dedicated political operative. But Horowitz has pointed out that one person's enthusiastic idealist is another's dangerous fool (and vice versa).[42]

Instead of grappling with the highly relativistic nature of his own viewpoint, Rourke comes perilously close to inviting us to think in terms of polarities advantageous to his profession. The governmental world according to Rourke seems vaguely Manichean: selfish politicians versus selfless professionals, expedience versus expertise, self-interest versus public interest. Though Rourke does not explicitly use these simplistic dichotomies, his discussion suggests them: the duality is necessary for the totality. Politics, a necessary vice required for public acceptance, versus administration, a necessary virtue required for public satisfaction. Now whether one agrees with the essential superiority of expertise over political ideology, this dichotomy successfully obscures the value loadings implicit in a scholarly article.

It is exactly the antidote to this self-serving ideology of knowledge that is one of Horowitz's important contributions to studies of policy-making and policy analysis. His notion of surrogate politics (which is one of his potentially fecund but underdeveloped and overlooked constructs) is also particularly relevant to this deflation. However, I should hasten to add that Rourke's article is commendable in that he brings forward some important cases of abusing authority and also raises significant questions. But the very foundation of his argument is based on a series of value premises, which are themselves as vulnerable to attack as are those of the political enforcers he criticizes.

Horowitz has been aware of public administration's lack of self-reflection. In his article, "Bureaucracy, Administration and State Power," he approvingly cites Samuel Bachrach's review essay critiquing leading public administration textbooks. Bachrach notes: "Only one author devotes much space to posing the question of which groups and social classes are best served by the administrative structure of the state."[43]

This question, and the general level of concern, is markedly absent from the sobering but circumscribed reflections of Rourke. Yet it forms a centerpiece of Horowitz's reflections. He recognizes that, as with any social institution, groups and interests are served at cost to other units. It is clear from Horowitz's writings that he does not oppose rationality or neutral competence as important factors in the policy equation. Indeed, he supports these, as well as democratic practices and the myriad of other values in the American creed. But he is also able to attain a reflexiveness that in general does not fit easily with the pre-existing perspectives of policy professionals and analysts. It is perhaps for this reason that while his overarching arguments and insights are often attended to, many of his subtler points escape the academic community concerned with policy studies. I examine this area next.

Engaging the Intellectual Community:
Three Worlds of Policy Development

Writers characterizing the role of social scientific information in policy tend to fall into one of three groups. First are savvy insiders who see as key the passions of the actors. Ideology, political advantage, socialization, and class service weigh heavily in the game and its scoring. Their work is not uncommonly found on the *New York Times'* best-seller list. Theirs is the stuff from which BBC documentaries are made.

Second are cool analytical types. They see the world in terms of mathematical games or systems largely devoid of impassioned actors. For them, process and payoff matrixes are key: actors with limited cognition or public choice rationales basically focus on inputs and outputs. When they look, they see the beauty of systems, whether they be "muddling systems," "trash-can systems," or utility-maximization systems. While often of central interest during panel discussion at academic meetings, they are remote even from consultants who peddle their wares to corporations. Yet their books are often found in the required reading areas of a campus bookstore's textbooks section. Theirs is the stuff from which journal articles are made.

Third are moralists, who fault policy for not serving their hobbyhorse. They rightly decry closed systems and cry out for justice on behalf of the cheated, abused, and disempowered. But their cries are often in the wilderness. Their work often appears in opinion journals and in ideologically oriented bookstores and are also made available for purchase through ads in small journals and gazettes. Theirs is the grist from which op-ed essays are ground.

Horowitz spans these three disparate groups. Perhaps no better example is his work on Project Camelot. This dramatic exploration was based on insider knowledge and careful investigation behind the scenes, so it appealed to the first group. Horowitz also made shrewd observations about the calculus of reward for the various players in this high risk game. His examination also encompassed institutions and actors as they did their "business as usual," following interests and operating along the guidelines and serving their clients. So in this way, it had appeal to the second group. And there was the drama, high politics, betrayal, and double dealing of real-life policy-making. The emotional pitch surrounding the project ran so high that it amounted to "hysteria."[44] This aspect of the case, combined with Horowitz's careful and close reading of moralities and teleologies, meant that it had much to offer the first and third groups.

Moreover, this 1965 article on "The Rise and Fall of Camelot" continues to affect discourse on the social sciences from ethical, historical, and operational perspectives. For example, it was cited in a 1992 essay on postmodernism in applied anthropology.[45] So the story remains a haunting one, and issues raised by it will doubtless return in other permutations.

Yet, despite Horowitz's relevance, gaps may occur between his approach and the rigid approaches of disciplinary subspecialties. To some extent this is partly due to his unwillingness, paraphrasing Lillian Hellman, to cut his conscience to fit the year's intellectual fashion. This also is due partly to his style, to what he refers to as his "predilection" for essays in which the "moral tail" steers "an empirical frame."[46] Yet what Horowitz has to say is not just a moral tail (or tale) but always morality inextricably linked with empiricism. This linking gives his arguments particular intellectual punch that is all the greater in contrast to the rising tide of some deconstructive and "mythopoetic"[47] discourse that has itself not only broken loose from empirical moorings but is even hostile to them.[48]

Moreover, his empirically based essays demand a great breadth of knowledge on the reader's part. He darts quickly among evidence, interpretation, and theory with celerity that can leave some behind. Thus, occasionally his intellectual nimbleness may reduce his connectedness with the first group of policy analysts I described. His essay style also precludes the traditional academic paraphernalia of hypotheses, integrated theories, and quantitative data. This reduces his work's appeal among the second group, the positivists.

Finally, Horowitz cannot whip himself into a lugubrious epiphany that seems so often necessary to fire the imagination of the third group. Hence, he rarely enamors himself to those who are interested in *Le dernier cri* from the intellectual fashion runways of Paris or Milan. As mentioned earlier, Murray Davis has a clever "debunking" schemata that is well within the tradition of Peter Berger, Karl Mannheim, and others. An important element in Davis's analysis is that the very grist of the sociological mill is finding "contrarian" results. For example, what seems to be a dysfunctional phenomenon is actually a functional one, and vice versa. Hence, some have argued that if people overthrow communist leadership, it shows not the bankruptcy of communism but rather its strength, value, and truth. Horowitz is willing to confront those who take this type of contrarianism too far, especially when done so in the name of a Procrustean ideology. Such a confrontational approach wins no acclaim from true believers.

Indeed, Horowitz has never been much for worshiping, to use Bacon's felicitous term, the *idols of the marketplace*. He is a man open to airing all viewpoints while holding that none is the ultimate. (This contrasts strikingly with Weber, who reputedly was "dangerously messianic in his readiness to turn the lecture hall into a rostrum for the propagation of conservative nationalist opinions.")[49] For his part, Horowitz uses formal lectures and presentations to provoke and stimulate, not inculcate. Hence, he declines to become a leader of a movement around which followers can congeal. The cumulative weight of these points means that Horowitz has foregone many opportunities to create his own school of thought and thence school of missionaries. Once again there are parallels to Weber: neither has an identifiable orthodoxy. Guenther Roth has made an interesting point in this regard about Weber. He noted that despite the enormous social scientific interest in his work, and in contrast to Karl Marx, Weber "never created an ism in politics or scholarship."[50] That seems equally true of Horowitz.

Technological Ecstasies, Technocratic Agonies

Among Horowitz's enduring interests has been technology and society. In fact, it was he who originally inspired me to work in this area (which has subsequently occupied much of my professional life). I have learned much from his generous sharing of insights about technological change and social processes, and he has been a helpfully critical reader of my work. In my view, one of his most acute insights here has been the impact of communication and information technologies on society, which he casts as a transformation from social classes into interest groups.[51] This insight captures what appears to be a profound change in the conduct of politics and the distribution of economic resources.

Yet, since others explore in detail Horowitz's evaluations of information technology and publishing, I would prefer restricting my consideration to his analysis of technology as a tool for class power and policy domination. Moreover, I would like to invite his additional consideration of selected topics of policy process. I will begin by pointing to an area where his analysis of class power modulated through self-interest, strategic alliances, communication technology, and narrowly rational tools has been path-breaking, and is worthy of additional scholarly notice.

Fascism and "Technification"

As mentioned earlier, Horowitz is able to see connections among phenomena that others miss. An example I would highlight here is his analysis of the social roots of the state, its ideology, power, and administrative bodies. Specifically, I have in mind his fecund demonstration that fascism is a coherent ideology rather than an opportunistic set of statist guidelines arrayed around a charismatic dictator. Further, he has demonstrated the technocratic means through which this ideology has been mobilized in Italy and Germany. At a general level he makes a persuasive argument that refutes the historically localized hypothesis,[52] outlined for instance by George Sabine and Thomas Thorson, which asserts that fascism and national socialism were "creatures of personal ambition forced on Italy and Germany by propaganda and terrorism."[53] In setting forth his thesis, Horowitz not only contradicts key actors, such as Benito Mussolini, who said fascism was nonideological and improvisational.[54] He also opposes those, like Seymour Martin Lipset, who, while admitting ideology and consistency, place it in a unique, time-specific context.[55]

Instead Horowitz argues that fascism is an explicit stage of advanced capitalism. He maintains that to believe that fascism "is less of an intellectual system than either socialism or liberalism, is a profound error."[56] Within this fascist stage, traditional class factors emphasized by Marx in the stratification and maintenance of society, such as control of the means of production, become less important. In their place are the factors of Weber—politics and power abetted by expertise and administration. Bureaucrats dictate to compliant capitalists, politics takes precedence over economics. This stage is a technocratically delineated creation of a pseudo-Gemeinschaft society that harks back to the feudal era of social organization. Laws are created without reference to justice, multiple forms are completed regardless of content, and artistic vision becomes merely political cant. This society with a black soul can occur whenever an advanced industrial society's "political goals are blocked by democracy and economic priorities are frustrated by the market network."[57]

But beyond the bureaucratic pivot lies the military's role. "The fascists created a network whereby they were able to use the professional military for various political ends and economic goals."[58] The newly professionalized military became an instrument of national mobilization, economic revitalization and rationalization, as well as social bonding and control. The fascists "directly linked militarism to the functions of an advanced technology...and harnessed the production apparatus to military ends."[59] Hence, technology becomes not just an artful tool for the administrative classes, but for the military ones as well.

Social control is exercised through the combined efforts of the administrative, military, political, and industrial communities. Key in his analysis is the national bureaucratic sector, which rose to "a place of primacy" within the society. This bureaucracy "had an allegiane only to the state and neither to the bourgeoisie nor to the proletariat."[60] For their parts, the party is to lead the government, and the military is to join the system of national bureaucratic administration. Not only is a professionalized military a vital ingredient in fascism and its support necessary for bureaucratic and economic control, it can also be a distinguishing characteristic. Thus, when he argues that Germany's Nazism was a special branch of fascism, he points to the role of its military. He sees the militaristic apparatus of Germany as a "critical feature" in differentiating its national character from the Italian model.[61]

In this manner, Horowitz is able to incorporate both general questions about the rise of fascism and also consider its regional variations. Overcoming this criticism of other theories is an important contribution.[62] At the same time he is able to link what others have characterized as rational decisions in light of "subjective expected utility"[63] with general social forces. In this manner, he is able to link the individual, almost psychological levels, with grand meanings of life and history.

Another noteworthy aspect of his analysis of fascism is its emphasis on technology. A prime goal of the fascists was to reduce individualism and synthesize a social bond among the people in the service of "a highly technological network."[64] And the fascists, as indicated above, fused technology and militarism in the service of an aggressive state.

His emphasis on technology is not unique to his analysis of fascism, for, as noted, it appears elsewhere in Horowitz's works. But it nonetheless acts in a unique way under fascism, according to Horowitz. Thus, "fascism is a stage in which class factors in themselves become less significant than the overall bureaucratization and technification of society."[65] So technification is a master societal trend in Horowitz's model of political sociology. In essence, then, the predominance of a technological mode is part of the nature of the advanced state. "The ultimate push and drive of the state is for technocratic expertise and hard data."[66] (I have reservations about this emphasis on technology's role in the modern state, which I describe below. At the same time, the Italian fascist celebration of modernism and technology, coupled with the German fascist achievements in technology—from jets and rockets to tank armor and atomic bombs—meshes well with his analysis.)

The possible resurgence of fascism, and the permanency of such threats are important, timely questions. Horowitz's analysis is particularly relevant today since so much of the rhetoric about the fate of the former Eastern bloc revolves around the relative standing of the free-market liberals versus former communists without explicit consideration of a fascist model (which was in fact often the predominating model during the interwar period). And even the "nationalists" of Russia are seen as rightists but not fascists. Yet Horowitz's concept of "left-wing fascism" and fascism as an advanced industrial class conflict speaks directly to these issues. In turn, it owes much to Weber's emphasis on class interests driven as much by political as economic interests. His interweaving of technology with these themes is quite admirable, and is achingly relevant to contemporary nation-based problems of social movements.

Progress, Administration, and Technology

Given these important insights about technology and sociopolitical power, Horowitz would clearly rank as an important thinker. Yet, there are some other areas that, based on my own assessments of the area (many of which were originally catalyzed by him), I would hope he might wish to reconsider. In particular I have in mind some of his positions on technology's impact on administration. As I read him, Horowitz shows great respect for technology in his analyses where it acts as a powerful locomotive to stratify classes. Weber, though, emphasized that "the rationalization of technique and of administration in an expanding hierarchical division of labor provides the underlying dynamics of contemporary society."[67] The distinction then is over the critical force in policy and social domination. Horowitz identifies it as technology—a *material product or tool*—whereas Weber identifies it as rational technique—a mental and social *process*. This divergence naturally leads us to look for two very different things under the distinctive theoretical perspectives.

For Horowitz, evolution in and differential distribution of technologies become important paths through which bureaucratic domination can be attained at both the tactical and strategic levels. As I understand his position, he interprets technology not just as an important factor in everyday "garden-variety" policy-making and implementation. He also assigns it a near transcendental force approximating the "means of production" in Karl Marx's theories, or the "looking-glass self" in Charles Horton Cooley's. He envisions technology's fruits as giving immense power to administrative classes, both East and West. To illustrate, he seemed to have interpreted Khrushchev's 1964 overthrow as a veritable "second Soviet revolution" in which autocracy gave way to technocracy.[68] (Note that technocracy and bureaucracy are not the same things.) As for the American context, he said in 1984 that "conflict between branches of government will remain in a technological context."[69] He asserts that computers reduce the public's ability to influence the administrative bureaucracy. Thus, in *Winners and Losers,* he states that "in a period of computer technology, administrative decisions by fiat become frequent."[70]

As I see it, there are some difficulties with how he interprets technology's real impact, particularly computers, on public administration and policy. For example, in 1984 Horowitz wrote, "Until now public administrators have focused on short-term uses of advanced technology. In the next round long-term planning is likely to prevail."[71]

My analysis differs with him on both the quotidian and cosmic levels of bureaucratic power. Let us look first at his assertion about long-term planning. Compared to prior years, it would appear that we are *less,* not more likely to use long-term planning. Indeed, "planning theory has never been under such attack," said Robert W. Burchell in 1988.[72] Part of the reason that we seem to be doing less long-term planning is not that computers are less powerful or useful. And it is not because knowledge about future conditions is less important to all concerned. Nor is it because we are less able to construct sophisticated models that can account for ever more factors. Rather it is because of a two-fold trend. First, decisions are becoming ever more atomized within our society at the very time that decision processes themselves are becoming more complicated. (Not, as Horowitz asserts, simpler and more likely to be delivered via fiat.) This trend builds in uncertainty to levels that make long-term planning seem less relevant and as likely to mislead as inform. Second, and related, there has been a shift away from futurology as a tool and from "social engineering" as an ideology. These trends reduce believability of and interest in long-term planning.

In particular many had pinned their hopes on the computer crystal ball that could "unlock" the future (and many continue to do so). Thus, Horowitz and others predicted a flourishing era of "future studies."[73] The institutional possibilities for such operations have shrunk as global economic relations have accelerated and control decentralized. Perhaps this is no more clearly illustrated than in the "social indicators movement," which has largely disappeared as an intellectual activity and completely disappeared from the White House, where it once enjoyed a momentary celebrity.

But in fairness to Horowitz, I have yet to find social predictions about the computer's impact that have not missed the boat.[74] Thus, rather than there being a few centralized and massive computer centers, as was often predicted in the 1950s, the technology's history has been one of increasing portability, diffusion, and user control. So, in a surprising way, computers themselves have added to uncertainty about the future, allowing more data to be crunched by more people, who then act upon their own results. Variation and independence offered by these systems are yet another source of perturbation in the carefully crafted models of would-be futurists.

We need only recall the debates of the 1970s, when global models of the Club of Rome[75] and others showed industrial civilization's last gasps were at hand, to feel skepticism about what the best and the brightest can provide for us in terms of auguring the future. These studies reached an epiphany of gloom at the end of the Carter administration when a *Global 2000* report[76] was issued warning of the impending exhaustion of natural resources and atmospheric carrying capacities by the end of the millennium. I in no way wish to appear sanguine about the urgent threats to global well-being, for I am deeply disturbed by them. Rather my point is that I believe we are further from, not closer to, a dehumanized computer-driven social policy process anticipated by numerous commentators, including Horowitz.

And certainly Horowitz stands in distinguished company with his positions. Carl Kaysen,[77] Robert E. Lane,[78] Jean Meynaud,[79] and Robert O. MacBride,[80] to name but a few, all came to similar conclusions. To further illustrate, RAND's David Ronfeldt coined the term "cyberocracy" in 1978 to describe this state of affairs,[81] and continues in 1992 to see looming what I might puckishly call the iron fist in a microchip-covered glove.

A full-scale assessment of how computers affect public administration is far beyond our present scope. But we can think about changes in computers over the past generation relative to the craft of public administration. Forty years ago, the first hydrogen bomb was designed and constructed using most of the world's computer capability.[82] That capability is significantly less than today's laptop computer. In contrast, how has the world of public administration changed?

I would invite readers to consider this question for themselves. Think about long-term planning today and then what it was like at the heydays of the Tennessee Valley Authority (TVA) in the 1930s and 1940s, the National Interstate Highway System's construction in the 1950s, Project Apollo in the 1960s. Think too about how public administration was conducted during the Great Society of President Johnson in the 1960s or the New Federalism of President Nixon in the 1970s versus what we have in the 1990s. The nature and types of public administration are not that different, I would aver, and to the extent they are, it is toward less, not more, long-term planning.

The absence of long-term, technology-based planning and bureaucratic investiture is all the more striking when one contrasts what has changed in terms of external mechanical transactions versus internal personal meanings. Has the relative status and role positions of the administrator and "client" changed since the TVA began building dams and displacing farmers or since social workers changed from typewriters and filing cabinets to computers? There have been some changes, but rarely have they aided bureaucratic classes to dominate others. But even if we grant that these changes have aided bureaucratic power, it still is unlikely that, as Horowitz claims, "advanced technology helps insure a simplified society more direct in its conflicts of choices and interests."[83] If anything, electronic bulletin boards, electronic mail, microtargeted advertising, 500-channel television, and telephone-bank empowered political candidates (witness the Ross Perot campaign of 1992) have added uncertainty and complexity, and have made conflicts more displaced, distorted, and surrogate in their nature.

But for me there is no clearer instantiation of the decoupling between the powers of technology and administration than by the ubiquitous calculator. In 1970, the premier office workhorse was a Wang calculator having six functions; its cost was over $300 in current dollars. Today, solar-powered calculators with superior functionality are typically given away free as an incentive for buying vitamins or magazine subscriptions.[84] Now of course there have been changes and efficiencies in public administration, but these changes have been diminutive compared to the changes in computer technologies and capabilities. My point is that I believe Horowitz and many others have been much too generous to the technological side of the equation in public administration. Simply, other forces operating on bureaucratic procedures and power are more important than technology.

Granted technology is changing swiftly; it allows us to do many things we could only dream about decades ago. And telecommunications played a role in galvanizing people to stop the Soviet coup plotters in August 1991, and gave strength to the protesters in China's Tiananmen Square.[85] But have any of these developments strengthened the bureaucracy's grip over subject classes?

For example, electronic mail and faxes allow us to communicate differently, and there is now even a Director of Electronic Publishing and Public Access Email in the Clinton White House.[86] But has this dramatic technological change made a dramatic life-style change? No, at least not nearly to the degree that the technology has changed. In fact, I would maintain that technology is a secondary (though interrelated) factor compared to ideologies, perceptions, and perhaps most centrally, values.

Was it the computer that brought equal opportunity legislation and statutory commitments to minorities and women? Has the space shuttle, personal computer, genetic engineering, voice-mail, or remote-control TV clickers affected dramatically daily bureaucratic politics?

Yes, the bureaucratic classes have gained power over other classes. But I would assert their gains have come through Weberian rationalization of technique and administration. They have not come via the

Horowitzian construct of superior ability to harness technology or manipulate information.

One reason for expressing a few reservations concerning Horowitz's arguments about technology is the hope that he may wish to reevaluate some of these issues from today's vantage point, thereby enriching us. Moreover, as Horowitz himself has said, "a Festschrift is a *Beruf*, a call to further work...a call to the improvement of learning."[87] And although he already has accomplished many times more than most scholars, given his enormous talent and energy, he may want to give additional attention to these questions.

The Policy Road Untaken

Beyond question, Horowitz has covered vast intellectual territory in the policy arena and contributed mightily thereto. And, perhaps equally important as his contributions to the then-current scholarly dialogue is the fact that his assessments remain relevant long after they have been penned. Plus, in some cases they anticipate intellectual discourse by years. This was already pointed out in terms of the Clinton administration, and another example germane at this point is his essay on the "two cultures of policy."[88] Though this was written in 1989, it addresses precisely the dilemma that decision makers confront today in the need to integrate domestic and foreign policy.

Yet, despite his towering achievements, as a researcher I want to know still more about a level of analysis that seems muted in his writings, namely, the fine-grained linking among policy players. In a sense the "street-level" of policy needs more coverage, a better feel for how for the details of various policy levels and sectors interact to produce policy. Certainly Horowitz is well-positioned to share this with us, given his firsthand experiences such as his service on a GAO board and involvement with the International Monetary Fund. It is obviously the case that he simply has not yet had time to tackle this aspect.

His analyses invariably show a subtle grasp of the pressures, policy objectives, values, and interest groups that are brought to bear on an issue. But once his policy pronouncements are made, the implementation issues are only superficially touched upon. So a valuable complement to give greater understanding of the policy process would be the tracing out of how each policy interfaces with the administrative procedures of implementing units, and, perhaps even more crucially, how each policy is received, modified, and embraced or rejected on the torturous path to becoming part of the ordinary life of an administrator. Finally, how does that administrator decide precisely how to apply or ignore rules and to what effect?

A particularly valuable addition to our understanding, which Horowitz would be well-placed to make, would be to amplify the social role and worldview, or canon, of each set of policy players that grasps and then amends a policy initiative. The role of the courts, which have a perspective much different than either the "administratively neutral competence" or the political ideology-driven perspectives of career and appointive bureaucrats, would also be worthy of his attention. Another area that would benefit from his detailed attention is state and local policies. He has a superb grasp of transcendental issues, and of the national and transnational systems. But the city and local dimensions to problems and resultant policies is much hazier, and less often described or delineated.

This is an extremely tall order, which could occupy several lifetimes. I myself think it the functional equivalent of the twelve labors Hercules undertook for cousin Eurystheus. But to the extent he might wish to pursue it, Horowitz's revelations about implementation and local policy processes would complete his policy "Ring of the Nibelung" cycle. And these efforts would leave rich intellectual veins for those who follow.

Conclusion

As a scholar, Horowitz has never forgotten that social action derives from beliefs and values. Horowitz embraces this multifaceted intellectual orientation and has used many venues to espouse it. In this way, he has been a professor in the truest sense of the word. He provokes and stimulates his audiences and colleagues, challenging them to think deeper, forcing them to push their analyses farther. Yet he never insists on winning arguments or concessions from his opponents, and is pleased to see vigorous intellectual competition among varying perspectives, provided it is based on evidence and logic rather than polemics and hyperbole. Yes, he asks a lot from those whom he intellectually engages, but demands more from himself. In this way he has been a teacher in the highest sense of the word.

Horowitz assesses technology as a powerful, transcendental force, almost an entirely abstract one. He attributes to it an important role in stratification and sees it as providing bureaucratic classes with a vital tool for social domination. Yet despite the fact that many other analysts agree with this perspective, I see some unresolved issues concerning it.

Social scientists, as much as anyone else, like surprise twists in plots. Horowitz is often able to provide these in his essays. He tracks policy winners and losers, revealing perspectives of those who act to make policy and those unto whom policy is done. His analyses reveal subtle ways policy players often end up with the opposite of what they thought they were getting. He also uncovers the politics of the process itself, showing not only the often sordid underside of motives but the unexpectedly altruistic side as well.

But overarching this is his interest in human freedom. Integrated into his analysis, particularly of fascism, are powerful insights about factors corroding freedom and, conversely, those sustaining it. Further, by his analysis of the policy role of social scientists, as well as the way social scientific knowledge alters and legitimizes policy outcomes, he has added important insight about how the craft socially constructs the world. These, a few of his enduring contributions, stem from explorations of linkages among values, social science, and policy. He demonstrates that these linkages form a dynamic eternal triangle that is not only morally necessary but also intellectually productive.

Irving Louis Horowitz has labored long, honorably, and prolifically in the intellectual tradition of Max Weber. There is an immense, invaluable body of work to show for his efforts. He has been an inspiration for students and colleagues alike; his words and ideas shall echo for generations to come.

Bell Communications Research (Bellcore)
Director
Multimedia Communications Research Division

Notes

1. Howard S. Becker, "The Three Lives of Irving L. Horowitz," in *Bibliography of the Writings of Irving Louis Horowitz* (Privately printed, 1984), ix–xi.
2. Nine-year supplement (1984–92) to *Bibliography of the Writings of Irving Louis Horowitz* (New Brunswick, NJ: mimeo).
3. Data drawn from the Social Science Citation Index (Philadelphia). I thank Martha Broad for her assistance in this accounting.

4. Irving Louis Horowitz, "Max Weber and the Spirit of American Sociology," *Sociological Quarterly* 5, no. 4 (Autumn 1964): 344.

5. Hence his term, "left-wing fascism." Irving Louis Horowitz, *Winners and Losers: Social and Political Polarities in America* (Durham, NC: Duke University Press, 1984).

6. Weber founded the *Archiv für Sozialwissenschaft und Sozialpolitk* with Werner Sombart and Philipp Jaffé; Horowitz founded *Transaction/Society* with Herbert Blumer and Alvin Gouldner. The two journals share strikingly parallel themes (though not style or audience).

7. Ilse Dronberger, *The Political Thought of Max Weber: In Quest of Statesmanship* (New York: Meredith Corporation, 1971). See also, for example, Irving Louis Horowitz, "Struggle among the Cuban exiles," *The New Leader* (19 March 1990): 9–11.

8. Dennis Wrong, *Max Weber* (Englewood Cliffs, NJ: Prentice-Hall, 1970), 14.

9. See for example Irving Louis Horowitz, *The Power Elite: A Critical Commentary* (New York: American R.D.M. Corporation, 1966), 29.

10. Walter Dean Burnham, "Foreword," in Irving Louis Horowitz, *Ideology and Utopia in the United States, 1956–1976* (New York: Oxford University Press, 1977), x.

11. Murray S. Davis, "That's Classic: The Phenomenology and Rhetoric of Successful Social Theories," *Philosophy of the Social Sciences* 16, no. 3 (1986): 285–301.

12. Charles A. Schwartz, "Research Significance: Behavioral Patterns and Outcome Characteristics," *The Library Quarterly* 62, no. 2 (April 1992): 123–49.

13. Hans Gerth and C. Wright Mills, eds., *From Max Weber* (New York: Oxford University Press, 1946), 95 (italics in original).

14. For example, see Reinhard Bendix, *Max Weber: An Intellectual Portrait* (New York: Doubleday, 1962), 440–41.

15. Gerth and Mills, *From Max Weber,* 39.

16. Max Weber, *Economy and Society,* ed. Guenther Roth and Claus Wittich (New York: Bedminster Press, 1968).

17. Gerth and Mills, *From Max Weber,* 77–158.

18. Irving Louis Horowitz, "Max Weber and the Spirit of American Sociology," *Sociological Quarterly* 5, no. 4 (Autumn 1964): 346.

19. Horowitz, *Winners and Losers,* 125.

20. Edward Shils, The Torment of Secrecy (New York: The Free Press of Macmillan, 1956), 58.

21. Gerth and Mills, *From Max Weber,* 137 (italics in original).

22. Jacob P. Mayer, *Max Weber and German Politics* (New York: Arno Press, 1979), 113.

23. Gerth and Mills, *From Max Weber,* 133.

24. Irving Louis Horowitz, "The Academy and the Polity: Interaction between Social Scientists and Federal Administrators," *Journal of Applied Behavioral Science* 5, no. 3 (1968): 309–35.

25. Gerth and Mills, *From Max Weber,* 233.

26. Ibid., 239.

27. Horowitz, "The Academy and the Polity," 315.

28. A. Hunter Dupree, *Science and the Federal Government* (Cambridge, MA: Belknap/Harvard University Press, 1940); see also Joseph P. Martino, *Science Funding: Politics and Porkbarrel.* (New Brunswick, NJ: Transaction Publishers, 1992).

29. Ibid., 41.

30. Weber quoted in Anthony Giddens, *Capitalism and Modern Social Theory* (London: Cambridge University Press, 1971), 216.
31. Reinhard Bendix, *Max Weber: An Intellectual Portrait* (Berkeley: University of California Press, 1977), 430.
32. David Osborne and Ted Gaebler, *Reinventing Government* (Reading, MA: Addison-Wesley Publishing, 1992). I thank Ray Rist for this point.
33. Ithiel de sola Pool, "The Necessity for Social Scientists Doing Research for Governments," in *The Rise and Fall of Project Camelot*, edited by Irving Louis Horowitz (Cambridge, MA: MIT Press, 1967), 267–80.
34. Irving Louis Horowitz, *Use and Abuse of Social Science*, 1st ed. (New Brunswick, NJ: Transaction Publishers, 1971), 4.
35. Judith Eleanor Innes, *Knowledge and Public Policy: The Search for Meaningful Indicators*, 2d ed. (New Brunswick, NJ: Transaction Publishers, 1990).
36. Kai Erikson, *The Wayward Puritans* (New York: Macmillan, 1968).
37. J. A. Barnes, *Who Should Know What? Social Science, Privacy, and Ethics* (Cambridge: Cambridge University Press, 1980).
38. Irving Louis Horowitz, "Review of J. A. Barnes, *Who Should Know What?*" *American Journal of Sociology* 87, no. 4 (January 1982): 1009.
39. See Frank E. Manuel, *The New World of Henri Saint-Simon* (Notre Dame, IN: Notre Dame University Press, 1963).
40. Francis E. Rourke, "Responsiveness and Neutral Competence in American Bureaucracy," *Public Administration Review* 52, no. 6 (November-December 1992): 546.
41. Horowitz, *Winners and Losers*, 122.
42. Irving Louis Horowitz, "The Limits of Pragmatism and Moralism in Politics," *New Literary History* 23, no. 3 (Spring 1982): 515–32.
43. Samuel B. Bachrach, "What's Public Administration? An Examination of Basic Textbooks," *Administrative Science Quarterly* 212, no. 2 (June 1976): 350, quoted in Horowitz, *Winners and Losers*, 119.
44. Horowitz, *Use and Abuse*, 1st ed., 240.
45. Agneta M. Johannsen, "Applied Anthropology and Post-Modernist Ethnography," *Human Organization* 51, no. 1 (1992): 71–81.
46. *Bibliography of the Writings*, xiv.
47. Ruth Rosen, "Stand by Your Woman," *Dissent* (Fall 1992): 540–42.
48. Irving Louis Horowitz, *Deconstructing Sociology* (in press).
49. Wrong, *Max Weber*, 4.
50. Guenther Roth, "Introduction to the New Edition," in Reinhard Bendix, *Max Weber: An Intellectual Portrait* (Berkeley: University of California Press, 1977), xiii–xxxiii.
51. Irving Louis Horowitz, "Dai mezzi di produzione ai modi di comunicazione: la trasformazione delle classi sociali in gruppi d'interesse," *Studi di Sociologia* 25, no. 2 (April-June 1987): 189–96.
52. G. Eley, "What Produces Fascism: Preindustrial Traditions or a Crisis of the Capitalist State," *Politics and Society* 12 (1983): 53–82.
53. George H. Sabine and T. L. Thorson, *A History of Political Theory*, 4th ed. (Hinsdale, IL: Dryden, 1973), 801.
54. Ibid., 818–20. Michael Ledeen, "Fascist Social Policy," in Horowitz, *Use and Abuse*, 91.
55. Seymour Martin Lipset, *Political Man* (New York: Doubleday, 1966).
56. Irving Louis Horowitz, *Foundations of Political Sociology* (New York: Harper & Row, 1972), 245.

57. Ibid., 246.
58. Ibid., 241.
59. Ibid.
60. Ibid., 245.
61. Ibid.
62. William Brustein, "The Political Geography of Belgian Fascism: The Case of Rexism," *American Sociological Review* 53 (1988): 939–50.
63. William Brustein and Barry Markovsky, "The Rational Fascist: Interwar Fascist Party Membership in Italy and Germany," *Journal of Political and Military Sociology* 17 (Winter 1989): 177–202.
64. Horowitz, *Political Sociology*, 242.
65. Ibid., 246.
66. Ibid., 247.
67. Maurice Zeitlin, "Review of A. Giddens' *The Class Structure of the Advanced Societies*," *American Journal of Sociology* 91 (November 1975): 661.
68. Irving Louis Horowitz, "The Second Soviet Revolution: From Autocracy to Technocracy," *The Correspondent* no. 33(Winter 1965): 4–7.
69. Horowitz, *Winners and Losers*, 124.
70. Ibid., 122.
71. Ibid., 123.
72. Robert W. Burchell, "The Incongruity of Theory and Practice," *Society* 26, no. 1 (January-February 1988): 6.
73. Horowitz, *Winners and Losers*, chap. 8. See W. Warren Wagar, "Tomorrow and Tomorrow and Tomorrow," *Technology Review* 96, no. 3 (April 1993): 50–59.
74. Why predictions about technology often go awry are discussed in Steven Schnaars, *Megamistakes: Forecasting and the Myth of Rapid Technological Change* (New York: Free Press, 1989). One might comment that futurology has become the true "dismal science" not because of the pessimism of its predictions, but because of its persistently inaccurate record. See also Linda R. Caporael, "Computers, Prophecy and Experience: A Historical Perspective," *Journal of Social Issues* 40, no. 3 (Fall 1984): 15–29.
75. Donella Meadows, *The Limits to Growth: A Report for the Club of Rome's Project on the Predicament of Mankind* (a Potomac Associates book) (New York: Universe Books, 1972).
76. *Global 2000 Report to the President*, 3 vols., report prepared by the Council on Environmental Quality and the Department of State (Gerald O. Barney, director) (Washington, DC: U.S. Government Printing Office, 1980).
77. Carl Kaysen, "Data Banks and Dossiers," *The Public Interest* 7 (Spring 1967): 52–60.
78. Robert E. Lane, "The Decline of Politics and Ideology in Knowledge Society," *American Sociological Review* 31 (October 1966): 649–62.
79. Jean Meynaud, *Technocracy* (London: Faber and Faber, 1968).
80. Robert O. MacBride, *The Automated State: Computer Systems as a New Force in Society* (Philadelphia: Chilton, 1967).
81. David Ronfeldt, "Cyberocracy is Coming," *The Information Society* 8 (1992): 243–96.
82. Compare with Ashton B. Carter, William J. Perry, and John D. Steinbruner, *A New Concept of Cooperative Security* (Washington, DC: Brookings Institution, 1992): 31.
83. Horowitz, *Winners and Losers*, 125.
84. It is perhaps worth pondering that it was believed that atomic power would create energy too cheap to meter. Clearly this prediction has not panned out. Yet techno-

logical change has rendered calculating ability almost "too cheap to charge." Many universities and libraries have freely available microcomputers allowing students and the public grind away as much as they want (provided they limit their consumption of paper!). Small calculators are given away by companies as prizes no more valuable than a ballpoint pen. So at least in this area we have seen the democratization of calculation. I would suggest that the impact of this little-noticed revolution is broader evidence of the decoupling between the power of our intellectual tools and our ability to address our social interaction and activity problems.

85. Craig Calhoun, "Revolution and Repression in Tiananmen Square," *Society* 26, no. 6 (November-December, 1989): 21-38.

86. Electronic mail message from: President-Elect's Office <75300.3115 @ compuserve.com > (14 Jan 93 19:02:40 EST); Message-Id: <930115000239_75300.3115_CHE66-1 @ Compuserve.COM>.

87. Irving Louis Horowitz, "The Place of the Festschrift," *Scholarly Publishing* (January 1990): 80.

88. Irving Louis Horowitz, "In Defense of Scientific Autonomy: The Two Cultures Revisited," *Academic Questions* 2, no. 1 (Spring 1989): 22-27.

2

The Moral Career of a Political Sociologist: Liberalism and the Democratic Spirit

Howard G. Schneiderman

The spectrum of contemporary political and intellectual life in America is composed of three ideologies: liberalism, radicalism, and conservatism. For most of this century liberalism characterized the real center of both politics and the life of the mind. But while the liberal center still holds, by and large, in American politics, the center of gravity in the intellectual and academic world has shifted, since the late 1960s, toward the radical pole. The reaction to this normalization of radicalism, which has been most prominent in the humanities and the social sciences, has played no small part in forming the moral career of Irving Louis Horowitz, one of our leading social scientists.

In this context I relate the following anecdotes about my first contact with Horowitz, and about a recent conversation between Horowitz and a colleague to which I was privy. They are indicative of Horowitz's changing reputation among his colleagues, or what I should like to call his moral career.

In 1971 I was a second-year graduate student in the sociology department at the University of Pennsylvania. Penn had developed one of the best graduate programs in sociology, with a teaching staff that included Digby Baltzell, Renee Fox, Erving Goffman, Edward Hutchinson, William Kephart, Richard Lambert, Otto Pollak, Philip Rieff, Vincent Whitney, Marvin Wolfgang, Charles Wright, and Samuel Klausner among other senior faculty members.

As part of the very vibrant intellectual discourse in the department, a series of colloquia had been arranged for the fall 1971 semester including lectures by both departmental professors and outside guests, including Horowitz.[1] Most of these colloquia, were well attended by both students and faculty, but one, Horowitz's, stood out from the others because it attracted more than the usual number of graduate students, and far less than the usual number of senior faculty.

On 5 March, at three o'clock one of the larger rooms used by the sociology department in the McNeil Building was filled with graduate students waiting to hear Horowitz, who had the reputation of being in the vanguard of radical sociologists. He was to present a lecture titled "The Impact of Radical Thought on Social Science Research." Arriving a few minutes late, Horowitz noticed that there were almost no senior faculty in attendance; in fact, Digby Baltzell and Otto Pollak were the only ones I saw there. He seemed genuinely offended, and he chided his absent colleagues for not being there. For a moment it looked as if he might leave without presenting his talk. He remained, however, and delivered a more reasonable and liberal, rather than radical, lecture than I expected to hear.

In the days after his presentation I asked a number of professors why Horowitz's lecture drew so few senior faculty, and the most common answer I got was that many of the older faculty saw him as a radical sociologist who had very little of interest to say to them. As it turned out, at least to my mind, Horowitz was not nearly as radical as he was supposed to be, and what he said was very interesting. My notes and diary entries concerning Horowitz's lecture confirm my suspicion that it was, by and large, drawn from a work then in progress, "Radical Politics and Social Research: Observations on Methodology and Ideology," an article coauthored with Howard Becker, and published in the *American Journal of Sociology* in July 1972. Perhaps it was the title or the subject of this presentation that helped foster the idea among the senior staff that Horowitz himself was an advocate of radicalism, but whatever the reason this idea seems to have kept many of them away.

This first memory of meeting Horowitz is in sharp contrast to a conversation I heard Horowitz participate in recently, in November 1992. By this time I knew Horowitz well; having served on the editorial board of *Society,* I was then book review editor.

After hearing Horowitz lecture on "Policy Research in a Post-Sociological Environment" to a large audience of social scientists at the Woodrow Wilson School at Princeton University, I was with him when he was approached by a well-known sociologist, who, after apologizing in advance for asking what seemed to be an impertinent question, proceeded to ask, "What happened to the young radical who you were in the 1960s?" He then continued to ask Horowitz why he had become a conservative .

I will not report Horowitz's reply, nor any of the rest of the conversation, both of which were couched in personal terms, but I was not at all surprised by the questions, for I have often heard it said by colleagues that Horowitz, having started out as a left-leaning radical, has undergone a sea change, and has become a right-leaning conservative. Depending upon the ideological orientation of the person making such a statement, this supposed change is met with either approval or disapproval, leading me to think that it has less to do with the subject of the remark, than with the politics of identity among social scientists, with Horowitz being an important focal point, or, perhaps better, a lightning rod.[2]

An Ideological Transformation?

This question of personal ideological transformation was addressed by Horowitz himself almost a decade ago. "Many times in recent years," he wrote,

> I have been asked how I changed over the years. The question about 'change' comes to mean more than simple alteration in my point of view. It is often asked in a testy way, suggesting changes for the worse: the cardinal sin, a failure to keep pace with progressive tides, or still more awful, a turn away from first principles with which I have long been identified." (Horowitz, 1984:xiii)

If such an ideological transformation had actually taken place, it would probably be relatively uninteresting, except on a personal and psychological level; after all, individuals sometimes do experience huge transformations of character and belief, and these are hardly unprecedented.

Horowitz's answer to his critics, however, is that he doesn't believe he has changed ideologically (Horowitz, 1984:xiii), and an examination of his writings from the early 1950s through today confirms his point, and clearly shows that his ideas about society and politics have, by and large, changed very little. From the beginning of his career Horowitz has been a free-thinking, liberal intellectual and so he has remained. By liberal, however, I mean to emphasize liberality; liberalism as toleration rather than liberalism as centrism. Throughout his career, Horowitz has emphasized the necessity for social science to get beyond the rituals and mantras of ideology, as well as the absurdity of radical doctrine whether it be on the left or the right. After all, social science demands analysis, not adherence to political doctrine. Put another way, it is not right or left that counts in social science, but right and wrong in terms of truth.

Liberalism, democracy, and social science are intimately connected for Horowitz as can be seen in the following passage from "The Pluralistic Bases of Modern American Liberalism," first written in 1972:

> Liberalism accepts the partiality of the world in a way that no other doctrine of the twentieth century does...what appears to critics as weakness is perhaps the ultimate strength of liberalism, for underneath the shibboleths and rhetoric of liberalism is something important. It is the assumption that one can live a life without knowing all the answers. The strength of liberalism is that it does not offer fanaticism, that it makes the assumption that the world is not always going to be fully known, and that men can yet act within a partial frame of reference. (Horowitz, 1977b:169)

As a believer in the pragmatic values needed to live in this world of partial knowledge, Horowitz has been a strong advocate of social science knowledge to help guide us through the maze of choices we face in a free and democratic society.

The remainder of this essay will examine the "moral career" of Horowitz's reputation within sociology, and following from that, his underlying liberal approach to the sociology of democracy and democratic politics.[3]

The Moral Career of a Political Sociologist

To begin, it should be obvious to any reader of this volume honoring him that Horowitz has been one of our most prolific and widely published social science writers, and as editor-in-chief of *Society* and president of Transaction Publishers one of our most important gatekeepers for, and disseminators of, social science ideas. Needless to say, he has been a highly influential and visible figure in sociology. That it is widely believed that Horowitz has traversed the political and professional continuum from the radical left to the conservative right, while actually remaining an old-time liberal committed to reason and truth from the start, is itself sociologically relevant, and raises the question of why so many social scientists have taken to thinking about Horowitz in this way.

In large measure this perception may be attributable to the professional sociological community's process of self-definition, which, in part, depends on the creation of collective representations of how sociology is "done," personified, sometimes totemically, in terms of "leading figures" or "big names." These leading figures, and I count Horowitz among them for at least the last thirty years, come to have pattern-setting moral careers in terms of the profession and its process of creating a set of professional identities for its members.[4]

In general terms, moral careers reflect the history of a culture's moral agreements and conflicts.[5] Here the idea of a moral career will be applied to Horowitz, whose symbolic life in the professional culture of sociology began in the 1960s when he played a leading role in revamping the profession under the banner "the new sociology." At that time he became a focal point in the soul-searching debate in the profession as to which is better: the "old" or the "new" sociology, the sociology of consensus or the sociology of conflict.[6]

The radical image attributed to Horowitz may be traced back to 1964, when in his introductory remarks to *The New Sociology: Essays in Social Science and Social Theory in Honor of C. Wright Mills,* Horowitz undertook a critical analysis of the state of his discipline, which, given the context, might well have been taken as a radical gesture. "There can be little doubt," he wrote,

> that the prevailing tendency in American sociology during the past two decades between 1940 and 1960 has put this discipline into a *cul de sac.* This tendency has been to package sociology, its tendencies, its tangents, and its theorists, in an institutional setting that is more concerned with the presentation of a social image than with the forging of a sociological imagination. (Horowitz, 1964:3)

Horowitz's main target in these remarks, indeed, in his editing of the entire volume, was sociological empiricism; his main goal was to infuse social science with a sense of social responsibility tied to social research. In 1964, such a critique of the status quo, combined with an advocacy of change, could easily be taken for radicalism, but was it really radical in any larger sense? I think not. A rereading of *The New Sociology* shows its contributors to be far less radical, and far more liberal, than they were said to have been. Ultimately, Horowitz was advocating the uses of sociology in the context of a democratic society that needed the proper discovery and analysis of the facts of social life in order to provide the basis for responsible decision making, or, as he put it, "the task of science is to lessen the pain of encountering the future by anticipating its problems" (Horowitz, 1964:37). Nevertheless, *The New Sociology* helped win for Horowitz a radical reputation, which in 1964 meant something quite different than it would four or five years later when the intellectual left went berserk.

But there is a larger irony to the professional perception of Horowitz as a radical at this time. Even as *The New Sociology* was coming out in a paperback edition a year later, in 1965, Horowitz was publishing "The Stalinization of Fidel Castro," a hard-hitting critique of the totalitarian tendencies to which the Communist revolutionaries in Cuba succumbed, (Horowitz, 1965). This was the first major Anglo assault on Castro's revolution and its aftermath, and as a result of writing and publishing this essay, Horowitz was called "the man who betrayed the legacy of C. Wright Mills," by some of his colleagues, and was almost persona non grata in the Latin American Studies Association of which he had been a leading member.

A Complex but Classical Liberal Worldview

We can see, therefore, that Horowitz had a complex view of the world. In terms of sociology he leaned slightly to the left, and in terms of the larger issues of world politics he leaned slightly to the right; but ultimately he never moved very far from the classical liberal ethos. This apparent inconsistency has never seemed to bother Horowitz, probably because consistency in these sorts of issues is the particular vanity of ideologues among whom he has never been numbered. Indeed, from the beginning Horowitz idealized science and reason, and had an aversion to ideological correctness and ideological hatred of the enemy, which characterized radicals of both the left and right. Looking back on the earliest phase of his career, Horowitz noted that for him "science was the harbinger of the open society, the source of democratic culture, the essence of a democratic style in which shared discourse rather than distilled hatred became the basis of policy," and, he added, "I still believe this to be the case" (Horowitz, 1984:xvi).

If the radical label didn't really fit in 1964, when he published *The New Sociology,* it is even harder to imagine why it still stuck after the late 1960s when Horowitz's criticism of the New Left was even sharper than had been his criticism of the old sociology. After all, whatever its

shortcomings, the old sociology was itself couched in a genuinely liberal context. It never did drift toward conservatism, but just the opposite. Ultimately it was the radical temptation that threatened to undermine
the positivistic and rational basis for sociology. Whereas the old left,
among whom were many sociologists, believed in organization, or "The
Party," the New Left believed in spontaneity, or "The Movement." In
response to all this, Horowitz wrote the following:

> The purpose of revolution is to create a society which is better than existing soci-
> ety. On the other hand, given the fact that few warranties can be made that this will
> in effect come about, the more proximate goal of revolution making is the thera-
> peutic values instilled in the participants, the revolutionists themselves. Therefore,
> the true change, or the essential condition for dramatic change, comes not with the
> triumph of one class over another, or the victory of one nation over another, but
> rather the victory that each individual gains in the act of revolutionary perfor-
> mance. (Horowitz, 1968a:ix–x)

If Horowitz appeared to be changing, however, one wonders why.
After all, his criticism of the radical left in the late 1960s was from the
same democratic, and liberal standpoint as had been his earlier criticism
of sociology. The belief that he was changing, while actually remaining
rock steady and true to his basic liberal beliefs, may be attributed to the
fact that the academic environment in general, and the social science
environmment in particular were changing around him, making it seem
as if he had moved from left to right. Thus, in Horowitz, and in perceptions and judgments about the changing character of his work, we have
a very interesting measure of social and cultural change, rather than a
case of personal and psychological transformation.

To examine the transformation of our academic and social science
cultures in this context, it will be necessary to look closely at Horowitz's
work, but since that includes over 600 published items, including books,
articles, and book reviews covering a remarkably wide range of subjects, this would be unwieldy in an article of this length. Thus, I have
chosen to concentrate upon Horowitz's writings about the relationship
of sociology to politics, and more specifically upon his unwavering liberal faith in reason and the search for truth (especially as these apply to
the enterprise of social science theory and research) as factors that might
strengthen democracy and foster freedom.

That this approach was once considered radical, or at least liberal,
and is now labeled conservative speaks volumes, not only about

Horowitz, but, even more important, about academic social science—where it once stood, where it stands today, and where it might be headed in the future.

Reason, Democracy, and a Shifting Academic Ethos

When Hoowitz began his career in the early 1950s America was in the midst of what, in political terms, many have described as a somewhat "conservative age," although we might do well to remember with Louis Hartz that the liberal tradition was really the only political tradition in America, (Hartz, 1955). Interestingly, in the same year (1955) that Hartz was publishing his great book, *The Liberal Tradition in America,* Horowitz was saying much the same thing in a brilliant critique of the new conservatism published in *Science and Society:* "The liberal belief is so profoundly rooted that the interesting question is how the triumph of liberalism took place so thoroughly" (Horowitz, 1977a:139). During this time the field of sociology was, as I have suggested above, profoundly liberal, even if it was dominated by the functionalist approach that seemed to many young Turks to promote the social status quo.

By the early 1960s, however, as Horowitz's career progressed, we were becoming an increasingly liberal society; and, within an already liberal sociology, functionalism was being further challenged by other approaches less likely to advocate stasis. In both American society and sociology the liberalizing trend became the norm by the late 1960s and early 1970s, and then actually tipped over into advocacy of radicalism among a large and well-educated portion of American society , including many, if not most, sociologists.

During this period the movement toward radicalism among social science intellectuals had far outpaced that of most other segments of American society in general, and of academia in particular. But many old-time liberals saw this radical movement as disastrous for both the universities and the larger society for which they provided future leaders. Sticking to liberal principles, these intellectuals were quickly and pejoratively labeled as "neoconservatives" by the more left-leaning radical elements of the intelligentsia for whom liberalism was too cautious, too compromising, too democratic, and too conservative.

By the late 1960s, Horowitz, who by temperament and intellectual disposition is a democrat and a liberal, was already established as one of our most prominent social scientists. Although he leaned slightly left in his sympathies, and was associated with radicalism because of his conflict perspective, his criticism of the war in Vietnam, his support for some elements of the student movement, and his exposure of Project Camelot easily places Horowitz among those strong-willed liberals who refused to betray their democratic and rational principles to the anarchic and antinomian forms of radicalism vying for supremacy in the academy and in American political circles.

In this context it is notable that the positive values expressed throughout Horowitz's work and career—democracy, freedom, rationality, autonomy, and decentralization of power and authority—are liberal values. Horowitz's work also reflects his aversion to absolutism, authoritarianism, communism, fascism, utopianism, terrorism, violence, secrecy, populism, war, civil disobedience, anarchism, and alienation. It also portrays conflict as a more important and integral element of democracy than consensus; significantly, Horowitz's work clearly had a greater affinity to Simmel's liberal theory of conflict, than to the more radical Marxian conflict theory. Indeed, of all the values that underlie his work, Horowitz's deep and abiding belief in the tenets and practices of liberal democracy, especially its constitutive elements of political conflict and freedom, are most characteristic of his thought, and best sum up the man and his ideas.

What then do we understand by the term *liberal democracy*? Although liberalism is essentially a nineteenth- and twentieth-century philosophy, it can justifiably be said to have its origins in the writings of John Locke in the seventeenth century. The hallmark of liberalism has always been its insistence that in and through politics, and the conflict of values undergirding politics, citizens should strive to "make their society rational, just, and capable of affording opportunities for everyone to develop his own potentialities" (Minogue, 1963:2). As such, liberalism was well suited to become the prevailing theory of democratic politics, for democracy, associated as it is with the ideas that governments should function with majority consent, but protect the rights of minorities, that they should insure the right of political parties to exist and to oppose each other, that they should not hamper the workings of a free press, nor the freedoms of speech, assembly, and movement, is really the only form of government suited to liberal doctrine.

All of these liberal democratic values inform Horowitz's work, but most of all Horowitz's political sociology is predicated on a belief in the liberal insistence on rationality as the basis for purposive political action, and as the basis of decision making in which the anticipatable consequences of political action are taken into account. It is hard to imagine why Horowitz was ever thought to be a radical, or why radicals would want to call him one of their own.

Advocating an Ethic of Responsibility

But such is the course of moral careers that advocates and opportunists who think that they can use a particular person as a symbolic collective representation of their group will appropriate whomever they see fit to play this role. Thus, they did see him in this light despite the fact that he criticized the new radicalism from the standpoint of an old-time liberalism. And, oddly, Horowitz was being referred to as a "radical authority on revolutionary thought" (Lipset, 1971:116) at about the same time as he was putting forth the following hard-hitting analysis of radicalism:

> This is the first generation in American society, at least in this century, to combine radicalism with irrationalism. As in the age of Sorel, reason has been displaced by passion...
>
> The current style of radicalism is abrasive, physical, impatient, and eclectic. It reflects a concern with the exercise of will over those objective forces which may exist in the world...
>
> The assertion of the priority of individual will assumes a strongly moralistic tone. The wills of individuals become objects to be mobilized into one total will. This moralistic style is a ready handmaiden to the "totalitarian democracy" that the historian Jacob Talmon spoke of. It is a fantastic attempt to impose a new social order upon the world, rather than to await the verdict of consensus building formulae among disparate individuals as well as the historical Muses. (Horowitz, 1968a:v–vi)

These are hardly the words of "a radical authority on revolutionary thought," they are the words of a liberal authority on radical thought. Horowitz, an admirer of Max Weber, the most important liberal democrat among the founders of modern sociology, certainly would have found Weber's distinction between those politicians who follow an "ethic of ultimate ends" as opposed to an "ethic of responsibility" in accordance with his own view of 1960s radicalism (Weber, 1946:120–26).

Extremists—utopians, revolutionaries, and radicals—of the left and right—tend to follow some variant or other of the ethic of ultimate ends. They believe so strongly in the value of their cause that they will do whatever they can to further it, no matter what the consequences. "If," as Weber said of those following this ethos, "an action of good intent leads to bad results, then, in the actor's eyes, not he but the world, or the stupidity of other men, or God's will who made them thus, is responsible for the evil" (Weber, 1946:121). Such an ethic has little to do with the liberal democratic imagination, nor with Horowitz's understanding of it.

In fact, it is the association of liberalism with what Weber called the ethic of responsibility that soured it in the eyes of 1960s' radicals. As Horowitz noted:

> [T]he modern Left movement...is not so much an attack on the world of ideas as it is an attack on the idea that reason is the only model of knowing. The suspicion is that reason is an ideology that teaches us to stand between two extremes, unable to act. This identification of liberalism with the spirit of judiciousness and prudence is precisely why liberalism, at the psychological level, continues to be the main target for radical jibes. (Horowitz, 1968a:xiv)

Liberalism is perfectly at home with an ethic of responsibility because those who follow such an ethic have to take into account the predictable results of their actions, and ultimately compromise their consciences to decide which action produces the least evil. Liberalism tends to balance reason and passion, while extremists on the left and right tend to allow passion to outweigh reason at every turn. "Fiat iustitia, et pereat mundus" (let there be justice though the world may perish) was, said Kant, the catchphrase of the extremist imagination (Kant, 1949:467). The same sentiment, but with regard to truth rather than justice, "Fiat veritas, et pereat mundus," was seen as the banner for extremists of a different stripe, by Hannah Arendt, whose name very appropriately graces the university chair that Horowitz occupies (Arendt, 1968:228).

Although Horowitz is obviously a staunch advocate of rationality, it is often unclear as to whether in itself reason is of more importance to him than simply minimizing irrationality, which he sees as a constant threat not only to democracy but to all forms of social order.

Radicalism and the Revolt against Reason

Even before *The New Sociology*, which seems to have established his reputation as a radical, Horowitz proved himself to be more of a critic of radicalism than a friend. In *Radicalism and the Revolt against Reason: The Social Theories of Georges Sorel*, Horowitz's fifth book, published in 1961, he analyzes the European roots of irrationalist radicalism and concludes that "our century bears firm witness to the fact that a radicalism founded upon irrationalism cuts two ways: it might serve as a decisive antiseptic to the infections caused by our inherited rational middle class civilization, but no less a poison which cures the infection by destroying the patient—civilization itself" (Horowitz, 1968a:195). In other words, in 1961, Horowitz, as a liberal, was of two minds about middle-class civilization. On the one hand he was left-minded enough to critique it; on the other hand, he was right-minded enough to warn against its destruction by irrationalist radicalism.

An objective reading of *Radicalism and the Revolt against Reason*, however, should make it plain that Horowitz himself was clearly no radical. In fact this book is an enormously important historical critique of radicalism, or at least the type of radicalism advocated by Sorel—one that glorifies violence, personalism, mysticism, and antinomianism. Nevertheless, it is interesting to note that during this time Horowitz was developing a reputation as a radical sociologist. Perhaps in a relatively conservative age, even within a liberal culture, such as our own, any criticism of the faults of middle-class civilization is considered radical, even when accompanied by a defense of its virtues.

In an insightful and analytical passage about Sorelian irrationalism, Horowitz presented both a critique and defense of democracy. "The appeal of Sorel's position," he wrote, "is evident to all who have been disconcerted by the division between liberal democratic pledges and practices. He made it clear that power is at the basis of political change. The force of democracy can be essentially conservative particularly when it obstructs the desire for change behind a veil of electoral procedures" (Horowitz, 1968a:76). But Horowitz went on to defend democracy in the face of the Sorelian radical critique:

> [S]urely the growth of civilization and the worth of democracy itself rests not so much on how it obfuscates conflict, but on how it points to a resolution of conflict within commonly accepted rules. Too often, critics of democracy call any non-violent resolution of differences obfuscation; this because they start with a definition of society as lawless. But democracy, in providing the rules of procedure offers a method of channeling and directing behavior, despite the contentions of critics. Democracy can clarify the relative strength of contending forces in a conscious way. *Democracy therefore is perhaps the most reasonable expression through which the issues dividing men can be resolved.* (Horowitz, 1968a:76–77; my emphasis)

Democracy and reason are therefore intimately linked for Horowitz, as they are for all liberals. But Horowitz is also a consummate realist as well as a liberal. From the beginning of his career as a social scientist he realized that democracy and reason are merely utopian concepts unless one understands them in terms of power and politics to which they are always linked in reality. Having lauded democracy as the most reasonable form of government, Horowitz contends with power:

> The fact that power remains basic political capital in all existing societies is no serious critique against the employment of democratic procedures. Quite the contrary. The abuse of democracy is perhaps the soundest argument for broadening the scope of human involvement in political processes.... What is needed at this juncture in history is not the overthrow of democratic procedures, nor the substitution of Sorel's method of direct violence, but a stipulation of the contents of democracy in functional rather than normative terms: that is, into terms which have utility and relevance for the masses of men in a scientific and technological civilization. (Horowitz, 1968a:77)

It is evident that Horowitz is saying that while Sorel's utopian, or better, anti-utopian, critique of democracy falls short of its mark, namely, the subversion of democratic procedure, some sort of reevaluation of democracy is needed, perhaps constantly, and that reason dictates that the social sciences are best poised to deliver such a thoroughgoing critique. We shall come back to this subject presently.

I have quoted at length from *Radicalism and the Revolt against Reason* because it demonstrates my thesis about Horowitz, namely, that in his more youthful writings he was never the radical he was said to have been, but merely a democrat and a liberal in a relatively conservative age within a historically liberal culture and a historically liberal social science environment. And, despite the popular perception among some intellectuals that he has become a conservative, Horowitz's later writings show that he has remained merely a democrat and a liberal in what is now a relatively radical age, and an infinitely more radical social science environment.

The Mills Biography and Critics on the Left

So why has Horowitz's reputation changed? Although there are great complexities involved in answering such a question, I think that the most telling reason is his publication of *C. Wright Mills: An American Utopian* in 1983. Mills was, and to some extent still is, one of the great iconic figures of the New Left. That Horowitz was his sociological heir after Mills's death in 1962 only enhanced, perhaps through the laws of charismatic succession, the radical reputation.

But *C. Wright Mills: An American Utopian* was not an uncritical biography; in fact, it was a penetrating liberal critique of Mills and his work. This was obviously too much for some of the most pronounced guardians of the radical spirit. This is best illustrated in a powerfully placed review of the Mills biography in *The American Journal of Sociology* by Lewis Coser, who wrote:

> [H]ad Irving Louis Horowitz written *C. Wright Mills: An American Utopian* in the years immediately following Mills's death in 1962 when he considered himself Mills's disciple and wished to emulate him, it would probably have been an uncritical hagiography. As it is, Horowitz has moved in the interim from a radical to a fairly conservative position and, as result, has gained critical distance from his subject. (Coser, 1984:657–658)

Likewise, Dan Wakefield, reviewing *C. Wright Mills: An American Utopian* in *The Nation,* said:

> Horowitz's opinion of Mills has shifted drastically. After Mills's death in 1962, Horowitz considered him "the greatest sociologist the United States ever produced," and in 1964, he described him as "the man whose spirit and zest for life inform the current political struggle for a better world." But the present volume calls him "a prophet and fanatic" whose "quite personal style led to a near-unanimous negative consensus about him" (Wakefield, 1984:212–13).

Although the Mills book received many glowing mainstream reviews, the pied pipers of the New Left played a different tune when reviewing it, and, parenthetically, its author. Thus, adding to Coser's view of Horowitz as a conservative, Mark Naison's review of the Mills biography for *Commonweal* suggested that Horowitz had integrated Mills's theoretical legacy "into a skeptical liberalism (or embittered neoconservatism)" (Naison, 1984:252–53).

The Collapse of Classical Liberalism

The New Left reception of Horowitz's biography of Mills necessitates that we confront the fact that the terms *radical, liberal,* and *conservative,* which once covered almost the entire political and social spectrum, have now been reduced to two: liberal and conservative. Horowitz realized the formerly tripartite nature of the political spectrum when he wrote that liberalism "offers a middle range between whatever is at one extreme end and whatever is said to be necessary at the other" (Horowitz, 1977b:169). That Horowitz himself saw and understood that the compression of the political spectrum was under way decades ago can be seen in his 1965 essay, "Radicalism and Contemporary American Society," where he remarked that "Classical Liberalism has no future" (Horowitz, 1970:563), by which he meant that it was being forced out of the political and social picture by both the radical and conservative movements. Horowitz came back to the same point, this time from a different angle, in 1992 in "Morris Raphael Cohen and the End of the Classical Liberal Tradition" (Horowitz, 1992), where, with the hindsight of more than two decades, he recognized that what he had predicted had come to pass, namely, that liberalism had no future. Before the 1960s, liberalism had been, in Horowitz's words "positioned *between* fascism and communism, or if one prefers, between the political right and left" (Horowitz, 1992:xv). But now "liberalism has become part of the polarity" (Horowitz, 1992:xv).

Another way to look at this process of terminological and philosophical compression is to realize that, in terms of politics, up to the 1960s most Americans could have been called, and probably would have called themselves, liberals. Relatively few would have fallen into the two polar categories, radical and conservative. Thus, Horowitz could write, in 1956, that "[e]verybody is a liberal. Everybody believes in the free exchange of ideas. Everybody believes in restricted planning, but not national planning. Everybody believes that democracy is a good thing, but not at the expense of social order" (Horowitz, 1977a:139). Not surprisingly, the inherently liberal nature of American society was understood perfectly by Franklin Delano Roosevelt in the 1932 presidential campaign:

> Say that civilization is a tree which, as it grows, continually produces rot and dead wood. The radical says: "Cut it down." The conservative says: "Don't touch it." The liberal compromises: "Lets prune, so that we lose neither the old trunk nor the new branches." This campaign is waged to teach the country to march upon its appointed course, the way of change, in an orderly march, avoiding alike the revolution of radicalism and the revolution of conservatism. (Schlesinger, 1960:648-49)

In many ways, Roosevelt, the epitome of American liberalism, struck a chord among a majority of Americans who responded by electing him to four terms in office.

But, as Horowitz has reminded us, since F. D. R.'s day we have drifted from this tripartite rhetorical structure, and today Americans talk about themselves in terms of being either liberals or conservatives, with the term *liberal* having taken on the meaning that the term *radical* used to have—at least when it is used by conservatives to characterize those they call liberal. The effect of this change has been to confuse people, most of whom still fall into what would have been the old liberal category, which no longer exists, and who no longer know how to characterize themselves politically and socially since they consider themselves neither new liberals, that is, old radicals, nor conservatives.

The rhetorical compression has lumped together those who had been radically left of center with the vast majority who had previously been properly characterized as liberals and who were at the center. The conservative category now encompasses not only traditional conservatives, but also many who had previously been cast as liberals, but who shunned the new more radical connotation of the term. These were dubbed neoconservatives by the left.[7] The overall result of this rhetorical compression was not merely to eliminate the old liberal category, which most Americans fit into, but to normalize the radical and conservative extremes, thus leaving the majority of Americans with no political and social category with which they identified.[8]

Conflict and the Moral Economy of Freedom

This brings us back to the nature of politics, and ultimately, at least for sociologists, back to Max Weber. In "Max Weber and the Spirit of American Sociology," Horowitz got to the bottom of the Weber puzzle, by showing how differently Weber had been interpreted by the three prevailing icons of sociology in the 1950s and early 1960s, namely, Talcott Parsons, Robert K. Merton, and C. Wright Mills. "Weber became in American sociological history," wrote Horowitz, "the form of legitimation for the conservatism of a Parsons, but no less for the liberalism of a Merton and the radicalism of a Mills" (Horowitz, 1968b:194). One might add, with hindsight, that Weber became a form of legitimation for the liberalism of Horowitz.

What Horowitz, following Weber, has stood for as a political sociologist is the primacy of politics and political conflict, for the creation and maintenance of freedom in a democracy. While politics is synonymous with conflict, both of these are equally synonymous with freedom. No politics, no freedom; no freedom, no conflict; no conflict, no politics.

The work of Horowitz, as well as that of Weber, is at once democratic, anti-utopian, and anti-totalitarian; it is predicated upon the idea that through political conflict a rational and informed citizenry can create a good society, or at least a tolerable one. The place of social science in a democracy is then clear: to help inform politicians and other policymakers, as well as the citizenry, about the problems their society faces and the possible consequences of making policies to solve those problems. If it does this well, sociology affirms the main Weberian lesson, which is, according to Horowitz, "that sociology is a human science and not merely a social science" (Horowitz, 1968b:194).

In a way, this Weberian lesson is also Horowitz's lesson , and it sums up his place in the moral economy of American democracy. In every democracy decisions have to be made, and they are regularly and necessarily more difficult to make than in totalitarian societies, or, indeed, than in any nondemocratic society. The majority decisions in a democracy cast a long moral shadow because they are made against the will of a minority that opposes them, but that must live under them, just as the majority that supported them must live under them. Hence, democracies operate under the conditions of a free market moral economy more so than any other form of government.

By advocating sociology with a human face, and through his place in social science publishing, Horowitz has helped make social science research an integral part of the policy-making process in America. He has proved himself to be an exemplary citizen and a liberal democratic voice among his social science contemporaries, and this, rather than speculation about his ideological stability, should be the essence of his reputation and moral career among sociologists today.

Lafayette College
Department of Sociology

Notes

1. Among the locals presenting lectures were Digby Baltzell, Renee Fox, Philip Rieff, Marvin Wolfgang, and Frank Furstenberg who was then a young assistant professor; the outside luminaries included Alasdaire McIntyre, Jackson Toby, Lee Rainwater, and Irving Louis Horowitz.
2. "A man's reputation is what is said about him. It is the overall response of people to both actor and role performance; an assessment not only of the results achieved

but also of the manner in which they were achieved...what is said about a man can serve to clarify and confirm both values and strategies among the discussants," John Hutson, "A Politician in Valloire," *Gifts and Poison: The Politics of Reputation*, ed. F. G. Bailey (Oxford: Blackwell, 1971), 79.

3. The term itself was first coined about thirty-five years ago by Erving Goffman who used it in "The Moral Career of the Mental Patient," *Psychiatry* 22, no. 2 (May 1959), where he wrote the following: "Traditionally the term career has been reserved for those who expect to enjoy the rises laid out within a respectable profession. The term is coming to be used, however, in a broadened sense to refer to any social strand of any person's course through life."

   Furthermore, Goffman, who was interested in the effects of a moral career on an individual's identity, suggested that moral careers were two-sided:

   > One side is linked to internal matters held dearly and closely, such as image of self and felt identity; the other side concerns official position, jural relations, and style of life, and is part of a publicly accessible institutional complex. The concept of career, then, allows one to move back and forth between the personal and the public, between the self and its significant society, without having overly to rely for data upon what the person says he thinks he imagines himself to be.

   Since individual social identity rather than the self definition of groups was his concern, Goffman stressed the "[m]oral aspects of career, i.e. the regular sequence of changes that career entails in the person's self and in his framework of imagery for judging himself and others." To understand Horowitz's place in contemporary sociology, however, I intend to use Goffman's concept in a different manner by stressing instead the career aspects of moral symbolism, that is, the sequence of changes that career entails, not in the person's self-conception, but in society's use of the person as a symbol to structure its framework of imagery for judging its range of actions and beliefs.

4. Some "moral careers" serve as unifying symbols that pull the various elements of a society together behind a single moral identity while others become symbolically divisive, splitting society into antagonistic moral camps each with its own particular moral identity, and each defining the other as a collective enemy held together by perverted or at least wrongheaded values. The later category is certainly germane to sociology in recent years.

5. For instance, in his lifetime Abraham Lincoln was referred to as a "despot" by some and as the "great liberator" by others, a "beast" as well as a "hero." But after his assassination on a Good Friday, Lincoln was quickly apotheosized and began a more unifying moral career in the American mind, leaving behind the more divisive one he had in life as president.

6. The term *moral career*, as used here, generally indicates a course of continued progress in, or beyond, the life of a person, place, event, or thing, which becomes the symbolic focus of public attention and debate pertaining to character, conduct, intentions, and social relations, viewed ethically, that is, from an evaluative and judgmental stand point. Viewed symbolically, or as a collective representation, a *moral career* says little or nothing about actual moral states, but only about the moral attitudes of the society, or those of social groups, within a society, which make use of a symbolic moral career to define the limits of its identity.

7. It is significant that Horowitz is not among those usually listed as neoconservatives, and that *The Neo-Conservatives* by Peter Steinfels, a prominent book about

neoconservatives, places *Society* (Horowitz's social science magazine) outside this camp.

8. To counter this recent rhetorical revolution I suggest we return, with some modification, to the Rooseveltian trichotomy: radical, liberal, conservative. The major modification here would be to add a fourth term, neoconservative. This would allow us to recognize that the right has its left, and the left its right. Put another way, conservatism, viewed as a continuum, can be seen as having a right wing—traditional conservatives-and a left wing—neoconservatives; the same applies, eo ipso, for liberalism, which also can be thought of as having a continuum, with a left wing—radicals—and a right wing—liberals. The advantage of viewing the spectrum of political and social sentiments in this way is that we can see that neoconservatives and liberals are really part of a third way of looking at the world, a middle category with liberals on the left and neoconservatives on the right.

References

Arendt, Hannah. "Truth and Politics." In *Between Past and Future*. New York: Viking, 1968.

Coser, Lewis. "Review of *C. Wright Mills: An American Utopian*." *American Journal of Sociology* 90, no. 3 (November 1984).

Goffman, Erving. "The Moral Career of the Mental Patient." *Psychiatry* 22, no. 2 (May 1959).

Hartz, Louis. *The Liberal Tradition in America*. New York: Harcourt, 1955.

Horowitz, Irving Louis, ed. *The New Sociology: Essays in Social Science and Social Theory in Honor of C. Wright Mills*. New York: Oxford, 1964.

———. "The Stalinization of Fidel Castro." *New Politics* 4, no. 4 (1965).

———. "Radicalism and the Revolt against Reason: Then and Now." In *Radicalism and the Revolt against Reason*. Carbondale: Southern Illinois University Press, 1968a.

———. "Max Weber and the Spirit of American Sociology." In *Professing Sociology*. Chicago: Aldine, 1968b.

———. "Radicalism and Contemporary American Society." In *Where Its At: Radical Perspectives in Sociology*, ed. Steven Deutsch and John Howard. New York: Harper & Row, 1970.

———. "The New Conservatism in America." In *Ideology and Utopia in the United States: 1956-1976*. New York: Oxford, 1977a.

———. "The Pluralistic Bases of Modern American Liberalism." In *Ideology and Utopia in the United States: 1956-1976*. New York: Oxford, 1977b.

———. "Democratic Societies and Their Enemies, 1950-1984." In *Bibliography of the Writings of Irving Louis Horowitz*. Privately printed, 1984.

———. "Morris Raphael Cohen and the End of the Classical Liberal Tradition." In *The Faith of a Liberal*, by Morris Raphael Cohen. New Brunswick, NJ: Transaction Publishers, 1992.

Horowitz, Irving Louis, and Howard Becker. "Radical Politics and Social Research: Observations on Methodology and Ideology." *American Journal of Sociology* 76, no. 1 (July 1972).

Kant, Immanuel. "Eternal Peace." In *Immanuel Kant's Moral and Political Writings*, ed. Karl Friedrich. New York: Random House, 1949.

Lipset, Seymour Martin. *Rebellion in the University*. Boston: Little, Brown, 1971.

Minogue, Kenneth. 1963. *The Liberal Mind.* London: Methuen, 1963.
Naison, Mark. "Populism, Pragmatism, and Activism." *Commonweal* (20 April 1984).
Schlesinger, Arthur M., Jr., *The Politics of Upheaval.* Boston: Houghton Mifflin, 1960.
Wakefield, Dan. "Before His Time." *The Nation* (15 September 1984).
Weber, Max. "Politics as a Vocation." In *From Max Weber: Essays in Sociology.* New York: Oxford, 1946.

3

Genocide and Social Structure: Reflections on *The Origins of Totalitarianism* and *Taking Lives*

Jeanne H. Guillemin

August 25, 1938. A Brechtian maxim: do not build on the good old days, but on the bad new ones.

—Walter Benjamin, *Reflections*

Mass murder is the one subject in contemporary society that should elicit universal concern, for who among us is free of the fear of an arbitrary, anonymous death? In addition, gruesome as it is, the organizational and technologic capacity of governments to mount genocidal campaigns is perhaps the most important political innovation of modern times.

Yet in 1976, when Irving Louis Horowitz was writing the monograph *Genocide: State Power and Mass Murder,* intellectuals and non-intellectuals alike were in a general state of denial. Somewhere in the national tumult following the Vietnam War and Watergate, we lost perspective on, of all things, the state. Ethnicity, decentralization, special interest groups—these were more than the talk of the moment; they were the ascendant political modes of self-identification and action. Within this context, historic cases of genocide became the provence of victim groups, a legitimate appropriation, but one that, insofar as it was exclusive, diminished understanding of genocide as a crime against humanity. If the Holocaust pertains only to Jews and can be understood and interpreted only by them, who else should care? That past atrocities became identified with present political agendas also troubled perspec-

tives on genocide. The Holocaust was linked to more than Israel's survival, but to its internal politics. The massacre of Armenians by Turks
early in this century was incorporated by Armenian Americans into their
platform to free Armenia from Soviet domination. Advocates for American Indian tribes commonly used the nineteenth-century decimation of
native populations to support the case for increased tribal autonomy from
federal jurisdiction. And the promotion of birth control among urban
and rural blacks was construed as genocidal.

Any transformation of victimization into political capital must be problematic. With genocide, it is doubly so. To begin, how does one shoe-
horn the hellish scenario of dehumanized executioners slaughtering
millions of innocents into the normative, competitive brackets of contemporary American politics? The public may feel sympathy or even
guilt, but have no clear sense of action demanded. In addition, when
resources are at stake, someone is bound to say, "Prove it!" and reduce
what should be of universal concern to a debate on numbers. Was it 6
million Jews annihilated by the Nazis, or 2 million? How many Armenians or American Indians must have died? In the most extreme rejection of guilt, a German historian argued that the Holocaust was entirely
a Zionist fiction (Butz, 1976).

Concerning the Stalinist purges, the denial evident twenty years ago
was of a different order. No other nation in this century has been more
mythologized by Americans than the former Union of the Soviet Socialist Republics. Geographically distant, often closed to Westerners, and
vast in its territories, the Soviet Union has at times been a complete
cipher to Americans.[1] Or our attitudes toward it have been shaped by
ideological swings that reflect the deep ambivalence of the United States
about both socialism (as repressive of individual rights) and individualism (as a threat to norms), as well as shifts in Soviet policy. In the aftermath of the McCarthy witch-hunts of the 1950s, for instance, and
following the relative thaw in the cold war that occurred in the 1960s,
Michael Parenti and other members of the New Left repudiated the significance of the purges, disputed the reported numbers of gulag victims,
and dropped discussion of genocide from their writings on the Soviet
Union (Whitfield, 1980:14–24), as if it would be impolite to raise these
historical events while pursuing detente, as if the loss of millions of
lives during the 1930s and 1940s was irrelevant to understanding the
contemporary Soviet state or Russian society.[2] During the early 1970s,

the publication in English of Aleksandr Solzhenitsyn's first volume of *The Gulag Archipelago* was a coup for the West and free speech, but the émigré author was more of a *cause célèbre* than the realities depicted in his books.

American resistance to confronting the facts of genocide also extended to contemporary occurrences. During this period, mass killings in Uganda, Indonesia, and Cambodia, matters of newspaper record, might as well have been taking place on another planet, for the extent that they perturbed American consciousness or provoked social scientists to infuse moral reactions with intellectual energy. Refusal to take the Third World seriously was part of the arrogance of the times, which was reinforced by the cold war emphasis on superpower relations. But it was also part of a general incapacity to perceive the many connections between and among nations, what we now call, for better or worse, the new global order. We had lost the war in Vietnam, proof enough of failure to construct a positive world role.

During this same period, the social sciences were in a kind of swoon. The happy policy niches they had enjoyed during the "Great Society" program had crumbled during the Republican administrations. Traumatic political events, such as the war in Vietnam and the resignation of President Nixon, were outstripping the ability of analysts to interpret them.

On a much deeper level, it was becoming obvious that our culture and civilization had failed to develop a critical history, in Nietzsche's sense of the strength to condemn the past while also understanding that we are the outcome of previous generations, their "aberrations, passions and errors, and indeed of their crimes" (1983:77). Locating evil in modern imperialism or Nazi Germany or even McCarthyism was easy enough; understanding the pervasiveness of human greed and brutality and our participation in it is much harder, and harder still when academic specialists obfuscate the problem. When Charles Dickens wrote *A Child's History of England,* which is replete with bloodbaths and mindless cruelties, only occasionally punctuated by valiant acts, he said more about human nature and politics than most contemporary texts in sociology, political science, or history. Where in scholarly works do we arrive at a better understanding of how people suffer or die, have good luck or bad, or love or hate enough to kill? Instead, we have relied on social models and that insipid composite called social problems. And yet without some approximate rendition of the human condition, how does one even begin to analyze society, let alone the nightmare of mass murder?

Genocide, which would in 1980 reach its final, augmented form as *Taking Lives: Genocide and State Power,* was a tour de force for its insistence that the state's capacity to do evil be confronted as a historical and global phenomenon. And the work remains so today. With the collapse of the Soviet Union, the reorganization of its satellites, and the reunification of Germany, both the specter and reality of mass murder are national concerns here and abroad. The rise of anti-Semitism in the newly united Germany has been accompanied by random attacks on the disabled and foreigners. The German government has struck a deal for cash with Romania for the deportation of Gypsies who are, if anything, more despised there than in Germany. How does one not think of the Third Reich? We look at the former Yugoslavia and see the brutal legacy of imperialism, Nazism, and communist dictatorship. Bosnian Serbs have embarked on wholesale destruction of Muslim communities in the name of "ethnic cleansing." In Serbian schools, children are educated with old photographs of the Ustase (Nazi-backed Croatians) torturing and killing Serbs, Jews, and Gypsies. Bosnian Croats, too, have their dreams, which also include the elimination of Muslims from their territory. Muslims, despite their limited resources, have apparently shown hatred in kind. In the Middle East, Israel expands, Palestinians resist, and *The Protocols of Zion* is a best-seller throughout the Muslim countries. The need for the kind of impassioned and informed perspective exemplified by *Taking Lives* has never been more clear.

In page length and detail, *Taking Lives* is hardly on the scale of Horowitz's contributions to theories of development or conflict. Rather, it emerged as a kind of a professional manifesto, as the author himself noted: "My early interest in social and philosophical ideas and ideologies of war and peace, and the attendant analysis of conflict, consensus, and cooperation, was itself a part of a basic commitment to a sociology which takes seriously the right to live as a determinant of other human rights and social alignments" (1980:186).

The work of philosophers (as well as novelists, playwrights, and poets) illumines *Taking Lives* (as well as Horowitz's other writings) and reflects the author's solid grounding in that field, as well as his ability to move beyond it. In fact, in his preface to the 1973 edition of *War and Peace in Contemporary Social and Political Theory,* Horowitz adds this note to his intellectual autobiography: "All that has really happened over time is a change in focus. I no longer emphasize philosophical themes as central, but rather see them as arising from the organizational frameworks in which men find themselves" (1973:ix–x).

Hannah Arendt

Among the philosophers cited in *Taking Lives,* Hannah Arendt is a primary influence and more footnoted in this book than sociologists, classical or modern. Her 1951 treatise *The Origins of Totalitarianism* brilliantly presented Nazi Germany and the Soviet Union under Stalin as historical innovations that, though their ideologic premises differed, still proved the violent capacity of the state to promote mass murder. The reflections in this essay will focus on the similarities and differences between Arendt's thinking on genocide and that of Irving Louis Horowitz and will conclude that these two are unlikely yet kindred spirits.

Arendt's work on totalitarianism is marked by a particular courage. If she had limited *Origins* to its first two parts, on anti-Semitism and imperialism, she would have made a solid contribution to the understanding of Western European political history prior to 1914. We would have better understood the Dreyfus case and the rise of pan-German movements. But it is with the third segment, "Totalitarianism," that she confronts the behemoths. Before the war was over, in 1944, Arendt had already presented an outline of the book to her publisher. At the time she was writing the final draft [from 1946 to 1949] Nazi Germany was only just defeated. Tons of records seized by the Allies and testimonies from every quarter were yielding detailed confirmation of atrocities against Jews and others. Although the U.S. government had during the war consistently downplayed information on the Holocaust, now the slaughter was undeniable. If Americans in general felt revulsion, and American Jews felt fear and anger, imagine the reaction of a German Jewish exile who, had she not escaped to France and then the United States, surely would have been sent to a concentration camp to die. Yet Arendt immediately began researching the available documents to discover how the Nazis engineered death, not just anyone's death, but potentially her own and certainly those of relations and friends. At the same time, she took on Stalin's Soviet Union as the corollary case to Nazi Germany, when Stalin's purge of dissidents, including intellectuals, was ongoing and his plans to exterminate Jews were in the making. Critics would fault her for having neither the Russian language skills nor the Soviet documents to balance this second case against the first, but she never wavered in her belief that Hitler's Germany and Stalin's Russia were comparable.[3]

That she as a Jew approached the subject of genocide is perhaps less extraordinary than her successful determination to impose upon the unthinkable the rigor of rational thought. For in daring to seize the phenomenon of mass murder and examining its political dynamic, she was also refusing to internalize the terror and be shut off from reasonable discourse with others. For Jew or non-Jew, the arguments are laid out. "Now what do you think?" was her question. Even though she died in 1973, one still hears the call for dialogue in the vivacity of her prose.

A parallel courage and the same faith in rational dialogue characterizes *Taking Lives* and is coupled with an exhortation to other social scientists:

> The mobilization of our resources to attack a problem such as genocide is not a risky artifact demanding a suspension of scientific judgment, but quite the reverse, an issue which all people of this century are common witness to, and hence an area of investigation which demands the fullest utilization of scientific judgment. (1980:xiv)

Arendt also eluded being characterized as a philosopher or any kind of academic specialist, in much the same way that she eschewed identification with any exclusionary group. Though she strongly identified with her Jewish background, she considered herself a citizen of the world and all her life abhorred the love and hate of collectives and "hatred of or blind allegiance to mankind collectively [which] is doubtless as predisposed to injustice as nations are" (1966:xiii). Intellectually, Horowitz has covered the field from philosophy to sociology to political science and history, without ever being captured by any specialization. Nor has he, despite the passion he has brought to his writings on Judaism, allowed himself to be identified with any group or movement, but only as an individual among friends and colleagues and, yes, adversaries. It was not for nothing, as the saying goes, that when asked to suggest a title for his professorship at Rutgers, Horowitz chose the name of this powerful and humane thinker or that the first edition of *Genocide* was dedicated to her memory.

Horowitz, though, is of another generation than Arendt and represents a distinctly American as opposed to European perspective. For instance, he neither limits himself to the principle cases of Nazism and the Stalinist era nor does he underestimate the role of technology, which Arendt, though she appreciated the power of science, tended to overlook. Rather, he understands the twentieth century for its having developed both the technological and organizational means to implement genocidal impulses in a variety of national contexts with varying ideologies and against various subgroups. Arendt well understood the beginnings of this trend. She knew the license for brutality inherent in imperialism and "law by decree" and she explained the alienated heroes of Joseph Conrad better than many literary critics: "The world of native savages was a perfect setting for men who had escaped the reality of civilization" (1973:190).

Yet the world grew more complex after the Second World War than she might have predicted and her subsequent work on the subject, such as *Eichmann in Jerusalem,* never took her far beyond her original arguments about the nature of totalitarianism. Indeed, her reliance on Nazi Germany and the Soviet Union under Stalin deeply influenced how she perceived both the role of ideology and its relation to the structure of the state.

Ideology and Political Structure

A major point in Arendt's analysis of both German Nazism and Stalin's Soviet Union is that totalitarian governments, in the aftermath of totalitarian movements, construct a novel relationship between party and state, generally enervating and perverting the latter in order to pursue the ideological goals of the former (1973:393–410). In a sense, the momentum of the movement makes the state the means to the end of ideological goals, rather than a stable system to protect citizens. The "planned shapelessness" of the Third Reich consisted of a proliferation of offices and divisions that duplicated each others' functions, so that no one, neither the ordinary citizen nor those who executed orders, knew whom to obey or whom to disregard. Arendt also pointed out that, distinct from authoritarian regimes where authority is filtered down a hierarchy of intervening offices to the body politic, the principle of the leader in the totalitarian state relies on destruction of a rational hierarchy and a substitution of power based on the changing will of the leader, from which subordinates derived their authority.

In the case of the Soviet Union,

...the ostensible power of the party bureaucracy as against the real power of the secret police corresponds to the original duplication of party and state as known in Nazi Germany, and the multiplication (of administrative offices) becomes evident only in the secret police itself, with its extremely complicated, widely ramified network of agents, in which one department is always assigned to supervising and spying on another. (1973:403)

In this totalitarian state, a constitution becomes irrelevant. Even ideological dogma may be discarded. The framework is set for terror because the government is "topsy-turvy." And the government is in disarray because the fiction of ideology is mobile. In Germany it was the evolutionary movement of nature that underwrote racism. In the Soviet Union, it was the movement of historical evolution that required purges. There lingers behind Arendt's interpretations of totalitarian and especially that of the Nazi state, the presumption that all would have been well had the government hierarchy been nonduplicative, if ideology had been restrained by reality, and if everyone had been free of loneliness and able to reason. For her, the genocidal state is an aberrant form of government, an irreality or a kind of monster, but the state itself is potentially good. Horowitz's views of the role of ideology and of the state are markedly different from Arendt's, in part because his approach comprehends the diverse strategies of nationalism. In the postwar world, non-European nations have proved perfectly capable of inflicting brutalities on their own people and subordinating populations in ways not easily identified with the specifics of either Nazi Germany or the Soviet Union under Stalin. Instead of ideology or the "shape" of government, he seizes upon the valuation of human life as the analytic measure of the state. He also circumvents the quagmire surrounding the use and abuse of totalitarianism as a descriptive category. Rather, he has decided that what the state effects is crucial, not its structure, which is a necessary but not sufficient condition for explaining the society as a whole (1980:180). Thus, when Horowitz categorizes the contemporary instances of genocide (Uganda, Paraguay, Indonesia, Cambodia, and others), he is reminding us of the multiplicity of political forms of mass murder. The world is armed and looking dangerous. Today we have not only camps, but killing fields. The ideological differences, for example, between capitalism and socialism, or between the revolutionary and the reactionary, have fallen by the wayside. In commenting on Third World development, for instance, he writes: "There are as many societies presumably following capitalist models of development practicing such mass annihilation as those following socialist models of development" (1980:81). Likewise, in considering Uganda, where in just a few years Idi Amin managed to kill hundreds of thousands, Horowitz concludes: "What is especially noteworthy about viewing Uganda primarily as a genocidal society is that one does not become encumbered with lengthy discussions about communism or fascism, and comparative governments of Europe and Africa" (1980:53).

From this decision to emphasize effects over structure emerge four categories of states, which range from genocidal states to those characterized by other strategies: deportation or incarceration, torture, and harassment. Deportation of undesirables characterized France in the nineteenth-century as well as Castro's Cuba. China uses imprisonment as a form of social control. Brazil is an example of a torture society that releases its victims so that they may act as examples of the risks of dissidence.

Horowitz wisely notes the qualitative distinction between societies that practice genocide, "the only form of rule which takes lives systematically" (1980:44), and those that do not, and recognizes the necessity of analyzing these most dangerous environments. Out of his succinct comparison of the Holocaust and the genocide of Armenians, for example, he develops a ranked order of common features. In line with Arendt, he gives primary importance to the "political parties (Young Turks and Nazis) which invested themselves with monolithic power and literally took over the functions of their respective states" (1980:48). He assigns secondary importance to the ministries of war and other subverted military organizations utilized for the ends of genocide, as well as to the minority status of the victim populations, whose elimination in various ways enriched officials. Of tertiary importance are the cultural, religious, and racial differences that separated victims from persecutors, as well as the bureaucratic machine and the sanctions by which all bureaucrats, military and civilian, were made to carry out the processes of genocide. This pairing of cases begins with genocide and proceeds from there to analysis. Nothing, therefore, restricts a reordering of elements in other cases and pairings, or the discovery of other features, as, for example, the actions of a host nation, Serbia, in supporting Bosnian Serbs.

In no way does Horowitz assume the beneficence of the state. In contrast to the duplicative, chaotic governments portrayed by Arendt, for him, the genocidal state is nothing if efficient. If it is not, as in the case of Colombia, where hundreds of thousands have died in chronic wars, it is anomalous:

> As in all high-level generalizations, one must account for sharp variations in political systems. The most extreme of these is a weak state, which underwrites mass violence and human genocide in order to foster its own survival. The most pronounced and unique illustration of this is Colombia throughout the twentieth century. Here we have a nation characterized by *la violencia* that demonstrates how weak state authority can be yet manage to foster its interests without alleviating mass destruction. (1980:51)

Ideology and structure aside, inherent in all states is danger to the individual: "As a general condition within a finite social system, more state authority means less individual capacity to survive, and a higher individual capacity to survive means less state authority" (1980:83).

Culture, Community, and the Individual

This positing of the survival of the individual as crucial to distinguishing more from less dangerous states raises the larger issue of causality. Why are some states genocidal and others not? Neither author can answer this question. From Arendt's point of view, a crystallization of historic events provokes a degradation of freedom that affects elites and ordinary citizens. In the totalitarian state, political chaos masquerades as political order and, by consequence, the leadership is free to pursue an ideology posited on ultimates, which actually have nothing to do with sustaining the nation-state. These are world domination and genocide, goals that may be at variance with national survival. Even the dogma of ideology may be dispensed with, if the leader so desires.

In her analysis, the precondition for this situation is the creation of the masses, those uprooted from tradition and without direction. Arendt's emphasis on disorder as a feature of totalitarian regimes is in line with her general interpretation of the immediate cause of evil. The root is social. People lose their social moorings, become part of the modern masses, and seek a consistent explanation for their condition: "They do not believe in anything visible, in the reality of their own experience; they do not trust their eyes and ears but only their imaginations, which may be caught by anything that is at once universal and consistent in itself" (1973:353).

This "escape from reality into fiction" also extended to her explanation of why bourgeois Germans denied or failed to react to information about genocide in the concentration camps. The breakdown of the bourgeois class had produced the philistine, the individual isolated from his own class whose "single-minded devotion to matters of family and career was the last, already degenerated, product of the bourgeoisie's interest in the primacy of public interest" (1973:338). By clinging to conventional domestic lives and their jobs, many Germans, including camp commanders, were able to retreat from grossly abnormal circumstances or find ways of rationalizing their participation in the Reich, so that evil was not admissible.[4] Arendt also quotes David Rousset's reflection on ignorance about the camps: "Normal men don't know that anything is possible" (1973:436). Conversely, ideologues believe that all means to their ends are possible and any can be imperative.

When Arendt ventured into the social psychology of genocide, she confined herself to the discussion of loneliness (1973:474–79). Employing Montesquieu's dictum that tyranny is based on isolation, that is, the rupturing of political contacts and the human capacities for action and power, she found that its corollary in "the iron band of total terror" leaves no space for private life. "What we call isolation in the political sphere," she wrote, "is called loneliness in the sphere of social intercourse" (1973:474). What is new about totalitarianism is it destroys private life as well as public bonds.[5]

In tracing the effect of totalitarianism on the person, she emphasized two losses. One is the loss of the ability to trust, which she linked to loneliness, "the experience of being abandoned by everything and everybody" (1973:476). While loneliness is a fundamental human experience, in the totalitarian state it pervades private life and lays the groundwork for terroristic control of the population.

The other loss happens when the individual replaces thinking with an undifferentiated reliance on logic. Truth is reduced to consistency; one literally cannot think, that is, spontaneously reason and reflect. What has been lost is the "mutual guarantee, the common sense, men need in order to experience and live and know their way in a common world."

In Nazi Germany and Stalin's Soviet Union, arbitrary arrest, incarceration, and anonymous (and therefore meaningless) death were tactics that inflicted isolation and the inability to think not just on target populations, but potentially on everyone. The camps were spaces where freedom for individual thought and action disappeared, but the totalitarian society in general seeks to destroy the individual as a political and moral actor because it strives for a system in which human beings are expendable, superfluous: "What makes conviction and opinion of any sort so ridiculous and dangerous under totalitarian conditions is that totalitarian regimes take the greatest pride in having no need of them, or of any human help of any kind" (1980:456–57).

The focus in *Taking Lives* is squarely on the problem of individual survival, rather than the social antecedents of totalitarianism. Horowitz thinks primarily of the latitude offered or denied the individual, who should be able to shun collectivities, not in the sense of being a philistine, but as a citizen of the world. His wish is for a cosmopolitan society that allows individual difference and draws no ultimate insider-outsider distinctions. At the far extreme of the genocidal society is the society that is civil and tolerant, that might be a refuge or a passage from danger. Hence, one of his statements against sociological model building for its own sake receives the metaphor of flight: "It is infinitely more important to know what country to travel in order to prolong one's life than to provide others with an abstract dictionary of social systems" (1980:184). A good government, therefore, is one that fundamentally gives the individual latitude either by its laws or by its lack of them. Thus, when Horowitz discusses the difference between Germany and Italy during the Second World War, he argues that Italian Jews fared better than German Jews because of a general tolerance that refused to create and dispense with an alien class. In contrast, when Arendt addressed this difference, she noted Italy's long humanistic tradition, but saw Mussolini's role as crucial, insofar as he was content with a dictatorship and thus kept Italy from reaching a complete totalitarian form until the war began.[6]

When it comes to the Soviet Union, though, Horowitz perceives that insider-outsider designations were not characteristic of the purges, rather "terror was self-inflicted, because Russians killed and maimed Russians" (1980:92). His analysis in *The Gulag Archipelago*, which then follows, is a virtuoso analysis of Solzhenitsyn's account as social fact (not literary event) and moral warning, for it reminds us that justification of the Stalinist purges in the name of industrial or national development deserves rejection:

> I submit that the special nature of Solzhenitsyn's impact derives from his keen awareness of the substitution of engineering for ethical criteria in evaluating the human soul. He does not speak against development, but rather for those countless millions who paid the price for development. And in compelling a fresh review of the actual costs paid and the dubious benefits received, he has restored the balance between political realities and moral possibilities. (1980:110)

Horowitz also placed Solzhenitsyn's work in the context of the transformation of Soviet society from totalitarianism to authoritarian modalities, with the rise of middle sectors (bureaucrats, teachers, party officials, technicians, and the like) creating "the seeds of a consumer society without a conflict society, a mass society without a mass democracy" (1980:96). In a similar vein, he noted the integration of the Soviet Union into the world economy and the breakdown of differences between American and Russian political and economic realities: "The United States and the Soviet Union may not be converging, but certainly there are parallels between their economic systems that make detente functionally as well as strategically plausible—if not downright inevitable" (1980:114). The comfort that might be taken in this dissolution of differences, which we have begun to witness, is little, unless the new Russia overcomes its history of terrorism and accommodates democratic processes.[7]

While Horowitz writes in the American conservative tradition of "the less government, the better," Arendt developed a vision of good governments and even good revolutions born of her émigré enthusiasm for the United States, but also of her European education and background. As early as her doctoral thesis on St. Augustine, written in the late 1920s, Arendt had wrestled with the Christian notion of community based on *caritas*[8] and eventually abandoned it for a celebration of a combination of the Greek *polis* and Roman legislation. If people act and speak in the public space of politics, they become actors in history and potentially immortalize the best of political forms:[9] "It is the publicity of the public realm which can absorb and make shine through the centuries whatever men may want to save from the natural ruin of time" (1958:55).

In his 1964 review of Arendt's book *On Revolution*, Horowitz aptly characterized her as a "revolutionary conservative."[10] She saw revolutions as a supreme example of the human ability to act, to interrupt the blind processes of nature and society. In this view she was much influenced by Rosa Luxemburg (Canovan, 1974:100; Young-Bruehl, 1982: 399–402). Yet Arendt expected, in the aftermath of revolution, for a federation of "popular councils" or other grass-roots political units to insure the rights of the ordinary citizen. Her firm belief was in a republic with a constitution that would promote rational, nonideological economic development (1963a:60). Though faulted by many, including Horowitz, for not supporting her ideas with facts, Arendt's goal was laudable. She was looking for an essentially populist way to secure justice. "I have a romance with councils," she told an audience in 1972 (Hill, 1979:327). In her thesis, Arendt also took up the Augustinian concept of natality (as opposed to mortality) and subsequently envisioned it as the foundation of human action.[11] Because each individual is unique, each new birth guarantees a new beginning, even a revolution. In this fact, Arendt found hope. It was with reference to natality that she ended *Origins of Totalitarianism*. She wrote that being able to begin is "the supreme capacity" of humans and politically identical with each individual's freedom. In the last line of the book, she affirms that this "beginning is guaranteed by each new birth" (1973:479).

Similarly, when Horowitz seeks optimism in and about this most dismal subject matter, he looks to "the final realization that 'types' of people are extremely resistant to their own elimination" (1980:64). If individuals are hardy, so, too, apparently are victim groups. The Jewish population survived and is equal to or greater in number than before the Second World War. With each successive census, American Indians seem to double in numbers. American blacks, whose subjugation was, if not genocidal, certainly brutal, are also increasing in numbers. The same figures can be marshalled for Armenians, Ugandans, and Vietnamese (1980:xv).

Both Arendt's reference to natality and Horowitz's to repopulation are like small candles in a terrible darkness. We still must ask ourselves what the world would be like now had the individuals murdered by states in the last hundred years or so been allowed to live in peace, if death had not conquered, if survivors had not been shamed, if entire cultures had not been brutalized and communities destroyed, if "radical evil," as Arendt called it, had not been invented.

The original edition of *Genocide* began with a quote from Elie Wiesel's *Messengers of God*, the essence of which was to ask how different the world would be if only Cain had chosen words and not violence. Suppose he had said, "I shall not kill!" and, instead of murder, there had been "a pure and purifying gesture" of love between brothers? Or suppose train station masters in the Third Reich had simply gone on strike or bankers refused to stuff the vaults with Jewish watches? Or Christians had understood the profundity of the concept of charity? Suppose a similar resistance had occurred in the Soviet Union? But Cain did not speak and humanity began its long acquaintance with murder. Now, by the most terrible failure of imagination, we have become well versed in genocide, and, as a result, we have all lost something of our humanity. To retrieve any of it requires memory and an appreciation of justice as our common resource, which, if lost to one, is potentially lost to all. Somewhere in our remembrance, it must be possible to put faces back on faceless victims, to deny their anonymity and the anonymity of their executioners, to retreat from the political bankruptcy of a world of saints and monsters and secure that place where the individual can live freely or travel through and the truly civic environment thrives.

Boston College
Department of Sociology and Anthropology

Notes

1. At Yalta in February 1945, President Roosevelt, in a toast, said,

   In 1933 my wife visited a school in our country. In one of the classrooms she saw a map with a large blank space in it. She asked what was the blank space, and was told they were not allowed to mention the place—it was the Soviet Union. That incident was one of the reasons why I wrote to President Kalinin asking him to send a representative to Washington to discuss the opening of diplomatic relations. That is the history of our recognition of Russia. (Quoted by Winston Churchill [1953:391])

2. Whitfield cites the misuse of the term "totalitarianism" in its application to many forms of tyranny and also, by Herbert Marcuse and Norman Mailer, to American society. This misuse occurred simultaneously with a general retreat from criticism of the Soviet Union, including its past.

3. Arendt was aware of the imbalance between her two cases, yet an urgency, encouraged by Karl Jaspers, led to the publication of *Origins* in 1951 (Arendt and Jaspers, 1992: 119). She had plans to extend her writings on Stalin and Marxism (Young-Bruehl, 1982:276-79). The book was never written, although part of it, "Ideology and Terror," later became an epilogue to the second edition of *Origins* in 1958.

4. The enormous literature on everyday life in Nazi Germany published in the last ten years supports this observation. Clinging to normalcy, when nothing any longer

was normal, was a retreat from reality. For example, Claudia Koontz's *Mothers in the Fatherland* (1987) elucidates the exclusion of women from politics (and their submission to Nazi ideology) and the subsequent perversion of the family as a function of the state. Everyone from villagers to civil servants to the commanders of concentration camps found solace in domestic order. Similarly (although Arendt associated the police rather than the military with totalitarian regimes), Omer Bartov's *Hitler's Army* (1991) thoroughly documents the German foot soldier's complete acceptance of propaganda, to the extent that, especially on the Eastern Front, the enemy was routinely considered subhuman, not as an abstraction but after having been met on the battlefield, on roads, in conquered villages and towns.

5. Arendt saw solitude as distinct from loneliness and an experience necessary for philosophers within the community. She herself depended greatly on a wide circle of friends. Note the personalization of this passage in *Origins*. "What makes loneliness so unbearable is the loss of one's own self which can be realized in solitude, but confirmed in its identity only by the trusting and trustworthy company of my equals" (1973:477).

6. In a footnote (1973:278), Arendt, with typical emphasis on juridical detail, points out that Italy was reluctant to deport even antifascist refugees or deprive them of passports, even though in 1926 it had enacted laws to do so.

7. Following a conference with Russian intellectuals in Prague in 1990, Horowitz expressed his optimism about this new, younger generation of thinkers, but warned, "Democracy is not a pleasant placebo. It does not make friends easily. But it permits enemies to exist, to thrive, to multiply, to have a tomorrow. It permits a world in which enemies become friends and friends become enemies" (1991:25).

8. Arendt's thesis was on the Augustinian concept of love as having its sources in human mortality, in true being, and in the community. Karl Jaspers, in his comments on her oral defense of the thesis in 1928, said that the discussion of the first source was "absolutely clear, in every point complete and flawless," but he faulted the second part of the thesis as uneven, and the last as unfinished (Arendt and Jaspers, 1992:689–90).

9. "For the *polis* was for the Greeks, as the *res publica* was for the Romans, first of all their guarantee against the futility of individual life, the space protected against this futility and reserved for the relative permanence, if not immortality, of mortals" (Arendt, 1958:56).

10. George Steiner (1963:43) in his review said Arendt seemed to be working toward a kind of Burkean Toryism "with overtones of nostalgia for an agrarian, hierarchic society of freeholders and eloquent town councils."

11. The miracle that saves the world, the realm of human affairs, from its normal, "natural" ruin is ultimately "the fact of natality, in which the faculty of action is ontologically rooted" (Arendt, 1958:247).

References

Arendt, Hannah. *The Human Condition.* Chicago: University of Chicago Press, 1958.
———. *On Revolution.* New York: Viking Press, 1963a.
———. *Eichmann in Jerusalem: A Report on the Banality of Evil.* New York: The Viking Press, 1963b.
———. *The Origins of Totalitarianism.* New York: Harcourt, Brace & World, 1966.

————. *The Origins of Totalitarianism*, 5th ed. New York: Harcourt Brace Jovanovich, 1973.

Arendt, Hannah, and Karl Jaspers. *Hannah Arendt Karl Jaspers Correspondence 1926–1969*, ed. Lotte Kohler and Hans Saner, trans. Robert and Rita Kimber. New York: Harcourt Brace Jovanovich, 1992.

Bartov, Omer. *Hitler's Army Soldiers, Nazis, and War in the Third Reich*. New York: Oxford University Press, 1991.

Benjamin, Walter. *Reflections Essays, Aphorisms, Autobiographical Writings*, ed. Peter Demetz. New York: Schocken Books, 1978.

Butz, Alfred. *The Hoax of the Twentieth Century*. Torrance, CA: Noontide Press, 1976.

Canovan, Margaret. *The Political Thought of Hannah Arendt*. New York: Harcourt Brace Jovanovich, 1974.

Churchill, Winston. *The Second World War, Vol. 6: Triumph and Tragedy*. Boston: Houghton Mifflin, 1953.

Hill, Melvyn A., editor. *The Recovery of the Public World*. New York: St. Martin's Press, 1979.

Horowitz, Irving Louis. "Review of *On Revolution*." *The American Journal of Sociology* 69, no.4 (1964): 419–21.

————. *War and Peace in Contemporary Social and Political Theory*, 2d ed. Atlantic Highlands, NJ: Humanities Publishers, 1973.

————. *Genocide State Power and Mass Murder* New Brunswick, NJ: Transaction Publishers, 1976.

————. *Taking Lives: Genocide and State Power*. New Brunswick, NJ: Transaction Publishers, 1980.

————. "The New Generation of Soviet Intellectuals." *Freedom Review* 22, no. 2 (1991): 22–25.

Koontz, Claudia. *Mothers in the Fatherland Women, the Family, and Nazi Politics*. New York: St. Martin's Press, 1987.

Nietzsche, Friedrich. "On the Uses and Disadvantages of History for Life." In *Untimely Meditations*, trans. R. J. Hollingdale, 59–123. Cambridge: Cambridge University Press, 1983.

Steiner, George. "Lafayette, Where Are We?" *Reporter* 37 (9 May 1963): 42–43.

Whitfield, Stephen J. *Into the Dark: Hannah Arendt and Totalitarianism*. Philadelphia: Temple University Press, 1980.

Young-Bruehl, Elisabeth. *Hannah Arendt for Love of the World*. New Haven, CT: Yale University Press, 1982.

4

Communication, Community, and Sociology

Abraham Edel

"Community" is probably derived from the Latin stem "com" (the Latin word "cum" means *with*) and "munis," fortifications or walls. A community is thus a group of people living within the same walled city. Every state, Aristotle tells us at the beginning of his *Politics,* is a community and every community is established with a view to some good. Much of his discussion deals concretely with the kinds of goods different communities aim at and how this depends on material resources available. He has in mind, of course, the city-state, not the global community; a good community should be small enough such that the voice of the crier can be heard from one end of the city to the other. Today, with varied modes of travel, and with radio, television, and computer devices as modes of communication, a global crier is possible, and, thus, so is a single community of the world forged by communication. It would not even matter what language the crier used, given the feasibility of concurrent translation today. Language, though an essential component of communication, is no longer a source of serious obstacles.

The worldwide spread of communication has not lessened the power of the audience. The simplest case is getting a letter in the mails. It may reach you quickly or slowly, but it is up to you whether you open it or throw it away unopened, as many do with advertisements. The same applies for radio and television: you can turn it on or not, and you can certainly turn off any given program. Even in listening or watching, it does not follow that what is advertised will be bought; advertising may be watched as an amusement. To know who gets affected, and how, requires a whole communications research industry, which nowadays

77

systematically investigates reading and listening habits. No uniformity in these habits can be taken for granted. What people watch depends on their interests, whether in music, nature programs, or situation comedies. How far programs follow the lines of popular interest, how far they help fashion interests, is a further problem of communication.

What have been the effects of these developments on democracy and its institutions on science, on economic and political life, on intellectual life? For example, scientists, however they work, require a knowledge of what advances are made throughout the whole world; there is no point in looking for what already has been found out. Where such communication is blocked for economic or political purposes science is the loser. Communication advances have thus made possible a world community of science.

Paradoxically, economic activity, although usually competitive among countries, is now forced into global relations. Technological requirements in raw materials as well as scientific knowledge in the earlier part of the century led to competition and even wars. For example, World War I began in part over the struggle between Germany and France for coal and iron; and later the discovery of oil in the Middle East contributed to the rivalries out of which World War II arose. Here scientific advance may diminish conflict by showing the possible development of atomic power or other universally available materials. This, however, may precipitate a race for developing atomic power with the aim of subduing a rival country by threat of complete destruction. These developments and the new technologies offer rich fresh opportunities for the publishing profession. It can take for granted a worldwide potential audience. But, as an economic activity, it is carried on from one country centrally or else from different countries separately. In either case it is entangled in the economic situation of particular localities. It can achieve success only to the extent that there is economic and financial stability and peace in the country or countries in which it publishes and sells. How the success is attained may also vary. For example, the U.S. government has at times subsidized American publishers for their foreign exports, selecting on grounds of foreign policy which publishers to support. This has involved ideological elements in selecting the materials (books, journals, newspapers) whose content or policies it has found congenial, for example, in the cold war situation of the 1950s. Such support is thus in the same position as foreign aid generally.

We turn now to the linguistic aspect of the global community. Whatever its economic and political base and whether carried by carrier pigeon between warships (such as during World War I, since telegraph and telephone could be caught by the enemy) or by drum or fire signals in African societies, it uses one or another language. And there is tremendous variety in the languages a person will know and the uses of those languages under existent conditions in his or her country. For example, in the earlier part of the century a German intellectual would probably understand (or even speak) French or Russian, certainly English. A Yugoslavian might understand all three. Political attitudes might, however, hinder communication. Starting early after World War II— and continuing as late as 1960—a Yugoslavian would often not answer a question in German, perhaps assuming that the questioner was German, but would readily respond even in broken French. Anti-German attitudes did not die easily in Yugoslavia, many of whose men and women had fought the Nazi invaders. Again, in the early years, a Rumanian intellectual might know several languages, including French, German, Russian, Hungarian, Czech, and Polish. By contrast, Americans were learning in their schools chiefly French. German had been boycotted during World War I. After World War II, however, the whole world opened up, and different American groups, with scientific or economic motivation or a desire to travel, studied languages of the Pacific Rim and Pacific Islands as well. The schools now added Spanish, with an eye on the Latin American trade as well as the problems of Spanish-speaking immigrants in the United States. And the Korean and Vietnam wars compelled some knowledge of those countries.

How complex the situation is can be illustrated by the spread of the English language in the second half of the century. Partly as a consequence of American expansion after World War II, and partly due to the previous expansion and colonization by the British empire, English became a lingua franca in the Middle East and the Pacific Islands, just as French had been in north Africa, Belgian in the Congo, and English in India. The diverse dialects, even in one country such as India, had been another reason for a supervening or secondary language, since the speakers of one dialect often did not understand the speakers of another. The need for a lingua franca had been shown in the Pacific by the phenomenon of "Pidgin English"—a limited vocabulary with a truncated syntax—that had grown up in trade between the various countries and islands.

What the future holds for a world language we cannot predict. Nor, for that matter, can a single nation with a desire to establish a language of its own be sure of success. For example, the attempt of Jews who spoke Yiddish to revive Hebrew proved successful—indeed Hebrew now flourishes in Israel—while Yiddish is gradually dying out throughout the world. Interestingly, the Jews in the diaspora remained in some sense a community, even while scattered all over the world. On the other hand, the attempt of the Irish in Ireland to revive Gaelic hangs thus far in the balance. In Belgium the rivalry of French and Flemish has divided the country into two linguistic areas; in fact, the University of Louvain has split into two campuses. In Canada, Quebec has compelled the use of French for all governmental purposes (including street signs); only the threat of moving to Ontario prevented the Quebec government from imposing French as the language of instruction on English-speaking McGill University. Such nationalistic efforts have spread to the large Indian and Eskimo groups in northern Quebec and Ontario, leading at times to armed conflict. Similar problems have beset the United States on native Indian territories, and on the West coast of both the United States and Canada where there has been a large migration from the Pacific Rim.

Indeed, while English is the primary language of the United States, in select urban areas, English speakers are now only 40 percent of the population. In the area of Los Angeles, as evidenced in the schools, there are today more than thirty or forty languages in use among the students. In California universities—particularly at Stanford and Berkeley—controversy has been strong about whether literature course requirements should consist of major Western writers (Shakespeare or the Bible for example) or whether students should have the option of focusing on, say, Indian or Chinese classics. Perhaps the test for the most desirable college requirements would be whether they *expanded* the individual's knowledge. A second criterion for decision would obviously be the field of intended work for the student. In the first half of the century, French and German were commonly required for the doctorate in the fields of chemistry and mathematics. In philosophy, Latin or Greek might be substituted if the student's doctoral dissertation was in the area and he or she did not know the language. (For example, a student might be required to learn Latin to do a thesis on Aquinas.) How complex such decisions may be, even within the history of one language, was evidenced on one occasion in Athens, where students went on strike for the right to read Homer "in translation."

Obviously, deciding on desirable or required learning of language is a function of what kind of life and social relations are envisaged for the country. The late Senator Hayakawa organized a movement to require the early use of English in the schools. Thus, in the Los Angeles area even where children (especially of recent immigrants) might only have spoken Spanish, teaching would be carried on in English after the second grade. This gave them two years to learn English. Such requirements show that the United States is obviously regarded as an English-speaking community. This was not the only context in which such a problem had arisen. In Pennsylvania there was, in the colonial period, the possibility that the state would become a German-speaking territory. When in the nineteenth century legislation required the use of English in schools, the Menonites, a large German-speaking religious sect, simply moved to the South, and thereafter to Brazil. Obviously English has had to struggle to remain dominant, and it is a continuous struggle.

In contemporary humanities there has been some concern over the relation of language and thought, in a special sense. Speech and reading entail one person understanding what another person has said or written. It is thus the personal aspect in communication that is the focus of attention. Some, starting from the issues of translation and believing the difficulties insurmountable, have even challenged the possibilities of interpersonal communication. For example, one group of literary critics, developing so-called "reception theory," have argued that later generations cannot understand the writings of earlier generations because they read them in altered social contexts. Quite literally, we cannot understand *Othello* because we interpret Othello's reactions in terms of the twentieth-century problems of blacks. Nor can we understand *The Merchant of Venice* because the picture of Shylock rests on seventeenth-century views of the Jews. Indeed, English audiences of Shakespeare's time could not know Jews because they were banned from England. Even in twentieth-century America, the second half of the century can hardly understand the first half. For example, "ghetto" in the first half referred largely to the still prevalent segregation, formally or in an informal but quite rigid social way, of the Jewish community. In the second half of the century, after World War II, if the concept survived, it referred to black areas of a city.

Other theorists have dealt with individual-to-individual aspects of communication. Again, it is the recipient to whom attention is paid. Presumably the speaker or writer knows what he or she is trying to say. But their ideas and beliefs, feelings and attitudes area always rich, reflecting the complex experiences of the person's past. The recipient's interpretation is construed in terms of his or her own feelings. Interpersonal relations are, it has been said, like two people trying to shake hands in the dark. This outcome has led some philosophers, particularly in the pragmatic tradition, to stress the importance of the social approach to language, and the socio-historical character of meaning and interpretation, and to regard the individual interpretation as derivative. Much the same conclusions as were reached earlier in the case of science and the scientist are taken to hold for the individual and the interpersonal.

We move now to problems of content in communication. On the American scene the most prominent have been questions of censorship and pornography. Here journals and magazines often have to make difficult decisions. Federal law has, on the whole, eased the difficulty through court decisions in favor of free speech and the press. But a particular magazine—such as *Society*—has to decide what it will accept or tolerate in theme and language within the broad scope of federal permission—in language, in pictorial representation, and in content.

On the whole, so far as I can see, Irving Louis Horowitz's policy as editor in chief has followed a path of moderation with respect to content. In the early days of the magazine, when issues of democracy versus fascism and communism were more critical, the magazine followed the familiar liberal solution (whether in editorial or acceptance of articles) of printing articles that favored American democracy against the Soviet Union, but also articles that posed a socialist solution for American socioeconomic problems. On one occasion, I recall, he printed an editorial against a position taken by the Moonies, and offered them space for a reply. They replied by threatening to sue the *Society* for use of a quotation from them without permission. The issue was compromised by a per-line payment for the material quoted! I do not recall whether there were any problems raised by verbal, nonpictorial material that might be construed as pornographic. Again, the interpretation of social theory has been broad, spanning not only the social sciences and history but occasionally philosophical theory as well, particularly problems of social morality. This range has been evident in books reviewed as well as in articles.

In many respects *Society* is unique among American publications. It is not a journal of opinion, as for example *The New Republic, The Na-*

tion, Commonweal, and *Mother Jones* are in frankly embodying a specific social value position. Nor does it occupy a specific point of conservatism or liberalism on the political spectrum, as does the *New York Times* or the *Washington Post.* By its very nature as a social science periodical it can treat all these value issues in the content of its articles. Its own values are seen in the range and scope of its materials and in occasional editorials. It does not shun value judgment.

By its character in these respects *Society* has won worldwide acceptance, and is now found in translation in many European and Asian countries. In part this is doubtless due to the pro attitude toward America found in many parts of the globe, but in part its quality doubtless contributes to the forming of that attitude.

Horowitz's own writings present an interesting array. They seem to me to fall into three periods. In the first, when he was a student of philosophy, he turned particularly to social philosophy. This is where *The Idea of War and Peace in Contemporary Philosophy* (1957) is found. He argued at that time that war and peace, so prominent in human life, must surely have found their way into philosophical writing, and he set his task as gathering the variety of views. In his subsequent graduate work he studied individual philosophers who played an active role in social affairs: Bruno (1952), Helvetius (1954), Sorel (1961). Soon he moved to analysis of the social scene itself: *Revolution in Brazil* (1964), *Masses in Latin America* (1970), *Latin American Radicalism* (1969). He examined several times the changing scene in Cuba (e.g., 1977). At the same time as he studied social practice—for example, military movements in the Third World (1982)—he paid attention to social theory (*Foundations of Political Sociology,* 1972; *Dialogues on American Politics,* 1978).

A particularly important period is described in *The Rise and Fall of Project Camelot* (1967). Here he had learned of the projected formation of a U.S. Army group in South America, under various excuses, intended to constitute a permanent military presence. He forced the War Department to provide public information by telling them of his intention to publish the partial (and possibly partly incorrect) information he had. The effect was that they abandoned the project. The episode about the Moonies recounted earlier belongs to the same period.

Further, it was clear that any examination of a movement involves its theory, and the account of its theory involves a conception of social theory (e.g., the study of C. Wright Mills, 1964, 1983), types of ideology even among social scientists themselves (e.g., *Sociological Self-Images*, 1969; *Science, Sin, and Scholarship*, 1978). At times his writing becomes self-probing, where the self is our social self (pre-eminently in the work on genocide, 1976; *The Use and Abuse of Social Science*, 1971).

I have known Irving Louis Horowitz since his college days; our personal contact has been continual in conversation and correspondence. The only part of his life I did not know was his childhood, and this I learned from his moving reflections in *Daydreams and Nightmares* (1990). It is a very special pleasure to write in this festschrift.

University of Pennsylvania
Department of Philosophy

References

Horowitz, Irving Louis. *The Renaissance Philosophy of Giordano Bruno*. Boston: Coleman-Ross Publishers, 1952.
———. *Claude Helvetius: Philosopher of Democracy and Enlightenment*. Paine-Whitman Publishers, 1954.
———. *The Idea of War and Peace in Contemprary Philosophy*, 2d ed. London and New York: Humanities Press, 1957, 1973.
———. *Radicalism and the Revolt against Reason: The Social Theories of Georges Sorel*. London and New York: Routledge & Kegan Paul Ltd., 1961.
———, ed. *The New Sociology: Essays in Social Science and Social Values in Honor of C. Wright Mills*. New York and London, Oxford University Press, 1964.
———. *Revolution in Brazil: Politics and Society in a Developing Nation*. New York: E.P. Dutton Publishers, 1964.
———, ed. *The Rise and Fall of Project Camelot*. Cambridge: Massachusetts Institute of Technology Press, 1967.
———, ed. *Sociological Self-Images*. Beverly Hills: Sage Publishers, 1969, and Oxford: Pergamon Press Ltd, 1970.
———, ed. *Masses in Latin America*. New York and London: Oxford University Press, 1970.
———, ed. *The Use and Abuse of Social Science*. New Brunswick, NJ: Transaction Publishers, 1971.
———. *Foundations of Political Sociology*. New York: Harper & Row, 1972.
———. *Genocide: State Power and Mass Murder*. New Brunswick, NJ: Transaction Publishers, 1976.
———. *Cuban Communism*, 3d ed. New Brunswick, NJ: Transaction Publishers, 1977.
———. *Dialogues on American Politics* (with Seymour Martin Lipset). New York and London: Oxford University Press, 1978.
———, ed. *Science, Sin and Scholarship*. Boston and London: Massachusetts Institute of Technology Press, 1978.
———. *Beyond Empire and Revolution: Militarization and Consolidation in the Third World*. New York and London: Oxford University Press, 1982.

————. *C. Wright Mills: An American Utopian.* New York: Macmillan Publishers/ The Free Press, and London: Collier/Macmillan, 1983.

————. *Cuban Communism,* 7th ed New Brunswick, NJ and London: Transaction Publishers, 1989.

————. *Daydreams and Nightmares.* Jackson: University Press of Mississippi, 1990.

Horowitz, Irving Louis, Josue de Castro, and John Gerassi, eds. *Latin American Radicalism.* New York: Random House and London: Jonathan Cape Ltd., 1969.

Section Two

The Sociology of Politics

5

Democracy as a Coalition of Cultures

Aaron Wildavsky

The shortest definition of democracy I can think of is willingness to leave office when defeated at the polls. Even shorter as a criterion of the existence of democracy is alternation of political parties in office. All models of democracy include competition for office based on civil liberties and fundamental freedoms. Beyond, that, however, they differ according to the major criterion used to assess the degree to which there can be said to be democracy. In contemporary discourse, both among political theorists and political activists, the basic split is between those who view democracy as a process, a self-organizing system, that enables individuals to carry out their plans, and those who view it as having a substantive purpose.[1]

When I grew up in the 1940s and 1950s, the line on democracy was pretty clear: because the American people (or, at least, those powerful and liberty-loving elites) agreed on the processes of democracy, unlike those forever petulant, quarrelsome, and, worse, ideological Europeans, we lucky ones could afford to disagree on what might otherwise be divisive policies. No more. Now there are demands that greater equality of condition be achieved before the processes of democracy are legitimated. Recall the cry of civil rights leaders that the needs of their constituencies be met before they would listen to the pros and cons of the Persian Gulf War. Listen to the voices stating that support for equal opportunity is a code word for racism (cf. the literature on symbolic racism). Or the accusation (which I heard over public radio and "CBS News" before I stopped counting) that opposition to hiring quotas by race and gender is

a cover for racism and, if possible, worse, Nazism in the guise of one
David Duke.

Cultures and Competition

Everyone agrees that, in democracies, citizens, as Robert Dahl wrote
in his seminal *Preface to Democratic Theory,* have to be able to gather
information and switch their support away. Thus, there also has to be a
range of choice available to them. Let us call this individualist democracy in which citizens bring government in line with their preferences
by (a) voting parties in or out, and thus (b) encouraging parties to compete for their votes.

Friedrich Hayek adds a criterion of neutrality of decision rules so that
legislation may not take from some groups to give to others. He is em-
phatic in stating that the rules are there to enable individuals to organize
themselves, not to give advantage to some over others.[2] His is the ultimate individualist position.[3] Opposition to individualist democracy comes
not from those who would reject it—all supporters of democracy agree
that these are necessary conditions—but from those who believe it is
insufficient. They call for much more widespread participation, from
activity in localities to voluntary organizations to interest groups to direct action. Let us call this egalitarian democracy. Its purpose is to form
governments that will pursue redistributive policies and to inform citizens who will exert influences on government. Their concern is about
the private inequalities brought into public politics. The gains they expect from egalitarian democracy range from greater governmental responsiveness to the worst off elements in society to inculcation of
democratic norms into citizens who learn to appreciate democracy by
practicing and extending it to many other spheres of life. The accusations leveled against proponents of egalitarian democracy—politicization
of what their opponents think of nonpolitical subjects—is due to the
egalitarian expansion of the political; all relationships that create or
maintain inequality, in their view, are power-laden, because of their conviction that all spheres of life impinge on the public sphere.[4] What is
properly deemed political, to be sure, not a pre-existing entity, but is
constructed through social conflict. Individualists counter with the explanation that egalitarians are looking in the wrong place; democracy
involving large numbers of people should not be sought inside organiza-

tions but outside in the competition between them. Economist Joseph Schumpeter made this view famous in his *Capitalism, Socialism and Democracy* by making democracy into a procedure. "The democratic method," he advised, "is that institutional arrangement for arriving at political decisions in which individuals acquire the power to decide by means of a competitive struggle for the people's vote."[5]

Though praising this procedural approach, which leads to a definition in which "[d]emocracy is a by-product of a competitive method of leadership recruitment," Giovanni Sartori, in his major work on democratic theory, is not entirely happy.[6] While he regards the view that *"competitive elections produce democracy"* as an accurate description, he declares that "[t]his is not, let it be stressed, an optimal state of affairs."[7] Why? "What makes democracy *possible*," Sartori replies, "should not be mixed up with what makes democracy *more democratic*."[8] Yet if more participation is in and of itself better than less, what is wrong with establishing the more egalitarian participatory democracy as the ideal toward which all who desire democracy should strive?[9]

The answers Sartori and others before him give is that the ideal of equal power is more appropriate for small governments where face-to-face relationships and relatively simple affairs lend themselves to participation in person rather than to large societies where the representative, not the in-person, method is the only feasible way.[10] How, Sartori raises the question rhetorically, can democracy as competition maintain itself "in the face of value pressure that evermore devalues" it? His solution, since everyone else insists on talking about equality, is to introduce it as "equality of merit" as opposed to leveling down, so that equality now means "each according to his merit,"[11] which our by-now practiced readers can see amounts to reintroducing individualist democracy in another guise. In appraising the dangers to democracy systems, Sartori does not in the future perceive risks to come from rule by minorities but rather "in loss of authority and clogged by too many demands they are unable to process."[12] Evidently, in his estimation, as well as those who worry about governmental "overload," there is too much of the wrong kind of participation and not enough of the right kind that shores up authority.[13]

The hierarchical counter to egalitarian democracy is not that it is too idealistic but that it is counterproductive, leading to worse choices and eventually to the destruction of democracy. The hierarchical model of democracy is competitive, to be sure, otherwise there could be no alternation in office, but competition with the principle of graded distinctions at the forefront. First of all, the competition is among hierarchies, so that, second of all, each victor is capable of governing. The opposition is a rival government temporarily out of office. The purpose of the election is to gain popular assent by conferring legitimacy upon governments that can govern. Popular representation, though important, is secondary to the capacity to govern. Participation is to be pluralized, channeled, deflected, so that it poses no threat to the government, except during election times, after which whoever gets in has the capacity to act. This stratified vision of participation is that, except for voting, seen as a civic duty and expression of allegiance, participation be confined to one's station in life. Those whose task it is in the division of labor ought to participate, others not.

The purpose of a stratified democracy is to preserve existing institutions. Hence, it sets out deliberately to duplicate itself in churches, schools, families, all sorts of associations, whom it co-opts by teaching its own sense of who is fit to rule—people of traditional (hierarchic) sensibilities, people who keep the well-known but not publicly advertised secret that institutions and their leaders are far from perfect.[14] That is why Sartori objects to the notion that "democracy seemingly demands transparence, that the house of power be a house of glass."[15] This is also Ralf Dahrendorf's position: "I submit that the permanent participation of all in everything is in fact a definition of total immobility...it would mean...permanent practical inaction."[16] Now if you were an egalitarian who believed that your governmental system was immoral because its hierarchies were coercive and its individualism was grossly inegalitarian, exposing its sins to public view might seem more desirable.

Openness comports as well with the common accusation made by egalitarians against corporate capitalism—that its operatives plot in secret to harm the health of the public by exposing them to toxic substances in order to make money.[17] To hierarchical supporters of democracy, however, weakening and delegitimizing government is anathema because they have institutions they wish to defend. Individualists would object to the hyper-regulation imposed by egalitarians.

Members of an inclusive hierarchy would favor something like Arendt Lijphart's model of consociational democracy characterized by endless bargaining, mutual vetoes, quotas by religion, race, language, and other deeply felt distinctions, to keep these diverse peoples together.[18] The exclusive hierarchy is incompatible with democracy because it will not accept the results of competition. Let us take a closer look at the cultural conditions for willingness to leave office so as to allow opposition parties and personnel to govern.

Reconciling Support and Opposition through Competition

If willingness to leave office is a key to democracy, then the idea and the practices of a "loyal opposition" are crucial. On one side, the government is loyal to the opposition by its willingness to leave office; on the other side, the opposition is loyal to the government by waging its electoral campaign peacefully and by signaling its willingness to concede if it loses. The two loyalties work together in what is hopefully a cycle of mutual reassurance. When party activists and other elites are disloyal to the idea of opposition, democracy often dies.[19]

On the sensible grounds that it is the existence of a legal opposition that distinguishes democracy from dictatorship, Robert Dahl investigated patterns of opposition. He finds that "[t]here is no single prevailing pattern of opposition in Western democracies."[20] Political parties and groups opposed to the government in power share neither goals, strategies, organization, nor competitiveness. Neither two-party nor multiparty systems seem more advantageous for the development of democracy. In some democratic nations it is easy to distinguish government from opposition, in others it is not.[21] Nor are there evident social or economic features they share in common.[22]

Yet it appears that the ten nations Dahl and his colleagues studied revealed "Widely Shared Cultural Premises." In system I, people are pragmatic, cooperative, allegiant, and trustful. Under system II, people are uncooperative, mistrustful, and alienated. From such characteristics, "[i]t seems reasonable," to Dahl, "to think that in the first system the opposition would wish to maintain the existing regime, stick to the prevailing rules for getting in and out of office, and make mostly marginal changes in policy. Those in the second system would behave quite differently, being quite ready to destabilize the existing regime, altering the rules of the game even if this will help achieve their policy objectives."[23] This is plausible; the trouble is that it is very close to the phenomena we wish to explain, namely, why some countries develop behaviors supportive of democracy conceived as alternation in office and others do not.

My suggestion is that the political cultural aspects of democracy be conceived in a different, albeit quite traditional, way. Stable democracy requires a willingness to *support authority;* a willingness to *oppose authority;* and a willingness to accept *alternation in office.* The principles are support, opposition, and competition.

More than one writer has observed that this compaction of opposites is difficult to reconcile. How might these evidently disparate qualities be reconciled and, more than that, be made to serve one another? The obvious solution is to have sufficient belief in competition to encourage leaving office, sufficient criticism to keep government responsive, and sufficient support to keep government going. All three active cultures, then, are essential to democracy. But in what proportions?

In a follow-up to his famous 1959 article, "Some Social Requisites of Democracy: Economic Development and Political Legitimacy," in which he argued that economic development and democracy were mutually reinforcing,[24] Seymour Lipset and his colleagues, adding new variables (like being a former British colony) and more countries, strengthened the old conclusions.[25] Cultural theory, I claim, can add something to the explanation. From a cultural perspective, market economics, polyarchic democracies, and science are essentially the same phenomena because they are based on competitive individualism. The more of one, therefore, the more of the others. The eleven communist command economies, as they were in 1980, had half of the world's scientists and engineers but only 2 percent of the world's patents. The more individualism, the political conclusion would be, the more polyarchy. However, if individualism were dominant over long periods, many citizens might become fatalists, unable to found networks of their own, so that competition would likely give way to some form of control. I conclude that without significant elements of egalitarianism to challenge inequality, without hierarchy to inculcate the norm that the parts should sacrifice for the whole, and without individualism to legitimize accepting the results of competitive elections, democracy is doubtful.

In moderation, egalitarianism is a tonic or, perhaps better, an astringent for the establishment cultures. Just as a balance between passivity and involvement is necessary for democracy, so is a blend of allegiance ("my country right or wrong") and skepticism ("question authority") healthy for democracy. A willingness to oppose authority is as essential as a willingness to support authority. Egalitarianism punctures authority's pomposity. It criticizes the establishment's connivances, exposing its hypocrisies and cover-ups. The incessant criticism of authority prevents governmental power from growing arrogant or domineering. Moreover, since there is always the danger that egalitarianism may grow by recruiting fatalists, the establishment has an added incentive to placate minorities to keep down discontent. The practices that we today identify as free societies—the rule of law, alternation in office, and the right to criticize—are a product of the interpenetration of hierarchy, individualism, and egalitarianism. The relationship of each of the cultures to democracy is curvilinear: Paracelsus's dictum, "The poison is the dose," applies to the body politic as well.

A considerable body of opinion among political scientists holds that democracy is safe as long as elites do most of the governing and they believe firmly in procedures facilitating competition, more firmly than do the general citizenry. A dash of cold water has been thrown on the elites-save-civil rights syndrome by Paul Sniderman and his colleagues who focus not on elite versus citizen but on rival elites. Studying these relationships in Canada and the United States, they conclude that "differences among elites in support for civil liberties eclipse, both in size and political significance, differences between elites and citizens."[26] From a cultural perspective, we would expect hierarchists to favor governmental intervention to protect society against what they perceive to be social deviance in personal behavior.[27] Egalitarians, according to cultural theory, are more likely to favor restricting speech and assembly they perceive to be anti-egalitarian, anti-minority, anti-women, anti-gay, etc. New speech codes on university campuses, for instance, are not directed against vulgarity but against speech believed to harm students in protected categories.

The idea that the balance between cultures is as important as the content in explaining democratic success has been most fully developed by Harry Eckstein in his classic *Theory of Stable Democracy*. He argues that democracy requires authority that "contains a balance of disparate elements." Like Almond and Verba, he points to Britain as an exemplar case that combines, among other things, popular participation, governing by elites, and the rule of law. Testing this theory, Eckstein concludes, requires "a much better set of categories for classifying authority patterns that we now possess." Such categories, he continues, "ought to be applicable to any kind of authority pattern not just to government."[28]

No one will be surprised to learn that I think that the categories of cultural theory fill the bill. They are built around authority relationships—subordination, equality, bargaining, coping—yet are sufficiently general to be applied in or out of government. By showing that all ways of seeing are biased, cultural theory provides an explanation for why balanced democracies do better. Excluding cultural biases, we can now see, weakens democracy by enlarging its blindspots.

University of California, Berkeley
Department of Political Science

Notes

1. This is usually done by defining equal opportunity not as the right to compete but as substantial equality of resources with which to compete. See, for instance, Robert A. Dahl's recent *Democracy and Its Critics* (New Haven, CT: Yale University Press, 1989):

    The criteria specify that citizens or the demos ought to have adequate and equal *opportunities* to act in certain ways. I can readily imagine two objections to this formulation. First, it might be said that "equal opportunities" can be reduced to nothing more than formal or legal requirements that ignore important differences—in resources, for example. Suppose Citizen P is poor and Citizen R is rich. Then (the argument might go) both P and R may have "equal opportunities" to participate in collective decisions, in the sense that both are legally entitled to do so. Yet because R has far greater access to money, information, publicity, organizations, time, and other political resources than P, not only will R probably participate more than P, but R's influence on decisions will vastly outweigh P's.

    The objection draws its force from the familiar fact that influence is a function of resources, and typically resources are unequally distributed. Nonetheless, it misses the point. For "equal opportunities" means "equal opportunities," and what the example shows is that R's and P's opportunities to participate are decidedly unequal. Though the idea of equal opportunity is often so weakly interpreted that it is rightly dismissed as too undemanding, when it is taken in its fullest sense it is extraordinarily demanding—so demanding, indeed, that the criteria for the democratic process would require a people committed to it to institute measures well beyond those that even the most democratic states have hitherto brought about. (114–15)

    Strong equality, in short, is equality of condition. See also Benjamin Barber, *Strong Democracy* (Berkeley: University of California Press, 1984); Gus diZerega, "Democracy as a Spontaneous Order," *Critical Review* (Spring 1989), 206–40; and Irving Louis Horowitz, "Unlimited Equality and Limited Growth," in *Winners and Losers* (Durham, NC: Duke University Press, 1984).

2. Friedrich Hayek, *Individualism and Economic Order* (University of Chicago Press, 1948); idem, *Rules and Order* (University of Chicago Press, 1973); idem, *The Political Order of a Free People* (University of Chicago Press, 1979).

3. See Augustus diZerega, "Equality, Self-Government and Democracy: A Critique of Dahl's Political Equality," *Western Political Quarterly* 41, no. 3 (September 1988): 447–68; and idem, "Elites and Democratic Theory: Insights from the Self-Organizing Model," *Review of Politics* (Spring 1991): 340–72, for a critique of Dahl's theorizing about democracy from the standpoint of an advocate of self-organizing systems.

4. For an excellent expression of this view, see Barber, *Strong Democracy*. I do not use his vocabulary because of the implication that other forms of democracy are "weak."

5. Joseph Schumpeter, *Capitalism, Socialism and Democracy,* 2d ed. (New York: Harper and Brothers, 1947), 269.

6. Giovanni Sartori, *The Theory of Democracy Revisited. Part I: The Contemporary Debate* (Chatham, NJ: Chatham House, 1987), 152.

7. Ibid., 152, 151, emphasis in original.

8. Ibid., 156.

9. Ibid., 169 and prior pages.

10. Ibid., "Vertical Democracy," chap. 6, pp. 131–81.

11. Ibid., 168–69.

12. Ibid., 170.

13. See Joseph White and Aaron Wildavsky, "Public Authority and the Public Interest: What the 1980s Budget Battles Tell Us about the American State," *Journal of Theoretical Politics* 1, no. 1 (January 1988): 7–31.

14. For a well-developed example of hierarchy in the United States, see Daniel Walker Howe's superb *The Political Culture of the American Whigs* (Chicago: University of Chicago Press, 1979). Supremely conscious of what they were doing and why, the denizens of the Whig party sought to inculcate obedience in children (taught to bow to their parents) so as to create a deferential citizenry. With the population at large, they never succeeded.

15. Sartori, *Theory of Democracy Revisited,* 144.

16. Ralf Dahrendorf, "Citizenship and Beyond: The Social Dynamics of an Idea," *Social Research* (Winter 1974): 691–92; quoted by Sartori, *Theory of Democracy Revisited,* 246.

17. See Aaron Wildavsky, "On the Social Construction of Distinctions: Risk, Rape, Public Goods, and Altruism," in *Toward a Scientific Understanding of Values,* ed. Michael Hechter, Lynn A. Cooper, and Lynn Nadel (Stanford, CA: Stanford University Press for Russell Sage Foundation, forthcoming).

18. Arendt A. Lijphart, *Democracy in Plural Societies* (New Haven, CT: Yale University Press, 1977); idem, *Democracies: Patterns of Majoritarian and Consensus Government in Twenty-One Countries* (New Haven, CT: Yale University Press, 1984).

19. See Juan J. Linz and Alfred Stepan, eds., *The Breakdown of Democratic Regimes* (Baltimore: Johns Hopkins University Press, 1978); John Higley and Michael G. Burton, "The Elite Variable in Democratic Transitions and Breakdowns," *American Sociological Review* 54 (February 1989).

20. Robert A. Dahl, *Political Oppositions in Western Democracies* (New Haven, CT: Yale University Press, 1966), 332.

21. Ibid., 335.

22. Ibid., 368-70.
23. Ibid., 352-56.
24. *American Political Science Review* 53 (1959): 69-105.
25. Seymour Martin Lipset, Ryoung-Ryung Seone, and John Charles Torres, "Comparative Analysis of the Social Requisites of Democracy," Typescript, 1991.
26. Paul M. Sniderman, Joseph F. Fletcher, Peter H. Russell, Philip E. Tetlock, and Brian J. Gaines, "The Fallacy of Democratic Elitism: Elite Competition and Commitment to Civil Liberties," *British Journal of Political Science* 21 (forthcoming): 349-70, quote on p. 349.
27. Confirmed in ibid. See also Karl Dake and Aaron Wildavsky, "Theories of Risk Perception: Who Fears What and Why," *Daedalus* 119, no. 4 (Fall 1990): 41-60.
28. Harry Eckstein, *A Theory of Stable Democracy,* monograph originally published in 1962, reprinted as an appendix to Eckstein, *Division and Cohesion in Democracy: A Study of Norway* (Princeton, NJ: Princeton University Press, 1966), Appendix B. Quotes on pp. 262-63, 284-85.

6

Politics in the West: Totalitarian and Democratic

Peter F. Drucker

Until recently, only Nazis and Stalinists spoke of "political correctness." It is indeed a purely totalitarian concept. It asserts the right of those in power to suppress all but the party line's official lies. But though the term is new in American usage, the present try to beat academia into the conformity of political correctness is not the first but the second such attempt in recent U.S. history. The first one was made by the Stalinists in the 1930s and early 1940s.

Both attempts are quite similar in their tactics: intimidation; character assassination; hounding of "resisters" and "reactionaries"; denial of discourse and of freedom of thought and of speech. Otherwise, however, in their goals, in their view of the university, of learning and of academia altogether, these two attempts are fundamentally different. But these differences are most instructive. They offer profound insights into the nature of the present attempt and into the crisis of learning that it exploits. A look back—more than fifty years back—to that all but forgotten first attempt to impose political correctness on American academia might therefore be the best way to start an analysis of the second, the present attempt—especially as I am one of the few eye witnesses of that first attempt still to be alive and still to be teaching.

I was quite young, of course—in my early thirties—when the first attempt reached its climax in the years of "Phony War" and "Blitzkrieg," that is, in the interval between the Stalin-Hitler Pact in August 1939 and Hitler's invasion of Soviet Russia not quite two years later. My main job then was not in the university but as American correspondent for a group of British newspapers. But I had started college teaching in 1939—at Sarah Lawrence College in Bronxville, outside of New York City—and my newspaper job, after all, was to study and to report on significant U.S. social and political developments, of which the communist attempt to control academia was surely one. I was thus in the middle of the action.

A Look Back

In the 1930s and early 1940s the Stalinists' main appeal to American academia—and to American intellectuals altogether—was, of course, that they claimed to oppose Hitler, and indeed to be the only ones to do so. Though it convinced many, the claim was fraudulent. Stalinist dogma actually welcomed Nazism. It was the "grave digger of Capitalism" as Stalin himself once called it, and the "final contradiction of Capitalism" that would inevitably usher in the "Revolution" and the "Classless Society" according to the "objective laws of history." But personally, Stalin also felt all along much closer to Hitler and the Nazis than he felt to the democratic West. And this was clear even in the 1930s. In my first book *The End of Economic Man*,[1] finished in 1937 (and published in the winter of 1938–39, that is, almost a full year ahead of the actual event), I had reached and published the conclusion that a Stalin-Hitler alliance was inevitable, and that, indeed, Stalin had been planning for one all along. And the same conclusion was reached about the same time (although I only learned that much later) and independently of each other, by three strategically well-placed European leaders, Heinrich Bruening, last democratic chancellor of the Weimar Republic; Kurt von Schuschnigg, last chancellor of independent Austria; and Jan Masaryk, son of Czecholovakia's founder, Czech Ambassador in London at the time of Munich, foreign minister in the first postwar government of Czechoslovakia, and murdered by the Stalinists when they established their dictatorship in Prague, in a terrorist coup in 1948. And, of course, Stalin all along was as much an anti-Semite as Hitler ever was. He might well have agreed with one of his best known spokesmen in the 1930s, the Belgian fellow traveler, Henrik de Man, who claimed, when turning quisling and arch collaborator as soon as the Germans occupied his country, that Nazism was "pure socialism only without Jews."[2]

Stalin's real enemy was the noncommunist left: social democrats, progressives, and liberals. In this he only followed Marx and Lenin. The noncommunist left was not only "insubordinate" and populated by "rebels." They, and they alone—Marx already argued in the 1870s—could slow down and perhaps even defeat the "Inevitable Revolution." For by improving the workers' lot they counteracted the "immiseration of the proletariat"—Marx's precondition for the overthrow of the "exploiters." And this is, of course, what actually happened after World War I. According to the Marxist Leninist canon, that war had to bring about the triumph of communism in the belligerent countries of the West. Socialist parties did indeed emerge after 1918 as the biggest political parties in all the Western countries. But they were *social democratic* parties, with their leaders—Friedrich Ebert in Germany, Leon Blum in France, Giacomo Matteoti in Italy, even the stridently militant Otto Bauer in Austria—uncompromisingly opposed to communism and committed to democracy.

It was then that Stalin made war against the noncommunist left the center of his theory, of his political strategy, and of his tactics. The resulting refusal of the German Communists to support the Weimar Republic, that is, to work with the noncommunist left in Germany, was surely a major factor in Nazism's triumph. There is also good reason to believe that Franco would have been defeated in the Spanish Civil War had the Communists, on Stalin's orders, not systematically killed off the men of the noncommunist left, the anarchists, social democrats, liberals, radicals. It was the Communists who brought down Leon Blum and with him the one strong socialist government in post-World War I France, thereby handing France to Laval and the appeasers, and ultimately to the Men of Vichy. But, from 1933 on, the main target of Stalin's war against noncommunists on the left and left-center was increasingly Franklin D. Roosevelt's America. Europe's social democrats were heretics who had to be *punished.* But the United States had to be *defeated.* For Stalin it was the "Evil Empire." Success of Roosevelt's America in maintaining, let alone in strengthening the civil order and moral authority of democracy—and with it of democratic capitalism—would, Stalin clearly understood, totally invalidate *all* of Marxist and communist theory. It would prove that there is nothing "inevitable" about the "collapse of Capitalism" and the coming of the "Revolution," and that, instead, democratic political order and society were viable by themselves rather than mere "superstructure" to "capitalist exploitation."

Political analysts—especially in Europe—often wondered during the 1930s why Stalin concentrated so much fire power on the United States where the Communist party was totally insignificant and even less competent. But from Stalin's point of view there was no other choice. Success of Franklin D. Roosevelt's America, he clearly thought, meant the end of communism as an effective ideology, and with it, ultimately, of communism itself—and by now we know that Stalin was right. And so, as soon as it had become clear, that is, from the end of 1933 on, that Roosevelt's America had regained social and political cohesion and had, indeed, become stronger socially and politically than it had been for long decades—despite being mired in the deepest Depression, if not because of it—Stalin made undermining America his first priority. The cold war, it was clear to some of us even then, did not begin in 1947 or 1948, with Stalin's almost successful attempt to grab power in Italy and Greece, with his establishing Communist dictatorships in Eastern Europe, with the Communist invasion of South Korea, nor with the atom bomb or the Marshall Plan. The cold war had begun in 1933.

Stalin's first target was America's black population. The black must have appeared to Stalin—as it did to most Europeans—as America's "soft underbelly." But the attempt to make America's blacks the 'vanguard of the revolution" (the slogan of those days) was a complete fiasco. However alienated and hostile to white society, black leadership had thoroughly learned the first lesson of black politics in America—the lesson that the 1990s are teaching again: blacks do not make gains in the United States unless the "establishment" (i.e., enough of the whites) supports them. By themselves they have neither the political strength nor (as Dr. Martin Luther King so forcefully pointed out) the moral strength. By 1935 the communist drive to gain control of America's blacks had failed.

Stalin then mounted a *Blitzkrieg* to gain control of the emerging mass union movement. At first he scored tremendous successes. But by 1937 a counteroffensive had been mounted, led by Sidney Hillman of New York's Amalgamated Clothing Workers, and soon supported by the emerging younger leaders such as Walter Reuther of the Automobile Workers, and—perhaps most strongly—by Phil Murray, the first head of the Steel Workers and then of the CIO (Congress of Industrial Organizations). In 1938 the unionization drive had largely succeeded. But the communists had been pushed out of the major unions and had become increasingly marginal.

It was only then that Stalin and his American henchmen—foremost among them Larry Todd, American correspondent of *Pravda* and Stalin's all but official U.S. deputy for cultural affairs—turned to academia as their target in the U.S. and as "beachhead of the revolution." The more communists and fellow travelers were losing ground in all other segments of American society (except in Hollywood where their influence continued to grow until World War II), the more did academia become important to them. It definitely was not their first choice. In Europe, for instance, neither the communists nor the Nazis had shown much interest in academia. Both were, in fact, openly contemptuous of it. They were quite sure—and subsequent events proved them right—that academia would not offer much resistance once the totalitarians were in power. But their failure in the United States to gain decisive support in any of the true power centers—as the Nazis had gained support of much of German business and of much of the German officer corps, and as the Communists had gained support (if not domination) of the unions in Italy (before Mussolini) and in France—left them little choice.

There probably never were a great many "card-carrying Communists" in American academia, if only because the Communists did not want any. They much preferred "fellow travelers"—and of those there was a substantial supply. Fellow travelers could be manipulated without exposing themselves—or the party—to publicity or to much knowledge as to what the party was after. Fellow travelers could be made to serve specific Communist causes and Communist front organizations without even suspecting who their real masters were or whose cause they served. They were thus available to form and to steer "front organizations" and to lend "bourgeois respectability" to Communist ventures. Outside of the United States, fellow travelers were almost unknown until after World War II—and even then were used in few countries except France. But in the United States, in the late 1930s and early 1940s they were ubiquitous—intellectuals, liberals, clergymen, writers and artists, newspapermen, but above all college and university professors. And for every fellow traveler in academia there were a dozen apolitical colleagues who were being sweet-talked into submission to the Communists' political correctness—by the fatuous though popular argument that, "there are no enemies on the left"; by their outrage and impotent fury about Nazism and anti-Semitism; by promises of jobs, promotions, and tenure—and in those depression days jobs in academic fields were scarce indeed, and tenure scarcer still. And if promises didn't work there were threats: resisters got fired;[3] they became the targets of systematic and unrelenting smear campaigns—often continued well into the 1950s; character assassination; whispered slander; being denounced as "fascists" or "re-actionaries" wherever they were being considered for appointment or for promotion; and having publication of their work in professional journals blocked systematically—that is, by all the same tactics of intimidation and persecution that the new politically correct groups use in today's academia.

The Stalinists were actually not a bit interested in academia itself and even less in students. No attempts were made to dictate what or how a faculty member should or should not teach. As one former fellow trav-eler—a distinguished literary critic—told me many years later: he did ask at a meeting of the "progressives" on his faculty how he might build a Marxist interpretation into his course on Dante. "We wouldn't want you to do this," he was told. "You teach your subject the way you al-ways taught it. What we want you to do is to head the Committee against Aid to Britain. And for this you better maintain your academic standing and the public's respect for your scholarship." Only after World War II, when most faculty members had, by and large, given up on communism (though not, for long years, on sympathy for Soviet Russia in a good many cases) were there serious attempts in a few places to spread communism among students. In earlier years they had been considered much too "immature." What the Stalinists were interested in were Ameri-can politics and American public opinion; academia was to them a "bully pulpit."

The Stalinists were defeated in the end. But they were not defeated by academia. There were a few courageous resisters, for example, the philosopher and lifelong social democrat, Sidney Hook. There were some equally courageous university presidents, Harry Gideonese; George Schuster, president of Hunter College in New York and then the only Catholic to head a non-Catholic college in the United States; and Robert Hutchins at the University of Chicago. But otherwise academia gave in or, at least, acquiesced. The Stalinist attempt to dominate American academia was defeated by Stalin's own acts, which, in the end, alien-ated even the most faithful and the most gullible: his purges; the pact with Hitler; his serving the Nazis slavishly until Hitler attacked him; and finally by his terror, aggression, paranoia, and faithlessness after World War II.

But precisely because it was not defeated by American academia stand-ing up for its values, its independence, and its integrity, the few years during which Stalinism exerted power had a traumatic impact. It is to a large extent responsible for the ease with which Joe McCarthy, a scant ten years later, terrorized the American university. It was from the Stalinists—and especially from the Stalinists in academia—that McCarthy learned his tactics of character assassination, of unproven and undocumented allegations, of persecution by lies, innuendos, and intimidation. And it was largely because academia had so ignominiously submitted to the Stalinists ten or fifteen years earlier that McCarthy knew that he could attack it without running much risk of its fighting back. Above all, American academia was so deeply imbued with guilty feelings for having submitted to Stalinist political correctness—and, in many cases, for having joined in denouncing, slandering, and persecuting non-Stalinist colleagues—that it cowered under McCarthy's scurrilous attacks rather than fought back, even though, as events proved soon enough, McCarthy was all bluff and just a lot of noise.

In 1927 a French writer, Julien Benda (1867–1956), published *La Trahison des Clercs* (The Treason of the Intellectuals) in which he castigated the scholars and writers who, out of cowardice, out of lust for power, or simply "to be with it," abdicated their duty, betrayed their values and joined the new barbarians of the left or the right. This, Benda warned, could only destroy the intellectuals themselves and any respect for them. The book was a best-seller when translated into English, especially in American academia. But not many heeded its warnings when political correctness came to the American campus ten years later.

A Look Forward

The most important difference between Stalinist political correctness half a century ago, and today's political correctness is in their view of academia and its position in society, of academicians, and of learning. The Stalinists had little or no interest in the university as an institution. They tried to control academicians and to use them for their political purposes. Today's political correctness is not at all interested in academicians. It ignores them as long as they keep their mouths shut. But it is making a determined effort to gain control of the institution, the university, and of higher learning altogether.

Half a century ago the university was not a power center in American society. It was still quite small, and very poor. And, of course, only a tiny minority had ever thought of attending a college, let alone actually attended one—or even thought of college for their children. No one in 1940 would have expected a GI Bill of Rights, which, a few years later, offered returning World War II veterans a free college education. Indeed, even in 1945, few people expected such a bill to have much effect—it was seen by practically everybody as pure public relations. President Truman regretted all his life that his father's bankruptcy prevented him from going to college before World War I. But even he would not have signed the GI Bill of Rights had he not been assured by all his advisers (foremost among them the then president of Harvard) that practically no one among the veterans would avail themselves of the bill's educational benefits—actually some 60 percent of all veterans did. In 1940, the university was still an "ornament." Except for professionals— doctors, lawyers, engineers—the college degree was not a "must." It did not control access to jobs and careers. On the contrary, in large parts of the country—the Midwest and the old South, especially—and in many segments of American society—manufacturing, retail, the railroads, even finance—it carried a real stigma.[4] By any yardstick, whether money, the numbers of students and faculty, or control of access to jobs and careers, colleges and universities in the America of the 1930s and early 1940s were marginal rather than central.

But while academia did not matter, individual academicians did. Prominent classicists or literature professors, philosophers, historians, anthropologists, sociologists, political scientists, psychologists, and economists were "personages," if not "celebrities." Their books were best-sellers. They were in constant demand on the lecture circuit—and in those days the lecture audiences were not, as they mostly are today, professional groups or trade associations. They were the students in the colleges and high schools, and the members of the churches, the women's clubs, the foreign affairs associations (which blossomed even in fairly small cities such as Akron, Ohio; Reading, Pennsylvania; Jackson, Mississippi; or Wichita, Kansas—to name a few for which I spoke in those days). Individual professors were constantly being interviewed by the press and appeared on the "serious" radio programs. Their names were household words. Altogether they were the "opinion leaders" of that period. And as many of them—if not more—taught at the good, undergraduate schools, such as Oberlin, Grinnell, or Mills, as at the "great" universities, such as Hazard or Chicago (which themselves, in those years, were still predominantly undergraduate institutions and had not yet turned themselves into "research universities"). Practically all of these luminaries were liberal arts people either in the humanities or in the social sciences. In fact, what gave them their visibility, their prominence, their influence was precisely that they were seen—and saw themselves—as representing the best of the great tradition. And this was, of course, the reason why the Stalinists attempted to gain control of them. They mattered because their discipline—and their disciples—mattered.

By sharp contrast, today's political correctness focuses on gaining control of the institution, the college and university. For colleges and universities have become power centers: in their control of the degree, which, in turn, controls access to jobs and careers; in their budgets, which rival those of big business; in the numbers of their students and their faculty. But academicians are dismissed by today's political correctness; they do not matter. There are almost no people in today's liberal arts faculties who are "personages." Plenty of books in the humanities and social sciences enjoy substantial sales, are widely read, and have considerable influence. But very few of these are authored by academicians—and even fewer by younger academicians. Everybody fifty years ago, for instance, who read more than the sports page, knew the names of the prominent anthropologists, sociologists, political scientists, historians, and economists. Few people today, outside the graduate economics seminar have even heard the names of today's economics Nobelists. Such professors who are likely to be known outside their own fraternity tend not to be liberal arts people but Harvard Business School faculty.

The common complaint in academia today—I have voiced it myself, I must admit—is that the new barbarians, such as the deconstructionists, the radical feminists, the gay and lesbian liberationists, are destroying the liberal arts. No, things are a good deal worse. The new barbarians triumph because the liberal arts have made themselves irrelevant. Some, academicians, of course, have become politically correct—but not too many, except in sociology perhaps, and in literature. But the great majority long ago fled their posts, long before the enemy appeared. Decades ago they abdicated their responsibility to create vision, to set standards, to give example, and to lead us out of our humdrum lives— which is what it literally means to be an educator. This is as much treason—if not more—as was *La Trahison des Clercs* in the age of the totalitarians of yesterday.

Academia itself argues that scholarship in the liberal arts never flourished more than it does today. But the task of the liberal arts is not scholarship—that is a means. The task is *leadership*—and that requires preaching and teaching. It requires making oneself heard and making oneself understood. It requires commitment, and it requires bearing witness.

It will be argued that the new barbarians in academia only reflect the condition of modern—and especially American—society. But the job of the liberal arts is not to *reflect* society. It is to hold up to it the ideal, the values, the order that ought to be—and above all, the enduring, the example of what is possible, the vision without which men perish. The liberal arts sixty and fifty years ago still did this, and in a society—and not only in the United States—that was as tortured, as distressed, as disturbed as ours, if not more so. This explains why the Stalinists thought it worth their while to gain control of them. The liberal artists today see themselves neither as leaders nor as vision makers. Nor are they seen as such. They can therefore safely be ignored by the new barbarians in their quest for power and for control over society.

Today's political correctness will not, I predict, succeed in its ultimate aim, which is to gain control of society. In fact I suspect that the backlash against it has already begun. I equally doubt that political correctness will have much impact on students. They are cynical about it and enroll in politically correct classes only because they clearly involve little work or effort. Above all, however, students are deserting the liberal arts because they are simply bored by a political correctness that has little intellectual content, or none. Disenchantment with the liberal arts may not be the only reason for the steady shift of student enrollment toward business, for instance. It may not even be a major reason. But it is surely a substantial contributor to the growing student rejection of the liberal arts as the center of their university experience and as their initiation into adulthood and citizenship.

The real danger—and it is far advanced—is that political correctness will make control of the university not worth having. Its triumph will have destroyed the university as we have known it for two hundred years, ever since Wilhelm von Humboldt, the last great figure of the European Enlightenment, designed in 1809 the first "modern" university in Berlin. Instead of the intellectual and moral center of society it may become a utility, a glorified junior high school that keeps adolescents off the street, or purely vocational. There are signs already that colleges and universities are losing esteem and support. Sixty and fifty years ago, in depression and war, university budgets were maintained better than the budgets of any other social institution and with full public support. Today university budgets are the first ones to be cut, and, politically, the easiest to cut—in the United States but also in the United Kingdom and in Germany.

Fortunately, there are signs that academia is beginning to realize the danger and is beginning to fight back, especially against the imposition of political correctness on freedom of thought and speech. But that is not nearly enough; indeed it is barely the first step. The real task is to restore the liberal arts to responsibility, to relevance, to commitment, to being "liberal" in other words. The real task is to pull them back from the obscurantism that they have embraced. To be sure, this will entail changes in substance and content. "Civilization" can surely no longer be equated with the "Western tradition" but must be restructured to include the art, wisdom, religions, and literature of the East as well. Technology surely can no longer be excluded from the humanities—it is, after all, the most specifically human activity of them all. But the biggest and the most crucial task is to call the liberal arts back to setting examples, to demonstrate and to embody values, to create vision—that is, to recall them to their responsibility to *lead.*

There is no place more appropriate to say all this than a *festschrift* that pays tribute to Irving Louis Horowitz. In his very early years he led the fight against the political correctness of the Stalinists. These last few years he has been leading the fight against the new political correctness. In his own scholarship and his own writings he exemplifies the true meaning of "liberal arts" and its commitment to create vision and responsibility. And as a publisher he has gone far to preserve the best work done in the social sciences and to make it accessible to scholars and laity alike as an enduring part of the great tradition.

Claremont Graduate School
Clarke Professor of Social Science and Management

Notes

1. Peter F. Drucker, *The End of Economic Man* (New Brunswick, NJ and London: Transaction Publishers, 1994); originally published in 1939.
2. In one of the ironies so beloved by history, his son Paul de Man began as propagandist for the Nazis only to end up as the founder of deconstructionism, which his father might have called "Lumpenproletariat Socialism."

3. As I was at Sarah Lawrence college when, in the spring of 1941, I refused—the only member of that faculty—to sign a Communist manifesto that viciously—and falsely—attacked the liberal president of Brooklyn College, Dr. Harry Gideonse—a distinguished economist and the first Jew to head an American college—who had committed two "crimes": refusing to accept a small Communist-led front organization as the sole representative of his large faculty; and calling for support of Britain when the Communist party line openly supported Hitler.

4. For an example from the early 1940s, see the chapter, "The Professional, Alfred Sloan," in my book *Adventures of a Bystander* (New Brunswick, NJ and London: Transaction Publishers, 1994); originally published in 1979.

7

Anti-Americanism: A Comparative Examination of Postwar Europe

Walter Laqueur

Anti-Americanism can be found among the left as much as on the right, in underdeveloped countries as in industrialized societies. It is perhaps a less unique phenomenon than commonly thought. It is easy to think of similar phenomena such as anti-Germanism; the British and the French not being universally popular at the height of their power in Europe, let alone in Asia and Africa; and anti-Russianism, which runs rampant in most of the former Soviet Empire, while the Russian right bitterly complains about Russophobia. Anti-Chinese attitudes are rampant in Southeast Asia and there was, of course, the "yellow peril." Small countries are likely to have fewer enemies than big ones, but this too is not always true.

Irving Horowitz has given thought to anti-Americanism specifically in one of his essays.[1] I became interested when, some eight years ago, I engaged in research resulting in a report on the political views of German youth, with particular reference to its attitude toward the United States. The subject has been of great personal interest to me, for earlier on in life I had been a student of that uniquely German phenomenon, the youth movement, which flourished from the turn of the century to Hitler's takeover in 1933. The book that ensued, *Young Germany,* was given a friendly welcome by the critics, and is, I am told, to this day the work most frequently quoted when referring to this subject.[2]

My interest in German youth was rekindled as new generations appeared on the scene, who, according to some observers, were wholly different in basic attitudes from their predecessors. This has been argued for about fifteen years, ever since the manifestations of youth protests in Europe and the United States.[3] There is, of course no denying that generations, more often than not, differ from the ones preceding them, sometimes radically. If this were not the case, the very concept "generation" would be largely irrelevant. But it is also true that total reevaluations of values, radical cultural revolutions, are exceedingly rare in the history of mankind, and that in a long-term perspective, the elements of change are less pronounced than those of continuity.

The purpose of my study on *Germany and Russia* in 1985–86—which was not intended to be published—was to find out how much radical, irreversible change had taken place. I am happy to see this study in print now for it provides the opportunity to reexamine its findings with the benefits of hindsight.

The most important event that has occurred since was, of course, the reunification of Germany. I believe I was correct at the time to point to the fact that the issue of German reunification did not figure highly on the agenda of West German youth. If young people went on the barricades fighting for unity, it was in East Germany rather than in the West. Equally, the disappointment that followed the wave of enthusiasm of 1989 was greater in East Germany than in West and also the upsurge of all kinds of extremist groups, mainly of the right. Many East Germans claimed that they had been relegated to second-class citizenship, that they had never imagined that unification would have such painful consequences, that West Germans would behave so tactlessly and without consideration. It is true that West Germans had underrated the economic and social difficulties, but then the peaceful transformation of a social system was a process virtually without precedent in history. One could feel sympathy for the East Germans who, having worked hard for decades, felt betrayed, but it was unjust on their part to make the West responsible for their plight.

It is as yet too early to generalize about the integration of East Germany. But there is some reason to assume that the younger generation in East Germany is psychologically better prepared for a transformation of the system than their elders who had grown up in the system and had accepted it even while they hated it. It could also perhaps have been foreseen that male attitudes would be more positive than female because there was more satisfactory work for male workers and employees. The abolition of certain East German social achievements such as the free care of small children, which had enabled young mothers to go out to work, further aggravated the situation of women in East Germany. But there could be other factors involved in shaping moods and attitudes which cannot as yet be properly assessed.

What of the changes in political attitudes of German youth in recent years? They have been relatively few but in some respects trends only dimly recognized in the middle 1980s have now become more pronounced.

The influence of the Greens, the ultra-environmental party in Germany, has stagnated and in many cases declined. This had partly to do with their internal splits, but perhaps even more with the absence of clear political concepts. To be "Green" was always more a mood, a mentality rather than a guide to political action. Above all, the movement was born out of the fear of a general military conflict—or to be more precise, out of the deployment of NATO forces on German soil. As this danger receded and virtually disappeared, as NATO forces were withdrawn from Central Europe, the Greens lost much of their political *raison d'être*. While it had been at one time the party of youth *par excellence,* fifteen years later it had become a party most of whose militants were in their forties. They still scored high in the smaller university cities but their hold on the younger generation had weakened. While at the height of the *Angst* wave in the early 1980s hundred of thousands had demonstrated in the streets of Germany, ten years later the eagerness to march had waned together with the fear.

True, the "without me" syndrome with a strong anti-American admixture had not vanished altogether as it again appeared during the Gulf crisis of 1990/91. The manifestations of fear, the warnings against a new world war, the protests against taking effective collective action against Saddam Hussein's aggression were so loud that the impression was created that Berlin and Bonn were threatened rather than Kuwait and Basra. Yet as the war came under way and as Saddam Hussein was defeated with almost contemptuous ease, it appeared that, as happens so often in recent German history, the media, in particular the electronic media, had conveyed an impression of German mood and reactions that was not accurate (56 percent of the public condemned the anti-war demonstrations even though they were, of course, a legitimate expression of opinion). While television and radio in their majority opposed and condemned allied military action, German public opinion (almost 70 percent) favored it, excepting only the extreme left and right. (Only 4 percent faulted the Americans for the Gulf War.) In brief, German views were more or less the same as in other European countries. Again, not for the first time, it appeared that there was no similarity of views between the German intelligentsia and the people at large. There was no difference in this context between the generations—a majority favored military action in all age groups.

Outside observers of the German scene have noted this phenomenon (the political isolation of the avant-garde) over the years; it has been striking, for instance, in the German cinema. While the films produced by Rainier Fassbender and his friends enjoyed huge acclaim among critics, the German movie-going public—predominantly young—voted with its feet against it. More than 80 percent of films shown in German cinemas were of foreign origin, most of them American, not necessarily of high quality.

It would still be a mistake to view German protests, Angst, and anti-Americanism as nothing but media events. There were some basic, inchoate trends in the mental makeup of the younger generation that had developed in the 1960s, which, to a larger or smaller degree, had become ingrained. Ecological concerns were perhaps taken more seriously in Germany than in other countries. True, the political importance of these concerns should not be exaggerated—partly because of the inability of the Greens to develop plausible alternatives and the fractiousness of their movement. Another noteworthy trend was the new nationalism on the left as much as on the right. This was only natural in the light of a changed world situation and Germany's growing weight in world affairs: The threat from the East had disappeared in the late 1980s and with it the necessity for an effective Western defense system. The new left wing nationalism was not aggressive as it had been in the 1930s but preponderately inward-looking. It did not demand expansion, frequently opposed international involvement, was often isolationist in character. It opposed Germany's role both as a policeman and paymaster in Europe. If the *Weltanschauung* of German youth in the 1930s had been largely "heroic" with the emphasis on the duty to make sacrifices, the new mood was definitely anti-heroic, hedonistic, averse to making sacrifices in money, let alone dying a hero's death for the fatherland. Opposition to German society was quite often coupled with a belief in German superiority at least in comparison with the United States. It is easy to see that some of these attitudes were contradictory, even mutually exclusive. But for all this they were (and are) quite real.

Similar trends can be detected in other parts of Europe and North America, but in Germany, they often seemed more pronounced. But for some unforeseen, cataclysmal development such as a deep and lasting economic crisis or war, these basic moods and attitudes, are unlikely to change dramatically in the near future. The unification of Germany has made it a bigger and stronger country, but it has also aggravated social and political problems and made the country, for a long time, become more inward-looking. Thus, the findings of 1985, by and large, still seem to apply seven years after, even though the specific problems facing the youth in the new regions (i.e., East Germany) are, by necessity, *sui generis* in character and deserve further study.

The political views of the young generation in the Federal Republic of Germany are of paramount interest for more than one reason. One is the importance of Germany in Europe. Furthermore, in Germany more than in any other country specific "youth attitudes" have crystallized. During the last decade the rise of the Green party was an obvious manifestation of this trend. Young people play an increasing role in German politics, their participation in elections is higher than in any other European country. Increasingly they are found in leading positions in political, social, and cultural life. Moreover, Germany has traditionally been a trend setter as far as her European neighbors have been concerned. This goes not only for Austria and Switzerland, but also for Scandinavia and Benelux. What happens in Germany is therefore of significance in a broader European context.

At the outset of our review an apparent paradox should be noted: Few topics in the modern world have been more thoroughly investigated than the attitudes and opinions of young people in Germany. There are massive multivolume studies on the subject (for instance by the German Bundestag). Many thousands of adolescents have been interrogated with regard to their views on all conceivable questions including whether they would like to live on a South Sea island. A leading expert on the subject (Klaus Allerbeck), following a visit to Harvard's Widener library has reached the conclusion that most of the international literature on "youth," "young generation," and "youth protest" seems to have been written by German authors or deal with the situation in Germany. This led him to ask the question: Are we (Germans) the only ones who have to face such problems? It ought to be added that the many investigations have by no means resulted in unambiguous findings. The facts and figures are often contradictory and the interpretations diverge widely; the diagnosis reaches from pointing to the total alienation of German youth from traditional values and orientations to assertions that there have been no significant changes at all.

It is not our endeavor to explain the reasons for these startling contradictions. It does appear that it is infinitely more difficult to assess the mood (often inchoate) and views of young people, partly no doubt because of their rapidly changing character, than the political party preferences of adults. It is more than doubtful whether even more wide-ranging and ambitious empirical studies will shed more light on this difficult subject. Some students of youth frustrated by the confusing and contradictory results of the polls have focused on the elite, the articulators of the young generation. This may be intellectually more satisfying but it can be even more misleading in the end. For these spokesmen represent only a small group of people, a committed avant-garde, not the many millions who do not write or make public speeches and whose organizational affiliation is usually limited to membership in a sports club.

We shall rely in the following primarily on our own observations, being guided, of course, by the experience and the research done by others. The present study focuses on German youth views on defense and foreign policy, with the emphasis on attitudes toward the United States. But this question cannot be approached in isolation from other, broader issues. The starting point must be a more general question: Has there been a secular change (as many have argued) in German youth views over the last twenty years, a "revaluation of all values" with regard to authority (family, the school, the state) and work ? Has a "postmaterialist generation transformed itself in a "new social movement" of major political significance? According to this school of thought, basing itself on the finding of various polls, the chasm between the generations is now much greater than a generation ago. Among the young, work is frequently regarded as a nuisance and a bore. Marriage is widely considered to be an outmoded institution, and religion is of little interest to the great majority. There is a greater desire to mix with another people, but this is mainly the result of young people being easily bored when alone and being afraid of loneliness. There is greater interest in politics than a generation ago but this is on a superficial level not matched by a willingness to learn about one's own society and the work involved to sustain its growth—a politicization not based on knowledge but on moods, on what others say and hence given to sudden and far-reaching changes.

According to these findings, youth sees the purpose of life in enjoying oneself. In school and at home discipline is no longer imposed, but neither is self-discipline expected or demanded. Seen in this light youth has lost its bearings, intellectually and morally, in a world that is becoming increasingly more complicated—hence the wave of protest. This, with only slight exaggeration, is the portrait of the youth that emerged from various studies. Some interpreted the changes in a positive rather than a negative light—the belated destruction of outworn institutions and shibboleths.

Ten or even five years ago most observers would have agreed that something in the nature of such a change had indeed happened or was about to take place. Today most are more skeptical. True, the existence of the Green party is a manifestation of youth disaffection—but many more young people still vote for the two major parties (CDU and SPD) than for the Greens who stagnate and may already be in a process of decline. True, some significant changes have taken place in attitudes but many more young people now want to make a career rather than to opt out of society; 81 percent feel rather optimistic about the future, which is more than felt that way twenty years ago—before the "cultural revolution."

German youth, like young generations in all other European countries, wants above all security and to "lead its own life." This mood is quite different from the romantic, emotionally high fever of fifteen or even ten years ago. But it is also true that many young Germans distrust state institutions and political parties. The fact that many more young Germans vote for the Christian Democrats and Social Democrats than for the "Greens" goes hand in hand with the belief that political parties are not very effective; they do not really represent the voters. Only one-third of those under age twenty-five trusts government, the army, and political parties; only 40–50 percent have confidence in the police and the courts. The more highly educated these young people are, the less confidence they express; negative views are quite strong with regard to national defense, Germany's place in the Western Alliance, and so forth. It ought to be noted in passing that the relevant figures among the older age groups are quite different: Distrust is nowadays a specific youth phenomenon and it has increased over the years.

At this stage observers confront a paradoxical situation: Young Germans in their overwhelming majority profess to be more or less content with the "system" or, generally speaking, the present state of affairs—as much as or more than in other countries. There is no general aversion against the "system" as many claimed in the past. But only 45 percent believe that democracy—with all its drawbacks—is the best political regime. The question then arises whether such relatively low support for a free order is rooted in the belief that democracy is not democratic enough—or that it is too democratic (and hence ineffective) or whether those concerned simply have not given much thought to the whole question?

Again, the evidence is contradictory: There is among the young great enthusiasm for more participation in the political process (such as various citizens' initiatives, demonstrations, etc.). But many of those who keep in close contact with the young report an ambivalent attitude toward freedom, a latent willingness to follow a leader provided he has an appealing message, which, at present, neither parents nor school nor others can provide. And lastly, there can be no doubt that there is a great deal of confusion with regard to the rights and duties of a citizen, and the alternatives to a democratic order. We suspect that if young Germans were confronted with a clear-cut choice between democracy and dictatorship they would overwhelmingly opt for democracy. The relatively low support for democracy stems not from the attraction of dictatorship but from the fact that they have not thought much about alternatives. Hence their confusion. But this muddle is an important political fact of life and must not be ignored.

In what way do German youth attitudes differ from those prevailing among the young generation of other countries? It has been frequently pointed out that only 21 percent of Germans are proud of their country (and an even smaller percentage of Japanese) in contrast to 80 percent of Americans. But it is also true that the term *very proud* is far more easily (and often) used in the American political language than in Europe. Patriotic upsurges occur quickly, and sometimes on slight provocation (Britain and the Falkland War). If the Los Angeles Olympic games gave a noticeable boost to American national pride, Boris Becker's Wimbledon victory had a similar effect in West Germany.

Nor can it be taken for granted that national pride more or less automatically manifests itself in a willingness to serve in the army or to defend one's country. With all the patriotism there is considerable resistance to the draft in America. According to many polls, Italians, who are very proud of their country, do not show equal enthusiasm for defending their homeland, whereas in the case of France the acceptance of the need to defend the country goes hand in hand with—in recent years— limited national pride. In Germany the number of conscientious objectors has significantly declined over the last ten years. But this is probably connected with the fact that opting out as become more difficult. Ten years ago a postcard was frequently sufficient for a young German to register his unwillingness to serve in the Bundeswehr. Today he has to do alternative civilian service for a period exceeding national service.

We ought to point to some other differences between Germany and other European countries which are not reflected in the facts and figures of the social science investigations but which are nonetheless real and of considerable importance. Traditionally, ideas—good, bad, and indifferent—have been taken more seriously in Germany than elsewhere and have had longer lives. The "quest for the absolute" has been, for better or worse, an integral part of German history; intellectual and political fashions have succeeded each other less rapidly than elsewhere. Germany has been the country of romanticism and philosophical idealism par excellence. This too may explain—together with the delayed psychological effect of World War II—the strong influence of pacifist and ecological groups, the radical position taken by some of the churches, and the fact that in Germany alone among all European nations, the "Greens" became (and, for the time being, have remained) a political factor of some consequence. It should be noted in passing that from the end of the war and up to the mid-1960s there was no significant divergence between the young people and the older age brackets. Such differences have been of some significance only during the last fifteen years. On the other hand, such divergences are by no means unprecedented: They were a pronounced feature of the political constellation in the Weimar Republic.

It ought to be mentioned in passing that up to the middle 1960s the Christian Democrats scored higher among young voters than among other age groups. From 1965 until recently there was a steady decline, which was only partly reversed in the last general elections. Even now polls show that the attitude of youths fourteen to seventeen years old is more positive toward the CDU than that of the age group over eighteen. It is thought that the very young become more critical vis-à-vis the CDU once they leave the parental home and are exposed to a higher degree to other influences, such as the upper forms of high school, college, and the media.

Lastly an interesting phenomenon should be mentioned which is of some importance with regard to the formation of public views among German youth being more effective in this role than anywhere else. This refers to the "clique," the peer group of friends and contemporaries, which, however inchoate and transient in composition, is more important in maintaining moods and views than either family or school. (On the impact of media on youth, see further below.) Groups of like-minded young and old people can be found, of course, in every society, but it seems to be more significant in Germany than elsewhere, just as a youth movement (*Jugendbewegung*) existed only in Germany (the "clique") as an important vehicle of socialization. If the classic youth movement was exclusively a middle-class phenomenon, the "cliques" in Germany transcend social class; they are found everywhere.

With all this, it is impossible to speak about a common political orientation, a consensus among the young generation in Germany as distinct from other age groups. There never was a consensus and there is none now. All knowledgeable observers of the German scene agree that the influence of the extreme groups of the left and the right is exceedingly small. It is believed that the extreme (antidemocratic, violent) left has about three times as many supporters as the extreme right. (As far as anti-Americanism and anti-NATO attitudes in these groups are concerned the differences between the extremes are insignificant even though the motivation is different.) But according to the annual reports of the regional offices of the Office for the Protection of the Constitution the membership of extreme right youth organizations is measured in hundreds, and at most a few thousands. On the university campuses they do not exist at all. On the left the (orthodox) communists have stagnated for many years, whereas the membership of the various sects of the New Left have sharply declined over the last years. Both extreme left and right have tried, not always unsuccessfully, to infiltrate "mass organization" in the universities, the churches, and elsewhere. The extreme left

Spartacus with (at one time) its 6,000 members had a disproportionately high representation in the students' parliaments. The extreme right, which is more "proletarian" in character has tried its luck mobilizing football fans and certain working-class gangs (Rockers). The extreme left publishes many dozens of magazines and newspapers for secondary school and college students. Yet in the final analysis all this does not really amount to much as the decline in violent demonstrations in the last three to four years has shown. The number of participants has steadily decreased even in cases when there was considerable public support for the cause—such as the protest marches against the stationing of missiles in the Bundesrepublik.

Terrorist and other violent groups in West Germany will be prominently featured in the media from time to time in view of the spectacular and sensational character of their exploits. Politically they are insignificant. Too much attention has been paid to them and any serious study on the political views of German youth must concentrate therefore on the overwhelming majority of the young generation.

The same is true with regard to the violent street demonstrations. It is possible to mobilize a few hundred, perhaps even a few thousand young men and women for such demonstrations on the slightest provocation in every major city. (Again it is interesting that some "bourgeois" cities such as Frankfurt score much higher in this respect than more "proletarian" towns such as Essen and Dortmund.) The heyday of such demonstrations is over but they still provide for some young people both excitement, which cannot easily be found elsewhere, and an outlet for excess energy. The policy forces have not been very energetic in suppressing such outrages but if they had been more effective (and, by necessity, more brutal) this could well have resulted in a strengthening of the terrorist scene.

To what extent do the views on national security and foreign affairs of the young generation differ from those of their elders and in what direction are these views developing? Most investigations have approached this question out of the historical context, and the general picture that emerged has been at best incomplete, quite often distorted. It is frequently forgotten that the consensus in Germany on NATO, indeed on a German contribution to Western defense *tout court,* is relatively recent : The Social Democrats and influential sections of the (Protestant) churches opposed such a contribution until about 1960. In the light

of the Nazi experience the danger of remilitarization loomed too large
on their political horizon: The cure (having a new army) seemed worse
than the disease (the threat from the East). The opponents believed that
there was a distinct danger that a German army would again become an
instrument of expansion and in the process subvert democracy. It is also
useful to recall that when Germany first polled in the late 1950s whether
they liked Americans and whether they would prefer the withdrawal of
American troops, the results expressed by no means overwhelming sympathy: Only 37 percent said in 1957 that they actually liked the Americans, and a majority thought that a neutral Germany, more or less like
Switzerland would be the best possible solution. In the 1960s and 1970s
the support for NATO rose to about 70 percent. As late as autumn 1982,
25 percent of all Germans said that America was their country's best
friend, and if only 35 percent maintained that they had great or considerable confidence in U.S. leadership, this was twice as much as other European countries had in U.S. leadership.

However, since the double track decision of 1979 to look in both
geographic directions, the number of those pressing for a dialogue with
the Soviet Union and a more reserved attitude toward the United States
with an emphasis on "specific German national interests" has increased—
as it has in most other European countries. Some have attributed these
reservations concerning solidarity with and support for the United States
to the "reckless" foreign policy of the Republican administration, which
allegedly frightened the more cautious Europeans. This argument seems
plausible at first sight; Europeans have been more cautious on the whole
and some have demanded the continuation of detente at almost any cost.
However, it is also true that in 1979, under President Carter, confidence
in the United States declined temporarily, not as the result of an overwhelming American show of strength but of perceived American weakness. On the other hand, as a result of President Reagan's Bitburg visit
in 1985 there was a sudden increase in support for the United States and
in the popularity of the president.

These figures are in no way conclusive; they only show that there are
no easy, straightforward answers to a complex phenomenon. If American strength has frightened some Germans, so has American weakness;
if a high-dollar exchange rate has provoked European complaints, so
has a low rate.

What are the specific attitudes of young Germans—those under thirty
years of age—in this respect? With all the discrepancies in research data

and their interpretation there is, broadly speaking, agreement along the following lines: (1) the importance of the reunification of Germany as a topmost concern besetting German youth was exaggerated; (2) the attitude of the present young generation toward the Western alliance is more skeptical than that of their predecessors, the older age group; (3) the more highly educated students take a more negative view toward the Western coalition than those already employed.

Beyond these general conclusions attitudes are often contradictory: More younger than older Germans maintained in the early 1980s that the threat to Germany from the East had increased in recent years. But at the same time the youngest age bracket is less worried by this threat, and sees in America a greater danger to world peace than their elders. The percentage of young people who believed in 1983 (at the height of the antinuclear, antimissile campaign) that the existence of the Western defense alliance has made world peace more secure was virtually as high as the rest of the population (about 60 percent). But the percentage of those actively supporting or at least in group sympathy with the peace movement (which opposed the Western alliance) was considerably higher among the young. Sixty-eight percent of the young believe that it is important that the German army should belong to NATO—almost as much as among the rest of the population. But only 49 percent think that a strong Bundeswehr is of any importance in the first place.

On the basis of such confused and contradictory statements, analysts, according to their party preferences, have reached opposite conclusions: The relative optimists emphasize the fact that with all the mutterings about neutralism the great majority of Germans do not want the withdrawal of U.S. troops from their country. They point to the fact that the big commotion over the INF deployment (1981–84) has not significantly affected German attitudes toward the United States. On the contrary (as Gerhard Schweigler has noted) among the young age group a significant change occurred between 1981 and 1984 inasmuch as it joined the rest of the population in the belief that security had actually improved or at least had not been impaired—hence the decline of the peace movement in West Germany.

All this may be true but it is only part of a more complex picture. In any case, the polls do not tell us much about deeper motives, about the intensity of belief and even less about future trends. Is the relative unconcern of large sections of the young generation about defense and the negative attitudes vis-à-vis the United States a passing phase or do they constitute the beginning of a major shift in orientation? If so, what are the origins? What are the causes of the great confusion among German youth?

It is emotionally torn in opposite directions: To do their civic duty (including national service) is time consuming and, on the whole, unpopular. A great majority of young Germans would, no doubt, greatly prefer their country to be located somewhere else, not in the very heart of Europe, where the two superpowers confront each other. They would like their country to be less vulnerable, less open to conflicting pressures. There is a vague feeling of helplessness facing much superior military powers, and the instinctive belief that peace has to be preserved at any price. All this is psychologically understandable, but how can these longings be translated into political action? It is a situation conducive to wishful thinking, leading to questioning the value of the Western alliance. For would not a country in a position such as Germany be more secure if it were truly neutral, without foreign bases on its soil? Young Germans would, of course, greatly prefer to live in freedom but if the choice is between peace and a free political order, should not peace take precedence? Such questions are hardly ever asked in such a brutal, inelegant way. In any case most of the young tend to take freedom for granted never having known any other political order and not having achieved it through their own effort.

This in turn leads to the rationalization of weakness and to more wishful thinking: Probably the greatest confusion prevails with regard to the Soviet Union. When asked in 1982 whether one could trust the Soviet Union, a relative majority of those under thirty (45 percent) declared that they could not make up their mind on this subject. This majority suspects that lack of freedom there and the expansive character of the Soviet system have been grossly exaggerated by American cold war propaganda. There is the belief that both big powers are essentially evil, and Germany's best bet—if it only had more freedom of action!—would be to preserve equidistance from both.

If German youth knows little about America, it knows virtually nothing about the former Soviet Union and has no interest in the subject. This topic is, after all, not taught in school. A few "ideologists" among the students may be avid readers of neo-Marxist philosophers, but their interest is on the level of theory and abstraction. About the realities of Communist rule they know no more than the rest.

It has always to be recalled that for those who are under thirty-five, not only the Second World War but also the cold war belongs to he distant past. They don't know how Eastern Europe was taken over by the Russians after 1945. Their first political recollections are the Vietnam War and detente. Afghanistan is a far away country, and they do not want to hear about Poland. Perhaps they feel instinctively that protests would make the Russians only more angry. While the great majority of movies shown in West Germany are of American rather than German origin, most young people in West Germany had never seen a Soviet film in their life. This nonexposure to the Soviet way of life—even in its censored form—was a blessing from the point of view of Soviet propaganda. Greater knowledge about "real socialism" would only have caused problems.

What has been said about movies applies to youth culture in general—rock music, sartorial fashions, and so forth. In this respect, the American impact on large sections of German youth is overwhelming, whereas there is no Russian influence worth mentioning. Yet the huge quantity of American cultural imports (often adduced as a proof that there is no anti-Americanism among German youth) does not translate itself into deeper political or cultural orientation. it is no more than the absorption and assimilation of an international style, American or mid-Atlantic in origin, without any significant substance—or, to be precise, with a form that can be filled with almost any substance.

With only slight exaggeration it can be said that the problem of the young generation in Germany is not the existence of a strong anti-American movement, but the absence of a party of freedom, or, to put it differently, the inability of Western democracy to imbue its children with its own values. Such bequests do not usually happen by way of indoctrination but come about through example. But it is also true that the self-confidence of the older generation plays an important role, and in the absence of such self-confidence, youth protest, always latent in society, is likely to recognize a vacuum and evolve its own alternative values.

The heyday of the protest movement of German youth was in the 1970s. Its motives and components were heterogeneous: It was in some respects a classical example of youth revolt such as has cyclically occurred in many countries in various times. It coincided with various movements of cultural reform or revolution and was in part rooted in genuine fear—of nuclear war and of irreparable ecological damage. To some extent this movement has run full circle with the generation that was its main carrier. The "ideas of 1967" are no longer seriously advocated by any significant group, and the violent demonstrations have greatly declined in frequency and intensity. The observers who at the time regarded the movement as quite distinct from all its predecessors and the changes it brought as irreversible ("postmaterialism", the concept of a "new social movement") no longer propagate their theses with equal conviction.

But it is also true that not everything the movement stood for has disappeared without a trace. The presence of the Greens is sufficient evidence to this effect. And even if the Greens should suffer further reverses in the years to come, some of their ideas will be absorbed by the established political parties, in particular the Social Democrats, and to a much smaller extent by the extreme right. There is a "protest potential" in Germany of perhaps 10-15 percent. This may be submerged for a while, but it will not disappear.

One of its components is anti-Americanism, which, of course, predates in time the youth protest by many decades, but which received from it considerable fresh impetus. The anti-American tradition in Germany (as in Britain and France) can be traced back well into the nineteenth century. It was spearheaded by thinkers of the right including, eventually, Nazis and was cultural as much as political in character. Its complaints focused on American excessive egalitarianism, dishonesty, superficiality, degeneracy, the absence of manners, and lack of cultural interests. The anti-American writings of Dickens and Mrs. Trollope in Britain had a parallel in Germany in Nikolaus Lenau and Kuernberger's *Der Amerikamuede* (The Man Tired of America). These books contain in essence almost all the negative things that have ever been said about the American way of life. However, attitudes to America were complicated by U.S. intervention in two world wars. As far as Germany is concerned, the United States played a decisive part in the defeat of Nazism, the plague of which the German people could not rid itself through its own strength. Such intervention was welcomed by some but resented by others. Not a few of the older generation, sharing the traditional anti-American biases, resented the victors, whereas some of the young radicals complained on the contrary that through their presence and policy the United States had prevented a true, radical transformation of German society, in other words a socialist or communist revolution.

But such feelings had to be suppressed in the early postwar period. During the first fifteen years after the war America could do no wrong as far as West Germany was concerned; open anti-Americanism was limited to the few communists and neo-Nazis. This began to change even before Vietnam and it has been explained as the inevitable reaction to indiscriminate pro-Americanism, with the rise of a new generation and the revolt of the (German) children against the (American) parents. There seems to be some truth in these contentions and it is also true that similar attitudes prevailed in most other European countries. There was envy vis-à-vis rich Americans at a time when Europe was still quite poor. There was, furthermore, the (inevitable) resentment of the weaker country against the powerful protector, the senior partner in the alliance, hence the psychological necessity to assert oneself, to show that one is not a vassal—a phenomenon that found near-perfect expression in Gaullism and in different guises could also be found in Germany and elsewhere in Europe.

All this does not however fully explain the growth of anti-Americanism in the 1970s when some of the conditions just described no longer existed: America was no more the rich relation; on the contrary, with the decline in the purchase power of the dollar in the early 1980s, Americans living in Germany—especially the armed forces—became frequently an object of pity rather than of envy. If so, how can we explain that during the 1970s almost half of those Germans in the universities and the upper classes of the gymnasium (senior high school) expressed the view that Germany would be better off leaving NATO? This cannot solely be explained with reference to a revolt against parental authority.

It is important to realize that German anti-Americanism is rooted not so much in the foreign or domestic policy of one administration or another; "Americanism" has become a symbol for some German ideologists. As one German once put it: "There is more culture in one Beethoven symphony than in all that has been produced so far by America." The German just quoted was Adolf Hitler, but a similar attitude can easily be found both before and after Hitler, on the left as on the right. F. Vulpius, a relative of Goethe, wrote in 1847 that America is the country of freedom for all robbers and scoundrels, a cliché that returned for a century in many variations including in some unlikely places. Thus, Hermann Hesse wrote in a letter to Thomas Mann exactly one hundred years after Vulpius: "It is good to know that the sadists, gangsters and speculators are no longer Nazis speaking German—but Americans." The anti-Americans of the left quote Marx and Engels who wrote that the Americans are "backward in all things theoretical," since they took from Europe (and never discarded) "all kind of medieval traditions, religions, superstition and other such nonsense." The same views could be found in the writings of the right and cultural elite. America has produced no proper philosophy—except pragmatism and Dewey—no literature, art, or music that could remotely be compared with the German cultural heritage. Again on the left American wholesomeness (patriotism, church attendance, family ties, etc.) is ridiculed. Both extreme left and extreme right complain about continued occupation of Germany by the aggressive imperialist cultural character of "Yankee Kultur" ("Ami Kultur"), hence the need to purge the country of the consequences of this invasion. If the left accuses America of having deprived Germany of its revolutionary tradition, the right makes the same claim concerning Germany's national tradition, which, they say, has been replaced by the intellectual interests and moral values of television serials.

The German anti-Americans complain that "Americanism" has become so all-pervasive that even the opposition to this phenomenon has already been preempted by Americans: They were in fact the most severe critics of U.S. culture, and hard as Germans may try, they find it next to impossible to think of anything detrimental about America that has not already been said by the anti-American Americans.

It remains to be added that views of this kind have been sharply contradicted even on the extreme left. Wolfgang Pohrt, the most brilliant essayist on the left, has drawn attention to the similarity in outlook between the anti-Americanism of the Nazis and today's "national left." According to Pohrt and others, hostility to President Reagan's policy stemmed from the secret power dreams on the part of those who attacked him most severely. The main motive of the peace movement, says Pohrt, is not the issue of rearmament, but the hankering after lost world power and the conviction (as exemplified in the relationship of Carter and Helmut Schmidt) that (some) Germans are much better equipped to give a lead to the world than the primitive and inexperienced Americans.

The phenomenon has to be considered in the general context of the Zeitgeist, the mood of the period, and also the degree of political education of German youth. The Zeitgeist of the late 1960s and the following decade was "anti-imperialist," in favor of liberation movements in all parts of the world. (It was militant-revolutionary in the Third World, but pacifist in orientation in Europe.) It was not pro-Soviet, but it was bound to turn anti-American. It was an elite phenomenon, restricted to the most articulate sections of those in higher education, it never affected directly the majority of German youth. But it has an indirect impact on the "silent majority" through the mass media, through educators, and social workers—professions in which many of the revolutionaries of 1966–70 made their career.

It cannot simply be written off as a phenomenon of the *Schickeria*— the radical chic section of the German intelligentsia; though there was a marked element of this too. The mood corresponded to a very deep longing (the *ohne mich*—without me—of the 1950s) to be left alone, not to be involved in the stupid quarrels of the global powers. Seen in this light the quarrel of the Germans (and particularly the young among them) is with their own geopolitical situation rather than with America.

But since the geographical location cannot be changed, the discontent found its way into other channels. Not a few young Germans have persuaded themselves that the cold war, and the present confrontation between the two superpowers have really nothing to do with Germany and Europe, but are somehow proceeding in a vacuum, are conflicts about abstract bones of contention. The lament: "Why don't they leave us alone?" is widespread, and the idea that both superpowers are equally to blame and that all would be well if they only left, can be found in the most unlikely places—for instance, in the best-selling unpolitical novels of Johann Mario Simmel (such as his recent *Die im Dunkeln sieht man nicht*—a quotation from Brecht). It is from this kind of television broadcast and mass literature—not reviewed in the quality press, not discussed in the histories of high literature—that millions of Germans draw their inspiration, not from the academic journals on world affairs. It has been a mistake to ignore these sources of information and indoctrination as far as German public opinion is concerned.

Many young Germans have strong opinions on a variety of subjects but they are not well informed about their own country and even less so about the world at large. Political education in Germany (as elsewhere in Europe) has been a near total failure. Schools and family have imparted little but a few stereotypes; few young people read serious newspapers. Television on the other hand, in particular ZDF, the second channel, is one of the major sources of anti-Americanism. The state of affairs in the press is more complicated. Weeklies such as *Spiegel* and *Stern* are by and large anti-American, whereas the daily newspapers take a different line. These striking divergences in the media are not the result of deliberate penetration by anti-Western elements—they just happened more or less by accident. Nor is this to imply that all TV stations and programs are consistently anti-American; since they are under political control (of the class gentry rather than the central government) a brake would be put to propaganda that is too blatant. Several anti-American programs will always be counterbalanced by one that is critical of the Soviet Union so that no one could charge the TV managers of lack of evenhandedness. Anti-Americanism on TV is seldom of the crude, all-out variety. The bias is less obtrusive; it is by insinuation and implication not only in comment but also the selection of news coverage and even in nonpolitical programs. The net result is quite frequently the image of a society poor in culture, replete with social injustice, corrupt, lacking political sophistication, and led by people both stupid and aggressive ("cowboy types"). French television, with its strong (cultural) anti-American bias, has shown in recent years, even under a Socialist administration, considerably more evenhandedness than Germans, and this is also true, by and large, with regard to British TV

Some social science investigations have claimed that television programs have little if any lasting political effect on the young or the public at large. This is not born out by our observations in Germany. There have been various studies on the effect of the media (and in particular of television) on the electoral behavior of voters. These investigations have dealt with the British general elections in 1961 and the European parliament elections . There have also been studies on the "agenda setting function" of the media. However, what may (or may not) apply to viewers in Syracuse, New York, (with a very different structured system of television programs) does not necessarily apply to West Germany. Even if it should be true—which is by no means certain—that the direct impact of television on young German voters on the eve of an election is negligible, the issue at stake in our context is quite different: It concerns not electoral propaganda on the part of political parties but television as a constant source of information (or misinformation) on a foreign country, which most young Germans have never visited. In fact, for many viewers, television is their only source of information.

Television programs reach a far wider public than all other media; they provide food for thought and topics of conversation for the masses. It may well be true that the TV public is more discriminating with regard to domestic issues simply because it is bound to be better informed. If viewers are shown a misleading program on a subject with which they are familiar—say the situation in their own town or region, they will not easily be influenced, and the program may in fact be counterproductive as far as the credibility of TV is concerned. But few German youngsters have first-hand experience of distant countries, and hence their greater readiness to believe reports on foreign parts.

Yet another aspect of anti-American propaganda is frequently overlooked; it takes place in the schools and aims at children aged twelve and above. *Englisch-Amerikanische Studien* (Anglo-American Studies), a journal by and for English teachers is most instructive in this context. It aims at imparting knowledge not about the gerund, questions of grammar, or a better understanding of Shakespeare or Charles Dickens. Its purpose is political-propagandistic. The articles published deal with the negative consequences of the policies of the United States and Great Britain. The main target is not even "U.S. imperialism" but the deeper issues at stake, the "nightmare" of the American dream, the mendacity of the American way of life, the melting pot, the "brutal egotism," rootlessness, bad taste, and mediocrity of America. These themes are dealt with at length not only in the tuition of the English language at school, but they also frequently appear in the radio broadcasts for schools to which hundreds of thousands of children and students regularly listen.

Against this it could be argued that not every German child studying the English language has to undergo such massive indoctrination. The majority has not. It could be said that young people do not slavishly accept what their teachers tell them but that, on the contrary, there is often an instinctive tendency to reject. But equally often there is an inclination, especially in the formative years, to believe what is said, to look for messages and to accept them—especially if the teacher is gifted and has the confidence of his pupils.

As for the substance of such propaganda little needs to be said. Few will deny the existence of a discrepancy between the American dream and American reality. But the significant feature of this kind of agitprop is the systematic attempt to focus on the negative sides of America, and to belittle, or altogether to ignore and deny the positive aspects. German "critical theory" suffers from tunnel vision. It would be only too easy to point to similar discrepancies elsewhere, for instance, between Soviet ideology and "real socialism." But only America undergoes such treatment. Few young Germans who have visited America or lived there will accept this kind of image. But most have not been to the United States, which makes the task of the propagandists much easier. German society is wide open; there are obvious limits to the effect of political propaganda. As a result, political indoctrination is a fairly rare exception. But in the final analysis it is a factor that should not be ignored.

Of those employed in television a high proportion sympathizes with the political forces at present in the opposition. While the Greens have been anti-American from the beginning, anti-Americanism was not widespread or deeply rooted in the SPD in the 1960s but made considerable strides since. This is hotly disputed by most Social Democratic leaders who argue that criticism of certain U.S. policies opposed to the interests of Germany and of world peace cannot fairly be equated with anti-Americanism; such opposition, after all, exists also inside the United States. But these arguments are true only in part. German Social Democracy is no longer what it was; there has been a shift away from support for America and the alliance. The traditional *Abgrenzung* (drawing a line) between the SPD, communism, and the Soviet bloc of the postwar period, which was once a fundamental tenet of belief, was considered largely outmoded in the 1980s. The United States is still considered a partner of the SPD in maintaining world peace—so was the Soviet Union while it existed. If the SPD were to return to power in Bonn, it would, of course, have to moderate the stand it took while in opposition. But it could not retreat altogether from some of the extreme positions taken in recent years. True, there are far-reaching differences among the Social Democratic leaders ranging from unabashed neutralism to traditional Atlanticism. But there can be no doubt that the center of gravity in the party (like that of sections of the churches) has moved in a direction critical of and opposed to America. There is no good reason to assume that any foreseeable change in U.S. foreign policy would decisively effect this, and lead the SPD back, toward wholehearted partnership with Washington. Like the trade unions and the churches, the SPD have all lost supporters among the younger generation during the last decade, their youth organizations are shrinking and they desperately wish to initiate a "dialogue with youth." But they still are a factor of considerable importance shaping the outlook of the young generation not so much as a party (or church) but through their contribution to the general political climate.

The issue of the missiles acted as a catalyst or mobilization factor as far as neutralist views in Germany are concerned. They reinformed in depth, not necessarily in scope, existing views or moods; polls only reveal the latter. Hence the paradox that while neutralism was more widespread in Germany in the 1950s and 1960s than today, it assumed a new intensity (which it did not have before) in the late 1970s and early 1980s, generating organized, fairly long-lasting political debate and behavior.

This set of "high-intensity" anti-American attitudes may have a left wing component but it is rooted in nationalist-cultural prejudices that have little to do with Marxist ideology. If leaders of the Green claim that the American people as a whole lack an ethnic identity and that, seen in this light, only the American Indians are entitled to a political existence on American soil, this argument can be traced back to Adolf Hitler, or, to take a more charitable view, to Karl May—the immensely popular (still widely read) thriller writer of the late nineteenth century who significantly wrote his books about the wild West without ever having been to America.

The anti-American mood in the successor generation encompasses three distinct groups: opinion leaders and holders motivated primarily by the immediate issue at hand (e.g., the missiles, or a vague longing toward equidistance and neutralism); fellow travelers, the *Mitlaeufer* joining, at least temporarily whatever political or cultural cause happens to be in fashion, but whose attachment is neither deep nor lasting; opinion leaders and holders deeply motivated by fundamental beliefs such as an extreme leftist doctrine with a strong admixture of German nationalism and a variety of cultural prejudices. This group is not recruited from the working class (let alone the Communist party) but the Protestant middle and upper class and from traditional professions such as clergy and teachers. If "class analysis" were applied to this group, it could be argued that this is an instance of an old ruling class having lost its traditional raison d'être and in search of a new one. This could be a return to Germany's old mission, its *Sonderweg*, the restoration of a united Germany restored in a nationalist mould, by necessity anti-American and anti-Western, for the road to German unity has to be traveled by way of Moscow. These are relatively few men and women but their views through media and mass organizations reach a great many, out of proportion to their number.

Attitudes such as anti-Americanism are normally short-lived even in their "high intensity" form unless underpinned by lasting political organizations and/or lasting behavior patterns. The behavior patterns of the mass of West German youth have largely been Americanized—even the most zealous anti-Americans go to McDonald's for a hamburger or watch American movies. Seen in this light the imposition of an anti-American life-style is a hopeless endeavor. However, it is also true that American behavior patterns do not necessarily make for pro-Americanism. To paraphrase a Soviet youth leader who said that the fact "that we wear jeans does not affect our political beliefs," it could be said that the influence of McDonald's and pop music does not necessarily translate itself into support for NATO.

Lastly, a factor frequently overlooked ought to be mentioned: a certain childish naughtiness and irresponsibility comparable to the boy cocking a snook behind the back of the teacher. The child knows that such an act of defiance is not dangerous and he expects that it will enhance his standing among his peers as a courageous, defiant little hero. The child also knows that there are some adults (or some world powers such as Russia) who take a dim view of such behavior, that punishment would quickly follow, and thus toward them he will not misbehave. Such behavior (like neutralism elsewhere in Europe) is based on the assumption that Germany is no longer a great power, that such escapades do not matter therefore, that America will defend Europe in any case, and that they are therefore in a position to behave irresponsibly without fear of grave consequences.

It cannot be repeated too often that the young generation in Germany has to be analyzed in a wider European framework. Anti-Americanism and the opposition to the alliance can be found to an equal (or higher degree) in many European countries. Sometimes this appears as a cyclical phenomenon. Fifteen years ago anti-Americanism was *de rigueur* among young Frenchmen and Italians. Since then there has been a marked decline in this respect in these two countries. Nor do the polls tell us much about the intensity of such feelings. A high percentage of German youth may utter doubts and misgivings about military service, but the overwhelming majority will serve in the army in the end.

If anti-Americanism and neutralism in Germany have been a cause of worry to America and other Western countries this has not been because what has happened so far in Germany in this respect has been somehow unique and unprecedented. There is the suspicion—and not entirely un-justified in the light of German history—that Germans have a tendency to take an idea, good, bad, or indifferent and pursue it to its last "logical consequences"—in other words, to exaggerate, to persist long after others may have discarded it. But so far such fears seem not warranted; if there is more apprehension about Germany in the West than about Sweden (where anti-Americanism is widespread among the intellectuals) it has, of course, mainly to do with the fact that Germany, in contrast to Sweden and most other European countries, plays a key role in European defense. A collapse in German self-confidence and a major resurgence of anti-Western moods would have incomparably more far-reaching consequences than similar trends in some Scandinavian or Benelux country.

Georgetown University
Center for Strategic and International Studies

Notes

1. Irving Louis Horowitz, "Latin America, Anti-Americanism, and Intellectual Hubris," in *Anti-Americanism in the Third World*, ed. Alvin Z. Rubenstein and Donald E. Smith (New York: Praeger/Holt, Rinehart and Winston, 1985), 49-66.
2. *Young Germany* was originally published in 1961, but has been reissued since with a new preface, in both the United States and Germany, most recently in the series "Classics of Sociology" by Transaction Publishers (New Brunswick, NJ) in 1984.
3. Again I would like to refer to Irving Louis Horowitz's analysis of "Youth as a Social Class." This happens to be the title of an essay in *The Knowledge Factory: Student Power and Academic Politics in America*, written by Irving Louis Horowitz in collaboration with William H. Friedland (Chicago: Aldine, 1970).

8

Organized Disorder: Terrorism, Politics, and Society

Martha Crenshaw

Terrorism is often presented to the public as inexplicable. The apparent arbitrariness of bombings, kidnappings, assassinations, and hijackings contributes to an impression of pointless destructiveness. The difficult task of scholars is to make this phenomenon understandable. Over the past twenty years Irving Louis Horowitz has contributed to this endeavor both as a writer and as a publisher. Since the early 1970s, before the literature on terrorism had swelled from a mere handful of citations to thousands of books, reports, articles, and chapters, he has been convinced that terrorism is understandable and that the concept can be an explanatory variable, not merely a political label.[1]

It has become fashionable to lament the absence of a universally accepted definition of terrorism and to regard the term as inescapably relativistic, a fault, incidentally, that Horowitz, specifically warned against in 1976. In a comprehensive research guide to the literature, which Transaction published and for which Horowitz composed the foreword, Alex Schmid (1984) devoted over a hundred pages to this problem and appended summaries of 109 different definitions offered between 1936 and 1981. The disagreements over meaning that his commendably thorough list reveals have several sources: the relative novelty, controversiality, and complexity of the subject; the genuine intellectual difficulty of establishing boundaries between terrorism and similar forms of political violence; and the paucity of testable theories in which the utility of different definitions could be assessed. Yet the concept must be specified if we are to reach an understanding of the phenomenon and if empirical research is to proceed.

Barriers to Understanding

A first source of confusion in trying to understand terrorism is the issue of whether we should apply the same term to actions that governments take to crush resistance from their citizens as we apply to antistate violence. Eugene Victor Walter (1969), for example, describes state terrorism as preventing resistance from society as a "regime of terror" theoretically comparable to oppositional challenges, and Thomas P. Thornton (1964) refers to both enforcement and agitational terrorism. The origins of the word *terrorism* lie in descriptions of the reign of terror of the French Revolution in 1793–94, a systematic effort by the newly installed revolutionary regime to consolidate its power in the face of external threat and internal unrest. Yet the magnitude of the potential destructiveness of modern governments may invalidate the comparison. Horowitz was one of the first scholars to point out, in an essay on terrorism and civil liberties (1977), that the power of the state is always greater than that of the opposition, so that asking who is at the root of violence may be futile. In a comparable vein, Richard L. Rubenstein (1975:78) had argued that official attempts at genocide are qualitatively as well as quantitatively different from terrorism: "The [Palestinian] terrorists at Maalot were capable of indiscriminate killing; they were neither capable of nor interested in organizing their victims into a society of total domination, as were the SS."

Governments normally possess not only superior resources but, especially in democracies, the presumption of legitimacy, a legacy and set of expectations that justify their actions to their citizens and to the world. Obedience, not disobedience, is the standard by which normal political behavior is judged. The claim that terrorism can be legitimate appears paradoxical, but Walter (1969:341) in his study of the Zulu kingdoms of nineteenth-century Africa contends that the victims of the highly arbitrary violence of the state accepted their persecution as right and proper. A shared ideology justified violence. "Legitimacy suppresses outrage." To Walter, government authority can be based on violence, which implies that violence from above is not an aberration or a sign of incipient breakdown or instability. Terrorism can be an integral part of the process of governing, firmly based on the consent of the governed. Horowitz, in Schmid (1984:xix), contributed to this insight the logical corollary that oppositional terrorism is also best analyzed as "part and parcel of the political process as a whole."

To be sure, opposition movements occasionally resemble governments, and the intelligence agencies of states often model their covert operations on the clandestine methods of undergrounds. National liberation movements may use violence in order to control a population they aspire to govern, typically in the context of rural insurgency. Oppositions often imitate the language and procedures of the state; the tiniest underground claims to execute prisoners after trials, for example, and organizes itself into armies, brigades, and battalions. Militants appropriate conventional military titles. Governments dispatch hit teams to assassinate dissidents in exile. Libya and Syria have been blamed for the bombing of Pan Am 103. After 1972, Israel established a special unit of the Mossad to track down and assassinate the members of the Palestinian Black September Organization who organized the attacks on Israeli athletes during the Munich Olympics.

Nevertheless, the analytical distinction between government and nongovernment is both well established in the mainstream literature on violence, protest, revolution, and conflict as well as an old source of dispute. In 1968, for example, Ted Robert Gurr felt compelled to defend the study of civil violence, which he defined exclusively as nongovernmental attacks on persons and property. He argued that nonstate violence was a significant topic for scholarly inquiry, not to be excluded from serious analysis because it was thought somehow to represent a "disfigurement" of the body politic. Little has changed in the interim.

Leaving aside the issue of duality between governments and their opponents, we must also consider the objections of critics who regard the word terrorism itself as polemical and unscholarly. Horowitz (1973:150–51) acknowledged that calling someone a terrorist can be a labeling device and he warned against allowing the term *terrorism* to become synonymous with social change. However, he contended that terrorism can be a useful analytical concept, not just a label to condemn anyone with whom one disagrees. In contrast, Austin Turk (1982:66, 68) believes that the term is unacceptable because it connotes moral condemnation of the practitioners of violence and reveals a bias against revolutionary change. He finds the concept conceptually arbitrary and confused, applied simplistically and disapprovingly to acts deemed particularly horrible. Similarly, H. C. Greisman (1977) argues that nonstate terrorists are viewed as bloody, vicious, and irrational, while the acts of agents of the state are assigned a favorable moral meaning despite their greater brutality. However justified these complaints, Horowitz would surely agree that the consequence of refusing to use the term is to leave the field to those most guilty of subjectivity and bias. If inappropriate usage is the problem, the answer is to provide a preferable alternative.

It would be naive to think of terrorism as a political activity as innocuous as voting or campaigning for electoral office, to assume that most people perceive a moral equivalence between defending order and destroying it, or to pretend that the language of politics is inconsequential. On the other hand, the concept of terrorism is not unusual in exhibiting both ambiguity and controversiality. Political discourse is filled with value-laden terms: imperialism, revolution, aggression, fascism, and even genocide can be used as pejorative labels. Thomas R. Conrad (1974:418-23) explained that "utterly pejorative" words such as coercion, assassination, and conspiracy—all minor terms of opprobrium compared to terrorism—are a cross that students of politics must bear. He finds it unfortunate that the emotionally charged character of these terms discourages analysis, to the detriment of understanding real political phenomena. Likewise James Farr (1982; see also Nardin, 1971) argues that an ideal language that could avoid emotional connotations is unattainable. There cannot be ahistorical concepts in political science; terrorism, like revolution, is bound to time and context, a "contested concept" subject to the changing practices and beliefs of political actors.

The meanings which actors themselves give to their actions express these contradictions. The People's Will in nineteenth-century Russia proudly admitted to the use of terrorism against the autocracy. Writing in 1883, one of their number (Stepniak, 1883:42) praised the terrorist in grandiloquent terms: "He is noble, terrible, irresistibly fascinating, for he combines in himself the two sublimities of human grandeur: the martyr and the hero." The successors to the People's Will, militants of the Combat Organization of the Socialist Revolutionary party, responded to criticism that terrorism was "pitiless" by claiming that, on the contrary, "The terrorists are the incarnation of the honor and the conscience of the Russian revolution" (Spiridovitch, 1930:386). As Horowitz (1973) rightly noted, within the early Marxist tradition, terrorism was not only heroic but moral to its users.

More recent examples of a similar self-presentation can also be produced. Although few people today would be inclined to link the antifascist partisan movements of the Second World War with terrorism, a member of the French Resistance titled his memoirs *Nous, les terroristes* (Leproux, 1947). J. K. Zawodny (1978), who spent five years in the Polish underground during World War II, has no qualms about identifying the company to which he belonged as a terrorist organization. M. R. D. Foot, writing in 1966 before terrorism and the study of terrorism became contentious subjects, specifically mentions terrorism as one of the activities of the French Resistance that the British Special Operations Executive (SOE) supported, although he adds that terrorism was by no means the primary function of the SOE and that the British military distinctly lacked enthusiasm for unconventional methods (439–40).

Ironically, in early 1947, the British army in Mandate Palestine banned the use of the term *terrorist* to refer to the Irgun zvai Leumi headed by Menachem Begin because it implied that British forces had reason to be terrified (Wilson, 1949:13). This proscription did not inhibit Geula Cohen, then a member of Lehi or the Stern Gang, who subtitled her autobiography *Memoirs of a Young Terrorist* (1966). However, by 1952 the British embraced the term, which was used to label the Mau Mau in Kenya.

In the 1960s, the Brazilian revolutionary theorist Carlos Marighela, author of the "Handbook of the Urban Guerrilla," a document since popularized as a guide to action in revolutionary circles, introduced his manual by saying (1971:62):

> The words "aggressor" and "terrorist" no longer mean what they did. Instead of arousing fear or censure, they are a call to action. To be called an aggressor or a terrorist in Brazil is now an honour to any citizen, for it means that he is fighting, with a gun in his hand, against the monstrosity of the present dictatorship and the suffering it causes.

It is thus a shift in the historical usage of the term when contemporary practitioners of the violence that others call terrorism tend to prefer different names, such as urban guerrilla or freedom fighter, to convey a positive image of combatting oppression and injustice. The West German Red Army Fraction (RAF), for example, claimed that the concept of terrorism was created by the government as a form of psychological projectionism (*Textes*, 1977:109–11). The West German policy of imperialism, they argued, was projected onto national liberation movements and used as reactionary counterpropaganda. The real terrorism was that of states acting to preserve the status quo. In the 1970s, Salah Khalaf (Abu Iyad), the Fatah leader reputed to be the head of the Black September Organization, insisted that he opposed terrorism, which he defined as nonpolitical, unconnected to organizational needs or strategic vision, and subjectively motivated. He insisted that "revolutionary violence," including assassinations of diplomats and government officials, is not terrorism because it is an auxiliary to mass resistance, used when mass action is no longer able to accomplish its goals. In his terms, Black September was not a terrorist organization (Iyad, 1978:155–56).

One reason for the changing usage of the term could be that the actions ordinarily referred to as terrorism seem to have become more arbitrary and destructive than in the past. Terrorism is no longer perceived as selective assassinations of heads of state but as random attacks on civilians and indiscriminate seizures of innocent hostages. Its victims are diplomats, anonymous foreigners, and civil aviation, not government, officials singled out for their position and past record. The willingness of oppositions to cause mass civilian casualties by bombing public places was associated with the social divisions as well as the repressiveness of colonial rule, when the entire settler community could be seen by indigenous nationalists as an undifferentiated enemy class. The bombings directed against Europeans that characterized the 1956–57 Battle of Algiers were symptomatic of this trend. Nevertheless, the idea of attacking classes of people was not novel at the time. Irish and Irish-American groups began bombing the British subway and railroad systems in the 1880s, and the anarchist movement of the same era became famous not only for the concept of propaganda but for the credo that there are no innocents among the bourgeoisie. Anarchists acted upon this belief in France, Spain, and Italy, bombing cafés, theaters, and restaurants in the 1890s (Maitron, 1955:158–62). Thus, while modern terrorism may be more indiscriminate and destructive than in the past, it is inaccurate to assume that it is unprecedented.

In explaining these changes, Horowitz (1976) was prescient in stressing that society's vulnerability to disruption has altered as much as the means available to terrorists. The complexities and interdependence of modern technological society have changed the patterns of terrorism, more so than the intentions or capabilities of the terrorists.

Defining Terrorism

If the concept of terrorism is to be defined in a way that will be useful in educating the public about risks and in providing a foundation for subsequent theoretical explanation, it must permit observers to identify the violence that constitutes terrorism and exclude that which is not. In order to identify sets of comparable phenomena, a definition should be as precise as possible in specifying the attributes that violent acts must possess if they are to be included as terrorism. Moreover, a plausible definition should not be incompatible with the ordinary language usage of a term.

As Alex Schmid (1984) demonstrated, it has proved difficult to formulate a definition of terrorism that satisfies these requirements. Arguments about terrorism are overlaid with questions of value, usually centered on the legitimacy of the use of violence. Attitudes toward terrorism are frequently based on deep moral commitments. The real issue, as Horowitz (1976) realized, is the morality of political systems and governments; one has to ask what values are to be defended against terrorism. That the issue is bound up with conceptions of justice is not irrelevant, but research cannot proceed without agreement on what is to be analyzed. Accepting a neutral definition as the basis for research need not preclude subsequent moral judgment.

The following distinctions provide some guidance in isolating terrorism from the general field of political violence and establishing homogeneity within the particular domain of terrorism. In brief, terrorism is clandestine violence organized systematically by small groups who seek a political and psychological impact out of proportion to the physical destructiveness of their actions. It resembles guerrilla warfare in all but the last of these characteristics. The instrumental goals of terrorism involve arousing or intimidating civilian audiences more than reducing an opponent's military effectiveness. Acts of terrorism are symbolic, unexpected, and fundamentally demonstrative. The relationship between victim and audience is critical to its distinctiveness. Victims are representative and symbolic. Their usefulness to the terrorist lies in the regard society has for them.

To elaborate on this definition, consider first the proposition that terrorism refers to acts of violence performed by small groups. It is not the product of direct mass participation and is thus not "collective" political action in a strict sense. The participation of the individual matters critically to a small-group effort, so the free rider problem introduced by rational choice theory can safely be disregarded. Horowitz (1977:290) refers to terrorists as believers in a voluntaristic conception of history. While they believe that mass action may in the end be necessary to bring about historical change, they are convinced that small conspiratorial undergrounds can lead the way. Obviously this condition does not mean that groups who use terrorism may not over time acquire popular backing. Most practitioners of terrorism consider themselves the representatives of an actual or potential constituency, however vaguely conceived. Terrorism may be intended to stimulate spontaneous popular support, acting as a catalyst to mass-based revolution. It may be an adjunct to collective political action, as it was for the Algerian Front de Libération Nationale or the Socialist Revolutionary party in the years leading up to the Russian Revolution. But even in large organizations, the auxiliary units responsible for terrorism remain separate and isolated for reasons of security and efficient decision making. They retain the psychological and organizational characteristics of a small group. The Combat Organization of the Socialist Revolutionaries operated autonomously from the parent organization, as did the FLN's Zone Autonome d'Alger during the Battle of Algiers.

A second attribute of terrorism, which Horowitz (1977) stipulated, is that terrorism is highly intentional or purposeful violence. It is not spontaneous or unplanned. Implementation of a terrorist strategy requires careful advance preparation and deliberate calculation of effect. This qualification suggests that terrorism may not always be an attractive outlet for the impulsively violent individual who seeks immediate gratification. However, Horowitz (1989) explains that terrorism does link structural and personality variables in political action; terrorism may not be just instrumental but a mechanism for acting out personal rage. Nevertheless, Horowitz (1973) suggested earlier that while terrorism may be intensive (sustained in frequency and destructiveness over time) or sporadic, it is always systematic. Mob violence, rioting, street fighting, individual assassinations without organized backing, and other possible exhibitions of spontaneous collective anger or expressive destructiveness cannot be counted as terrorism. The single act of terrorism is part of a coordinated and sustained political strategy. Each act of terrorism must be interpreted in the context of the sequence of actions of which it is a part. The appropriate unit of analysis is the campaign of terrorism, not the single act.

As befits a form of violent coercion, the magnitude of the physical destructiveness of terrorism is small compared not only to other forms of political violence such as civil wars or communal rioting but also to other sources of casualties in modern societies. The public perception of risk from terrorism usually far exceeds the reality. In Israel, car accidents, criminal violence, and labor accidents routinely produce far more numerous casualties than terrorism (Alon, 1980:93-94). In the period 1967-78, terrorism caused 1,856 out of 337,172 total casualties, or .55 percent. There were 272 deaths from terrorism, 2.9 percent of the 9,424 deaths from all sources. In West Germany in 1977, the so-called "year of the terrorist," a total of 17 deaths were associated with left wing terrorism, including both victims and perpetrators, whereas 14,978 deaths resulted from automobile accidents (Sobel, 1978:250-59). In 1990, 37,000 deaths in the United States were caused by firearms, while 200 deaths were caused by international terrorism (*New York Times,* 29 July 1993, p. 22). Figures from the Department of State and from the Jaffee Center for Strategic Studies at Tel Aviv University show that from 1985 to 1992 roughly 3,600 deaths were due to international terrorism.[2] In contrast, Melvin Small and J. David Singer (1979:69) estimate 133,250 battle deaths per year worldwide in the 1966-77 period. Over a million people were probably killed during the four years of Khmer Rouge rule in Cambodia (1975-79) and a similar figure is usually given for the Iran-Iraq war (1980-88).

Terrorism and Guerrilla Warfare

Both terrorism and guerrilla warfare are forms of what is currently called "low intensity conflict." Both involve actions of relatively small forces, commitment of limited resources, and reliance on elusiveness and mobility. Both are important strategies for political change by those out of power. Also, where circumstances are appropriate, oppositions can use both, either simultaneously or sequentially. Analyses of counterinsurgency typically list terrorism as the opening stage of revolutionary conflict, which then is presumed to move through guerrilla warfare to conventional warfare and eventual victory. In practice, difficulty in distinguishing terrorism from the general idea of national liberation struggle has impeded international cooperation and frequently driven the framers of international treaties to forsake the term *terrorism* altogether. Urban violence further complicates the issue. In Latin America, the attempt to transplant what seemed to be the successful methods of the Cuban Revolution to the cities of Brazil, Argentina, and Uruguay resulted in the concept of "urban guerrilla warfare." Richard Gillespie (1986:152) explains that terrorism can be one form of urban guerrilla warfare, but that the two concepts are not identical. He sees urban guerrilla warfare as more discriminate and predictable, but also as a strategy that tends to be dominated by military rather than political considerations.

It is thus important not to blur the two concepts. In conceptual terms, the ends and means of guerrilla warfare and terrorism are distinct. *Guerrilla warfare,* a term that originated with the Spanish popular resistance to Napoleon in 1808–1809, is intended to damage the military potential of the enemy, albeit in unconventional ways that are dictated by the disparity of forces. It is, as the word implies, a "small" war typically conducted by nationalist forces against foreign military occupation. Indeed, Horowitz (1973) has long emphasized the distinction that the participants in guerrilla warfare are typically nationals, not foreigners. On the other hand, terrorism often features what we might call transnational participation (the Popular Front for the Liberation of Palestine joined by the Japanese Red Army in shooting Puerto Rican pilgrims to Israel, for example, at Lod airport in 1972). As Horowitz also stressed, guerrilla warfare is a rural activity because it is a method of seizing territory in order to challenge government control. Targets possess a military value or relate directly to the government's claims to territory or people. The mobilization of rural populations is considered essential to the eventual seizure of power, and guerrilla forces are much larger in size than organizations devoted exclusively to terrorism. There is consequently a need for a more complex and specialized organization.

Rural-based nationalist or revolutionary organizations who rely primarily on guerrilla warfare can also use terrorism to intimidate populations and to compel obedience as part of a campaign to secure control of people and territory and undermine government control. Horowitz (1983), who was one of the first scholars to draw attention to the outcomes of terrorism, argued that such terrorism is more likely to succeed, because it is linked to national and territorial claims. Here terrorism and guerrilla warfare are closely linked, since the purpose of terrorism is to secure popular support, however reluctant. But paradoxically, this form of terrorism also resembles state terrorism since its goal is to prevent resistance to insurgent authority. Terrorism as an adjunct strategy becomes a substitute for genuine popular acceptance of the insurgents' cause.

Psychology, Symbolism, and Intentionality

Irving Louis Horowitz (1973) has described terrorism as a form of advertising discontent. It influences the political behavior of actors through psychological manipulation of their choices, an accomplishment that need not diminish military capability in any way. The significance of terrorism cannot be measured by amount of territory held or number of cadres deployed in the field. The tactics of terrorists are intended to demoralize, disorient, shock, or frighten civilians, in order to dominate them or to bring public pressure to bear on government decisions. Terrorism communicates a political message. The appeal to propaganda of the deed, introduced by the nineteenth-century anarchists to call for acts that are understandable in themselves, remains central today. The standard repertory of terrorist acts, including bombings, armed attack, assassination, sabotage, and hostage taking, are most likely to be directed against noncombatants precisely because violence against civilians creates public distress and consequently pressure on governments. Terrorism is a play on emotions and symbols. Harold D. Lasswell (1978:255) once observed that "terrorists are participants in the political process who strive for political results by arousing acute anxieties."

The acts of violence that comprise a terrorist campaign become meaningful not only because of their symbolism but because of the systematic and sustained purpose they represent in the eyes of audiences. The meaning of an act of terrorism is derived from the pattern it exhibits and from the interpretation the perpetrators of violence themselves give it. The act of terrorism is meant to reveal its political motivation and to threaten more violence to come. Thus, terrorism strikes victims who represent social and political categories or who symbolize the power of elites. The effects on the victims themselves are secondary to the intended effects on attentive audiences. Lawrence Z. Freedman (1983) described acts of terrorism as possessing the quality of resonance. Harold Lasswell (1978:258-59) called this quality evocative, and defined terrorism as reliance on the symbolic enhancement of instruments of destruction in order to achieve an evocative form that would arouse general apprehension, leading to politically significant consequences. The act itself must create a sense of fearful apprehension in other potential victims who have the same social characteristics or political affiliations, as well as in observers who are not personally at risk. It is the expectation of continued terrorism and the pervasiveness of perceived risk that influence behavior. As Thomas C. Schelling (1966:3) noted, "Unhappily, the power to hurt is often communicated by some performance of it."

Horowitz (1989:390–91) has written of "dramaturgical" terrorists. Terrorism can be interpreted as a socially constructed theatrical event, with a sequence of acts or phases, a discernible plot, and a dramatic resolution (Wagner-Pacifici, 1986). Hostage takings in particular can assume the characteristics of melodrama or tragedy, depending on how closely the audience identifies with the victim. Most audiences for hijackings and kidnappings are psychologically and geographically distant from the stage on which violence is enacted. The emotions a terrorist drama arouses will vary according to several factors: the distance between action and audience, the predispositions of the audience, the dramatic power of the events, and the public interpretation of terrorism. The physical victims of terrorism may be no more real to the audience than are the actors in a theater. Terrorism becomes a macabre form of mass entertainment. The personal histories of victims are inconsequential, except as they reinforce the drama by adding an element of pathos.

It is worth noting that the personal identities of the terrorists may be no more important than those of victims. Horowitz (1977:293) points out that not all terrorists seek publicity or "self-celebration"; their anonymity is also symbolic. This assumption is supported by the empirical evidence, since many incidents remain unclaimed, such as the bombing of Pan Am 103 in 1988.

What traits designate the victims of terrorism? There appear to be two dramatic models: representatives of the established order, considered guilty by virtue of responsibility or position, and sacrificial victims, who are representative of classes of people but otherwise innocent. The tragedy is intensified by their innocence. As common citizens came to be valued by democratic governments, both because of the accountability of leaders to the public and their replaceability and the generalized acceptance of the principle of protection for the rights of the individual, attacks on ordinary people became useful to terrorists as a way of manipulating the emotions of audiences. Democracies can survive the assassinations of leaders, as Horowitz (1983) noted, but they cannot tolerate public insecurity.

Effects of Terrorism

The idea that the purpose of terrorism is to produce these psychological and political outcomes is critical to understanding its form. Intentions, of course, should not be confused with results. Terrorism need not produce the consequences its users anticipate. While the concept of revolution implies success, the definition of terrorism does not require that its objects actually be terrorized. Whether terrorism succeeds or fails is a question that should be answered by comparing intentions with outcomes.

Horowitz (1973 and 1977) has stressed that terrorists seek not physical destruction but the unraveling of the fabric of society; nevertheless, their disruptions of modern society are highly transitory. They often fail to predict audience reactions. Terrorists may think that the uncommitted will withdraw support from the government, whereas the opposite usually happens—the public rallies behind the threatened government. In fact, many of the most enduring consequences of terrorism, such as the strengthening of the state's security institutions, the rallying of public opinion behind threatened democracies, and the growth of international security cooperation, are counterproductive from the point of view of the practitioners of terrorism.

Horowitz (1973 and 1977) also argued that any government that is willing to abandon restraint can eradicate terrorism, but that we should not exaggerate the menace to democratic societies. The existence of terrorism may actually be an indicator of social health rather than a sign of the breakdown of democracy. Despite the popular assumption that democracies are uniquely threatened, the dislike of terrorism is not confined to democracies; socialist states also find terrorism intolerable. Horowitz warned that while democratic governments should not be indecisive, they should be cautious about responses to terrorism that undermine civil liberties. Terrorism has never directly resulted in the overthrow of a democratic government. It has more often provoked military intervention in politics. The greatest danger may be overreaction.

Forms of Terrorism

An extremist group that intends to produce psychological effects that are disproportionate to the amount of destructive force employed has an interest in economizing on the means of violence. Economy is dictated by the small size of the typical extremist organization and its lack of active popular support. According to James DeNardo (1985), terrorism is one way of compensating for lack of numbers. The imperative of economizing strongly affects the form taken by terrorism. One way of compensating for small size is to surprise one's opponent. The time, the place, and the personal identity of victims are unexpected. Terrorism disrupts normally peaceful relationships and seizes on victims, whether military or civilian, who are unaware and unprepared. Terrorists rarely attack well-defended targets. The two factors of weakness and the desire to excite passions encourage terrorists to attack ordinary civilians rather than government leaders, who are surrounded by well-armed bodyguards and conveyed from place to place behind bulletproof glass. Terrorism inclines naturally against the most vulnerable and defenseless elements of society, especially those most valued by its members, such as schoolchildren.

At a time when most authors were calling our attention to the spectacular dimensions of terrorism, Horowitz (1983) reminded us of the possible routinization of terrorist violence. Terrorism, he said, can lose the power to shock. Thus, if victims are to be surprised and audiences outraged or horrified, terrorism must be innovative. As violence becomes routine, audiences adjust psychologically, the abnormal becomes normal, the press ceases to put terrorist incidents in the headlines, and governments mobilize to put effective security measures into place. Groups who resort to terrorism are compelled by the logic of their methods to seek out the defenseless and to invent new tactics, such as kidnapping diplomats or hijacking cruise ships. Yet innovation is limited by the requirement that victims possess symbolic significance if the act is to be understood by audiences.

The possibility that, because it is technically possible, future terrorism will escalate to unprecedented levels of destructiveness must be evaluated in view of these limits to political effectiveness. In the early days of terrorism analysis, Horowitz (1977:294) warned scholars of the perils of "anticipatory socialization" in predicting the future of terrorism. The alarmist scenarios that permeate popular treatments of the phenomenon are not only unrealistic but may be dangerous.

The unexpectedness and dramatic tension necessary for terrorism also require concealment. Clandestinity is essential to terrorism. In many forms of civil violence—street fighting and paramilitary activities, for example—the actors seek visibility. Terrorists, in contrast, do not wear uniforms or insignia unless they are disguises. E. V. Walter (1969:87-108, 341) has pointed out that terrorists resemble the members of early African secret societies, who wore masks to conceal their personal identities when acting in the name of the group. The robes and hoods of the Ku Klux Klan similarly hide the commonplace identities of its members and enhance their frightfulness. We are reminded again of Horowitz's point about the symbolism of anonymity. In general, potential victims cannot distinguish the terrorist from the crowd or recognize the danger that other members of society pose for them. The possibility that the members of terrorist organizations are not psychologically different from the rest of us only makes terrorism more disturbing. The very ordinariness and indistinguishability of terrorists are tacit forms of concealment and deception. The fear that terrorists are genuinely anonymous—that they are no different from the rest of society—may partially explain the persistent and undocumented tendency to attribute terrorism to mental illness. Disguise may also allow the perpetrator to escape normal moral inhibitions by assuming a new identity.

The forms of terrorist violence—bombings, kidnappings, sieges, or armed attacks that catch their victims off guard—and the targeting of civilians are shocking in their unacceptability to society. To many authors, including Horowitz, cultural unacceptability is a hallmark of terrorism. For example, David Rapoport (1977) defines terrorism as the politics of atrocity, a refusal to accept the conventional moral limits on violence that bind military action, including guerrilla warfare. Rapoport's interpretation of terrorism assumes that terrorists, victims, and audiences share a moral sensibility, a common understanding of the appropriate limits to political action. His argument suggests that the effectiveness of terrorism may depend on the existence of norms to be violated and thus on social context. The more normal and routine violence becomes, the less effectively it communicates its message. Escalation to a new level of unacceptability is required in order to maintain the same level of psychological effect. It is in this sense that terrorism is, in Thomas P.

Thornton's words (1964), extranormal and extraordinary. To produce outrage, terrorism depends on a system of shared beliefs, a condition for audiences to perceive acts of terrorism as the terrorists wish them to. Terrorism is thus highly context-dependent. In consequence, as terrorism reaches out to secure a reaction from global audiences, becoming a transnational phenomenon, it must violate universal norms, such as diplomatic inviolability. Yet it is still clear that what is outrageous in one situation or to one audience is not necessarily so in different contexts or before different audiences.

Paul Wilkinson (1986:54–57) defines terrorism as violence that is not only indiscriminate and arbitrary in form but also inhumane and barbarous. In his view, terrorism is always characterized by rejection of universal moral constraints. He thus concludes that the analysis of terrorism must be based on an evaluative concept, an explicit judgment that order and normalcy are to be valued over the type of social change favored by the proponents of terrorism. This linkage of ends and means is common in attitudes toward terrorism.

Nevertheless, however reprehensible we find terrorism, the commission of atrocities—the perpetuation of barbaric crimes against humanity—is not exclusive to terrorism. Communal violence driven by rivalry between ethnic, religious, or kinship groups, for example, is often extraordinarily brutal and destructive. The use of torture by governments is cruel and inhumane. The perception of terrorism as more barbarous than government atrocities may be due to its personalized quality. Institutionalized and bureaucratic violence may indeed seem less offensive to society, regardless of number of casualties or indiscriminacy. But cruelty cannot be considered unique to terrorism.

The characteristic that is probably most strongly associated with the perceived outrageousness of terrorism is indiscriminacy in selection of victims. But as we have noted earlier, terrorism is not *necessarily* indiscriminate or random. Degree of discrimination is relative; it is a variable that must be explained rather than a condition to be assumed. Horowitz (1983) has argued strongly in support of maintaining this distinction between discriminate and indiscriminate terrorism, to be used as a basis for predicting the success or failure of terrorism. His view is that the less focused terrorism is, the less likely it is to change the basis of law and society or to separate society from government. Instead it produces a popular backlash.

Not only is terrorism not always indiscriminate but lack of discrimination is hardly unique to terrorism. Conventional military operations cause *collateral damage,* an antiseptic term that means civilian casualties. The term *surgical strike* only makes us feel apprehensive. The policy of nuclear deterrence is based on a "countervalue" retaliatory strike, with the enemy's population centers as targets. In civil conflicts in Guatemala and elsewhere armies have massacred civilians by the hundreds and thousands.

Conclusion

It is clear that this conception of terrorism depends on understanding the intention behind violence. For at least fifty years terrorism has been considered as part of a coordinated political program that can be known to observers. Terrorism is assumed to be an activity with a political purpose. However, other scholars have responded that it is empirically unsound to define terrorism in terms of a political intent that limited information prevents the observer from knowing with any certainty (e.g., Gurr, 1979). One reason for this difference of opinion is the distinction between the long-term goals of terrorism, the political program that it ultimately serves, and its short-term objectives, which consist of the immediate effects on audiences and on governments. The search for precise evidence of instrumental goals is frustrating. The propaganda statements that accompany terrorist actions cannot be considered reliable indicators of intent, especially if terrorism is regarded as manipulative and deceptive.

Yet theories of politics cannot escape dependence on imperfect knowledge of the purpose behind political action. Comprehensive and accurate information about political motivation is rarely available. Distinguishing rationalization from motive is always problematic. In the case of terrorism the observer can often infer intent from the nature of behavior, while recognizing that many obstacles lie between the intentions of actors and the outcomes of their actions. Terrorism is a rare form of political behavior precisely because its form does reflect its general purpose. It is a specialized category of organized political violence, limited in its physical destructiveness but expansive in its power to draw attention. The actors responsible for oppositional terrorism are usually small conspiracies who seek to impress their claims on the pub-

lic mind and so influence the behavior of governments. The nature of
their influence is both psychological and political. Terrorism is characterized by stealth and secrecy, as well as by disproportion between the
magnitude of physical and psychological effects. Material weakness leads
radical oppositions to rely on unexpectedness. Their defiance of conventions is conscious and calculated. Terrorism is more than a violation
of standards: it symbolizes rejection of the rules that apply to the conduct of both war and peace. It is designed to be excessive, meant by its
very excess to expose the desperation behind the act, whether that desperation is real or false, the despair of the oppressed or the subterfuge of
the ideological fanatic.

The works of Irving Louis Horowitz have contributed to making the
study of terrorism both more scholarly and more balanced. He has argued that terrorism can be defined as an analytical concept and that
while we should be sensitive to the implications of political language,
we should not dismiss the term as useless. Terrorism, furthermore, should
be considered part of the political process, not an aberration. The users
of terrorism may see themselves as society's heroes, not society's vil-
lains. We must ask ourselves not only what conception of history terrorists hold and what they intend but also what values terrorism threatens
and why societies are vulnerable. Horowitz's approach to terrorism thus
links the concepts of individual agency and social structure. Furthermore, this interpretation leads him to caution us against exaggeration
and overreaction. Terrorism, he notes, succeeds only under special sets
of circumstances. Its effect are often ephemeral. In our fear of disruption, we should not undermine the values we are defending.

Wesleyan University
Department of Government

Notes

1. Lakos (1991) lists 5,850 citations. Works on terrorism by Irving Louis Horowitz include "Can Democracy Cope with Terrorism?" *Civil Liberties Review* 4 (May-June 1977): 29–37; "Political Terrorism and State Power," *Journal of Political and Military Sociology* 1 (Spring 1973): 145–57; "The Routinization of Terrorism and Its Unanticipated Consequences," in *Terrorism, Legitimacy, and Power: The Consequences of Political Violence,* ed. Martha Crenshaw (Middletown, CT: Wesleyan University Press, 1983), 38–51; "Transnational Terrorism, Civil Liberties, and Social Science," in *Terrorism: Interdisciplinary Perspectives,* ed. Yonah Alexander and Seymour Maxwell Finger (New York: The John Jay Press, 1977), 283–97; "The Texture of Terrorism: Socialization, Routinization, and Integration,"

in *Political Learning in Adulthood: A Sourcebook of Theory and Research,* ed. Roberta S. Sigel (Chicago: University of Chicago Press, 1989), 386–414; and "Unicorns and Terrorists," a review of *International Terrorism,* ed. Yonah Alexander, in *The Nation* (20 March 1976): 341–44.

2. U.S. Department of State, Office of the Ambassador at Large for Counter-Terrorism, *Patterns of Global Terrorism* (an annual publication). The Department of State defines international terrorism as "premeditated, politically motivated violence perpetrated against noncombatant targets by subnational groups or clandestine state agents, usually intended to influence an audience" and involving citizens or territory of more than one country. Horowitz (1976) has expressed some doubts about the usefulness of this concept. "International terrorism" may be a unicorn, not a social reality. Terrorism is a local, national, or regional phenomenon, not global.

References

Alon, Hanan. *Countering Palestinian Terrorism in Israel: Toward a Policy Analysis of Countermeasures.* Santa Monica, CA: Rand, 1980.

Cohen, Geula. *Woman of Violence: Memoirs of a Young Terrorist, 1943–1948.* New York: Holt, 1966.

Conrad, Thomas R. "Coercion, Assassination, Conspiracy: Pejorative Political Language." *Polity* 6 (Spring 1974): 418–23.

DeNardo, James. *Power in Numbers: The Political Strategy of Protest and Rebellion.* Princeton, NJ: Princeton University Press, 1985.

Farr, James. "Historical Concepts in Political Science: The Case of 'Revolution'." *American Journal of Political Science* 26 (November 1982): 688–708.

Foot, M. R. D. *SOE in France: An Account of the Work of the British Special Operations Executive in France 1940–1944.* Frederick, MD: University Publications of America, 1984. Originally published in London by H.M.S.O. in 1966.

Freedman, Lawrence Z. "Why Does Terrorism Terrorize?" *Terrorism: An International Journal* 6 (1983): 389–401.

Gillespie, Richard. "The Urban Guerrilla in Latin America." In *Terrorism, Ideology, and Revolution,* ed. Noel O'Sullivan. Boulder: Westview Press, 1986.

Greisman, H. C. "Social Meanings of Terrorism: Reunification, Violence, and Social Control." *Contemporary Crises* 1 (1977): 303–18.

Gurr, Ted Robert. "Psychological Factors in Civil Violence." *World Politics* 20 (January 1968): 245–78.

———. "Some Characteristics of Political Terrorism in the 1960s." In *The Politics of Terrorism,* ed. Michael Stohl. New York: Marcel Dekker, 1979.

Horowitz, Irving Louis. "Political Terrorism and State Power." *Journal of Political and Military Sociology* 1 (Spring 1973): 145–57.

———. "Unicorns and Terrorists." A review of *International Terrorism,* ed. Yonah Alexander, in *The Nation* (March 1976): 341–44.

———. "Transnational Terrorism, Civil Liberties, and Social Science." In *Terrorism: Interdisciplinary Perspectives,* ed. Yonah Alexander and Seymour Maxwell Finger. New York: The John Jay Press, 1977.

———. "The Routinization of Terrorism and Its Unanticipated Consequences." In *Terrorism, Legitimacy, and Power: The Consequences of Political Violence,* ed. Martha Crenshaw. Middletown, CT: Wesleyan University Press, 1983.

————. "The Texture of Terrorism: Socialization, Routinization, and Integration." In *Political Learning in Adulthood: A Sourcebook of Theory and Research*, ed. Roberta S. Sigel. Chicago: University of Chicago Press, 1989.

Iyad, Abou. [Khalaf, Salah]. *Palestinien sans patrie: Entretiens avec Eric Rouleau*. Paris: Fayolle, 1978.

Lakos, Amos. *Terrorism, 1980–1990: A Bibliography*. Boulder: Westview Press, 1991.

Lasswell, Harold D. "Terrorism and the Political Process." *Terrorism: An International Journal* 1 (1978): 255, 258–59.

Leproux, Marc. *Nous les Terroristes: Journal de la section spéciale de sabotage*, 2 vols. Monte Carlo: Raoul Solar, 1947.

Maitron, Jean. *Histoire du mouvement anarchiste en France (1880–1914)*, 2ème ed. Paris: Société universitaire d'editions et de librairie, 1955.

Marighela, Carlos. "Handbook of the Urban Guerrilla." In *For the Liberation of Brazil*. Harmondsworth: Penguin, 1971.

Nardin, Terry. *Violence and the State: A Critique of Empirical Political Theory*. Beverly Hills: Sage, 1971.

Rapoport, David. "The Politics of Atrocity." In *Terrorism: Interdisciplinary Perspectives*, ed. Yonah Alexander and Seymour Maxwell Finger. New York: John Jay Press, 1977.

Rubenstein, Richard L. *The Cunning of History: Mass Death and the American Future*. New York: Harper and Row, 1975.

Schelling, Thomas C. "The Diplomacy of Violence." In *Arms and Influence*. New Haven, CT: Yale University Press, 1966.

Schmid, Alex P. *Political Terrorism: A Research Guide to Concepts, Theories, Data Bases and Literature*. New Brunswick, NJ: Transaction Publishers, 1984.

Short, K. R. M. *The Dynamite War: Irish-American Bombers in Victorian Britain*. Dublin: Gill and Macmillan, 1979.

Small, Melvin, and J. David Singer. "Conflict in the International System, 1816–1977: Historical Trends and Policy Futures." in J. David Singer and Associates, *Explaining War: Selected Papers from the Correlates of War Project*. Beverly Hills: Sage, 1979.

Sobel, Lester A., ed. *Political Terrorism, Vol. 2: 1974–78*. New York: Facts on File, 1978.

Spiridovitch, Alexandre. *Histoire du terrorisme russe*. Paris: Payot, 1930.

Stepniak (pseud. for Kravchinski). *Underground Russia: Revolutionary Profiles and Sketches from Life*. London: Smith, Elder, and Co., 1883.

Textes des prisonniers de la "Fraction Armée Rouge" et dernières lettres d'Ulrike Meinhof. Paris: Maspéro, 1977.

Thornton, Thomas P. "Terror as a Weapon of Political Agitation." In *Internal War: Problems and Approaches*, ed. Harry Eckstein. New York: Free Press, 1964.

Turk, Austin T. *Political Criminality: The Defiance and Defense of Authority*. Beverly Hills: Sage, 1982.

Wagner-Pacifici, Robin Erica. *The Moro Morality Play: Terrorism as Social Drama*. Chicago: University of Chicago Press, 1986.

Walter, Eugene Victor. *Terror and Resistance*. New York: Oxford University Press, 1969.

Wilkinson, Paul. *Terrorism and the Liberal State*, rev. ed. New York: New York University Press, 1986.

Wilson, Ronald D. *Cordon and Search: With the 6th Airborne Division in Palestine*. Aldershot: Gale and Polden, 1949.

Zawodny, J. K. "Internal Organizational Problems and the Sources of Tensions of Terrorist Movements as Catalysts of Violence." *Terrorism: An International Journal* 1 (1978): 277–86.

Section Three

Social Research and Professional Ethics

9

Policy, Social Science, and Action

Anselm Strauss

In response to Irving Louis Horowitz's remark to me that a festschrift shouldn't be just thirty papers in search of a hard cover but should address the recipient, I am tempted to begin this paper with a Dear Irving caption. We have been dear friends, via correspondence and business dealings (Transaction Publishers and *Society*) for many years, and have been collegially intimate a couple of times when writing respective introductions to books. Though our careers have been conspicuously different, occasionally he reminds me of the many overlaps in perspective, aim and mood. One such intersection is on the vital significance of applied social science, "policy" being perhaps his preferred term for that conjunction. So it is to policy and Horowitz on policy that this paper is addressed.

One way of reading Horowitz's intellectual life is that it can't be separated, without immense distortion, from his moral life—from his sense of moral justice and injustice; nor are his beliefs, ideas, research, and writing clearly separable from his actions. In this sense he reminds me of one of my own heros, John Dewey, because of this unity of morality, thought, and conduct. Many items in his long bibliography are striking evidence of the not so usual combination of an always thoughtful and often profound social scientist who almost always writes with the aim of encouraging reform action. As he remarks, "[M]y predilection over the years for the essay form, a style of writing with a moral tail steering an empirical frame, continues unabated" (1984:xiv).

A central enterprise in his life, the long-lived and astonishingly successful Transaction Publishers, is eloquent testimony to both sides of his nature; yet we all know it is much more than that, for this publishing company engages its authors and readers in a direct dialogue about major issues of our day. This persistent application of social science addresses policy and reform issues. Whether called applied science, reform, or policy, what is important is the thrust and meaning of that thirty-year flow of books and articles.

What I am leading up to is the general topic of this festschrift paper, namely, Irving Horowitz's general conception of policy and its intersection with social science. The paper is divided into several sections. First, he and I will engage in a kind of question and answer session, where he will answer questions (through his writings) about policy and social science. Then, I will present a brief analysis of the premises behind his characteristic phrases, for they can tell us a great deal about why he has the courage to say the things he says and to do many of the things he does. Then a central policy issue raised by him, in a recent article on AIDS research (1988), will be discussed, namely, how to make sensible and effective policy when dissensus rather than relative consensus predominates. In considering this, I will attempt to show both the success of his policy views as applied to this issue of descensus, but also to suggest how these might be strengthened.

Some Questions, Some Responses

QUESTION: In the special thirtieth anniversary issue of *Society* (1992), I was struck by the forceful language in your introductory article ("Social Research and the Culture of Society"). There is a certain directness, in fact passion, when you talk about social science. This seems not to be just a set of information-collecting fields or even just one among a number of fields of knowledge.

IRVING LOUIS HOROWITZ: "[S]ocial science is the jewel in the crown of contemporary democracy.... Like...democracy itself, the social science vision is ever skeptical about institutions, ever respectful of individuals.... the social sciences are a twentieth century phenomenon...something quite recent in human affairs.... [They] represent a third realm of human activity, one that is now broadly, if hesitatingly, regarded as a beacon to humankind and a light to nations. It is within this context, and as part of a global effort to establish the discursive terms of a twentieth-century rationality, that *Society* was established" (1992:7–8).

QUESTION: So, you are asserting that social science exists for its contributions to, or perhaps more accurately phrased, for its crucial role in a democratic social order?

ILH: "One might say of social science what Walter Lippmann long ago said of democracy: it is not a very good instrument for the making of public policy but it is about the best one available. In the absence of a mass outpouring of democratic persuasion, and in the presence of political corruption in high office and political apathy among the ordinary citizens, the social sciences essentially perform the role of cementing American goals and presenting them in such a manner in which, at the very least, if it does not provide rational solution to social problems it prevents an irrational solution from being adopted toward these same problems" (1975a:134).

QUESTION: Are you claiming this for all the social sciences, all the work of social scientists?

ILH: "At their very best, the social sciences have inherited the classical sensibility...to understand that a victory over a specific tyranny is just as likely to open the way for worse tyrannies as it is to permit the evolution of new freedoms; the ability to understand that in a world filled with competing moral claims, as well as scientific rationales, a choice of preferences may be painful and difficult. But it is also a window of opportunity offering a potential for action" (1992:9–10).

QUESTION: Tell me a little more about your conception of democracy vis-à-vis the social sciences. You make a linkage there more directly than most of us, though probably just about every American social scientist assumes that connection.

ILH: Because we need "[t]o promote human equality, to advance human reason...to stand firm and clear against the forces of darkness. For such forces are not in outer space or inner earth, but part of the everyday conduct of human affairs" (1992:9).

QUESTION: I sense you think of this as a struggle (your word) against the forces of actual or potential tyranny, as you say "part of the everyday conduct of human affairs."

ILH: It "is not an easy task to navigate between those who identify science with raw matter, energy, and formal rules of grammar, and those who identify culture with theology. Neither will pause to reflect that convictions extrapolated from the soil of nature and society can be sources of murder and mayhem as well as workable belief systems.... Every despot in this most contentious of centuries has tried to capture the social sciences, and failing that, to destroy what could not be coopted. We cannot compromise in our resolve to prevent cheap victories to fanaticism" (1992:9).

QUESTION: Most of the social scientists whom I know are more or less comfortably lodged within universities and colleges, teaching and doing research. Do you think they should be addressing policy issues or holding down policy positions in government?

ILH: "For the most part, [these] social science personnel are book-keepers of the soul. They are involved at the level of generating data, compiling facts, monitoring programs, and evaluating results: they are not central figures in the policy process or in decisions affecting future policy. Nonetheless, it is clear that a qualitative new era in social science has begun, and requires careful analysis in order to establish a better appreciation of the contours of social science [for now and in the future]."

"The central advance of our times over social science in the first half of the twentieth century...is the role of policy as a guiding instrument for politics as a whole. [But also, there] "is an equally powerful method-ological reformation of social science: a belief that policy recommenda-tions are frequently, if not always, the touchstone of a sound social science research project, and should therefore be built into the structure of sci-ence itself" (1979:3).

QUESTION: Earlier you said the government policy scientists were not necessarily of the highest quality, but also faulted the universities for often not including nor usually emphasizing policy in their training pro-grams. What's your reasoning about policy scientists' relations with so-cial science itself?

ILH: "Policy makers live in a world once removed from the proper rank order of professional achievement in the social sciences. Rarely do they gain access to high office in the major organizations in [their re-spective disciplines]...status derives directly from participation in the policy process" (1979:2).

Also, they "are distinguished by a three-set process: confronting old theory with new data for the purpose of arriving at new theory. In this they differ from the classical model of European social science in which theorist battles theorist and where the scholar most nimble with word manipulation triumphs. They also differ from the contemporary bureaucratic model in which data speak for themselves.... [Policy] Researchers test theory against evidence; and they create new forms of testing through implementation of policies, which in turn, are monitored and evaluated. In this way the cycle of evidence comes to include policy making as an organic component of social science itself" (1975b:126–27).

QUESTION: Except for the policy lingo you sound very much like us "grounded theorists," with theory and data in close choreography.

ILH: "The worst reason for using social science talent more widely is to avoid or bypass the democratic processes—a situation in which the role of expertise comes to displace the will of the people on major issues. Between these two poles the tightrope must be walked...populism can degenerate into jingoism, just as assuredly as social science can issue into elitism. [Also I should point to] the essential role of criticism performed by the social scientists. In this context [I] would urge...the widest possible training for policy making roles in counterestablishment institutions no less than in established institutions...advice and support of industrial unions, ethnic minorities, and special interest-interest groups (such as women, the aged, or youth)" (1975b:164–65).

QUESTION: I was waiting somewhat anxiously for you to get away from federal or any governmental policy advising to address the more grass-roots, community, and social movement orientations. I wish generally in your writings you'd say more about those in relation to policy. However, next I want to ask about the antagonism between scientists in government and those in academia.

ILH: The "problems of fusing university and policy life are many, but the problem resulting in a bifurcation of such a relationship are insoluble; drawing apart leads to arrogance, presumptuousness and hardheadedness, and ultimately to a negation of science as an instrument of criticism as well as construction.... The growth of social science for policy purposes will require a large-scale shift in the understanding of what science in general is all about. Models of science that frankly take into account the role of advocacy procedures, the place of social forecasting, and the need for large-as well as small-scale planning mechanics must begin to augment the traditional empirical and historical forms of description. The present division between 'pure' and 'applied' science only serves to permeate and prolong the myth of dualism.... The need for cross-fertilization has never been greater, and the rise of policy-making roles for the sciences only points out further this need to maintain a balance between scientific theory and scientifically-based action" (1975a:167).

"[T]hose in the academic world have only vague and indirect impact on the policy process, while those working within the policy apparatus itself are clearly limited by their bureaucratic frameworks and their levels of appointment. Is there anything specifically that can be done by the scientists themselves to bring this greater awareness to the larger body politic?... We are...not simply dealing with the problem of the relationships between the university and the bureaucracy. What the points of leverage are, no less than the committing of a greater portion of our time and energies to policy matters, itself becomes problematic, requiring careful analysis" (1979:136–37).

QUESTION: Among your most passionate and effective books is the one on genocide, in which you talk directly to and about social scientists. You are very critical of them, there. Why? Isn't genocide merely an esoteric, though admittedly terrible phenomenon among all the others that cry for our attention?

ILH: "It is a sad truth that issues of great magnitude, like genocide, have passed from social theorists in the nineteenth century to theologians in the twentieth century. The impulse to know more about less has not simply invaded the social sciences, it is an impulse which offers guidance to such supposedly human sciences. If there is a higher purpose to this [book on genocide] it is to remind my brethren that the unity of social science, if it is to be more than a pious phrase, rests on the unity of human existence. The mobilization of our resources to attack a problem such as genocide is...an issue which all people of this century are common witness to, and hence an area of investigation which demands the fullest utilization of scientific judgment.... Because the tendency to emotivism is so tempting it should not be permitted to preempt what is essentially an analytic examination. The hideous features of genocide are grave enough not to cheapen the phenomenon by pandering to oversimplified visions of good and evil. Yet one can hope that moral concerns will be strengthened by the explanations and evidence herein adduced" (1980:xiv).

"Too often, social science resorts to the tyranny of impersonal deterministic forces to explain major events. [Social scientists need to] reintroduce the person as a central factor in understanding a phenomenon such as genocide.... A political psychology must accompany any sound political sociology. For motives of rulers at one end, the behaviors of masses at the other, and the decision makers all along the stratification line give meaning to terms like genocide" (1980:177–78).

"My early interest in social and philosophical ideas and ideologies of war and peace, and the attendant analysis of conflict, consensus and cooperation, was itself part of a basic commitment to a sociology which takes seriously the right to live as a determinant of other human rights and social alignments. Questions of social structures, cultural orders, and military regimes, ultimately reduce to living and dying.... A naturalistic sociology must take its stand with life and the living. The collective imposition of death by a state must be seen as a common ground at which the needs of sociology and morality interact and intersect. One cannot have a democratic ideology outside the rule of law nor a democratic sociology without the bold assertion of the right to live.... To presume obligations to the state is not to assert simply a theory of obedience, but rather that the state must insure the right to live without presuming the reasons for living. The record of the twentieth century is soiled by a juridical standpoint that asserts obligations to serve the state without any corresponding sense of right to life within a state" (1980:186–87).

"In the long swing of the twentieth century, Chicago-style work has rested not only on theories of society, but on policies for society.... [This work] entails an entire set of moral premises about the worth of all people embodied in the theme of self and other. [It] deals with the human soul and its inviolabilities. I realize that, in introducing such a notion as the soul, I can be accused of importing Horowitz into Strauss. But I suspect not" (Horowitz, 1991:xiii).

Basic Assumptions

Horowitz's suspicions of kinship are quite accurate. Yet, the intellectual core of every social scientist is different from every other. It takes close reading sometimes to get at that core and then one must still write persuasively to make the discovery believable. To make it believable even to the one who is under the sociology of knowledge microscope!

Let me begin with a strange comparison involving perspective and style. Morris Janowitz's writing often struck me as that of a man anxiously looking over his shoulder at threats to the fragile island of social order on which he was (and we were) standing. He even wrote a brochure, I believe, for the police on how to handle domestic terror during the 1960s. Now Horowitz was born and raised in Harlem and he talks about the real dangers besetting children and their literal struggle of survival. But his writing in *Daydreams and Nightmares* (1990), despite all the pain and struggle he endured, and its frequent linking of the polar terms "death" and "life," of "living" and "dying," is far from pessimistic. (Who could miss that wonderful sentence descriptive of Horowitz's life, after leaving Harlem, where experiences in a Brooklyn school "all confirmed a world to win beyond the physical: a triumph not of will, but of mind; of giving scope to imagination and liberating children from the terrible scourges of life and death, focusing our innocent attentions on the wonderful things in between" (1990:97). He writes so enthusiastically about childhood scenes, such as: going to the movies, listening raptly to wonderful jazz at the Apollo theater, learning to find his way in a world that imposed defeats but allowed victories, and developing self-reliance in the face of persistent adversity. Indeed, Horowitz's style reminds me a bit of the wonderfully vigorous, even dare I say it muscularly energetic work by my favorite American sculptor, David Smith.

But to get back to the comparison with Morris Janowitz, I feel that at the heart of Horowitz's sociology there is also deep concern for the fragility of social order. Yet metaphorically speaking, instead of a beleaguered island there is a solid rock on which we stand, fighting off the forces of evil (tyranny of any kind). Perhaps instead of a rock I need to change the metaphor to a dazzlingly precious city, since it is one our ancestors built and we are continuing to build, defend, and hopefully extend—despite totalitarianism, ideological deluge, special interests that continue to be out of control, and other forms of tyranny and nonrationality. It is my belief that anyone who does not understand that this is at the core of Irving Horowitz's being cannot understand him.

So, a social order, because it is constructed, is also fragile. Perhaps there exists something like progress, but not in the vulgar sense usually assumed; rather any incremental improvements in the human condition must be eked out in the face of the continual flow of detrimental contingencies. (For, "the human race—the only race that has moral standing—moves backward as well as forward, and most often sideways" [Horowitz, 1992:8].) This social order, this challenge to all of us,

Horowitz equates with democracy. To my delight he does not just refer to the noun, but often uses it as an adjective: democratic culture, democratic action, democratic sociology. Democracy for Horowitz is shared discourse, among individuals whose collective nature is inseparable from themselves. (In one place he harshly names "shared discourse" and "distilled hatred" as alternative bases for policy [1984:xvi].) This democratic discourse is not just talk, a play of ideas for its own sake, but carried out in the service of civic ideals, and ultimately human rights, in the face of the very real threats to them. Such a democratic society, one "must fight for with the same passion and conviction as those who would 'shut it down'" (1984:xviii).

Democracy also stands for rationality, the life support against (again I will switch metaphors) a sea of potentially engulfing waves. Horowitz makes so much of rationality, speaking of it so frequently, that a skeptical reader might wonder at his faith in it. But he is, I feel, very much in the line of Jefferson, Madison, and later Americans like Dewey, with a similar profound enlightenment-derived faith in reason. (I have it myself.) Horowitz is like them, though one shouldn't perhaps make too much of the specific comparisons, insofar as rationality is conceived of as in the service of democracy, civic ideals, human rights—or life itself. He does not concern himself with the postmodern question, nor share its frequent anxiety, about "what do we do since there is no real world out there, but only one that is constructed by us?" Having grown up in Harlem, having studied genocide, the world out there is real enough! One doesn't have to be insensitive to epistemological insights about reality and construction, to make the theory-of-action assumption that "yes we construct the world through our actions but not entirely."

Perhaps it is time that I said something about morality, though Horowitz's stand on this is pretty obvious, both from his own writings and from what has just been said. That central concern of his about social order is, said in less sociological terms, a passionate concern for the best (actively fought for) human condition possible. Democratic actions involve moral decisions. Democracy if it is a real democracy is a matter of morality, not just of clear thinking. A democratic social science is not in the least free of moral judgments and moral implications for action and social structures. To ignore this aspect of our social science work is to underestimate its potential for society, to run the risk of formalism on the one hand and nit-picking empiricism on the other.

Morality as well as rationality—indeed both together, hand in hand—embody our potential for building a more livable human existence. Yet, Horowitz does not use morality and rationality merely as nouns, but as verbs: He is not only a man of action but a theorist who assumes action. Action stands strikingly at the heart of his sociology, both in the theoretical and pragmatic senses.

So, Horowitz's criticism of sociology and the other social sciences is often likely to rest on their failures with respect to one or another counts, or both. Here he is in the best pragmatist tradition, for he even speaks of a damaging dualism. His antidualism, it is plain to see, is also a methodological position. He may not say much specifically about the range of social science methods and techniques, but he thinks of these as instruments leading to knowledge, which in turn leads to action, and also vice versa! This conception portrays a seamless web, though alas in the real world this ideal is often not reached, is indeed often corrupted by human hubris and stupidity.

Thought and action brought together, fused, are characteristic of our greatest sociologists. Thought stands for abstraction, for maintaining a certain distance from the tempestuous Hogarthian drama, which it is our business to understand, portray, and yes to tell the actors what we think they are doing. In this sense we are mirrors, reflecting back representations of their world of "concreteness"—picturing something they recognize and yet did not quite know, or at least know its deep significance. The action aspect of sociology is linked with employing knowledge in the service of desired change: that is, reform or policy. But this action aspect, as the foregoing sociologists exemplify, involved an immersion, directly or indirectly, in the human drama itself and certainly a profound grasp of the experiences of the actors whom they studied. Thus, I find Horowitz, unknowingly of course, echoing my point in the closing pages of the book on his childhood: "It is only now, or in the relatively recent past, that...a balance of sorts has been struck between the abstract and the concrete" (1990:101–102). (This he attributes to his original immersion in a Harlem childhood and a later more civically responsible and introspective life.) In his writing, at least after the first years of scholarship, I think that Horowitz has always had that balance: the ability to grasp the perspectives of people or organizations and to formulate analytic abstractions about them and their actions—as well as to commend them or take them to task. Horowitz commends and critiques in terms of his lifelong premises.

Horowitz sometimes reminds me of Ulysses steering between Scylla and Charybdis, between scientific elitism, and mass irrationality or ignorance. Ultimately his style of writing and action conveys, as I said before, the optimism of self-conscious heirs of the enlightenment. Yet it is not a naive optimism that the world will be or become right without plenty of action by doughty fighters. Human rights and civic orders are threatened on many fronts. So I see Horowitz writing and speaking and in other ways acting on many fronts, and in direct but informed confrontation with the forces of actual or potential tyranny and evil. Too passionate for some of his colleagues, too combative for others, too quick sometimes to react to suspected or clearly defined wrongs—yet shame on those who would have it otherwise.

Additional Comment: Descensus Arenas

Perhaps it is too much to ask for, but sometimes I wish Horowitz would push the implications of his assumptions and insights one analytic step further. Quite possibly he has in some writings, as in the book on genocide or in his frequent writing on international policy, but in an area in which I am especially interested he has stopped short. I will describe his 1988 paper on AIDS, an arena evincing great descensus, to show the strengths of Horowitz's policy writing and suggest where it might be extended.

All the premises and many of the policy themes alluded to above are present in "The Limits of Policy and the Purposes of Research: The Case of AIDS." The very title characteristically reflects Horowitz's views on the bipolarity of policy and research, also the limits and possibilities of policy. This paper suggests to me how he—without the all too frequent hand-wringing and fighting through by participants of personal dilemmas yet with a great deal of detailed spadework about the area itself—lays out what he considers the major policy features of an area and then makes clearly stated recommendations.

Interested readers can, if they have not already, read this paper for those points and for specific details about the AIDS arena circa 1987. Horowitz mainly wrote about AIDS then because he was intrigued, and still is, that there's "[h]ardly any policy consensus on what should or could be done. It is this disjunction between knowledge as public awareness and knowledge as policy correction" that would summarize the paper's basic message (1988:35–36). The phenomenon of AIDS and public responses to it had raised a crucial issue: How can effective policy be formulated and carried out when descensus rather than relative consensus obtains in a given public arena? As always Horowitz is concerned about the tendency by participants, be they governmental or communal, to jump the gun, ignoring any relatively solid research information. (I find this reminiscent of the older Chicago sociologists' credo: research before reform action, otherwise action may only make matters worse.)

Horowitz also criticizes a conservative approach to AIDS which he labels as an antipolicy practice: concern with protecting the exposed rather than the victims of AIDs, hence advocating the victims' isolation from the rest of the population. Rather, "a society still needs a set of policies on how to quarantine the victims, how to identify the victims from the non-victims,...on forms of indemnification for victims of AIDS and...types of punishment for carriers who spread the disease knowingly" (39).

What then can social scientists contribute in this kind of climate of descensus? First, we must "subject all efforts at policy to empirical scrutiny, avoiding the extremes of pure optimism and undiluted pessimism in which prudence and natural law are invoked with impunity." Horowitz criticizes the role of special interests in San Francisco, the city in which I live, since those "inhibit policy from being articulated even timidly." Though there is a moral center of gravity revealed and furthered by the public debate, special interests interfere with the clarity of policy-making. We need "to achieve a balance between pressures for reform, called policies, and compliance with long standing standards, called ethics," which AIDS dramatically highlights. Happily, the epidemic is likely to refocus our attention from moral codes or recipes to moral decision making and what policies are needed." So, we are likely "to reformulate the processes by which moral behavior is defined" (40, 42–43).

Horowitz concludes on a note now familiar to us, noting the distinction between "the development of social science and the manufacture of public policy. This does not imply a contradiction...or an antagonistic relation, only that the realms of discourse are distinct, and that one cannot simply, in the name of policy, invoke social science" (43). And again, in conclusion, "in the absence of noticeable consensus or majorities in viewpoints at least, the issue of policies...should be seen within a larger context of scientific, political and moral considerations. That panoply of concerns is what the social scientific study of public policy addresses"

(43). Thus, he characteristically brings together social science and policy even in those typically contentious modern political debates and maneuvers that have received the name of policy or issue "arenas."

His general framework is reflected clearly enough in the implications he draws for this situation of massive uncertainty. What Horowitz doesn't do is give us a more directed answer and certainly not a conceptualization about descensual arenas. For me to offer one here would be presumptuous, but allow me at least to suggest a direction that is consonant with Horowitz's position (see Strauss, 1993; Wiener, 1992).

To begin with, one should not overlook the amount and degree of descensus among the multitude of different kinds of scientists involved in studying AIDS, nor how this disagreement spills over to affect policy-making at every level of political action, from federal to grass-roots organizations. The interplay of scientists and AIDS organizations is, in fact, a conspicuously significant factor in all policy arenas—it is only the specifics of which scientific discipline or subdiscipline is prominent in a given arena.

Also, my own propensity for conceiving of the actions of all participants, whether they are organizations or organizational representatives, is to relate these to the issues they deem important and the actions they take when defining, monitoring, evaluating, maintaining, or altering the issues. The organizations operate not only with a context of usually evolving sets of issues, but are participants of or related to determinable social worlds. Of course, Horowitz needn't accept this way of analyzing situations of multiple issues and massive descensus. But a conceptualization there must be or our prescriptions will be exactly as he fears—action performed in relative (even descriptive) ignorance. This is not at all a counsel of delay, "wait until we are sure of the evidence." This is based on the same premise of social science's rational intelligence and its relationships to effective policy. Furthermore, this conceptualization needs to be based on close examination of social movements, community organizations, and grass-roots sources of emerging and evolving policy. AIDS and environmentalism have each brought this to vivid public attention. National policy is not all, nor at any rate needs to be, analytically scrutinized for its relationships with local policies. These are not necessarily in neat coordination, but as with those AIDS policies that have emerged in various cities, they are most certainly "policies," although not "policy." Sometimes these are broadly effective, sometimes not at all. We need to know how and how not, and why.

That said, I cannot refrain from quoting from a recent letter Horowitz wrote to me where he referred to this proposed paper on his own work in the policy arena. "You are on target in noting that a big part of my work has been to distinguish between policy and social science." This statement of fact is followed by a typical Horowitzian sentence:

> We are heirs to a set of false options: pure empiricism which drowns the critical role of social research into preordained tasks; and...the denial of any sort of practical uses in the name of pure theory.... It is far less important to have agreement [between us] than to stimulate among the young a sense of living concerns in social science.

Beyond his own research and thinking, Irving Louis Horowitz is a passionate and invaluable spokesman.

University of California, San Francisco
Department of Social and Behavioral Sciences

References

Horowitz, Irving Louis. *Social Science and Public Policy in the United States.* New York: Praeger, 1975a (especially pp. 125–41 and pp. 162–67).

———. *The Use and Abuse of Social Science, Behavioral Research, and Policy Making,* 2d ed. New Brunswick, NJ: Transaction Publishers, 1975b (especially the reprinted Preface to the 1st ed., pp. ix–xxi and pp. 110–35).

———. *Constructing Policy: Dialogues with Social Scientists in the National Political Arena.* New York: Praeger/Holt, Rinehart and Winston, 1979 (especially pp. 1–10 and 121–40).

———. *Taking Lives: Genocide and State Power.* New Brunswick, NJ: Transaction Publishers, 1980.

———. *Bibliography of the Writings of Irving Louis Horowitz.* Privately printed, 1984.

———. "The Limits of Policy and the Purposes of Research: The Case of AIDS." *Knowledge and Society: An International Journal of Knowledge Transfer* 1 (1988): 35–46.

———. *Daydreams and Nightmares: Reflections on a Harlem Childhood.* Jackson: University Press of Mississippi, 1990.

———. "Foreword." In A. Strauss, *Creating Sociological Awareness.* New Brunswick, NJ: Transaction Publishers, 1991 (pp. xi–xiii).

———. "Social Research and the Culture of Society." *Society* 30 (1992): 7–11.

Strauss, A. *Continual Permutations of Action.* New York: Aldine de Gruyter, 1993. (See the chapter on scientists and arenas.)

Wiener, C. "Arenas and Careers: The Complex Interweaving of Personal and Organizational Identity." In *Social Organization and Social Process: Essays in Honor of Anselm Strauss,* ed. D. Maines. New York: Aldine de Gruyter, 1992 (pp. 175–88).

10

Professional Sociology:
The Case of C. Wright Mills

Howard S. Becker

The Story of C. Wright Mills

Mills's famous dictum holds that personal troubles are public problems. What seem to be the private troubles of a single person are the result, at the individual level, of solving the problems of the society that person lives in. Being without a job is a terrible personal trouble, but it is neither the result nor the fault of anything the unemployed have done. Rather, it is the working out, for them, of society's inability or unwillingness to provide full employment.

Mills's dictum was never more true than in his own case. His professional problems were the outcome, on the personal level, of the general directions and troubles of American sociology during his lifetime. Using his dictum as an analytic research tool, we can inspect Mills's professional life and intellectual career to see what it reveals about the public (or, better put, the institutional and organizational) problems of sociology (and, especially, American sociology) in the middle of the twentieth century. This is the fruitful perspective from which Irving Louis Horowitz approached Mills's life; this essay is an appreciation and retelling of Horowitz's analysis.

As Horowitz tells the story, in *C. Wright Mills: An American Utopian*[1]—any quick summary must necessarily do an injustice to his massively detailed, heavily documented, and insightful biography—Mills was always an intensely American sociologist, steeped in the perspec-

175

tive of philosophical pragmatism from his college days at the University of Texas onward, and holding that point of view, in one form or another, throughout his short, eventful, troubled life. Almost always in conflict with colleagues and bosses, he produced a body of work—especially the trilogy on stratification (*The New Men of Power, White Collar,* and *The Power Elite*[2]) and the handbook of sociological practice he called *The Sociological Imagination*[3]—which still excites sociologists, professionals, and students alike.

Mills's professional troubles reflected a fork in the road of sociology's disciplinary development. It had once been possible for an American sociologist, as it had been for sociologists in other countries at other times and is for some even today, to be admired by colleagues for serious professional work and simultaneously be a voice in the major political and cultural dialogues of the day. Max Weber did it, producing works that were scholarly to a fare-thee-well and also speaking out on such contemporary German political problems as nationalism. Raymond Aron did it, with scholarly works on politics and regular political writing in such major Parisian papers as *Figaro* and *l'Express*. But no American sociologist had pulled this off in a long time (we might have to go as far back as E. A. Ross to find anything similar) and those who had tried it (e.g., David Riesman) were often unfairly criticized by colleagues as "popularizers."

But that was what Mills wanted to do. He wanted to be a respected professional, in a field in which professionalism was coming to be defined in a narrowly disciplinary way,[4] and a speaker on the big contemporary issues, at a time when success with those narrow disciplinary concerns disqualified you as such a speaker, almost by definition.

Mills thus had a double dilemma. On the one hand, he wanted to be more than just another political thinker. Although he admired the New York intellectuals associated with the influential journals of opinion of the day, he wanted to be something they were not and did not want to be: a social scientist. He could not be satisfied to be just another Dwight Macdonald writing essays, however insightful, in the pages of *Politics*. He wanted to bring something special to this kind of engaged political writing: the fruits of the historical tradition of social science, as that tradition was personified by Max Weber and other classical sociological thinkers.

It is implicit in Mills's understanding of the relation between public issues and private troubles that society changes continuously and that, therefore, people's personal problems will change as the society around them changes. This thought can be applied to the problem of a scholarly and political career of the kind Mills wanted. George Kubler, the art historian, has suggested—the idea converges nicely with Mills's—that an artist's (substitute thinker or social scientist) reputation and professional fate are a function of when in the development of an institutionalized sequence of thought and work that person appears. Appearing at the beginning of a sequence of work in a certain line, for instance, has great advantages, for you will not be held responsible for the same things someone who appears in the middle or at the end must attend to.[5]

Mills appeared at the height of the "professionalizing" of sociology and his problems are thus the problems of someone trying to put together things that could have gone together easily earlier, and might well go together later, but not when he tried it.

Theory, Contemporary Problems, and Professionalism

Scientists always conceive of their disciplines as universal; they would not like to think that French chemistry deals with the same questions differently, and produces different answers to them, than Russian or German chemistry. Similarly, social scientists want social science to deal with universal problems, to produce universally accepted propositions. Only by so doing, they typically think, can they achieve a true science. Since social science is an international enterprise, social scientists everywhere try to keep in touch with the universal concerns of their disciplines.

But social science, because its most general concerns are embodied in particular cases, necessarily deals with problems of serious and immediate concern to the members of the societies in which it develops. So, as sociology has developed in different countries, it has inevitably taken on a national character, devoting itself to the historically specific problems of each country. Those problems are not universal, though they have family resemblances.

American sociology, in its beginnings, thus devoted itself to the problems of its own society, the rapidly expanding America of the late nineteenth and early twentieth centuries. The problems it addressed included integrating the immigrants who were then flooding the country, teaching them to be "good Americans"; the racial problems that began with slavery and took a new turn with emancipation; and the massive dislocations and reorganizations created by urbanization. Indeed, Robert E. Park, one of the architects of the new discipline, defined the major problem of the modern world in terms he had learned by observing the quintessentially American city of Chicago: "All the world now either lives in the city or is on its way there."

Brazilian social science, to take a case described in detail by Mariza Peirano, reflected a different set of concerns. Because social science developed in international metropolitan centers (for Brazil until after World War II the preferred center was Paris), it dealt with issues that, while relevant to the concerns of those centers, were not germane to Brazilian national concerns. Brazilians, intellectuals and lay people alike, wanted answers to such questions as: What is a Brazilian (as opposed to a European or, later, a North American)? How should they conceptualize the mixture of the three races—white, black, and Indian— that made up Brazil's population? Was that mixture an advantage in the contest for international recognition or a disgrace to be apologized for and overcome? In our own time, Brazilian social scientists asked a question of great national import: how to overcome the relation with Europe and America that resulted in underdevelopment. What they came to want was what they called a *sociologia-feita-no-Brasil,* a sociology-made-in-Brazil, relevant to their problems, not to those of France, Germany, or the United States.[6]

National sociologies also develop distinctive emphases, in part, because their makers want what they do to appear different from dominant trends in the discipline seen internationally. Thus, according to Jean-Michel Chapoulie, French sociologists, after World War II, shaped their work in part to make clear that it was different from the sociology made in the United States (partly, too, to situate themselves vis-à-vis the workers' movement and the associated political debates).[7]

So national sociologies oscillate between a concern with national problems and national emphases, a sociology-made-in-Brazil or France or wherever, taking its shape from those distinctive nationally based concerns, and a concern with the development of a style of thought that is "universal," or at least transnational, capable of dealing with and being relevant to the concerns of all the particular countries in which it develops. This can take the form of an abstract theoretical concern with problems defined, at least on the surface, wholly within the discipline, in the manner described by Thomas Kuhn as characteristic of the development of any scientific discipline.[8] System builders like Talcott Parsons exemplified this tack. The impulse to universality at other times takes the form of a history of the world cast in sociological terms, which to some seems to offer the possibility of satisfying both the demand for generality and the need to deal with specific problems, which can be seen to embody general trends in world history.

When social scientists concern themselves with contemporary questions, their disciplines become less autonomous and self-contained, more responsive to people who are not professional colleagues, less "universal," more attuned to broader intellectual currents in their own society. They confront other currents of thought, other theoretical stances, other styles of work, which are very often not respectful of sociology and its autonomy.

Horowitz, always attentive to the international character of social science, nevertheless does not put such comparisons at the center of his analysis of the case of Mills, a case we can perhaps understand better by considering it comparatively. American sociology, when Mills entered the picture, was moving away from "problems" and toward a more autonomous and "professional" orientation, away from the concern with contemporary politics that so attracted him and toward an esoteric body of questions that signified, to its developers, the achievement of truly professional status. And that vision drew him too.

How Many Hours a Day?

Horowitz has distinguished between occupationalism and professionalism in mainstream sociological work—between those who want to tie the discipline to established institutions and those who, letting it develop according to its own logic, are quite happy to see in it a critique of existing institutions. He identified Mills as an occupationalist, and cited *The Sociological Imagination* as a classic exposition of that point of view.[9] But these categories do not do justice to his later analysis of Mills's career. (In fact, toward the end of his career, Mills certainly approached the ideal type Horowitz calls the *antisociologist*, who "owes a functional allegiance...to a set of ideas that is outside the control system of sociology.")[10]

Although Horowitz has never published the concept I'm about to quote now, I distinctly remember the conversation in which he distinguished between eight, sixteen, and twenty-four hour a day sociologists (a temporal rather than a spatial distinction).[11] He did not mean simply to make a quantitative distinction, to count the number of hours a day a person devotes to professional work and use that number as a "variable" that might predict something else about people who so spend their time. He meant, more imaginatively, to distinguish between different orientations to the organized profession of sociology, different ways of letting it invade and take over one's life, or, conversely, ways of keeping the potentially corrosive effects of sociological thinking within limits. That is, when people take up a line of work, one aspect of the "taking up" is deciding how far to allow its demands to intrude on your life. Perhaps very little: members of some occupations (prison convicts are a good example) try hard to keep their work from invading their personalities and constricting their lives. Other kinds of work, however, make more substantial invasions, whether or not they are welcome. Work may fill your time, as the families of doctors and lawyers, with good reason, complain. More to the point of Horowitz's distinction, work can become the major focus of your attention, taking over emotions, fantasies, dreams, providing the metaphors that shape your view of the world.

Work fills the consciousness of many scholars and thinkers, dominating their inner lives. That is what interests Horowitz: Does your intellectual work shape your waking thoughts? Does it take over your dreams? Does it become the way you see the world? Do you use its language to describe events and people? Some sociologists see sociologically, filtering everything through that lens. Others stop seeing that way at five o'clock. And some, a few, are possessed totally—their reflexes and dreams are sociological.

Thinking about Mills turns us away from Horowitz's spatial metaphor, and its identification of Mills as an occupationalist, and toward his temporal metaphor. Mills is perhaps better described as a twenty-four hour a day sociologist, one who thought sociologically, saw the world sociologically, dreamed sociologically.

Being such a person in a time of professional change creates distinctive problems. There is a strong sense in which the twenty-four a day sociologist is too sociological for the organized discipline. Interpreting the events of daily life in a university department or research institute as sociological phenomena is not palatable to people who run such institutions or to those who live by them and profit from them; for, like all institutions, universities and institutes have sacred myths and beliefs that their members do not want subjected to the skeptical sociological view. So the institutional settings a twenty-four hour a day sociologist finds himself in will not be, as for Mills they certainly were not, hospitable to his vision.

Mills: Professional Manqué/Big Thinker

Mills wanted very much to be a professional (not in the specialized sense Horowitz delineates but in the looser, commonsense version), to be part of the everyday, ongoing business of the discipline. He made great efforts to do what it took to reap the rewards of being a well-integrated professional: the reputation, the good position in a great university, the salary that went with it. He even worked, in a way that only Horowitz's revealing dissection of his motives and activities could make intelligible,[12] on Paul Lazarsfeld's projects, trying to run large-scale survey operations and produce the reports to sponsors that they required. That style of work was not congenial to Mills. He chafed under the discipline and the responsibility to outsiders it entailed. But he did it, with the help of some devoted assistants; Horowitz singles out Rose Goldsen, especially, as someone who made it possible for Mills to survive in this kind of work as long as he did.

Perhaps as a result of his ambivalence about whether to be an engaged political thinker or a professional sociologist, Mills never did what he would have had to do to make the sociological world accept him as a topnotch professional. His research, even in such major works as *White Collar* and *The Power Elite,* as well as in his most conventionally sociological research monograph, *The New Men of Power,* seldom displayed the tight coupling of assertion and evidence that the sociological world of his time required of "real research." Horowitz's analyses of these works makes clear how cavalier Mills could be in putting together empirical reality and his own ideas. He was often led, by the prospect of rhetorical flourish or a fine-sounding phrase, to assert what the materials he had at hand did not warrant.

Nor did he refrain from doing the things that kept that world from accepting him fully. Temperamentally a smart aleck and "difficult," he didn't do what the people who controlled the rewards he so much wanted required of him. For a long time he got away with it. Even though he mouthed off to his professors as an undergraduate, they all wrote strong recommendations on his behalf so that he could get into the graduate program at Wisconsin. He refused to make the changes his dissertation committee insisted on, but they finally gave him his degree anyway. He missed deadlines for research reports and did not do the research Lazarsfeld had contracted for and then put him in charge of, but he managed to keep his job at Columbia.

As sociology evolved and became more and more "professional," it focused increasingly on its own autonomously defined and, in the strict sense, esoteric questions, questions that arose in the context of the history of the discipline rather than that of the questions of the day. And one of the worst of Mills's sins, from the perspective of the scientifically mobile profession, was that he did not deal with those questions, or not very much. He dealt with the questions he thought were important. It is a token of his intellectual power that he could make such a mark on the sociology of his day when its leaders found his concerns so uncongenial.

We can return to the question: in Horowitz's hours-a-day typology, which kind of professional was Mills? Though I guessed just above that he was a twenty-four hour sociologist, it's not so clear. And here is where an ambiguity perhaps arises in Horowitz's analysis. Mills was certainly a sixteen-hour sociologist—one who took the New York Times apart with scissors every day in order to file the resulting confetti in appropriate sociological categories. But his case suggests another typological dimension, not fully accounted for in An American Utopian (though perhaps captured in the notion of the antisociologist), in which the desire to be a Big Thinker, to look the part and be recognized as one by other Big Thinkers, became a major focus of his effort. (Capitalizing the phrase has a somewhat satiric overtone, as I mean it to. There was an element of posturing in Mills's activity that Horowitz makes clear and that, at this remove, makes you wonder how he could have been so naive and unself-conscious about it.)

The Big Thinkers for Mills, the men (and his heroes were, of course, all men, thus reflecting the times as well as his own undoubted machismo) he wanted to be like or surpass, took on the Big Questions: the direction of history, the deep fractures of class and ideology that gave an age its distinctive character. His heroes were, preeminently, Max Weber and Karl Marx, as they so often are for people who want their names inscribed in the history of intellect and ideas. This tendency in Mills's thought went off the deep end in the last years of his life, when he planned gigantic, undoable comparative sociologies of the entire world.

The Big Thinker dimension is, perhaps, orthogonal to the hours-a-day dimension. One doesn't preclude the other. (We might think of Robert E. Park as someone who had somewhat similar desires, though he kept them to more modest dimensions, thinking of the sociologist not so much as a Big Thinker as a Big Reporter, someone who studied the major trends of modern society.) But the desire to play the part, to be that kind of person, certainly interacts with the hours-a-day style. Wanting to be recognized as a Big Thinker makes one sensitive to the opinions of nonprofessionals, which in turn makes it imperative or at least desirable to think in short-run terms. Professional Big Thinkers have to respond to the events of the day, the news, with opinions and analyses. They have to "know what it all means" and have an opinion on every subject. A Big Thinker can never say, as a social scientist might, "I don't know" or "That's out of my field."

Professional Big Thinkers of this kind are, in effect, newspaper or magazine columnists, whose readers look to them for direction. A successful contemporary practitioner of the style is, I suppose, Garry Wills, who manages a highly successful scholarly career, is well-respected by historians, political scientists, and literary scholars, and yet deals with current events routinely in a syndicated column (and does not affect the Big Thinker style personally). Mills never found so successful an accommodation.

Mills: Man at the Intellectual Heart of Things

In an odd way, Mills's view of the organization of intellectual life coincided with that of Edward Shils, whose thinking was otherwise quite different from his and whose review[13] of *The Sociological Imagination* in *Encounter* was one of the most vicious denunciations in the history of the discipline of one of the best books the discipline ever produced. What the two agreed on—and it is one of the signs of Mills's closet elitism, which Horowitz brings to the surface, though he doesn't remark on it—was the importance of the "center," as opposed to what Shils called the "periphery" (though it has always been clear that what he really meant was the provinces).[14] For Shils, the center is the place where major social values are concentrated, where legitimate authority resides, the place to which the provinces look for guidance, the place with a numinous aura of the holy. In his hands, the emphasis on the center is, as he would no doubt proudly insist, profoundly conservative.

For Mills, the emphasis is somewhat different and, of course, not conservative. For him, the center is where it's happening, where the Big Ideas come from, where the major advances in thought and culture are made. The center is where you must be if you want to take part in the important intellectual debates of your time. If you want to be an intellectual somebody, you must have access to the center, must be *there*.

For Mills, the center was New York, as it might have seemed to someone coming from a small city in Texas, and as it mostly did to serious intellectuals of his generation, wherever they came from. In fairness, this view, which in the face of the institutional and geographical changes in America in the last forty years, now seems only quaint, still had some truth left in it during the years of Mills's active career. Major magazines were published in New York; it was the center of serious book publishing, a somewhat incestuous intellectual world operated from there; Broadway had not yet lost its place as the center of American theater.

One of the oddities of Mills's professional life, which can only be accounted for by his firm belief that you had to be in New York to be an important intellectual, was that, though he was treated badly, even shabbily, at Columbia, though he was not allowed to teach graduate students, even at the height of his reputation, nevertheless he would not leave New York, so deep was his belief in the myth of New York as the center of American culture, his belief that you had to be there to be in touch with the main currents of intellectual, political, and cultural life. He seems to have thought that to move, say, to Chicago, where he had friends (Milton Singer, who had known him in Texas, and perhaps David Riesman, who might well have thought him a perfect recruit for the faculty of the University of Chicago's innovative multidisciplinary program in social science) would have left him outside the magic circle. And so he thought of himself as wronged, because he could not get the one university job he really wanted, which was to be a "real" professor at Columbia.

He looked to the circle around the left intellectual magazines of the day (*Dissent, Commentary, Politics, The New Leader*) centered in New York for an intellectual world to belong to, a world that would validate his claim to be an important intellectual. This world seemed to him far removed from the university world, though it was not all that removed, as the eventual settling of so many of its major figures in professorships demonstrated. Still, it is the looking to this world that most marks him as partaking in some part of the antisociologist.

What was perhaps saddest about Mills's belief in the center and disdain for the provinces was that, even as he lived and worked, the whole thing was breaking down. Though, as I said, there was a time when the myth was more or less true, from the 1950s on the cultural and intellectual life of the country became far less centralized. Shifts in population, the westward tilt that made Los Angeles and San Francisco major financial, intellectual, and artistic centers, the rapidly increasing ease of communication via long-distance phones, more rapid mail, and the increasing dependence on the airplane for the movement of people and things—all these made it increasingly easy for people to be important cultural actors whether or not they lived and worked in New York.

So it became less and less true that New York, or any other single place, was "the center," in the sense that Shils had described. What replaced such a center was a network of regional communities of intellect and art. The network itself was the "center," or as much of a center as there was, rather than any of its nodes. To take an example I am familiar with, as late as 1950, American theater was as centralized in New York as it still is in London or Paris: to make a career as an actor, director, or designer, you went to New York. If you wanted the play you had written to be a hit you went there to find a producer who would make your dream come true by producing your play on Broadway.

Since the 1950s, however, the major development in American theater has been the growth of regional theater. The major developments have not happened in New York, but in San Francisco, Minneapolis, Chicago, Seattle, and a network of smaller, active, urban theater worlds. The three major American playwrights of the 1970s and 1980s have been David Mamet (who got his start in Chicago), Sam Shepard (much of whose major work was written and premiered in San Francisco), and August Wilson (who became known when he worked in Minneapolis and St. Paul and later moved and continued to work in Seattle).[15]

Once there is no center, only a network, you can no longer situate yourself in the center, because there is no center to do that in. It is not just that you needn't live in New York to be a central figure in the intellectual world. Rather, living in New York no longer has anything to do with being central. It is a major irony of Mills's life that he did not foresee that he could have taken the jobs offered to him outside New York and sacrificed nothing in centrality.

Further, the intellectual center he wanted to be part of was, from the point of view of the world of professional sociology to which, remember, he also wanted to belong, not the center. For many years, the unquestioned center of American sociology was at 1126 E. 59th Street, the social science building of the University of Chicago. That unique dominance ended with World War II. Among the claimants to the succession were Columbia (the wagon Mills hitched his star to), but it was only one of eight or ten (Harvard, Michigan, Wisconsin, and Berkeley, among others, had as good a claim as Columbia), and only a claimant, never the actual successor to Chicago—the position of undisputed leader no longer existed.

Mills: Personal Troubles and Institutional Change

Mills's troubles were the personal side of a shift, in the field he had taken as his own, to a professionalism and scientism that had no room for the kind of work and career he wanted to do and have. American sociology went, for a while, down the road, laid out by the pioneers who produced *The American Soldier* and similar works that purported to turn sociology, finally, into a real science. It turned its back, for a while, on the road of Weber and Marx. These pioneers didn't succeed in their venture. The results that such real science ought to produce still elude their successors, and Marx and Weber and the big thinking they exemplified is stronger than ever. But the pioneers did succeed in turning the part of sociology Mills wanted to inhabit into a place he could not live in, though he could not leave it either.

In the same way, he wanted to be at the center of a world that was coming to have no center of the kind in which he envisioned being a major actor. The breakdown of New York as the intellectual center of the country produced that irony.

So Mills's unhappy career and the wrecked personal life that accompanied it, as Irving Louis Horowitz has laid them out in *An American Utopian*, embody his own dictum. It is one of the many virtues of the

Horowitz biography that it keeps both elements—the personal and the institutional—in focus throughout.

The University of Washington
Department of Sociology

Notes

1. Irving Louis Horowitz, *C. Wright Mills: An American Utopian* (New York: The Free Press, 1983).
2. C. Wright Mills, *The New Men of Power: America's Labor Leaders* (New York: Harcourt, Brace and Co., 1948); *White Collar: The American Middle Classes* (New York: Oxford University Press, 1951); and *The Power Elite* (New York: Oxford University Press, 1956).
3. C. Wright Mills, *The Sociological Imagination* (New York: Oxford University Press, 1959).
4. Horowitz has dealt with the professionalization of sociology in a number of places. See, for instance, "Establishment Sociology: The Value of Being Value-Free," in his *Professing Sociology*, 159–67 (Chicago: Aldine Publishing Co., 1968), and other essays in that book.
5. George Kubler, *The Shape of Time: Remarks on the History of Things* (New Haven, CT: Yale University Press, 1962), 87–88.
6. Her ideas are laid out in Mariza G. S. Peirano, "The Anthropology of Anthropology: The Brazilian Case," (Ph.D. diss., Harvard University, 1981), and in several of the essays in her *Uma Antropologiano Plural: Três Experiências Contemporâneas* (Brasília: Editora Universidade de Brasília, 1992).
7. Jean-Michel Chapoulie, "La seconde fondation de la sociologie française, les Etats-Unis et las classe ouvriére," *Revue Française de Sociologie* 32 (1991): 321–64. Chapoulie's argument is considerably more complex and sophisticated than the simple summary I have made of it.
8. Thomas Kuhn, *The Structure of Scientific Revolutions* (Chicago: University of Chicago Press, 1970), 35 ff.
9. Irving Louis Horowitz, "Mainliners and Marginals," in his *Professing Sociology*, 195–220. The reference to *The Sociological Imagination* is on p. 216.
10. See the description of the antisociologist in Horowitz, "Mainliners and Marginals," 212–14. Mills fits the description quite well.
11. Horowitz, when I consulted him for a citation to this idea, thought that it was in the essay just cited, but couldn't find it there. In fact, there is one sentence in which it is mentioned: "The mainline members of a scientific community embrace both those who believe in sociology as an 8-hour a day profession and those who believe in it as a 24-hour a day occupation" (206). But the point is not developed.
12. Horowitz, *C. Wright Mills*, 80 ff.
13. Edward Shils, "Imaginary Sociology," *Encounter* (June 1960): 77–80.
14. Edward Shils, *Center and Periphery* (Chicago: University of Chicago Press, 1975), passim.
15. The world of regional theater is described in Howard S. Becker, Michal McCall, and Lori Morris, "Theatre and Communities: Three Scenes," *Social Problems* 26 (April 1989): 93–112.

11

Policy-Making and the Quest for an Autonomous Social Science

William A. Donohue

It is the purpose of this chapter to trace the patterns and tensions in the writings of Irving Louis Horowitz as they bear on policy issues. After considering decades of his work, it seems clear that the pattern that most clearly emerges is his unabiding commitment to the integrity of the social sciences. From his searing indictment of Project Camelot to his more recent criticisms of the politicization of the social sciences, Horowitz has spared no quarter in critically assessing departures from objectivity, whether they be foisted by government (as in Camelot) or crafted from within (as in the politicization of scholarship). The chief tension in his work springs from his basic humanism, as reflected in his concern for social equality, and in his intellectual recognition of the limits of policy.

"It might well be that the goal of value-free social science is unattainable," comments Irving Louis Horowitz. But no matter, "we are still compelled to aim for the same canons of objectivity in the social sciences that are presumed to be present in the natural sciences" (1987a:54). Horowitz's Weberian quest for a value-free sociology might mean less if it were coming from one of those dispassionate social scientists busily engaged in quantitative research projects. However, Horowitz is anything but that kind of sociologist. He is passionately committed to the object of his intellectual pursuit and passionately engaged in the defense of objectivity.

At the heart of Horowitz's intellectual concerns is the poor. Whether it be in his writings on underdevelopment, or in his analysis of domestic programs, the lot of the poor has always been central to him. It may be that the experiences of his youth touched him in a way that has had an enduring effect on his scholarly interests (1990). Whatever the source, Horowitz's engagement with the poor has never stood in the way of critical analysis, either of the poor or of the programs designed to serve them. And that alone puts him in rare company.

Project Camelot and Its Progeny

Horowitz's first major undertaking in policy issues was his analysis of Project Camelot. Conceived in late 1963, and implemented in 1964, Project Camelot was a governmental-academic attempt to investigate counterinsurgency potentials in the Third World, with a special emphasis on developments in Latin America. The brainchild of the army's Special Operation's Research Office, Camelot hired social scientists to do the investigatory work and to provide a social systems model that would enable the U.S. government "to predict and influence politically significant aspects of social change in the developing nations of the world" (1967:5).

Most of the academics who worked on Camelot never raised serious questions regarding the propriety of the project; they were too taken by the opportunity to partake in unrestricted research, and too enthralled with the prospects of virtually unlimited resources, to bother with such distractions. True students of the Enlightenment, their notions of human perfectibility allowed them to see the Pentagon as an institution capable of dramatic reconstitution. But in the end the obsequiousness of the academics wasn't enough to stop the project from disintegration: in less than a year, Camelot was dead, the victim of traditional Washington turf battles, this time between the State Department and the Defense Department.

For Horowitz, the most troublesome part of Project Camelot was the extent to which trained social scientists were willing to compromise their principles in exchange for the chance to affect public policy. The tough questions never got asked, much less answered. Was it really the duty of social scientists to let army bureaucrats determine the nature of their research? Was it possible for social scientists to know enough about the conditions of Third World nations to advise the authorities on what to do about internal warfare? Was it correct to assume that it is the business of the U.S. government to determine the political outcomes of foreign nations? If stemming revolution is the goal, would that also apply to staving off the efforts of anti-Communists? Was it proper for American University (it played an integral role in the supervisory aspects of Camelot) to involve itself in an incestuous relationship with the government, without even addressing questions of responsibility for the project?

The appeal of Horowitz's criticisms is that it reaches the scientific issues, clearly transcending the important, but nonetheless separate, matter of political efficaciousness. The ambiguities of the research design, complete with contrasting and eclectic methodologies, should have caused concern. So, too, should have the use of a highly antiseptic vocabulary, designed more to conceal than to reveal. But by acceding to the army's authority, the academicians abandoned their status and became little more than hired guns.

If Horowitz had written a tirade against the right of academicians to help the government resolve international problems, it would merit no attention, except in the quarters of political correctness. But that most certainly is not the case. "It is important that scholars be willing to risk something of their reputations in helping to resolve major world social problems" (1967:32). Horowitz is quick to point out, however, that the "autonomous character of the social science disciplines" must not be compromised in the process.

What is even more commendable is Horowitz's willingness to shed his own bias without letting it affect his analysis. He admits that "Project Camelot was intellectually and from my own perspective ideologically unsound" (1967:40). But that doesn't stop him from complaining about the way Camelot was terminated. Horowitz is quick to add that "the cancellation of Camelot, however pleasing it may be on political grounds to advocates of a civilian solution to Latin American affairs, represents a decisive setback for social science research" (1967:41).

A few years after Camelot came the *Report of the Panel on Defense: Social and Behavioral Sciences*. This 1967 project was the effort of a high-ranking science advisory group of the Defense Department; it was established to discuss ways in which the social sciences could benefit the Department of Defense. "What we have in this Report is a collective statement by eminent social scientists," Horowitz contends, "a statement that can easily be read as the ominous conversion of social science into a service industry of the Pentagon" (1968a:30).

The parallels with Camelot were striking: the belief in human perfectibility allowed the social scientists to entertain the possibility that they were going to remake federal policy; the lack of any coherent methodological focus created scientific problems of considerable magnitude; and the willingness of social scientists to compromise their autonomy left serious questions regarding the objective basis of their claims. Horowitz notes approvingly, however, a list of recommendations set forth by the State Department's Foreign Area Research Coordination group (1968a:38). It is striking to note that the reform proposals, which gave deserved recognition to the autonomy of social scientists, emanated not from the academy, but from government.

Throughout the 1970s, Horowitz expanded on the themes that ignited his responses to Camelot and the subsequent *Defense Department Report on the Social Sciences*. Beginning with his work on Project Camelot (1967:42), Horowitz repeatedly warned against the corrupting influence that money can have on the autonomy of social scientists. It is one thing to enter into a contract with government, he advises, quite another to pursue a grant; the former requires the greatest surrender of autonomy, while the latter (because it is initiated by social scientists) offers greater insulation from compromising influences (1969:311–13; 1975a:112–13; 1979a:131).

Secrecy is another problem with government research that merits concern, especially as it runs against the grain of what is expected from scientists (1969:313–16; 1971:449–51; 1975a:113–15; 1975b:116–17). It also makes it more difficult to assess the research design (1975a:114). In essence, Horowitz recommends that autonomy can best be preserved when social scientists address policy issues from their independent base at the academy, rather than accepting the role of a "nonpartisan" expert employed at the behest of government (1984:258).

Ideology and Power in Social Science Research

There are other, perhaps more serious ways, that the autonomy of the social sciences is compromised. One way is through the presentation of data known to be weak and yet offered to policymakers as if it were convincing. Similarly, the objectivity of the social sciences is jeopardized when scholars rush forward to craft policy absent sufficient data to support their intervention. Worse still is the flight from objectivity and crass politicization of scholarship that has become all too common in recent years. All three examples are taken up by Horowitz.

As a person who believes in the ideals that the nation was founded upon, Horowitz applauds the 1954 *Brown v. Board of Education* decision. But unlike some of his colleagues, Horowitz does not shy away from scrutinizing the evidence that was used to legitimate the decision. He flatly says that the proponents of segregation were not wrong in criticizing the data that had been submitted by social scientists on behalf of the plaintiff: the data were weak, inconclusive, and arbitrarily selected (1975b:131). And this indictment extends to Kenneth B. Clark as well, the psychologist who had the greatest impact of any social scientist on the court decision.

Dr. Clark, who purported to show that segregation caused irreparable mental damage to black children, was less than forthcoming in his testimony. The "black doll" test that he employed actually demonstrated that black children in integrated schools were more likely to suffer from "negative self-identification" than their segregated cohorts in the South. But since he wasn't asked about this aspect of his research, Dr. Clark remained mute. Had he offered full disclosure of his research findings, it would have undermined the basis of his testimony, and thus have jeopardized the desired court decision.

For Horowitz, the fact that the data were not strong, and the fact that it had not been proven before *Brown* that segregation caused academic impairment, does not mean that the court decision was wrong. The high court weighed the testimony of the social scientists as it related to the requirements of the Fourteenth Amendment. Moreover, *Brown* did not turn on social science evidence; its role was ancillary.

With good reason, Horowitz sees the Supreme Court as "a policy-making body" (1975b:132). It is also true that the value of social science research is contingent on its use by political operatives, but it is not certain why we should greet with dismay, as Horowitz does, the failure of presidents to implement the recommendations of presidential commissions (1975b:132–33). Such bodies are virtually never staffed exclusively by social scientists (lawyers tend to predominate), and even if they were, it is not at all clear why objectivity ought to be assumed. Furthermore, presidents, being politicians, cannot be expected to implement the results of research that are counterproductive to the agenda that they were elected to promote. And it is a matter of some significance that oftentimes a commission's findings are presented to a president who had nothing to do with the creation or staffing of the commission in the first place.

None of this is said as a justification for political chicanery, but as a way of addressing another one of Horowitz's concerns, namely, the use of social science for legitimizing purposes (1975b:49–50). It is just that legitimatization cuts both ways, as research can be selectively employed or ignored, depending upon the politics of the moment. Rare is the policy that was written as a result of social science research: its role is hardly ever determinative. For those social scientists who function as policymakers, this is not generally seen as a problem. As Horowitz details, policymakers "are more nearly identified with transmitting ideas than innovating them," which is one reason why they are so at ease with the distinction between the expert and the elect. What keeps them on board is "their belief that the political arena as a whole is where the action is" (1979a:2–3).

This attraction to be "where the action is" is fraught with difficulties. In times of political unrest and social upheaval in particular, the temptation to do good frequently comes at the price of scientific rigor. This is exactly what happened during the 1960s, the heyday of social scientists *qua* policymakers.

Midway through the 1970s, Horowitz saw the war on poverty "as a remarkable era of experimentation in the public uses of the social sciences" (1975b:68). Experimentation there was, and in abundance. Unfortunately, as Daniel Patrick Moynihan pointed out, the war on poverty was based purely on theory, and not on empirical evidence (1970:170). The costs today seem excessive. Aside from the progress that the elderly have witnessed, there is little to the entitlement programs that merits admiration. As Charles Murray has documented, "We tried to provide more for the poor and produced more poor instead" (1984:9).

The position that Horowitz held in the mid-1970s—that the war on poverty was "denied adequate resources for its mission" (1975b:137)—is not supported by Murray's research. But unlike Michael Harrington, who went to his grave thinking that more money would have made a decisive difference, Horowitz, upon looking at the evidence, moved more closely to Murray's position. By the mid-1980s, Horowitz was ready to charge that President Johnson's initiative "proceeded with practically no aggregate data identifying who the poor were, why they were poor, or what might best be done about it" (1984:260).

Letting ideology dictate policy is expected of politicians, but not scientists. Yet in virtually every major social policy reform effort there has been no shortage of social and behavioral scientists ready to cut corners in order to justify desired programs. As Horowitz has written, "There has always been a wing of social science quite close to its social engineering inheritance" (1975b:55). The deinstitutionalization of the mentally ill is a case in point.

Tragically, as E. Fuller Torrey shows (1988), the data were not there to support massive deinstitutionalization, yet the experts advised the elected to go forth anyway. Drugs that were supposed to make a difference weren't sufficiently tested. There was no plan or procedure whereby the newly discharged patients were to be received into the community health centers. And "there was no evidence that poverty *per se* caused mental disorders" (1988:122). But none of this mattered. Psychiatrists were convinced that social inequality lay at the root of the mentally ill. Yet as Torrey contends, "there was no more scientific basis for psychiatrists to assume a leadership position on social problems than for anyone else to do" (1988:128). The result is only too well known: the homeless mentally ill are a staple in urban America, a tribute to ideology disguised as science.

The Politicization of the Social Sciences

If it is indefensible for social scientists to engage in policy-making before they have accumulated sufficient data to warrant intervention, then it is simply unprincipled and unprofessional for social scientists to summarily dismiss the canons of objectivity that they were pledged to uphold. There is by now, thanks in part to Irving Louis Horowitz, a considerable body of evidence that details exactly how this intellectual corruption has taken place. In Horowitz's writings, in his role in the National Association of Scholars, and in his founding role of the NAS journal *Academic Questions,* there is evidence of a strong commitment to principle, born of a long-standing dedication to an autonomous social science.

There were signs that by the late 1970s, Horowitz had already had enough with the assault on the integrity of the social sciences. The vicious attack on James S. Coleman, a sociologist as ethical as Horowitz, meant not only the return of witch-hunting, it meant the loss of status for sociologists working in policy studies. The lesson to be learned from Coleman's ordeal with the American Sociological Association, Horowitz informs, was that "when social scientists fly in the face of established wisdom, they are treated differently. The demands for new kinds of evidence become much more stringent" (1979a:126).

In 1981, Horowitz noted that "the politicization of the social sciences [is] a fact we all live with" (1981a:11). In the same year, with Reagan in the White House, and with the traditional association of social scientists with the Democratic party still largely intact, Horowitz announced: "It is time for a declaration of independence from one party, and an equally firm pledge to participate actively in the political process as a whole" (1981b:129). (The latter point addressed Horowitz's interest in seeing social scientists employed in as many sectors of government as possible.) A few years later, Horowitz admitted to "a disenchantment with political tests for social science values and a corresponding enchantment with social science as an end in itself" (1984:ix). And in his seminal piece, "Disenthralling Sociology," Horowitz makes a major attempt to recall sociology to its first principles, after decades of politicization (1987a). His book on the subject is by now much anticipated.

None of this is to say that Horowitz expects policy to be made in a vacuum of values. At the same time that he was criticizing the politicization of the social sciences, he was stating that it was only in the light of "the value context" that "issues of policy relevance can be raised and measurements can be made." That is why he could declare that the issue of child labor was a measure of the quality of our society, and as such could not be treated independent of its value context (1981c:10). Horowitz's participation in the creation of social accounting, especially his role in developing quality-of-life surveys (1979a:116), shows his interest in seeing sociologists addressing issues of value. Indeed he readily admits that "[t]he ultimate purpose of this kind of social accounting would be to provide the nation with the great equalizer" (1971a:454). Horowitz's only insistence is that social scientists refrain from letting their personal preferences color the outcome of their research.

Equality versus Equity in Policy-Making

Horowitz's basic humanism, as expressed in his writings on the poor, and in his commitment to social melioration in general, not only provides a certain tension with his dedication to an autonomous social science, but also leads him to come to grips with the question of the limits of policy. It is because his passion for objectivity supersedes his political predilections that the tension is resolved favorably in behalf of science. But how he works this tension out is a most fascinating intellectual exercise.

The demand for equality, especially as ventilated since the 1960s, has been a demand for group rights. As Horowitz notes, no segment of the population has been left out, as the demands of short people and fat people compete with the demands of cancer and diabetes patients. He finds no problem with any of this: "All of these demands are perfectly reasonable; none save those who are without human compassion could deny the legitimacy of such demands" (1977:11). But the state, and only the state, is in a position to grant relief to these demands, and that raises questions not only of delivery but of the effects on liberty. Unrestrained demands on the state create as many problems as they pretend to resolve, and it is this issue that Horowitz is forced to come to grips with.

Policy-oriented social scientists, Horowitz observes, are split between a commitment to equity and a commitment to equality, properties which, though related, are nonetheless discrete (1979a:9, 45). Horowitz himself seems sometimes to be pulled both ways, as his desire for equality of opportunity is rivaled by his dissatisfaction with unequal results. There are times when these leanings unite in troublesome fashion: "U.S. society presents a major inconsistency: a near unanimous belief in the value of equity and a constant of income and occupational differences" (1977:1).

But why should a commitment to fairness (equity) entail leveling (equality)? If we can assume that the distribution of individual abilities, industry, and preferences are not uniform in the population, why should we not expect this unevenness to be reflected in the distribution of social and economic status? Moreover, the unequal distribution of income that Horowitz identifies (1977:10–11; 1979a:31) masks the reality of mobility that most people experience. Most people, as Eli Ginzberg says in his exchange with Horowitz, do not remain forever fixed in the bottom quintiles. Nor do income distribution figures tap the effects of transfer payments and taxes, two measures that considerably decrease real inequality. And as Ginzberg instructs in his dialogue with Horowitz in *Constructing Policy,* no matter what policy is followed, "You will always have a lowest quintile" (1979a:31).

It is the demand for equality—cast as equal results—that gives Horowitz pause. He prefers, as do many liberals of his generation, a society where economic mobility is open to all, as opposed to "a notion of ethnic homogeneity, or religious homogeneity that espouses the larger national culture." Not to concern ourselves with this new equality is to risk "the breakup of our national culture through disintegration rather than breakup through revolution" (1979a:54). Speaking of the revitalization of an ascriptive society, where everyone references his ancestry or anatomy as a basis for rewards, Horowitz poses the kind of question that cries out for a response: "How can a society withstand, much less satisfy, all competing demands; and more, how can a society sort out its priorities if everyone is speaking on behalf of a special interest, and few, if any, are asserting conditions of growth for the general interest?" (1979a:149).

Striking a Consensus

Horowitz's ability to address social issues and remain nonpartisan (at least with regard to his assessments of those issues) is a trait that he did not have to cultivate: it was evident at a young age. Indeed, it was evident at a time when he took his most adversarial stance against the social order. To read Horowitz's account of the need to appreciate the merger of social deviance and political marginality (1968b), or his analysis of the drug problem (1972), and then see him conclude with a statement on the resiliency of American society and the necessity of resolving the drug problem without decriminalization, is to witness a temperance of mind not shared by most of those who were caught up in the fever of the late 1960s and early 1970s.

Similarly, it would be a mistake to say that Horowitz came late to the realization that policy has limits. Certainly in this regard, there is no such thing as an "early Horowitz" and a "late Horowitz." He has always recognized the limits of policy. And the central limit to all policy, as Horowitz has long acknowledged, is consensus. When it exists, successful policy-making is possible; when it is absent, policy-making is doomed (1975b:139). This is as true of foreign policy as it is of domestic policy. It was dissensus that killed the prospects of Project Camelot (1979a:235) and it is dissensus that is standing in the way of a coherent policy on AIDS (1989:40–41).

One of the early lessons that Horowitz learned about the need for consensus and the limits of policy came from his study of urban politics. The problems he identifies are by now well known: the flight of the white middle class to the suburbs; the shrinkage of the city's tax base; increased demand on city services; urban renewal and the construction of housing projects; growing poverty; mounting crime; and a failing educational system—all combined to convince Horowitz that by the late 1960s the reigning political response was already obsolete (1970). Quite simply, city mayors were in over their heads, and this was nowhere more true than in New York.

"The crisis of our cities," Horowitz argues, "is perhaps best understood as part of the crisis in the federalist system of representative democracy." What drove him to this conclusion was his observation that the cities had simply become too big to govern. Representative government works well in small communities, but "when one man represents one million people, any notion of democracy becomes strained and tenuous, and ultimately it must break down" (1970:302). Looking at Horowitz's analysis from the vantage of the 1990s, his recommendations on what should not be done are as illuminating now as they were then. Even more instructive are his proposals for reform.

What won't work, Horowitz maintains, is making states out of big cities or extending the boundaries of the cities to include the outlying areas. Both schemes, he holds, would have the effect of further bureaucratizing urban areas, thus adding to the nature of the problem. And "to argue the case for an enlarged bureaucracy seems ingenuous if not worse" (1970:301). As important as any proposal that Horowitz rejects is the perennial favorite of raising taxes: "The solution is *not* an increase in taxes people pay—either on income or property. These are already at maximum figures and serve to further drive the much maligned middle sectors to the suburban regions" (1970:307). While this position is hardly unique today, there were relatively few in the social sciences—and almost none in sociology—who voiced this idea in the late 1960s and early 1970s.

What was needed, Horowitz advised, was community control. For New York, this meant division of the city into five separate cities, one for each borough. Subdivision from that base would then take place, with each borough being split into organic neighborhoods. As Horowitz saw it, there were simply too many competing interest groups—cut along lines of class, race, and ethnicity—for any city mayor to cope with. A decentralized structure would allow for the one variable that was uppermost in Horowitz's mind: consensus (1970:302–308).

Community control means small-scale planning. It means that competing interest groups would all be housed in the same neighborhood, making a consensus easier to achieve. It means that the Harlems of New York would actually be able to wield political clout, something denied under the present structure. It would not mean that the federal government would lessen support, only that in the long run the cities might need less help from Washington. "Community control is not a panacea," Horowitz cautioned, "and not without risks" (1970:310). But it did allow for the cities to be governable.

One of the major problems confronting reform, as Horowitz saw it, was that "most liberal-minded people [desire] the goals of big government but would like to see that they are brought about through community control." Horowitz's reply is telling: "This is not to be. One has to accept certain bridling of enlightened policies if one wants community control; whereas one has to accept the bureaucratic apparatus if we want certain welfare programs" (1970:309). Horowitz realizes that there will be no progress without reform, and no workable reform without a consensus. That means community control, and that means giving up the pipe dream of trying to orchestrate reform from above.

New York is today more ungovernable than ever before, having ignored the advice of social scientists like Horowitz. The welfare state continues to expand, especially in New York: in 1992 more than 1 million New Yorkers were on welfare, out of a total population of 7.3 million. The family breakup and dependency that have become the trademark of welfare have not been overlooked by Horowitz (1984:129), and neither has the increasing chasm between the working class and the lower class.

Though hardly new, in recent years working-class resentment has increasingly been expressed toward both the rich and the poor. The upwardly mobile yuppies who climbed faster than the working class could ever dream, and the poor who have inched closer to the standard of living enjoyed by blue-collar workers, have left the working class increasingly bitter (1984:129). As Horowitz sees it, "What began with the New Deal as a broad-based rebellion against privilege has now concluded as a class-based rebellion against a different set of privileges accruing to the welfare underclass" (1984:154). This can partly be explained by the extent to which the working class have been ignored by policymakers: they simply don't count (1979a:26–27; 1984:129). It is impressions like these that lead Horowitz to question the wisdom of contemporary public policy.

The Pitfalls of the "Limits to Growth" Model

Even when policy is well crafted, Horowitz suggests, it doesn't follow that a measure of equity and equality will follow. For that to happen, there must be economic growth. The demands that are levied on the state, he advises, cannot be satisfied within a democratic system unless there is real growth (1977:14). It is this conviction that leads Horowitz to look critically upon the limits to growth thesis as propounded by the Club of Rome.

Horowitz is duly suspicious of accepting the zero-sum world of economic development as posited by the Club of Rome. Why accept a no-growth model? Does not the image of a "fixed pie" assume limits on technology and resources that are at least contentious? Is a final collapse inevitable? Horowitz's principal concern in all this is the sociological implications of the limits to equity model (1980:939). It goes to the heart of his interests, and to the heart of American society.

As always, Horowitz's quarrel is not with the evidence, it is with the unexamined assumptions of those who interpret the data. To be sure, the 1970s was a decade of stagflation. The struggle for federal monies between the snowbelt and the sunbelt is real. Those who have been left out of Washington's deliberations, namely, those who live in small towns and rural areas, are becoming more vocal, looking for their fair share of the pie. Special interests are growing and are much better organized than in the past, upping the ante of demands (1980:938). It appears that something has to give, lest the overload causes the system to short-circuit.

To acknowledge certain systemic strains, however, is not to uncritically accept the limits to growth model. Horowitz is not only leery of the model, he is concerned that if policymakers were to take it seriously, certain negative social consequences would be unavoidable. Class conflict would certainly increase, possibly to threatening levels. Government would be induced to pull back on its commitment to the poor, thus further increasing polarization. Repression might follow and that in turn might engender problems of isolation within the international community. But "the ultimate consequence of a limits to growth policy would be an absolute decline in the United States as a world power," a prospect that would allow new potentates to "act with impunity against the United States" (1980:955). Those interested in preserving a base where equality and liberty can be furthered deserve to ponder the implications of Horowitz's concern.

Horowitz understands that economic growth is a necessary predicate of the equity and equality that he champions. Between 1950 and 1970, there was a doubling of the median family income in the United States. This paid dividends in policy as well: "When there is high growth, there is a greater capacity to absorb social welfare programs and social costs" (1984:151). Given this observation, it might seem that Horowitz would accept the position of Peter Berger (1986) that a market economy is the best bet for the poor and best tonic against inequality. But he stays removed from this issue, owing possibly to his disaffiliation with the ranks of the well-to-do. If there is one animus that Horowitz carries it is his animus against exploitation, and true to his nonpartisanship, he evenhandedly criticizes any social system that allows for its triumph. But he also criticizes any social system that makes a fetish of equality, to the detriment of other noble and competing values, such as liberty.

Threats to Liberty

Threats to liberty are multiple, but it is Horowitz's special interest to show how policy can contribute to liberticide. He targets two areas in particular: (a) programs that enlarge the powers of the state, and (b) judicial decisions that jeopardize the existence of the social order. In doing so, Horowitz gives tribute to Madison's admonition that "liberty may be endangered by the abuses of liberty as well as by the abuses of power" (1961).

The threat to liberty that the state poses comes by way of an expansive welfare bureaucracy. It has long been maintained that there is a point where equality and liberty part ways, moving in opposite and contradictory directions. But it was not until the twentieth century that the state would enter the picture, complete with an administrative apparatus that cast a pall over liberty. As Horowitz sees it, "the price of social welfare is political anomie for the masses. The equation that emerges is as painful as it is incontestable: libertarian goals tend to vanish as the range of federal social welfare programs expand" (1977:16).

The equation is particularly painful for Horowitz because of his real interest in addressing the conditions of the dispossessed: his basic humanism clashes with his understanding of statist prescriptions and the need to maintain liberty. Policy has limits, then, not only in the sense that the ambitions of policymakers typically exceeds their reach. In free nations, policy is further limited by the need to reconcile equality and liberty. The need to balance, to strike a consensus, while acceptable to Horowitz, has been resisted throughout the twentieth century by egalitarians and libertarians alike, as well as by those rationalists who seek a final harmony of values. That they have little of merit to show for their efforts only strengthens Horowitz's position.

If the equity and equality that Horowitz seeks is tempered by the limits of policy and the need to maintain liberty, the quest for freedom that he heartily endorses is tempered by liberty's excesses. To those of an absolutist persuasion, liberty for Nazis is as unexceptional as liberty for Boy Scouts. But Horowitz will have none of it. To defend Nazis in the name of liberty is to counsel the possibility of liberticide. "To argue that law must sanction lawlessness," he writes, "or that the right of free speech can be proven only by defending the rights of those who would suppress speech, is to place a burden on a legal code that is objectively implausible and logically self-contradictory" (1979b:343).

There is something perverse at work when, as Horowitz argues, advocates for civil liberties are transformed into advocates of civil disorder. "Under this view," he says, "since every act is permissible as long as it carries a political or ideological label, society can retaliate but can never anticipate disaster" (1987b:537). But waiting for liberty to dissolve is not recommended by Horowitz. What is missing from the ACLU view of law as policy is any recognition of the responsibilities that liberty entails. There is a dialectic between rights and obligations, the content of which Horowitz holds "is the limits of law itself as actual events come upon the extralegal, or social, requirement that a democratic society, no less than any other society, seek its own survival" (1987b:536–37).

Staking a Claim

The problem with the ACLU view of liberty, as Horowitz sees it, is the same problem that afflicts egalitarians: a fixation on one value to the exclusion of all others. Such a stance is not only philosophically wanting, it is problematic from a policy-oriented perspective as well.

Horowitz's dictum that successful policy-making is conditioned on consensus requires something less than the asymmetrical program afforded by the ACLU. At bottom, a consensual approach admits to a not-having-it-all approach to policy issues. Couple this orientation with Horowitz's commitment to an autonomous social science and the result is a scholarship that is rich, mature, and laced with integrity.

In looking back at Horowitz's contribution to policy studies, the mind is drawn to the incredible range of his interests and his unyielding demand for objectivity. This is not to say that all has been constant. Like Sidney Hook before him (with whom he shares a number of impressive characteristics), Horowitz has experienced an intellectual migration to the center. And as with Hook, the misgivings that Horowitz has about the nature of our economic order has never been enough to challenge his commitment to country. For when all is said and done, Horowitz has no stomach for those who would junk liberty for equality, or the promise of the United States for some abstract utopian ideal.

Finally, it is especially noteworthy that Horowitz's work shows that his essential nonpartisanship has never been used as a guise for avoiding big questions. When choices are critical, he is prepared to make them: "The good social scientist is obligated to stake a claim . . . for the better social and political system against the lesser social and political system" (1984:xvi). It is our good fortune that Horowitz found his obligation in the United States of America.

Catholic League for Religious and Civial Rights
Office of the President

References

Berger, Peter. *The Capitalist Revolution*. New York: Basic Books, 1986.

Horowitz, Irving Louis. "The Rise and Fall of Project Camelot." In *The Rise and Fall of Project Camelot,* ed. Irving Louis Horowitz, 3–44. Cambridge: Massachusetts Institute of Technology Press, 1967.

———. "Social Science Yogis and Military Commissars." *Transaction/Society* 5 (May 1968a):29–38.

———. "Social Deviance and Political Marginality: Toward a Redefinition of the Relation between Sociology and Politics" (with Martin Liebowitz). *Social Problems* 15 (Winter 1968b): 280–96.

———. "The Academy and the Polity: Interaction between Social Scientists and Federal Administrators." *Journal of Applied Behavioral Science* 5 (July-August 1969):309–35.

———. "'Separate but Equal': Revolution and Counter-Revolution in the American City." *Social Problems* 17 (Winter 1970):294–312.

————. "Social Change, Social Control and Social Policy." In *Handbook on the Study of Social Problems,* ed. Erwin O. Smigel, 435–78. Chicago: Rand McNally and Co., 1971.

————. "The Politics of Drugs." *Social Policy* 3 (July-August 1972):36–40.

————. "Conflict and Consensus between Social Scientists and Policy-Makers." In *The Use and Abuse of Social Science: Behavioral Research and Policy Making,* ed. Irving Louis Horowitz, 110–35. New Brunswick, NJ and London: Transaction Publishers, 1975a.

————. *Social Science and Public Policy in the United States* (with James Everett Katz). New York: Praeger, 1975b.

————. "Social Welfare, State Power, and the Limits to Equity." In *Equity, Income, and Policy: Comparative Studies in Three Worlds of Development,* ed. Irving Louis Horowitz, 1–18. New York: Praeger, 1977.

————. *Constructing Policy: Dialogues with Social Scientists in the National Political Arena.* New York and London: Praeger/Holt, Rinehart and Winston, 1979a.

————. "Skokie, the ACLU, and the Endurance of Democratic Theory" (with Victoria Bramson). *Law and Contemporary Problems: Duke University School of Law* 43 (Spring 1979b):328–49.

————. "Economic Equality as a Social Goal." *Journal of Economic Issues* 14 (December 1980):937–58.

————. "Is Social Science a God That Failed?" *Public Opinion* 4 (October-November 1981a):11–12.

————. "Social Science and the Reagan Administration." *Journal of Policy Analysis and Management* 1 (September-October 1981b):126–28.

————. Introduction to *Public Policy and the Migrant Child,* ed. Cassandra Stockburger. New York: National Organization for Migrant Children, Inc., 1981c.

————. *Winners and Losers: Social and Political Polarities in Present-Day America.* Durham, NC: Duke University Press, 1984.

————. "Disenthralling Sociology." *Transaction/Society* 24 (January-February 1987a):48–55.

————. "The ACLU and Politics: First Amendment Blues." *American Bar Foundation Research Journal* 1986 (Summer 1987b):533–45.

————. "The Limits of Policy and the Purposes of Research: The Case of AIDS." In *Policy Issues for the 1990s (Policy Studies Review Annual:9),* ed. Ray C. Rist, 35–46. New Brunswick, NJ and London: Transaction Publishers, 1989.

————. *Daydreams and Nightmares: Reflections on a Harlem Childhood.* Jackson: The University Press of Mississippi, 1990.

Madison, James. Federalist Paper 63. In *Federalist Papers.* New York: New American Library, Mentor Book ed., 1961.

Moynihan, Daniel Patrick. *Maximum Feasible Misunderstanding.* New York: Free Press, 1970.

Murray, Charles. *Losing Ground.* New York: Basic Books, 1984.

Torrey, E. Fuller. *Nowhere to Go.* New York: Harper and Row, 1988.

Section Four

Nation-Building and Development

12

Worlds of Development: The Sociological Perspective

John D. Martz

Over the past four decades, international development and social change have been writ large in the intellectual evolution of sociology and of related disciplines. Countless scholars have attempted to produce new paradigmatic fibers from which to weave richly varied conceptual fabrics in the quest for theoretical explanation and practical wisdom. Definitional criteria have been progressively enlarged. In one sense this has been a finite process, for there are obvious limits imposed by a global system that embraces all the regions of the world. Irving Louis Horowitz was among the first to acknowledge the existence of such a world system, believing that the developmentalist perspective provides the truest approximation to the very structure of the social scientific community. In a long and distinguished career, he has consciously undertaken the continuing effort to go beyond a single systemic component of particular personal interest—Latin America—in the quest for a broad and fundamental cultural convergence. In so doing, he has also breathed fresh air into a field of study and a discipline seeking to break out of traditionalistic bonds.

From the late 1950s on, a small but vigorous group of scholars had increasingly raised questions about the innate conservatism of the social sciences, as well as its perception of the political world. There was a preoccupation over the threatened transformation of political theory into methodology, accompanied in many instances by sharp questioning of U.S. politics in both its domestic and international manifestations. A

prime champion of this outlook was C. Wright Mills, as amply documented in the Horowitz collection of Mills's essays appearing in 1963.
Horowitz himself shared many of these views concerning both the social sciences and the international realities into which this realm of inquiry was attempting to probe. A revealing statement of his professional
concerns at a relatively early juncture in his career was "Sociology and
Politics: The Myth of Functionalism Revisited."[1]

Observing the unsettled question of the place of political belief in
sociological analysis, Horowitz objected to the contention that functionalism had resolved the issue of the relationship between sociology and
class bias. He was unpersuaded by the structural-functionalist argument
that a strict separation of facts and values would assure that sociology
be scientific. Such an attitude, as exemplified by Robert Merton's classic 1957 formulation that functionalism was without basic political or
ideological commitments, struck Horowitz as flawed. Rejecting that
"secularization" of the discipline suggested by those proclaiming an end
to ideology, he suggested that functionalism had merely shifted the lo-
cus of the ideological dialogue. Sociology had divided into rival camps
over their inability to resolve the relationship of political beliefs to sociological inquiry. In the final analysis, he insisted that functionalism
lacked a capacity to proclaim itself the bearer of neutral scientific trust.
It was to be from this intellectual foundation, then, that the young
Horowitz approached the study of development as the best means of
merging a valid intellectual disciplinary outlook by the sociological and
social scientific community with the needs of political policy goals.

The Sociology and Ideology of Development

While sociological research and theorizing became fundamental to
the study of international development, it had been preceded by the contributions of several other disciplines. To a considerable degree, historians were the early pioneers, to be followed by economists and then by
anthropologists. The first of these dealt with broad-based change, often
realized over extended periods of time, while the economists engaged in
a different set of variables as a means of examining social transformation. It then followed for the anthropologists to introduce broad cultural
dimensions in the wake of World War II, after which political scientists
brought to bear their own experience in studying authority, state power,

and policy-making. What remained for the sociologists was the need to enrich empirical studies through the articulation of theoretical perspectives. This they have done, exploring and articulating three orientations toward the study of development, as Horowitz has explained in the process of thinking through his own interpretation. These three theses he labeled as modernization, developmentalism, and dependency. Given the ambiguity and occasional sloppiness with which such terms have been used, it is important to clarify their meaning in Horowitz's eyes in order better to focus on his own study of development.

Sociology's oldest and earliest position was embraced in the concept of modernization, which assumed an inevitable historical transition from tradition to modernity. A prominent version stressed the shift from feudal, landed agrarian economies to urban industrialized economies. This and other variations relied upon Keynesian economics in which a mixture of public and private sectors injected new and sophisticated mechanisms of communication and transportation. Bargaining and negotiation were to become hallmarks in the policy process; thus, modernization represented a means of achieving change without societal violence, eschewing destructive revolution or counterrevolution. Social mobility and a democratization of the social system were necessary byproducts. Modernization consequently found as its model the advanced Western powers—those presumably capitalist democracies reflecting the American century as characterized by achievement-oriented societies.

The modernization school was championed by such eminent figures as Kingsley Davis, Bert Hoselitz, Alex Inkeles, Daniel Lerner, Seymour Martin Lipset, and Edward Shils. Much of their primary field research was conducted in the decade of the 1950s, informed in graduate school and beyond by patterns of international relationships spawned by the cold war. There was an ideological assumption, sometimes verbalized or muted, that modernization and Americanism were inextricably linked. The modernization school was inclined either explicitly or otherwise to join the struggle presumably pitting a democratic West and a totalitarian East. Modernization generally viewed the Third World through similar political optics. As Horowitz commented, it was remarkable that the modernization position so long maintained its primacy in American social science, given its reliance on a single set of political and economic experiences. In due course, however, a younger generation of theorists emerged to challenge modernization theory, including Horowitz himself. They became responsible for the formulation and articulation of a second intellectual orientation, one designed to recognize and respond to the shortcomings of the modernization school.

Developmentalism was the work of scholars who were of the 1960s more than the 1950s. In addition to Irving Louis Horowitz, they included Fernando Henrique Cardoso, Celso Furtado, Pablo Gonzalez Casanova, Samuel Huntington, Alejandro Portes, and Luis Ratinoff. Significantly, participation by Third World scholars was prominent in fashioning new ideas. As Horowitz noted, attention shifted from value theory to interest theory, as structural factors were emphasized over personality factors. The dichotomous implications of the evolution from traditional to modern societies—from colonialism to independence—gave way to more complex perspectives. Greater attention was directed to Asia, Africa, and Latin America. Policy considerations also became more important, for the nations of the Third World were in a position to make their own decisions about strategies and tactics, not merely imported European patterns of change. In Horowitz's view, the developmental process was triangular: economic, political, and military classes shared in the evolution and development of the Third World.

In all of this, the developmentalist model was embodied by those Third World nations that had gained independence after World War II. This permitted the inclusion of one-party rule, military authoritarianism, and a newly emergent, developmentally oriented bureaucratization of the state. Democratic values were not rejected, but the developmentalists accepted and responded to the emergence of a wide variety of authoritarian and totalitarian regimes. The Third World was more than a transitional phase marking the passage from traditionalism to modernization. Instead of being susceptible to inexorable historical and societal forces, it was viewed as pursuing choices, decisions, and options springing forth from its heritage as based upon fundamental regional and national experience. There was recognition that a greater sensitivity to internal forces was necessary, replacing the earlier assumption that these nations were simply battlegrounds on which surrogates for the cold war powers competed. In short, structural variables received far more penetrating attention than had previously been the case.

Developmentalism, initially a phenomenon of the 1960s, was to be followed duly by a third school, dependency. Stimulated by a reemergence of Marxism, it criticized both the bifurcation into traditional and modern sectors found in the modernization school, and the tendency toward a tripartite profile in the writings of many developmentalists. While sharing with the latter a holistic view of the world, dependency spokesmen envisaged this world system as the historic consequence of capitalist expansion from dominant to subordinate states. They stressed the so-called core, semiperiphery, and periphery of power and dominion. Ascribing the general cultural backwardness and economic deprivation of the Third World to manipulative domination by advanced capitalist nations, *dependentistas* in effect extended Lenin's theory of imperialism to the postindustrial era. To understand the problems of development required an identification of historical patterns of colonialism, which in contemporary times led to a focus on Western economic forces and multinational corporations. Among the more widely read exponents of the dependency school were Samir Amin, Paul Baran, Susanne Bodenheimer, Ronald Chilcote, Theotonio Dos Santos, and Andre Gunder Frank.

With the major exception of Amin, advocates of the dependency school of sociology drew primarily upon the Latin American experience. For some, this meant extended historical analysis of Western exploitation during the colonial era, particularly stressing the Iberian role, but also including England, France, and the Netherlands. The greater emphasis, however, was placed upon the twentieth-century relationship between Latin America and the United States. This first embraced the economic imperialism of dollar diplomacy while later being extended to such manifestations of anticommunist crusading as intervention in Guatemala (1954), the Bay of Pigs fiasco (1961), and the Dominican invasion (1965). Given the dependentista belief in revolution as a precondition for significant change anywhere in the world, Cuba became a central concern. The long involvement of the United States in Vietnam and its eventual withdrawal, coupled with the stubborn survival of the Castro regime in Havana, seemingly provided grist for the mill of the dependency school. Certainly it sensitized developmental studies in general to the importance of global power in its many and diverse manifestations. Yet with time, systemic capitalism displayed a resilience that gave the lie to many of the assumptions of the model, never more so than with the ultimate collapse of international communism.

In Horowitz's view, all three sets of attitudes toward development contributed to an improved understanding of the functioning of the world.

He has repeatedly argued that developmental studies constitute an important case in the sociology of knowledge; moreover, the discipline has made a sustained contribution to the study of international development. As among the three distinctive perspectives, of course, his preference has remained that of developmentalism. While conceding to critics that it says relatively little regarding the explanatory power respectively of social, economic, and political factors, he nonetheless contends that it represents an expression of eclecticism that is superior to the more exclusivistic alternatives. Modernization remains a model in which the measurement of development is inescapably reliant upon the manifestations of Western capitalism, often immune or insensitive to the needs and realities of the developing areas. Dependency, on the other hand, offers a model that, until recently, was linked to the social organization and economic techniques of the more advanced socialist countries. Here too, the result is too often extrinsic to the nations of the Third World. Only the developmental conception of change, in contrast, accepts and studies an emerging partnership between the developing and the developed nations, with the former adapting the institutional forms of the latter to their own cultural traditions.

In *Three Worlds of Development: The Theory and Practice of International Stratification,*[2] Horowitz laid out in detail his theories of developmentalism. Carefully defining the sociological meanings of each of the three worlds, he examines their interrelationships as influenced and shaped by the emergence and development of international stratification. Characteristically adopting a multidisciplinary approach, he integrates relevant categories from economics, history, political science, and social psychology. The result is a sociological framework, which is uniformly stimulating and thought-provoking, if sometimes more impressionistic than systemic. This is nowhere better exemplified than in the closing twenty-two page listing of propositions concerning social development wherein he bedazzles the reader while simultaneously frustrating him by its conceptual and organizational complexity.

Ten years later he again offered an extended consideration of his developmental preoccupations in *Beyond Empire and Revolution: Militarization and Consolidation in the Third World.*[3] Repeating his insistence on the essential integrity of the Third World, Horowitz again denied the contentions of those who saw it as following a path toward either First World modernization or Second World socialization. He also subdivided the Third World, thereby recognizing a Fourth World of some forty or more nations perpetually suffering from insufficient energy, food, and natural resources. In considering the changes that had recently transpired, he argued that historically, a new developmental stage was emerging. The first two, previously set forth in Three Worlds, embraced the collapse of nineteenth- and early twentieth-century empires and then the subsequent turmoil and revolutions in the new nations of Africa and Asia, as well as the upheavals in Latin America. By the 1980s, however, a new set of issues and policies was growing out of the legacy of empire or revolution. Thus, the developing areas were seeking alternatives to either Western or socialist models, with new routes for the expression and realization of true independence. Foremost among these choices— and receiving the greatest attention from Horowitz—were military-dominated systems.

A military formula was set forth as maximizing national control in the developing areas. This led in turn to the controversial notion that militarism was potentially beneficial for the achievement of stability, which in turn promoted growth and an ultimate transition to democratic politics. Horowitz drew heavily upon the Latin American states in arguing this position. Despite his overall incorporation of all the Third World, only limited attention was dedicated to African and Asian nations. With the former, for instance, Nigeria was the only nation to receive much attention. Thus, the weight of his arguments rested heavily upon Latin America. It is within that context that he presented militarism as a viable means of socioeconomic progress and political maturation. Consequently, his writings on Latin American development constitute a basic underpinning to his sociological conceptualization.

Patterns of Development: The Latin American Experience

The theoretical net cast by Horowitz in his developmental writings is characteristically broad and far-reaching. His qualitative analysis in *Three Worlds of Development* is illustrative. Much of the vision is decisively informed by the experience of the Third World and it is variously derived from Asia, Africa, and Latin America. It is the last of these, however, that most deeply reflects his own research and field work. A significant influence came from his time in Argentina, where Gino Germani was creating an organizational and intellectual sociological tradition in the post-1955 period. Having received a chair at the University of Buenos Aires, Germani proceeded to develop national research capabilities. The economist Jorge Graciarena became his key associate for administrative responsibilities; Torcuato di Tella was another important colleague. Germani also invited a number of talented young foreign scholars to join in the enterprise. Among these were Luis A. Costa Pinto of Brazil and, from the United States, Kalman and Frieda Silvert, Rose Goldsen, and Irving Louis Horowitz.

Intellectual exchanges with these and other talented scholars, in addition to direct cultural and societal exposure, were inevitably manifested in research and publication. A prime example was *Revolution in Brazil: Politics and Society in a Developing Nation.*[4] As I myself wrote in a review at the time, it constituted a brilliant and challenging documentary collection, which, while concentrating on Brazil, was carefully located within a comparative context.[5] Writing at a time when revolutionary tides were sweeping the Third World, Horowitz sought not only to correct fundamental North American perceptions of Brazil, but also connected movements in that country with those common to other developing countries. A sympathetic and informed treatment of Brazil's peasant leagues was related to similar movements in the Americas. His own contributions also included a splendid discussion of the institutional facade of Brazilian constitutionalism. The fundamental soundness of his analysis was strikingly documented in the fact that although the book was prepared prior to the military ouster of constitutional government on 31 March 1964, it was no less valid when published later in the year. Indeed, it was both a historical document and an insightful set of heuristic guidelines for future research and investigation.

In terms of Horowitz's Latin American perspectives on development in the early 1960s, it was noteworthy that while the book's subject index lacked listings on development, modernism, and modernization, it did include such items as the military and industrialization. These latter were to assume greater significance in forthcoming publications. An important statement came in his "The Norm of Illegitimacy: The Political Sociology of Latin America," which introduced the section on "The Socioeconomic Pivot" in *Latin American Radicalism,* coedited with Josue de Castro and John Gerassi.[6] He insisted upon a conceptualization of developmentalism that comprehended both modernization and industrialization. The former was tied to the urban style of life, implying a functional rationalization of this particular life-style. Yet it constituted a posture for the consumption of ideas and commodities that was dependent upon industrialization. This was described as a developmental factor related not only to the technology of production, but to decisions on savings and investment as well. The notion was also advanced that industrialization was necessarily linked to participational variables in the overall process of political institutionalization.

Beginning the essay by drawing a distinction between legitimacy and violence, Horowitz described legitimacy in Weberian terms as the perception of the state as a service agency, not Marx's image of an oppressive mechanism dispensing power. Illegitimacy was the perception of the state as relying on illegal means to hold and to exercise power; for Latin America, this had deep roots in colonial history and in the basic role of the military. In examining what were termed the *imperial dynamics* of illegitimacy, Horowitz reiterated concerns also expressed in *Three Worlds of Development*. These included criticism of the common interchangeable usage in the social science literature of that day of the terms *modernization, industrialization,* and *development*. As already noted, he saw modernization as linked to the urban process, and indeed to industrialization. The former incorporates such indicators as literacy, life expectancy, transportation, and communication; for the latter, relevant measures include per capita national production, energy consumption, and percentage of population engaging in business, commerce, and the service industries.

Development, as he put it then, "might be said to encompass a double interchange—the interaction of modernization and industrialization forming the core problems of developmental processes and strategies alike." In terms of policy, strategies of growth were multiple; modernization and development did not proscribe revolutionary alternatives. Horowitz saw the probability of popular frustrations resulting from hopes and aspirations unrealized; this in turn permitted the introduction of influences from the United States, incorporating a norm of illegitimacy into the new imperialism. In his view, any theory of Latin America would necessarily be incorporated into a larger framework spawned by the interplay of nationalism and colonialism. In an appendix Horowitz noted the absence of an adequate general social theory for Latin America. His bibliographic review of Merle Kling, John J. Johnson, Rodolfo Stavenhagen, Pablo Gonzalez-Casanova, Celso Furtado, and others was not unsym-

pathetic to individual contributions but lamented the failure of area specialists to articulate broader theoretical statements.

Perceiving the so-called new imperialism as embracing a norm of
illegitimacy, Horowitz went further by insisting that any meaningful
theory of Latin America—a desideratum that he often reiterated—would
necessarily be incorporated within a global framework marked by the
interplay of nationalism and colonialism. He was prescient in concluding that military or quasi-military rule could well become a surrogate
for legitimate authority in Latin America, while adding that this did not
necessarily promote modernization or industrial growth. Thus, it was
possible—even probable—that a norm of illegitimacy would be fos-
tered and promoted from the cosmopolitan center. This further encouraged the spread of that form of imperialism that inevitably inhibited the
establishment and maturation of pluralistic governmental forms. For
Horowitz, it suggested preoccupations that emerged elsewhere in his
writings, one important source of which was "State Power and Military
Nationalism in Latin America," written in collaboration with Ellen Kay
Trimberger.[7]

The basic thrust was to assess the role of the state in Latin America in
the light of approaches toward the achievement of autonomous development. Noting that a "barrage of sociological theories has been put
forward...to show that Latin America is exempt from general laws of
social and economic development," the article examines the major theoretical paradigms of the moment in seeking more satisfactory bases for
generalizing about the region within a comparative global context. A
particular preoccupation over the manifest doctrines of "exceptionalism,"
which "plagued" Latin America, stimulated a renewed examination of
the dependency model. While praising the effort to break out of
exceptionalist bonds, Horowitz and Trimberger fault its global emphasis for failing to recognize important forces in Latin America itself. Consequently, the universality of dependency makes few provisions for
national diversity within the region.

The emphasis of dependency theories on internal class and political
relations as structured primarily by external capital not only ignored
national differences, but underlined the necessity of examining the Latin
American state via the relationship of its apparatus to class structure.
Historically, it is argued, class barriers must be broken down in order to
promote industrialization and either create or strengthen an independent

entrepreneurial class. It is the state—ultimately indispensable for economic development—which must foster the necessary internal mobilization of capital and human resources.

In so doing, the state must turn inward to mobilize capital, in the process becoming efficient, centralized, and autonomous. It is the necessarily bureaucratized state apparatus that becomes autonomous under two basic conditions. First, the bureaucrats themselves are not to be recruited from the dominant landed commercial or industrial classes; and second, they must at the same time be independent of either parliamentary or party machinery, which similarly represents dominant interests. In short, the autonomous state must differentiate clearly between state and class power. Ultimately, control of the governing apparatus must be a source of power independent of that held by a dominant class through its own control over the means of production.

The fundamental argument, then—not unrelated to broader and more general discussions of sociological theories of development—holds that neither Marxist nor functionalist perspectives have properly considered the relationship between state apparatus and dominant classes as an independent variable determining the type and rate of economic development. All of this leads to a closer treatment of an autonomous military bureaucracy as the potentially pivotal element in society. Doubtless influenced by the rise of military intervention and authoritarian rule in Latin America of the 1970s, there is an assumption—over which debate continues to the present—that military bureaucrats are more likely to produce economic development. In further detailing this contention, Horowitz and Trimberger identify three patterns that illustrate the potentials and problems in Latin American countries. First comes state-initiated national capitalist development. Second is state-initiated dependent capitalist development, while the last is designated as state-directed socialist development.

Without entering into a lengthy discussion of the specifics here, suffice it to say that, for Horowitz, in each of the three models, military and civil-technocratic elites have more political and economic power than their counterparts in earlier developed states. With the first, military and civil bureaucrats conduct a revolution from above in the approach to state-initiated national capitalist development. In contrast, state-initiated dependent capitalist development is controlled by a coalition of military and civil bureaucrats who have broken the traditional power of the landed bourgeoisie. Last is state-directed socialist development, led by military bureaucrats who seize power via mass revolution, break the power of the landed and national bourgeoisie, and take control of foreign investments. This overall perspective thus identifies a potentially unique mission for military sectors in seeking the goal of national cohesion and integration. In conjunction with the bureaucracy, it becomes capable of managing state power and its coercive apparatus.

Within this theoretical context, the reader is conducted on a swift flight across Latin America, touching down at Brazil, Argentina, Cuba, and Mexico. While individual situations varied, in each nation the role of the state was becoming ever more prominent, while the military itself resided at or very near the center of national nerve. It also bore substantial responsibility for a new consciousness of approaches, which might remedy critical economic stagnation. The military in Latin America, in short, constituted a crucial element in developmental theorizing. It was increasingly inclined to seek entry to the modern world despite heavy costs of social change and even heavier costs in political liberties. Granting the pessimism inherent in such a major emphasis on the role of the military, this "at least provides a ray of hope in that the fundamental loyalties of Latin America to the development process have finally replaced the illusions of North America as a basis for further analysis and political practice."

Unlike so many observers, whose theorizing has slavishly followed the political headlines and intellectual fads of the day, Horowitz has sought more lasting and universalistic developmental truths. At the same time, changing hemispheric trends have not been irrelevant for his emphases and inquiry over time. He inevitably found it necessary to recognize and to confront the implications of the Cuban Revolution through the decade of the 1960s. In similar fashion, the dramatic spread of authoritarianism in the 1970s in a host of nations—at least symbolically originated as early as 1964 in the Brazilian military seizure of power—also required careful attention. By the close of that decade and the initiation of the 1980s, further shifts were occurring. These received their due when, fifteen years after the initial publication of *Three Worlds of Development, Beyond Empire and Revolution* appeared. Here Horowitz reiterated but further refined his earlier attention to military regimes, arguing that militarism retained the capacity to achieve that systemic stability necessary for economic growth and, moreover, an ultimate transition to democratic politics.

With the work significantly subtitled "Militarization and Consolidation in the Third World," Horowitz again articulated arguments that incorporated events and analyses from across the globe. For Latin America in particular, he was explicit in conceding that in some senses it constituted an exception to the other developing areas. He built upon and extended his 1976 treatment of Brazil, Argentina, Mexico, and Cuba, as well as dwelling on the relationship with the United States. This buttressed his contention that a period of consolidation and structural unification was under way—a historical transformation, the outcome of which was undetermined. In Latin America as well as elsewhere, modernization continued to clash with traditionalism on several levels. A series of real-world processes marked this struggle over compatibility, and in the final analysis would (and will) prove decisive in sketching and establishing the "limits of modernity," as he put it.

Looking at the Latin America of the 1990s, a critic might readily and conveniently remark that the spread of at least formalistically democratic regimes gives the lie to the Horowitz treatment of the military, so essential to his prescriptive vision of development in the Americas. Yet this would be a superficial argument that does not stand up to closer consideration, one that fails to recognize the timeless power and influence of the armed forces in Latin American politics and policy-making. Argentina, Brazil, Chile, and Uruguay, for example, are among the nations at this writing where democratic regimes with variable degrees of systemic fragility are heavily dependent upon military approval and, equally important, of both subtle and unsubtle participation in national affairs by the armed forces. Venezuela—putatively the most participatory and institutionalized democracy on the South American continent over the last third of a century—has undergone two major military rebellions early in the decade. Moreover, in Venezuela as elsewhere, development is powerfully if negatively affected by the problem of popular frustrations arising from hopes unrealized. Horowitz has written at length of the perils inherent in nations whose stability and accompanying capacity for growth and progress are undermined by governments too myopic or incompetent to adopt measures consistent with the needs, demands, and expectations of the citizenry at large.

It might more defensibly be argued that Horowitz's description of the military role in development, as linked with civilian technocrats, was realized in such instances as Chile under Pinochet but is now passé, for such regimes no longer dot the landscape. There is some justice to this observation, although, here again, it does not vitiate Horowitz's writings on the subject. Granting that there are relatively few cases at present of the so-called bureaucratic-authoritarian regimes that bore a resemblance to the Horowitz position on the military and developmentalism, this is not to say that prevailing political reality in contemporary Latin America displays a fundamental reduction or diminution of the military role in public affairs. Furthermore, present-day conditions also confirm the broader Horowitz belief that neither modernization nor dependency models would ultimately prevail. As the Brazilian political sociologist Helio Jaguaribe once remarked,[8] Horowitz was prescient in recognizing as early as the mid-1960s that the societies of the Third World as a whole would adopt neither the modernization school's macromodel of Western Europe and the United States, nor the dependentistas' Eastern European and/or Chinese versions of socialism.

Essays on Latin America and on Cuba elsewhere in this volume go further in confirming the wisdom of Horowitz's judgment over time. Even more important for an assessment of his thought about development, however, is the broader thrust of his writing over the course of the past three decades. In the final analysis, he has unwaveringly depicted the study of international development and change—and especially of what he understands as developmentalism—as the dominant paradigm for sociological research and analysis. In all of this, his contribution to fundamental theory in social development has been profound. Perhaps most importantly of all, it represents his unparalleled personal commitment to scholarship at the service of society as well as the academic profession. Some years ago, writing in the wake of the disastrous Camelot research project, Kalman Silvert eloquently insisted that basic societal issues transcended the controversy of the moment. The grounds for that disgraceful episode, he wrote, were well prepared "by the ethical incomprehension, cavalier attitudes, and tolerance of ignorance manifested by American universities and scholars for many years."[9] It is against such ethical and intellectual nightmares that Irving Louis Horowitz has fought throughout his career—nowhere more eloquently nor tellingly than in the study of development and change.

The Pennsylvania State University
Department of Political Science

Notes

1. Irving Louis Horowitz, "Sociology and Politics: The Myth of Functionalism Revisited," *Journal of Politics* 25, no. 2 (May 1963): 248–65.
2. Irving Louis Horowitz, *Three Worlds of Development: The Theory and Practice of International Stratification,* 2d ed. (New York: Oxford University Press, 1972).
3. Irving Louis Horowitz, *Beyond Empire and Revolution: Militarization and Consolidation in the Third World* (New York: Oxford University Press, 1982).
4. Irving Louis Horowitz, *Revolution in Brazil: Politics and Society in a Developing Nation* (New York: E. P. Dutton & Company, 1964).
5. John D. Martz, Review of *Revolution in Brazil, Social Forces* 43, no. 3 (March 1965): 453.
6. Irving Louis Horowitz, "The Norm of Illegitimacy: The Political Sociology of Latin America," in *Latin American Radicalism; A Documentary Report on Left and Nationalist Movements,* ed. Irving Louis Horowitz, Josue de Castro, and John Gerassi (New York: Random House, 1969), 3–29.
7. Irving Louis Horowitz and Ellen Kay Trimberger, "State Power and Military Nationalism in Latin America," *Comparative Politics* 8, no. 2 (January 1976): 223–45.
8. Helio Jaguaribe, *Political Development: A General Theory and a Latin American Case Study* (New York: Harper & Row Publishers, 1973), 204.
9. The Silvert chapter is included in Irving Louis Horowitz, ed., *The Rise and Fall of Project Camelot: Studies in the Relationship between Social Science and Practical Politics* (Cambridge: Massachusetts Institute of Technology Press, 1967). This collection, which includes cogent contributions from the editor, remains the best single source for understanding the Camelot affair, its complications, and its implications.

13

The Sociology of Truth and Its Consequences

Simon M. Fass

Irving Louis Horowitz makes his mark on progress through his influence on the thoughts and attendant actions of those who by design or good fortune come to be his apprentices, be they other scholars, development practitioners engaged policy and program work, students in the classroom, or anyone else that shares with him the conviction that the purpose of understanding the conditions of the present is to try to make the future a trifle better (Horowitz, 1992). He instructs all of us in fundamentals.

Out of his daydreams and nightmares of survival in the developing country of Harlem, study of Plato, and the struggle to link these experiences, Horowitz teaches that truth has consequences (Horowitz, 1990a). It is important to understand this relationship because we live in a world that seems always to need some kind of generalized wisdom about collective, imminent, and miraculous redemption (Horowitz, 1975). In this world there is danger of straying from the precepts of scientific inquiry. Removed from them, scholars may act as theologians, and practitioners as missionaries, in the service not of explanatory theory but of ideological or utopian canons that undermine the cause of understanding (Horowitz, 1981a). And because ideas influence strategies of action, prescriptions that flow from untutored doctrine masquerading as truth have the power to impede progress and inflict harm (Horowitz, 1966).

Explanations that rest more on the presumption of historical authority than on characteristics of the relationships that require explanation are especially dangerous because they act as self-evident truths and not,

225

as science insists, as theoretical postulates subject to proof or disproof. The circular and self-reinforcing logics that implant themselves in these truths do away with science and therefore the possibility of achieving either meaningful analysis of the processes of social change and development or meaningful action to husband improvements in the human condition (Horowitz, 1976).

Horowitz illustrates this phenomenon through exploration of the consequences of two truths that at one time dominated thought and action with respect to social development in the Third World. One, sanctified by presumed authority in Marx and Lenin, is the gospel of dependency theory (Horowitz, 1979). The other, consecrated in the presumed authority of Durkheim and Weber, is modernization theory (Horowitz, 1992). If dependency and modernization are of science rather than faith, Horowitz asks, where is the evidence to sustain the thesis that elites are either radical or modern and ordinary people either conservative or traditional (Horowitz, 1966)? If these are scientific theories, why is there no sign even of effort to gather evidence that could test their truth content by the degree to which they correlate with objective circumstances (Horowitz, 1962a)? Why, if they adhere to science, are so many of the scholars and practitioners who engage in Third World activities content to remain removed from the objects of their attention, to have little first-hand experience with the actual data of their trades, or to know so little about the human beings, social institutions, and communities about which they proclaim expertise (Horowitz, 1963)?

These are not the behaviors one expects of scientists, nor of most theologians and missionaries for that matter. They are the conduct of people who, like the charming bourgeoisie of Miranda that Horowitz describes so well in his review of Bunuel's film, are simply too detached from the harsh realities around them and the sufferings and needs of societies to recognize that their truths, at best, make little difference to people in the Third World (Horowitz, 1973). At worst, by maintaining ideological embers of nineteenth-century (and earlier) doctrines long after they have run out of intellectual steam, on the eve of the twenty-first century these truths also fuel nineteenth-century modes of action that often cause needless pain (Horowitz, 1987).

Much has changed in the developing countries since these theories first attracted Irving Horowitz's attention. Although variations on the theory seem to have acquired currency (and Horowitz's ire) in

American sociology, dependency has for the moment faded from view (Horowitz, 1987, 1990b, 1992). Modernization theory, a framework that often sustained perspectives that according to Horowitz viewed peoples of the Third World as too sick, immature, and retarded to freely steer their own destinies, is no longer fashionable for describing the evolution of whole societies or for devising policy prescriptions for them (Horowitz, 1968).

The reasoning that sustains this second theory, if not the thesis itself, is also well on its way to being expiated from thought and action at the sectoral level. Compelled to discover solutions to the population explosion and its perceived threat to the entire planet, for example, the field of demography has achieved much success in distancing itself from eighteenth-century, Malthusian premises (e.g., that high fertility stems from traditional or other irrational behavior), and in impeding coercive actions that flow from such assumptions.

Unfortunately, progress is still quite slow in other sectors, such as education. I discovered this while working with several African, European, and American colleagues in a two-year study, recently ended, of prospects for harnessing education to further the emergence of participatory democracy in francophone west Africa (Fass, 1992). Our work, commissioned by branches of the U.S. Agency for International Development (USAID) and the Organization for Economic Cooperation and Development (OECD) that concern themselves with the region, found most actors in the political classes that influence thought and action in education to be suffering from what Horowitz labels ideological, ethnocentric, temporally self-centered, chauvinist, racist, colonialist, and moral assumptions and predilections (Horowitz, 1967, 1975, 1979, 1981b).[1]

By defining educational progress as First Worldization (i.e., as Westernization) they sustain a human tragedy of long duration that is directly attributable to the same factors that sustained modernization theory. For almost two centuries this definition has aborted possibilities for education systems in Africa, as Horowitz puts it, to modernize on their own terms and thereby contribute to social progress (Horowitz, 1984). Intentionally or no, it has also helped to keep majority populations economically and politically subordinate (Horowitz, 1966).

This circumstance might have gone unnoticed had fortune not put the study and preparation of this homage to Irving Horowitz into the same slice of time. At the beginning, no less captive of self-evident truths than other actors, we might not have questioned our premises had Horowitz's writings not insisted that we should. We might not have searched for evidence to sustain these premises or, more important, followed his dictum to search for new ideas by studying ordinary people as well as elites, farmers as well as city people, the interests that shape how people act at the individual and family level as well as the national level, structural relationships within Third World societies as well as between these societies and the First World, and other important things (Horowitz, 1970, 1971, 1979). And of course, had we not followed his guidance to study developing societies on their own terms and the interest-group strategies and tactics that circulate in them, we might not have identified courses of future action that, by diverging from traditional practice, might eventually accelerate Africa's movement from colonialism to independence (Horowitz, 1984).

Initial reactions to our study range from delight by our immediate sponsors through consternation by all those we implicate as active contributors to the tragedy. This outcome as well as my own personal development as researcher and practitioner owes much to Irving Horowitz. Because the subject matter highlights much of what he has strived to accomplish during his career, and because he, in any event, says (and amply demonstrates through his own explorations of the military) that it is best to analyze and generalize about discrete processes rather than make monastic claims about whole societies, it seems only fitting to present some of our findings (Horowitz, 1972). To this end I now explore the relationship between self-evident truth and irrationalities in the practice of analysis and policy.

The Meaning of Education

The education sector in francophone west Africa, as elsewhere in the Third World, consists of several systems that, for present purposes, can be assigned to one of two domains: African (or non-Western) and Western (or non-African). The African sphere circumscribes a rich array of instruction systems that were present in the region before the arrival of Europe, including Islamic education dating from the twelfth century, animistic instruction, which preceded Islam, and, most important, various community systems that now as always transmit vital knowledge and values from one generation to the next. Observers with Western outlooks call these systems religious, nonformal, traditional, indigenous, and the like.

The Western sphere contains all schools in the state-controlled and supported public system of each nation. These relay one or another variant of the secular instruction and value sets that, for several centuries before colonization brought them to the region, evolved out of Christian and communal educational foundations in step with economic, social, and political transformations taking place in France. Some westerners call this formal education. Most Africans refer to it as white man's schooling.

Systems in both domains serve important purposes for the segments of society they serve, dissimilarities between them reflecting differences in the social, economic, and political environments in which people live and the fortunes of history that produced these differences. Because each system is in principle inferior to what it may become in the future, educational modernization can be viewed as a process wherein each social group adjusts features of its system in response to autonomous discoveries and/or change in its environment over the course of time, including the flow of new information and understanding. This is more or less the way in which different systems developed in Europe, America, and Japan until, toward the end of the nineteenth century, they began fusing together within and between nations to become what we now call Western education.

This definition of modernization, borrowed from Horowitz's use of it to describe improvements in technology, has the useful property of placing all systems on an equal analytical footing (Horowitz, 1982). As a conceptual device it has the further advantage of offering wide latitude for prescriptive action. If reason and means exist to husband the modernization process, then policy can address one or all systems and one or all the different publics that manage them.

The concept does not, for example, preclude from the purview of policy the community instruction that Mbaïosso (1990) reports for Tchad. This curriculum now offers rural boys initiation to religion; morals and social conduct; use of farm and hunting implements; nature and the physical environment; production of traps; management of animals; crop production techniques; social convention and law; geography; history and culture; participation in community affairs; verbal expression and debate; and intellectual refinement. Girls, in addition to religion, morals, and conduct, receive guidance in household production activities; personal hygiene and health; posture and physical comportment; culture; pounding of grain; production of thread; sewing and knitting; preparation of meals; hairdressing, cosmetics, and dress; sex; and mastery of aphrodisiacs.

Together with others similarly well-adapted to their milieus and to the probable life courses of the young, this curriculum has successfully transmitted the wherewithal to assure livelihood and survival for a very long time in very hostile environments. In Muslim areas that benefit from competent Islamic teachers, it may sometimes also supply rudimentary literacy in Arabic if there is interest in extending past memorization of prayers to read the Prophet's word in the Koran or, in the rare instances where these opportunities exist, to engage in commercial transactions too large to account for in one's head.

The content of community and other African instruction has ample scope to bring itself up to date, of course, if not with respect to aphrodisiacs then perhaps with respect to traps, grinding of grain, and hygiene. Still, given what the curriculum does for people it earns the privilege, if there is need to assign the word, to be viewed as one of the region's most basic forms of education.

Most governments, donor agencies, scholars, and others in the political classes do not see African or other non-Western systems in the developing countries as basic, however, or for that matter even as education. They made this plain at the 1990 "Education for All" conference in Thailand, which by concentrating most Third World education ministers, bilateral donor and nongovernmental agency delegates, and representatives from the United Nations Development Program (UNDP), UNESCO, UNICEF, and the World Bank in one place, was the largest meeting ever assembled of individuals and institutions that deal with education research and policy in developing countries.

As approved by participants, the final declaration of the conference defined basic education as that which provides the skills, knowledge, values, and attitudes that a person needs to survive, develop his abilities, live and work in dignity, improve the quality of his existence, take enlightened decisions, and continue to learn (CMET, 1990). With allowance for different interpretations of terms such as survival, ability, dignity, quality, enlightenment, and learning in different social and economic milieus, this definition could cover any system of instruction. By retaining the possibility that everyone already possesses a basic education of some type, it could also make room for policy or other actions that address all systems.

But a gathering that organized itself around the premise that all do not yet have education used enrollment rates in primary schools of the Western system to quantify the scale of the problem, while making no mention of non-Western instruction. This makes clear that most participants did not view this last as education or, if they did, saw schooling as the only means to improve upon it. Modernization meant enrolling all children in Western schools, improving the quality of these schools, realizing universal literacy, and doing everything else required to make education sectors in the Third World look like those of the First World. It meant Westernization.

Thought and action in the sector suffer from many shortcomings as a result of this ideological basis for defining modernization. Not least of these faults, one to which Horowitz attaches great importance, is denial of the right of people to interpret the meaning of events and name the world for themselves (Horowitz, 1983b).

This is not to suggest that everyone was satisfied with the characteristics of schooling. The open and highly general definition of education resulted from the requirement that competing views about purposes, financing, priorities, and other things achieve a minimum of consensus. First Worlders, for instance, were especially insistent on the need to change curricula in countries, like those of francophone Africa, where the content of instruction has too much of what some call an urban or academic orientation and too little of practical value in agrarian societies. But only a very few, free of the intellectual trap of making schooling and education isomorphic, noted that the urban-academic content of public schools serves important economic and political purposes in the historical circumstances of places like Africa and, as such, is relatively impervious to change.

Fewer still were those who mentioned that agrarian societies already possess pertinent and practical non-Western systems, or that these societies might need or want something other than change in school curricula when their milieus lack industrialization, urbanization, agricultural surpluses, and the other factors that stimulated economic demand for literacy and led education systems in the West to acquire their particular features. With respect to this last, there was also little mention of the useful parallels and concomitant guidance that can be extracted from the ways in which schooling evolved before these factors became important in Europe or America. A prime example of this is the correspondence between the Muslim interest in access to the Koran and the Puritan imperative for everyone to have access to God's word in the Bible, which, in the seventeenth century, yielded America's first compulsory education law and near-universal literacy in the colony of Massachusetts shortly thereafter (Ulrich, 1967).

Nor, obviously, were there many who remarked that an alternative path to improving education might lie in helping African systems modernize on their own terms, or that efforts to broaden the definition of public to include them as legitimate subcomponents of national instruction systems worthy of the name might offer greater long-term promise than changing school curricula.

These ideas were absent not only from the conference. They have been missing from the agendas of the political class ever since the first Western school opened in Senegal in 1816. Colonial authorities and Christian missionaries saw little merit in them, among other reasons because the fact that Africans did not already have literacy, Christianity, or other practical or academic Western knowledge and values meant that they were primitive, backward, uncivilized, unenlightened, underdeveloped, and, in a word, uneducated. The only way to extract people from this condition, therefore, was to endow them with either a secular or a Christian version of the white man's schooling.

The talk of postcolonial authorities and education missionaries, in Thailand and elsewhere, indicates that the Third World's movement from colonialism to independence has not been accompanied by noteworthy change in dominant reasoning. In fact, there has been no change. Guizot, when he was minister of education in 1833, adopted a definition almost identical to that of the conference when he launched a program of basic education for all in France (Maynes, 1985). This stasis is unfortunate because the persistence of old logics in the political class has and continues to compel African systems that serve the majority of people to fend for themselves in discovering additions to their repertoires of instruction.

The spread of pan-Islamic nationalism, which at the turn of this century sent Muslim missionaries into the region to compete with Christians for animistic souls, followed in more recent times by some financial support from nearby countries such as Sudan, Egypt, and

Saudi Arabia, allowed Islamic education to make a bit of headway for urban populations in spite of energetic French and state efforts to suppress it (Brenner, 1989). This led to slow emergence of Islamic facilities called Medersas that, like parochial schools in America and Europe, combine religious instruction with other social and technical subjects. But these aside, African systems and the environments with which they interact are much the same today as they were before colonization two hundred years ago.

One may suppose that if traditional reasoning continues to dominate thinking in the political class it will continue to contribute to the inability of African societies to build upon their existing educational foundations, to emulate the evolutionary processes of trial and error that led to the emergence of integrated systems of public education in the West, and to enable the education sector as a whole to equip each succeeding generation with the capacity to contribute more to economic and social progress than its predecessor. It follows that if education in Africa is to have the opportunity to modernize itself on its own terms and thereby contribute more in the future than in the past, traditional logics in the political class, especially in the parts occupied by non-Africans, must also find ways to modernize. These logics need to bring themselves into the modern age by incorporating the one thing that our present era suggests (and Irving insists) offers at least some chance of contributing to progress—principles of scientific analysis.

This is hard for a number of reasons. One reason is that every form of logic, as the term itself implies, is perceived as rational by those who subscribe to it. Reasoning is reasonable because it derives from a coherent and meaningful universe founded on doctrines of shorter or longer duration, in this case something to the effect that we are better than they, which has sustained not only Westernization but also colonization, Christianization, islamization, barbarization, romanization, and hellenization, to name but a few. So long as a logic is under no pressure from within or without to reconcile its internal contradictions—Heraclitus's axiom according to Horowitz—it persists (Horowitz, 1966).

For example, when invited by Brecht's Galileo to peer through a telescope and see moons rotating about Jupiter, a finding inconsistent with Aristotle's explanation of movement in the heavens, the Florentine court's philosopher and mathematician refuse (Brecht, 1972). Their reasoning is sound. Such planets cannot exist according to the prevailing view.

The writings of Aristotle are themselves strong empirical evidence of their impossibility. Contradiction of these writings would put into question not only this evidence but also the reputation and divine authority of Aristotle. Logically, and scientifically, if moons are visible in the telescope then there is something wrong with the lens.

Galileo responds that there is a difference between observable facts and belief in authority; that truth is the child of time and not of authority, and that given a chance to whittle away just one cubic millimeter of their infinite ignorance, it is unclear why scholars should still want to be so clever when they have a chance to be a little less stupid. Reasonably, the scholars reply that what matters is not truth but its consequences. Similarly, as Horowitz himself discovered, one cannot easily challenge dependency theory if it means casting doubt on the authority of Marx and Lenin, or on modernization if the reputations of Durkheim and Weber are to be dragged through the mire.

Another reason is that many scholars and practitioners, though they may be well-schooled in the social sciences, cannot distinguish between ideology and scientific explanation because they have yet to master the principles. Thus, if they see the play most of them side with Galileo and cannot conceive the possibility that they might be acting the roles of the philosopher and mathematician. This allows nasty things to happen, such as pseudo-science and what Horowitz calls untutored empiricism (Horowitz, 1990b). It also allows actors guided by this authority to claim with good conscience that they are struggling, as Horowitz suggests they should, to understand the present in order to better the future.

No less than in the theories of societal modernization that precipitate Horowitz's ire, the problem here stems not so much from the overarching we-they dichotomy, though this can be a problem, as it does from the arrogance and ignorance that interprets this to mean a rational (us)-irrational (them) dichotomy. This teleology turns on its head a fundamental precept of scientific inquiry (i.e., the null hypothesis), makes it virtually impossible for those who subscribe to it to recognize empirical evidence when it confronts them in analysis or policy, and, in an odd twist, impedes achievement of many of their stated goals. Working in perfect harmony, these things make the traditional reasoning that guides far too many scholars and practitioners almost impervious to change and prevent the modernization of education in Africa.

Irrational Analysis

Scholars and development practitioners that deal with education sincerely believe their thoughts and actions to be grounded in something that looks like empirical evidence. This faith is sustained by statistical studies suggesting that schooling is indeed superior to all other forms of instruction, at least for economic purposes. One recent review of these studies, for example, concludes that there is now a persuasive body of theoretical and empirical evidence that investment in schooling of the labor force plays a crucial role in economic development (Haddad et al., 1990). Another review argues that the literacy, numeracy, and problem-solving knowledge that schools provide have direct positive effects on earnings, farm productivity, and human fertility, as well as indirect intergenerational effects on child health, nutrition, and education (World Bank, 1990).

For better or worse, however, the actual evidence is less convincing than these reviews suggest. Excellent econometric analyses, for instance, demonstrate that most of the studies contain serious technical and conceptual flaws, that claims about the positive effects of schooling that flow from them are exaggerations at best and that the causes of differences in productivity and in intergenerational effects are still unknown (e.g., Glewwe, 1990; Behrman, 1990).

The claims also run counter to the findings of many careful historical analyses of the spread of literacy and schooling in the First World (e.g., Cipolla, 1969; Cubberly, 1919; Furet and Ozouf, 1977; Graff, 1987; Kayashima, 1989; Maynes, 1985; Resnick, 1983). These show that after financial and institutional constraints on schooling children disappeared in Europe, America, and Japan, even after governments began to compel parents to school them, rural families were the last to show interest in doing so. That is, such positive effects as schools may have engendered, if any, were not apparent to most rural parents or, if apparent, were offset by higher social or economic costs.

Further, these analyses show that the less the likelihood that a child could eventually take advantage of opportunities such as urban wage employment or expanded rural trade that required language, literacy, certificates, or other things that schools offered and the greater the difference between the content and character of public schools and those of existing systems, the lower their interest. Sociological surveys in Togo by Lange (1987) and in Benin by Akpaka and Gaba (1991) come to the same conclusions.

Indeed, it seems clear from these surveys that state schools are often regarded as a tangible threat to welfare in milieus where the work of children is crucial to assuring the older generation a longer life expectancy. Besides compromising the future capacity of children to support parents because they offer no knowledge of productive economic value, schools undermine intergenerational cohesion and thus their future willingness to provide support—an effect that De La Chatolais, a French reformer, noted when he wrote in 1762 that schools taught children to despise the occupations of their parents (Cippola, 1969). The notion of sending children to school thus makes no more sense to people living in these milieus than the idea of adopting family planning practices, which would prevent them from having sufficient children in the first place.

The weight of available econometric, historical, and sociological evidence of quality should therefore indicate that schooling, at the very least, is not a universal good. If they nevertheless insist upon the inherent goodness of schools, it may perhaps be because scholars and practitioners find difficulty interpreting this type of evidence or are not yet aware of it. A high level of mathematical sophistication is required to assess the quality and correctly interpret statistical analyses. And it takes a great deal of time to filter through the large inventory of historical tracts about education in the First World, to find the few rigorous, empirical analyses pertinent to developing countries, and to discover unpublished work about less-studied places such as Africa.

Ignorance is not a satisfactory explanation, however, because scholars and practitioners stare at other, more compelling evidence every day. An obvious piece of evidence is the enrollment rate itself. If one accords parents a minimum degree of respect for their intelligence, understanding of their own circumstances, knowledge of what is required to survive in these circumstances, and their capacity to make rational decisions through a reasonably accurate calculus of the social and economic benefits and costs to themselves, children, families, and communities, then it necessarily follows from the observation of low enrollment (i.e., where schooling is available) that schools are not good for these parents and therefore not good for everyone.

Alternatively, if one interprets this evidence through a lens that accords parents little or no respect, for example, by drawing from historical and sociological studies the conclusion that the evidence shows only that cultural or other impediments among rural populations everywhere always prevented and still prevents them from appreciating the productive values of schooling, then it is easy to insist that schools are inherently good in all circumstances. In this instance logical necessity demands that low enrollment be interpreted in the same manner as did a French school inspector one hundred and fifty years ago when he had to explain low enrollment and absenteeism to his superiors. He reported that the problem had to do with the negligence, ignorance, greed, lack of appreciation of knowledge, and the indifference of some parents who did not want for their children a benefit whose advantages they could not comprehend because they themselves were deprived of it (Maynes, 1985).

The issue at hand therefore turns not on ignorance of the evidence but on its interpretation. The question that immediately presents itself is: Which interpretation is better? Subscription to what we normally understand as rules of science would suggest that an explanation based on respect is better than an interpretation based on arrogance. It is better because disrespect implies the need to turn hypothesis testing on its head. That is, the null hypothesis is that schooling is good. One must disprove this statement rather than disprove the claim that schools are not good. This is the same as saying that one must disprove the thesis that people are irrational rather than the inverse, fundamental to economic theory, that they are rational. This failure to understand the implications on rigor of presuming irrationality traps analytic reasoning in a circle that curtails the very inquiries that might put current theses to any sort of meaningful test.

For instance, the presumption implies that there is little need to understand the characteristics of consumers and of their demand for schools or other forms of education because the explanation is self-evident. There is therefore also no need to search either for other factors that may constrain enrollment or for methods to deal with these factors. The truth, as understood by Guizot, French inspectors, participants in Thailand, and authors of the vast majority of scholarly works that touch on education in developing nations, is simple and straightforward. People who have not attended a public school are uneducated rather than unschooled. The share of an adult population that spent time in school or is literate represents a reliable measure of the quantity of human resources in a society. The level of school attainment measures the quality of these resources. Change in enrollment rates is a measure of educational progress. Since these and related statements are not only true but also backed by the authority of prior work on the subject, the utility of testing them is not apparent.

More obvious are the policy prescriptions, also simple and straightforward, that flow from this truth—children must go to school. As set down in almost all project documents that have been put forward in recent times by agencies such as UNESCO, USAID, and the World Bank, the proper tactic to reach this goal is to convince parents, nowadays with an emphasis on girls, of the benefits of schooling. Together with coercion, when schools did not satisfy their enrollment quotas, this is the same procedure that authorities and missionaries used in Africa before independence, and that governments in America and Europe adopted before they acquired sufficient power to enforce compulsory schooling laws in the nineteenth century (Capelle, 1990).

That there seems to be no sense of something dreadfully amiss in the logic that compels adoption of nineteenth-century and earlier practices on the eve of the twenty-first is not surprising. Harmony and order of the universe require old ideas and old tactics . Nor, for this same reason, is it surprising that the doctrines that produce this result not only defeat the policy goals of those who subscribe to them but also make them oblivious to this fact. The results of efforts to reform the curriculum of public schools, providing scholars and practitioners with yet another piece of evidence about the soundness of their premises, is a case in point.

Irrational Policy

Many First Worlders, as I indicated earlier, believe that the content of public schooling needs drastic change. They say that superimposition on Africa of an urban-academic form of instruction that derives from the experiences of France forces schools to be divorced from the realities in which most people live. Parental interest in schooling cannot be high when the knowledge they transmit is unintelligible or, if intelligible, is of no practical social or economic value in rural milieus. Curriculum and language thus serve as unnecessary impediments to enrollment.[2] And by both compromising learning outcomes and contributing to high repetition and dropout, they also constrain expansion of literacy (e.g.,

Belloncle, 1984; Botti, 1978; Heyneman, 1983; IIEP, 1989; Lockheed and Verspoor, 1992; World Bank, 1988, 1990).

This argument is old. Self-anointed reformers have made it and have tried to alter the content of schools ever since Catholic missionaries first attempted to elicit interest in what they surmised was practical rural instruction in 1840. But all efforts failed.

When governments rejected proposals for change after independence, reformers accused officials and the political classes they served of indifference to the basic needs of ordinary people or, worse, of deliberate effort to subordinate them. When governments permitted pilot projects and ordinary parents rejected new curricula and languages, demanding return to the standard format even though the new approaches clearly demonstrated their capacity to improve literacy, reformers assailed parents with the usual array of disparaging adjectives I've already listed. The evidence clearly pointed to something fundamentally wrong with the entire society. Since this was the Third World, such a conclusion was plausible.

Diarra (1991) counters that it would be more accurate to suggest that there was and remains something very wrong with the reformers. The "Achilles heel" of all efforts to alter curricula during the past half-century, not to mention since 1840, stems from their insistence that it is somehow better for children to go to schools that lead to nothing than to schools that offer at least a slim chance of something. This insistence stems partly from inattention to differences in structural features between public systems in the First World and Africa, and partly from inattention to African systems and what they already supply in rural milieus.

One important structural difference between the two worlds is that while systems in the First have evolved to the point where their main economic function is to respond to demand by whole societies for a stream of (properly) socialized labor ranked by level of school attainment and corresponding credentials, those in Africa restrict themselves to supplying the needs of a very small segment of the economy, mainly the state sector and a few other urban activities.

This restricted supply function results from three colonial legacies: disinterest in promoting broad economic development (and, as noted, improvements in the non-Western systems that sustained production in rural areas); centralization of political authority in an administrative apparatus and thus in townspeople that worked in or attached themselves to it by other means; and use of the French metropolitan system not only as the method of recruiting and screening cadres for the apparatus but also, after 1946, as the method to ration opportunities for temporary or permanent emigration to the urban, secular societies of the West. Reinforced after independence by the tendency of external aid agencies to channel all assistance to or through governments, colonization thus endowed the region with a circumstance in which the state apparatus and emigration offer the only unambiguous paths to higher economic and political standing and, within this context, with a public system that resists change because it still serves as the only route to the apparatus and to the ultimate prize—escape to France.

Though any hierarchical scheme of instruction with almost any content or language could allocate domestic rewards, such as scholarships and state or other urban employment, the paramount goal demands that the entire system, from primary schools through universities, offer opportunities to master the French language and literacy, and to acquire values and behaviors consistent not only with the expectations of those already in the apparatus and other segments of the political class but also with expectations of schools and employers in Europe. Further, in order to function properly, the system must balance a credible promise of large rewards with assurance that only a small fraction of a society's children obtain them.

This is especially important in Africa because the state, with limited resources at its disposal, must do double duty as both the supplier of schooling and the main consumer of its final products (i.e., graduates). The same as in lotteries, the system would cease to be viable if a limited number of prizes had to be divided among a large number of winners. This would dilute the value of each reward and undermine the broad support the system now receives inside and, much more important, outside the political class.

Curriculum and language inadvertently help in this regard by creating what looks like a natural barrier to enrollment. It works by narrowing the difference that parents perceive between future benefits and present costs. Since schools offer little practical value for life in rural areas, failure to reach a diploma means that a child acquires nothing that can enhance its capacity to support itself or its parents in later years. If probabilities of reaching a certificate seem low, as would be the case when language and content are alien, rural parents have little incentive to school their offspring. Then there are the social risks. Schools can undermine the willingness of offspring to provide support for their parents by encouraging divergence between the attitudes and behaviors of children and their families. The idea of secular education is no less alien and worrisome to many Muslim and animistic families than Islamic and animistic education to most French or American parents.

Through this and other mechanisms the public system protects itself by presenting higher costs and risks and lower benefits to rural families in the majority than to urban families in the minority. This restrains enrollment and demand for schools, prevents dilution of state budgets, and stems the rate of increase in numbers of graduates and competition for scholarships and employment.

The adjective public thus circumscribes a population that, though fluid, at any one moment includes only those that expect or want their children to access the apparatus, other urban activities, or emigration, that do not see in the white man's school a threat to parental welfare, and the relatively few that can make practical use of French literacy by other means. Although probabilities of success vary substantially across this population, almost all its members see the main purpose of schooling as one of giving offspring a shot at a prize. Reform of curriculum or language would thus defeat the purpose of the public system for almost everyone that wants to play the game. The same applies to every other proposal for change that, by promising wider access to schooling, increases in the rate at which students move from one grade and level to the next, or other outcomes that threaten the system's capacity to serve as an effective social, economic, and political screening device and make the game worthwhile.

At the same time, parents outside this circle are indifferent to the public system. Their demand for practical instruction has always been much better supplied, notwithstanding its limitations, by their own systems than by any reformed white man's school. And because history did not present them with the idea or the possibility of state assistance to help modernize these systems or, alternatively, to incorporate this instruction into the state system along the lines, for example, of the independent communal schools of nineteenth-century France noted by Michel (1992), they never had and still do not have reason to demand such things.

First Worlders have thus impeded achievement of their missionary goals by relying on a form of reasoning that does not permit them to see that the education sector in Africa, as in the developed nations not long ago, has more than one education system, and that for more than a century they have tried to supply a product for which demand does not exist. Absent the instantaneous feedback hat business people receive about the merits of this approach to marketing, they have been under no internal pressure to discover that each system serves as a self-contained method to achieve a universal social purpose, namely, to transmit the willingness and capacity of younger generations to produce and share income with older generations. Nor have they been compelled to discover that abandonment of their premise of parental irrationality and revision of their concurrent definition of modernization might get them further than insisting that one system is modern and others, to the extent that they bother to call them anything, are traditional.

Conclusion

The education situation in Africa is the same as Horowitz confronted with respect to ideas about the development of whole societies. Though I've not mentioned them because they occupy a small place in the greater scheme of things, some scholars insist via the dependency thesis that the problem will resolve itself when revolutionary action flows from peasant and working-class awareness of the role of education in their exploitation by international capital, the formation of cheap labor for export being a glaring example. Africa will then come to resemble (what until recently was called) the Second World. The prescription, logically, is to transform schools into hotbeds of popular discontent by engaging in a pedagogy of the oppressed to raise consciousness and speed the day of revolution.

Modernists, in turn, insist that the complementary interaction that exists within public education, leading, on one side, to modernization of traditional values and attitudes as well as productivity enhancements in the population and, on the other side, to industrialization and urbanization, which make use of and reinforce these new values and attitudes, will lead African societies to resemble the First World. The prescription here, as we have seen, is to do everything humanly possible speed the day by striving for universal schooling and literacy.

Time alone will assess the predictive accuracy of these theories. But the prescriptions that flow from them, as I have illustrated with respect to the second (and could have done for the first had there been something concrete to look at), leave much to be desired. The challenge confronting people in the Third World, especially in rural Africa, is about the basics of life and livelihood today. The prescriptions are irrelevant in this regard, as the responses of people to actions in education demonstrate. The ideas behind these actions do not contribute to an understanding of the present that can make the future better. They cause pain.

Direct costs to the population of past and present thoughts and actions in education are small, more in the nature of nuisance than anything else. But the opportunity costs of foregone knowledge that might have contributed to progress, now accumulated for a long time, seem exceedingly high. Lack of resources may partly explain why schools are scarce. But they do not explain why traps, farm and hunting implements, techniques of animal husbandry and cropping, thread and nutrition production, or understanding of health, hygiene, and nature have not changed for almost two centuries while malnutrition has become prominent and the environment has deteriorated.

Horowitz says that this situation stems from corruptions in the conduct of the enterprise we call scientific inquiry that, as I mentioned earlier, help old ideas to persist long after they have run out of intellectual steam and old actions to persist long after their era has passed. But he also says that what needs explaining are the factors that permit these corruptions to exist in the contemporary period. Guiding us toward a key factor, he reminds us of Mannheim's caution that the focus and form of intellectual activity is shaped by self-interest (Horowitz, 1962b). This is crucially important.

Every reasoning will persist so long as it is under no pressure from within or without to resolve its internal contradictions. Once in motion it will stay in place until change in the calculus of self-interest demands that it reform itself. Selfless pursuit of science in the name of science may sometimes husband this process through demonstration. But the heroisms of Galileo, and of Horowitz with respect to the modernization thesis, indicate that it is usually too weak by itself to challenge the power of prevailing wisdom and recognized authority. No less in the politics of truth than in other politics, the mathematics of historical progression assure that a minority must always confront a majority. Odds for change are rarely favorable.

In this context Horowitz emphasizes the importance of understanding that the persistence of old logics is a symptom of a larger problem—the absence of broad participatory democracy in Africa and elsewhere in the Third World (Horowitz, 1983a). However else one might choose think of it, and regardless of its methodological shortcomings, this type of democracy remains a basic mechanism for improving the quality of social science because the definitive empirical test of the veracity of theory lies in the feedback that flows from its application to policy. Life is an exacting laboratory.

Old ways of reasoning were dominant in Europe until progress in participatory democracy in the last century made them increasingly untenable. Though many in these societies continue to subscribe to these ways, one need only sample from the stream of ideas about what education should be in the First World to see that they are no longer dominant. This is partly because participatory democracy has made it difficult for one group to accuse another of ignorance or irrationality without risk of penalty, especially when the irrational have power, and partly because the failure of policy prescriptions based on flawed reasoning are plain for all to see, assess, and debate. That is, ideas in the First World have changed because parents and communities have much greater voice in matters of education and, for better or worse, are much more powerful than self-anointed reformers. They do not accept pain because they do not have to accept it.

Thus, the essence of the problem is that the environment that sustained traditional reasoning in the industrial societies before the advent of economic and political democracy continues to sustain it in Africa. Or, to put it in Horowitz's terms, the definition of educational modernization has remained impervious to change because there is neither a sense of inner strain among its adherents nor external pressures to which it must respond (Horowitz, 1979). Unlike the facts of political life that confront their counterparts in the West who must answer to elected education officials (and who, in turn, must answer to parents), the professional welfare of practitioners inside and outside governments and donor agencies, and through them the ideas of scholars that shape policy actions, does not depend on the opinions or preferences of consumers, voters, or anyone else in the majority of the population.

Participatory democracy is still a long way off. But I am optimistic that reform of ideas will come sooner than political change. This optimism draws from the transformations to which I alluded at the outset concerning change in the field of demography. The urgency to find solutions to the population explosion, a perceived threat to the First World, demanded policy solutions that worked. And because ideas flowing from the presumption of irrationality did not work, there was also an urgent need to understand population dynamics on its own terms, including the rational reasons for which parents have children. Though change in thinking has not necessarily improved fertility statistics, harmful policies such as involuntary sterilization have largely disappeared.

Though no comparable concern exists in education, there is growing urgency among First World actors to bring a semblance of democracy to Africa (as much or more from frustration that nothing else seems to have worked to alleviate its misery than from moral compulsion). This has moved issues such as political decentralization and participation to the front of the agendas of many of these actors. Along the way it has also spotlighted the inherently nondemocratic nature of decision making by the First World's own actors in different sectors, and the ideological premises that sustain this behavior among individuals and institutions that claim to be democratically inclined. The study from which I extract this paper is one spotlight. The work of Akpaka and Gaba (1991) and of Diarra (1991) are others.

The important thing, I think, is that the request for our study came from within USAID and the OECD. When political exigency asks research to produce ideas and recommendations that, as our sponsors put it, are more effective than dominant ideas in the existing literature, then no matter the quality of the response I become optimistic. The asking of important questions that have not been previously asked by major First World institutions of other First World agencies strikes me as a sign of substantial progress in the circumstances I describe. I cannot predict the eventual outcome of this process. One thing certain is that my colleagues and I are in debt to Irving Louis Horowitz for having given so much of himself to producing the scholarly wherewithal that I believe helped us become better researchers and actors in the process of social development.

University of Texas, Dallas
Department of Social Sciences

Notes

1. I use political class to distinguish between the array of competing social groups in each society that have the will and capacity to influence the policies of the state and groups that do not have this will or ability. Though it is fluid, expanding in step with economic growth, membership in the class in Africa still limits itself

to a small minority that for the most part live in towns and derive their livelihood from employment or other close associations with the state apparatus. I include in this minority non-African scholars and practitioners directly attached to foreign agencies or, indirectly, who influence policy ideas from afar.
2. Primary school enrollment figures in francophone west Africa run from national averages of 30 to 70 percent for boys and 20 to 50 percent for girls, while adult literacy rates range between 20 and 40 percent.

References

Akpaka, O., and L. Gaba. "Les aspects socio-culturels de la frequentation scolaire des filles au niveau primaire au Benin." Cotonou, Benin: UNESCO, May 1991.

Behrman, J. R. "The Action of Human Resources and Poverty on One Another: What We Have Yet to Learn." Living Standards Measurement Study Working Paper No. 74. Washington, DC: The World Bank, 1990.

Belloncle, G. *La Question Educative en Afrique Noire*. Paris: Karthala, 1984.

Botti, L. *Basic Education in the Sahel Countries*. Study prepared for the World Bank by the UNESCO Institute for Education, Hamburg, 1978.

Brecht, B. *Collected Plays*, vol. 5. New York: Vintage Press, 1972.

Brenner, L. "Two Paradigms of Islamic Schooling in West Africa." Paper presented at the colloquium on "The Modes of Transmission of Religious Culture," Princeton University, 27–30 April 1989.

Capelle, J. *L'education en Afrique Noir a la veille des Independences*. Paris: Karthala, 1990.

Cippola, C. M. *Literacy and Development in the West*. Baltimore: Penguin Books, 1969.

CMET (Conference mondiale sur l'education pour tous). 1990. "Repondre Aux Besoins Educatifs Fondamentaux: Document de Reference." Commission Interinstitutions (Banque Mondiale, PNUD, UNESCO, UNICEF) de la Conference Mondiale sur l'Education pour Tous, New York, 5–9 March 1990.

Cubberly, E. P. *Public Education in the United States*. Boston: Houghton Mifflin, 1919.

Diarra, I. "Le travail productif a l'ecole primaire: une analyse de l'experience malienne." UNESCO-Institut international de planification de l'education, Paris, 1991.

Fass, S. M. "Democracy and Political Participation in the Sahel: The Place of Education." Study prepared for the U.S. Agency for International Development and the Club du Sahel-OECD, Washington, DC, August 1992.

Furet, F., and J. Ozouf. *Lire et Ecrire*. Paris: Editions de Minuit, 1977.

Glewwe, P. "Schooling, Skills, and the Returns to Education: An Econometric Exploration Using Data from Ghana." Living Standards Measurement Study Working Paper No. 76. Washington DC: The World Bank, 1990.

Graff, H. *The Legacies of Literacy*. Bloomington: Indiana University Press, 1987.

Haddad, W. D., M. Carnoy, R. Rinaldi, and O. Regel. "Education and Development: Evidence for New Priorities." World Bank Discussion Paper No. 95. Washington DC: The World Bank, 1990.

Heyneman, S. "Improving the Quality of Education in Developing Countries." In *Education and Development: Views from the World Bank*, ed. A. Habte. Washington, DC: World Bank, 1983.

Horowitz, Irving Louis. "Consensus, Conflict and Cooperation: A Sociological Inventory." *Social Forces* 41, no. 2 (December 1962a): 177–88.

―――. "Social Science Objectivity and Value Neutrality: Historical Problems and Projections." *Diogenes* no. 39 (Fall 1962b): 17–44.

―――. "Anthropology for Sociologists: Cross-Disciplinary Research as Scientific Humanism." *Social Problems* 2, no. 2 (Fall 1963): 201–206 (book review).

―――. *Three Worlds of Development.* New York: Oxford University Press, 1966.

―――. "The Search for a Development Ideal: Alternative Models and Their Implications." *The Sociological Quarterly* 8, no. 4 (Autumn 1967): 427–38.

―――. "The Political Ideology of Political Economy." In *Cultural Factors in Inter-American Relations,* ed. S. Shapiro, 285–312. Notre Dame, IN: University of Notre Dame Press, 1968.

―――. "Masses in Latin America." In *Masses in Latin America,* ed. Irving Louis Horowitz, 3-28. New York: Oxford University Press, 1970.

―――. "Sociological Priorities for the Second Development Decade." *Social Problems* 19, no. 1 (Summer 1971): 137–43.

―――. "Qualitative and Quantitative Research Problems in Comparative International Development." In *Social Development,* ed. Manfred Stanley, 6–38. New York: Basic Books, 1972.

―――. "Movie Review: Bunuel's Bourgeoisie." *Society* 10, no. 5 (July-August 1973): 70–74.

―――. "Sociology and Futurology: the Contemporary Pursuit of the Millennium." *Berkeley Journal of Sociology* 19 (1975): 37–54.

―――. "Introduction: National Realities and Universal Ambitions in the Practice of Sociology." In *Sociological Praxis,* ed. Elizabeth Crawford and Stein Rokkan, 11–28. Beverly Hills: Sage Publications, 1976.

―――. "The Sociology of Development and the Ideology of Sociology." In *Societal Growth: Processes and Implications,* ed. A. S. Hawley, 279–89. New York: The Free Press/Macmillan, 1979.

―――. 1981a. "International Studies and the Pursuit of the Millenium." *International Studies Notes* 8, no.1 (Spring 1981a): 11–12.

―――. "Military Origins of Third World Dictatorship and Democracy." *Third World Quarterly* 3, no. 1 (January 1981b): 37–47.

―――. "Tradition, Modernity and Industrialization: Toward an Integrated Developmental Paradigm." In *Tradition and Modernity: The Role of Traditionalism in the Modern Process,* ed. J. G. Lutz and S. El-Shakhs. Washington, DC: University Press of America, 1982.

―――. "Democracy and Development: Policy Perspectives in a Postcolonial Context." In *The Newer Caribbean: Decolonization, Democracy and Development,* ed. P. Henry and C. Stone, 221–34. Philadelphia: The Institute for the Study of Human Issues, 1983a.

―――. "Language, Truth and Politics." *The Washington Quarterly* 6, no. 1 (Winter 1983b): 71–77.

―――. *Winners and Losers.* Durham, NC: Duke University Press, 1984.

―――. "Disenthralling Sociology." *Society* 24, no. 2 (January-February 1987): 48–55.

―――. *Daydreams and Nightmares: Reflections of a Harlem Childhood.* Jackson: University Press of Mississippi, 1990a.

―――. "A Third Way?" *First Things* 1, no. 3 (May 1990b): 57–59 (book review of Alan Wolfe's *Whose Keeper? Social Science and Moral Obligation*).

————. "The Decomposition of Sociology." *Academic Questions* 5, no. 2 (Spring 1992): 32–39.

IIEP. "L'education de base en Afrique." Institut international de planification de l'education. Paris: UNESCO, 1989.

Kayashima, N. "Le developpement de l'education au cours de l'ere Meiji (1867–1912): modernisation et montee du nationalisme au Japon." Cahiers de l'Institut international de planification de l'education. Numero 78. Paris: UNESCO, 1989.

Lange, M-F. "Le refus de l'ecole: pouvoir d'une societe civile bloquee?" *Politique Africaine* 27 (September-October 1987): 74–85.

Lockheed, M., A. Verspoor, and associates. 1992. *Improving Primary Education in Developing Countries*. Washington, DC: The World Bank, 1992.

Maynes, M. J. *Schooling for the People*. New York: Holmes and Meier, 1985.

Mbaïosso, A. *L'education au Tchad*. Paris: Karthala, 1990.

Michel, G. 1992. "Les orientations de la Cooperation francaise dans le domaine de la scolarisation primaire." *Marches Tropicaux* 24 juillet, 1944–1946.

Resnick, D. P., ed. *Literacy in Historical Perspective*. Washington, DC: Library of Congress, 1983.

Ulrich, R. *The Education of Nations*. Cambridge: Harvard University Press, 1967.

World Bank. "Education in Sub-Saharan Africa: Policies for Adjustment, Revitalization, and Expansion." World Bank Policy Study. Washington, DC: World Bank, 1988.

————. "Primary Education." World Bank Policy Paper. Washington, DC: World Bank, 1990.

14

Three Worlds of Development: An African Context

Tunde Olatunde Odetola

As a title for my essay I have finally settled on "Three Worlds of Development: An African Context." This I do for a number of reasons. First, Horowitz's conceptualization of "development" is in broad and global terms. Change and development occur structurally in societies and must be viewed in ecumenical and catholic terms. The consideration of development and change even for single societies must carry the wide consciousness of a global imprint. Change within Africa or Latin America can best be comprehended in terms of the changes observable in the relationships of man to the rest of his society. The activities within social institutions affect and are affected by the structure of societies.

Thus, it is possible to study the development of the structures of societies with sociological tools from one society to another. Societies differ, but the sociological consciousness or imagination is an eminently viable tool for making comparisons, for generating theories, or even for accounting for singular differences within social structures. This truly "world" perspective gave rise to "The Three Worlds of Development" in which categories of societies are stratified for comparison and for analysis. This breadth of vision in comprehending development in global terms, and the scholarship of "Third World" studies it has given rise to, emphasize the worldview of development held by Horowitz.

The second reason is a product of the first. Man is the center of his own universe, the pinpoint of his own world. He has impact upon the structure of society, which in turn acts to shape him. Thus, changes in the structure of society, which this relationship produces, reflects the level and direction of development of the society. While Horowitz has deep concern and sensitivity for man in his society, his approach and orientation are in no way psychological. They reflect a deep inner humaneness about the nature of societies and man and are truly reminiscent of C. Wright Mills. The proper conceptualization of man in his own world, that is, human beings in the context of their own societal development constitute a global view of the relationships of man in society. This focus is thus at another conceptual level from the first, although theoretically related to it.

My third reason is a product of the first two—an intelligent recognition of the role of structures in the development process. Horowitz has consistently emphasized that this recognition leads to the identification of new and emerging structures and the roles they lay in national development. Thus, it has been important to understand the relationships among the bourgeoisie, the bureaucracy, the military, and other classes in the process of nation building. The interplay of the weakness of the national bourgeoisie, the need for development, the absence of clearly defined classes, and the early beginnings of the emergence of state power have all contributed to the emergence of a bureaucratized centralized force—the military.

The occasion we are celebrating here calls for a frank review of this great scholar's contribution, his legacy with some of us who were his students, the directions in which he has led us, and what we assess our own development to be over and against what we learned in his class. Has he left us with certain eternal truths or with certain controversies we are still battling to resolve? Or with theories that sometimes explain or sometimes fail to explain in the spirit of all true theories? What are these contributions and what are our assessments.

We propose to examine Horowitz's contribution to development theory under the three-part thematic scheme outlined below:

1. Globalism versus exceptionalism in development theory;
2. The process of development in the Horowitzian perspective; and
3. Horowitz and general theories of development.

Globalism versus Exceptionalism

The works of Horowitz (*Three Worlds of Development, Masses in Latin America,* and even *The New Sociology*) all reflect an international, comparative perspective from which he has derived his theoretical perspectives. Comparative analysis of economic growth, first among Latin American nations and then among African and Asian countries as well, yielded fruitful ideas about the role of structures or agencies that generated accountability. He has discovered that centralized, bureaucratic structures tend to be more positively associated with rises in economic growth figures than are the more liberalized (sometimes democratic institutions) of civilian regimes. From this approach has come what we regard as the theory of coercion.

Horowitz argued in *Beyond Empire and Revolution*, "The doctrine of exceptionalism does not yield a general theory to explain events." He believes that the more exceptional cases there are, the fewer will be the opportunities for establishing a rule. There will be exceptions, he agrees, but individual cases of development and underdevelopment can be explained only by considering both a country's relationships to the world economy and internal variables, particularly the relationships of the state apparatus to the class structure of that society. A different theory is certainly not needed for every nation. Otherwise, with multiple theories at the national level, parsimony will be reduced and we will begin to substitute nationalism for science as a basis for political analysis. His overachieving perspective on development is essentially that Third World nations are trying to industrialize "in a world economy shaped and controlled by those countries—capitalist and socialist—already developed" (1982).

There are two clear issues involved in the controversy between "globalism" and "exceptionalism." The first relates to the focus by American scholars on Latin American nations and the struggle by these scholars to individually influence government policy by establishing intellectual riches in the sociology of knowledge. The same situation has gradually asserted itself over studies in Africa. While Horowitz himself made specific studies on Latin American issues (*Latin American Radicalism* and *Revolution in Brazil*), he had revolted against basing social science theory on individual national case studies, which in their conduct shy away from comparative analysis.

This leads to the second and equally, if not more, important point: To what extent can single case studies lead to general theoretical principles? This issue in the sociology of knowledge should be treated with caution. Horowitz has not himself argued against making generalizations from single case studies. He had said: "The National factor does indeed organize the economic, legal and linguistic aspects of social life" and that "the class base of the state has varied between countries and within a given nation over time" (1982). This gives ample evidence of his belief that knowledge is best derived from grass-roots, local, in-depth analysis of given societies. The Horowitzian approach, however, insists that a more substantive understanding would be achieved only when the knowledge so gained is held in the light of comparison with others that have had effects on the generation of such knowledge. It is then and only then that generalizable knowledge across wide areas or examples can be made over uniform or even disparate cases.

For example, a study of the emergence, strength, and roles of the national bourgeoisie in national development can best be undertaken in a comparative approach in the Third World because these structures have developed in similar circumstances over many areas and have been subjected to fairly similar external influences from the same or similar external forces. Indeed, it is only such comparisons that will adequately yield whatever differences exist and assist to explain why Ghana has successfully implemented the Structural Adjustment Programme (SAP) for economic development while Nigeria is failing or still struggling to achieve some measure of success.

Scholarship on Third World development had been influenced rather negatively by single scholars with expertise in single disciplines and who have focused on single countries. They have come up with equally poor and unfruitful studies that have not yielded any understanding of how structures emerge, how relationships have been built on such structures, and how development has been influenced by the totalities of such influences. In *The Three Worlds of Development,* Horowitz has written: "Almost unfailingly, development is written about from the particularized standpoint of the science of politics, economics, sociology, anthropology, or psychology. The standpoint is derived from the author's professional commitments rather than from the development process as a whole" (1968:ix).

It is his view that only the more comprehensive social science approach can explain the development process. As an integrated approach, social science enables a comprehensive collection of information, leads to sounder methodologies and theories, and allows the researcher to concentrate on problems of development in general. Horowitz had warned that most literature on development is nation-centered: "There is an absence of data on comparative rates of growth, or on unique historical aspects of area clusters which make for contrasting concepts of what is considered development" (1968: x). The purpose for writing *Three Worlds of Development,* according to him, "is to etch the elements of favorable or invidious contrast as we move from nation to nation, or even continent to continent."

His purpose was eminently achieved judged by the acceptability and popularity of this work, even in far away Nigeria. It has led to the social science categorization of a group of countries as the Third World and has considerably influenced further studies, no less than First and Second World international policies, on aid and development. We now argue, with the advantage of hindsight, and with Horowitz, that "[d]evelopment studies need increasingly not only analyses in depth but also in scope. By focusing on multi-national (no less than sub-national) characteristics of development, further studies along historical as well as analytical lines can perhaps be stimulated" (1968: x).

Having been his student, I became enamored by this approach and subsequently wrote the book *Military Regimes and Development: A Comparative Approach in African Societies.* I based my study on a comparison of Ghana, Nigeria, and Ethiopia. Historically, Nigeria and Ghana were British colonies while Ethiopia was not. All three nations were under military rule. The Ethiopian military were wrestling power from an ancient feudal monarchy while in Nigeria and Ghana democratic civilian regimes had lost power to the military. Ethiopia had gone socialist while Ghana and Nigeria remained essentially within Western orbits.

The work has yielded a significant body of knowledge and has received favorable international reviews. The work has been designed as building on an earlier in-depth case study of Nigeria, from which we have also derived what can be modestly regarded as useful theoretical insights. As a faithful student, I want to say that Horowitz's lectures in class, coupled with his personal commitment to the intellectual progress of his students, have been significant in determining my own intellectual orientations, which I have, in turn, passed on as an enduring legacy to my own students.

Having said all of the above, attention must now be turned to far more critical reviews of this approach. My argument has always been (even in class) that this approach may tempt its adherents to adopt wider and wider geographical scopes as basis for study under the false assumption that the wider the scope the more fruitful the generalizations derivable. It also runs the risk of underestimating the usefulness of theoretical insights derived from serious case studies. Horowitz himself supports case studies. My doctoral dissertation was a case study of Nigeria. The argument here that an uncritical acceptance of the doctrine of "scope leads to greater comparability" or its inverse can each lead the unwary scholar to methodological ineptitude.

A second point of concern is that uncritical adherence to large global scopes have led to aggregated studies that generalize across boundaries, but are useless explanatory tools for events in any single nation that forms part of the aggregate. Therefore, the larger the scope, the greater the danger of ignoring within-nation variations and of imposing explanations derived from general situations, but which have little relevance and applicability to specific nations. Social science literature is full of studies of this kind.

The international stratification depicted in *Three Worlds of Development* has stood the test of time only to the extent that it provides a basic framework for explaining such stratifications. The text has lumped together nations that were very far apart developmentally in 1968, and seem no closer at present. Horowitz had himself admitted that there is a fourth world based upon the demands and rationalization efforts of the First World upon the Third World through the activities of international organizations such as the World Bank. The question should be asked: Can we group Brazil and Saudi Arabia into the same third world category as Gabon, Nigeria or Haiti.

Even within the First World, new developments in information technology or in the advancement and application of the concept of "productivity" can make for and explain differences in development (both in rate and character) between Japan and the United States of America. Such fine distinctions are necessary and only a continuous refinement of the tools of social science can yield such explanations. For example, we would argue that technology in its more modern variants is playing an independent role, as much as any other variable of the social structure. Any development theory that today does not recognize technology's autonomous role (not just its existence) can explain only little. It is perhaps as autonomous in influencing the development of the state in the Western world as the military has been in influencing development in the Third World .

This approach would help us to distinguish between categories within the Second World of development. By way of extension of the imagination, we can ask what the differences are between Romania, Saudi Arabia, South Korea, and Argentina? Into what "world" would they be classified? Hence, the first chapter in the book *Beyond Empire and Revolution* (1982) is titled "Three Worlds of Development Plus One." In another decade, with the exponential rate at which Ghana and Nigeria are leaving Niger and Somalia behind, we may have "Three Worlds of Development Plus Two" and so on. This is why we have argued that the 1968 book provides only a guideline for international stratification.

Recent changes in the world, which have resulted in increased nationalism, raise serious challenges for development studies. The character of the challenge lies in greater comparability a la Horowitz, but supplemented by serious in-depth case studies. This, to me, is the only way that recent trends will be best explained and grounds properly laid for future development efforts. It will also lay foundations for the future of social science, which depends for its explanatory tools on products of human action.

The Development Process

According to Horowitz, it is necessary to take account of the relationships between internal and external influences as they produce structures that determine development. In this way, he has identified multiple processes and structures, four of which we will focus upon: emergence of agencies of development; legitimation and institutionalization; coercion as development process; and state power and military nationalism.

The Emergence of the Agencies of Development

According to Horowitz, the *economy, polity, society,* and *military* are the four major pillars of national systems in the Third World. The military is treated as an institution here and its influence extends far beyond its organizational limits. He has further argued that the structural framework provided by sovereignty defines the central role of national development and the place of the economy, polity, society, and the military in the delineation and definition of the nation.

A centralized, bureaucratic system is basic, he says, to development in the Third World. Hence, the emergence and role of the state as the focal point of development is crucial. In those instances where the national bourgeoisie is weak and economy is sluggish, the state is unable to effectively perform the role of the absolute provider of capital that it has taken upon itself. The interaction of a weak economy, an unmobilized polity, and an inept national bourgeoisie result in the establishment of a weak state. Coupled with the absence of class cohesion, the military then frequently intervenes. In so doing, it assumes the role of an autonomous and independent agency of national power. Third World development rests, he further argues, on the military determination of power. Military rule becomes important, therefore, not merely to satisfy economic, social, and political claims, but to satisfy the structural conditions of twentieth-century nationalism. Upon assumption of power, the military attempts to build a broad-based class consensus through its centralizing apparatuses.

Horowitz's positions have aptly explained several Latin American and African situations. In Nigeria, the national bourgeoisie has been very weak, ridden by religious, ethnic, and educational differences and antagonisms. For almost half a century, the state has assumed the role of the entrepreneur. Similar situations have occurred in Ghana, Sierra Leone, and other places where the military subsequently took over power. But there have been significant exceptions to this interplay of forces. For example, Zimbabwe, Tanzania, Ivory Coast, Zambia, Kenya, and Cameroon have never come under military rule, but have been ruled by dictators. Historically, Zimbabwe passed through a long period of guerilla warfare; Tanzania went through a long period of "socialism" under one-man rule; while the Ivory Coast, Zambia, Kenya, and Cameroon have come under strong one-man rule. What explains such significant within-continent differences where the military never emerged as the fourth pillar, let alone as an independent and autonomous source of power?

We explain such differences by the characteristics of leadership, with particular emphasis on charisma. Nyerere was charismatic and so was Kaunda to a lesser extent. We also argue that the size of the military in those nations had been small. The following issues then arise: Was Nkrumah not as charismatic as Nyerere? But why did the military take over power in Ghana and not in Tanzania? Also, is the size of the military in Niger larger than in Kenya? And if so, why was there a coup in Niger and not in Kenya? Answers to these questions can be gotten only by in-depth studies of the situations in each country. For example, the elite structures in Ghana developed faster than in Tanzania, which remained largely rural for a considerable period. It can also be argued that the guerrilla war waged by the Mau Mau in Kenya, the subsequent absorption of the guerrillas into the regular army, and the repressive rule of Kenyan leaders had all interacted to render the military incapable of seizing power. Micro-data collected across nations will lead to more meaningful generalizations than those derived from or even imposed by observations leading from macro-level information, even if this were done on a comparative basis.

The emergence of structures will naturally result in new forms of relationships and interactions, which require institutionalization and legitimacy. The form that these processes take is a significant indicator of the direction of development. The rise of the military in the Third World is thus, for Horowitz, both a mechanism for and a consequence of social change (1982).

Legitimacy and Institutionalization

The emergence of a national bourgeoisie has not resulted in growth for the Third World. The ineptitude of the national bourgeoisie and lack of class cohesion has frequently resulted in military intervention. The pattern of military intervention and the nature of military rule have given rise to what has been characterized as the "norm of illegitimacy." It is to Horowitz's credit that ideas have been developed around the issue of legitimacy. But I find the concept of the norm of illegitimacy to be of doubtful relevance. First, norms represent acceptable guides of behavior or, in their simplest form, standards regulating procedures. Such a definition appears to create a contradiction vis-à-vis illegitimacy. Granted, criminals have norms of behaviors. But criminal behavior is a substantive activity that has referents in terms of concrete human products. Legitimacy (or illegitimacy) is a concept derived from a quality or standard of a particularly defined behavior. It is a normative concept that describes the quality of substantive activities beyond itself. We therefore cannot have norms of (normative) illegitimacy. The propositions derived from it can only lead to a cul-de-sac.

In reexamining the concept of legitimacy over the years, I have come to the conclusion that it is only when it is viewed as a dynamic concept—a living one—can it really have meaning in development. For example, a military junta that seizes power begins as an illegitimate ruler (based on standard democratic procedures). If the ensuing regime governs well and provides what the people want, it becomes increasingly acceptable over the years. That is, its legitimacy increases. Its performance level may be so high that it is positively regarded as progressive. On the other hand, a democratically elected government may gradually lose its legitimacy as it performs poorly. Therefore, legitimacy is a concept that can be measured, that grows or declines depending on the acceptability of actors in the system.

If then, we are to understand development, legitimacy must be conceived of in these dynamic terms. The norms of illegitimacy can convert to the norms of legitimacy. It makes it difficult to assess military contributions to development without this possibility. So it is in the consideration of whether violence contributes to development. The Western literature regards violence as abhorrent and nonlegitimate. It was the analysis of Hannah Arendt that illuminated a much clearer understanding of violence. "Machismo," a cultural value in Latin America, is inherently riddled with violence, yet generates positive orientation and achievement in that society. Therefore, viewed as a dynamic concept, legitimacy helps us to understand how structures grow or die, gain or lose viability, and strengthen or weaken relationships.

A useful concept derivable from the work of Horowitz is the relationships between legitimacy, institutionalization, and succession. The gap between legitimation and institutionalization phases is where the riddle of succession is resolved. One strategy of institutionalization is the regulation of the political process. If the military was in power, then it would proceed to establish its own hegemonic rule. However, direct evidence of attempts by the military at transition from military to civilian rule demonstrates that the military does not always establish hegemonic rule. Horowitz doubts whether the military can successfully handle transition from military to civilian rule, because they are caste-like in character. In Nigeria, the military has done it once and is doing it again a second time. Ghana has also gone through such a transition (even though this needs to be qualified since it is the former military leader that is now also heading the new civilian government).

During military rule, the government strives to achieve legitimacy by instituting a strong measure of discipline as a norm of accountability and as a key strategy of economic performance. As a result, productivity tends to go up and the economy tends to grow faster during military than during civilian rule. The capacity for discipline and accountability derives from the authoritarian and coercive nature of the military organization.

The Theory of Coercion

It has been argued that the development impulse is so strong among the military officer corps that the military has become identified with the capacity to increase productivity. The military successfully imposes harsh conditions for the realization of increased productivity. It imposes norms of output and productivity upon both management and labor. The military becomes repressive where these norms are broken. As I have argued elsewhere, "From the working class they extract high level output in exchange for highly charged nationalistic rhetoric. From the entrepreneurial class they extract high taxes in exchange for anti-communist rhetoric" (Odetola, 1982). Several examples had been given by Horowitz from Latin America to support this view (1968, 1982). We have also found strong evidence of support from African examples.

In enunciating this position Horowitz had been careful to separate the use of sheer organizational force in enforcing discipline from the norm of accountability prescribed by the military and deriving from its own organizational characteristics. This is the strength of the theory. Or, in other words, this is the point at which it would have collapsed if such fine distinctions were not made.

However, a number of questions remain: Can not the same goals be achieved by civilian authoritarian regimes who have disciplined political party apparatuses? Can unscrupulous military leaders seize the opportunity offered by their organizations to accumulate wealth at the expense of the masses and ignore the norms of productivity? Many authoritarian regimes have increased productivity and raised economic growth in their nations. However, the one-party system in Africa, which represents the equivalent of the military organization, has proved to be totally inept in mobilizing resources and raising productivity. Rather, its officials have roamed the countryside in search of spoils.

We have also seen examples of military regimes that adopted strict socialist structures and yet failed to raise productivity. The example of Ethiopia readily comes to mind. The problems Ethiopia had were two-fold. First, it was prosecuting a long internal war, which devoured the bulk of its resources. Second, and equally important, the officials charged with the responsibility of administering the new socialist structures were corrupt.

In establishing hegemony, the military seizes the opportunity that it is offered in order to establish consensus by mobilizing all available resources and laying down norms. It is this principle of governance that assists the military to move quickly in the establishment of state power.

Military Nationalism and State Power

The epitome of the Horowitzian contributions to development studies has come in his later writings, which center on the roles and functions of the military. His masterful stroke in this regard has been to assess other emerging elite structures in comparison with the military. His conclusions have influenced Third World studies of the military as well as Third World development in a unique manner.

His concern has been the necessity for the development of an autonomous state capable of determining the type and rate of economic growth. He believes that the state that has the potential for playing an innovative economic role is bureaucratized, centralized, efficient, and, most important, autonomous. The state must play an active role in economic development. The later the stage of economic development, the more necessary is state direction and control of the economy. From history, it is possible to see that the state was more important in German economic development than was the case in Great Britain or the United States and it is even more important in Japan, Russia, and China.

The autonomy of the state is determined by the distance between the state power holders on the one hand and vested interests of classes on the other. It is the duty of the state to foster mobilization of capital and human resources and to break down class barriers to industrialization and either create, greatly strengthen, or substitute for an independent entrepreneurial class. Because Horowitz has considered how the apparatus in a bureaucratized state relates to other sources of power, it has been possible for him to critically examine the dominant classes. The military stands out as the structure that is most independent of class forces and functions as the pivotal element in society guaranteeing state autonomy. "The military sector of the bureaucracy becomes the national sector, the epitome of the state itself" (1982). He has argued that the rise of military intervention in many Latin American and African nations "is a function of the general law of statim—the increase of centralized power at the expense of separatist class, ethnic and religious interests" (1982).

In considering the above, several issues arise: First, to what extent do we have coherent classes in the Third World, particularly in Africa? Is the military itself independent of ethnic and religious forces? What is the trend in the role of the modern state in development?

The answer to the first question is negative, but explains why the military still finds it easy to assume power. The lack of class cohesion renders the national bourgeoisie incompetent and always paves the way for military intervention. Second, the African military is not free from religious and ethnic affiliations and has the problem of developing a truly autonomous state. The conclusion still remains valid, however, that until viable state autonomy is created, the military will continue to intervene. Third, recent trends in international economics and the development of democracy across the world put into some jeopardy the development of a strong state in the Third World. International funding agencies are demanding the liberalization of trade, privatization of enterprise, and reduction in state control of the economy. This is coming at a period when African and other Third World nations are struggling to build a strong state. Contradictory as this development appears to be, I believe it can only strengthen the polity. It will speed the development of the national bourgeoisie, increase class cohesion, and reduce dependence on the military structure as the pivot of state power.

Horowitz and General Theories of Development

We shall focus here only on Horowitzian perspectives on the dependency theory. The school of dependency theory grew to be a formidable body of scholars in the 1960s and early 1970s. Its popularity waned considerably in the early 1970s and the progress of its decline had been hastened by the collapse of the socialist world. The theory has collapsed as have the states that were founded upon it. Horowitz had condemned the dependency theory as belonging in a waste paper basket.

We will not go so far as to do that. A body of knowledge has emerged from this field capable of explaining in part some of the structures, however small, that have developed in the Third World. The inability of many African nations to establish an industrial base has been, in part, historically due to the forced dependence of those nations on the goods from Europe and repression of innovative productivity that accompanied it. A consumption pattern that reflected the dependence on those goods, euphemistically termed the *colonial mentality,* has been bred, for example, in Nigeria. Africans were arrested for brewing any liquor that was similar to British imported liquor. This, coupled with myriad other examples, was responsible, in a small measure (there were other reasons), for the sloth of the development of process technology in the food and other industries.

Where a theory offers an explanation in even a small measure, it should not be rejected out of hand. The problem with the dependency school has been its preoccupation with this concept. Theorists in this school sought the explanation of every human action and the development of all structures, including their interactions, within this theoretical perspective. Its explanatory value has been so ever extended by Marxist scholars that large parts of it have clearly become meaningless.

Conclusion

I want to conclude briefly by paying my respects and expressing my gratitude to this great scholar whose works have so informed and illumined the world of development scholarship. Irving Louis Horowitz stands out as an independent thinker, a close observer of societal processes and their interactions. He is one of the most astute observers of the human society, one of its most humane critics.

His scholarship on the military in the Third World has moved thinking away from "the man on horseback" and placed it squarely in the orbit of modern social science scholarship focusing on the state and its actors. The analysis of the state will continue to dominate Third World scholarship for a long time to come and his works will remain central. As a prolific writer, his contributions will continue to illumine our thoughts.

One final note, I have found Irving Horowitz to be a good friend and senior colleague who may wish to irk his companions occasionally, but who is one of the most gentle and humane scholars there has ever been.

Obafemi Awolowo University, Nigeria
Department of Sociology

References

Horowitz, Irving Louis. *Three Worlds of Development: The Theory and Practice of International Stratification.* New York and London: Oxford University Press, 1968.
———. *Beyond Empire and Revolution: Militarization and Consolidation in the Third World.* New York and London: Oxford University Press, 1982.
Odetola, T. Olatunde. *Military Politics in Nigeria: Economic Development and Political Stability.* New Brunswick, NJ: Transaction Publishers, 1978.
———. *Military Regimes and Development: A Comparative Analysis in African Societies.* London: Allen and Unwin, 1982.

15

Three Worlds and One Future?
The Korean Case of Social
Development Theory

Byoung-Lo Philo Kim

In recent years, we have seen the massive popular rejection and the collapse of communism in the Second World. Following the fall of the Berlin Wall in late 1989, East and West Germany achieved a historic unification in October 1990. All the countries in Eastern Europe broke the shackles of the old ideology and strove for political dignity and ethnic solidarity. The Soviet Union and Gorbachev give us already a sort of nostalgic feeling, and strange new names, such as CIS and Yeltsin, now became ordinary words.

With the end of the cold war in sight, people are anxious to reappraise the structure of the three worlds. Horowitz correctly foresaw the fate of socialism more than a decade ago, analyzing that the overwhelming myth of socialism so long dominant in the century after 1848 had been broken down into fragments that could not be reassembled. The solid framework became loosened and has dramatically changed. Socialist economic system, based on public ownership, is only moderately accepted, and the one-party politics became totally obsolete in holding socialism.

As the external threat decreases, the Third World is moving away from a highly politicized military government to a limited civilian democracy. There is no doubt that the Second World as a viable political system collapsed, and that the democratization transition and liberalization process in the world stimulated a dialogue concerning multiparty democracy throughout the Third World. South Korea, once dominated by an extremely anti-Communist regime, has now opened official diplomatic relations with East European countries and even won a substantive recognition from Russia and China, offering them economic funds. As a result, much of the dictatorial element done under the pretext of the cold war ideology has vanished in the political process of South Korea. The recent presidential election held on 18 December 1992 reflected this changing atmosphere, just as that of United States did.

The dramatic moves toward freedom in Eastern Europe and the former Soviet Union had, however, little direct impact on the Communist regime in North Korea in the early 1990s. Only declining Russian support of oil and weapons left North Korea with little choice but to try to improve relations with the capitalist world. North Korea's moves has had little immediate political ramification; an opening to the capitalist world, including the establishment of a free economic zone, will probably be an essential condition for internal political ferment to begin.

In the euphoria of the lagging communism in certain countries, the focus has shifted to Asian communism such as China, Cambodia, and North Korea. Why does the communism in these areas persist ? Here I raise the problem of the Third World in which a societal development is deeply involved with its historical situation.

It is somewhat difficult to locate the two Koreas in the map of the three worlds since a more in-depth analysis is needed. The term *Third World* was, as Horowitz explained, sociologically created since the original industrial forms covered too broad a range for just two worlds. The Third World is continually searching for specific ways in which some sort of "mixture" between the two giant social structures can be brought about without destroying either the vitality or integrity of their national development as such. From this viewpoint, both Koreas are without doubt categorized into the Third World. The economy of South Korea had been operated by a sort of state capitalism until a liberalization measure was attempted in the 1980s. North Korea has also developed a quite unique economy , becoming the most coal-dependent industrial economy in the world. It is estimated, for instance, that coal accounted for 77 percent of primary energy consumption in North Korea, with hydro-electric power accounted for 18 percent, and oil for only 5 percent. North and South Korea cannot be oversimplified as having a market or a planned economy, nor as being democratic or totalitarian.

Nevertheless, South Korea and North Korea hold much of capitalism and socialism in their essence. In ideology, two Koreas have been drawn closer to either capitalist or socialist bloc countries on the basis of common political rhetoric and common strategies for dealing with larger states. It is no doubt that North Korea was as much a part of the Second World, at least until recently, as South Korea was of the First World. North Korea remains dedicated to the ideals and principles of, if not Western Marxism, than Asian communism, particularly that of China. Similarly, South Korea may be considered not very much outside the U.S. power bloc.

With the awareness of the world's problems, I would like to review in this article the two great books on development written by Horowitz: *Three Worlds of Development*[1] and *Beyond Empire and Revolution*.[2] I will discuss whether their frameworks, concepts, and analysis are relevant in the Korean context, and whether the explanations can be extended to the recent changes, since these two books are universal in scope and were written ten to twenty years ago.

Diverging Korean Development

Horowitz's two books on development begin with what he believes the Third World psychology and mentality should express. The developed nations show to the less developed the image to be imitated, creating particularly the conditions for rebellion and revolution. The "demonstration effect" allows for the most developed to show in advance the face of the future to the least developed. Unlike its unconscious and spontaneous generation in the advanced nations, "development" means for the less developed an intentional and planned change toward a desirable goal. The core values of development for these countries are, therefore, modernization or socialist nation-building of their motherland.

Korean development is none other than the process of catching up to the advanced nations. The division of Korea into two ideologically opposing camps is a sheer reflection of the divided world at large. The postwar decade was characterized by a radical realignment of the balance of economic and political power, with the ascendancy of the United States as the dominant power of the capitalist world and the concomitant consolidation of the power of the Soviet Union and the victory of the Chinese Communist party. In that period the powerful resurgence of the national liberation movement and the dismantling of the colonial system became central. Historical evolution was presented in terms of movement from colonialism to independence. The newly born nations were especially vulnerable to involvement in the ideological conflict of the superpowers, a conflict between the United States and the Soviet Union, involving competing concepts of development between the Keynesian concept in the West of modernization based upon consumer satisfaction and the Marxist concept of industrialization based upon principles of national security and self-sufficiency. And national liberation took one of two directions. There were countries where liberation took the form of a radical break with the framework of world capitalism and with an effective social revolution of varying characteristics and internal dynamics. Independence movements in other countries did not try to break with the institutions and the international framework of the capitalist world or radically overturn their own class structure. North Korea followed socialism of the former, and South Korea adopted capitalism of the latter.

Development in the Third World should be analyzed by ideology and psychology. Entering the Third World means in general an announcement of independence from established power blocs. In this regard, North Korea can be incorporated into the Third World whereas South Korea is placed in the First or Second World and the Third. Horowitz defines what development means for the Third World in the context of ideology: Human development reflects at some level culture and consciousness. Development can be seen as an aspect of human will. It can be viewed as a particular kind of planning aimed at transforming an underdeveloped country into one that will eventually resemble the First or Second World or some combination of the two. All planning is done by a dedicated development-oriented elite supported by local, self-sacrificing masses. It attempts to determine in advance not simply the goals but the instruments, tactics, and strategies of planning social change. It contains a pragmatic dimension that enables it to shift its theoretical focus if plans do not work out in practice. Developmental ideologies tend to compel types of change along predirected channels. Although the problem of development has to be considered in terms of various methods, rates, directions, and consequences, it is also a matter of national pride for being a part of the Third World.

Psychology seems much more important in understanding the development of Third World countries, for example, attitudes, spirits, and personalities. According to the psychological concepts Horowitz carved out, North Korea is characterized by the attitudes toward traditionalism, mass type, innovation, and the spirit of revolution. North Korea emphasizes the development of a communist type of man, which is to be done under the name of self-sacrifice and altruism. Responsibility for welfare in the society shifts from the individual to the collective society. South Korea is, in contrast, characterized by modernism, managerial type, imitation in their take-off period, and the spirit of work. In fact, South Korea even introduced a mass type of development called the *Saemaeul* (New Community) Movement during the 1970s.

Psychological characteristics of the people of a developing nation directly affect the economic take-off point in that there must be a cognitive awareness of the backwardness. Risk taking does indeed seem characteristic of rapidly developing countries. North Korean Communism has attempted to develop citizens characterized by self-sacrifice, altruism, dedication, and patriotic madness. Language becomes an useful vehicle for that purpose.

Juche and *mobang* are exactly the proper vocabularies to portray the internal dynamics of the two Koreas' development. The strategy of capitalist South Korea for development is characterized by its *mobang,* or modeling or intensive imitation of, particularly, Japan. Japan itself is called the excellent nation of *mobang.* The strategy has been: "Do what the Japanese have done, but do it cheaper and faster."[3] South Korea has imitated whatever it can produce at a cheap price. South Korea has also extensively imitated the Japanese from long-term plans to a short-term marketing.[4] The strategy of *mobang* has been driven by the Korean spirit of "that's good enough" policy and by the aggressiveness of "first start and then let's see" practices.[5]

The strategy of Communist North Korea for development has stubbornly been guided by, what it calls, *juche,* or the ideology of self-identity, creativity, and autonomy. This model encompasses two parallel concepts: the idea of *charip* (self-sustenance) in economic endeavors and the idea of *chawi* (self-defense) in military affairs. The strategy of *juche* is defined as a line of economic construction for meeting by home production the needs for manufactured goods and farm produce necessary to build one's country with one's own labor and one's own national resources. For this goal, agricultural industries have been encouraged by putting 40 percent of the entire population of North Korea into it. The basic strategy claims that "without building an independent national economy, it is impossible to establish the material and technological foundations for socialism and build socialism and communism successfully."[6]

The *juche* itself, however, came into being from the cunning imitation of the Chinese and of the former Soviet Union. The idea of national self-sufficiency is always desirable and has been the ultimate answer for development as such, but the outcomes of the strategy are striking. The diverging outcomes are not unlike those of the advanced nations. During only the early years of its existence, North Korea had developed rapidly with the help of mass mobilization techniques, transforming a backward agricultural country into a relatively strong industrial state.

In contrast, South Korea since the mid-1960s has been successful in generating high rates of economic growth, industrializing the economy, and achieving a significantly high standard of living for its people. The size of the South Korean economy is eight times larger than that of North Korea, and the per capita GNP (gross national product) of South Korea is four times larger than that of North Korea. North Korea had earned higher marks than South Korea for generating per capita economic production until 1975. Five years before and five years after the 1975 reveals an important aspect in Korean development. Higher per capita material production, which encompasses, what it calls, "productive" services from the GNP, has been matched by South Korea only since 1980; better living standards of the people had already been achieved by South Korea in 1970.

North Korea was prosperous at least during the very early period, adopting the strategy of, what Horowitz called, "expropriation," which referred to land reform and urban renewal; the country also abolished its tax system in 1974. On the other hand, South Korea followed the road of "taxation," which referred to forced saving, guided investment, and reallocation of profits. In South Korea, the system of private ownership of land was not only retained but emphasized, despite the fact that genuine attempts at land reform were made by the American military government and by the Rhee regime. In sharp contrast, the Communist pattern in North Korea viewed the reform movement as a means to abolish the existing land-tenure systems and collectivize the agricultural sector.

Structural development in the two Koreas shows an irony: North Korea achieved a higher level of industrial structure. The proportion of industrial production in the North Korean GNP is about 70 percent, doubling that of South Korea. On the other hand, service sector in North Korea is extremely small, only one-tenth that of South Korea. Trade shows a far greater contrast: The North Korean trade volume explains only 12 percent of its GNP; the South Korean one, 75 percent of its GNP.

Development differs, as Horowitz mentioned, from industrialization, change, growth, or externally induced transformation. Development implies a new technology , in other words, "new methods of production," to make available consumer goods. Innovation is the near-exclusive property of the First and Second Worlds, because innovation must be based upon the existence of political and cultural variety. But, it seems that the imitative elements are more basic in developmental process of the Third World. What was formerly a product of change now becomes a matter of planning. It becomes increasingly apparent that there is a great deal of tension between imitation and innovation in the take-off period. Innovation has been attempted, and moderately achieved, in South Korea by imitation. Innovation in North Korea has been sublimated into the spiritual level, but not incarnated into the physical level of new technology.

Some Theoretical Thoughts

One of the three tactics for development of the Third World delineated by Horowitz more than two decades ago is the use of developmentalism against modernization and dependency. His position is most persuasive in explaining the Korean case than that of any other country. From the modernization perspective, the prediction turned out to be right. Some critics point out the South Korean success vis-à-vis North Korean failure as living proof that capitalism works, that integration into the world market, on the basis of comparative advantage, is the only way forward. However, there are numerous flaws in that explanation. Foreign capital was important, but the role of the South Korean state was equally important in the process of rapid economic development. And the state's guidance of the capitalist class and the state's exploitation of proletarian workers are also among the reasons for the South Korean success that weaken a modernization explanation. The early success of North Korean development cannot be explained by this theory.

Moreover, some disparity exists between economic development and social modernization in the two Koreas. That is, high levels of social development did not create the basis of economic development as modernization theory posits. Social development has been achieved at the same pace in both Koreas regardless of the differences in the level of economic development. Certain social achievements such as adult literacy, infant mortality, education, and health care do not appear to lead to economic development. Rather, political and institutional mechanisms could be a factor to bring about social improvements in health care and infant mortality. On the other hand, high levels of education and adult literacy could be diverted into the wasteful indoctrination of political ideology.

From the viewpoint of dependency theory, it was very difficult for both Koreas to be developed. Korea, before its division, was a Japanese colony for thirty-six years with extreme forms of dependency, and with human and cultural loss due to ruthless rule. However, we also have to painfully accept that these costs were offset, at least in part, by the construction of factories, roads, railroads, and administrative services under colonial power. North Korea, in particular, benefited from the division in its early development during the second half of the 1940s.

Cutting economic ties with developed capitalist countries, as dependency theory recommends, is more likely to inhibit than expedite the development of struggling countries. To be sure, China and the Soviet Union were not much hurt by a policy of economic self-sufficiency itself because they had a large resource base, but self-sufficiency is often costly for small countries.[7] Thus, North Korea as a small country suffered from the strict policy of self-sufficiency.

Dependency has taken new forms in the last quarter of the twentieth century. Like any late developer, South Korea has perforce relied on technology. Closer examination of this process reveals a determined and largely successful effort to ensure that technology really does become a significant aspect of the country. The manufacture of televisions, VCRs (video cassette recorders), and many other electronic products began with the purchase by Korean firms of Japanese technology, with Japanese firms withholding a key component. But, putting their own scientists to work, the Korean firms in each case developed the missing part of technology themselves, forcing the Japanese to cede the patent.

The solution to the underdevelopment is not to withdraw from a world capitalist system, but rather to generate a more selective policy in dealing with capitalist countries. South Korean economic growth was achieved with increasing dependency on trade with Japan and the United States, but the state of South Korea managed to develop in spite of multinational corporations by using local capital. The state severely limited the entrance of the multinationals to South Korea; only joint ventures with local partners have been permitted. The state preferred public and commercial loans to direct investment, which was seriously restricted. The state monopolized agricultural products, banks, financial institutions, railways, and communications. The state also runs many state industries including defense industries. Half of government revenues came from the public sector. The state controlled local capital through banking and financial institutions, which were nationalized after the Japanese colonial period.

More importantly, the solution largely depends on the policy option concerning domestic resources. Dependency theory has been inadequate in examining national and domestic structures, which are more fundamental than the problems of external dependence. The self-reliant model of North Korea needs to concentrate on heavy industry and agriculture rather than service industries. This imbalance of allocation of labor and capital does not help development at all.

The dependency tactic proves that it is not only inadequate in explaining contemporary Korean development, but has been all but invalidated by the diverging experiences of the two Koreas. A valid point of the dependency framework is, however, that the socialist alternative appears to effect more income-equalization than does the capitalist one, because income inequality is lower in North Korea than in South Korea. North Korean income ranges from 7 to 55 percent of that of South Korea, and the average income of North Korean workers is located in the lowest 15 percent of the South Korean income range.[8] Only 7 percent of South Korean people who are supported, due to absolute poverty, by the South Korean government fall below the lowest level of North Korean income. Although the level of income in North Korea is far lower than in South Korea, the income inequality is in general lower in North Korea than in South Korea.

This tells us that there is no automatic solution regarding the problem of equity in development. A socialist alternative suggested by the dependency tactic has at least challenged developmentalism to tackle the problem of injustice in income distribution. As Horowitz recognized, the ultimate duality in the Third World is the deadly competition between liberty and equality. Capitalism and socialism were hardened into an ideological controversy over man's essential nature. The natural "egotism" of men became identified with the forms of capitalist production, while the "altruism" of men became identified with socialism. This schism between egotism and altruism, between capitalist and socialist ideologies, initiated the present competition between liberty and equality.

Bureaucratic authoritarianism and dependent development theories do not address what we call the "comparison effect," that the two Koreas are mutually stimulated by awareness of each other. Bureaucratic authoritarianism has explained that a "deeper" level of industrialization accompanies the authoritarian state in Third World development. But authoritarian transformation could take place not only at the initial stage of this "deeper" level, but also at the stage of economic downturn. Both Koreas had experienced authoritarian transformation in 1972. In South Korea, economic development was on the rise and it needed social stability to attract more international capital when it entered a deeper level of expansive development, which necessitated a more authoritarian state.[9] On the other hand, North Korean economic growth slowed down during the 1960s. The stagnant economy, driven by mass mobilization, needed revitalization through the introduction of Western capital, which led, in turn, to further authoritarianism and surveillance to prevent popular exposure to the external world.

In addition, bureaucratic-authoritarian theory overlooked the so-called "comparison effect" in the authoritarian transformation of the two Korean states. The authoritarian adaptation of both Koreas in 1972 was in part a result of the awareness of each other. North Korea's introduction to Western technology during the early 1970s was stimulated by the rapid economic development of South Korea in the late 1960s, where substantial development was achieved with the help of Western technology and capital. South Korea needed more extensive control in introducing a mass mobilization measure, the New Community Movement, which was stimulated by the nature of the early success of North Korean development based on mass mobilization techniques. South Korea's timely introduction of the mass mobilization measure during the 1970s contributed significantly to its success.

The success of mass mobilization technique is the area that dependent development theory generally overlooks. The theory explains Third

World development within the framework of the triple alliance between the state, local capital, and multinationals.[10] Nor does this theory focus on the structure of resource allocation including labor force, military expense, and trade.

The implication of Korean development for the sociological theories of the Third World is that capitalism works for generating national development in general, but not for bringing about income equalization. In this sense, the Marxist theory of market expansion by the bourgeoisie and resulting working-class exploitation as well as a theory of state domination appear to provide reasonable explanations for the divergence of the two Koreas' development. Unlike dependency theory or dependent development theory, the primary agent in South Korean development was not the multinationals, but the domestic bourgeoisie as classical Marxist theory maintained. However, unlike modernization theory, bourgeois entrepreneurship is not the sole motivation. Rather, the state guided the domestic bourgeoisie, affording them sufficient capital and guaranteeing a low price of labor; it even employed mass-mobilization measures, which were the developmental engine of socialist North Korea.

Converging Korean Development

Third World was a popular phrase on college campuses in Korea in the 1970s and the early 1980s. The compartmentalization of world into three was fashionable, and recognized as a solid reality. The impact of Horowitz's two books on the Third World was serious. The immediate result was that the Three Worlds were created in concrete form on the earth. The concept of Third World was very attractive particularly because it came in the middle of military dictatorship.

Militarization of society is the common characteristic of both Korean states during the postwar period, and military leadership has exerted powerful influences, controlling every corner of their civil society. The rise of guerrilla activities during the Japanese colonial period was an attempt at consolidating power on both sides. Kim Il Sung of North Korea participated in guerilla activities as a commander in the Second Army of the First Route Army of the Northeast Anti-Japanese United Army in Manchuria. He also received military training in the Soviet Union near Khabarovsk. The guerilla group has been used as an effective power in the process of consolidating his supremacy in the North. He was well aware of his lack of a political base inside Korea. The most important element of consolidating his political power was the control of the military and security forces.

As soon as Kim Il Sung returned to North Korea, he began to organize a security unit. All military and internal security posts were taken by Kim's partisans. The first Provisional People's Committee organized in February 1946 was dominated by the partisan group. Kim emphasized the special mission of the army in the creation of the people's government in North Korea. Kim's takeover of North Korea was in a sense a military takeover under Soviet tutelage. His partisans and the Soviet-Koreans controlled every military and security unit and they supported Kim's consolidation of political power. The army did in fact enjoy a special status, primarily because it was led by the partisans and Soviet-Koreans, the military phalanx of the party.

Since the early 1960s, partisans began to rise to the top of the political scene in North Korea, deeply influenced by the external cold war environment such as the Cuban missile crisis and the military coup in South Korea. They stressed the military capabilities and fought to maintain peace even at the cost of compromising and limiting economic development.[11] Several military attacks were in fact implemented by these groups during the late 1960s including the command raids on Blue House, the seizure of the Pueblo, and the shooting down of a U.S. Navy EC-121 reconnaissance aircraft.

Unfortunately, however, their cause of South Korean revolution failed and the partisan power was purged in the early 1970s. Instead, a new strategy was sought in order to consolidate the power of Kim Jong Il, son of Kim Il Sung. Three Great Revolution Team Movement was launched under the direction of Kim Jong Il. Since then, he has controlled North Korea. This long effort paid off in 1992 when he became the supreme commander of the North Korean Army.

In South Korea, likewise, political leadership all came from the military: Park Chunghee, Chun Doowhan, and Rho Tae-woo were all former military generals. In the early years, the rudimentary military establishment set up by the American military government was transformed into the regular Korean Armed Forces when South Korea proclaimed its independence formally in 1948. A military leadership assumed political control of the government since 1961 after a period of ineffective civilian parliamentary leadership. It created a powerful party organization, the Democratic Republic party, and General Park reigned until his assassination in 1979. Many military officers have been converted into high-ranking governmental officials, diplomats, and top managers of public corporations. The military has emerged as a crucial institution and power group, forming a new power structure.

The armed forces are a major instrument of socialization in both Koreas. At no other time in the history of Korea has military organization been such an influential institution in determining the direction of national development in both Koreas, and the presence of the military has had an enormous effect upon socialization. Every male must by law serve in the military approximately two and one-half years in the South and five years in the North. During this duty some experience the tension of the demilitarized zone (DMZ). After their mandatory military duty, they are sent to the reserve army. This, combined with the all-encompassing military requirement, makes for a society that operates well with the "aggressiveness" of top-down leadership. Not only is there the guerrilla background of some of the country's top leaders, but also the vivid experience of the Korean War. The confrontation between the heavily armed condition of both countries has kept them in a state of permanent militarization.

North Korea probably has more of its citizens under arms than any other country in the world, except Iraq and Israel. In North Korea, life in the armed forces may not be particularly different from that in civil society, in which nearly all able-bodied men and women are organized into a people's militia. There is also a militia of perhaps 6 million people. North Korean society is thoroughly regimented and the entire country is organized like military units. Work teams and universities are divided into platoon, company, and so on, and their leaders are called platoon leader, company leader, and so on. The North Korean government still keeps reminding people of the morale of anti-Japanese guerrillas in the workplace. Life has been likened to a military campaign with people urged to set new records in production through ceaseless "speed battles." Under the social system, North Korea has been portrayed to its people as engaged in a continuing war with imperialism that requires a wartime spirit of dedication and sacrifice. This type of behavior often manifests itself in the industrial arena. They command speed and aggressiveness.

It is also noticeable that reforms were executed as rapidly as possible by both Korean states. In North Korea, the property of landlords was confiscated and distributed. The peasants did not acquire the rights of ownership but merely a title to use the property. The redistribution of the land did not result in an increase in the income of North Korean peasants nor in their having a feeling of ownership.

Unlike the observations of socialist economies in Eastern Europe and the former Soviet Union, the size of firms and factories are generally small in North Korea. Giganticism is one of the distinguished characteristics of the Soviet and East European experiences. However, many medium- and small-scale factories and industries have developed, and are evenly located throughout the country. This has a military purpose because in that way the total demolition by an air raid can be avoided.

Military readiness continues to be the principal preoccupation of the two Koreas' development. Modernization of South Korean armed forces proceeds steadily during the early 1990s, giving South Korea a qualitative edge in certain weapons systems, particularly in aircraft, but leaving North Korea well ahead in numbers of weapons. In 1992, North Korea still had a quantitative advantage of two to one in tanks, assault guns, personnel carriers, artillery, and combat aircraft.

South Korea is disturbed not only by North Korea's growing quantitative edge over South Korea in weapons and equipment but also by other military preparations. North Korea has continued to construct underground factories and hangars for aircraft, as well as adding to its underground fortifications along the DMZ. It has converted several infantry divisions into mechanized or motorized divisions. North Korea continues intensive training for special forces numbering 100,000 men, some of whom could rapidly infiltrate South Korean lines by numerous fast patrol crafts or by 250 slow and low-flying AN-2 aircraft. It is now believed that North Korea has a capability of making nuclear weapons.

The Korean War had contributed to a rapid military buildup, accelerating the pace of the initial effort. It was the first war triggered at the climax of cold war times, and left deep scars on the process of both Koreas' development, physically and psychologically. Except the material loss caused by the war, human casualties were heavy on both sides. It is estimated that over 2.5 million North Koreans died, and that 1.1 million South Koreans were lost. The South Korean Army had been reinforced from 60,000 to 600,000 during the war period. The war also led the North Korean Army to increase from 40,000 men to 400,000.

The cold war is not over yet on the Korean peninsula. The growth of military spending and militarization is still one of the most salient phenomena in the development of divided Korea, exceeding the pace of general militarization of the world. No less than 25 percent of the GNP has been spent in various activities of military buildups in North Korea. The two states have developed into two of the most militarized societies in the world today by any measurement, and, combining the two, they have the world's fifth largest military personnel and are thirteenth in military spending. While much of the rest of the world has been slowing down its military spending and rate of armament procurement since the collapse of the communist world, both North and South Korea have continued to invest more into preparations for war and measures to prevent war. North Korea's overriding commitment of resources to military expansion at the expense of the civilian economy is a key reason why North Korea has lagged behind South Korea in developmental outcomes since the mid-1960s.

In the euphoria of colonialism and war, socialism meant to these nations social justice, rather than economic affluence, from the beginning. Socialism in its origin emerged as the effective economic organization against wasteful capitalism. As Horowitz mentioned, even Stalin claimed that the Russian revolutionary sweep must also include a place for a capitalist efficiency. Stakhanovism is little more than an adaptation of Taylorism to Russian industrial conditions. Socialism in the Second World began in its start with the idea of economic rationalism of planning, not with the "social" rationalism of justice characterized by the socialism in the Third World.

Concluding Remarks

The Korean divergence has been the subtle reflection of the larger world. Although much of capitalism and communism is contained on each side, the two Koreas are more likely to be Third World countries, rather than First or Second. Since extensive nation-building in Korea has been attempted in the cold war environment, physically and ideologically, military power has indeed steered the process. The very nature of military "readiness" has played a major role in the rapid construction of both Koreas. Unfortunately, however, as the new detente between the First and Second Worlds spreads over, a vulgar military confrontation between the two Koreas has now become a problematic obstacle in the course to move forward.

What makes the Korean case more unique and essential is that the nature of militarization and aggressiveness, which once played an important part in Korean success, is now as a hurdle to overcome for possible future unification in the post-cold war era. Military characteristics have become hypertrophic in both Korean societies, so that, unlike the convergence of the First and Second Worlds, it is likely to be a great impediment for peace between the two states. In this sense, the tripartite conceptual map is still valid, as Horowitz thought, but the Third World has strayed too far from the convergence of the first two worlds, and the future of a single Korea is now less promising.

Sung Kyun Kwan University, Korea
Department of Sociology
and The Embassy of The Republic of Korea,
Moscow, Russia

Notes

1. Irving Louis Horowitz, *Three Worlds of Development: The Theory and Practice of International Stratification*, 2d ed. (New York: Oxford University Press, 1972).
2. Irving Louis Horowitz, *Beyond Empire and Revolution: Militarization and Consolidation in the Third World* (New York: Oxford University Press, 1982).
3. T. W. Kang, *Is Korea the Next Japan?: Understanding the Structure, Strategy, and Tactics of America's Next Competitor* (New York: The Free Press, 1989), 23.
4. Peter A. Petri, "Korea's Export Niche: Origins and Prospects," *World Development* 16, no. 1 (1989): 47–63.
5. Kang, *Is Korea the Next Japan?* This learning process among major Korean companies was well researched by Alice H. Amsdan, *Asia's Next Giant: South Korea and Late Industrialization* (New York: Oxford University Press, 1989).
6. Foreign Languages Publishing House, *Our Party's Policy for the Building of an Independent National Economy* (Pyongyang, Korea: FLPH, 1975), 7.
7. E. Wayne Nafziger, *The Economics of Developing Countries*, 2d ed. (Englewood Cliffs, NJ: Prentice Hall, 1990), 94.
8. See Byoung-Lo P. Kim, *Two Koreas in Development* (New Brunswick, NJ: Transaction Publishers, 1992).
9. Guillermo O'Donnell, "Tensions in the Bureaucratic-Authoritarian State and the Question of Democracy," in *The New Authoritarianism in Latin America*, ed. David Collier, 285–318 (Princeton, NJ: Princeton University Press, 1979).
10. Peter Evans, *Dependent Development: The Alliance of Multinational, State, and Local Capital in Brazil* (Princeton, NJ: Princeton University Press, 1979).
11. Dae-Sook Suh, *Kim Il Sung: The North Korean Leader* (New York: Columbia University Press, 1988), 213.

Section Five

Cuba, the Caribbean, and Communism

16

Conscience, Courage, and the Cuban Revolution: Studying Thirty-Five Years of a Failed System

Ernesto F. Betancourt

When I was asked to make a contribution to a festschrift for Irving Horowitz's sixty-fifth birthday, I felt honored and happy. It gave me the opportunity of expressing my gratitude to him, first, as a Cuban American for his dedication to Cuba, and second, as an individual who has enjoyed his friendship and generous encouragement to do research on Cuba. At the same time I felt overwhelmed, because I don't know of any non-Cuban who has made a more prolific contribution to scholarly work on Cuba. His published work over the last thirty years, written from the perspective of a sociologist, covers many dimensions of Cuban life and contemporary history.

For this great sociologist has addressed subjects that go from the Stalinization of the Castro regime and its militarization to its practice of deportation-incarceration as a form of genocide. He has also discussed the Cuban Revolution from the perspective of Marxism-Leninism and the so-called dependency theory, not to mention legitimacy and charisma, as well as its impact on Latin America.

Irving Horowitz's contribution to the understanding of this dramatic contemporary event has gone beyond the scope of his own scholarly research—a remarkable accomplishment by itself—to include a significant publishing effort, which allowed other scholars, particularly Cuban-American social scientists, to have their research known and disseminated throughout the academic community. This he did mostly through the publication by Transaction Publishers of seven editions of the anthology entitled *Cuban Communism,* which he edited, and of the five volumes of *Cuba Annual Reports* generated by the Radio Martí Office of Research.

But Irving Horowitz did not limit himself to the pursuit of academic or publishing endeavors in relation to the Cuban Revolution. In addition, he engaged in lively controversies with fellow social scientists who, he rightly considered, sacrificed their scholarly integrity to ideological bias in their writings on Castro and his revolution. As an exuberant Jewish scholar raised in Harlem, Horowitz relishes a good fight and we have shared a few on the issue of Cuba, fortunately for me on the same side. Finally, he has also been willing to generously contribute his wisdom and political savvy to operational efforts such as the Radio Martí External Research Advisory Group and, through countless articles and testimonies, to the policy debate on what the United States should do about Cuba.

To comment on such a formidable contribution is an overwhelming task indeed. Under such circumstances, selectivity becomes mandatory. Although this paper will be basically limited to a review of the evolution of Irving Horowitz's thinking about the Cuban Revolution as reflected in his comments in the introductions to the volumes of *Cuban Communism,* it will also draw on other writings and comments at various anniversaries of the revolution, as well as his most recent research for the Bacardi Lectures at the University of Miami.

An Early Commitment to Unbiased Social Research

In the postscript to the seventh edition of *Cuban Communism,* Irving Horowitz provides a glimpse of how he became involved in the study of the Cuban Revolution. In early 1959, the year of Castro's emergence as a revolutionary leader and shortly after returning from teaching in Buenos Aires, Horowitz was approached by C. Wright Mills with a request to review the proofs of *Listen Yankee.* He agreed, but to his disappointment he found Mills's work not sound social science but sheer advocacy. This was probably his first experience with the leftist bias among many social scientists dealing with the Cuban revolution. At that time, he was under the impression, gathered from his students and colleagues in Argentina, that Cuba's revolution was Marxist from its beginnings.

Three years later he was again asked by Mills to do some research on Cuba for a TV debate with Adolf Berle, and to his surprise, which was shared by Mills, he discovered that Cuba "was the most advanced nation in the Caribbean in 1959."[1] This early discovery influenced the position of Horowitz on the Cuban revolution throughout the years. It made him one of the first liberal intellectuals to take a skeptical view of the claims of Castro's regime at a time when many intellectuals were still blindly praising its accomplishments and ignoring its totalitarian bent.

In 1964, while lecturing in Mexico, he engaged in a public dialogue with Carlos Fuentes over whether the Cuban Revolution had enhanced or reduced the possibilities for hemispheric revolution.[2] Horowitz's position, which events have confirmed to be correct, was in essence that the possibility of revolution had been diminished precisely because Cuba had become aligned with the Soviet Union. That made replication of the Cuban model less likely at the national level in Latin America and repetition of U.S. passivity in relation to Cuba highly unlikely. This dialogue was published in *Excelsior*, a Mexican newspaper, and provides a context for the first expressions of Horowitz's evolving sociological analysis of what had happened in Cuba, as well as of its impact on U.S. influence in Latin America.

The *Excelsior* dialogue centered on whether U.S. policy and capitalism were to be blamed for the situation in Latin America at the time. Fuentes advanced the typical Latin American intellectual argument placing the burden of responsibility for what was wrong in the region on the United States. However, he was forced to back out of this categoric position in response to the arguments marshaled by Horowitz for a more balanced approach. One running theme in Horowitz's work on Cuba, as well as on Latin America in general, is that, although he is willing to acknowledge what has been wrong with U.S. policies, he is not willing to join the self-flagellation on U.S. behavior that prevails among many left wing intellectuals.

An Attempt to Fit Castro into a Marxist Framework

In 1965, Horowitz published his first work on the Cuban Revolution: "The Stalinization of Fidel Castro."[3] In this article, Horowitz makes an effort to apply to Cuba a formal framework for the analysis of its Stalinist characteristics: in essence, the move toward building socialism in one country at the expense of promoting it regionally, the loss of diversity through the bureaucratization of the regime that restricts consideration of more than one viewpoint, and, finally, the introduction of dictatorial rule of a party leader and his henchmen. The article is the first of several attempts by Horowitz to fit Cuba within a model of sociological inquiry and, particularly, to see if it fits the mold of the Soviet socialist experiment.

The analysis relies on the issues that emerged during the Marxist debate that took place around Stalin's policies to consolidate his rule and attempts to fit publicly available data on Cuba into the resulting framework. As a result, it does not give enough weight to the impact of Castro's personality on the inner workings of the regime. Instead, it gives more weight to the role of the old pro-Soviet Communist party figures than they ever had in reality. The impact of Castro's personality is dismissed in a comment on the split with China by saying that "the idea that Castro's critique is a psychological phenomenon can be accepted only as a last resort."[4]

However, Horowitz perceived, quite correctly, that Cuba was abandoning the policy of exporting revolution for the sake of consolidating Castro's dictatorial rule. Being the image maker he is, Castro continued his revolutionary posturing for the benefit of his followers. This discrepancy between words and action is commented on by Horowitz: "The more conservative its practices, the more noisy are its ideological pronouncements."[5]

As Horowitz was to conclude later, the use of conventional categories for a comparative analysis between Cuba and the Soviet Union, for example, in terms of the feasibility of industrialization and the existence of a proletariat, had limited the ability to understand Castro's behavior. In his later writings, Horowitz refers to Castro's personality and charisma as decisive factors in determining policies and events.

In reality, Castro is more of a traditional Latin caudillo—remarkable indeed in his reach and audacity—than is realized even today. His resorting to Marxism-Leninism responds more to his opportunism than to a thorough ideological internalization of that doctrine. Castro has been a Fidelista more than anything else.

At that time, Castro was reacting to the harsher U.S. policy toward Cuba under President Johnson, reflected in the U.S. invasion of the Dominican Republic. He was also reacting to the pressure from his Soviet allies who were committed, under the Khrushchev-Kennedy exchange of letters that ended the Cuban Missile Crisis in 1962, not to allow Cuba to promote revolution in the Americas. Castro was personally thwarted under those restrictions—agreed to without his consent—which limited his ambitions for a worldwide role. His chaffing was all the more so, in view of the competition coming from the aggressive Chinese promotion of revolution in the Third World to gain support in the Sino-Soviet conflict.

This explains the repeated accusations of Trotskyism, using the label applied by the Soviets to the Chinese, against those Latin American revolutionaries who were demanding that Castro live up to his words. The Soviet leashing of Castro led to the departure of Guevara from Cuba and, after his death in Bolivia, to the ignominy of Castro's support for the Soviet invasion of Czechoslovakia in 1968. In that year, Cuba's dependency on the Soviets was conveyed to Castro in brutal terms: suspension of oil shipments until he complied with Soviet demands to toe the line in form as well as in substance both in domestic and foreign policy.

Expanding Social Research on Cuba

As Castro was falling more and more into dependency on the Soviets, and Cuba was being brought into Soviet bloc orthodoxy, Irving Horowitz got deeper into the study of the Cuban Revolution. He extended his reach beyond his own research and edited the first volume of *Cuban Communism,* which appeared in 1970, and the second, which was published in 1972. These were the years during which Castro failed completely in his make-or-break effort to expand sugar production to 10 million tons, leading to a severe loss of popular support for the revolution and to 30 percent absenteeism at work centers. Meanwhile, the Soviets were living up to their side of the agreement to bring Cuba into the COMECON on the condition that Castro geared the Cuban economy fully into its integration with the Soviet bloc. Cuba was assigned the role of the sugar bowl of the Soviet bloc, bringing to an end any hopes of fulfilling nationalist revolutionary promises about product and market diversification.

In the introduction to the first edition of *Cuban Communism,* Horowitz does not expand on his thoughts on the revolution, limiting himself to state that the regime had attained stability and that "in Cuba self-determination is a reality." However, he included several of his articles on diverse aspects of the Cuban revolution, which reveal that by that time he had already become a prolific member of the so-called Castrologist social science researchers. This is a label he may not like to be applied to himself since he disagreed with many of them over their uncritical approach to Cuba's revolution.

The volume came one year ahead of the work edited by Carmelo Mesa-Lago, *Revolutionary Change in Cuba,* and the one by Rolando E. Bonachea and Nelson P. Valdés, *Cuba in Revolution.* Both were anthologies of scholarly writings on Cuba that coincided more or less with the tenth anniversary of the revolution. In the introduction to the second edition of *Cuban Communism,* published in 1972, Horowitz explains that he decided to go ahead with that edition despite those two volumes because "the need for a systematic social science examination of the Cuban regime remains." This was the beginning of his role as publisher of social science research on Cuba, which has lasted for the last twenty years.

The Research Focus Shifts to Castro's Impact

In the second volume, Horowitz starts focusing his own comments more sharply on Castro himself. He states that during the period since the first edition, the Cuban leadership seemed to have realized that they were facing more complicated problems than they had assumed, concluding that the "most significant development is the recognition that the art of governance is considerably more complex than is the art of insurrection."[6] Horowitz discusses the difficulties Castro faced in his dealings with the bureaucracy he had created, expanding on his initial perception that the bureaucratization of the revolution was a consequence of Castro's Stalinization. Judging Cuba from what emerges as a social democratic perspective, Horowitz continues to express concern for the lack of political controversy prevailing in Cuba—a reflection of the totalitarian nature of Castro's rule—while recognizing Castro's predicament should political controversy interfere with the priority need for economic performance.

In addition, for the first time, he addresses the issue of dependency on the Soviets, which by then had become evident due to the increased Sovietization of Cuba and the growing reliance on Soviet trade and financing. In contrast with Castro's apologists, Horowitz saw from the beginning that there was symmetry between that relationship and other colonial relationships of dependency, pointing out that "it is clear that dependence upon the USSR is not any better than dependence upon the USA."[7] This concept set Horowitz on a crash course with leftist intellectuals.

Finally, according to Horowitz, the need to continue relying on a single crop economy, which was determined by Cuba's small size, further complicated the situation. His conclusion was that the three factors—the centralized ruling style, the increased dependency on the Soviets, and the inability to attain economic diversification—led to worker demoralization and loss of productivity. Horowitz quite correctly states that the dilemma facing the regime was either to restore material incentives or to resort "to terrorism against the very classes on behalf of whom the revolution was made."[8]

Despite this depressing assessment, the optimist in Horowitz prevails and he ends expressing the view that the regime "shows a capacity to learn from error no less than to celebrate ideology." Later events revealed this was a premature judgment, as was his statement at the time that "Cuban communism seems destined to help shape hemispheric politics and economics for the decade ahead, no less than the decade just completed."[9]

Castro Retrenches in the Americas and Reaches for Africa

This last prediction fell short of the mark. In the next decade Cuba crossed the Atlantic as a Soviet surrogate to play a decisive military role in Africa and in the war against apartheid. It was concurrently becoming less relevant in the hemisphere. Castro became president of the Non-Aligned Movement in October 1979, after hosting its meeting in Havana. This diplomatic success was to be spoiled two months later by the Soviet invasion of Afghanistan, which prevented Castro from becoming one of the members of the United Nations Security Council, a position that Castro coveted because it would have enabled him to speak in that forum as the spokesman for the Non-Aligned.

In this hemisphere, the Allende regime was overthrown in Chile, the Tupamaros failed in Uruguay, the Dirty War crushed the Montoneros and the ERP in Argentina. The left wing military dictatorship of Velasco

Alvarado in Perú, the so-called Nasserites, also failed and Michael Manley, Castro's friend and admirer, lost the 1980 election in Jamaica. On the positive side, in 1979 Castro could rejoice on the Sandinista victory in Nicaragua, which reopened the prospects for promoting revolution in the Americas and the Maurice Bishop coup in Grenada, which he had also supported.

At the domestic level, Castro was unable to capitalize on the highest prices sugar had ever enjoyed in the world market due to his commitment to be the Soviet bloc's sugar bowl. So, for a brief period, the Soviet subsidy to Cuba in sugar prices turned negative. In 1975, Cuba held its First Party Congress and, in 1976, a new socialist constitution was enacted, as Cuban society was being remade to fit the mold of Soviet bloc regimes. Castro was so confident that the revolution was consolidated and in process of institutionalization that he even allowed a mass visit of the despised exiles, the so-called worms. The impact of that visit on Cuban society triggered the Mariel exodus in 1980, which made dramatically evident the failure of the Cuban model.

And, to Castro's chagrin, in 1980, the American electorate voted Ronald Reagan into power, a hardliner who decided to challenge the evil empire on all fronts, including launching a military competition in space, which the Soviets were unable to match. It was this challenge that, in the end, freed Fidel from his dependency on the Soviet Union: Cuba's third metropolis in a century just ceased to exist.

Challenging the Institutionalization Myth

Despite these clear signals that the Cuban revolution was facing some difficulties, the prevalent notion among Castrologists was that the revolution was institutionalized. It is in this context that Horowitz commented on the twenty years of the Cuban Revolution. The comments appear in the introduction to the fourth edition of *Cuban Communism* and in a brief paper entitled "Institutionalization as Integration: The Cuban Revolution at Age Twenty."[10] Since the second paper was written before the Mariel exodus in 1980, it is advisable to consider first that source of Horowitz's thoughts on Cuba and then comment on the introduction where Horowitz addresses the impact of Mariel.

The discussion on institutionalization reflects a keen perception of the real nature of the process Cuba was undergoing. At a time when, as has been mentioned above, Castro was confident the regime was consolidated and becoming institutionalized and many social scientists in the United states were promoting that view, Horowitz saw clearly that the so-called institutionalization was shallow indeed.

He starts by pointing out that the militarization of Cuban life was no different than the one prevailing in other Third World societies and that Castro's main concern was basically to ensure his tenure in power by preventing a coup. He added this dimension of Cuban life to the prevalence of single-crop production and political dependency, as he had done in his earlier writings, to reach the conclusion that what existed in Cuba was not compatible with "an advanced form of socialism."[11]

In evaluating the process of institutionalization, Horowitz elaborates on the fact that Cuban foreign policy had become subordinated to Soviet strategic interests and expansionism in Africa, particularly in the role of provider of a surrogate military force. He delves into the relationship between a real institutionalization and the process of succession, reaching the conclusion that in Cuba, succession in the party leadership had not even reached the stage it had attained within the Soviet Union. He also makes the very perceptive distinction that in Cuba "the official Communist Party, the chief organ of political power, was not the vanguard but the tail of the Cuban revolution,"[12] an observation that reflects his downgrading of the party leaders as he became aware that the old Communist party leadership had not played a significant role in the struggle against Batista. In conclusion, the regime had not attained legitimacy despite the party congress and the enactment of a new constitution.

Horowitz also observes that institutionalization requires the subordination of the military to civilian authority, a characteristic absent from the Castro regime, in which all aspects of national life are penetrated by, and subordinated to, the military. Rather than institutionalization, he perceives a process of integration of military and civil functions to ensure control from the top, stating that, in Cuba "[i]t is clear that institutionalization means quite simply authoritarianism."[13] This was a clear and unmistakable diagnosis of the stage attained by the Cuban Revolution as of 1979.

In the introduction to the fourth edition of *Cuban Communism*, Horowitz concentrates on the impact and meaning of the Mariel exodus stating that there can be scarcely any doubt it is "the most significant event in recent years."[14] Then, he goes on to analyze the anticipated impact of this event on the policies of the regime, and radical movements in Latin America, the United States, and the Soviets.

He also makes a damning indictment of a revolution betrayed, reiterating that institutionalization has really meant acceptance of authoritarian rule as a permanent feature of the system. To the surprise of Castro and his admirers in academe, that was the real meaning of the Mariel exodus. However, contrary to many of the hopes expressed at the time, he advises caution on what it means in terms of Castro's tenure in power: "Cuban communism will hardly come to an end as a result of constant Cuban exodus; migration is as much a 'safety valve' for Cuban communism as it is for Chilean fascism."[15]

The fifth edition of *Cuban Communism*, published in 1984, coincided with the twenty-fifth anniversary of the Cuban Revolution. In its introduction Horowitz follows up on the theme of institutionalization that he had developed in the previous anthology. Broadening his analysis, he makes the distinction between institutionalization and routinization, pointing out that "devices ensuring legitimacy (such as elections, oppositional parties, or a free press) are absent."[16] Then, he moves to the issue of the lack of changes in the revolutionary leadership, which he perceived as a symptom that routinization had not attained normalization. He expands the concept of routinization of authoritarian rule to that of a paranoid style of ruling.

In this case, "the political functions of the paranoid style are numerous and complex, but above all can best be viewed as the essential mechanism of mass mobilization."[17] And, in Cuba, the paranoia has been based all along on keeping alive the external threat by the United States. This leads to the very perceptive observation that, as is the case with apocalyptic religious cults, when cataclysmic events fail to materialize, the followers react either by questioning the leadership, and turning away from them, or reaffirming their faith and moving closer around them, while many just become cynical. To a great extent this describes the behavior of Cubans in recent times, as Castro's decisions bring disastrous results.

In this introduction, Horowitz expands on his previous comments on another important issue in relation to Castro's regime: the lack of a workable succession mechanism. He makes a comparison with the case of Franco in Spain, which leads to a dead end since Castro is not Franco and the institutional framework of Cuba differs completely from that of

Spain—there is no monarchy in Cuba, although willing candidates to start one could probably be found. The succession topic was raised by Castro himself when he speculated on retiring from daily management of the government to address international issues and rumors were spread on the possibility of his brother Raúl becoming prime minister.

Lacking in this introduction, however, is any reference to the impact of the 1983 invasion of Grenada, an event that shook up the regime's confidence in its international importance and the willingness of the Soviets to come to the support of its client's states. Another Grenada-related factor leading to loss of confidence was the poor performance of the Cuban military. But the most damage was done to the credibility of the leadership. This resulted from an announcement in which Cubans were told by the official media that the last Cuban combatants had died embraced in the flag—an uncomfortable battle position indeed—to find a few days later that the overwhelming majority returned safely and the wounded had been given excellent medical attention by U.S. forces.

Cuba's Impact on Social Science Research

Returning to a theme that runs throughout his work on Cuba in the last three decades, in the preface to the sixth edition of *Cuban Communism* (1987) Horowitz commented mostly on the development of social science research on Cuba and the impact this research had on the contents of this volume of the anthology. In this respect, there is a very significant statement that reflects the change over the years in Horowitz's perception of how to conduct research on the nature of the Cuban regime. Horowitz writes:

> I have increasingly come to believe that as the Castro era inevitably draws to its conclusion, developments in Cuba since 1959 will be perceived as having a profound role in transforming theories about societies even more (much more) than a particular society as such. Indeed, increasingly one must account for the political psychology of absolute rule rather than laws of history to explain Cuban developments. Political mutation, even accident, comes to loom larger than economic determinism or iron necessity.[18]

In this paragraph Horowitz recognizes that conventional sociological analysis or traditional Marxist conceptual schemes developed in Europe and the United States were inadequate instruments to engage in social science inquiries on the Castro phenomenon. There was something unique in the nature of the Cuban regime and its origins that could not be explained through established social science approaches. Perhaps social science could develop from the study of Cuba other approaches suitable to deal with such situations. If anything, the emergence of Castro contradicted many of the tenets of Marxist-Leninist dogma and, precisely for that reason, the leaders of the old pro-Soviet Communist party of Cuba questioned Fidel Castro's strategy against Batista; to be proven wrong is the acid test of historical reality.

Impact of Glasnost and Perestroika on Castro's Regime

In the second half of the 1980s, the situation for Castro took a turn for the worse in several directions. The relationship with the Soviet Union turned increasingly antagonistic with the deaths within a few years of Brezhnev, Andropov, and Chernenko and the emergence of Gorbachev and his advocacy of *glasnost* and *perestroika*. In foreign policy, this meant the abandonment of the Brezhnev Doctrine on the irreversibility of communism and the end of Soviet expansionism, thus depriving Castro of the Soviet strategic umbrella that had allowed him to pursue his policy of "internationalism" and project Cuban military power throughout Africa.

Gorbachev's position implied initially, and made explicit later, that politically and economically the Marxist-Leninist doctrine had failed and that democracy and capitalism were the wave of the future. Gorbachev was pulling the ideological rug from under Fidel Castro. Consequent with the new foreign policy and economic realism, the Soviets started using international market prices for the goods exchanged and enterprise-to-enterprise transactions rather than state-to-state global agreements. This meant a total change in the trade relationship with Cuba. Castro was deprived of the so-called subsidies he was receiving in exchange for his providing cannon fodder for Soviet expansionism.

The empire was collapsing, leaving its most remote colony to fend for itself in the pursuit of Castro's war against the United States. Castro's big gamble in siding with the Soviets in the cold war ended in a foreign policy disaster for his regime. This forced Castro to repatriate his overseas expeditionary force from Angola and Ethiopia at a time when the Cuban economy could not absorb them. For Cuba was bankrupt due to excessive investment in military expenditures and the capricious economic decision making of Castro himself. By 1986, Cuba had been forced to stop payment of interest and principal on its foreign debt to the West. This default closed the possibility of further external financing from the Paris Club.

The totalitarian nature of the regime was depriving it of international support as democracy and freedom became fashionable even in the Third World. Defections of high-ranking officials in the economic area, in the military and in the intelligence apparatus revealed cracks in regime ranks. Voice of America's Radio Martí broke the state communications monopoly, offering an alternative source of information and making knowledge of events and discussion of ideas accessible to the population. This created conditions for the emergence of a public opinion other than the one manipulated through state media. A dissident movement emerged, basically demanding respect for human rights, to offer for the first time alternative organizational means within Cuban society to channel the increasing popular disagreement with official policy. As Castro was unable to prevent the introduction of diversity of ideas—a basic requirement for a totalitarian or theocratic society to prevail—an incipient civil society was emerging.

Horowitz's Views on Castro's Reaction to Glasnost and Perestroika

It is in this context that the seventh edition of *Cuban Communism* was published in 1989. Horowitz's views of the Castro regime at this time are reflected not only in the introduction to this edition but in his comments during a conference sponsored by the Cuban American National Foundation on the thirtieth anniversary of the revolution.[19] In the introduction, Horowitz reiterates his previous perception of the relationship between the lack of change in the leadership and the rigidity of the regime's reaction to the sweeping changes under way at that time in the Soviet bloc.

Taking into account Castro's increasing international isolation, Horowitz offers a possible explanation for his inflexible behavior on the basis of four reasons:

Castro's absolute belief in the correctness of his strategic and tactical reasoning.... Further, his years as a guerrilla leader have given him a sense of being a military strategist of a special sort.... There is also Castro's long-held belief in his world

leadership role at the head of the nonaligned powers.... Finally, to accept Chinese
or Soviet styles of reform is to set in motion certain menacing administrative and
military trends that could topple his personalist style of rule.[20]

In the rest of the introduction, Horowitz provides a summary review
of the situation of Cuba economically, politically, and internationally. It
is interesting to point out that at this stage in the evolution of his approach toward the study of Cuba, Horowitz bases his discussion more
on Castro's own statements than on the use of a formal sociological or
Marxist framework as in his early works. Will is recognized to prevail
over determinism. He follows his own conclusion about social science
research on Cuba, quoted above, and his comments and analysis are in
essence based "on the political psychology of absolute rule." He ends
by indicating that this is, hopefully, the last edition of *Cuban Communism*.

In the Cuban American National Foundation-sponsored conference,
Horowitz was asked to comment on Jaime Suchlicki's political assessment and my economic assessment of the revolution after thirty years.
Reacting to our presentations from a sociological perspective, he opened
the discussion by raising the issue of the emergence of deviance as a
consequence of economic development, saying that the intolerance of
deviance in Cuba is a manifestation, and quite possibly a cause, of its
lack of development. He also provided an excellent summary of what
the Cuban people had lost in these thirty years: "a sense of vivacity of
the private life, a life that is not subject to block-by-block, house-by-
house, inspection by keepers of the ethical flame. In short, a sense of
deviance goes along with a sense of development in an open society—
yes, like Miami!"[21] Then he proceeded to discuss our presentations.

The humane person in Irving Horowitz rebelled against the inhuman-
ity of the system Castro has imposed on the Cuban people. In the end,
the sociologist is telling us that politics and economics are means, but
that ends in a society should include the right to be oneself, which is the
essence of happiness and freedom.

Afterwards, in response to a question on how to explain the length of
Castro's stay in power, Horowitz made a very valid argument against
the notion that longevity may be an indication of regime success:
"[D]urability at the personal level is really symptomatic of failure...In
a democratic society, the idea of a person being in office for thirty years
is viewed as a danger signal to the character of the society itself. It is
often viewed as a systemic breakdown."[22]

Beyond the Soviet Collapse

After the seventh edition of *Cuban Communism* came out in 1989, events in the Soviet bloc took a turn that nobody had anticipated, except Fidel Castro. He predicted in his speech on 26 July 1989 that *glasnost* and *perestroika* could end in the collapse of communism not only in the Eastern bloc, but in the Soviet Union itself, leading to its disintegration. By the end of 1989, the Berlin Wall had been demolished; Honnecker, the hardliner who shared with Castro serious misgivings about *glasnost* and *perestroika,* had to flee to Moscow and eventually was returned to a reunited Germany to be tried. In Rumania, Ceausescu, who acted with an independence from Moscow similar to Castro's, was also overthrown, tried, and executed.

Castro himself faced a threat from disgruntled high-ranking officers in the military and the security apparatus, which led to the trial of General Arnaldo Ochoa, the hero of the Ogaden War in Ethiopia and of many other battles in Angola at the service of Castro's internationalist ambitions. Not too much attention has been given to the fact that the Ochoa trial took place three months after Gorbachev's visit to Cuba but, taking into account how Gorbachev undermined Honnecker and Ceausescu, it is not too farfetched to raise the hypothesis that Ochoa acted with at least some encouragement from the Soviets. To this day, former Soviet—or now Russian—officials respond very evasively to any inquiry on this issue.

Castro's initial response to the new situation was to hint at the possibility of some concessions. The Fourth Party Congress in October 1991 was billed as the opportunity for definition of Cuba's own version of communism in view of the evident failure of other formulations. Carlos Aldana, who was in charge of ideology within Cuba's Communist party, encouraged the notion of possible openings in economic management and political participation.

But the collapse of the Soviet Union after the failure of the August 1991 coup by Castro's hardline friends within the Soviet Union Communist party, the KGB, and the military left Castro with a much more threatening situation than the changes in Eastern Europe: The metropolis had collapsed and Cuba's external sector with it. Besides the loss of strategic support and a serious weakening of ideological credibility for Marxism, this meant a massive and severe decline in the economic capability of Cuba. Castro opted for a harder line of no concessions in ideology, economic reform, or party control, while at the same time resorting to increasing repression to ensure his personal rule. As a corollary, Cubans have been forced to return to living conditions prevalent in the last century.

At this time, we do not have any more introductions to *Cuban Communism* from which to draw Horowitz's thoughts on Cuba, Castro, and his revolution. As mentioned before, Horowitz has concluded there will be no need for another edition, although wisely has refrained to predict a precise timetable for Castro's demise. His notion is that at this stage U.S. policy may be as much of a factor as the regime's internal dynamics, in particular its pervasive repressive nature.

However, we are fortunate to have his 1992 lectures at the Bacardi-Moreau Endowed Chair on Cuban Studies at the University of Miami. They have been published by the North-South Center under the intriguing title *The Conscience of Worms and the Cowardice of Lions: The Cuban-American Experience, 1959–1992.*[23]

The Wizard of Oz, Castrologist Behavior, and the Past and the Future

In the preface to this collection of lectures, Horowitz explains that, in the title, "conscience of worms" is meant to honor Cuban exiles by referring to old Spanish and Jewish roots respectively of the words as burrowing "through the mind to find what is true and ethically appropriate" or to "a small worm that was used by King Solomon to break rocks"; and "cowardice of lions" is associated with the lion in *The Wizard of Oz,* who although cowardly is eventually redeemed, which offers hope "for those Castrologists who roared their collective disapproval of critics of Cuban communism."[24] Evidently, in these lectures Horowitz decided to take a conciliatory stance.

In the first lecture, Horowitz discusses "American Foreign Policy Towards Castro's Cuba: Paradox, Procrastination and Paralysis."[25] He is pessimistic about the possibility of Castro's regime coming to an end soon because U.S. policy is saddled by ambiguity and guilt, which leads to inaction. To the intellectuals from the left who have defended Castro in the past and advocated nonintervention and normalization of relations, he adds the isolationists from the right, a la Pat Buchanan, to conclude that they are bringing immobility to our foreign policy.[26] He expresses the hope that eventually the United States will awaken to the fact that it is also a Latin country, due to the high proportion of our population with a Latin origin, and take a more assertive stance.

He ends his lecture with an eclectic comment:

> Cuban communism will be an acid test of American foreign policy. The outcome in Moscow favored the democratic gods; the outcome in Beijing favored the totalitarian demigods. What takes place in Havana over the proximate period of time will tell us much about an American policy that simultaneously appears impatient to observe the positive changes in Cuba and yet seems to be too exhausted by recent world events to help bring about such desirable outcome.[27]

In the second lecture, Horowitz discusses the Castrologists who became apologists for the Castro regime. Since events have proven Horowitz right and his social science critics wrong, the lecture provides a well-documented list of flawed analyses of what really was happening in Cuba by Castro apologists within the ranks of Castrologists. Toward the end he concludes,

> In point of fact, the work of social scientists on Cuba represents a fundamental betrayal of the critical tradition, one demanding examination of events based in a framework of analysis first and foremost and in a valuation framework last and tentatively. Such work also pitted domestic American sociologists against the new immigrants. And in academic life, unlike anywhere else, this older nativistic tradition was powerful enough to block routes of access to academic higher stations.[28]

In the third lecture, Horowitz discusses the work of those immigrant social scientists who used their professional skills to try to elicit the truth about what was happening in Cuba.[29] He equates the contribution of Cuban exile intellectuals with that of two previous waves of intellectual political exiles, the first from Russia after the Soviet Revolution and the second from Germany under Nazism. He identifies three broad categories of professional backgrounds for these Cuban social scientists: economists, lawyers, and historians. These initial immigrants were joined by a generation of younger professionals trained in American universities.

In discussing the contributions of this new wave of immigrant intellectuals, Horowitz points to the fact that they did not enjoy formal support for their research and in many cases were rejected within academe precisely for their critical stance toward Castro. This lack of financial and institutional support forced many to link their research on Cuba to their operational responsibilities, in other words, to the policy process in their respective professional disciplines.

As to the resulting perspective of the efforts of these social scientists, Horowitz states:

> Cuban intellectuals in exile, far from being parochial, limited or narrow are in fact the third great wave of social researchers to these shores in the present century. They share with the Russian migration a deep disdain for totalitarian solutions. They share with the German-Jewish migration a feeling for the universal nature of political issues. But they are also different. They have stayed focused on Cuba and the Hemisphere.[30]

In the fourth lecture in this volume, "What Have We Learned from 33 Years of the Cuban Revolution? The Myth of Theory and the Theory of Myths Revisited,"[31] Horowitz updates his assessment of the Castro regime in the light of the existing situation and the new social science approach he has already indicated may be necessary to deal with regimes such as Castro's. He discusses five myths that have emerged in relation to the Cuban revolution.

The first is the myth of eternal development associated with Marxist-Leninist doctrine, which empirical evidence shows has not worked. He elaborates this failure in terms of the Cuban regime pointing out that Castro "reverts to a solution predicated on the return of Cuba to primitive agrarianism."[32] He also comments on the ability of Castro to make a virtue out of necessity by turning these adversities into heroic sacrifices for the fatherland.

The second is the myth of revolutionary will versus determinism, the role of the great man. In the Cuban case, Horowitz refines his earlier comments on the issue to reach the conclusion that to discuss the time of Castro's conversion to Marxism is "essentially silly." Rather, the important factor is the set of convictions guiding Castro's actions, which he relates to the Sorelian response to orthodox Marxism. In this belief system, which ruled the actions of 26 July during the insurrection and afterward, "leadership and will, mobilization and charisma, are at least as important as history and economy."[33]

Starting from that basis, it is Horowitz's contention that Castro was also helped by external factors, in particular the passive, and perhaps even supportive, U.S. response to his coming to power. He considers that the ease with which Castro attained power led people like Regis Debray to the naive notion that it would be easy to export the revolution to Latin America. It also resulted in the formulation of the myth of the "foco" as the revolutionary strategy to attain that goal. This led to a series of revolutionary failures and, according to Horowitz, to a lesson for social science research: "The use of a single victory as a model for behavior is risky, and the assumption that any one path to national change is the correct path is ludicrous."[34]

Third, he discusses the myth of national liberation in a very incisive analysis that may well explain one of the roots of Castro's ability to retain the loyalty of many of his followers. Going back into the last century, Horowitz comments on the collective sense of colonial dependency developed by the Cubans, which Castro exploited very effectively. "The revolutionary act, whatever its consequences, was seen as a unique ability to throw off the past, to eliminate a tradition of dependence upon foreign powers. This was heady wine."[35] It should be mentioned that, despite the fact that Cuba was more dependent on the Soviets than Castro and his admirers were ever willing to admit, this factor or myth may make the collapse of the Soviet Union a favorable force for Castro's leadership at present, despite the hardships that entails. It reinforces Castro's image as the symbol of Cuba's independence and nationalism, a factor that still plays an important role in Castro's appeal to many in Cuba.

The fourth myth commented on by Horowitz is that of the social accomplishments of the revolution. As he has done in previous essays, he points out that Castro started from a fairly advanced social base, at least in the context of Latin American development. Then, he goes on to point out some facts about health and educational attainments that raise some questions on the magnitude of the revolution's accomplishments in these aspects of Cuban society, without ignoring that significant progress has been attained.

Finally, he discusses the myth of moral man. After commenting on the exploitation of Guevara's death as a symbol to encourage sacrifice, he goes on to point out that this is used to extract more labor without pay from the population and to justify the loss of autonomy and freedom in a paralysis of political activity. In conclusion, Horowitz states that

> the myth of moral man remains a way to mobilize people, even as a general demobilization takes place in the political realm.... The resilience of twentieth-century totalitarianism, a century in which heroes are suspect and expectations have turned sour, inheres in the ability of leaders such as Castro to convince the masses that suffering is divine while affluence is sinful.[36]

Since Castro has tried to portray mobilization as the equivalent of political participation, and many intellectuals of the left have been willing to accept such an interpretation, Horowitz has made a substantial contribution to the demythologizing of Castro's regime with this formulation.

This lecture provides us the last chapter in the evolution of the thoughts of Irving Horowitz on the Cuban Revolution. Although this document contains some themes that have been present throughout his coverage of the Cuban Revolution, it constitutes a totally new presentation of Horowitz's thoughts on the subject, enriched by his own research and learning from the revolutionary process. In that respect, it is an excellent example of the impact the Cuban Revolution has had "in transforming theories about societies," as Horowitz commented in the preface to the sixth edition of *Cuban Communism*.

This review of the evolution of Irving Louis Horowitz's writings on Cuba and its revolution covers only a portion of his work. Space and time limitations do not allow a deeper coverage of Horowitz's prolific output on Cuba. Therefore, this is far from an exhaustive treatment of the subject. There are other Cuba-related topics that he has discussed in depth, which are only mentioned in passing here, such as militarization, and others that have not even been discussed in passing, such his expansion of the concept of genocide to include imprisonment and forcing people to live in exile,[37] in which Horowitz's contribution is extremely relevant to an understanding of the magnitude of the tragedy that has been the Cuban Revolution.

Finally, many Cuban-American social scientists have benefited from Irving Horowitz's generous support and encouragement. We have always found him willing to contribute gladly his time and efforts to enlighten us on the issue of Cuba from the broad perspectives of sociological research. Let this contribution to his festschrift be a modest expression of our gratitude. I hope it does justice to his work.

Trade and Economic Development Associates, Washington, D.C.
Office of the Director

Notes

1. Irving Louis Horowitz, "Looking Backwards: A Postscript to the Seventh Edition," in *Cuban Communism*, 7th ed., ed. Irving Louis Horowitz (New Brunswick, NJ: Transaction Publishers, 1989), 841.
2. Ibid.

3. Irving Louis Horowitz, "The Stalinization of Fidel Castro," *New Politics* 4, no. 4 (1965): 61–69.

4. Ibid., 67.

5. Horowitz, "Stalinization," 63.

6. Irving Louis Horowitz, "Introduction: Second Edition," *Cuban Communism*, 3d ed., ed. Irving Louis Horowitz (New Brunswick, NJ: Transaction Publishers, 1977), 12.

7. Ibid.

8. Ibid., 14.

9. Ibid.

10. Irving Louis Horowitz, "Institutionalization as Integration: The Cuban Revolution at Age Twenty," in *Cuban Studies/Estudios Cubanos* 9, no. 2 (July 1979): 84–90.

11. Ibid, 85.

12. Ibid., 86.

13. Ibid., 89.

14. Irving Louis Horowitz, "Introduction to the Fourth Edition," in *Cuban Communism*, 4th ed., ed. Irving Louis Horowitz (New Brunswick, NJ: Transaction Publishers, 1981), 2.

15. Ibid., 3.

16. Irving Louis Horowitz, "Introduction," *Cuban Communism*, 5th ed., ed. Irving Louis Horowitz (New Brunswick, NJ: Transaction Publishers, 1984), 2.

17. Ibid., 3.

18. Irving Louis Horowitz, "Preface," in *Cuban Communism*, 6th ed., ed. Irving Louis Horowitz (New Brunswick, NJ: Transaction Publishers, 1987), xiv.

19. Cuban American National Foundation, *The Cuban Revolution at Thirty* (Washington, DC, 1989), Occasional Paper #29.

20. Irving Louis Horowitz, "Looking Forward," in *Cuban Communism*, 7th ed., ed. Irving Louis Horowitz (New Brunswick, NJ: Transaction Publishers, 1989), xv.

21. Ibid., 16–17.

22. Ibid., 24–25.

23. Irving Louis Horowitz, *The Conscience of Worms and the Cowardice of Lions: The Cuban-American Experience, 1959–1992* (Miami: The North South Center, University of Miami, 1993).

24. Ibid., i.

25. Ibid., 1–13.

26. Ibid., 10.

27. Ibid., 11.

28. Ibid., 28.

29. Ibid., 35–52.

30. Ibid., 41.

31. Ibid., 53–71.

32. Ibid., 55.

33. Ibid., 57.

34. Ibid., 60.

35. Ibid., 61.

36. Ibid., 69.

37. Irving Louis Horowitz, *Genocide: State Power and Mass Murder* (New Brunswick, NJ: Transaction Publishers, 1976).

17

Successful Inferences and Mutating Views: Horowitz's Writings on Socialist Cuba's Domestic and Foreign Policies

Carmelo Mesa-Lago

Cuban studies and immigrant scholars are in debt to Irving Louis Horowitz. He was an early critic of some flaws of the revolution at a time when such criticism was virtually nonexistent and considered anathema by the left. His analysis contributed to the legitimization of the work of Cuban-American academics, which was then rejected outright as biased or inconsequent by uncritical supporters of the revolution: "Any analysis is suspect and scrutinized from the standpoint of the analyst instead of how well it explains the Cuban system" (Horowitz, 1975a). He also opened the door of *Society* and *Studies in Comparative Development* to Cuban-American scholars and praised our work, favorably contrasting it with that produced on the island and that of many U.S. and European intellectuals (Horowitz, 1975b, 1989a, 1993). Last but not least, part of Horowitz's oeuvre has stood the passage of time; this is remarkable in view of the numerous zigzags of Cuban policy in thirty-five years and the radical transformation of the socialist world in the last quinquennium.

Personally I have several reasons to be grateful to Horowitz. He published (and reprinted) one of my first essays on Cuba in a collection that included articles by well-known U.S. liberal social scientists and sympathizers of the revolution, such as Maurice Zeitlin, Richard Fagen, and Joseph Kahl. My piece was the most critical in that collection, but in that company I earned the reputation of being *un gusano inteligente* (a shrewd worm—in reference to the pejorative term applied to exiles by the Cuban government and sympathizers abroad). Horowitz (1975b) also authored the most favorable review published on one of my books—although it was not exempt from criticism (which will be further discussed later). Finally, he has been a contributor to my edited books and the journal/yearbook *Cuban Studies,* while various essays of mine have been reprinted in the seven editions of his successful compilation *Cuban Communism.*

In view of what I've said above, the temptation to write a eulogy of Horowitz's work was compelling and it was reinforced by the persuasive fact that he is a formidable opponent in debate. In a recent article on festschrifts, Horowitz recommended that if the contribution to such book was "contentious and argumentative, then the person being honored should have the right of rebuttal and response." And yet, in the same piece he showed that the festschrift could be boring, an editorial failure. He therefore exhorted the contributors to such endeavor to stimulate "further work, effort and energy" by the honored author, which could result in "the improvement of learning or an intellectual position" (Horowitz, 1990). In the end I decided to evaluate his work with a critical albeit friendly eye: praising significant contributions but identifying flaws in his work as well.

Three salient characteristics of Horowitz's work are: the enormous variety of the topics he has studied, his habit of rapidly putting his thoughts into print instead of waiting until "everything is perfect," and his tendency to discuss sensible topics with self-confidence and daring—even irritating—views (Becker, 1984). The application of such approach to the highly politicized and ideologically polarized subject of the Cuban Revolution, with its numerous shifts in doctrine and domestic-foreign policies for more than three decades, logically led Horowitz to success and notoriety but also to errors and controversy, as well as changes in his viewpoints.

Horowitz has addressed some of those thorny issues sometimes candidly, other times humorously and also cryptically. In a recent publication on Cuba he stated: "In doing my work...I have been guided by [the] motto: To err is human but it feels divine! I mean this motto in a literal sense. The preparation of seven editions of a book *[Cuban Communism]* should convince anyone that events change and alter opinions and appraisals.... [I]deologies like research require modification"

(Horowitz, 1989b). Referring to the same issue in a global review of his work, he acknowledged that: "Many times...I have been asked how I have changed over the years." He then specified that such a question implied, more than a simple alteration of his point of view, "a failure to keep path with progressive tides" or even worse "a turn away from first principles." Although he rejected that charge, he now acknowledges the viewing of his earliest principles "as covering a much wider and different terrain than I first imagined." And he concludes : "What changes over time is to which individuals or collectives one or another set of terms of opprobrium or approval is applied, but not the passionate convictions as such" (Horowitz, 1984).

Major Themes in Horowitz's Work

In 1965–93 Horowitz published more than forty works on Cuba, counting translations, reprints, and multiple editions. He has indeed covered much terrain and a wide diversity of topics, which could be divided into two major clusters: (1) analyses of internal features of the revolution, such as Stalinization, militarization, institutionalization, and authenticity versus autonomy; and (2) studies of Cuba's foreign policy, particularly the exportation of the revolution and its relations with the United States.

The Stalinization of the Revolution

Stalinization was the topic of Horowitz's first essay on Cuba, published in 1965 and updated in 1971. According to him, between 1966 and 1969, Castro's statements and policies bore the contention that he accepted the premises of Stalinism. This was mainly a result of Castro's own personality but was exacerbated by the hostile U.S. policy against the island, which provided the milieu for such negative features to flourish (Horowitz, 1965, 1977a). To prove his hypothesis, Horowitz pinpointed several common features of Castro's Cuba and Stalin's Soviet Union:

- The shift to left wing domestic nationalism: the survival of the revolution in both countries required its consolidation and development at home at the price of abandoning revolution abroad. In addition, Castro's attitude toward other revolutionaries in Latin America also resembled Stalin's:

patronizing when they agreed with him and censorious when they did not.

- The bureaucratization of the Cuban Communist party (PCC) personally controlled by Castro who became the party's exclusive spokesman and also concentrated the top positions in the government and the army, as well as the subordination of society to the party state and this, in turn, to Castro.
- The politics of purge, dismemberment of any possible opposition, elimination of politico-economic debate and socialist democracy (both subordinated to a single developmental strategy set by Castro) and the militarization of society and institutions including the party.
- The removal of the heads of the right and left wings of the revolution and the centralization of control by the Maximum leader: in Cuba the dismissal of pro-Soviet economist Carlos Rafael Rodriguez and the departure of Guevara—Cuba's Trotsky—in the mid-1960s.
- The surrounding of the revolutionary state by powerful hostile forces (the United States in the Cuban case) and the impossibility of normalizing trade with the capitalist bloc; these two factors provided a rationale for the inward concentration on development and defense, as well as the repressive measures.
- The politics of massive labor mobilization of a military type in both countries (toward industry in the Soviet Union and sugar in Cuba) regardless of their economic costs and consequences.
- Finally, Castro's attack on and break with China in 1966, which took place at the same time that Soviet ideologists were resuming their condemnation of both Trotskyism and the need for permanent revolution (an idea then supported by the Chinese leadership) while arguing that the peaceful coexistence strategy did not imply capitulation.

But Horowitz noted differences between Castro and Stalin, for example, charismatic versus bureaucratic styles. Furthermore, he identified a series of unique physical conditions in Cuba that led to more divergent outcomes than in the Soviet Union: Cuba is a small island facing severe limits on key natural resources (e.g., oil and coal) and lacking the basis for heavy industrialization and crop diversification. (In addition, he noted questionable sociological barriers, such as the absence of a strong proletarian tradition and peasant dominance.) These restrictions forced the abandonment of the first industrialization program (1959–63) and a return to agricultural prominence and the central role of sugar ("single-crop socialism"). These problems—Horowitz argued—would impede the economic development of the island and increase the potential for extreme repression over time. Furthermore, Cuba's domestic limitations would restrain its external involvement as well: while the Soviet Union has had "immense international significance," Cuba has "little possibility of performing a world role"; the Cuban Revolution has a poor "chance of becoming hemispheric in nature."

Horowitz's essay was criticized by Ian Lumsden (1966) who, although accepting a few of his points (the bureaucratization of the party and Castro's control), unsuccessfully tried to disprove the alleged features of Stalinism in Cuba. Some of Lumsden's marginal arguments, however, were well taken: (*a*) there was a strong proletariat in Cuba even prior to the revolution (shown by a high degree of unionization and urbanization) instead of a "peasant dominance" (an aspect proven in Zeitlin's work and my own); (*b*) terror under Stalin had no parallel in the Cuba of the 1960s; (*c*) Castro's internationalism was proven by its solidarity with Vietnam; and (*d*) Cuba had indeed attempted to trade with capitalist countries as a means of reducing dependence on the Soviet Union, thus in 1964 one-third of Cuban trade was with market economies (40 percent in 1975; Mesa-Lago, 1993).

Lumsden's points were dismissed by Horowitz (1966) in a rebuttal in which he sustained that: (*a*) his opponent confused industrialization with urbanization, not the same in Cuba, which remained an agricultural society; (*b*) Horowitz's position did not rest on the quantum of terror as uniquely defining Stalinism, but moved beyond it to focus on structural politico-economic factors; (*c*) support to faraway Vietnam hid the fact that Castro had failed to support the 1965 insurrection in the Dominican Republic and condemned Guatemalan and Venezuelan revolutionaries because they did not agree with him; and (*d*) one-third of Cuba's trade with market economies was measured in cash transactions but would be less if barter trade with socialist countries had been taken into account. I disagree with most of these counterarguments, particularly the last one, because Cuba's barter trade with socialist countries was indeed measured in both pesos and rubles. But I tend to concur with Horowitz's blunt conclusion: what made his opponent so upset was not principally a matter of fact but sentiment; Lumsden disliked the analogy between Castroism and Stalinism in the same manner that communists in the 1930s criticized the comparison of Stalin and Hitler (Horowitz, 1966).

Horowitz's rebuttal to Lumsden prompted threats of ostracism, accusations of betrayal, and admonitions from the left that his criticism was premature. Reflecting on that last point twenty-five years later, he ruminated: "For such cautious, timorous voices who speak with the spent force of a dead metaphysic, the time for criticism or breaking ranks is always premature" (Horowitz, 1989b).

Even before the collapse of socialism in Eastern Europe and the Soviet Union, Horowitz's first essay on Cuba proved to be correct on two points: the failure of the revolution to diversify the economy and break away from "single-crop socialism," and the increase in domestic political control and repression. In the early 1990s the grave economic crisis on the island had exacerbated those two problems (which will be discussed below in the section entitled "Authenticity and Autonomy of the Revolution"). But Horowitz's assertion that Castro had halted the exportation of the revolution (actually this happened in 1970-75 not in 1966-69, as he argued, see below the section entitled "The Exportation of the Cuban Revolution") and his prediction that the island would not play a significant world role were contradicted by actual events from the mid-1970s through the end of the 1980s: for instance, Cuba's military victories in Africa, its support of the triumphant Sandinista revolution in Nicaragua, and Castro's leadership in the Non-Aligned Movement. These events would force Horowitz to change his interpretation and acknowledge Cuban support for insurgency in Latin America and elsewhere. Still his forecast that the revolution would not spread throughout Latin America was on target. Furthermore, in the long run, Cuba's costly military interventions and subversion abroad proved to be helpless in maintaining sympathetic regimes or leading revolutionary movements to power except for a short period .

In one of his most recent works Horowitz (1989a) maintains that Castro is the last Stalinist and pure Leninist, and properly argues that the Cuban leader's stubborn resistance to Gorbachev-style politico-economic reforms is explicable by his fear that they would put in motion forces threatening both his personalistic style of rule and the revolution itself.

The Militarization Process

In several essays Horowitz (1965, 1967, 1971, 1975a, 1977b, 1983) argued that there has been an increasing militarization of the revolution, government, party, and society, and that such a process has been more important and occurred faster in Cuba than in any other nation in Latin America.

Both domestic and external factors—according to him—explain the militarization process: (*a*) the origin of the revolution mainly fought by military or paramilitary guerrillas; (b) the fact that Cuban society is part of the Third World (and particularly Latin America) where militarism is a common element; (c) the limitations of the Cuban economy (single-crop socialism in a small island); (d) the need to defend the revolution against U.S. hostility and threats; (e) the military support of revolutionary movements and regimes abroad (this factor, however, is not always included by Horowitz); and (f) Cuba's role as an "outpost of the USSR, or agent of Soviet foreign policy."

I do agree with Horowitz's central hypothesis (militarization) and its causes, except for the last one. Actually, Horowitz's stand on this issue has not been consistent; for instance, he has also said that after the missile crisis of 1962 the Soviet Union and the United States realized that "Cuba was not a pawn...but a sovereign power in its own right" (Horowitz, 1977b). There is a fair scholarly consensus in the sense that, until recently, Cuba was one of the socialist countries most economically dependent on the Soviet Union, but at the same time one of the most politically independent. Domestically, Cuba confronted the Soviet Union in 1966-70, enforcing an antagonistic economic model (resembling Mao's), claiming that the island was more advanced in the construction of socialism than the mother of communism, and imprisoning pro-Soviet prerevolutionary communists (the "microfaction"). In military affairs Cuba's involvement in Latin America and the Caribbean was done with a high degree of autonomy, and, in some periods, against the local pro-Soviet Communist parties (the last point has been acknowledged by Horowitz, 1967). Although Cuba's involvement in Africa was performed in conjunction with the Soviet Union, the initiative was taken by the Cubans in the case of Angola, although probably by the Soviets in the Somali-Ethiopian war. One could agree that Cuba's actions in Africa contributed to an increase of Havana's leverage in economic dealings with Moscow, but it would be hard to accept Horowitz's stance that the demilitarization of the island could occur only if called for by the Soviet Union. I will grant, nevertheless, that in 1971-85 (the "Sovietization" period) Cuba's model of economic organization, its political structure and voting pattern at international organizations (e.g., at the United Nations) became quite close to those of the Soviet Union. And yet, even in this period, Cuba had more political independence from Moscow than the Eastern European regimes, except for Romania, and Castro continued to dominate the political system of the island. Finally, in 1986-92 Castro rejected glasnost and perestroika while his economic and military links with the former Soviet Union steadily declined and virtually vanished. At the same time, the process of domestic militarization increased, obviously not as an outpost of the Russians but to control any potential internal rebellion (Mesa-Lago, 1978, 1982, 1993).

But if I disagree with Horowitz on the point discussed above, I basically concur with the elements that he earlier identified as proof of both the existence of militarization and its growing trend in Cuba: (a) the enormous size of the military forces, both in absolute and in per capita terms (he estimated a total of 250,000 men in the mid-1970s (the largest in Latin America after Brazil but the latter's population is more than ten times that of Cuba); (b) the significant growth in military professionalization and specialization since the early 1970s (e.g., the elimination of the nonprofessional militia, the increasing number of domestic military academies and Cuban military personnel trained in the Soviet Union and other Eastern European countries, and the establishment of a military hierarchy as well as ranks equivalent to those in the Soviet armed forces and other countries); (c) the quantity, sophistication, and increment in military hardware supplied mostly by the Soviet Union as well as East Germany and Czechoslovakia; (d) the militarization of the party and practical fusion of the armed forces, the government, and the party (at the end of the 1960s Horowitz calculated that 66 percent of the Central Committee members were military and all except two were members of the Politburo); (e) the militarization of agricultural work in 1966–70; (f) the use of militarized micro brigades in housing construction (this practice was discontinued in 1976–85 but reintroduced in 1986); (g) the establishment of militarized elementary and secondary schools ("Lenin" school being the most outstanding example) and the organization of a "Youth Labor Army" to work in agriculture and other tasks; and (h) the intervention by military means—directly or through subversion and aid—in other countries of Latin America, Africa, and Asia (an extraordinary role in relation to Cuba's population).

In the 1980s and early 1990s, there has been significant new elements of militarization that could not be accounted for by Horowitz in his earlier works. For instance, the share of defense and security expenditures in the Cuban budget increased from 5.4 percent to 10.2 percent in 1981–89. In 1991 the armed forces had grown to 300,000 members, the Ministry of Interior had another 83,000, and the territorial troop militia (created in 1981) counted 1.5 million members, for a total personnel close to 2 million, roughly one military person per five inhabitants of the island (excluding the Committees for the Defense of the Revolution, which perform spy functions). All the "forces of order" were unified in 1992 into one single command under Castro. In addition, there has been: a revival of the construction of micro brigades and the establishment of new militarized work "contingents"; the organization of "rapid response brigades" to physically attack opponents; the use of military troops to protect food warehouses and crops from robbery by the population; the increasing use of students—organized, controlled, and sanctioned in military fashion—to work in key crops and the construction of hundreds of tunnels for defense; and the presentation as a model for the civilian sector of the experiments on enterprise reform in manufacturing plants of the Ministry of the Armed Forces ("integral system of enterprise improvement"). This reform strengthens the power of state managers as "production sergeants" and reduces the role of workers to fulfill their labor duties. In the early 1990s, however, Cuba's military involvement abroad has diminished to a trifle (Mesa-Lago, 1993).

Institutionalization versus Castro's Personalism

In 1970 the failure of both Cuba's development strategy (the nonfulfillment of the 10-million ton sugar harvest goal and subsequent economic chaos) and the model of economic organization pursued since 1966 (the Guevarist dream of forging a "new man" through mobilization, education, and moral stimulation) led to a severe economic crisis. Castro's charismatic personalistic and centralized style of government was tainted by such double failure and hence politico-economic changes began to take place.

A good number of experts on Cuba, including myself, sustained that in the 1970s Cuba appeared to be moving toward a more pragmatic and institutionalized form of government and policy-making. I identified a series of elements that seemed to indicate an institutionalization process: the enactment in 1976 of the first socialist political constitution; the introduction of Soviet-style elections (at the national, provincial, and local levels) to select delegates to the newly established Organs of Popular Power or OPPs (including a new National Assembly); steps to separate the administration, party, and armed-forces functions; reorganization of the party, expansion of its membership and celebration of its first congress; revamping of trade unions and other mass organizations, such as the National Association of Private Farmers (ANAP) and the Union of the Communist Youth (UJC); professionalization, specialization, and introduction of new ranks in the armed forces; institutionalization of relations with the Soviet Union (Cuba's entry into the Council of Mutual Economic Assistance, establishment of permanent bilateral commissions with the Soviet Union); reestablishment of relations with several Latin American countries and opening of diplomatic conversations and exchanges with the USA; and launching of a new model of economic organization, the System of Planning and Management of the Economy (SDPE), fundamentally based on the Soviet model. The SDPE was directed by technocrats and relied on more "objective" mechanisms such as material incentives and a limited use of market tools (Mesa-Lago, 1978, 1981).

Horowitz (1979) focused on a different set of elements to assess institutionalization: (a) existence of a mechanism to guarantee a stable succession; (b) change in the political leadership and allowance of new political parties as well as mass political participation; (c) transfer of power from military to civilian authorities; and (d) more independence from the Soviet Union. He then rejected the existence of these four elements in Cuba: (a) Castro continued to be the undisputed leader (Horowitz dismissed the legalization of Castro's brother Raul as his successor for being "a short-term solution"); (b) there was neither party plurality nor mass political participation; (c) the military prominence continued unabated and there was no separation but integration of a modernized military and the party apparatus; and (d) Cuba's dependence on the Soviet Union reached new heights. According to him, it was only the political culture that became institutionalized as the regime stopped being experimental and was "locked into the Soviet model" leading to the emergence of a new technocracy, concentration of authority in the military-party, authoritarianism, and intolerance with any opposition.

One could argue that Horowitz's set of elements was more adequate to judge democratization—within the framework of a multiparty system and political freedoms—than institutionalization. For instance, the now defunct Soviet regime was indeed institutionalized (within a totalitarian framework) but it provided a proper mechanism neither for succession nor for party pluralism or mass participation in politics. Equally, increasing Cuban dependence on Moscow could hardly be used as a measurement of institutionalization except for Horowitz's idea—which I share—that such dependency led to Cuba's locking into the Soviet bureaucratic-totalitarian model and alas institutionalization albeit not democratic.

Horowitz (1975b) criticized my work on Cuba's institutionalization as "naive and romantic" because—according to him—I suggested there was "a slow transformation from socialist dependence [on the Soviet Union] to a democratic independent system." This assertion is surprising as my book reached precisely the opposite conclusions. Half of the first chapter was devoted to prove that, since 1971, Cuba became increasingly economically dependent on Moscow—the so-called "Sovietization of the Cuban Revolution" thesis, that thereafter became a subject of criticism by Cubans and foreign Marxist scholars alike. The bulk of the book discussed which type of institutionalization was really taking place in Cuba; for that purpose, I contrasted two opposite trends: one toward decentralization and democracy and another toward centralization and rigidity. In order to answer which of the two trends was prevailing, I studied the most important Cuban institutions, reaching the following conclusions: (a) both in the Constitution and in practice, Castro's central political role was confirmed as he concentrated the direction of the state, the government, the party, and the armed forces; (b) the new institutions established were remarkably similar to those in the Soviet Union but with more concentration of power in Cuba; (c) the National Assembly was a rubber-stamp agency of the executive and the OPPs' functions at the provincial and local levels were significantly limited; (d) there was no true popular representation in the party, as 80 percent of the population was neither a member of the PCC nor the UJC; (e) the power of state managers was strengthened, the unions' least important function became the defense of workers' interests, and state control over the workers was tightened; (f) government pressure on small private farmers increased and their fate was total absorption by the state; (g) control of youth behavior, fashions, ideas, and political views was toughened; (h) military camps were used to clamp down on "antisocial behavior"; and (i) the Congress on Education and Culture introduced a more dogmatic line and ended with the imprisonment and ultimate confession of the famous poet Heberto Padilla, followed by a clamp down on intellectuals and artists. My final conclusion was that despite the new institutions and rules, Cuban institutionalization followed in real life the Soviet model, characterized by central control, dogmatism, administrative-bureaucratic features, limited mass participation, and strengthened government controls over workers, small farmers, the youth, and intellectuals (Mesa-Lago, 1978).

In summary, I agree with Horowitz that since the 1970s Cuba became increasingly dependent on the Soviet Union (particularly on economic grounds) and copied many of that nation's politico-economic institutions. But I also believe that in 1971–85, there was a process of institutionalization in Cuba, casted in the Soviet die and characterized by continued centralization of decision-making power and without a democratic opening (these last two features accepted by Horowitz). And yet, a comparison of Cuba's institutions and style of government in 1966–70 (the idealist period), 1971–85 (institutionalization a la Soviet), and 1986 on (Rectification Process) are significantly different. In 1966–70 Castro practically directly controlled the economy, there was virtually no planning, and key decisions were made in a personalistic and subjective manner. Conversely, in 1971–85 Castro's economic powers were somewhat reduced: there was an increasing control of the economic apparatus by the technocracy, the central plan became the key economic tool, and there was a modest process of decentralization in economic decision making. The Rectification Process set in motion in the mid-1980s has been the instrument used by Castro to get rid of the technocracy, reverse the institutionalization process, and fully retake his personalistic control of the economy, as he did in 1966–70, leading the country to a grave crisis (see next section).

Authenticity and Autonomy of the Revolution

In an attempt to produce a general assessment of the nature of the Cuban Revolution, Horowitz (1976) identified internal and external factors that respectively determined the authenticity of such a revolution and the limits to its autonomy. Five domestic conditions found in Cuba differentiate an authentic revolution from "spurious political alterations" as a coup d'etat: (*a*) the destruction (actually exile) of a social class (the bourgeoisie) and transfer of its power to the revolutionary state; (*b*) the elimination of "social evils" such as prostitution, drug traffic, gambling, illiteracy, and poverty; (*c*) the eradication of huge class differences and universalization of employment, health care, education, and social security, social services that became the responsibility of the state; and (d) the elimination of racial supremacy and drive toward racial equality (Horowitz correctly acknowledges, however, that although "now blacks have some leadership...the Cuban government is still predominantly white.")

Horowitz concluded that the Cuban Revolution is authentic, but its autonomy is limited by factors that are beyond or outside the control of its leaders: (a) being relatively small in size and an island, Cuba has not been capable of exercising significant influence and hemispheric expansion; (b) both goals were made even more difficult to reach in the 1960s by the shift of the largest Latin American countries—Brazil and Argentina—to the right (in contrast, the Soviet Union and China, being the largest nations in Europe and Asia, were able to reach those goals); (c) Cuba's adventurism and romanticism about the replicability and exportability of its revolution did more to frighten off Latin American support (and increase U.S. opposition) than to get new adherents; (d) the revolution's confinement to Cuba, the single-crop island economy and the U.S. threat forced Cuba to compromise its autonomy in exchange for military and economic protection from the Soviet Union (hence Cuba shifted from the American to the Soviet orbit with only marginal improvement); and (e) because of such dependence, Cuba became increasingly identified with Soviet foreign policy (e.g., breaking diplomatic and economic relations with Israel, supporting the Soviet invasion of Czechoslovakia).

At the beginning of this chapter, I contested Horowitz's view that the Cuban Revolution was a Soviet outpost unable to exercise significant influence abroad. I concur with the rest of his 1976 analysis on autonomy, but both internal developments in Cuba and the collapse of communism in Europe have changed somewhat his conclusions on the authenticity of the revolution (he briefly touches on some of these changes in Horowitz, 1989a, 1993). In 1986 Castro launched the Rectification Process (RP), which has set Cuba against the worldwide socialist trend of market-oriented reform. The RP lacks an integrated economic-organization model but has further restrained the tiny domestic private sector (albeit encouraged foreign investment, particularly in tourism), curtailed material incentives, tightened labor controls, and expanded mobilization for agricultural work. Although the RP has not moved Cuba completely back to the idealistic approach of 1966–70, it certainly has placed that country in the most antimarket stand in the world today.

Between 1989 and 1992 Soviet and Eastern European economic aid to Cuba sharply declined and ceased altogether, while trade with Eastern Europe virtually stopped and commerce with the Soviet Union and then the Commonwealth of Russian Republics was reduced to probably one-third. The Council for Mutual Economic Assistance (the Soviet-dominated CMEA in which Cuba was a member) disappeared in 1991 and with it the "socialist world market," leaving only one (capitalist) world market. Cuba's trade with CMEA reached 84 percent of its total trade in 1988 (70 percent with the Soviet Union), while Soviet cumulative aid to Cuba alone in 1960–90 was $65 billion. The combination of the antimarket RP domestically and the halting of aid and trade with its former socialist partners has proven fatal to the Cuban economy. Although official estimates are not available, the economic decline in 1989–92 has been estimated to be from 30 percent to 50 percent. Soviet supply of oil and oil by-products declined at best to one-third in 1987–92. Half of the Cuban industrial plant is paralyzed, as well as from 75 percent to 90 percent of transportation in Havana (bicycles and oxen are now used for transportation and agricultural work). Rationing has been extended to all consumer goods and the rations reduced dramatically. Unemployment increased from 3 percent to 6 percent in 1981–88 and must be much higher now due to the economic paralysis (there is unemployment compensation but it is suspended if an offer to work in agriculture is not accepted). The most cherished social services provided by the revolution are now in jeopardy; for instance, there is a severe scarcity of drugs and other medical goods as well as of spare parts for equipment—which has affected the quality of health care—while pensions are grossly insufficient to buy goods in the black market (Mesa-Lago, 1993).

In trying to cope with the worst crisis under the revolution, the leadership in desperation has opened up the country for foreign investment especially in tourism. With the latter, some of the social evils of the past have returned, such as prostitution. Furthermore, hotels, restaurants, and beaches for foreign tourists are banned to the island's population thus creating an irritating inequality. Paradoxically, the Cuban leaders allow private ownership and the market to function in the foreign enclaves but stubbornly reject such practices in the domestic economy—another source of tension and discontent. The severe food scarcity has provoked a significant increase in crime, corruption, robbery and black-marketing. In the latter, prices are ten to twenty times the official price, hence, the lowest income groups cannot supplement their meager rations, buying in the black market. Conversely, the elite still maintains access to special stores, separate hospitals, cars, social clubs, recreational villas, and trips abroad. In 1989 the trial of General Ochoa and other top military and national security officers not only revealed the wide drug traffic but the appalling privileges enjoyed by the elite (Oppenheimer, 1992; Mesa-Lago, 1993).

In conclusion, dependency (poor autonomy) of Cuba on the Soviet Union partly made possible the exalted "authentic" features or social gains of the revolution but the new "independence" and subsequent crisis has harmed, reversed, or put in jeopardy many of those gains.

The Exportation of the Cuban Revolution

As in domestic affairs, Castro has followed zigzag policies on the exportation of revolution. In 1959-60 Cuba's ill-prepared expeditions sent to some Latin American countries were defeated. In 1961-63 Cuba was ousted from the Organization of American States (OAS) and became increasingly isolated in the Western Hemisphere; Castro reacted by supporting guerrillas in the region and collided with some Communist parties there. In 1963-66 Castro's more compromising attitude toward Communist parties led to an agreement on where to export the revolution and his inaction vis-à-vis U.S. counterrevolutionary activities in Latin America. In 1966-69 the theory of the rural guerrilla foco as the only path to revolution was elaborated, the Tricontinental Conference and the Organization of Latin American Solidarity (OLAS) were established to support revolution abroad, and Guevara organized a guerrilla foco in Bolivia, which he hoped would become the Cuban Sierra Maestra of the Andean mountain-range countries. In 1970-75 the exportation of the revolution virtually ended, nonguerrilla roads to socialism were accepted (the democratic election of Allende in Chile as well as the inception of left wing or nationalistic military regimes in Panama, Peru, and Bolivia), Havana reestablished relations with several Latin American countries of diverse ideologies, and the OAS freed its members to resume ties with Cuba (but also in this period Allende was over-thrown and leftist military regimes faded away). In 1975–89 Cuba militarily intervened in Angola and Ethiopia, sent military advisers to other African and Asian countries, supported the Sandinista insurrection in Nicaragua, as well as guerrillas in El Salvador and other Central American countries, and provided military aid to Grenada and Panama. In 1990–91 Cuba withdrew its troops from Africa, the Sandinistas were defeated in free elections, the regimes of Grenada and Panama were overthrown by U.S. intervention, and the guerrillas in El Salvador signed a peace pact with the government. Currently, Cuba is quite isolated and incapable of exporting revolution because the downfall of communist regimes in the Soviet Union and Eastern Europe has halted the supply of weapons and logistic support, and due to the island's grave economic crisis as well as the universal process of democratization and disarray of the left in Latin America (Mesa-Lago, 1978, 1982, 1983).

Horowitz has dealt with the issue of Cuba's exportation of the revolution in several essays but concentrated on the second half of the 1960s. In 1964, while in Mexico, he was engaged in a debate with Carlos Fuentes. Against the Mexican novelist's opinion that the Cuban Revolution would enhance a similar process throughout Latin America, Horowitz correctly maintained that Castro's increasing identification with the Soviet Union plus U.S. fears of a spreading revolution on the continent would make such a possibility remote. The *World Marxist Review* subsequently published an article accusing Horowitz of being a counterrevolutionary and defeatist (Horowitz, 1989b). In his first article published on Cuba, Horowitz expanded his previous views: The revolution would become more costly and difficult in Latin American countries because the Cuban threat has led to heightened counterrevolutionary programs by the United States and its Latin neighbors. The U.S. invasion and occupation of the Dominican Republic in 1965 to defeat a military insurrection allegedly of leftist ideology (an important point never fully proved) was intended also as a lesson for other potential revolutionaries in the region. Castro's response to the critiques about his lack of support of the Dominican leader Caamao during the U.S. intervention was that a Cuban action would have prompted a U.S. invasion of Cuba as well, and that every nation had to come to its own revolution in its own way, and in its own time. Horowitz ironically commented that Cuba had thus become a paper tiger, which made the real tiger (the

United States) more alert and effective. He also argued (as we saw earlier) that—in Stalinist fashion—Cuba had abandoned the support of revolution abroad in order to consolidate and develop its revolution at home (Horowitz 1965). Note that when this article was published, Cuba had taken (1963–66) a more compromising position and agreed to only selectively support revolution abroad, that is, in those countries where the probability of success was highest. But that policy would radically change with Castro's radicalization of the revolution in 1966–70. At that time he endorsed the idealistic Mao-Guevarist model of a "moral economy" (opposed to the mild market-oriented economic reform introduced in the Soviet Union in 1965), and became much more active in supporting revolution abroad (Mesa-Lago, 1978).

In his third article on Cuba, Horowitz (1967) explored the causes of the island's "immense tactical shift toward belligerence." It contradicted his previous assertion that a key element of Castro's Stalinization was the abandonment of the principle of "permanent revolution." Castro realized, argued Horowitz, that the traditional Communist party orthodoxy (in Cuba and Latin America) was an obstacle to accomplish his ideals, as it frustrated rather than fomented revolutionary action because of the following reasons: the party bureaucracy threatened the charismatic basis of Castro's leadership; the party orthodoxy would lead him not only to economic but ideological dependence on the Soviet Union (at a time when he was following a different economic model); the party's caution to get involved in real action would isolate Cuba from Latin American revolutionary movements; and the party's rigidity would smother revolutionary will and creativity while stressing doctrinal blueprints. Cuba's isolation in the hemisphere and the effective U.S. action in the Dominican Republic, as well as the increasing U.S. threat to Cuba, thought Horowitz, led Castro to change his belief in the viability of a revolution confined to the island and to reactivate the exportation of the revolution.

Following the previous reasoning, Castro liquidated the pre-revolutionary pro-Soviet old communist guard of the Cuban party. In the mid-1960s he started to remove the old communists from key positions of power and, in 1968, he put on trial, discredited, and imprisoned the so-called microfaction, thus completing his objective.

Castro confronted the Soviet orthodox long-range view—expressed by history rather than by action—that the deterioration of capitalism would take place as its own internal contradiction became aggravated. (At the time Khruschev's doctrine of peaceful coexistence was reinforced by Brezhnev.) He held instead an unorthodox short-range view of revolutionary action to accelerate the process of capitalist downfall (what happened in Cuba could be replicated in Latin America). Hence, Castro opposed historical determinism ad inaction with free will and action. Mao-Guevara-Debray's theory of the guerrilla rural foco would provide him with the doctrinal basis for his strategy. The insurrection would be led by a vanguard elite with a highly developed consciousness (the guerrillas) instead of the urban party bureaucracy; once the revolution triumphed, the guerrillas, instead of the party bureaucracy, would control power. Such approach was labeled "revolution within the revolution." Guevara and Castro also called for "many Vietnams" in Latin America to make more difficult a victory of U.S. imperialism over revolutionary forces (Horowitz, 1967, 1975a).

The above explained strategy would alienate the Communist parties of Latin America and significantly contribute to Guevara's isolation in the Bolivian mountains and his eventual defeat by the local army that was trained in antiguerrilla warfare by the United States. Other Cuban-supported guerrillas also failed in Argentina, Guatemala, Peru, and Venezuela. Furthermore, an important belief, noted by Horowitz (1967), would not materialize: "that the USSR will never willingly stop supporting Cuba—no matter how resentful orthodox Latin American communist parties may become—or, for that matter, the Soviet Union itself." In 1968 the Soviet Union reduced the committed delivery of oil to the island, a clear indication that the Soviet leaders' patience had a limit. The Soviet invasion of Czechoslovakia provided an opportunity to Castro to mend the deteriorated relationship: he endorsed the invasion, although with rhetorical reservations. The Soviet Union reciprocated with increased aid and formalization of economic ties with Cuba. In 1970–75 Cuba's support of the revolutionary movement would virtually stop and, after 1970 (with the failures of the "moral economy" and the 10-million ton sugar production goal), there would be a gradual approximation to the Soviet economic model (Mesa-Lago, 1978).

Horowitz could have argued that Cuba's Stalinization feature of abandonment of the revolution abroad reappeared in 1970–75, but the new change in that Cuban policy in 1975–89 would have led him to another reversal in position. In fact, this issue is not readdressed in his later works. I have also contested his prediction that Cuba would not play a significant role in the world but praised his long-run correctness in forecasting the confinement of the revolution to Cuba. The point he made in 1967 is still valid in 1993: Despite all Cuban efforts and heavy costs, no government in Latin America has fallen so far as a result of guerrilla activities. Nicaragua was an exception for one decade, but the Sandinistas were voted out of power.

U.S. Relations with Cuba: To Normalize or to Harden

This is probably the issue on which Horowitz's views have changed most dramatically: from an early stand in favor of normalization (1969, 1971, 1977a) to one criticizing that side and endorsing the fulfillment of preconditions for that move (1978), to the most recent position advocating a tightening of the embargo (1993).

At the beginning of the Nixon presidency, Horowitz (1969) published his first article on U.S.-Cuban relations, proposing a program for normalization. At midpoint in Nixon's first administration (when detente with the Soviet Union and the rapprochement with China were taking place) Horowitz (1971) advanced the idea that an agreement between Nixon and Castro might occur—shocking from the point of view of revolutionaries but not from the logic of Cuba's Stalinist position. Actually, this view—which appears so odd today—might have resulted from Castro's early hope for the possibility of a change in U.S. policy with the new president (an attitude he has normally taken each time the U.S. administration has changed except for Reagan's). Furthermore, among some U.S. political circles it was speculated that Nixon was in a good position to reestablish relations with Cuba—as he was doing with China—because being a conservative Republican, his intentions could not be suspect. But subsequent events resulted in a frontal confrontation between the two leaders, eliminating any possibility of rapprochement.

During the Ford presidency, there were secret diplomatic negotiations between the two countries. In 1975 the U.S. Congress lifted a previous ban on subsidiaries abroad to trade with Cuba, and the OAS freed their members (with U.S. acquiescence) to reestablish diplomatic and trade relations with the island. The trend toward rapprochement was stopped because of Cuba's intervention in Angola. When President Carter took over, he resumed (openly) the negotiations with Castro and, as a result, "interest diplomatic sections" were opened in both countries. A third essay by Horowitz on this subject was completed in 1975 but not published until two years later (Horowitz, 1977a).

The first and third articles already cited basically reinforced and complemented each other, and there were no significant differences between them, except that the third was slightly more cautious and less optimistic. Horowitz sustained that the principal arguments against normalizing U.S. relations with Cuba did not hold: (*a*) Castro had not been successful in exporting the revolution to Latin America, and there were even doubts that he was trying to do so at the end of the 1960s; (*b*) the U.S. embargo had not succeeded in overthrowing the Cuban regime and, since 1975, it had been relaxed; and (*c*) Cuba was no longer a significant threat to the United States. Normalization of relations, Horowitz argued, would benefit all three parties involved. The United States would gain a reduction of Cuban dependency on the Soviet Union and a nonmilitary solution to the confrontation with a hostile power close to home. Cuba would see an easing of trade and travel restrictions, a reduced military budget (based on the assurance of no U.S. aggression), and a lessening of dependence on the Soviet Union. And the Soviet Union would profit from a reduction of its costly aid to Cuba. But he noted some obstacles to rapprochement within the United States: the powerful lobby of 1 million Cuban exiles who "clearly confine if not define" the U.S. posture toward Cuba, and American fears that Castro might continue a close relationship with the Soviet Union and reactivate his support to revolution in Latin America. There were also obstacles within Cuba: the extraordinary animosity of their leaders against the United States, and reluctance to allow the latter to go back to Cuba, via trade and tourism, because it would erode the anti-imperialist spirit of the revolution. The cornerstone of any future U.S. policy should be—said Horowitz (1969) supporting the view of liberal Brazilian Archbishop Helder Camara— that Cuba is "reintegrated into the Latin American community with due respect for her political option and acceptance of her autonomy as a sovereign nation." Finally, Horowitz outlined five steps to be taken under a scenario of normalization of relations: (*a*) reestablish U.S.-Cuban flights; (*b*) lift the U.S. ban on exports/imports to and from Cuba in exchange for indemnification to U.S. corporations' property confiscated by Cuba; (*c*) trade off the U.S. Navy base in Guantanamo for complete dismantling and removal of Soviet surface-to-air-missiles still installed on the island; (*d*) discuss, within the OAS, the reincorporation of Cuba and review the Inter-American Defense Treaty (perhaps including Cuba as a member); and (*e*) hold talks leading to full resumption of diplomatic relations (Horowitz, 1969). In the third article he expected the detente movement to be done with reserve and caution, and predicted a lengthy period of normalization intersected by continued ideological debate between the two sides (Horowitz, 1977a).

Castro's military intervention in the Ethiopian-Somali war was a slap in the face to the Carter administration as such action undermined the position of those U.S. officials who supported normalization while giving ammunition to those who argued that Cuba could not be trusted. Furthermore, Cuba's military support of Ethiopia allowed the latter's troops to crush the antigovernment Eritrean guerrillas who were fighting for independence and had previously been aided by Cuba. These events led to a U.S. halt in the process of rapprochement and a chilling in the relations between the two governments. (Later, the discovery of a Soviet military brigade in Cuba and the Soviet invasion of Afghanistan would revive the policies of hostility and confrontation.)

Horowitz's fourth article (1978) was published when the normalization trend had been already halted and he showed a dramatic shift in his position. He described a U.S. "Cuba Lobby" (in favor of normalization) as made up by two ideologically divergent groups: liberal senators and congressmen, and conservative businessmen. The latter were "the paramount group" whose only interest was to profit from Cuban trade. One senator even accepted, said Horowitz, that the U.S. resumption of diplomatic and trade relations would not alter Cuba's positions with respect to military intervention in Africa, close ties with the Soviet Union, and reluctance to fully pay for confiscated U.S. property.

Horowitz then proceeded to systematically present and criticize the arguments of the Cuba lobby in favor of normalization but, in doing so, he contradicted some of his own arguments published in 1969:

1. Normalization would open trade for the U.S.: He rejected it on the ground that Cuba's percentage of trade with capitalist economies was only 30 percent and declining (actually 40 percent in 1975 but 24 percent in 1980); the U.S. would have to fight for that small fraction.
2. The U.S. image in Latin America would be improved: He argued that some of the Latin countries (Bolivia, Guatemala, Venezuela) would not

like normalization and hence that such a decision should be discussed within the OAS.

3. There would be a free flow of people between the two countries: He contended there was "not one iota of evidence" that the Cubans would permit such a flow (from December 1978 to April 1980, however, the Cuban government allowed the visitation of 125,000 Cuban Americans and, in the spring of 1980, permitted an equal number of Cubans to leave by the Mariel port).

4. A reduction of Cuban military intervention abroad could result: He sustained that Cuba had repeatedly asserted its right to intervene on behalf of revolutionary movements and governments that called for its assistance (more to the point, Castro's massive intervention in Africa had taken place precisely when he was negotiating detente with the Ford and Carter administrations).

5. An opening of Cuban domestic politics could take place: He said that normalization would not automatically lead to political pluralism and civic freedoms in Cuba.

6. A turn in Cuba's tide, in favor of the United States and against the Soviet Union, could occur: He argued that Cuban policy of intervention in Africa was subservient to Soviet foreign policy and advanced Soviet influence in that continent, and hence, there was no reason for Castro to change it.

On the opposite side of the fence was an "anti-Cuba lobby" made up by a group of conservative senators who—according to Horowitz—conditioned the lifting of the U.S. embargo and resumption of diplomatic relations with Cuba to the previous fulfillment of four conditions: compensation of U.S.-confiscated property; withdrawal of Cuban military troops and advisers from Africa; release of U.S. prisoners and progress in the observance of human rights on the island; renewal of the 1973 antihijacking agreement (repealed by Castro); and provision of guarantees of future security for the U.S. Navy base in Guantanamo. He agreed with that stand and repeated his 1969 reasons for Castro not accepting a full normalization of relations, adding one more: with the disappearance of the U.S. threat and embargo, the Cuban leaders would lose a scapegoat for their domestic failures and a motive to rally the population against the Yankees (Horowitz, 1978).

In a series of lectures at the University of Miami in 1992, Horowitz presented his toughest stand against normalization. He said that the U.S. policy toward Cuba suffered from "procrastination and paralysis" due to the following five reasons: (a) a general U.S. public disdain for intervention especially in light of the Vietnam experience, as well as guilt over past adventures in the hemisphere combined with neo-isolationism (supported by the extreme left and right), all of which have led to a rejection of Monroeism; (*b*) the belief that Latin American countries are in control of their own destinies and that democracy will solve the Cuban threat by cauterization; (*c*) the idea that the U.S.-Soviet agreements reached during the Missile Crisis of 1962 impede the United States from intervening in Cuba; (*d*) the hope that Castro will fall as a result of the collapse of communism in Eastern Europe and the Soviet Union plus the grave economic crisis at home; and (*e*) the view that Cuba is no longer vital to U.S. interests and a threat to hemispheric peace. Horowitz argues that as long as the current paralysis continues, Castro will survive; hence, there should be an active, tough U.S. policy against Cuba based on three fronts: reassertion of the U.S. implacable opposition to Castro, tightening of the U.S. embargo, and constant struggle until the Communist regime is overthrown on the island (Horowitz, 1993).

One could argue that the U.S. policy toward Cuba—particularly under the Reagan and Bush administrations—has not been "paralyzed" but has become increasingly tougher: to the ban on travel to Cuba (except for humanitarian and research purposes) the U.S. Treasury added (early in the 1980s) the prohibition to spend money on the island; the U.S. government has put pressure on other countries to stop trade dealings with Cuba, particularly the buying of Cuban nickel and sugar; the United States has led an international campaign against Cuba's violation of human rights that culminated in a recent UN resolution condemning the regime; U.S. economic pressure on the Russians to stop all economic aid to the island was finally successful in 1992 when such aid was terminated; ; the amount of monetary remittances of Cuban exiles to their relatives in order for them to escape from the island as well as food packages have been limited; and in the fall of 1992 the U.S. Congress passed a bill signed by President Bush reintroducing the ban on U.S. subsidiaries abroad to trade with Cuba (Mesa-Lago, 1993).

Another debatable point in Horowitz's argument is that the United States is not intervening abroad because of the Vietnam syndrome and guilt resulting from past adventures in the hemisphere: the U.S. invasions of Grenada and Panama City (to abduct Noriega) as well as the Gulf War are contradictory evidence. And with the disappearance of the Soviet Union, the Kennedy-Khruschev agreements would not technically impede the United States from military intervention in Cuba. But such an action—virtually the only one left—not only would be extremely costly for the United States, as Horowitz acknowledged in the past, but could create a blood bath in Cuba, destroy a good part of whatever resources are left on the island, and provoke tremendous hostility against the United States, thus making the future transition to democracy extremely difficult.

The Cubans should solve the impasse by themselves and, as the economy deteriorates, Castro's image and his regime would suffer even more, hence increasing the possibility of a revolt. And yet, the current policies of the U.S. government and attitudes of the exile community do not help in achieving that end. Many in Cuba fear that Castro's downfall could result in the return of both U.S. domination and the social situation that existed in 1958. Those inside the island who could potentially lead a rebellion or a military coup do not really have an alternative vis-à-vis Castro: why should they risk their lives if there is no assurance that the powers to be would deal with them in a fair manner? And the majority of the population is afraid that the end of the regime would result in widespread unemployment, inflation, and even loss of the extremely poor housing they have. Cuban news media has widely diffused the problems confronted by the former communist countries in Eastern Europe and the former Soviet Union as well as the vindictiveness among some groups of exiles and their overall desire for restitution (for instance, the opening of a "real estate registry" in Miami for those who have claims, led to Cuban propaganda that the exiles would take away the homes of Cubans living on the island). Finally, even some Cuban dissidents have been critical of the embargo because of the hardships—such as food scarcity—that they attribute to it; the recent moves by the United States to cut food packages are resented even by opponents of Castro. Obviously, there is room for a more innovative and effective U.S. policy vis-à-vis Cuba but not necessarily in the direction of an indiscriminate tightening of the embargo or military intervention (Betancourt, 1992; Mesa-Lago, 1993).

A Final Assessment

Horowitz's contributions on Stalinization, militarization, and Sovietization of the Cuban Revolution have not only stood the passage of time, but have been reinforced by subsequent historical events. Some of his predictions have materialized; for instance, the revolution will become increasingly repressive and will not expand to the hemisphere, both trends explained by factors he identified quite early. His other forecasts were not as successful, for example, that Cuba did not have the capacity to exercise international influence; although in the last instance, he proved to be right on that score. In my view, the features he used to assess institutionalization were more adequate to measure democratization. And he erred on his assessment that Cuba was a Soviet outpost or was completely dominated by the Soviet Union; on this front, history seems to be on my side as Cuba has become the last communist warrior after the disappearance of the Soviet Union.

His views on domestic policies have been more stable than those on foreign policies. He quickly shifted his stand on the subject of the abandonment of Cuba's exportation of the revolution (to support revolution at home), but that was not surprising in view of Castro's zig-zag policies. Horowitz, however, did not modify his analysis of Stalinization of the revolution after such crucial feature was no longer present in Cuba. A more intriguing question pertains to the reasons for Horowitz's dramatic shifts on his position on U.S.-Cuban relations. The increasing authoritarian and repressive nature of the regime, as well as its Stalinization and militarization, could not be explanations because when he published his article in favor of normalization (1969), those features were obvious and had been previously analyzed by him. It is true that those negative features became even more salient thereafter, but that did not change the nature of the Cuban regime to justify his radical change in policy outlook. The increasing dependence on the Soviet Union was also pinpointed in Horowitz's writings in the 1960s, but the decline in "autonomy" became much more dramatic in the 1970s as he reported in 1976 and 1979. Finally, Castro's intervention in the Horn of Africa, in the midst of his negotiations with Carter, could have been another important factor in Horowitz's shift as the timing of his 1978 article suggests. Hopefully, he will clarify this issue in this festschrift or in his future works.

In summary, his balance sheet is positive. No minor accomplishment in such a difficult subject where so many "experts" have been seduced by mirages or have dreamed of miracles. He undoubtedly has been on the side of those who have been more critical than laudatory of Cuban socialism, and history and world opinion have ultimately joined our ranks.

University of Pittsburgh

Department of Economics

References

Becker, Howard S. "The Three Lives of Irving Louis Horowitz." In *Bibliography of the Writings of Irving Louis Horowitz,* pp. ix–xi. Privately printed, 1984.

Betancourt, Ernesto. "Prepared Statement…Before the Committee on Foreign Affairs U.S. House of Representatives." Washington, DC, April 1992.

Horowitz, Irving Louis. "The Stalinization of Fidel Castro." *New Politics* 4, no. 4 (1965): 61–69.

———. "Castrologists and Apologists: A Reply to Science in the Service of Sentiment." *New Politics* 5, no. 1 (1966): 27–34.

———. "Cuban Communism: Revolution within a Revolution." *Transaction/Society* 4, no. 10 (October 1967): 7–15, 55–57.

———. "United States-Cuban Relations: Beyond the Quarantine." *Transaction/Society* 6, no. 6 (April 1969): 43–47.

———. "The Political Sociology of Cuban Communism." In *Revolutionary Change in Cuba,* ed. Carmelo Mesa-Lago, 127–41. Pittsburgh: University of Pittsburgh Press, 1971.

———. "Military Origins of the Cuban Revolution." *Armed Forces and Society* 1, no. 4 (August 1975a): 402–18.

———. "Cuba Libre? Social Science Writings on Postrevolutionary Cuba, 1959–1975." *Studies in Comparative International Development* 10, no. 1 (Fall 1975b): 101–23.

———. "Authenticity and Autonomy in the Cuban Experience." *Cuban Studies/Estudios Cubanos* 6, no. 1 (January 1976): 67–61.

———. "Deterrence, Detente and the Cuban Missile Crisis." In *Cuban Communism,* 3d ed., ed. Irving Louis Horowitz, 106–16. New Brunswick, NJ: Transaction Publishers, 1977a.

———. "Castrology Revisited: Further Observations on the Militarization of Cuba." *Armed Forces and Society* 3, no. 4 (August 1977b): 617–31.

———. "The Cuba Lobby." *The Washington Review of Strategic and International Studies* 1, no. 3 (July 1978): 58–71.

———. "Institutionalization as Integration: The Cuban Revolution at Age Twenty." *Cuban Studies/Estudios Cubanos* 9:2 (July 1979): 84–90.

———. "Cuba and the Caribbean." *Worldview* 26, no. 12 (December 1983): 19–22.

———. "Democratic Societies and Their Enemies, 1950–1984." In *Bibliography of the Writings of Irving Louis Horowitz,* pp. xii–xviii. Privately Printed, 1984.

———. "Looking Forward: An Introduction to the Seventh Edition." In *Cuban Communism,* 7th ed., ed. Irving Louis Horowitz, xiii–xix. New Brunswick, NJ: Transaction Publishers, 1989a.

———. "Looking Backward: A Postscript to the Seventh Edition." In *Cuban Communism,* 7th ed., ed. Irving Louis Horowitz, 839–46. New Brunswick, NJ: Transaction Publishers, 1989b.

———. "The Place of the Festschrift." *Scholarly Publishing* 21, no. 2 (January 1990): 77–83.

———. *The Conscience of Worms and the Cowardice of Lions: The Cuban-American Experience, 1959–1992.* Miami: The North-South Center, University of Miami, 1993.

Lumsden, I. C. Ian. "On Socialists and Stalinists: A Rejoinder to Irving Louis Horowitz." *New Politics* 5, no. 1 (1966): 20–26.

Mesa-Lago, Carmelo. *Cuba in the 1970s: Pragmatism and Institutionalization.* Albuquerque: University of New Mexico Press, 1978.

———. *The Economy of Socialist Cuba: A Two-Decade Appraisal.* Albuquerque: University of New Mexico Press, 1981.

———, ed. *Cuba in Africa.* Pittsburgh: Latin American Monograph & Document Series, no. 3, 1982.

———, ed. *Cuba After the Cold War.* Pittsburgh: University of Pittsburgh Press, 1993.

Oppenheimer, Andres. *Castro's Final Hour.* New York: Simon & Schuster, 1992.

18

The Courage of a Real Lion: Horowitz's Contributions to Cuban Studies

Jaime Suchlicki

As a young doctoral student in Texas some three decades ago, I longed for the time when I would enter the "academic world." My first real experience with the academic community occurred when my professor invited me to attend with him the yearly meeting of the American Historical Association. Here, I reasoned, would be an opportunity to meet some of those luminaries I knew only by their writings. In particular I was eager to meet a famous U.S. historian of Argentina, Arthur P. Whitaker. After all, Argentina was a subject close to my heart since my mother had been born in Buenos Aires and I also had been doing research on the Peronista movement. I asked my mentor to introduce me to Professor Whitaker as soon as he could. The second day of the meeting we were lucky to find Professor Whitaker and I was duly introduced as one of Don Worcester's finest doctoral students in Latin American history. To my surprise, Professor Whitaker hardly said hello and instead continued talking to other colleagues.

To a young, somewhat idealistic student this was a crushing blow. Yet I justified this arrogant and somewhat selfish behavior as a passing flaw in a professor too busy to talk to a lowly graduate student. Little did I know that I would encounter this attitude over and over again throughout my academic career. Contrary to the idolized castle that most people think of the academic world, this sector of society is inhabited primarily by an arrogant species that thinks they are smarter and better than the rest of society and that, therefore, they know best. Instead of a community of scholars striving for knowledge, this is by and large a dysfunctional group of jealous, petty, insecure, and selfish individuals.

Lest I be accused of unfair generalizations, it is clear that there are many devoted, unselfish scholars that deserve admiration and respect. I, however, find this group to be in the minority. Irving Louis Horowitz belongs to this select minority. Over the decade that I have known him, my respect and admiration for him has grown. He is one of those special individuals—unselfish and caring, a friend ready to help when you need him, but more important, a man of conviction and fairness. What he believes in, he defends with a passion; what he cares for, he cares for intensely.

The plight of the Cuban people is one of those subjects that Horowitz has embraced passionately. Early on, when most American academics were defending the Castro regime, he saw the malevolence of a regime that violated the most fundamental rights of its people and established a totalitarian society. Instead of the freedom that Castro had promised, he imposed a dictatorship that has spanned over three decades. Hunger, misery, and exile has been the fate of this once happy and prosperous people.

Horowitz's denunciations of the excesses of Castroism brought him in conflict with the American left. And they haven't forgiven him yet! The defection of a brilliant intellectual from the ranks of the admirers of the Caribbean Stalin rattled liberal academia. While Horowitz was exposing the true nature of Castro, liberal academics continued to justify Castroism, perhaps longing for the same sort of authoritarianism in America that would create a society devoid of democracy and capitalism and directed by an elite who "knows best" what is best for America.

Even when the worst excesses of Castroism became known, primarily in the past two decades, and the thin veil of anti-Americanism and nationalism was swept aside to reveal the true nature of the regime in Havana, these apologists have kept silent. One would have expected, at least, claims of ignorance and deception and some words of rectification for past adulation. Worse yet, they are now proclaiming that the United States is to blame for all the problems of Cuba and are advocating that the American government should lift its economic embargo and negotiate with Castro. The same voices who claim that economic punishment hasn't worked in the past are now advocating economic incentive to "democratize" Castro. Neither punishment nor incentives have worked with Qaddafi or Hussein. They didn't work with Hitler in the 1930s. They are not likely to work with Fidel Castro now.

It is a measure of the strong and pervasive economic determinism in the American outlook that we still tend to assign priority to economics in trying to understand the motivations of revolutionary Marxist-Leninist regimes, like the one in Havana. The history of the past three decades offers clear proof that economic considerations have never dominated Castro's policies. On the contrary, political considerations usually dictate economic policies. Many of the initiatives and actions that the Cuban leadership has undertaken abroad, such as involvement in Angola, Ethiopia, Grenada, and Nicaragua, as well as constant mass mobilizations at home, have been costly, disruptive, and detrimental to orderly economic development. If the economic welfare of the Cuban people had been the *leitmotif* of Castro's policies, we would be confronting a totally different Cuba today.

And it is this American psyche toward Cuba, one of the main themes of Horowitz's most recent book *The Conscience of Worms and the Cowardice of Lions*.[1] Delivered originally as the Emilio Bacardi lectures at the University of Miami, this short but powerful book explores the mindset of the American academic community toward the Castro phenomenon and the role played by exile writers in denouncing Castroism. "Worms" refer to the latter, those *gusanos de conciencia* that burrow beneath the surface for truth. The "cowardice of lions" refers to those North Americans who mindlessly roared in favor of Castro only to lapse into a protracted silence when the excesses of the Communist regime became evident.

Horowitz has the courage to speak out. He chastises both the extreme right and the ultraleft for urging immobility to justify a policy of nonintervention in Cuba. "The defensive posture of American foreign policy," Horowitz warns, "will be sorely tested and quite possibly be found wanting." Like a skillful surgeon, Horowitz cuts through the nonsense of social science in the United States and its continuous justification of Castroism to link it to the eternal search for paradise. "If ideology is the curse of the masses," he points out, "then utopia is the bane of the intellectuals." It is this myth of Castroism's utopia that still sustain those who refuse to accept the true nature of the leader in Havana and, for that matter, of totalitarian leaders elsewhere.

All of us, Cuban exiles, U.S. social scientists and humanists, and the Cuban people once liberated from the present regime, owe a debt of gratitude to Irving Louis Horowitz for speaking out against oppression. In a world where hypocrisy and double standards abound, Horowitz stands out as one of those rare human beings committed to fairness and truth. His intellectual contribution stands out as an example for younger scholars to admire and emulate.

University of Miami
Department of History

Note

1. Irving Louis Horowitz, *The Conscience of Worms and the Cowardice of Lions: The Cuban-American Experience, 1959–1992.* Miami: The North-South Center, University of Miami, 1993.

Section Six

Religion, Culture, and the Jewish Enigma

19

Reflections of a Jewish Traveler: An Intellectual and Personal Odyssey

William B. Helmreich

Having known Irving Louis Horowitz for more than twenty-five years, it would be both impossible and unfair to write this essay without incorporating my personal knowledge of him. Impossible because Horowitz's writings on Jews are related to his own experiences as a Jew, unfair because to ignore them would deprive the reader of basic information. Since Horowitz has written a moving and candid autobiography of his early years in Harlem, doing so is all the easier. But first an explanation of my own connection to Irving Horowitz.

I first came to know Irving Horowitz during my graduate student days at Washington University in 1967. At that time the department was one of the most outstanding in the country, including among its luminaries Jules Henry, Lee Rainwater, Alvin Gouldner, David Pittman, and many others. It was a place where sociology was discussed and analyzed with passion and precision, not only in seminars, but in the dining halls and local bars, often until the wee hours of the morning. Since the university was a hotbed of 1960s activism, the theory and praxis of the classroom acquired special relevance.

Within such a context, our professors came to be seen as larger than life figures, representations of worldviews whose intricacies and contradictions were in urgent need of resolution. "After all," we thought, "the revolution is coming!" Probably no professor embodied these perceptions more than Irving Louis Horowitz. In the fall of 1967, I was one of a group of students (Mary Curtis among them) in his Latin American

Development course. The class size meant that "you couldn't run and you couldn't hide." You simply did not show up to his seminar unprepared, at least not if you wanted to remain in the class.

Having worked on a kibbutz that summer, I chose to write a paper comparing Israeli kibbutzim with Cuban collectives, an ambitious project to say the least. When it came my turn to present, I rambled on for about thirty-five minutes. When I finally finished, Horowitz delivered a scathing critique of my efforts that lasted about as long as my presentation. I was crushed and entertained the notion of dropping the course while there was still time. Imagine my surprise when, as I walked out of the room, he pulled me aside and said: "Not a bad job, Helmreich." "Why didn't you say so right away then?" I blurted out. "Oh, that's just my way of teaching," he replied with a chuckle.

True words. Horowitz became my adviser, mentor, and for the last twenty years, my close friend. Throughout that period, he has often used that device to stimulate my thinking—criticism tempered with encouragement. For this he has both my deepest appreciation and affection.

Marginality

Marginality and its relationship to the Jewish experience has been one of the dominant themes in Horowitz's writing throughout his career.[1] This interest may stem from his own experiences as a Jewish child growing up in Harlem. Unlike most Jewish residents who resided there in its heyday as a Jewish community, Horowitz lived there in the 1930s, by which time most Jews had already departed. He was clearly sensitive to that, as he writes in *Daydreams and Nightmares*: "The Jews of Harlem, if my extended family was any barometer, were viewed as dregs—social scourges and economic failures—simply by virtue of the fact that they remained."[2] As a result, Horowitz learned early on what it was like to be an outsider, not only among blacks in his own neighborhood but among Jews in general, observing that his upbringing was "very remote from that of other white Jewish children of the middle classes."[3]

Beyond his own experiences, Horowitz clearly saw marginality as integrally related to his family history, describing his father as: "[t]he grandson of a rabbi cut adrift from moral law; the son of a soldier in a world of urban guerillas; an anti-Jewish Jew in a world of pious Christian blacks—my father's world had gone astray. All previous norms had failed him. He was trapped by tradition rather than liberated by modernism."[4]

As we shall see, when Horowitz writes about Jewish marginality, he refers to the classic condition of the Jews as a people and their relationships with other nations. Nevertheless, the personal marginality that characterized his family may have kindled his general interest in the subject.

The establishment of the state of Israel has probably done more to reduce Jewish marginality than any other event in the last two thousand years. Besides giving Jews self-respect and a feeling of "a place among the nations" it has provided them with a certain degree of control over their destiny. Even so, it has not eliminated the wish among anti-Semites to marginalize the Jew by marginalizing Israel. This desire is primarily responsible for the tendency to hold Israel to a higher standard, to blame it for behavior not criticized elsewhere in the world. Horowitz argues that the existence of Israel as a nation-state challenges the Jewish stereotypes of court Jews and kabalistic Jews, both of whom flourish in the Diaspora context. As he puts it: "Mystery yields only to the ordinary, rarely to counter claims."[5]

The Six Day War is seen by Horowitz as a watershed event with respect to the above because it decisively transformed the Jew from victim to victor.[6] For Horowitz this distinction is part of a lifelong interest in the dual role of Jews as victims and as agents of social change, a point he makes with respect to Jews under the czars and the communists in his introduction to Jacob Talmon's, *Myth of the Nation and Vision of Revolution.*[7]

While acutely aware of the negative consequences of Jewish marginality, Horowitz is by no means oblivious to its benefits: "Marginality is a consequence of a people dispossessed, displaced and well-travelled. But, more pointedly, marginality is also a condition which makes possible the maximum amount of objectivity toward facing problems of the world with a minimum amount of undiluted fanaticism."[8] He also observes that marginality has played a role in determining where Jews live, namely, in those places whose systems of government permit them the greatest degree of freedom. This is why, he says, virtually all German social scientists who fled the Nazi onslaught, marginal Jews mostly, migrated to Western democratic countries and not to the Soviet Union.[9] If there seems to be an implied criticism here of the Soviet Union, it is not accidental, for, as Horowitz points out: "I inherited my father's life-long ambivalence toward Soviet power."[10]

The Working Class, Blacks, and Black-Jewish Relations

Horowitz's father, a disciplinarian, was far closer to the Russian peasant tradition than to the education-oriented Jewish tradition. "There is a tendency to mystify Jewish life, to assume that every family from Eastern Europe celebrated the values of education, philanthropy, and good food," Horowitz wryly notes. "In my family, these values for the most part were ignored."[11] What emerges here is a self-portrait of a family marked by adversity and of an individual sensitive to what that meant. The way out, in his father's eyes, lay, not in education, but in adopting working-class values: "He was the perfect Sombartian man—the Calvinist Jew, convinced that the road to heaven involved good work and no nonsense.... Perhaps Werner Sombart was right in suggesting that the Jews were the highest contemporary expression of Calvinism."[12]

Horowitz, like his father, is fiercely independent and respects hard work and success. At the same time, his respect for education, as exemplified by his choice of a profession and his value system, is in sharp contrast to his father's. Possibly it was a reaction to the hard times of his childhood, a feeling that lack of education may have been what held the family back, as opposed to most Jews of that era. There is another aspect too that must be considered here. Throughout his life Horowitz has championed the causes of underdogs, be they Indians in Latin America or blacks in the United States. Perhaps this involvement was a way of balancing his rejection of his working-class father's lack of emphasis on education, for in so doing he was demonstrating to his father that one could still care about the plight of the poor masses even with an education.

At Washington University my choice of a dissertation topic was to study firsthand a black militant organization. Horowitz enthusiastically endorsed the idea but expressed concern for the dangers involved. Reading his autobiography it is clear why this project was so close to his heart. The members of the organization, mostly teenagers, and the experiences I had with them as a participant observer, must have reminded him of his own days. Describing his life then, Horowitz wrote: "We never walked through the streets of Harlem. We ran."[13]

The nexus between Jews and African-Americans in Horowitz's writings is revealed most clearly in his discussions of the relations between the two groups. He was sensitized to this early on:

> The experience of Harlem convinced me that the relationship of blacks and Jews in America has special historical significance.... These two distinctly different peoples tell us much about the moral status of this nation at any given moment in time. They tell a story of aspirations realized and thwarted, cultures transmitted yet bowdlerized, and groups seeking security in race or religious solidarity up against individuals seeking to escape the boundaries of group life as such.[14]

It is here that Horowitz touches on a most important issue in minority relations: To what extent does the group as a whole have a right to compel its members to do its bidding? Does it have a right to ask its members to identify with the group if they wish only to advance as individuals and express no interest in racial or ethnic solidarity?

While not insisting on such unity, Horowitz provides a strong indication of his position in a critique of Emil Fackenheim's view of the Holocaust that appeared in *Modern Judaism* in 1981.[15] Responding to a statement by Fackenheim that the Holocaust was not racism but rather anti-Semitism, Horowitz says that not considering the Holocaust as racism is "to reject the special bond that oppressed peoples share, the special unity that can bind Blacks and Armenians and Jews."[16] Recognition of this bond influences his perceptions on other issues too. In *Israeli Ecstasies/Jewish Agonies,* Horowitz proposed that Israel raise its profile with African lands and argued that this would help black-Jewish relations.[17] In this light, it would be interesting to see whether the welcome given Ethiopian Jews by Israel has changed any minds in the black community when it comes to Jews in general.

Part of Horowitz's concern is no doubt rooted in his macro view of society, one that includes a strong concern about state-inspired genocide. When motivated by an interest in consolidating and maintaining power, the identity of a scapegoated minority is not so important to the state as the *need* for such a group, be they blacks, Jews, Gypsies, Armenians, or whatever. In addition, Horowitz also understands that separating racism from anti-Semitism often increases the likelihood that blacks and Jews, historically insecure, will be tempted to turn against each other. In this context he notes that there has always been a strong tendency on the part of these two peoples to view each other through somewhat stereotypical lenses. In Harlem, he writes, blacks thought Jews had money and power and were "strongly attracted to the Jewish ethic of family solidarity and social concern." For their part, "Jews viewed black physicality with more fear than respect. They also saw black argot, humor, and frank sexuality as a danger and risk."[18]

Horowitz's own thoughts on the subject over time demonstrate the importance of taking the long view when evaluating how ethnicity and group identity develop and change. In 1972, a time of serious conflict between Jews and blacks in the United States, he observed that the Jewish model of making it through education had proven less relevant for postwar blacks than the Third World model of revolution. During the same time period certain segments in the Jewish community turned to ethnic alliances such as the Jewish Defense League with the Italian-American League. Realizing the fluidity of such connections and commitments, Horowitz acknowledged that it would be difficult to say what the future held in store, pointing out that "the ethnics themselves often define the Jews as outside ethnicity."[19]

Although predicting the future is again difficult, his reservations about the permanence of these trends were correct. Today, it is clear that, however fractious relations between the two groups, neither model has been seriously adopted by either side. More and more African-Americans have identified themselves with mainstream American goals and life-styles and Jews have remained distinct from the attitudes and behavior patterns of white ethnics.

Anti-Semitism

Anti-Semitism, its manifestations and underlying causes, is a theme that runs consistently through much of Horowitz's writings about Jews and even those not about Jews *per se*. It makes its first appearance chronologically in his autobiography. He is cautioned by his mother not to accept the *"goyish"* Christmas presents that the hospital gave to its outpatients. Ignoring his mother's advice, he accepts the gifts and is subsequently robbed of them by neighborhood bullies. Unsympathetic, his mother tells him: "I told you Christmas isn't a Jewish holiday."[20] One clue about his feelings regarding his helplessness in such situations emerges in his ambivalent response to a childhood friend's beatings at the hands of anti-Semites: "I was filled with admiration for his courage and loathing for his infinite capacity for defeat."[21] Admiration must have been the more dominant emotion since *Israeli Ecstasies/Jewish Agonies* is dedicated to the friend, Arthur Grumberger, with the following poignant inscription: "To my dear departed friend from a Harlem childhood, who in his piety never lost his humanity and who in the process of growing up taught me daily lessons in courage."

While Horowitz clearly values physical courage and aggressiveness (as anyone who has ever played basketball with him knows!), his view of how Jews should respond is much more sophisticated, always accompanied by an understanding that there are different ways to resist, not all of them physical. Rejecting the "sheep to the slaughter" stereotype about Jews during the Holocaust, he wrote: "One cannot help but be impressed by the dignity of Jews sewing their yellow armbands with the Star of David and publicly announcing an identity with a Jewishness that many had forgotten and even abandoned."[22]

The most highly developed discussion of anti-Semitism probably appears in an essay called, "Philo-Semitism and Anti-Semitism," that appeared in the May 1990 issue of *Midstream*. In it Horowitz writes of a disturbing tendency by some Christians to compliment Jews on how wonderful they are so that Jews will be convinced that such beneficent Christians are worthy of "joining." However, when the public expression of such attitudes by Christians fails to produce either "conversion or cultural absorption, the usual canards of anti-Semitism are trotted forth: from Jewish clannishness to Jewish conspiracies." In this way, he notes, it becomes possible for philo-Semitism and anti-Semitism to co-exist within the same individual.[23]

This explanation reminds me of a story told to me by Rabbi Marvin Tokayer who served for a time as chief rabbi of Tokyo. On one occasion he was invited to receive an award at the University of Kyoto. The "award" turned out to be a gilt-edged copy of the infamous *Protocols of the Elders of Zion*. Amazed, the rabbi asked his hosts: "Do you realize what an anti-Semitic book this is? It's a fraud of the most outrageous sort." The Japanese were equally surprised by Rabbi Tokayer's protests: "What's wrong with it?" asked one. "It talks about how smart and cunning the Jews are, how much power they have, how they control everything. We think it's wonderful and proves your greatness." Horowitz succinctly explains the dangers inherent in such seemingly sincere praise: "When Jews achieve great success, philo-Semites point to them as proof of Jewish superiority. But this very superiority fuels anti-Semitism because it makes the anti-Semite feel threatened and jealous."[24]

Although he sees them as strongly connected, Horowitz does not see anti-Semitism and philo-Semitism as the same and he therefore concludes that while they "share a disquieting set of features, they do not merit the same level of opprobrium."[25] Both anti-Semites and philo-Semites want to understand the "secret" of Jewish survival, asserts Horowitz, and for the same reason—they fear Jews. Moreover, he argues, the Final Solution constituted an admission by anti-Semites that the "secrets" of Jewish success and survival could never be uncovered. Therefore, to eliminate Jews as a threat, it was necessary to kill all of them.[26] This idea of extermination figures very strongly in the mind of the modern-day anti-Semite. Such an individual does not, like the white racist, dream of a world in which Jews can be subjugated, but rather of one in which Jews *can be completely eliminated*. This is why, as Norman Cohn has pointed out, Jews have often been depicted in classic anti-Semitic literature as "vermin" or a "cancer," something that needs to be eradicated, not simply controlled.[27] In this context, the idea of portraying Jewish survival as a deep unfathomable mystery, plays into the hands of the conspiracy-theorist anti-Semites, for it means that the secret "must be pried loose for the world to achieve true tranquility."[28]

In his efforts to provide a more encompassing explanation of anti-Semitism, Horowitz returns to a favorite theme: "The Jewish tradition of social marginality, or reticence to participate in nationalistic celebrations, makes anti-Semitism a universal phenomenon, as characteristic of France as of the Soviet Union."[29] Does this not seem contradicted, however, by the case of Germany, where Jews were very patriotic and fought gallantly in World War I? Not really, because the Jews were also accused by Germans, as in the other countries, of refusing to assimilate. The sad reality is that, because of the many psychological and social functions served by anti-Semitism, it becomes quite possible to hate Jews for manifesting seemingly contradictory traits. Horowitz recognizes this problem, observing that Europeans could not handle a situation where Jews became the spokespersons for forces contesting each other. He is referring to the fact that Jews became both bourgeois adversaries and communist enemies within the same Europe.[30] What the anti-Semite often does is to find different Jews for each category, something that, given the fact that Jews are not monolithic in their views or behavior, is relatively easy to do. These same psycho-social needs are at least partially responsible for the behavior of many who today deny that the Holocaust ever occurred. Among the accusations leveled by Holocaust deniers is that it is all "a Zionist/nationalist plot." In this regard it is worth mentioning that Horowitz was one of the first to recognize the dangers of Holocaust denial, making mention of it in 1981.[31]

Horowitz takes issue with Fackenheim's position that the Jews were not merely a scapegoat, but were targeted for destruction because of virulent anti-Semitism. He points out that Gypsies, Slavs, Poles, and Jews were *all* singled out, albeit to varying degrees. While not ignoring the passion that the Nazis displayed when it came to killing Jews, Horowitz thinks that greater emphasis needs to be placed on the *rational* reasons that motivated the Nazis.[32] By liquidating the Jews, the Nazi bureaucrats fatally wounded both the bourgeoisie and the proletariat (since Jews were influential in both groups), thus allowing them to consolidate state power.[33] Their task was made easier by the fact that there were relatively few Jews within German bureaucracy.[34]

In another instance it becomes clear that to Horowitz, anti-Semitism is not simply a matter of concern for Jews. It is a threat to the survival of a democratic society. This is why he felt that the Jewish community's sensitivities superseded the issue of free speech when the American Nazi party attempted to march in the largely Jewish Chicago suburb of Skokie. In an essay on the subject, Horowitz argued that once the neo-Nazis chose Skokie as their stage they proved that they were not primarily interested in presenting ideas but rather in provoking violence, a clear threat to democracy that needed to be stopped.[35]

In addition to the intellectual issues, it is apparent that anti-Semitism is something that Horowitz personally feels must be identified and fought. As a result, he does not hesitate to speak out when he sees it occurring within the sociological community. In a trenchant observation, he reminds us that at the turn of the century Jews were seen within the profession as marginalized outsiders. Today, however, they have come full circle and are criticized as self-serving members of the establishment. In addition to the irony of such attacks, Horowitz points out their falseness, citing as examples of anti-establishment figures such prominent sociologists as Bennett Berger, Alvin Gouldner, and Immanuel Wallerstein.[36] He demonstrates clearly the one-sidedness of the writings of academics such as Ali Mazrui, and concludes, with evident regret, that in view of its ideological biases (perhaps because of them), the recent declining participation in professional sociology meetings may not be such a bad thing.[37]

Given Horowitz's extensive writings on Latin America, it is to be expected that he would have something to say about Latin American Jewry and indeed, he does. In *Israeli Ecstasies/Jewish Agonies,* he presents a complex analysis of Jews in Latin America (especially in Argentina) and of the dilemmas facing them. The immigrant generation, he says, possessed a "shallow commitment" to Judaism out of a desire to adapt to the new ways as a "survival mechanism." The second generation had a

> shallow secularism since once a modicum of integration was achieved, economic pursuits became dominant. Thus, for third generation Jews to become truly radical means an abandonment of Judaism altogether, while to remain overtly and manifestly Jewish implies an identity with the exploiting middle sectors.[38]

In this stereotype of the "exploiting middle sectors" we see again the problem of anti-Semitism. Linking it with Jewish marginality, Horowitz argues that "[i]t is the estrangement, the alienation of Jews in the Diaspora from the sources of State power, that is responsible for their special connection with the spirit of capitalism."[39] In fact, the rise of nationalism in Latin America causes suspicion of Jews in terms of dual loyalty, a suspicion fueled by a very strong Catholic culture. Proof of their lack of influence is the relative absence of Jews in politically influential positions anywhere on the continent. Although written twenty years ago, it is an analysis, as confirmed in a recent discussion with Horowitz in the summer of 1993, that still holds true today.[40]

The Holocaust

Explaining the Holocaust has always posed tremendous difficulties for theologians who are at great pains to understand how a caring and just God could allow such terrible events to happen. Even when theologians have offered explanations they are still forced to admit that the answers can, almost by definition, never be certain.[41] Horowitz, however, approaches the issue from an empirical social science perspective. He does not question how human beings could have been allowed to act in such fashion, but rather what their motivations might have been to carry out acts that they were clearly not prevented from committing. In his view:

> To incorporate into the Jewish psyche the phrase "never again," requires an antecedent commitment to explain why genocide happened in the first place. Theologians must not presume an exclusive monopoly on meaning by insisting upon the mystery and irrationality of taking lives. The task of social science remains in this area, as in all others, a rationalization of irrationality.[42]

In his distaste for such a "monopoly" Horowitz takes an Aristotelian or Platonic approach to reason. The answer comes in *Taking Lives: Genocide and State Power,* a full-fledged analysis of the state's central role in allowing the official destruction of its own people. Along the way Horowitz notes that the Germans went to great expense in their efforts to exterminate the Jews.[43] Most importantly, he differentiates between murder and genocide in that those who commit genocide often see themselves simply as instruments for state-sanctioned policies. In this way, the act is a collective one and the individual can disclaim responsibility.[44]

The many examples given in *Taking Lives* provide ample evidence that the Holocaust was not an event unique to the Jewish community. Among the cases cited are Armenians, Gypsies, Cambodians, Colombians, Indians, Biafrans, and Paraguayans. The Armenians, he notes, lost 50 percent of their total population, compared to 60 percent for the Jews. Rather, he says, "The special Jewish triumph is life."[45]

Horowitz again takes sharp issue with Fackenheim on the Holocaust, challenging a number of the latter's propositions about the event. He disagrees with Fackenheim's assertion that the Holocaust was not "a war" because the Jews were a powerless civilian population. "A war of annihilation is a war," Horowitz says. "To deny the warlike character of genocide is to deny its essence: the destruction of human beings for predetermined nationalist or statist goals." This is not a matter of semantics, for, in Horowitz's opinion, the fact that the Jews were a threat to the Nazis' *legitimacy* gave them a certain degree of power.[46] It would appear that Horowitz is not alone in his position. No less an authority than Lucy Dawidowicz titled her landmark book on the subject *The War against the Jews.*[47]

Fackenheim also believes that the Holocaust hindered the overall aims of the war and that it was not directed by "passions that wars unleashed."

As a result, it was not really a war but rather a methodically executed policy. But Horowitz points out that in terms of slave labor and the theft of Jewish property, valuables, and so forth, it is an open question whether the Nazis' attacks upon the Jews were a loss. Moreover, if it was not a war of passion, then why did the Nazis pursue it even after it became clear following their 1943 defeat at Stalingrad that they had lost the war?[48] Finally, Horowitz disagrees with Fackenheim's claim that Hitler was not interested in exporting National Socialism, but rather anti-Semitism. What about the Nazi puppet regimes set up in Norway, the Ukraine, Rumania, and elsewhere?[49]

Having posited the view that the actions taken against the Jews must be seen within a larger framework and that it was not a unique phenomenon, Horowitz presents arguments supporting the idea that *certain aspects* of the Holocaust were, in fact, unique. These were its systematic nature, the technological refinement, and the ideological single-mindedness: "So intent were the Nazis on their policy of extermination of Jews, that they dared contact other nations, especially axis powers and neutral countries, to repatrite Jews back to Germany to suffer the ultimate degradation."[50]

Jews and Politics

Because of the era in which he lived, Irving Horowitz's Jewishness commingled with other values that, while not synonymous with Judaism, were synonymous with Jews—FDR, socialism, and the Democratic party. "Republicans were all anti-Semites," he wrote in his memoir, "worse, bad for the poor."[51] One can also see who influenced Horowitz in his development as a concerned Jew interested in social justice by looking at whom he praises and for what reasons. More than anyone perhaps, Morris Raphael Cohen who taught at Horowitz's *alma mater,* City College, fit his idea of how a Jew blended his identity together with his philosophical approach to life.[52]

Despite his strong views about many things, the portrait that emerges from Horowitz's writings is that of an eclectic liberal, suspicious of both labels and extremism. Whether conservative or liberal isn't the point so much as "the profound attachment of Jews to American ideals," he wrote in an article that appeared in *Forum* in 1980.[53] And again, in a 1986 essay on Sombart, Horowitz discussed the apprehension Jews in general feel about extremism of any sort, especially because they rarely benefit from such tendencies: "In any social order where collective guilt is an acceptable mode of reasoning, the Jews as a persecuted group fare poorly. Thus individualism becomes a Jewish mode of survival far beyond anything envisaged by the Yankee pioneers of individual redemption."[54]

In the contemporary American context, Horowitz sees a "magical combination" that, if followed by politicians, will garner them Jewish support—strong support for Israel and liberal positions on domestic issues. In 1980, Horowitz expressed the view that the relatively strong Jewish vote for Reagan at the time did not necessarily signal a permanent shift in Jewish allegiance from liberal policies or the Democratic party.[55] Rather, it was due to the perceived anti-Israel position of Jimmy Carter. In this he was prophetic as witnessed by the 90 percent level of support Clinton received twelve years later from the Jewish community. Of course, the unprecedented high level of support may have been due more to hostility toward Bush and Baker than love for the Democrats. Whatever the reasons, Jews are still not as liberal in their attitudes as they were in earlier years. Horowitz attributes this, in part, to the leftward movement of certain elements in the Democratic party. As he put it: "Jewish voting patterns are centrist in policy and universalist in principle."[56]

Jewish Identity

In the introduction to *Israeli Ecstasies/Jewish Agonies,* Horowitz wrote: "This volume is built on the belief that plural identities are possible, even necessary, as a survival mechanism for any ethnic or racial group in American life."[57] This essentially positive outlook on the importance and benefits of ethnic identity stands in sharp contrast to the assimilationist pattern or, at best, muted identification that characterizes so many Jewish sociologists. There is no question that Horowitz is intensely proud of his Jewishness. Though he does not identify religiously, he is deeply religious about the importance of identifying with the Jewish people.

Even as a child Horowitz saw identification in a hostile environment as something courageous. Writing about a boyhood friend in Harlem who wore a yarmulke and had earlocks, or *peyes,* he stated: "It took guts to be so self-identified." Still, he was not oblivious to the disadvantages of doing so: "I grew up with an image of Judaism fixed by Arthur—by his tenacity and willfulness and, at the same time, his inability to develop any strategy other than to lose."[58] This observation, when juxtaposed against the following comments about Israel in *Israeli Ecstasies/ Jewish Agonies,* makes for interesting reading: "The test for a State is its ability to maintain its power. While suffering may be a value and a positive attribute to Jewish solidarity, it comes perilously close to making powerlessness an equivalent to virtue."[59]

In Horowitz's opinion one of the most important lessons of the Holocaust is that ethnic pride is crucial to survival and that such survival is an important value in and of itself. He argues that the considerable power of the neo-Orthodox in Israel is rooted in the collapse of the European Enlightenment (whose values Zionism shared) in the face of fascism. In short, one cannot displace ethnicity with ethics and survive as a group.[60] While he would probably say that America is different, Horowitz's words constitute a cautionary note to Jews everywhere: "The ideals of enlightenment remain intact, but its cultivated bearers had disappointed Jews for the last time. Nationhood became the last gasp of a shattered Diaspora."[61]

To Horowitz, being an authentic Jew involves not only consciousness of ethnicity, but also having a sense of social justice, and an attachment on some level, to the state of Israel. For this reason he is highly critical of Will Herberg's conception of Jews as part of a nondenominational mosaic of American religions, an approach he attributes to Herberg's "desperate impulse for acceptance."[62] In his essay on the politics of centrism, Horowitz presents an excellent model for understanding Jewish concerns—Israel (secular nationalism-Zionism), Torah (religion), and God (Jewish moral values and norms of behavior). Because almost all identifying Jews fall into one or more of these categories, they cannot be seen as simply another interest group with a narrow perspective or agenda.[63] And "Jewish concerns" are no longer limited to those living in the Diaspora. In a prescient remark that appeared in 1977, Horowitz touched on the emergence of a need among Israelis to explain the role of Jewishness in their lives. That trend has accelerated over the years to the point where it is now seen as one of the many "social crises" within Israeli society.[64]

Israel

Horowitz's own upbringing reflects a fairly prevalent view of Zionism among American Jews before 1948. Reminiscing about his father, he said: "He was not prepared to risk his hard-won Americanization for a one-way ticket to Zion and Palestine."[65] It must be remembered that the socialist Bundists, whom Horowitz's father admired, were strongly anti-Zionist. In his own work, however, we see that Horowitz is a classic Zionist. He does not merely invoke the Holocaust as a justification for the Jewish state but uses the traditional arguments as well:

> The Jewish people had not only maintained their spiritual contact with Palestine throughout the centuries in the *Galut* but also that Jews have been continuously an indigenous, though a minority, population of Palestine. In some areas of the country, such as Peki'in in the Galilee, there are even families (about fifty) which trace their genealogy directly back to the Hebrews; in Jerusalem and Safed they were a majority throughout this century; and they formed substantial communities in Tiberias and Hebron.[66]

Israeli Ecstasies/Jewish Agonies sets down Horowitz's most extensive views on Jews and much of it deals with Israel. Although most of the essays were penned before the 1973 Yom Kippur War, many of their unusual and interesting insights have withstood the test of time. While the high moral ground that Israel occupied after that war has been weakened by the Lebanon incursion and the Intifada and while the religious sector is far more involved with the government, other significant features remain essentially unchanged. For example, the Israelis and Arabs still feel they are being manipulated by forces outside the region, and Israel's position vis-à-vis nations in Africa and Asia is still ambivalent, despite some improvement in the situation.

Horowitz points out that as a small nation Israel has "limited room for maneuvering at international levels of power."[67] It is further hamstrung because it "belongs neither to the highly developed nor to the underdeveloped sectors of the world political economy." Nevertheless, he argues, it has not been as "timorous" in its foreign policy as some have claimed. As examples he cites Israel's having distanced itself from South Vietnam in the 1960s despite its close relationship with the United States and its having voted in 1962 for China's admission to the UN.[68] While these examples may seem somewhat dated they are actually part of a continuing pattern in which Israel, probably because of its fear that one day it may be all alone in the world, must demonstrate its independence. Other instances include its unpopular relationship with South Africa and its refusal to give in to demands by Bush and Baker for the sake of obtaining the loan guarantees.

Some of the most interesting connections made by Horowitz concern Arab-Jewish relations. For example, he recalls that both Arabs and Jews are involved in "restorations" of cultures that were once much greater and that Islamic and Hebraic traditions do not separate religion from the state as does the United States. While this might create more antagonism between the two cultures it has the advantage of enabling participants in these societies to see politics as having a potential for moral good. Socialism, he reminds us, is viewed primarily as economic in Israel, but in Arab lands it is "a term of consensus and integration rather than a rallying cry for revolutions yet to be fought."[69]

A reading of Horowitz's book is retrospectively valuable. Lest we forget, Israel, in the aftermath of the Six Day War, was largely interested in *de jure* status. Today, the Arabs are willing to give that but the Israelis are unwilling to settle for it. The experiences of the last two decades have made Israel feel that it needs to have security arrangements such as buffer zones as well as full diplomatic relations to insure that peace will not merely be an empty word.

Writing prophetically, Horowitz notes (actually the piece was written jointly with Maurice Zeitlin) that Israel has inherited a degree of danger that only an "enemy within" can provide. The choice therefore is between a "left" solution giving the Arabs full equality or a "right" solution giving them some form of autonomy.[70] Although reprinted in *Israeli Ecstasies,* these words first appeared in *Judaism* in 1967; yet they are quite relevant today. Horowitz was also correct in identifying Egypt, almost twenty years ago, as a key to peace in the Middle East.[71] Although there can be no true solution without the Palestinians, the "cold peace" with Egypt has held up and has greatly reduced the Arab military threat to Israel.

Naturally, as an American Jew, Horowitz pays attention to relations between American Jews and Israelis. He thinks it is nonsense to perceive Israel as an outpost of America or the West, or as a transplanted European democracy.[72] While recognizing the interconnections, he asserts that American policy toward Israel "ultimately is distinct from the

Jewish question in America."[73] And, of course, he is right on target. The two societies have evolved in different ways over time, with different priorities and different ways of looking at things. Israelis are most concerned with survival in the Middle East. American Jews worry about assimilation, intermarriage, affirmative action, and domestic anti-Semitism, all rather irrelevant in the Israeli context. Moreover, they give increasingly tepid support to the concept of *Aliyah*. The only time Israel becomes a central issue to American Jews is when it is endangered.[74]

Horowitz is also concerned about Israel's relationships with other countries, particularly those in the Third World. He sees Israel's economy, political structure, and struggle in the 1940s against British colonialism as qualifying it to be a model for other developing nations. He thinks that when it identifies too strongly with the West, it damages that image and that such an image is inconsistent with its location in the Middle East.[75] In the long run, he feels, Israel will have to adopt a perspective more in tune with the Third World. This observation, made in 1976, rings true today, as Israel continues to expand its contacts with more and more African and Asian nations.[76]

Conclusion

Taken as a whole, Horowitz's writings present a personal and intellectual portrait that is extraordinarily rich in breadth and scope. No area of importance in Jewish life and culture seems to have escaped his interest and scrutiny. Israel, the Holocaust, anti-Semitism, Jewish identity and marginality, Jews and politics, all these and more are brilliantly discussed and analyzed in his writings. Moreover, within these areas there is also remarkable diversity. In his analyses of the Middle East, for instance, he focuses on both global issues, Arab-Jewish relations and the Third World, and also micro issues, such as how Israelis in their daily lives identify both as Jews and as Israelis.

There are also topics such as Latin American Jewry, in which Horowitz's interest is linked to his broader focus on the general topic of development. In those instances he is able to bring to bear the full power of his encyclopedic knowledge and insights about the subject as a whole.

Sociologists have for many years emphasized the importance of a person's personal life history in assessing his or her intellectual contributions. The debate about the ability of social scientists to be truly objective has been going on for decades but few would deny that a person's experiences have *some* effect on their writings. This is most likely to occur when an individual writes about a group to which he belongs and even more so when he is a strongly identifying member of that group.

Irving Louis Horowitz is a Jew whose connection with Jewishness is unquestioned. While his evaluations of Jewish issues never fail to be critical when that is called for, he *feels* for Jews, their suffering as well as their dreams. He fully appreciates their unique history while at the same time knowing where that history is not unique but rather a part of human history as a whole. His own experiences growing up as a Jew have clearly affected his choice of topics and also the way in which he looks at Jewish issues, but they have never influenced his ability to see Jews as a complex people deeply affected in many ways, some positive and some not, by what they have gone through.

As a student of Horowitz I probably owe him a greater debt than I can fully articulate, simply because I cannot say for certain that I am fully aware of all the ways in which he has influenced me. This is especially true because our friendship has deepened and grown in the years since I completed my studies and I maintain constant contact with him. There is, however, one thing about Irving Louis Horowitz that stands out for me: his deep commitment to scholarship, one that never fails to take into account the human dimension of what one is doing.

City College of the City University of New York
Department of Sociology

Notes

1. Personal correspondence, 19 April 1988.
2. Irving Louis Horowitz, *Daydreams and Nightmares: Reflections of a Harlem Childhood* (Jackson: University Press of Mississippi, 1990), 5.
3. Ibid., 6.
4. Ibid., 63.
5. Irving Louis Horowitz, "Philo-Semitism and Anti-Semitism: Jewish Conspiracies and Totalitarian Sentiments," *Midstream* 36 (May 1990): 21.
6. Irving Louis Horowitz, *Israeli Ecstasies/Jewish Agonies* (New York: Oxford University Press, 1974), 4.
7. Irving Louis Horowitz, "On Jacob L. Talmon," an introduction to Jacob L. Talmon, *Myth of the Nation and Vision of Revolution: Ideological Polarization in the Twentieth Century* (New Brunswick, NJ and London: Transaction Publishers, 1991), xxii.
8. Irving Louis Horowitz, "Israel-Diaspora Relations as a Problem in Center-Periphery Linkages," *Contemporary Jewry* 3 (Spring-Summer 1977): 36.

9. Irving Louis Horowitz, "Between the Charybodis of Capitalism and the Scylla of Communism: The Emigration of German Social Scientists, 1933–1945," *Social Science History* 11 (Summer 1987): 128, 130, 132.

10. Horowitz, *Daydreams and Nightmares*, 65.

11. Ibid., 61.

12. Ibid., 63.

13. Ibid., 5.

14. Ibid., 2–3.

15. Irving Louis Horowitz, "Many Genocides, One Holocaust?: The Limits of the Rights of States and the Obligations of Individuals," *Modern Judaism* 1, no. 1 (1981): 74–89.

16. Ibid., 79.

17. Horowitz, *Israeli Ecstasies*, 84.

18. Horowitz, *Daydreams and Nightmares*, 3. In a June 1963 letter that appeared in *Commentary* (it was also reprinted in Eldrigde Cleaver's *Soul on Ice* [New York: McGraw-Hill, 1969], 191), Horowitz proposed the following: "The solution is thus not the direct liquidation of the color line, through the liquidation of color; but rather through a greater physical connectedness of the whites; and a greater intellectual connectedness of the blacks."

19. Irving Louis Horowitz, *Foundations of Political Sociology* (New York: Harper & Row, 1972), 531–32.

20. Horowitz, *Daydreams and Nightmares*, 78.

21. Ibid.

22. Horowitz, *Israeli Ecstasies*, 183.

23. Horowitz, *Philo-Semitism*, 17.

24. Ibid., 20.

25. Ibid., 22.

26. Ibid., 19.

27. Norman Cohn, *Warrant for Genocide: The Myth of the Jewish-World Conspiracy and Protocols of the Elders of Zion* (New York: Harper & Row, 1966).

28. Horowitz, *Philo-Semitism*, 20. Actually, some Jews do believe, albeit in a quite different way, that there is something almost supernatural in the fact that Jews have survived as a people for so many thousands of years. Thus, Rabbi Isaac Hutner, a prominent Orthodox leader, observed, when asked about the survival of the yeshiva (rabbinical seminary) for so many centuries: "They'll give you all sorts of reasons, but in reality it's a mystery just like the mystery of the Jews.... The Jew has a deep, mysterious connection to Torah that we don't fully understand although we know it's there." Clearly, as Horowitz indicates, it's the *motive* for asking the question that counts, not the question itself. See also William B. Helmreich, *The World of the Yeshiva: An Intimate Portrait of Orthodox Jewry* (New York: The Free Press, 1982), 320.

29. Horowitz, "Many Genocides, One Holocaust?" 80.

30. Horowitz, "On Jacob L. Talmon," xviii.

31. Horowitz, "Many Genocides, One Holocaust?" 86.

32. Jean Paul Sartre has also written about the "passion" of the anti-Semite. See *Anti-Semite and Jew* (New York: Schocken, 1966, paperback ed.), 18.

33. Horowitz, "Many Genocides, One Holocaust?" 83–84.

34. Horowitz, *Foundations of Political Sociology*, 237.

35. Irving Louis Horowitz and Victoria Curtis Bramson, "Skokie, the ACLU and the Endurance of Democratic Theory," *Law and Contemporary Problems* 43 (Spring 1979): 334.

36. Irving Louis Horowitz, "Jews, Anti-Semitism, and Sociology," *Congress Monthly* 53 (November-December 1986): 5.
37. Ibid., 6.
38. Horowitz, *Israeli Ecstasies,* 122-23.
39. Ibid., 125.
40. For other writings on Latin American Jewry by Horowitz, see "The Jewish Community of Buenos Aires," *Jewish Social Studies* 24 (October 1962): 195-222; "Jewish Ethnicity and Latin American Nationalism," in *Ethnicity in an International Context,* ed. Abdul A. Said and Luis R. Simmons (New Brunswick, NJ: Transaction Publishers, 1976), 92-109.
41. William B. Helmreich, "Making the Awful Meaningful," *Society* 19 (September-October 1982): 62-66.
42. Horowitz, "Many Genocides, One Holocaust?" 87.
43. Irving Louis Horowitz, *Taking Lives: Genocide and State Power* (New Brunswick, NJ: Transaction Publishers, 1980), 36-37.
44. Ibid., 81.
45. Ibid., 75.
46. Ibid., 76-77.
47. Lucy S. Dawidowicz, *The War against the Jews 1933-1945* (New York: Holt, Rinehart and Winston, 1975).
48. Horowitz, "Many Genocides, One Holocaust?" 77-78.
49. Horowitz, "Many Genocides, One Holocaust?" 82-83.
50. Ibid., 86. See also Irving Louis Horowitz, "Hitler, History and the Holocaust" (a review of *Forever in the Shadow of Hitler? Original Documents of the Historikerstreit, the Controversy Concerning the Singularity of the Holocaust,* trans. James Knowlton and Truett Cates [Atlantic Highlands, NJ: Humanities Press, 1993]), in *Jewish Quarterly* 40, no. 2 (Summer 1993): 68-71.
51. Horowitz, *Daydreams and Nightmares,* 44.
52. Irving Louis Horowitz, "Introduction," in Morris Raphael Cohen, *The Faith of a Liberal* (New Brunswick, NJ: Transaction Publishers), xii.
53. Irving Louis Horowitz, "The Politics of Centrism: Jews and the 1980 Elections," *Forum* 30 (Summer 1980): 35.
54. Irving Louis Horowitz, "The Jews and Modern Communism: The Sombart Thesis Reconsidered," *Modern Judaism* 6 (February 1986): 18.
55. Horowitz, "The Politics of Centrism," 37.
56. Ibid., 38.
57. Horowitz, *Israeli Ecstasies,* vii.
58. Horowitz, *Daydreams and Nightmares,* 78.
59. Horowitz, *Israeli Ecstasies,* 79.
60. Ibid., 186.
61. Ibid., 191.
62. Irving Louis Horowitz, "Rediscovering Jewish Conservatism" (review of *From Marxism to Judaism: The Collected Essays of Will Herberg,* ed. David G. Dalin), *Jewish Quarterly* 37 (Winter 1990-91): 68.
63. Horowitz, "The Politics of Centrism," 39-40.
64. Horowitz, "Israel-Diaspora Relations," 34.
65. Ibid.
66. Ibid., 13.
67. Horowitz, "On Jacob L. Talmon," xxii.
68. Horowitz, "Israeli Ecstasies," 27-28.

69. Ibid. 63.
70. Ibid., 33–34.
71. Irving Louis Horowitz, "The Middle East Terror: A Global Estimate," *Sh'ma: A Journal of Jewish Responsibility* 4 (25 January 1974): 41–43.
72. Horowitz, *Israeli Ecstasies,* 76.
73. Ibid., 102.
74. Horowitz, "Israel-Diaspora Relations," 29–30.
75. Horowitz, *Israeli Ecstasies,* 78.
76. Irving Louis Horowitz, "From Pariah People to Pariah Nation: Jews, Israelis, and the Third World," in *Israel and the Third World,* ed. Michael Curtis and Susan Aurelia Gitelson (New Brunswick, NJ: Transaction Publishers, 1976), 385–87.

20

Israel and the American Diaspora

Michael Curtis

In a lecture in 1969, Gershom Scholem confessed he had not previously spoken on the relationships between Israel and the Diaspora, partly
because of the difficulty of saying anything new, and partly because of
his own contradictory thoughts about it. Indeed, the relationships,
troubled, complicated, and historically unique, is more likely to raise
questions, which can be presented with clarity, than to lead to clear or
definitive answers. Can there be a dialectical process between a community that has miraculously survived and remains, with its complicated religious, ethnic, and national characteristics, scattered through
the world, and a part of that community that now comprises the majority
of the population in a sovereign state?

In a number of his writings, especially in his book *Israeli Ecstasies/
Jewish Agonies* and in an essay in 1977,[1] Irving Louis Horowitz has
touched on the questions not only of whether Israel was central or peripheral to the Jewish Diaspora, but also on whether Judaism was central to what he termed Israeli marginality. At an early stage Horowitz
correctly appreciated that Israel was central to the world Jewish experience when its survival was threatened and that its centrality might be
seen as less significant after the minimum conditions of Israeli security
had been met. His argument became more challenging and problematic
in positing that Israel does not play a central role in Diaspora affairs in
normal circumstances, and therefore one can fairly ask whether it is the
Jewish rather than the Israel question that is central to Jewish experience. For anyone who, like Horowitz, in his own words, is "a spiritual

holder of volatile national stock," the complex and unique relationships between the independent sovereign state of Israel and the Jewish Diaspora requires serious reevaluation.

At the outset of this discussion of the relationships and tension between Israel and the Diaspora three points might be made. The first is that, with the exception of some French intellectuals and, in a different way, of Soviet activists, most of the contemporary debate on the interaction is between Israel and the American Jewish community, with only occasional reference to other areas of the Diaspora as some specific problem arises there. The second is the question of who is to be regarded as the American partner: the majority of Jews in the United States, rabbinical groups, major organizational bodies, the federations, the Conference of Presidents, the members of the international organizations (WZO, Jewish Agency, World Jewish Congress). Attitudinal surveys over the last decade indicate, not unexpectedly, that different sections of American Jewry disagree or vary significantly on some issues, as is shown by the beliefs of younger or older people, members of the Orthodox, Conservative or Reform congregations, and the Jewish community as a whole or the leaders of professional organizations.

Third, one is drawn into the discussion of related issues such as the complex interrelationships between Judaism, Zionism, and the reality of Israel as a pluralistic society with a significant and increasing minority of Moslems and Christians. Recent poll surveys illustrate the problem. While 86 percent of the American Jewish community think that being Jewish was either very or fairly important in their lives, and while a considerable majority support Israel, only 27 percent consider themselves as Zionist, however that is defined. The majority American position at present would thus be a pro-Israeli stance in which the state can be regarded and supported as an end in itself, either the fulfillment of a historical dream of the Jewish people or as insurance against future anti-Semitism. But at the same time it would not regard Israel as the embodiment of a particular Zionist vision, and would reject the more complex Zionist concepts of the destiny of the Jewish people, including that of *shlilat hagolah* (negation of the Diaspora).

The Historical Battle

For almost a century an intellectual battle, sometimes bitter in character, has been waged over solutions to "the Jewish problem." Some, like Simon Dubnow and the Bund, argued the secular case while some Orthodox argued the religious case for communal autonomy in the Diaspora. Others, like Salo Baron, discussed emancipation without assimilation. And still others, like Moses Hess in one way and Ahad Ha'Am in another, stressed the importance of Jewish culture and education, and saw Palestine as the spiritual center for the maintenance of that culture in the Diaspora.

Within this intellectual debate, the territorial Zionists, whether Herzl, Nordau, or Jabotinsky, assumed that a self-governing political entity was essential for the survival of the Jewish people, and that its creation would likely end the Diaspora. With the establishment of Israel, the question of the perpetuation of the Diaspora was raised. At its most extreme, as with Arthur Koestler, the answer was that anyone who wanted to remain a Jew or have a Jewish identity should emigrate to Israel and that others should no longer consider themselves as Jews. The contrary position, argued forcefully and often polemically by Simon Rawidowicz, is based on the intriguing historical and contemporary parallel of Babylon and Jerusalem. Jews have usually lived in a Diaspora as well as in the land of Israel, and comprised different parts of the organic unity called "the people of Israel," one and indivisible *(yisrael ehad)*. Both parts were engaged in the same process of Jewish creativity; the state of Israel was neither a condition for Jewish survival, nor could it claim hegemony in the relationships with the Diaspora.

After 1948, the debate centered on the viability of the Diaspora and on the right of Israel not only to act as a sovereign state and determine its own fate but also to see itself as the center of the Jewish people. The sharp correspondence between Ben-Gurion and Rawidowicz heralds the tension inherent in the Israel-Diaspora relationships. Ben-Gurion, in a letter to an American rabbi in January 1953, had already asserted that "the meaning of Zionism is life in the land of Israel, not affiliation with a Zionist organization." Ben-Gurion, on 24 November 1954, writes that "[t]he Jew in the *golah*...is not able to be a complete Jew, and no Jewish community in the golah is able to live a complete Jewish life. Only in the State of Israel is a full Jewish life possible." The Rawidowicz rejoinder, here and elsewhere, is that the Diaspora consists of vibrant, creative communities with their own intrinsic value, striving to create a Jewish life to the extent they can. Where Ahad Ha'Am spoke of a spiritual center and a periphery, Rawidowicz speaks of an ellipse with two foci, the land of Israel and the Diaspora, equally partners in "the people of Israel", and in the preservation of a common people. The question now is whether the relationships is more properly seen in terms of bipolarity and mutuality than in centrality and subordination.

Within the American Jewish community as a whole, the commitment to Zionism was always a minority view. Not until the 1967 war did the Jewish people almost unanimously become involved not only in political and financial support of the imperiled state struggling for survival, but also in virtually automatic acceptance of its policy decisions to ensure that survival and the political stability of Israel. But, increasingly over the last decade, those decisions have been assessed more soberly, and the hegemony of Israel has become subject to challenge. Political, social, and ideological factors have all contributed to this end. The rise to power of Likud in 1977, the Lebanese imbroglio of 1982, the Iran-contra affair, the Pollard case, the riots in the territories, the continuing division in political leadership resulting in immobility, and a hesitancy about the peace process have all taken their toll and led to significant differences, both procedural and substantive, between the two communities. Crisis empathy may not become enduring solidarity.

Social and demographic changes in Israel, now with an Oriental-Jewish majority and a rapidly increasing Arab minority, presently 17 percent, and suffering from a hemorrhage of yordim, who often provide and exemplify a negative image of Israel, suggest a mosaic less attractive for Ashkenazi Americans. At the same time, the prosperity and growing prominence of Jews in almost all areas of American life in an open and tolerant society with little overt anti-Semitism, have given the Jewish community a greater self-confidence and status than ever before and an influence it has not been loath to use. The community has not accepted the European nineteenth-century premise that emancipated Jews were obligated to an unspoken social contract, to become assimilated except for strictly religious beliefs and observances, or to become "Englishmen of the Mosaic persuasion."

Between Israel and the Diaspora, the relationship is at once unique, because of the Law of Return and the automatic citizenship granted to Jews immigrating into Israel, and also filled with a special emotional intensity. Both sides are still deeply concerned about both the survival and condition of world Jewry, and about the state of Israel. A 1986 poll shows that 63 percent of American Jews agree that "caring about Israel is a very important part of my being a Jew." Caring generally increases with older people, who have memories of the Hitler era and virulent anti-Semitism, affiliation with Jewish organizations, or degree of religious Orthodoxy. Two warning signs at this point. In 1983 a similar poll showed 15 percent more who cared. Also, about a third of the Jewish population today do not feel any special deep concern for Israel.

The two communities are bound in a host of ways: familial relationships; personal friendship; professional association; public religious, cultural, and economic connections; children and students spending time in Israel; philanthropic contributions; and, in a more ambiguous way, the growing present of yordim. Fund-raisers now play a role in supervising some of Israel's social and educational programs. Business people are involved in Israeli industrial and commercial development. A high proportion of American Jews (85 percent) pay attention to news about Israel. About three-quarters would not vote for a political candidate unfriendly to Israel. Over 90 percent think U.S. support for Israel is in America's self-interest. Is Israel therefore the major binding force of American Jewry, at a historical moment when other ties of Jewishness are less cohesive? Can Jewish identity survive without the existence and example of Israel?

Three points are pertinent here. The first is that the majority of American Jewry is neither Orthodox nor Zionist, the two groups that are the strongest supporters of Israel. Young adults, Reform believers, and secular people are less involved with Israel. And over 60 percent of Jewish school-age children presently get no formal Jewish education. Second, the numerically declining American community (low birth rate and high and increasing rate of intermarriage, especially among professionals and graduates), the growing professional class character of a society where barriers have fallen, more divorce, greater physical mobility increases the risks for a Jewish presence. Apart from the Orthodox minority, those of Jewish extraction are less likely to participate in Jewish life in the future and less likely to feel deeply attached to Israel. The third fact, shown by polls, is that the Israel response to American Jews is less warm than the reciprocal feeling.

A New Zionism?

Despite doctrinal and personal differences, the cardinal assumption of traditional Zionism was that, with the establishment of a Jewish state,

Diaspora Jews would make aliyah to it. Zionist theorists could not anticipate that few of the now 5.5 million American Jews would be prepared to emigrate. Only 22 percent of the world's Jews live in Israel, although 40 percent of new births of Jewish children occur there.

The harsh reality is that aliyah has been rejected by the most powerful part of the Diaspora, as well as by most Jews elsewhere free to choose. Algerian Jews went to France, South Africans to Australia, and Latin American and Soviet Jews to the United States. A 1986 poll shows that over 80 percent of American Jews reject the idea of aliyah, and only 10 percent think they can live a full Jewish life in Israel.

Disturbed by this development, Zionist intellectuals, in the United States and elsewhere, have attempted to reexamine the fundamentals of Zionist theory. Over the last decade, greater prominence is now accorded Ahad Ha'Am and his belief in a *merkaz ruhani*, a spiritual center in Israel that would be an inspiration for the continuing Diaspora, and would embody concepts of justice and right action, provide a basis for Jewish identity, and lead to the psychological reconditioning of the Jewish people. Israel would become a kingdom of priests and a holy nation. Simply formulated, where Herzl was concerned with the problems of Jews, Ahad Ha'Am was interested in strengthening Jewishness. Yet, even conceding that inherent ambiguity was always present in Zionist writings, the significant role recently given to Ahad Ha'Am seems more a post facto rationalization of reality, as seen in the lack of aliyah and the increase of yeridah, than the logical conclusion to be reached from those writings. After all, it is Herzl who is seen in Israel's Declaration of Independence as "the spiritual father of the Jewish State."

Of course, Zionist theorists should decide their ideology appropriate to changing circumstances and attitudes. But inevitably this revisionism, resulting from the persistence and vitality of the Diaspora, raises problems. In the Diaspora what meaning is to be given to Jewish culture and to Jewish identity? Can that identity have any real content other than religion? What can the concepts of the centrality of Israel or of Israel as a spiritual center now mean? Does the state of Israel exist more for the sake of the Jewish people than for its own sake?

Jewish Identity

Defining "Jewish identity," whether seen as religious, communal, or cultural in character, is a rather difficult task. Alternatively, it can be understood as a way of life regulated by *Halakhah* and ethical norms, adherence to basic ideas and values, commitment to essential principles of justice and humanitarianism, belief in a vision of national redemption, acknowledgment of historical pedigree, membership of a collective entity, attachment to synagogue, common folkways and life-style, fear of anti-Semitism, or simply a feeling of Jewishness.

Polls of American Jewish observance indicate that identity is now overwhelmingly celebratory, when at a festival, and domestic, rather than devout and public. The Israeli view is more intricate. About two-thirds think, as do American Jews, of the Jewish people "as an extension of my family." Indeed, it is interesting that in recent years some Israeli parents have returned to the practice of giving Jewish names to their children. But the same number cannot think of being a Jew without thinking of the land of Israel and the state of Israel, and half agree that their basic sense of identity and commitment is to Israel and Israelis rather than to Jews and Judaism. Persons under forty, especially those of Oriental origin, generally believe that being Jewish is less important than do their elders. All the same, Israel is unlikely, under present conditions, to witness the reemergence of the "Canaanites," the small group that argued after 1948 that the new Israel should be differentiated from Jewish life in the Diaspora, and related to the land and its people.

However "Jewish identity" is defined, the Jerusalem Program of the World Jewish Congress in 1968 states as one of its five aims, "the preservation of the identity of the Jewish People through the fostering of Jewish Hebrew education and of Jewish spiritual and cultural values." The crucial fact is that only in Israel do all Jewish children receive a Jewish education. The need for American Jewish education has been appreciated on both sides. Some 500 Jewish day schools now exist with a claimed total attendance of 100,000. Institutions or centers of Jewish studies have been established, and over 250 colleges have courses in Judaica.

Whether the effect of these educational programs can overcome the disintegrating forces of intermarriage and assimilation and can maintain Jewish identity in some meaningful fashion, or whether much of the content of that identity will derive, in the absence of any anti-Semitic manifestation, from adherence to Israel, the front line of Jewish survival, by non-Orthodox Jews, remains an open question. The irony here is that secular Israeli culture is conceivable while a long-term secular Jewish culture in the Diaspora is improbable, especially if the emotional memories of the Holocaust dim.

Negation of Aliyah

The negation of aliyah as a fundamental requirement began soon af-ter the establishment of Israel. In his celebrated encounter in August 1950 with Jacob Blaustein, then president of the American Jewish Com-mittee, Prime Minister Ben-Gurion was obliged to agree that the deci-sion on emigration to Israel "rests with the free discretion of each American Jew himself...the essence of halutziut is free choice." Ten years later, in his address to the 25th World Jewish Congress, Ben-Gurion, portraying his true feeling, stated that "every religious Jew has daily violated the precepts of Judaism and the Torah by remaining in the Diaspora." After protest by Mr. Blaustein, Ben-Gurion in April 1961 again agreed that "it was perfectly natural for differences of view to exist on the essence and meaning of Judaism and Jewishness...in particular between the Jews who live in the independent State of Israel and Jews living in other countries." At other times Ben-Gurion sug-gested second-best alternatives to aliyah: study of the Bible and He-brew, visits to Israel, investing capital, sending children to high school or college. Nevertheless, for Ben-Gurion, with his fundamental concept of "statism," "everything done by Jews in Israel is central, vital, critical for the Jewish people and for Jewish history...what is done by Jews in the Diaspora is secondary."

The debate on aliyah is inextricably linked with that on the Diaspora. On one side is the view that Diaspora life is second-rate and derivative where Jews live under the authority of a non-Jewish state and cannot control the forces that surround them. The *galut* is punishment, a mani-festation, in A. B. Yeshoshua's formulation, of a national perversion of a neurotic people who wish to dwell apart. In the midst of the Pollard affair, Shlomo Avineri harshly remarked that the American condition, comfortable though it might be, was "exile nonetheless." Elsewhere, Avineri has spoken of the lack in the Diaspora of a public, corporate Jewishness that is the state.

On the other side of the argument is the moderate view of Salo Baron who in 1958 rejected what he called "the lachrymose conception of Jew-ish history," and did not see any pressure that could lead to mass emi-gration, a view that has amply been borne out. An extreme position, in the polemics of Jacob Neusner, argues that "if there ever was a prom-ised land, we American Jews are living in it."

Recent polls indicate the differences between the two communities. Israelis, by a two to one margin, think that "American Jews who refuse to seriously consider aliyah are doing something wrong," and a majority feel that those Jews could "lead a fuller Jewish life in Israel than in the US." American Jews are more anxious about present and future anti-Semitism than are Israelis, and recognize that current rates of assimilation and intermarriage pose serious dangers to American Jewish survival. Nonetheless, overwhelmingly they see American Jewish life as vital and dynamic, and do not believe they can live a fuller Jewish life in Israel than in the United States.

Indeed, the concept of *shlilat Hagolah* (negation of the Diaspora) stems from the experience of Eastern Europe where Jews could not lead a viable life or develop fully. But the Diaspora is now voluntarily chosen. It may be modern Babylon; it is certainly not nineteenth-century Minsk. The danger to Jewish identity is assimilation, not oppression. If the Jewish people are not now prepared to emigrate to Israel, do they see themselves as peripheral to the Jewish state?

Centrality of Israel

The centrality of Israel enunciated in the 1951 Jerusalem program and reemphasized in 1968, is problematic both in theory and practice. At its most exalted, centrality implies a spiritual and cultural center providing a light unto Jewry as well as the nations, and , in Alfred Gottschalk's words, "must remain sacred in the consciousness of the Jewish people." In a more secular vein, Israel, embodying communal cohesiveness and national continuity, or performing a symbolic function, is to ensure the survival and the self-awareness and the identity of Jews in the Diaspora. Some, like Gerson Scholem, hold that the state is meant to serve the Jewish people, and would lose its meaning if deprived of this goal. Many others believe that without Israel, the Jewish people would soon disappear.

The opposite intellectual argument has been made by scholars from Israel and the American Diaspora like Simon Rawidowicz and Gerson Cohen. Zionists should stop speaking of Israel as the spiritual center; it must not be made a condition for Jewish survival, it has no right to claim hegemony of the Jewish people, it has no automatic right to control the religious and personal life of Jews in the rest of the world but has to earn that right by its performance.

Centrality depends on respect and that will stem from perceptions of Israeli actions and the nature of its society. Israel has to earn that respect, politically by a legitimate leadership capable of making decisions, diplomatically by pursuing the path to peace, and spiritually and culturally by Jewish scholarship, ethos, and its definition of a Jewish state. Others, more harshly, have suggested that Israel has yet to prove by concrete example that it provides a spiritually or culturally creative light that can be a beacon for the Diaspora. Whether Israel has or has not produced those concrete examples in the fields of Jewish scholarship and literature or raised the Jewish spirit or renewed Judaism is a matter of professional judgment.

As an abstract concept, centrality, or priority to use a more moderate term, is difficult to address because it relates differently to the complex nature of Jewry in its ethnic, religious, and national aspects. Empirically, Conservative, Reform, and secular American Jews, will not accept the authority of the Chief Rabbinate, nor do American organizational leaders view Israel as a cultural or ideological center. The problem is compounded by cultural differences. The Rabbinate in Israel is seen as a political body as well as a spiritual leadership. But for most American Jews, separation of church and state is not simply instrumental but is an important value in its own right.

Since the formula "we are one people" was propounded, "centrality" has often given way in practice to a partnership in which mutual concerns and benefits, and sometimes costs, have been present. Salo Baron, in a speech in 1959, had a picturesque image for this. The Diaspora, he wrote, is simultaneously Israel's daughter, getting spiritual sustenance from Israel, and her mother, lavishing bounty and tenderness. Indeed, the Diaspora has been made proud of and basked in the reflected glory of a democracy's determination to survive against innumerable odds. It has gained content for its own survival by welcoming Israeli rabbis and teachers to help foster Jewish culture and education. And Israeli statehood has, to some extent, enhanced the acceptance of the exercise of power by American Jews, both directly and as a lobby.

Israel has benefited in a variety of ways. Economically, it has been aided by American financial assistance, business involvement, and provision of technical and professional knowledge. Administratively, fundraisers and the new Jewish priesthood have helped plan and supervise Israel's social and educational maturation. All Jewish organization have set up educational programs in Israel and have taken part in discussion of spiritual and cultural matters. Project Renewal connects local federations with neighborhood development programs in Israel. At least two federations, Los Angeles and San Francisco, have offices in Jerusalem that attend to the efficient operation of their Israeli programs.

Above all, Israel has benefited from the constant and skillful use of American Jewish political influence and pressure, by nearly forty organizations, on both the president and Congress. American decision makers have responded to the urging of economic and military aid for Israel, which has been recognized as a strategic asset and the only real friend of the United States in the Middle East. This has probable been the most successful sustained lobbying effort in recent American politics and has been the object of both admiration and envy. But it has also now led to a certain concern, expressed in a number of recent books, that the lobby has been too manipulated by Israel and too automatically supportive of its policies. Within the Jewish community a minority view argues that the needs of Israel preoccupy leaders of organizations to an unwarranted degree and that other internal Jewish issues have been neglected. Nahum Goldmann in 1980 thought Jewish pressure and American support "was now slowly becoming something of a negative factor." But the prediction of that permanent pessimist has not been validated, either in the attitude of the general public, policies of support for Israel, or increase in anti-Semitism.

Problems Over Centrality

The whole issue of centrality compels one to raise a number of questions on issues such as ethical standards, yordim, dual loyalty, the role of Israel in world Jewry, the right of criticism, as well as the concept, already discussed, of Jewish and Israeli identity after the emergence of a pluralistic society in Israel.

Ethical Standards

Centrality imposes an unwarranted moral burden on Israel, which is still uncertain whether to be a state, like all others, or a light unto the nations, but which is expected to adhere to a higher standard than the norm in its ethical behavior and pluralistic tolerance. Yet, even admitting this inequity, American Jewry, expecting Israel to be based on Western norms, has become increasingly disturbed by some facets of Israeli society: the growth and increased demands of the Orthodox—with consequences for education, the army, personal choice, and political moderation—the more strident note of the ultra-Orthodox (shown in the recent dispute over schmitta), the lack of civil marriage and divorce, the Orthodox view of the role of women, the raucous political fundamentalism of a small minority, the place and rights of the growing Arab minority, as well as the political divisions that on some issues have resulted in immobility. These factors do not make Israel a Third World society, but neither are they appealing to an American Jewry that is Ashkenazi, more highly educated, more liberal on civil rights, less Orthodox, more concerned with democratic norms or religious pluralism; it is thus less likely to accept guidance on ethical issues.

Yordim

The numbers of those who have left Israel are uncertain, perhaps half a million in North American alone. A 1983 poll showed that only 16 percent of American Jewry agreed that Israelis who emigrate are doing something wrong (compared with 70 percent of Israelis); at least 20 percent of Israelis thought of leaving. Three matters cause concern. The Israeli rate of disapproval of *yordim* fell from 70 percent in 1982 to 55 percent in 1986. The rate of disapproval is lowest among young adults, the group most likely to go. To some extent the stigma formerly associated with emigration has declined. And about half of the 65,000 American *olim*, the best educated group, have returned to the United States, allegedly for economic and family reasons. Whatever the reasons, the *yordim* constitute a poignant example of the rejection of centrality. It can be argued that the general attrition figures compare favorably with those countries, such as the United States or Australia, to which emigration has taken place. But the telling figure is that of emigrating sabras, born and educated in Israel. A society that cannot hold its natives can hardly make claims on outsiders.

Dual Loyalty

The charge of dual loyalty, with its implication at the most extreme of potential treason, has troubled some in the Diaspora. The anti-Semitism index, drawn up by Gertrude Selznick and Stephen Steinberg in 1964, indicates a link between beliefs that Jews "stick together too much" and that they are "more loyal to Israel." Indeed, polls of American citizens over the last twenty years show that the proportion believing Jews are more loyal to or feel closer to Israel than to the United States has varied between 20 percent and 37 percent, figures that move in relation to attitudes to Israel itself.

Coincidentally, these figures are strikingly similar to the proportion of American Jews who have an unquestioning devotion to Israel or who think that devotion may come into conflict with devotion to the United States. The rest of American Jewry feel differently. Polls in 1981 indicate that only 7 percent of Jews agree that most Jewish people feel closer to Israel, and 72 percent disagree that their feelings for Israel come into conflict with devotion to America. American Jews thus agree with Ben-Gurion's 1950 statement that "the Jews of the United States...have one political attachment and that is to the United States. They owe no political allegiance to Israel."

Some do not accept this view, as Gore Vidal showed in his attack on Norman Podhoretz and Midge Decter in 1986 for their support of Israel with his implication that their first loyalty would always be to Israel. But warm friendship, close ties, and efforts to gain support for Israel, as the ethnic groups have done for their peoples, do not constitute disloyalty. Espionage, of course, is a different matter, but is the result of individual, not communal action. The case of Jonathan Pollard caused needless concern for some Jewish leaders. It may have given some fuel for those critical of the role of American Jewry in influencing American policy. But the limited repercussions both in Washington and among the general public over the matter suggest it has been commonly regarded as an aberration, not as a norm. However, the Pollard case, like the Iran-contra affair, also suggests that the interest and objectives of Israel and the United States may not always coincide.

In particular, the Pollard case did not, apparently, increase anti-Semitism in the United States. Certainly one of the ironies of the creation of Israel has been that it affords an opportunity for a disguised form of anti-Semitism. Classical Zionism, failed to envisage the possibility that it might become a cause of, or at least an excuse for, anti-Semitic feelings. Criticism of Israel has sometimes been accompanied by undertones of prejudice. At the United Nations, particularly since the infamous Zionism-as-racism resolution of November 1975, this prejudice has even been overt. During the war in Lebanon, the media on-slaught against Israel, going far beyond reasonable commentary, again suggested deeper emotions at work. As Leon Poliakov pointed out, the effect of the war was to create not so much a rekindling of anti-Semitism as a weakening of the taboos that have surrounded it since World War II. Theoretically, one might be able to distinguish between anti-Zionism—whatever that means at present—and anti-Semitism. But in reality, one suspects that the intensity of the attack on Zionism or the Zionist entity betrays the feelings of traditional anti-Semitism.

Israel's Protective Role

Should Israel have the central role in speaking or acting on behalf of Diaspora Jews? It has certainly acted in what it perceived to be the Jewish interest as well as in its own interests as a sovereign state. On some issues—Operation Babylon in Iraq, the capture of Eichmann in 1960, the Entebbe raid in 1976, the Demjanjuk case today, Operation Moses in Ethiopia, protests against bombings of Diaspora Jews—few will be troubled by Israeli activity.

On the other matters—tactics at a given moment about Soviet Jewry, the issue of *noshrim*, relations with Latin American countries in the past or with South Africa and Iran more recently—the Israeli position does not necessarily coincide with that of American Jewry. Over the years Israel has necessarily acted as a sovereign state: attempting, because of friendship with France at the time, to influence American Jewry on the Algerian question in the late 1950s; under pressure from President Lyndon Johnson, trying to moderate Jewish opposition to his Vietnam policy; registering support, as did Ambassador Rabin (though he was repri-manded by Golda Meir for doing so), for the reelection of President Nixon in 1972.

On some issues differences exist between the two communities and must be accepted, though attempts have been made to mitigate them. The exercise of power, realpolitik, by a sovereign state is based on self-interest and expediency more than on ethical principles. No doubt, Is-rael takes the views of American Jewry into account to some extent in formulating its policies. Similarly, American Jews may be conscious of Israeli concerns in the outcome of some political questions: relations with blacks, alliances with Hispanics, location of the American embassy in Israel, U.S. arms sales to Arab countries, decisions made under the Gramm-Rudman law, resolutions of the United Nations.

Some, like Nahum Goldmann, Arthur Hertzberg, and Alexander Schindler, have argued for the creation of a consultative assembly representing both sides. Even apart from the difficulties in deciding on the modalities of representation, a formal process of this kind seems both unworkable and undesirable. Such a body would not help dispose of he phantasmagoria of a worldwide conspiracy, which has recently surprisingly reemerged in a Japanese form in works by Masami Uno. A consultative assembly might well reinforce the delusion that international Jewish capital already functions as a global shadow government, manipulating everything that happens in the world.

Moreover, organizational links already exist, particularly through the WZO and the Jewish Agency, with economic and cultural functions overlapping those of the state institutions, and which provide a structure for political leadership. In addition, elections to the top positions of the WZO result from agreements made between American groups in the organization and Israeli political parties.

The Right of Criticism

Is public criticism of Israel desirable, and to what degree should American Jews and groups enter into the policy-making debate? The first question cannot be categorically answered in the abstract, but only in expedient relation to specific issues, both because political issues are inextricably interrelated with others, and because the long-term consequences of action can rarely be foreseen.

Recognizing that public criticism might provide fuel and ammunition for opponents of Israel, as well as reduce its self-confidence, three working rules might be appropriate. Public comment on Israeli policies and actions is admirable, indeed desirable, except on those matters where the survival of Israel is endangered in a clear and present fashion. Any criticism should be circumspect both in character and in the choice of arena or public space in which it is made. And third, Israel should not be held to an intolerably high standard of perfection, but rather compared with other democracies, such as the United States and Britain, in wartime.

American Partisanship

Should American Jewry enter into the partisan debate in Israel? In 1987 both the American Jewish Congress and the Union of American Hebrew Congregations did this by offering their advice on the nature of the peace process. From the beginning of the state, different American groups have taken positions or been implored to do so by like-minded Israeli groups to provide political support.

This has particularly been the case with Orthodox groups. Since 1949 they have engaged in debates, including those on education of immigrant children, national service for women, Kashrut on the ship "Shalom," autopsy, and naturally, "Who is a Jew?" There is nothing inappropriate about legitimate expression of this kind and indeed it is incumbent on American Jews to make known their views on general ethical issues or to form coalitions with Israeli groups. But, at least two problems exist. The first is that on these particular questions, touching on religion and on the turf of religious groups, the American Reform and Conservative groups have less opportunity than the Orthodox to act as a counterweight pressure on Israel. A second is that the secular community is even more at a disadvantage, having no representative organized counterpart in Israel. Parenthetically, this group is handicapped in another sense: The area of foreign affairs, in which it may have particular interest, is the one that is most circumscribed for public comment.

The Future

A final word on the last two issues. Public utterance or attempt to influence Israeli policy could be related to the opportunities available in private to American Jewish leaders, most of whom have easy access, to Israeli decision makers both on visits to Israel and during the appearances of Israeli officials and party heads before Diaspora groups.

What is likely to be the future of the relationships? After the experience of its virtual isolation in 1967, and 1973, apart from the support of Diaspora Jews, Israel is understandably anxious about it. Much will depend on the nature of the two communities and on the state of the peace process. An Israel in which tension between the Ashkenazi and Oriental communities is reduced with intermarriage and mutual toleration, in which the Orthodox minority does not militantly try to coerce the majority, and in which the Arab community has assured civil rights, is likely to maintain American affection and good will. But the intense enthusiasm of the American community in the decade after 1967 is not likely to be easily rekindled. The community is aging, and its younger members have been moving to the sunbelt states and from large to smaller towns bringing with it two problems for Israel. One is a probable change in allocation and priority of philanthropic expenditure from Israel to internal needs of the aged and new settlements. The other is that younger people are less likely to feel emotionally attached to or to identify with Jewry, to join Jewish organizations, or to support military action or the use of force by Israel. Already, at least one-third of the nominally 5.5 million Jews have nothing to do with Jewish affairs. Under present circumstances that proportion will continue to increase, and participation in American Jewish life will decline. The effective American community will thus be not much, if any, larger than that of Israeli Jews.

Finally, if the peace process moves forward successfully, will the bonds between the Diaspora and Israel be strengthened or weakened? The answer is problematic—one can argue either way about it—but the need for peace is not. The very least all of us can do is to foster the search for peace in the best way we can.

Rutgers, The State University of New Jersey
Department of Political Science

Note

1. Irving Louis Horowitz, "Israeli-Diaspora Relations as a Problem in Center-Periphery Linkages," *Contemporary Jewry* (Spring 1977): 28–37.

21

In Pursuit of Objectivity

Raymond Horricks

I am not a professional sociologist, nor even a self-proclaimed one. The nearest legitimate entitlement I can make is that Hannah Arendt's *The Origins of Totalitarianism* has been, together with Veblen's economics, first a formative, and since then a lasting influence upon my adult life. I suppose, too, I can claim that anyone who writes about *real* people—as has always been my intention—becomes a sociologist of sorts. My relationship with Irving Louis Horowitz has been based upon friendship and upon his being the publisher (at Transaction) of myself as a writer. But I have not been unaware of his own personal distinction as both sociologist and writer; and if this is not unique for a publisher, it is nevertheless rare.

I am also aware of the wide variety of his interests, which in turn has been an important fueling component of his work as a publisher and in the field of sociology. But one item sticks with me from the variety of his curiosity and subsequently gained knowledge, which might otherwise appear butterfly-like—albeit of a butterfly with a clear sense of direction and sureness in the local air currents. And this is his inherent, unfailing objectivity at all times, which I suppose is really the main quality allowing a prominent sociologist to rise above the mediocre. What one expects from modern sociology (I know I do) is painstaking research, hinged upon both instinct *and* inquisitiveness, a genuine concern for humanity and, eventually, lucid presentation. But if any one of these things is not accompanied by overall objectivity, then his most precious ingredient of all, the Truth, will almost certainly become muddied—even distorted. Leading on the one hand to fanaticism, be it political or literary (Lenin or Leavis), and on the other to that particular kind of "thesis grinding" which Cyril Connolly accused American scholarship of adopting apropos the works of James Joyce,[1] and Gore Vidal has damned more forcefully still in his essay "The Hacks of Academe: Our New Novels are Being Written for Teaching Rather Than for Reading!"[2]

Irving Horowitz's own objectivity is something reassuring, therefore. I first noted it in person, at a seminar in Rotterdam in 1992, when the subject of Ronald Reagan's presidency cropped up. (I am writing here of the time when George Bush was still the White House incumbent.) Prior to this I'd marked my companion of the day for a liberal, if not necessarily a card-carrying Democrat. (Probably I was right, although I never did get around to asking him.) But when someone—one of my fellow Europeans—launched a verbal attack upon the Reagan years *in toto,* Irving was swift to respond. Not as an American patriot, but as an objective analyst. He simply would not accede to a blanket put-down of the two-term presidency, instead enumerating, with firmness and speed, the social benefits and other achievements that had gone on steadily behind all of the 'film star' politics and general saber rattling.

Following which, it is in pursuit of objectivity that I now move more directly into Irving Horowitz's writings. These writings again cover a wide variety of subject matter, and I cannot bluff that I have read them all. But just a random glance at the titles tells its own story: *Rock, Recording and Rebellion; Rock on the Rocks: Bubblegum Anybody?; Ideologies and Theories about American Jazz; Solzhenitsyn: Revolution, Retribution and Redemption; Orwell: Language, Truth and Politics; The War Game: Studies in the Civilian Militarists; The Rise and Fall of Project Camelot;* and a collection of his single papers, *Professing Sociology.*

But the theme of objectivity takes me by choice to a paper entitled "On Relieving the Deformities of our Transgressions," written for and published in 1979 by the magazine *Society.*[3] This piece is, in fact, a film review of *The Deer Hunter,* the Universal/EMI production starring Robert DeNiro, Meryl Streep, and Christopher Walken, written by Deric Washburn, directed by Michael Cimino, and including a "hit" record (an acoustic guitar solo composed by Stanley Myers) as part of its soundtrack. The film itself was a hit too, in the terms of awards gained and money earned. But I still remember coming away from it after a second viewing and, while agreeing that its success was deserved, disagreeing with what most national and international reviewers had assumed in praising it as an antiwar film. By doing this they had inadvertently lumped it together with such skillfully made, but essentially anti-American films as *Apocalypse Now, Platoon,* and later, Kubrick's *Full Metal Jacket.* By anti-American I mean stating that U.S. entry into the Vietnam War was morally wrong or, at best, mistaken. True, *The Deer Hunter* can be interpreted in this way; but I think to do so is to miss out on its more important truths. And it is precisely such truths that I can pick out from the Horowitz review, and underline as a tribute to their objectivity.

Objectivity is not something naturally held or there by instinct. It has to be worked for. Also, its very clear-sightedness can only be arrived at when passions have cooled. Above all it has to *allow* for much. To quote from Irving's review, "Creativity invariably displays near-universal ambiguity."[4] As a result of which, he writes, "*The Deer Hunter* is not simply another film, or solely a work of art. It is these things, and more; it is a political statement. This combination of art and politics lends this destined-to-be classic both its volatility *and its ambiguity*" (my italics).[5]

For me the most strategic breakthrough of *The Deer Hunter* was its managing to be antiwar without being necessarily anti-American. Admittedly American (or, if you like, Kennedy) involvement in Vietnam began as something decidedly tacky; and while a cliché, it also happens to be correct that militarily the United States did not learn from previous French mistakes, but proceeded to reproduce them on an ever-expanding scale. Given the benefit of hindsight though, it is no longer possible to look back on that particular war as a strictly black and white affair, a "goodies and baddies" war like some glorious John Ford film. For in reality the Socialist Republic of Vietnam was (and is) far from glorious.

A distinguished antiwar campaigner while the fighting continued in Vietnam, the folk singer Joan Baez more recently has felt compelled toward the following dramatic outburst:

> Instead of bringing hope and reconciliation to war-torn Vietnam, your government [the Hanoi Regime] has created a nightmare of appalling dimensions.... The jails are overflowing with thousands upon thousands of "detainees." People disappear and never return. People are shipped to re-education centers, fed a starvation diet of stale rice, forced to squat bound wrist to ankle, to suffocate in connex boxes. People are used as human mine detectors, clearing live mine fields with their hands and feet. Torture is rampant, life in general is hell, and death prayed for.

All of this and much more was anticipated by *The Deer Hunter.* The film does not whitewash America's contribution to the war, but it does lift some of the covers off the other side. And this much Irving Horowitz has seen with both clarity and acute sensitivity in his perceptive and (at the risk of laboring the word) objective review. He in turn quotes the French antiwar writer Jean Lacouture, also speaking from a position given hindsight: "People like myself...have become vehicles and intermediaries for a lying and criminal propaganda, ingenuous spokesmen for tyranny in the name of liberty."[6]

The Horowitz review goes on to explain, convincingly to my mind, a walkout by the then-Stalinist Soviets and their Cuban acolytes during the Cannes Film Festival showing of 1978: "For *The Deer Hunter* is a film about free Russians living in a free nation,"[7] and grateful at that time for being just that. As he points out, a good deal of the first portion of the movie is taken up with the wedding of one of the three young men who go to war!

The scenes of the old Russian women bringing the wedding cake to the hall where the reception is to be held could easily have been taken from any town and country scene in the Ukraine. The physical qualities and properties are clearly Russian and Eastern European. Many members of the second generation reveal themselves as generous, big-hearted, and with broad grins. Their emotions are transparently honest. The lovely ceremony in the church and its beautiful old Russian hymns, followed by the reception and a series of folk songs that anyone with a Russian ancestry is familiar with, sets the tone for a film that is unmistakenly ethnic, and in this case unmistakenly Russian. For this film of grizzly proportions involving Americans in Vietnam remains throughout a film of Americans from old Russia.

We should not lose sight of Irving's own Russian ancestry here, nor of his Americanization by a process of growing up in one of the poorest areas of New York City. Even so, the writing combines a rare balance and insight with observation of the highest order, as does this:

> [T]he most devastating aspect of the film...is...from the point of Soviet ideology. One of the "heroic" victims of the war (Christopher Walken), when asked if his name is Russian, answers laconically: "No, America." But, in fact, his name is of Russian derivation; and he and his friends are free Russians. It is inconceivable that any citizen of the Soviet Union could say the same. And it is an irony of history, no less than a quirk of fate, that such people bore the American burdens of the Vietnam War.[8]

Again, this was written before the Gorbachev reforms and the subsequent internal Russian collapse under Boris Yeltsin. Nevertheless the writer poses what is, in a sense, a timeless dilemma.

The essential tension of *The Deer Hunter,* and what makes it work, is a combination of antiwar feelings with potent rejection of anti-American feelings. The film's subjects are, after all, working-class people with strong allegiances and commitments to what Louis Adamic called their native land. They believe in the legitimacy of the system, and its right to call upon its young for military duty. Those who do not go feel this need to apologize to those who do. But only those who go to Vietnam shared the utter sense of tragic waste that this war represented.

Is genuine patriotism so very wrong, therefore? And isn't it a good thing when scales fall from the eyes of former sincere antiwar protesters (like Joan Baez) once the real and cynical nature of Hanoi's despotism is revealed? "The film," his review concludes:

> presents a working-class which fought the war but did not want the war; who, nonetheless, as participants, understood the nature of that conflict far better than those who opposed it on ideological grounds. This was a working-class war, opposed by a middle-class intelligentsia: two worlds that did not meet a decade ago, and which, in the aftermath of the film, still seem unable to comprehend what each side was doing in the last decade. The moral guilt Americans have universally laboured under is finally being lifted as a result of the manifestly oppressive nature of these Asian mini-despotisms. This awareness may not bring back the dead, but at least it does attenuate our collective suffering. And with this watershed film we can move about our lives with greater attention to fundamentals, less arrogance, and more appreciation for those who fought in this made, undeclared war.[9]

Of course the working class had to fight the war, as is true of Northern Ireland and has now proven to be so in Bosnia. I have to add a more modern point here: Nowadays generals generally die in their beds. Of the twenty-six marshals created by Napoleon, three died on the battlefield; and of those who survived Oudinot received twenty-two wounds and Ney, I believe, fourteen—not counting the eleven bullets from his execution squad. In our present century the avoiding of personal danger by the top brass is taken for granted. As for the politicians, who actually start the wars, well . . .

I regard *The Deer Hunter* as the most important American film of its decade, just as David Lynch's *Blue Velvet* was probably the most revolutionary new film of the 1980s (and *Easy Rider* that of the 1960s). But *The Deer Hunter,* because of, rather than despite its variable ambiguity, still succeeds in being objective: in political, social, and even in the most basic human terms. It has been fortunate to receive from Irving Horowitz a most lucid *apologia*. Such occasional pieces are also a key to his larger writings. Which leads me on to examine the objectivity contained in a second piece of Horowitz's writing, entitled "Winners and Losers."[10] Again this is in concentrated essay form, in the style descended from Michel de Montaigne, which the author confesses he prefers to "lengthy tomes." But it is in turn included in a book of twenty-four essays given the same name and divided under the three headings of "Society," "Polity," and "Ideology." I have found much absorbing reading in this volume (collected and published in 1984 by Duke University Press), especially the pieces on "Transnational Terrorism," the more recent outbreaks of "Left-Wing Fascism," and, in the light, still more recently, of the Soviet Union's disintegration, on the "Multiplication of Marxisms." For where now, one wonders, is there left in our modern world for orthodox Marxists to go?

Even so, it is the title-essay itself that has gained my closest attention, not least because it confirms how, to retain true objectiveness, a sociologist must be at the same time empirical, that is, empirical in the speculative sense, of a preparedness to revise his theories (be they formerly adventurous or longstandingly held) in view of subsequent events. Also, it is interesting to discover the author, for the purpose of this essay, showing a readiness to move his ground from war and militarism (as of *The Deer Hunter*) to the shifting sands of politics, a field within which, to quote a previous (and these days somewhat tarnished) British prime minister, "a week can be a very long time."

Winners or Losers is addressed to the subject of politics and morality, from which other matters quite naturally arise: How does one reconcile pragmatism (so important to any would-be victor) with morals? Or when can a genuine and sincere ideology ever hope to succeed?

Four real politicians of historical significance have been chosen for examination under his intellectual microscope: Joseph Stalin, Leon Trotsky, George W. Plunkitt, and Thomas Hutchinson, all of whom were themselves empirical in the opportunist sense, but only two were victors in the pragmatic, temporal sense, while the other two have been frequently judged losers because their empiricism was qualified by idealism and/or morality. But is this straightforwardly true? Shouldn't we now be regarding all four as winners *and* losers?

The author has clearly researched his chosen figures with the utmost care. Historically, Stalin and Trotsky require no further introduction from me here. But Plunkitt and Hutchinson are less well known to us today (although it could be claimed their personal importance deserves to be better known), so that a thumbnail sketch about each might not go amiss.

George W. Plunkitt, as a result of his considerable pragmatic abilities, became the very darling of Tammany Hall (New York) Democratic politicians during their most halcyon days around the turn of our present century. He was not an evil man as such (in the Hitler or Stalinist sense), and was even known to argue against corruption, certain forms of corruption, that is. "The politician who steals is worse than a thief. He is a fool," he once said. "With the grand opportunities all around for the man with a political pull, there's no excuse for stealing a cent!" On the other hand, he himself was a man who never missed a trick. His philosophical handbook was *The Prince* by Machiavelli rather than the thoughts of Plato. Advancing toward a stage when he could speak kindly of his opponents, he once noted: "Me and the Republicans are enemies just one day in the year—election day. Then we fight tooth and nail. The rest of the time it's live and let live with us." He also believed in social reforms for the benefit of the people, *but only after being elevated to office*. First become attuned to what ordinary people want. Then get out the vote. Then give the people what you can afford to. But let them have it *from a position of power*. All economic theories must become subservient to the latter.

And, of course, he was wildly successful. Within a time span of under two hundred years Jeffersonian concepts of democracy in the United States had progressed politically to a heyday for the smoke-filled rooms. With just the lone voice of the Reverend Charles Henry Parkhust raised in criticism of Tammany methods and its fat cats, Plunkitt could afford to light yet another cigar, stick his thumbs into his waistcoat pockets and wax moral, albeit self-righteous moral:

> The civil service gang is always howlin' about candidates and officeholders putting' up money for campaigns and about corporations chippin' in. They might as well howl about givin' contributions to churches. A political organisation has to have money for its business as well as a church, and who has more right to put up than the men who get the good things goin'. Take, for instance, a great political concern like Tammany hall. It does missionary work like a church, it's got big expenses and it's got to be supported by the faithful. If a corporation sends in a check to help the good work of the Tammany Society, why shouldn't we take it like

other missionary societies? Of course, the day may come when we'll reject the money of the rich as tainted, but it hadn't come when I left Tammany hall at 11:25 today.[11]

In contrast, on paper (historically) no one could appear to have been a bigger loser in his own lifetime than Thomas Hutchinson, the last royal governor of the state of Massachusetts. A good man and a humane one, it can be argued he was particularly naive in allowing his very qualities of compassion and wanting a fair deal for the American colonists to take second place to his loyalty to George III's incompetent conservative government in London. There is no evidence that Hutchinson even admired England's monarch personally, while there is ample evidence that he would have made an excellent first leader for an independent Massachusetts. His public principles were those of the English constitutional system as defined by John Locke; and in this instance loyalty triumphed, his rigidity increased, and in the end he suffered both defeat and exile. In the words of his chief biographer, Bernard Bailyn:

> For all (Hutchinson's) intelligence, he did not comprehend the nature of the forces that confronted him and that at a critical point he might have controlled, or if not controlled then at least evaded. He was never able to understand the moral basis of the protests that arose against the existing order. Committed to small, prudential gains through an intricate, closely calibrated world of status, deference, and degree he could not respond to the aroused moral passion and the optimistic and idealist impulses that gripped the minds of the Revolutionaries that led them to condemn as corrupt and oppressive the whole system by which their world was governed.[12]

Irving Horowitz does not entirely agree with this proposition. "I am not certain that Hutchinson's position can be described as myopic or self-serving," he writes.[13] Quite the contrary: from Bailyn's own testimony one should have to say that the total disregard of what was in his personal interests, interpreted as utilitarian, ultimately led to his rigidity. In this way, Hutchinson proved himself a moral force of considerable note even though he was of less significance as a political being: a politician eliciting some support although sadly out of step with historical progression.

I will return now to deal briefly with Stalin and Trotsky. The former was supremely successful by his own standards and via pragmatic methods within his living time span. The victor over Hitler's ambitions and invasion, undisputed overlord of the Russian people, scourge of the West, he died in his own bed and at the zenith of his powers. Trotsky, on the other hand, while no less an extremist (in his aims for communism), but in their confrontation neither pragmatic nor even practical, suffered flight and then eventually assassination on the orders of his rival, a point arrived at by the disillusioned end of George Orwell's *Animal Farm*. But what a difference Orwell would witness if still alive today! The crash and abandonment of Stalin's empire, with the dictator himself in the light of history almost totally revised; while Trotsky's teachings, ideals, and moralistic approach are all that any self-respecting communist has got to cling on to, be this right or wrong.

Thus, we are back with a quadrature. Four people in a sociological square, each in his own separate corner both a winner and a loser. Plunkitt a winner in his own lifetime, and a loser afterward, because Tammany hall eventually had to become to the Democratic party an Augean stable. Hutchinson an undoubted physical loser while he lived, but now something of a winner because he is respected for his integrity and principles. Stalin a monstrous winner until his death in 1953, but ever since a toppled effigy. Trotsky a losing martyr to his beliefs, now accorded a grudging respect even by his most implacable adversaries for being sincere in those beliefs. It all adds up to an ongoing conundrum. But it forces me to accept the premise that there are no *outright* winners and no *everlasting* losers. Not in historical terms anyway. And I have been helped along the way to realizing this by the objectivity within the Horowitz essay.

It also causes me to reiterate the earlier claim that his objectivity has been empiric in its revisionism. He would not have been able to write this piece in 1953—although he may even then have had glimmerings about it. However, he now has history and the subsequent reputations of Stalin and Trotsky on his side to amplify the comparison with Plunkitt and Hutchinson and bring it up to date. History, be it of sociology or any other subject or persona will always fail to be interpreted correctly if the interpreter is not sufficiently flexible to turn newly discovered facts into newly objective words. Even if this sometimes means eating earlier words.

But it takes courage to do so, because no writer (on any subject) finds it easy to declare his earlier published work invalid. While some have preferred to fight tooth and nail to discredit the new evidence, it is to Irving Horowitz's great credit, therefore, that in the light of what is fresh and has convinced him, no previous reputation, no matter how all-bestriding, can be excluded from revision—even when this involves his own chosen subject matter in the face of disconfirming evidence, I believe he would always opt for saying: The daughter of time is the truth, and must be recognized as such.

Independent broadcaster and producer
United Kingdom, Isle of Wright

Notes

1. Cyril Connolly, *Previous Convictions* (London: Hamish Hamilton, 1963).
2. Gore Vidal, *Matters of Fact and of Fiction* (London: William Heinemann, 1977).
3. Irving Louis Horowitz, "On Relieving the Deformities of Our Transgressions," *Society* 16, no. 5 (July-August 1979): 80–83.
4. Ibid., 80.
5. Ibid., 81.
6. Ibid., 81.
7. Ibid., 82.
8. Ibid., 83.
9. Ibid., 83.
10. Irving Louis Horowitz, *Winners and Losers* (Durham, NC: Duke University Press, 1984).
11. William L. Riordan, *Plunkitt of Tammany Hall* (New York: Knopf, 1948), 65.
12. Bernard Bailyn, The Ordeal of Thomas Hutchinson (Cambridge: Harvard University Press, 1974), x–xi.
13. Horowitz, *Winners and Losers*.

22

Six Deconstructionists in Search of a Preferred Reading and One Sociologist Discovered to be a Deconstructionist

Arthur Asa Berger

> HAMLET: *Do you see yonder cloud that's almost in shape of a camel?*
> POLONIUS: *By th' mass, and 'tis like a camel indeed.*
> HAMLET: *Methinks it is like a weasel.*
> POLONIUS: *It is backed like a weasel.*
> HAMLET: *Or like a whale?*
> POLONIUS: *Very like a whale.*
> —William Shakespeare, *Hamlet*

> *But don't you see that the whole trouble lies here. In words, words. Each one of us has within him a whole world of things, each man of us his own special world. And how can we ever come to an understanding if I put in the words I utter the sense and value of things as I see them, while you who listen to me must inevitably translate them according to the conception of things each one of you has within himself. We think we understand each other, but we never really do.*
> —Luigi Pirandello,
>   *Six Characters in Search of an Author*

A number of years ago I participated at a conference on culture and society held at Stanford University. I was a last-minute substitute for a scholar who was snowed in somewhere in the Midwest, and happened to spend a few minutes chatting with Melvin Tumin, another presenter at the conference.

"What are you interested in?" he asked.

"Popular culture," I replied.

"Popular culture," he repeated, smiling. "I usually take care of it in about a half hour in my seminars. That's about what I figure it's worth."

Things have changed a good deal since then, and popular culture, especially in its mass-mediated aspects, has become a subject of great interest to social scientists and scholars of all persuasions. But there have been some changes. Many people (myself included) who work in what we used to call popular culture now describe themselves somewhat differently.

One reason for this is that popular culture is a rather vague term and nobody is sure exactly what popular culture is and isn't. Where do you draw the line between popular culture and elite culture? Or can you draw a line that means anything? I generally argue that it is only at the extremes that one can make distinctions. Thus, professional wrestling on television in unabashedly (actually, there's a lot of bashing going on in televised wrestling) popular culture and James Joyce's *Finnegans Wake* is obviously elite culture. But in the middle of the continuum it's hard to see significant differences and popular culture and elite culture often seem to be different sides of the same coin. If a television network puts on a production of *Hamlet* and 30 million people see it, does the fact that so many people see it mean it is popular culture? Or that it has become popular culture?

As I use the term, I see popular culture as somewhat broader than what is found in mass media. Popular culture also involves fads, ceremonies, humor, food preferences, fashion, material culture, public rituals, and other phenomena that often are not mass-mediated (but which can often become mass-mediated).

The Great Transmogrification

Because popular culture is so vague a term, and the term *popular* has negative connotations, many scholars who are interested in this area now say they work in communications, in media studies, or, and this seems to be the current identification of choice, in cultural studies. Popular culture, we must remember, *is* a kind of culture. It is the culture of the common man and woman (and child and senior citizen), the hoi polloi, those who make up our so-called mass society and who, we are told, absorb this "mass culture" and, as a result, end up, to varying degrees, ideologized, hegemonized, dehumanized, moronized, alienated, decentered, and so on.

This language comes mostly from Marxist European intellectuals who must watch, with horror, as American films and television shows (*Alien, Terminator II, Dallas,* etc.) "overwhelm" their native societies. American scholars who work in cultural studies (and this includes literary theorists, literary critics, communications scholars, rhetoricians, cultural anthropologists, sociologists, and psychologists) have been profoundly influenced by European thinkers—thinkers who are generally on "the left" such as Barthes, Foucault, Derrida, Levi-Strauss, Lacan (to cite many in the French connection). This has led to a number of dilemmas involving the decline (if not death) of Marxism and the problem posed by deconstruction, topics I will address shortly.

Let me return to the question: Why is popular culture so unpopular? Or, to be more precise, why is it so unpopular with certain segments of the population? Is the opposite of popular culture "unpopular" culture, and if something is unpopular does that mean it is good (and that something popular is bad)? I raised this question years ago and suggested the answer was that since, in America at least, it is no longer acceptable for elites to insult members of the lower classes (the "masses") directly, elites can get a measure of comfort by attacking the tastes of these elements.

These left wing elites also see the media and popular culture as instruments of cultural manipulation and repression by conservative elite elements in societies so one can argue that if the tastes of the masses are depraved, it is because they are victims of a ruling class that is using control of the media as a means of maintaining political stability or, in Marxist terms, *hegemonial ideological domination.* In recent years Marxist critics have abandoned the manipulation thesis in favor of the hegemony thesis, which argues that the fabric of everyday life and the essential thought processes of ordinary people are controlled by the capitalist system of beliefs and values. There is, then, a culture of capitalism that is found in our belles lettres and comic books and everything in between.

The terms that are used are instructive and the frames of reference are often interesting. For example, because I wrote about popular culture, many people thought I was, or had to be, an "appreciative" critic. They assumed I "liked" it. Why else, they thought, would anyone bother with that junk? And much of it is junk, to be sure. In some cases I was "appreciative" and in other cases I wasn't. (I actually spent more time being negative about popular culture than being positive, but that's not what is important.) It is the logic of people's presuppositions that is interesting. This logic escapes me. It would suggest that oncologists study cancer because they "like" it and criminologists "like" criminals.

And think of the negativity involved with terms such as *mass* culture, *mass* media, and the *mass* arts. Where are these *mass* men and women we hear so much about? If people can be manipulated into easily controlled masses as easily as they are supposed to be, why is it so hard to get people to do anything (like vote or stop smoking) and why do advertisers talk about running things up flagpoles to see whether anyone salutes? Why not use terms such as *vernacular* arts or *public* arts or *public culture,* terms which are not so negative and which may even be more accurate?

Studying Public Culture

I like the term *public culture* because it doesn't have negative connotations and it is much more inclusive than the terms using *mass*. Literature, arts, media, all forms and levels of expression fit under this rubric, and work on public culture is done by scholars in many different disciplines. Generally speaking, those who study public culture use some mixture of semiotics, Marxism, psychoanalytic thought, sociological thought, feminist thought, anthropological thought, and literary theory and linguistics.

You have to learn an arcane language to communicate, on a scholarly level, in studies of public culture—and use words such as signifier, iconicity, indexicality, deconstruction, dialogism, unconscious, metonymy, metaphor, hegemony, heteroglossia, ideology, formalism, phallocentrism, postmodernism, intertextuality, deep structure, *differance,* syntagmatic and paradigmatic structure, and so on. These terms come from thinkers such as Ferdinand de Saussure, Charles Peirce, M. M. Bakhtin, Sigmund Freud, Jacques Derrida, Roman Jacobson, Roland Barthes, Umberto Eco, Juri Lotman, Jacques Lacan, Julia Kristeva, and others. Most are men and all, with the exception of Peirce, are Europeans.

All disciplines have their jargons and there's no reason why people interested in cultural studies shouldn't have one since technical terms facilitate communication among people working in the field. There is, of course, a great deal of argumentation among scholars in cultural studies about how to define terms, but that's nothing new. Academics who do cultural studies tend, often, to take themselves very seriously (even though some of them make puns and love to play around with language) and thus set themselves up for ridicule by people in the "real" world, especially journalists and writers. There is a genre of journalism that might be called academic (and in this case cultural criticism) bashing that consists of poking fun at the jargon that scholars use and listing some of the titles of papers they give and essays they write, which are displayed for public ridicule.

William Safire, in his 1991 essay published in the *New York Times* entitled "You May Write Your Own Headline Here" satirizes culture studies scholars and their jargon, though he focuses on literary theorists, who are only one segment of the culture studies field:

> Welcome, semiotics fans, to lit-crits glorious new era of *post-deconstuctionism*. This epoch, which could last six months to a year, has been named here today. *Post-deconstructionism,* which I will define in due course, is coined on the analogy of *post-modernism,* the label that architexts and decorative artists put on their complex and classic shapes evocative of historical periods.

He defines deconstructionism as follows:

> This is the philosophy that makes the reader more important than the author, placing the interpretation higher than the text. That word *text* is central; in the old days, a flesh-and-blood author created a *work;* nowadays, a critic studies a stand-alone *text.*

> Decon[structionism] is a way of analyzing literature [and popular culture, the mass media, etc.] by denying the traditional meanings of words, breaking their link with real things and insisting that they have significance only in relation to other words or sign. Author's intent, agreed upon meanings of words, historic or cultural settings—all go by the boards.

Safire is making fun of literary theorists and other people in the cultural studies movement, but he has put his finger on an important notion—the critics now have elevated themselves to a position of primacy and suggest, it would seem, that texts exist only so ingenious critics can deconstruct them. Safire also, as might be expected in a hatchet job, oversimplifies things a good deal.

If I had to nominate one passage in the writings of semioticians and literary theorists that led to the notion that relationships are primary I would cite one in Ferdinand de Saussure's *Course in General Linguistics* in which he writes "concepts are purely differential and defined not by their positive content but negatively by their relations with other terms of the system" (Saussure, 1966:117). Later he adds, "the most precise characteristic [of concepts] is in being what the others are not." This notion, that the mind tends to find meaning by establishing binary oppositions, led to Claude Levi-Strauss's analysis (we might now call it "deconstruction") of myths and to the achievements (or aberrations, some might say) of semiotic analysis. In *Mythologies,* one of the most important semiotic texts, Roland Barthes analyzes everything from detergents to steak, from Greta Garbo's face to Einstein's brain. He also devotes the second section of his book to a Marxist analysis of myth in contemporary society.

Cultural studies deal, then, with many different levels of analysis. The categories listed below are analogous to such levels of analysis:

World (Humanity)

Regions:	North America, Asia, the Mideast, etc.
Countries:	France, Italy, Thailand, USA
Sections of countries:	West Coast (USA)
States:	California
Sections of states:	Bay area
Cities:	San Francisco
Sections of cities:	Downtown
Streets:	Market Street
Buildings:	Nordstrom's Department Store
Areas in buildings:	Necktie store

One can deal with topics that involve all human beings (such as the way we find meaning in things) to those that are very narrow (such as a necktie at a department store in San Francisco). It is possible, also, to deal with texts (radio and television programs, works of one sort or another) at different levels. *Dallas* has been broadcast in many countries and cultural studies scholars have examined it in terms of how it is perceived in various countries and from international perspective. Movies circulate all over the world and are studied by critics with different perspectives on things and various techniques of analysis.

The Discreet Charms of the Bourgeoisie: A Case Study

Irving Louis Horowitz wrote a brilliant analysis of Bunuel's surrealistic comedy, *Discreet Charm of the Bourgeoisie,* that, though it has a sociological and political focus, has a good deal of we might describe as the deconstructive virus in it. He points out that the film is divided into eight eating-dining segments and that it is full of comic errors:

> Here the joys of the feast are punctuated by a comedy of errors: missed cues, coming to eat at an associate's house on the wrong day, going to a restaurant and finding a funeral, and experiencing sexual desire at a socially embarrassing moment. But in the end, Hogarth is displaced by Mao. The feast is disrupted by the slaughter of the meat eaters.

He discusses the significance of these curiosities and various other bizarre events in the film. Note, at the end, the way he plays with the numbers 27 and 72, as deconstructionists are wont to do:

> What is special about surrealism in the seventies is its subtlety. No longer are temporal and causal time reversals done primarily for shock value. Rather, they illustrate the pretentiousness of bourgeois discretion; the impossibility of reconciling every trifling incongruity into a polite middle-class framework, and the need to try. Here, too, art and criticism intersect with more telling effect than in previous films. A foremost member of the Spanish "generation of 27" has evolved into a "revolutionist of 72."

His analysis is also structured around conceptual polarities, some of which I have taken from his essay and listed below:

Humans	Beasts
The fantastic	The real
Shock	Subtlety
Spanish passion	French civility
Sensual pleasure	Violence and death
Dreams	Everyday life
Privatism	Politics
Metaphorical aims	Empirical terms

If Horowitz's essay seems predeconstructionist, it is because, as Saussure argues, the mind works in terms of oppositions and critics who analyze the meanings found in texts are all (and have always been whether they realize it or not) decontructionists. Like Moliere's Monsieur Jourdain, we all write prose when we're not writing poetry.

Horowitz also deals with the Oedipal themes found in the film as well as its ideological and political meanings. He cites the dream sequences in the film in which "neo-Freudian Oedipal complexes compete with neo-Marxian social messages for attention." We find in Horowitz's review of this remarkable and "difficult film" many of the techniques or methodologies used by those doing cultural studies—employed, as we might expect, in an extremely sophisticated manner.

Horowitz on Music

Horowitz has also written a number of articles on music, and I would like to focus on two essays—one on rock and roll music and another on jazz. His essay "Rock on the Rocks or Bubblegum, Anybody?" appeared in *Psychology Today* in January of 1971. In it he dealt with what he believed would be the forthcoming "death" of rock music and its resurrection as something new. As he wrote: "Rock 'n' roll is dying. It is now going through the terminal symptoms that jazz went through in the forties and early fifties. And it will die the same way jazz did—by growing up, by being transformed."

He suggests that there is a parallel between jazz and rock, and, in this respect, discusses "alligators," jazz fans who knew and appreciated the music the jazz musicians were playing and the movement of jazz "from the dance floor to the concert hall."

Now, he suggests, the technology involved in making rock music has become extremely complicated and sophisticated and it has taken rock artists away from their roots—the song and the beat. As a result, he argues, rock music concerts have entered the "sit-and-listen" stage; fans don't dance the way they used to but concentrate on the music, the way people do with jazz and classical music. When this happens, Horowitz suggests, when music moves to the sit-and-listen stage, the music changes: jazz becomes modern jazz and rock become *hard* or *acid* rock. Then it fails to pick up a new audience and starts dying. Horowitz saw bubblegum music, or soft popular melodies, as taking rock's place because young men and women don't like to sit, but want to dance and there was one thing you could say about bubblegum music that was of importance—"It's got a good beat. You can dance to it." You used to be able to say this about rock, he suggests.

Horowitz's predictions about rock dying were, it turns out, premature. All art forms evolve, so it was not particularly risky to suggest that rock would evolve, but what could not have been predicted was that a number of the most important rock groups of the 1970s would still be around or that young people would still dance, or start dancing again, at rock concerts. It is, I should add, a risky business to predict what young people will or will not do, and how entertainment forms will change.

Interestingly enough, we find Horowitz still pursuing his thesis about musicians evolving and in certain ways leaving their fans behind, twenty years later. In a letter to the editor printed in the *New York Times* in September 1992, Horowitz chides Keith Jarrett, whom he greatly admires, for having lost his way. Jarrett had written an article about the music industry in which he had complained about, among other things, technicians wandering off and reading newspapers while he was recording. Horowitz writes: "With every Jarrett recording revealing longer, more amorphous 'solos,' with an absence of structure becoming a celebrated norm, it is little wonder that the studio technicians were wandering off reading newspapers. Indeed, the recording technologies have been a distinct disservice to Mr. Jarrett."

Horowitz is beating his same electronic drum (I was going to say horse) here—that technological developments in recording have led musicians to become too arty. They have become, he suggests, too self-conscious and this is leading them, if it has not led them already, to self-destruct.

This perspective is the basis of another article on music by Horowitz, "On Seeing and Hearing Music: Nine Propositions in Search of an Explanation." This essay appeared in the 1982 *Annual Review of Jazz Studies*. In it he asks the following question: "In the age of electronic recording, the sound of music has become astonishingly precise and higher in quality then [*sic*] live performances; why then should anyone go to hear music in person?" There is some question as to whether Horowitz is right about this, about whether recorded music is, in fact, "higher in quality" than live performances. He is rather vague on what "quality" is. (Some critics, as a matter of fact, have attacked digital compact disc records as being sterile and not as satisfying as regular records.)

He then offers nine reasons why people might go to concerts, discussing everything from wanting to see interactions between musicians and what he terms *extramusical elements* (wanting to see a "failed note") to having one's social status verified (to show one has good taste) an comparing the technology of live and recorded sounds. What is interesting about Horowitz's list is what is not on it. Why is there nothing specific about sociability and the need people have to be together in groups or the desire they have to entertain themselves and have fun? Why nothing about youth culture and rock? Why nothing about rock and politics?

Listening to a record in a room may, perhaps, yield acoustic ecstasy but it also can be alienating, as well. The point Horowitz raises is an important one, however, but more so for films, I'd say, than records. Young people don't like to sit and do like to dance, so there is every reason to assume that they will continue to attend rock concerts. But increasingly larger numbers of people, especially those over the age of thirty, either tape films off television or rent films at video stores, even though the experience of seeing a film at a theater is considerably different from seeing one at home.

Is Horowitz a technological determinist, a writer of jeremiads, who sees the new recording technologies as inevitably leading musicians (jazz and rock) to self-destruct? Or is he a voice in the wilderness warning us, and musicians, about the dangers new recording technologies pose for them? I would say the latter, but there are, it would seem, Luddite elements to his thinking about music. It is curious that Horowitz is open to experimentation in film and is very positive about Bunuel's surrealism, but somewhat conservative about musicians and downright negative in his letter about Jarrett's experimentation and his "amorphous" solos that are characterized by an "absence of structure."

Perspectives of Cultural Critics

On this note, let us return to our considerations of cultural criticism and of the role that semiotics and related concerns have played in the analysis of texts and popular culture in general, with particular reference to films and humor. In the discussion to come, I make use of M. M. Bakhtin's theories, which focus, in part, on the importance of folk cultures and the way they use humor (and popular culture in general) as a means of resistance to power and authority. Bakhtin also explains the carnival-like aspects of medieval culture, a concept that helps explain, I would suggest, the role of rock concerts in American culture.

Before the development of semiotic analysis and the various offshoots from it, such as deconstruction, film analysis tended to focus on the social and political messages carried in films and performance qualities and tended to neglect the way the film generated its meanings. After the development of semiotics, film critics had a new subject—how a film, by its use of visual language, dialogue, and structure conveyed its meanings. (It is Horowitz's focus on the structure of *Discreet Charms* that led me to suggest he's a bit of a deconstructionist.) Much of the theory behind this was done by French scholars who teach us how to find meaning in books characterized by opaque, almost unintelligible styles of writing (some say purposefully so).

The only problem is that deconstruction and the notion that texts have no intrinsic meanings led to a problem for Marxist critics. For if a text only exists, so to speak, in terms of the "readings" given it by various people, how can it be argued that the media can be used to brainwash people into accepting certain disguised ideologies. The old hypodermic theory of communication argues that we all get the same message. That would make media domination quite possible. But the argument now is that there is no message other than what viewers, readers, and others make of it, based on their social class and worldview, and, as Umberto Eco has argued, most of the decodings of messages found in the mass media are "aberrant."

Some critics now argue that there are "preferred readings," and that it is not quite "everyone for himself or herself" when it comes to interpreting and understanding texts. This preferred reading is not necessarily what the creators of the texts had in mind, I should point out. (Authors, critics argue, don't understand what they are doing and how they did it; if they did, they could write a short essay at the end of each work and we wouldn't need all the literary critics and media analysts we have.) Some scholars describe the controversy over semiotics and deconstruction in terms of two competing theories—"God's Truth" and "Hocus-Pocus." The "God's Truth" notion is that semioticians and those doing culture studies find what is hidden in texts and thus reveal what is there. The "Hocus-Pocus" notion is that semioticians and others create ingenious structures which they "read into" texts and this criticism is, essentially, "Hocus-Pocus," or, in other words, a sham.

Deconstructing a Joke

In order to let you evaluate deconstruction and related forms of criticism for yourself, I will deconstruct a joke. But before I do, let me say something about the role of humor in cultural studies and, in particular, the work of the latest big "discovery" for those in the field, Mikhail M. Bakhtin.

In the introduction to *The Dialogic Imagination,* a collection of Bakhtin's essays, the editor of the book, Michael Holmquist writes: "Mikhail Mikhailovich Bakhtin is gradually emerging as one of the leading thinkers of the twentieth century. This claim will strike many as extravagant, since a number of factors have until recently conspired to obscure his importance" (1981:xv).

He mentions that Bakhtin spent many years in exile, that his writing style is highly idiosyncratic and that he interprets Western European culture in unfamiliar ways. But he was continually working on what, Holmquist suggests, is "the central preoccupation of our time—language," and in that field he made major contributions, on a par with Saussure, Jacobson, and a few others. One of Bahktin's most important concepts is that of "dialogism," which involves the relationship between our speech and the speech of others (from the past or anticipated) or the inner dialogue we carry on with ourselves. Just as concepts have meaning relatively (as Saussure pointed out in his book, published posthumously in 1917, that I quoted earlier) so does speech. As Krysyna Pomorska points out in the foreword to Bakhtin's *Rabelais and His World*:

> Another of Bakhtin's outstanding ideas connecting him with modern semiotics is his discovery that *quoted speech*...permeates all our language activities in both practical and artistic communication. Baktin reveals the constant presence of this phenomenon in a vast number of examples from all areas of life: literature, ethics, politics, law, and inner speech. He points to the fact that we are actually dealing with someone else's words more often than with our own. Either we remember and respond to someone else's words (in the case of ethics); or we represent them in order to argue, disagree, or defend them (in the case of law); or, finally, we carry on an inner dialogue, responding to someone's words (including our own). In each case someone else's speech makes it possible for us to generate our own and thus becomes an indispensable factor in the creative power of language. (1984:ix)

This passage suggests that in addition to our being sign-generating beings we are also dialogic ones—responding to the words others have spoken or written and anticipating what they may speak or write.

The second concept from Bakhtin I would like to discuss is that of "carnival." *Rabelais and His World* discusses the role humor played in the folk culture and everyday life of the Middle Ages and Renaissance and offers the principle of carnivalization as central to understanding the importance of this humor. As Michael Holmquist explains it in his introduction to the book: "This carnival is the people's second life, organized on the basis of laughter. It is a festive life. Festivity is a peculiar quality of all comic rituals and spectacles of the Middle Ages" (1984:8). These carnivals were all connected to folk feasts, Holmquist adds, which were used to unite the world of mundane events and the world of spiritual ones.

What was central, Bakhtin writes, was the importance of humor. As he explains things in *Rabelais and His World,* there was a "medieval culture of humor" that was universal (connected to the feasts and to the carnivalization of life) and was linked to freedom. It was also connected, Bakhtin suggests, to the people's victory over fear and terror, oppression and guilt (generated by the Church). "Medieval laughter," he writes, "is not subjective, individual...it is the social consciousness of all the people" (1984:92).

According to Bakhtin, this culture of laughter was eventually "degraded" in the eighteenth century, but it was never destroyed, and one might argue that even though the culture of laughter may not exist as it did in the Middle Ages, remnants of it still can be found in our folklore, popular culture, mass media, and elite literature. This discussion of the importance of humor leads, logically and dialogically, to the matter of jokes and to my example of how a joke might be deconstructed by various cultural critics and analysts.

Metaphornication and Metonymphomania and Other Approaches to Jokes

I will conclude this essay with the "deconstruction" of a joke, which will show how different perspectives in the cultural studies field lead to different "readings" of this text and insights about it and its psychological, sociological, and political implications.

A man goes to Miami Beach for a week's vacation. Everyday he gets into his bathing suit, goes out on the beach, applies sunscreen and tanning lotions, and sits in the sun. After a few days he has a beautiful tan. One evening, after his shower, he looks at himself in the mirror and notices his tan covers every part of his body except for his penis. He decides to remedy this situation. The next day he gets up early, goes to a deserted part of the beach, strips naked, and then flicks sand over every part of his body until all that remains exposed to the sun is his penis. A few minutes after he has done this, three little old ladies are out walking on the boardwalk. One notices the penis sticking up out of the sand. She points it out to her friends. "Funny," she says. "When I was twenty, I was scared to death of them. When I was forty, I couldn't get enough of them. When I was sixty, I couldn't get one to come near me...and now they're growing wild on the beach!

Let me suggest, now, how different analysts would "deconstruct" this joke.

Interpretation 1: A semiotic analysis. A semiotician would see the joke as involving a set of polar oppositions between culture and nature. That is how the joke generates its meaning:

Culture	*Nature*
Public beach	Private parts
Sexuality at age 20, 40, 60	Growing wild
Society	The beach
Repression	Freedom

The man's penis, semiotically speaking, is an example of metonymy, in which meaning is based on association, and, in particular, a form of metonymy known as synecdoche—in which a part of something stands for (literally, here) the whole.

Semioticians might also study the joke as a narrative with a number of different elements and analyze how the elements are put together, leading to a punch line. I have made an analysis of the forty-five techniques found in all humor (*Journal of Communication*) and would suggest that this joke is based upon the following techniques: mistakes penis wild on the beach, not attached to a man; stereotypes lack of sexuality of the aged; absurdity covering self with sand so only penis shows.

Interpretation 2: A psychoanalytic perspective. A psychoanalytically inclined deconstructionist would be interested in the attitudes toward sexuality revealed in the old woman's speech: scared at twenty, full of desire at forty, deprived at sixty. There may also be an element of wish-fulfillment—the fantasy of abundant sexuality promised in the punch line, "and now they're growing wild on the beach." Penises are dissociated from male bodies and, it is suggested, "grow wild" on the beach. They are, therefore, in abundant supply. There is also an element of compulsive behavior and narcissism in the man's behavior—in his desire to be tanned all over so he'll be perfectly tanned. There may also be a bit of exhibitionism in the man, in that he is willing to display his private parts in public. Finally, a psychoanalytically inclined critic might point out that many American jokes are about sexuality because that still remains a subject over which there is a great deal of anxiety and many hang-ups of one sort or another. Americans, the argument goes, tend to be repressed sexually (especially around twenty, so the joke tells us) and thus we make jokes to help us deal with our problems in this area.

Interpretation 3: A Marxist perspective. From the Marxist perspective, the joke shows the degrading nature of American bourgeois society. The focus of the joke is on the private desires of the man, for his perfect tan, and the frustration of the women, who mature in a society full of repression. The focus on sexuality is caused by a society in which widespread alienation has turned people away from social and political matters to the only area where they have any power and a degree of control—their own bodies and their ability to engage in sexual relationships. When he covers himself with sand he displays his alienation from his own body and, by implication, his alienation from his own sexuality.

Miami Beach is, also, we must remember, a center of American popular culture and self-indulgent hedonism where those who can afford it enjoy vacations while those who serve them, people of color for the most part, are exploited. This underclass, we notice, is not mentioned in the joke; it is invisible in the joke just as it is invisible, generally speaking, in society at large.

Interpretation 4: A sociological analysis. A sociologically informed critic would focus on the relationship between attitudes toward sexuality and age as well as the matter of the absurd stereotypes held by people about the sexual lives of old people (or senior citizens as they are now designated). The matter of tans is also of interest. Tans used to be a sign of the working classes (who got tans from working outdoors, in fields, etc.) but tans were changed into signifiers of middle and upper-class life-styles, of people who went on vacations to sunny places. In recent years, now that we recognize sun as a danger, tans have been returned to signifying working classes, rednecks, and so forth.

The sun and the whole matter of leisure are also of interest to sociologically oriented critics. Miami Beach is connected in the popular imagination with leisure, vacations, hedonistic values, and with the elderly—retired people from cold climates who come to Miami to spend their last years, soaking up the sun. Many of these retirees are Jewish, and there is good reason to believe that these little old ladies out for a walk are Jewish. This is because one of the stereotypes of Jews held by the general public is that they are materialistic, are overly concerned with money, and are cheap. Thus, getting penises "free" would be of particular interest, so this theory goes, to Jews.

Interpretation 5: A feminist analysis. For a feminist critic this joke shows the domination of the male phallus over women. Talk about a "phallocentric" culture! This joke revolves (as American culture does, the feminists argue) around the male phallus and reflects the degraded status of women in contemporary American society. Notice, for example, that the old woman who describes her sexual development does so in terms of the all-powerful phallus, not in terms of her relationship with men.

Women can talk about men as phalluses, one might argue, because men, as a rule, think of women in reductionist, anatomical terms, and this reductionism by the dominant figures in a patriarchal society establishes the way in which women think of themselves and of members of the opposite and dominant sex. In the same light, we have here a reversal of the "male gaze," which is the way men look upon women as primarily sexual objects, designed, so to speak, primarily for their pleasure and sexual gratification. Instead of repudiating this "male gaze," women have acquiesced and done all they can to become sexual objects. This is a reaction caused by female powerlessness and those who acquiesce are, from the feminist perspective, unknowing victims of the phallocentric society (as well as a Euro-centric society dominated by DWEMs—Dead White European Males) in which they are brought up. (For more on this last topic, see my forthcoming book, *The Interpretation of DWEMs.*)

Interpretation 6: A multidisciplinary analysis. In this mode of criticism, we combine the elements from the five discussed above and any other modalities that interest us (myth-ritual-symbol, Jungian, historical, etc.) and use them to explain the text in a "gestalt" that leads to the most comprehensive manner possible.

It is often the case that critics use a number of different approaches, so one might find critics who identify themselves as semioticians, Marxists, and feminists or psychoanalytically inclined semioticians. This is because, I would say, texts are extremely complex and no single discipline or approach is adequate to deal with their complexity. It also may be that the different critical approaches complement one another and are needed to deal with the richness of texts and the problems generated by our having given new "roles" to readers, especially of texts found in popular culture and the mass media, which often have visual and performance components to them.

A Concluding Question

We have had six culture analyses of the deconstruction of a joke, and each reveals something different . A question comes to mind: Which analysis is right? Or, if they are all right, we are left with a dilemma—are some critical perspectives "more right" than others? That is, do some perspectives have more interesting things to say about more of the text (and its relation to culture and society) than other perspectives?

My approach to popular culture, mass media, and what is termed *cultural studies* is to use a variety of approaches, letting the text more or less suggest the critical method or methods to be used. I would describe this approach as multidisciplinary, interdisciplinary, or perhaps pandisciplinary. Or, now that we are supposedly in a postdeconstructionist era, maybe it is postdisciplinary. Some, who are convinced of the primacy of their particular discipline and their perspective on things, might call it undisciplinary.

Whatever the case, I have spent close to thirty years and written more than twenty books working on a subject that a reputable sociologist—Melvin Tumin, who taught at a reputable and distinguished institution, Princeton University—told me was only worth thirty minutes. I often wonder what I might have accomplished had I chosen a really important subject—one that he devoted one or two weeks to, such as deviance or roles.

San Francisco State University
Department of Broadcast Communication Arts

References

Bakhtin, M. M. *The Dialogic Imagination.* Austin: University of Texas Press, 1981.
———. *Rabelais and His World.* Cambridge: The Massachusetts Institute of Technology Press, 1984.

Berger, Arthur Asa. *Media Analysis Techniques* (revised edition). Newbury Park, CA: Sage Publications, 1991.

Horowitz, Irving Louis. "Rock on the Rocks or Bubblegum, Anybody?" *Psychology Today* 4, no. 8 (January 1971): 59–61, 83.

———. "On Seeing and Hearing Music: Nine Propositions in Search of Explanation." *Annual Review of Jazz Studies*, vol. 1, ed. Charles Nanry and David A. Cayer. New Brunswick, NJ: Transaction Publishers, 1982.

———. "Personal Loss" (Letter to the Editor). *The New York Times*, 6 September 1992.

Safire, William. "You May Write Your Own Headline Here." *The New York Times*, 14 June 1991.

Saussure, Ferdinand de. *Course in General Linguistics*. New York: McGraw-Hill, 1966.

23

"You Know Something Is Happening, but You Don't Know What It Is"

R. Serge Denisoff with George Plasketes

Must we become a tail-end discipline gaining a public hearing by virtue of our superb journalists? Instead of sniping at the sociological "populariz- ers" and "journalists," we might well start appreciating them.

...the very idea of imputing negative values to journalism is a grotesque misreading of the essence of good sociology. The journalist is a good chronicler of events. When he is successful, he offers the sociologist an enormous amount of data.

The main drift of C. Wright Mills' work is linked to the practical importance of an ethically viable social science. This is so because such a sociology confronts the facts with integrity by doing something about the facts. This then is the "message" of the greatest sociology the United States has ever produced.
> —Irving Louis Horowitz,
> *The New Sociology,* 1964

C. Wright Mills died on 21 March 1962. Three months prior to Mills's untimely demise, activist Tom Hayden was appointed to write a mani- festo for the Students for a Democratic Society (SDS) convention at the United Automobile Workers camp in Port Huron, Michigan. The sixty- three-page document, which came to be called "The Port Huron State- ment," had a special appeal for middle-class intellectuals and university students. The statement criticized mindless anticommunism as well as the Soviet ideology and social structure.

The document stresses alliances with middle-class, ideologically leftist organizations such as the "liberal" wing of the Democratic party, labor, and Americans for Democratic Action. The growing civil rights movement also was perceived as a potential ally.

The so-called New Left disclaimed the demigods of the Old Left, partially due to the internecine battles of "progressives" in the 1930s and 1940s. As activist Todd Gitlin recalls,

> The future New Left read David Riesman and C. Wright Mills and Albert Camus, and found them in warrants for estrangement, but nothing influenced me, or the Baby Boom generation as a whole, as much as movies, music...did. On the big screen, on posters, and in popular magazines, America was mass producing images of white youth on the move yet with nowhere to go.[1]

The members of SDS were determined to create their own pantheon of intellectual and cultural heroes. Thus the elevation of C. Wright Mills.

Like Bob Dylan in his early years, C. Wright Mills was the ideal antihero. "Mills was a hero in student radical circles for his books, of course," Gitlin continues. "But it was no small part of the person for which he was cherished—that he was a motorcycle-riding, cabin-building Texan, cultivating the image of a gunslinging homesteader of the old frontier who springs into virtuous action crying, "Don't tread on me!"[2]

The movement lacked intellectual heroes, having rejected Marx, Lenin, and Leon Trotsky. "Ah, but I was so much older then, I'm younger than that now," wrote Bob Dylan in "My Back Pages." This was his rejection of the Old Left, which had viewed him as the heir apparent to Woody Guthrie.

The Old Left and the Progressive Labor party, called "tight-assed Stalinists" by Students for a Democratic Society, originally made overtures to the middle-class university students, but with little success. Theoretician Herbert Aptheker attacked Mills for concentrating on the ruling class and ignoring the proletariat and its historical mission. One can only imagine his reaction to Mills's thoughtful analysis of Marxism.[3]

The Power Elite by Mills rose from the critical ashes in the early 1960s. Young assistant professors were assigning the book in their classes. Phrases like the "power structure" and "power elite" entered the campus lexicon, especially among students. Mills, also, could not be accused of being "a leftist Commie pinko" with books such as *The Marxists* and *Causes of World War Three*. The death of Mills left a void, particularly in the ranks of the New Left.

New Directions

Irving Louis Horowitz, a native of New York City, had received prestigious university degrees in the United States and abroad. By 1963 he had published four books concentrating on theory, the sociology of knowledge, and politics. He was hardly a "newcomer" to the world of C. Wright Mills. Horowitz had planned a volume of essays dealing with the Millsian tradition. The collection would be tentatively titled *The Sociology of Our Times: Critical Appraisals of the Work of C. Wright Mills*. Mills suggested the title in March 1960. The project was not to be as Mills died in the spring of 1962. In 1964, Horowitz published two anthologies devoted to Mills while at Washington University—*The New Sociology: Essays in Social Science and Social Theory* followed by *Power, Politics and People: The Collected Essays of C. Wright Mills*. The books were well received by budding scholars and those interested in social change and the sorry state of sociology.

In the introduction to *New Sociology*, Horowitz expands, with revisions, Mills's key themes in his book *The Sociological Imagination*. In essence, Horowitz deals with the ivory tower posturing of the social sciences and the need to transform private troubles into public issues. For Horowitz, sociology should be socially responsible. The introduction struck a dissident chord with the elite in corporate boardrooms and at the Pentagon, but also in the hallowed halls of academe. The status quo was being challenged and vested interests became defensive.

The war in Vietnam and the civil rights struggle found the word "relevance" being thrown about with abandon. The student portents, university sit-ins, and campus unrest that included violence, all highlighted the "irrelevance" of the establishment, including the university system, with the exception, of course, of progressive junior professors and a few gray beards.

In *The Greening of America*, Charles Reich attempted to define the new generation as possessing Consciousness III. Con III, according to the author, was a holistic belief that the "goals of status, a position in the hierarchy, security, money, possessions, power, respect, and honor [are] not merely wrong, they are *unreal*."[4]

The language of the Con III generation was rock music, but *not* the material found on "Boss" or Top 40 radio, instead album cuts beamed on low, poor, "underground" or FM stations. A key term became *alternative*. Working or spending leisure time had to be achieved *outside* of established institutions.

One of the offsprings of the campus protests was the open air; when possible, outdoor teach-ins, where opponents of the war gathered within earshot of dusty lecture halls, were conducted. It was clear that the desires of students, those opposed to the "dirty little war," were not being met by standard course offerings. Disaffected faculty members began to discuss alternatives to standard curricula with generally little success. Except for the introductory 101 level, alterations in courses surfaced with glacier-like speed. Ray Browne's experiences at Bowling Green State University in Ohio were typical of the movement. Hired by the English Department, Browne was able to pursue his pioneering interest in literary popular culture. However, by the early 1970s "the Department saw the whole popular culture movement as much more of a threat than they had anticipated, and they were prepared to work against it. And they did…they did not want me in the Department any longer."[5] In time, and after significant drawn out strife, popular culture became a separate department at Bowling Green. Being recognized as a separate entity was a giant step toward the legitimation of popular culture as an academic discipline.

Publishing and Legitimation

Another consequence of the radical or alternative approach to higher education was the growth of specialty journals allowing some esoteric topics to appear in print. This was a particularly important outlet for younger professors with less traditional interests and perspectives on research and writing. Textbook publishers in the humanities gradually began to issue special volumes appealing to the so-called radical professors, including sociologists. University presses, however, did not follow suit. Indeed, it would take President Nixon's curtailment of the library subsidy, the economic backbone of academic presses, for these entities to liberalize.

It is within this environment and set of circumstances that Horowitz began to coedit *Transaction,* a social science version of *Scientific American,* in 1963. The name change to *Society* came in 1971.

The Transaction Periodicals Consortium in 1974 had seven publications listed in their catalogue, including *The Journal of Jazz Studies,* edited by Charles Nanry and David A. Cayer. This journal first appeared in October 1973. The editors described the endeavor as designed to meet a specific need. That need was "for a multidisciplinary and interdisciplinary publication for scholarly articles about jazz and related to music."[6] In 1982, the journal became *The Annual Review of Jazz Studies.*

In 1972, Transaction Publishers released *American Music: From Storyville to Woodstock,* edited by Charles Nanry. Horowitz introduced the anthology as "experimental and engaging."[7] The collection reflected, not surprisingly, the jazz interests of the editor. Horowitz contributed "Rock, Recordings and Rebellion" to Nanry's collection. "Music expresses its times and anxieties," he wrote, "...hard rock is a sound apart: white, youthful, disengaged, sexually blunt and for the most part closer to pantheism than socialism."[8]

Three years later, Transaction published *Solid Gold: The Popular Record Industry* by R. Serge Denisoff. Horowitz characterized the monograph as "a fundamental contribution to the theory and practice of mass culture and mass communication."[9] Since *Solid Gold,* Denisoff and Transaction have enjoyed a working relationship for nearly twenty years that has resulted in a trilogy of landmark studies on the popular recording industry, television (particularly MTV), and film.

Horowitz's diligent scholarship, leadership, and advocacy in book publishing have all but obscured his contributions to the development of lesser writers especially in esoteric areas of inquiry. Horowitz has been nurturing in that regard. *Solid Gold,* for example, was one of the first sociological treatments of the rock culture and the music business or industry itself. A reviewer in *Contemporary Sociology,* the book review arm of the American Sociological Association, closed by saying, "Sociologists who would follow will find it virtually impossible not to refer to *Solid Gold.*"[10] The publication of the book by Transaction, and the complimentary introduction and support by Horowitz legitimized the effort. The "when are you going to do some *real* sociology?" school of critics was temporarily silenced.

Horowitz has made the sociological inquiry into popular music more respectable. Yet there remain further steps to be taken in the path he has helped pioneer. For example, *The American Sociological Review* has never printed a qualitative piece on popular music since its inception. Such critical essays have been largely the domain of *Popular Music and*

Society, a journal conceived and edited by a Horowitz disciple. Journals in mass communication, popular culture, and youth norms and values are all vehicles of exposure lacking the widespread visibility and acceptance of "mainstream publications."

Conclusion

Irving Louis Horowitz is to be commended for his contributions to the field of sociology, and broadening its parameters to embrace American culture, music, mass media, and its industries. His book, *Communicating Ideas: The Politics of Scholarly Publishing,* is a revealing treatment of perishing and publishing, as well as the cultural and communication gatekeeping process. That is to say, writing is no guarantee of academic security. What counts is what one writes. At the same time, Irving Horowitz must also be praised for his personal vision, his faith in alternative approaches and those who pursue them, and his understanding of the essence of good sociology.

Bowling Green State University
Department of Sociology

Auburn University
Department of Communications

Notes

1. Todd Gitlin, *Sixties: Years of Hope, Days of Rage* (New York: Bantam Books, 1987), 31.
2. Ibid., 34.
3. Herbert Aptheker, *The World of C. Wright Mills* (New York: Marzani and Munsell, Inc., 1960).
4. Charles A. Reich, *The Greening of America* (New York: Bantam Books, 1971), 257.
5. Ray B. Browne, *Against Academia* (Bowling Green, OH: Popular Press, 1989), 17.
6. Charles Nanry and David A. Cayer, "Editor's Notes," *Journal of Jazz Studies* 1 (1973): 2.
7. Charles Nanry, ed., *American Music: From Storyville to Woodstock* (New Brunswick, NJ: Transaction Publishers, 1972), xii.
8. Irving Louis Horowitz, in Nanry, ed., *American Music,* 274.
9. R. Serge Denisoff, *Solid Gold: The Popular Record Industry* (New Brunswick, NJ: Transaction Publishers, 1975), xiv.
10. Peter Hesbacher, "Review of *Solid Gold,*" *Contemporary Sociology* (1976): 567.

Section Seven

Publishing and the Craft of Writing

24

The Scholar as Publisher

Mary E. Curtis

The breadth of Irving Louis Horowitz's scholarly interests and accomplishments is truly prodigious. Those who know him can attest to his ability to grasp the essence of an idea or a situation with intimidating speed and skill. Not only is he a perceptive observer, but he also links his observations to a formidable array of knowledge about any number of topics, and couples it with a solid grounding in the foundations of twentieth-century social thought.

The world of publishing is one he inhabits as well as observes. As is well known, for more than thirty years Horowitz has been editor-in-chief of *Society* (originally *Transaction*) magazine and president of Transaction Publishers. Under his leadership, Transaction evolved from a single publication to a full-fledged publisher of more than one hundred books annually and nearly thirty journals. And along the way he has played an active public role in the publishing industry, especially in the area of copyright and technology.

My role is unique among those who are contributing to this festschrift. In addition to working with Irving Louis Horowitz at Transaction, as I have done since 1987 (and before that from 1968 to 1974), I am his wife. Critically assessing his work in and on publishing has been more complicated than I anticipated; for, as Irving has observed in his preface to *Communicating Ideas,* much of his work on publishing reflects our shared discussions and perspectives. In addition, we have coauthored articles.[1] Achieving the appropriate degree of psychological distance and objectivity has been a challenge.

As did all of the contributors to this volume, I reviewed his bibliography and reflected upon where his writings on my assigned topic, in this case publishing, fits into the panorama of his work. Fortunately, Irving provided guidelines. Not only has he written about the festschrift as a publishing genre,[2] but he has also edited a memorable festschrift, *The New Sociology*.[3] For a generation of sociologists, this book indelibly associated C. Wright Mills with a brilliant cast of sociologists carrying on the legacy of his work. This present festschrift is, of course, very different. Mills died prematurely; Horowitz is very much alive. In addition, Horowitz has already organized and published much of his principal work (a task he also performed for Mills in several posthumous books). This has vastly simplified our task.

Horowitz's principal articles on publishing have been assembled in a single volume, the second edition of *Communicating Ideas*.[4] As an analytic tool for those interested in the evolution of his thinking on publishing, however, the book has some limitations. It does not reference sources of original versions of the chapters, so one does not know precisely when or where they initially appeared. His bibliography fills these gaps, and I have chosen to reference these original versions as well as the chapters in *Communicating Ideas* in this chapter.

A Chronology of Irving Louis Horowitz on Publishing

One might logically link Horowitz's scholarly work on publishing with his writings on music and other cultural matters. This festschrift does not do so, perhaps because of the sheer volume of his work on publishing. More important, I would argue, is that publishing occupies such a central role in his life that it merits this individual attention.

Horowitz's first published article on any subject appeared in 1951, when he was only twenty-one (his first book was published one year later). His first publishing-related article did not appear until twenty-one years later, in 1972,[5] but even then, the publishing emphasis was secondary to a continuing interest in conflict, evident as far back as his 1957 book *The Idea of War and Peace in Contemporary Philosophy*. A review article of a textbook appeared that same year, colorfully entitled "Packaging a Sociological Monsterpiece."[6] Again, it focused mainly on the content of the volume, rather than on publishing issues, although he did critically assess the publisher's approach in what then was one of the earliest "managed textbooks." In 1974, he discussed the role of "mediating journals" such as *Society*.[7] In 1977, "Autobiography as the Presentation of Self for Social Responsibility" appeared,[8] interestingly just after he signed an agreement to write a biography of C. Wright Mills (not to appear until 1983).

Horowitz's most significant work on publishing spans the decade of the 1980s, starting in 1978, when he wrote an invited article about advertising and publishing for the Council of Better Business Bureaus.[9] The two of us contributed to a *Nation* symposium, "On Truth in Publishing," that same year, a contribution that he expanded for *Communicating Ideas*. In 1979, he wrote "Marketing Social Science" for an International Sociology Association panel.[10] In 1980, he wrote three articles on publishing-related topics, and from that point until 1990, at least one, and more often several, a year, ranging from occasional pieces to major statements. His scholarly writing on publishing has diminished since the 1980s.

A Scholar/Publisher at Work

Horowitz is more than a publisher who writes about publishing; he is also a scholar who brings to the subject an established reputation in other fields. Although writing about publishing by publishers has not been particularly distinguished, there have been a few publishers who have written in learned ways about publishing. In the United States, most such publishers have been associated with university presses. Few have brought to their writing about publishing deep scholarly knowledge from other fields. More characteristically, most publisher/authors have fallen prey to the twin pitfalls of partisanship and pedestrian thinking.

Horowitz's writing is all the more unusual because there has been so little good scholarship on publishing from those in academic life. Historians, biographers, and social scientists have made very little effort to analyze the world of publishing. In a sense, this is surprising, given publishing's importance in their careers. Certainly a few scholars have contributed an insight or two and sometimes more—one thinks of Lewis Coser's "gatekeeper" concept[11]—but in general those scholars who have tried to write about publishing have failed either to surprise publishers by what they knew about their world, or to tell them things they did not already know. Some of their observations have simply been off-base. It is interesting to speculate about why this is so. Perhaps because of their proximity to the industry as authors, many scholars overestimate what they know about publishing. For their part, publishers have done little to fund or otherwise encourage research on their industry by outsiders, perhaps because like people in many businesses, they are not particularly interested in being studied.

Why have scholars initiated so little research on an enterprise that, after all, plays such a large part in the cultural life of Western civilization? Part of the answer may be that it is difficult to obtain comprehensive information about the industry. No single trade association represents all, or even most, of the companies in the industry. Membership of the Association of American Publishers (AAP) does not include many smaller publishers and only a few university presses. Most of the latter belong instead to the Association of American University Presses (AAUP). Even some major trade publishers, like Harcourt Brace, Jovanovich, remained aloof from trade association involvement for many years. Overseas the situation is not much different. Although European publishers appear to be better organized, like their American counterparts, they operate with little comprehensive industry data beyond basic statistics. Even this information may not be publicly known.

Perhaps because of his unique position as an "inside outsider"—a scholar/publisher—Horowitz's work has been treated seriously by all groups with an interest in publishing issues. Not only is he a founder of his company, he has remained actively involved with the business. Consequently, what he has to say about publishing carries with it a high degree of credibility. Equally importantly, he brings to the world of publishing rare theoretical sophistication. This unusual combination of perspectives has made him an influential spokesman for the industry and an influential force among his peers in publishing.

More provocative than the question of why there is so little sound scholarship on publishing may be why so few scholars have involved themselves with publishing as a business. There have been other academics who have founded publishing companies or important publications—one thinks especially of Irving Kristol with Basic Books and *The Public Interest*—but very few have stayed with it, certainly not for their entire professional life, as has Horowitz. This may be because many academics have an aversion to the idea of a life in business. More likely, it is because publishing requires commitment to work other than one's own. To be a successful publisher, one must be prepared to recognize and publish quality work of others, even if one does not necessarily agree with it. One has to genuinely believe in a "marketplace of ideas," which implies competition and choice. Scholars may give lip service to the concept, but more than that is required. Egotism may keep them from full-scale commitment to publishing as a worldview and a life-style.

In contrast, from his earliest days, scholarship and publishing have been intimately linked in Horowitz's life. His autobiographical description of how he first entered the world of publishing in the 1950s is a fascinating saga.[12] This young entrepreneur learned by doing, taking risks (without fully understanding them), and inventing ways of doing things because no one told him they wouldn't work. Reading between the lines, one realizes that in the McCarthyite world of the 1950s, an unusual group of distinguished noncommunist left authors were accessible to an undercapitalized new publisher. Perhaps publication of such works even helped change the climate of those times.

Certainly by the end of his tale of the brief life and early retirement of his company, Paine-Whitman Publishers, this young scholar/publisher had moved from the margins to a major university, Washington University. A measure of the recognition he had achieved was an invitation to become a social science editor at Oxford University Press (succeeding Robert Nisbet), a position he held until 1972, when Transaction developed its own book publishing program. Horowitz's early experience with publishing undoubtedly taught him the importance to the world of ideas of an outlet for good scholarly work, regardless of ideology. The result was a lifelong commitment to what others undoubtedly see as a dual career—but which he sees as an integrated life.

Much of Horowitz's writing on publishing concerns topical issues that have been of deep concern to publishers. Some articles were written as a result of invitations to speak on particular topics. Others resulted from his participation in ongoing dialogue on such issues. Still others undoubtedly were influenced by his involvements with publisher organizations. In some sense, they all reflect his commitment to a role for social science in the public discourse.

In this chapter, I will discuss Horowitz's work on several subjects that have occupied much of his attention. They are also of key importance to publishers. The first of these is copyright, an issue of central importance to the publishing industry and that has been part of public policy debates since the copyright law was revised in 1976. After publication of his earliest article on the subject, Horowitz was invited to serve on the AAP's Copyright Committee (one of the few nonlawyers in the group). He addressed the second subject, the impact of technological change on publishing, in a number of articles. This, too, has been a subject of great interest within the industry, although it lacks the obvious public policy significance of copyright issues.

Horowitz has also written on a number of other subjects, ranging from author-publisher relations, to journals publishing, to publishing about philanthropy. In these more random articles, as well as those in the two subject areas mentioned earlier, there have been two strong subthemes: (1) competing rights in the international arena, and (2) the relationship of publishing to democracy. Undoubtedly those who are aware of other aspects of Horowitz's work will perceive that these subthemes are echoed elsewhere in his work .

In the pages that follow, I want to discuss these central subjects and themes and how Horowitz has addressed them. Most of his writing has been confined to scholarly publishing, and consequently there are inevitably some omissions and oversights. These will be discussed in a final section on the business of publishing.

Copyright: A Balance of Rights

For publishers, some of Horowitz's most significant writing is on copyright issues. With a few exceptions, discussion about law is the province of lawyers, and copyright law is no exception. Writing as a publisher, not a lawyer, he challenged fundamental assumptions about the Copyright Act of 1976 and its implications, charted grounds for possible cooperation among contentious parties, and placed the discussion in a broad intellectual context.

Mainstream thinking sees copyright's purpose to be the encouragement of creativity, by permitting the creator a time of exclusive ownership and right to compensation. Horowitz shares this position, but goes beyond conventional thinking in a number of areas. In one of his earliest articles on copyright, "Corporate Ghosts in the Photocopying Machine,"[13] he addressed the issue of photocopying. Publishers were concerned about the erosion of copyright through widespread unauthorized reproduction. Although it was not widely understood as such at the time, the photocopying machine was one of the earliest "new technologies" to challenge the copyright status quo. Awareness of the difficulty of controlling reproduction of copyright materials on photocopiers led legislators to give explicit recognition and legal status to the previously unwritten concept of "fair use" in the Copyright Act of 1976.

The rather narrow criteria established for "fair use" in that legislation did not resolve the disputes. Librarians, claiming to represent users, moved to broaden the criteria, claiming almost all photocopying by libraries or their users to be "fair use." Publishers were indecisive and initially unable to develop a strategy to counter librarian efforts. To counter claims that clearing permission was excessively burdensome, they established the Copyright Clearance Center (CCC) as an independent body to collect royalties. Publishers registered serial publications with CCC, generally journals, and established a fee for copying the publication. Users were permitted to copy these publications without prior authorization. As one of the first Reproduction Rights Organizations (RROs), CCC was modeled after ASCAP (the American Society of Composers and Performers), which collects royalties for the playing of music without prior authorization.

Launching CCC required an unprecedented commitment on the part of publishers; but it was not greeted with enthusiasm by librarians, despite the fact CCC had been set up in response to complaints voiced in hearings on the 1976 law. Meanwhile, William and Wilkins, a publisher of medical journals, independently filed legal action against the National Institute of Health for systematic photocopying, which was expressly forbidden by the Copyright Act. When that suit was decided in language unfavorable to publishers, they became uneasy about pursuing further legal actions, and were undecided about an appropriate and effective strategy. Librarians, meanwhile, proceeded as if there were now no impediments to broad-scale copying.

In this context, Horowitz presented a number of radical ideas. He argued that publishers should hold the manufacturer of photocopying equipment liable, not the person or organization making copies. He argued that publishers should also give librarians incentives for enforcing copyright law and collecting fees, and urged publishers to permit them to share in revenues collected. Realistically, he said, it was impossible to sue all people and organizations engaged in illegal copying; the practice was too widespread. It would be better to challenge those companies that produce the photocopying equipment and profit from copies made. While this argument may seem akin to accusing the manufacturer of a gun used in a murder, it is a provocative idea. And civil law on occasion holds the party providing the means for injury responsible for injury. Equally radical was Horowitz's public criticism of the ineffectiveness of CCC. Despite its lack of public acceptance and its continuing inability to become self-funding (and pay publishers royalties it had collected), major publishers had been reluctant to face up to growing publisher dissatisfaction with the organization.

In arguing for a technological solution to problems created by technology, Horowitz anticipated strategies of other copyright industries faced with similar problems. Record companies have argued for a royalty on sales of cassette tapes (to compensate for taping of music); software producers have used encoding and similar approaches to control unauthorized duplication of their products. Cable companies and networks use complex codes to thwart unauthorized capture of their signals by satellite-dish owners. While these efforts have had mixed success, the debates surrounding them have raised public consciousness about copyright. However, the AAP did not adopt the approach Horowitz advocated in its legal strategy. Perhaps for understandable reasons, publishers were reluctant to confront major corporations with deep pockets in a legally cloudy area.

The AAP chose a different strategy: select, highly visible, and potentially precedent-setting legal suits against major violators in key areas of systematic photocopying. It filed suit against Texaco, which had made only token payments to CCC for the photocopying of journal articles by its researchers. It also filed suit against Kinko's, which sold professors photocopies of publications for use in courses, but made only token payments to copyright holders. The publicity value of this strategy and its impact on the behavior of other violators has had a major impact. As demonstrated by the aftermath of successful actions against Kinko and Texaco, selective legal action, widely publicized, can change behavior. Permissions are now being sought for a large proportion of educational photocopying, and the potential impact of the Texaco suit is even greater. Not only are more corporations now registering with CCC, but libraries and universities seem to have seen parallels between their practices and Texaco, and are rethinking their positions.

Horowitz's forthright comments on CCC helped focus attention on the need to simplify CCC procedures to make it effective. Since the mid-1980s, CCC has developed new approaches to encourage respect for copyright. Most notably, it developed a site license approach to permit organizations to make a single annual payment and avoid the burdensome record keeping required by the older "transactional" system. CCC has also worked out collateral agreements with other RROs to encourage reporting and payment for transnational copying. Most importantly, by giving voice to widespread discontent among publishers, Horowitz encouraged CCC to become more responsive rather than taking publisher support for granted. In 1992 CCC disbursed $6 million in royalties to publishers, a vast improvement from its reported six-figure deficit in the mid-1980s.[14]

Our coauthored article "Fair Use versus Fair Return: Copyright Legislation and Its Consequences"[15] had an even greater impact. It charted a far more rigorous line of argument against "fair use" than publishers had thought possible, suggesting that in its lack of precision, the concept constituted a loophole that threw open the door to widespread transgression of publisher rights by users of copyright materials. It is fair to say that a more narrow interpretation of "fair use" has been articulated by Judge Lasker in his decision on the Texaco suit.[16] Moreover, a more vigorous, confident assertion of publisher rights is echoed in virtually every article in a recent special issue on international copyright in *Publishing Research Quarterly.*[17]

The tide has turned. In fact, publishers now face a different kind of risk. If their business practices fail to acknowledge that copyright is intended to balance the rights of users and proprietors, they may erode the public support they have gained with such difficulty, and success (or failure) in court, as we know, often reflects changes in public opinion as well as legal precedent. Publishers should support new approaches to satisfy the needs of users within the bounds of law, such as document delivery services. To oppose these new developments through exorbitant royalty demands for copies made or, worse, nonparticipation, is to invite failure in future litigation. As the Texaco decision makes clear, a critical factor in the court's decision was that it was not an "undue burden" for users to pay royalties.[18]

What accounts for the dramatic shift in publisher fortunes from William and Wilkins to the Texaco suit? In part, publishers have now developed a body of evidence, presented in writing and research, that supports their arguments against uncompensated reproduction. In part the decision to challenge Texaco, a major private enterprise organization, was simply a better choice than the decision to take on the National Institute of Health, an institution so close to the U.S. government. Even more important is increasing awareness of the importance of the intellectual property industries to the American economy and the balance of trade. Publishers successfully linked up with other industries suffering from assaults on their copyrights (both nationally and internationally), notably the computer software, motion picture, and music and sound recording industries. Instead of arguing that publishing, print, and the book and journal are exceptional products, publishers successfully positioned themselves alongside other intellectual property industries.[19]

In 1984, major copyright industries affected by international piracy (the illegal use of copyrighted materials in an international context) joined together to form the International Intellectual Property Alliance (IIPA). Their purpose was to educate the U.S. Congress as well as the executive branch about the economic importance of these industries, and to identify nations whose practices represented threats to them. For the first time, the U.S. government began to challenge the primarily Third World countries engaging in piracy, through the General Agreement on Tariffs and Trade (GATT), with some success. The domestic climate began to change as well; if piracy abroad is indefensible, surely piracy at home is too.

It would be naive to argue a direct relationship between scholarship and policy consequences. It is fair to say, however, that Horowitz's positions on copyright came at a fortuitous moment. AAP appointed a vigorous new director, Nicholas Veliotes, early in 1986. With solid experience in Washington, he quickly helped forge a more assertive policy stance for the association on copyright as well as other issues.[20] Horowitz's fresh views on copyright helped clarify publisher thinking. The legal strategy that became the bulwark of the AAP effort was not an approach he envisioned or even particularly favored; but he deserves credit for helping create a climate of understanding for publisher positions that made success possible.

Technological Change and Social Consequences

Another major theme in Horowitz's work on publishing has to do with the impact of technological innovation on publishing. This is also a theme in development research, of course, and Horowitz applied insights derived from his work in that area to the field of publishing. The interaction between his broad understanding of socioeconomic development issues and his specific understanding of how publishing works made his assessments of technology's likely impact on traditional publishing practices unusually on target. His articles on the impact of technology on scholarly publishing[21] correctly anticipated major changes whose impact is only now being felt.

For example, Horowitz correctly predicted that the publisher's "gatekeeper" function—deciding what to publish and how to publish it—would become increasingly important. He also made a perceptive distinction between "active" and "passive" publishing. "Passive" publishing is dissemination on demand; databases and bibliographic services communicate availability and leave it up to the user to obtain what they want from the publisher. The "publisher" may be a research center or any kind of organization, but it is generally not an individual, because an independent party must authenticate the value of the publication. In more "active" publishing, the publisher invests time, energy, and money in marketing the product, so as to make it known to audiences that may wish to purchase it. This does not, of course, mean that such material is excluded from databases. The difference is that the publisher actively strives to generate sales and ensure maximum distribution of the publication.

Horowitz is particularly interested in the impact of technology on the editorial process. He emphasizes the increased importance of the publisher's "gatekeeper" function in a world where technology makes it possible for writers to communicate with others instantly about works in progress. He speculates about the consequences of overload of the system of evaluation and peer review prior to publication. His discussion anticipates some of the issues raised by the widely accepted government-sponsored Internet system.[22] Scientists and others who use the system to disseminate their work and communicate with fellow professionals about it know that work on the system has not been evaluated or peer-reviewed. Anyone can put virtually anything on the system provided it is in an appropriate format, and much of the information is available at no charge. The acceptance of Internet suggests that in some circumstances the need for rapid communication can be so acute that individuals are prepared to forego the usual apparatus of scholarly publication, perhaps even credit for publication. The unanswered question is, will this persist as Internet expands? Use is currently estimated to be doubling each year, and has exploded since early 1993.

It will be interesting to see how Internet changes as use strains the capacity of the system. It may be necessary to introduce some control as to what is permitted to be entered onto the system. Who will make these judgments, and who will decide who the judges are to be, raises interesting new questions.

There has been a good deal of discussion about a National Education and Research Network (NREN), widely characterized by its proponents as an "information superhighway," that will store and transmit vast networks of government-generated information and other databases, perhaps including even the resources of the Library of Congress. This seems visionary, but it has been discussed seriously as one of many possible "infrastructure" investments that might be made in the Clinton administration. Librarians and some sectors of the federal government are quick to argue for a predominant role for the federal government in building such a network, which they see as a dramatically expanded version of Internet. Leaving building of the network in private hands, they assert, would be tantamount to having left building the U.S. highway system in private hands. A predominantly governmental role will ensure a "safety net" of public access.

Industry is divided on the question of how a national information network should be funded. Owners of private databases and computer companies are open to a large public role so long as the system is built. Private contenders to build an "information superhighway"—such as AT&T—vigorously argue that they are best positioned to build the system, expanding on their voice communication capabilities. Given the magnitude of the commitment that would be necessary for a national information network, it seems a likely candidate for public/private partnership. The participation of such players as the regional telephone systems, the so-called Baby Bells, is predictable; the role of publishers is unclear. Not least of the questions is how publishers are to be compensated if vast quantities of the world's literature are scanned and digitalized into electronic libraries, and, as librarians envision, libraries themselves generate databases of their holdings.[23]

Although he has not addressed these specific new questions, Horowitz's attitude toward the impact of technology on publishing has been fairly clear. In assessing the probability of broadscale adoption of new technology, he has been cautiously optimistic. He has observed a number of possible constraints. Some of his insights are derived from his awareness of how technology has been accepted (or rejected) in developing countries. In these countries, social and political factors often intervene: Nationalism sometimes conflicts with technology of foreign origin; there may also be conflict between the need for control and the need for openness inherent in periods of rapid development.

Horowitz's observations about publishing in the international arena are equally applicable domestically. He foresees a "new class struggle" between those who are technologically literate and those who lack the skills necessary to use new means of communication. Economic constraints may not stem innovation, but they may interfere with their application. Horowitz knows that technology is neither good nor evil, but offers new options; these in turn bring new dangers and opportunities. His perspective provides much-needed balance to the assessments— both pro and con—of possible changes in the world of communication, and their impact on publishing. For Horowitz, progress is generally beneficial, but he does not believe that the old will be completely replaced by the new. He sees systems as coexisting. What he does not make explicit is that new technology may not replace the old, but it most assuredly will transform its use. The decision for or against a technology is an economic decision, in which the marketplace sometimes decides to maintain the old technology rather than take the new. However, in certain situations, the preference of the marketplace may not be the deciding factor.

In publishing, this may occur when a producer has monopoly control of a body of scholarly information. That producer may unilaterally choose a single format to disseminate the information. The decision may be made for economic reasons—or sometimes for ideological reasons. We have seen this occur in the case of government information. To the dismay of librarians, print formats have been unilaterally discontinued without public input into the decision. The case of *Chemical Abstracts* (CA) is also instructive. *Chemical Abstracts* is a publication of the American Chemical Association (ACA), a not-for-profit professional association that has a monopoly of information about chemical research. When CA went online, for a time it was available in both print and electronic formats. Economic disincentives were introduced to wean users away from the print versions; and finally, users were no longer able to purchase print subscriptions at all. The ACA simply decided to discontinue the print version—not in response to marketplace demands, but because it genuinely believed that electronic information was the future. In an environment of increasing monopolization of scholarly information—particularly in the sciences—we may see other instances in which such nonmarketplace decisions are made.

Competing Rights in the International Arena

Part of the reason for his success in articulating publisher concerns on copyright matters was Horowitz's sensitivity to the need for balance between competing rights: the public's right to know (access) and the publisher's right to compensation (property). Similarly, he approaches issues of technology and publishing with a sense of balance. His ability to acknowledge multiple objectives serves him especially well in his work on issues in international publishing.

Horowitz's sophistication on development issues and theory makes him particularly effective in dealing with well-meaning arguments on behalf of Third World countries that have a great need for information (and almost everything else) but limited capacity to pay. Most publishers are liberal in inclination and share a commitment to a vision of worldwide cultural and intellectual enrichment. Consequently, publishers have been more vulnerable than many other business people might be to arguments that access to their products is a basic human right. In his article "Expropriating Ideas—the Politics of Global Publishing," Horowitz identifies these arguments as political: "What is at issue is nothing short of political responsibility for the present imbalances in the input and output of literary product, and the rights and obligations of publishers and readers to each other and to the community of scholarship as a whole."[24]

Posing the issue thus, Horowitz clarifies the positions of both sides. He distinguishes the First World's desire to control the flow of certain information for security reasons from the demand of publishers who simply want to be paid for use of their products. He observes that the positions of governments and proprietors cannot be equated. He perceives uncritical adoption of the Leninist doctrine of imperialism in arguments of some Third World advocates. He turns these arguments on their head by observing that effectively they deny the right of compensation for their labor to those who work in the creative industries, noting with irony that these same advocates would not deny compensation for manual labor. And he notes that there has always been a class basis of learning, whatever the technology of dissemination.

Instead Horowitz constructs a different kind of rationale for freer flow of information from the developed countries to the underdeveloped. Essentially, it is an argument for self-interest. He notes that an environment in which communication is free and open is also one that is hospitable to a democratic culture. In short, encouraging a free flow of information is likely to breed a more democratic environment, and ultimately a freer world. He even suggests a policy objective for those who want to see this occur: increased international support by governments of advanced nations for dissemination of information.

Essentially, Horowitz argues for a marketplace orientation, with government support to enable poorer countries to participate. The decision to publish should be made between publishers, and information should be provided in whatever formats are desired by users. Horowitz has been forceful on this point and on one or more occasions has made this case with high-ranking United States Information Agency (USIA) officials.[25] Whether one can argue the case for cause and effect or not, it is the case that this position has been reflected in USIA programs since the mid-1980s. USAI has moved away from an orientation toward high-technology approaches that were not compatible with the needs of many Third World countries. High technology is still supported; but more traditional translation and book purchase programs are again being funded.

Some positions Horowitz argues have not yet been taken up by either publishers or policymakers. Observing that information is never free, that it is always paid for, he has compared public lending right legislation (which requires lending libraries to pay publishers royalties based on use) in countries like the United Kingdom with the concept of the free (taxpayer-supported) public library in the United States. Public lending right legislation was on the agenda between 1973 and 1983; it may not have gained support because it became intertwined with arguments for and against public education. Nonetheless, one would think the enormous expansion of videocassette and audiocassette rentals in the United States might stimulate a demand for compensation based on use, despite librarian opposition. Publishers have quite clearly not made such an approach a priority. Perhaps they consider institutional subscription fees for journals a de facto multiple use charge, and for other publications, royalty inclusive licenses cover such instances.

Whatever the reasoning, publishers should make a case for public lending right legislation in the United States. At the very least, such legislation would undermine librarians' arguments that their purchase of journals and books gives them "ownership" rights, and they are therefore free to optically scan contents of publications and include them in databases for further dissemination. If librarians are in fact "owners" of what they have purchased, it would follow that they are free to "lend" the publications (or copies) to other libraries (or users), and charge for the service. In this perspective, there would be no requirement to share any fees collected with publishers. Public lending right legislation would eliminate this argument.

As noted earlier, publishers have linked up with other intellectual property industries to press their case through efforts such as GATT negotiations; the more rapidly developing Third World countries, unwilling to risk loss of access to U.S. markets, have begun to respond to trade pressures. The problem of piracy is not just confined to the Third World, however. Some relatively developed countries fully understand and have previously respected copyright, but are now finding it difficult to control their newly liberated publics. As they undergo rapid political and economic change, the former Soviet Union and Eastern Europe are experiencing rampant entrepreneurship, unleashing pirate publishers that compete with legitimate publishers who try to acquire rights lawfully.

This is a case where the economic interests of copyright proprietors may not always be synonymous with political interests of the United States. Writing before the breakup of the Soviet Union, Horowitz anticipated these situations in a discussion of copyright violations in Poland.[26] As in Russia in 1992, piracy in Poland then made it impossible for legitimate publishers who respect copyright to compete with those who operate illegally. The problem was not lack of knowledge of the law, but perceived ability to adhere to it. Horowitz's analysis of these tensions offers still-relevant guidelines for the publishing and policy-making communities. Such countries need financial assistance through USIA or other agencies to support legitimate publishing activity and translation efforts. The will is there; the money to pay for rights is not, at present.

Publishing and Democracy

While he has never written explicitly about the role of publishing in a democratic civilization, belief in this relationship permeates every aspect of Horowitz's work on publishing. One could go so far as to say that his deep commitment to publishing is one with his deep commitment to democratic values. In a few instances he has made his belief in this relationship explicit, most notably in his observations on publishing in an international context, and most broadly and provocatively in his article "New Technologies, Scientific Information, and Democratic Choice."[27]

Horowitz's sensitivities to the relationship between publishing and democracy in part account for the special character of his perspective on such issues as copyright, for example. His clear distinctions between the right to know and the right to property are both presented as central to democratic culture. As he observes, some would have it that only the right to access (know) is a part of our democratic civilization, but so too is the right to compensation for one's labor. ("The right to know does not entail a denial of payment for food.")[28]

These sensitivities are also evident in a brief but insightful article on the place of standards in advanced industrial societies, originally presented as an address before NISO (the National Information Standards Organization).[29] NISO develops voluntary standards for the publishing, library, and information science communities. Such standards represent a society's agreement that it will adopt uniform ways of working in specific, defined areas. As Horowitz notes, standards are essential rationalizing tools in advanced societies. But he draws an interesting distinction between standards that are imposed by the state, "top down" standards, and those that are developed and adhered to on a voluntary basis, as is characteristic in the United States and as is perforce necessary in an international context. What is unusual about Horowitz's approach is that he sees the process followed by NISO almost as a shorthand way of describing the process of democracy itself. Complex and messy, democracy is ultimately stronger and more effective because it has the commitment of all parties ("the consensual development of standards is part of the long tradition of democracy").[30]

Horowitz's sense of the symmetry between publishing and democracy is also evident in his frequently expressed observation that knowledge is power. By this he simply means that a level of knowledge is essential if one is to have power over technology rather than vice versa. But he also sees the knowledge/power link as double-edged. That is, access to information is essential for a society to fully participate, but a society must on occasion protect certain knowledge from becoming available to those who would do it harm, so as not to give those others power over it. In other words, knowledge (and power) needs to be broadly shared in a democratic society; but that society does not have an absolute obligation to make all knowledge (and all power) available to everyone at any time. Discretion is sometimes justified.

Horowitz's belief that publishing is central to democracy is also reflected in his frequently expressed belief in the appropriate role of the editorial decision maker. While acknowledging that partisanship exists—both within the publishing enterprise and the communities it serves—he sees this not as something to be quiescently accepted, but as something to be overcome "to maintain and extend the open society." This classically liberal sense of publishing, and his own role in it, is explored at some length in several chapters in *Communicating Ideas*.

The Business of Publishing

Throughout, Horowitz's explicit or implicit emphasis is on scholarly publishing, with a focus on the social sciences. This is what he knows about and cares about. With a few rare exceptions, he does not seem particularly interested in textbook publishing or general (trade) publishing, except insofar as these areas affect either scholarly publishing or the social sciences. Consequently, when he writes about textbook publishing, it is usually only in a book review of a sociology textbook. Although the review may not warrant inclusion in *Communicating Ideas*, he might have used it as a starting point for a discussion of textbook publishing in the social sciences, or of changes in textbook publishing per se, but tellingly chose not to do so. It is not lack of personal experience that keeps him from writing about textbooks. Although he has never written a major textbook, he has advised both publishers and textbook authors, and he has been pursued by major publishers to write a textbook, any textbook. As a faculty member, he has received unsolicited samples of texts. Whatever the reason, this is one area of publishing that has never really captured his attention.

Horowitz is fond of saying that he learned from his years with Oxford University Press that the dichotomy between a trade and a scholarly book is false; there are only good books and bad books. This may once have been true, but it is no longer. Despite the very rare serious book that becomes a best-seller, one thinks of Allan Bloom's *The Closing of the American Mind,* for example, scholarly books are produced and distributed quite differently than trade books.

Jason Epstein has recently noted critical changes in trade publishing.[31] Although it was not his intent, his observations also underline differences between trade and scholarly publishing. By the mid-1970s the distribution of trade books began to change with the advent of bookstore chains (such as Dalton and Walden), which assumed a critical role in distribution. Their proliferation in malls brought in substantial new business for best-sellers, but not other kinds of books; the chains also had a destructive impact on independent bookstores. A federal antitrust suit against six major publishers' preferential policies toward chains was resolved in 1992 with the publishers' agreement to discontinue such practices. However, bookstore chains will still be able to order in quantities large enough to guarantee them maximum discounts from publishers, enabling them to offer books to customers at prices lower than the competition.

Epstein also notes the ascendance of "star" authors in trade publishing, akin to Hollywood personalities (or, one might note, today's professional baseball players). These "stars" demand royalty advances that far outstrip probable sales; they are able to get what they demand because their public visibility is entirely independent of anything the publisher can add. As Epstein sourly notes, "star" authors use the publisher's human and financial resources to bring their book to market, assuming none of the risk but taking most of the reward.

It appears that mainline trade publishing has taken on many of the worst characteristics of mass market paperback publishing: dependence on a distribution system controlled by a handful of players, and reliance on a small group of proven authors. These authors' high demands have to be met if the publisher is to obtain the equivalent of shelf space and position for its list in the bookstores. In consequence, trade publishing has become a high risk, uncertain return. And scholarly publishing is increasingly low risk, low return.

How do changes in trade publishing affect scholarly publishing?[32] There is no doubt that the further demise of independent stores would be

a blow to scholarly publishers. Scholarly books do not generate significant enough sales to be of interest to the chains, and in any case the
discounts and return policies of the chains are onerous. The "star" system undoubtedly affects scholarly publishing as well, contributing as it
does to the decline of the mid-list prestige book—the kind of book
Horowitz is thinking about in his "good books, bad books" statement.
For every Allan Bloom, there are hundreds of scholars who have written
serious books that are taken on by trade publishers simply to fill out a
seasonal list. These books are not expected to be successful; the publishers spend little energy in publicizing such books. The trade publisher's
investment in a mid-list book is modest and their expectations low; the
investment in a "star" book, on the other hand, is so significant that the
book may well be a failure if it does not reach the best-seller list—and
stay there. In consequence, the disjunction between trade publishing and
scholarly publishing in the United States has become even wider than it
was in the late 1970s. The implications for scholarly publishers have
still not received sufficient attention.[33]

As the preceding discussion suggests, Horowitz has paid scant attention in his written work to publishing as a business. It is not that he lacks
experience with the business requirements of publishing. Transaction
faces all of the business challenges of larger publishers (and some they
do not face). It is true, however, that Horowitz has never had to be accountable to someone else if Transaction fails to meet its financial goals,
nor need he respond to public inquiry about shortfalls in profits. Transaction is simply not that kind of business. It is not under obligation to a
parent company or the banks, and it is free to make major decisions
without justifying them to external overseers. It is difficult to imagine
the management of many other publishers with similar freedom of action.

The ultimate accountability at Transaction is what it should be for all
publishers, in an ideal world: to the company's employees, its authors,
and the public, all of whom depend on management to make wise decisions so that the company survives and thrives. Unfortunately, these ac-
countabilities, in a conventional business environment, are too often put
aside in favor of this quarter's results. The short-sighted decisions that
are taken in consequence are difficult for a largely self-financed entrepreneur like Horowitz to imagine. This is not necessarily a weakness—
there are more than enough second-rate business analysts in and about
publishing. But it does occasionally make it difficult for him to under-

stand the internal dynamics of decision making within other kinds of publishing companies.

When he does address business-related topics, Horowitz has generally done so critically and without much empathy. An article on "the bottom line" challenges conventional assumptions by which corporations measure performance, and bemoans the incorporation of this way of looking at the world into the public discourse.[34] In his article on marketing scholarly books, he argues that the usual marketing rules do not apply.[35] He has been critical of market-oriented business concepts as applied to publishing. Specifically, he took exception to McGraw-Hill's mid-1980s announcement that henceforth it would not produce products (books, magazines, and information services), but service markets (groups of customers with shared interests).[36] He publicly criticized the decisions of major publishers to discontinue business in South Africa.[37] While I am sympathetic with most of these positions, I also suspect his arguments might have been even more effective if he squarely confronted the business assumptions undergirding them.

Horowitz's antipathy to such approaches may be simply visceral. For someone who sees a key role of publishers as shaping the market rather than responding to it, the idea that books or other journals might be developed to satisfy needs identified by market research is probably disturbing. Horowitz discounts the idea that the editorial decision is often a market-oriented decision, in which the editor decides that the market (or "the public" or "the student") needs a book by a particular author, or a book on a particular topic, and tries to sign a contract for such a book. Such decisions may not be particularly rigorously researched and are often based on intuition and knowledge, but they are a kind of market-oriented decision. The difference is the underlying philosophy; and this is what he has difficulty accepting.

Although one would hope for a more empathetic vision of publishing as a business, its absence has generally not had a negative impact on his analysis. About all that can be said in criticism is that he has missed opportunities: to challenge publishers' business decisions on their own terms, where they are sometimes vulnerable, and to help nonpublishers better understand the rationale for publisher decisions. Better understanding might generate more support for publishing as an industry, and more reasonable expectations from the public. On the other hand, public perception of publishing as just another business might weaken its moral force, and publishers' ability to speak persuasively on such critical issues as First Amendment concerns.

Last Thoughts

Writing about publishing is not often noted for its profundity. The depth of insight, the analytic skills, and the originality Horowitz brings to his work on publishing has elevated the level of discourse. As in his work in many other areas discussed in this volume, Horowitz has been sensitive to the policy choices and the social and political implications of the issues he addresses. Consequently, his writings do not simply defend publishers and their positions. To the contrary, he brings to the public debate a fair degree of criticism. On such matters as copyright, he reveals as much concern about the rapacious consequences of unfettered free markets as the controlled environments of totalitarian states. He is no more confident that publishers will act in the public interest (if it conflicts with their business needs) than he trusts the state to protect the interests of individuals if it has monopoly control of information. Horowitz is never pedestrian; but it is his lack of partisanship that ultimately makes his work on publishing so convincing.

Horowitz's contributions to scholarship on publishing transcend what he himself has written. Publishers now write about their environment more often and more eloquently than they once did. He helped institutionalize serious discussions about publishing with the launch of the award-winning journal *Book Research Quarterly* (since 1990 retitled *Publishing Research Quarterly*). Enough good writing about publishing now exists to fill the pages of several important new journals devoted to publishing in the 1980s. *Scholarly Publishing*, of course, has existed since the early 1970s; but in addition to it and *Publishing Research Quarterly* we also have *Logos*. There are any number of newsletters and less formal means of communication as well. Such publications do not exist because people in publishing must write in order to secure their employment. Writing has few tangible rewards for most publishing professionals, and it takes time away from tasks for which they are held strictly accountable. Attitudes have changed. In part, publishers now see the benefit of creating a body of literature that helps others to understand their business, and that also presents their perspectives on public issues of importance.[38]

The contribution of Irving Louis Horowitz to such developments within the publishing industry and to what it values are no less important than his specific contributions to the debates on the critical issues of the 1980s. If there is any regret, it is that his writing on publishing has diminished in volume in recent years. The reasons are complex; in part he has intellectually moved on, and in part his diminished involvement with publishing organizations may have removed him from some of the critical internal debates in the industry. Irving Horowitz would be the first to say, "Where I have lapsed, let others step forward." Let us hope they do so. There would be no greater tribute to him.

Rutgers, The State University of New Jersey
Transaction Publishers

Notes

The author wishes to express gratitude for the wise counsel of Ray C. Rist in his editorial review of this article.

1. Irving Louis Horowitz and Mary E. Curtis, "On Truth in Publishing: A Response," *The Nation* 226, no. 21 (3 June 3 1978): 660–61 (an expanded version appears in the second edition of *Communicating Ideas* [New Brunswick, NJ: Transaction Publishers, 1991] as chapter 13, "Gatekeeping Functions and Publishing Truths," pp. 162–68); "The Impact of the New Information Technology on Scientific and Scholarly Publishing," *Scholarly Publishing* 13, no. 3 (April 1982) 211–28 (in *Communicating Ideas* as chapter 3, "Technological Impacts on Scholarly Publishing," pp. 30–44); "Fair Use versus Fair Return: Copyright Legislation and Its Consequences," *Journal of the American Society for Information Science* (JASIS) 35, no.2 (March 1984): 67–74 (in *Communicating Ideas* as chapter 5, "Copyright Legislation and Its Consequences," pp. 56–71); "The 'Bottom Line' as American Myth and Metaphor," *Chronicles: A Magazine of American Culture* 15, no. 4 (April 1991): 26–31; and "Scholarly Book Publishing in the 1990s," *International Encyclopedia of Book Publishing,* ed. Philip G. Altbach and Edith S. Hoshino (New York: Garland Publishing, Inc., 1993).
2. Irving Louis Horowitz, "The Place of the Festschrift in Academic Life," *Scholarly Publishing* 21, no. 2 (January 1990): 77–83 (in *Communicating Ideas* as chapter 20, "The Place of the Festschrift in Scholarly Publishing," pp. 234–40).
3. Irving Louis Horowitz, ed., *The New Sociology: Essays in Social Science and Social Values in Honor of C. Wright Mills* (New York: Oxford University Press, 1964).
4. Irving Louis Horowitz, ed., *Communicating Ideas: The Politics of Scholarly Publishing,* 2d expanded ed. (New Brunswick, NJ: Transaction Publishers, 1991).
5. Irving Louis Horowitz, "The Sociology Textbook: The Treatment of Conflict in American Sociological Literature," *Social Science Information* 11, no. 1 (February 1972): 51–63.

6. Irving Louis Horowitz, "Packaging a Sociological Monsterpiece: Society Today," *Transaction/Society* 9, no. 8 (June 1972): 50–54.

7. Irving Louis Horowitz and Paul Barker, "Mediating Journals: Reaching Out to a Public beyond the Scientific Community," *International Social Science Journal* 26, no. 3 (1974): 383–410.

8. Irving Louis Horowitz, "Autobiography as the Presentation of Self for Social Responsibility," *New Literary History* 9, no. 1 (Autumn 1977): 173–79.

9. Irving Louis Horowitz, "Advertising Truth, Propaganda, and Consequences," *Proceedings of the Council of Better Business Bureaus on the Responsibilities of Advertisers to Society* (Washington, DC: Council of Better Business Bureaus, 1978), 58–71 (in *Communicating Ideas* as chapter 12, "Advertising Ideas and Marketing Products").

10. Irving Louis Horowitz, "Marketing Social Science," *Transaction/Society* 17, no. 1 (November/December 1979): 12–19.

11. Lewis A. Coser, Charles Kadushin, and Walter W. Powell, *Books: The Culture and Commerce of Publishing* (New York: Basic Books, 1982).

12. Irving Louis Horowitz, "Scholarly Publishing as the Word Made Flesh," chapter 24 of *Communicating Ideas.*

13. Irving Louis Horowitz, "Corporate Ghosts in the Photocopying Machine," *Scholarly Publishing* 12, no. 4 (July 1981): 299–304 (in *Communicating Ideas* as chapter 6, "The Reproduction of Knowledge and the Maintenance of Property").

14. These figures were reported by Eamon Fennessey, former director of CCC, in a telephone conversation with the author in December 1992; the $6 million figure was confirmed by a CCC representative in January 1993.

15. See note 1 above.

16. Irving Louis Horowitz, "Texaco Decision and Publishers Rights," memorandum to the International Publishers Copyright Council by Jon Baumgarten of Proskauer, Rose, Goetz & Mendelsohn, 24 July 1992.

17. Special issue on international copyright, *Publishing Research Quarterly* 8, no. 2 (Summer 1992). Compare the assertiveness of contributors to this issue with the far more tentative and problematic tone adopted by contributors to a special issue on new perspectives on copyright, *Book Research Quarterly* 2, no. 2 (Summer 1986).

18. "The publishers have persuasively shown that there exist convenient and reasonably priced procedures by which Texaco could obtain the necessary additional copies for its scientists" (pp. 39 of the decision, quoted in Baumgarten memorandum [see note 16 above]).

19. For a discussion of publisher strategy on copyright issues under the leadership of AAP Director, see Nicholas Veliotes, "Copyright in the 1990s: A New Round of Challenges for American Publishers," *Publishing Research Quarterly* 4, no. 1 (Spring 1988): esp. p. 7 on the AAP's role in creation of the International Intellectual Property Alliance.

20. See, for example, the Washington Update on the Status of Key Publishing Issues Before the 102nd Congress (1991–92) (Washington, DC: Association of American Publishers, 1993). The report, issued to members of the AAP, lists federal legislation enacted and proposed but not enacted of particular interest to the publishing industry. The report provides an analysis of AAP positions on the legislation, analyzes the consequences of action taken or not taken, and reviews other areas of concern. It indicates a more vigorous sense of the industry's participation in the policy process than was evident prior to Veliotes becoming director of

the organization. John F. Baker also discussed key policy issues confronting the industry in "Outlook 93: Anxieties and Openings," *Publishers Weekly* 240, no. 1 (4 January 1993): 40–41.

21. See our article cited in note 1. Also, Irving Louis Horowitz, "A Pessimistic View of New Technology," *Information Age* 6, no. 3 (July 1984): 186–87 (which appears as a portion of chapter 1 of *Communicating Ideas,* pp. 3–12); "The Political Economy of Data-Base Technology," in *Information and Behavior,* vol. 1, ed. Brent D. Ruben (New Brunswick, NJ: Transaction Publishers, 1983) (which appears in *Communicating Ideas* as chapter 4, with the same title).

22. The *Chronicle of Higher Education* provides excellent coverage of developments on Internet, and addresses some of the issues. See, for example, David L. Wilson, "Acceptable Use Policy on Internet Prompts Confusion Over Commercial Activities," *The Chronicle of Higher Education,* 20 January 1993, pp. A-17, A-18. For a discussion of private-public issues see John Markoff, "Building the Electronic Superhighway," *The New York Times,* Sunday, 24 January 1993.

23. The public/private debate is currently being expressed in terms of who shall build (and profit from) the electronic network. The publishers' concern is how copyrighted materials are to be protected in a digitalized environment. For a recent discussion, see Paul Hilts, "Through the Electronic Copyright Maze," *Publishers Weekly* 239, no. 26 (8 June 1992). Librarian perspectives on these issues are well covered by *College and Research Libraries News.* The Association of College and Research Libraries (ACRL) has taken a strongly supportive position on NREN (the National Research and Education Network), the so-called electronic superhighway.

24. The article was originally published in *The Bookseller,* no. 4206 (2 August 1986): 528–32. The quotation is from chapter 9, which bears the same title, p. 115.

25. This is an example of a situation in which Irving's multiple roles beneficially interacted. As a member of the Advisory Council to USIA's Radio Martí, he interacted with the senior eschelons of USIA. As a member of the Board of Directors of the Professional and Scholarly Division of AAP, he was aware of publisher concerns about USIA's abandonment of support for book programs in favor of high technology approaches. He made an effective case for the reinstatement of these programs in 1986.

26. Irving Louis Horowitz, "The Reproduction of Knowledge and Maintenance of Property," *Communicating Ideas,* chapter 6, p. 820.

27. Irving Louis Horowitz, "New Technology, Scientific Information, and Democratic Choices," *Information Age* 5, no. 2 (April 1983): 67–73 (in *Communicating Ideas* as chapter 2, pp. 13–29).

28. Horowitz and Curtis, "Copyright Legislation and Its Consequences," see note 1, p. 70.

29. Irving Louis Horowitz, "Forms of Democracy: The Place of Scientific Standards in Advanced Societies," *Information Standards Quarterly* 2, no. 1 (January 1990): 8–12 (chapter 22 in *Communicating Ideas,* pp. 245–51).

30. Ibid., 251.

31. Irving Louis Horowitz, "The Decline and Rise of Publishing by Jason Epstein," *The New York Review of Books,* 1 March 1990, pp.8–12.

32. For a discussion of the impact of superstores on small presses, see Joseph Barbato, "Chain Superstores: Good Business for Small Presses?" *Publishers Weekly* 239, no. 49 (9 November 1992).

33. For a discussion of the distinction between scholarly and trade publishing in the 1970s see Mary E. Curtis, "The Informational Basis of Social Science Publish-

ing," *Society* (November-December 1979): 25–31. An expanded version appears in *Communicating Ideas* as chapter 8, "Scholarly Communication and Academic Publishing," pp. 97–114.

34. See note 1 above.
35. Horowitz, *Communicating Ideas,* chapter 12, "Advertising Ideas and Marketing Products, pp. 154–61.
36. Ibid., chapter 7, "From Computer Revolution to Intellectual Counterrevolution," pp. 84–93.
37. Irving Louis Horowitz, "Between South African Rocks and Publishing Hard Places," *The Bookseller* (26 June 1987): 2403–04.
38. This position is argued most explicitly by Charles Clark, "Copyright and the Publisher in a Market Economy," *Publishing Research Quarterly* 8, no. 2 (Summer 1992): 79–85. Mr. Clark is general counsel to the International Publishers Copyright Council.

25

Planning Expeditions into
Uncharted Territory

Beth Luey

Academics and other scholars take the outcome of the publishing process very seriously. One's own books, articles, offprints, reviews—all of these are the scholar's life blood, the source of professional connection, economic security, status, even identity. The published works of others are also important, providing information, inspiration, contact, and—more practically—a basis for teaching one's courses. Until very recently, however, few academics considered the process itself worthy of study. Publishing apparently held no mysteries, especially for the successful. Nor have publishers themselves studied the field. As Irving Horowitz has noted, "professional publishing is a strangely anti-intellectual environment dominated by individuals often remote from the publishing product" (Horowitz, 1991:xiv–xv). Publishers either do not believe that their work has social, cultural, and political implications, or they do not care to investigate these implications very closely.

Perhaps because Irving Horowitz is both a publisher and a scholar, he has taken the process of publishing seriously. Along with other sociologists, he has looked inside the house at editorial decision making, the impact of technology, and other operational concerns. Unlike most other sociologists who have written about publishing, though, he does not suffer from what he has called "an editorialist bias, the presumption that problems connected with decisions to publish or not to publish a book or a journal are uniquely decisive, whilst by implication all other facets of publishing are secondary" (Horowitz, 1991:xv). This is clearly the view of the experienced publisher, and the message has been validated by recent historical studies that point out the importance of studying not only editorial, design, and marketing decisions, but even transportation and distribution when analyzing the spread of literacy and literature.[1]

Most important, Horowitz has examined issues that link publishers to the rest of the world: copyright and questions of ownership of intellectual property, more generally; the role of publishing in education; and publishing and democracy, for example. As he remarks in writing about social science publication, the discussion

> quickly becomes entangled in a web of commercial, political, and technical considerations.... [S]ocial scientific publishing immediately raises questions about the organization of the academy, the processes of communicating ideas, and the constraints of the marketplace. The sheer attempt to disaggregate and distinguish these different parts of the puzzle moves us also into areas as wide-ranging as class stratification and personal stress. (Horowitz, 1991:187)

Most of Irving Horowitz's studies of publishing are gathered together in *Communicating Ideas* (1991). The title is significant: one of the vital functions of the publisher is to make possible communication between author and reader; the subject matter of these transactions is ideas as well as data, knowledge as well as information, a distinction Horowitz develops in his essay "From Computer Revolution to Intellectual Counter-revolution" (Horowitz, 1991:84–94).

The attempt to study publishing in a scientific way is relatively new. For a long time, scholars viewed the process of publication as trivial and the world of publishing as unworthy of study. Textual scholars and literary critics found writing worthy of study; some historians investigated printing history; educators tried to understand how reading occurs; publishing was largely ignored.

In recent years, however, scholars in these fields and others have begun to understand that publishing is neither trivial nor passive. Literary scholars pondering texts have come to realize that the physical presentation of the text affects who reads it and how; that the marketing of books helps determine the size and nature of the audience; that publishers shape or even create genres.[2] Historians have looked at the impact of print on society (particularly in Europe) and are beginning to investigate the role of publishers in shaping opinion and culture.[3] Educators trying to understand how children learn have begun to recognize that the role of textbook publishers is more complex than they once believed.[4] Sociologists have studied editorial decision making, peer review, and evaluation of journals.[5] At their best, such studies have begun to achieve what Horowitz has called "symmetry" in their research: that is, just as industrial sociology must not be merely managerial sociology but must include the sociology of labor, the sociology (and history) of publishing must include among its subjects authors and readers as well as publishers (Horowitz, 1967:32).

It is my hope that scholars in all these disciplines are on the verge of taking on some unanswered questions about the role of publishers in communicating ideas. These questions can be approached both theoretically and empirically, and although micro-level research is needed, such "local" research must be located in a broader context for it to be significant.

In this essay I will look at one of the many unanswered questions and propose methods by which it might be studied. How do academic disciplines evolve and become part of the culture? Of the many issues in need of investigation, this seems to me to be important because, rather than viewing publishing as a system that can be studied in isolation, it recognizes the importance of publishers' intellectual and social role in the larger society, a point Irving Horowitz has made repeatedly. And, as we shall see, this question is linked inextricably to issues Irving Horowitz has examined, not only in his studies of publishing, but in his works about sociology as a discipline and about the academy.

Scholarly Disciplines in the Academy

During the last half of the twentieth century, academic disciplines have divided, sprung into existence, evolved, and died with little understanding among the participants of how these processes occur. Division is the most widely recognized and discussed phenomenon; those in both research and publishing circles discuss the "twigging" of scientific disciplines with facility. Yet some disciplines have emerged, not through twigging, but through other phenomena.

One phenomenon to which the discipline of history seems particularly susceptible is what we might call grafting—the adoption of a theoretical or technical approach used in another discipline. Psychohistory and quantitative history are good examples.

Besides twigging and grafting, we must look at hybridization, the creation of new disciplines by combining existing ones. Women's studies, African-American studies, and multidisciplinary approaches to the study of various ethnic groups are a useful example. Women's studies is not a twig of anything else; even women's history is not a twig of history. Nor is it simply a coalition of scholars with similar interests from various disciplines. In fact, we know very little about where such enterprises come from. Twigging, which seems generally to occur when a subdiscipline reaches a critical mass and secedes, is a phenomenon internal to the relevant discipline. But women's studies and its parallel disciplines seem to have arisen as much from social forces outside the disciplines—indeed, outside the academy—as from intellectual needs internal to any discipline.

Having emerged in some manner that we do not understand, areas such as women's studies have evolved in ways that are in some ways parallel to the development of traditional disciplines and in other ways very different. Their politicization, for example, is much more extreme than that of many other fields. The accoutrements, however, are identical: departments, associations, journals, book series, and the like.

Other disciplines are disappearing or are on the lists of endangered or threatened species. Many women now attending their fiftieth college reunions find that their major is long gone: few universities boast departments of home economics. In some cases, remnants can be found under new names, but usually the subject has simply vanished. Numerous departments of geography have been abolished, along with a few departments of sociology. How and why does this happen?

Certainly it is possible to echo conservative commentators on education and dismiss all disciplines more recent than the classics as fads. New disciplines are merely trendy responses to irresponsible social movements; these faddish disciplines disappear because they were never valid in the first place. These explanations—if they can be called that—are simplistic, if not question begging. To find genuine answers, and to gain true understanding of how disciplines arise, mature, or fail, will require a great deal of study and thought. A clearer understanding of the role of publishing should be a fascinating part of such work.

How might such multidisciplinary studies be done? Here I must stress the importance of methodological variety, a point Horowitz develops in his work on the sociology of knowledge:

There is no objection to using various types of evidence in order to explain social events. To argue that the existence of a multiplicity of laws and levels in social theory would leave unresolved the ultimate problems of men is not to take seriously the fact that mankind is not a discoverable essence but rather the general symbol for concrete men. Men have problems, not functional or historical abstractions. The validation and verification of data may rule out inspirational solutions to the "perennial" questions; but in breaking down monumental questions into manageable proportions, and in weeding out perennial nonsense from perennial questions. (Horowitz, 1961:128)

How, then, might we understand the phenomenon of twigging, for example? First, it is important to remember one of the basic focuses of Irving Horowitz's work in this field: no matter how narrow our component studies may be, the complexity of the environment remains a central fact. In this case, as he notes,

specialization within the scientific community has encouraged smaller, more specialized forms of scholarly publishing and the development of specialized units within larger publishing houses. Both have close relationships with subsets of the scholarly community, and their publishing activity both supports and is supported by these subsets. (Horowitz, 1991:33–34)

So let us begin with the scholarly community. The general catalogue of my university—which fifty years ago had a department of biology—now lists departments of botany, zoology, and microbiology. These offer courses in subfields, including lichenology, plant ecology, mycology, palynology, phycology, paleobotany, physiology, genetics, biogenetics, anatomy, entomology, sociobiology, neurophysiology, ornithology, mammalogy, ichthyology, herpetology, bacteriology, immunology, virology, and neuroimmunology. Each of these subdisciplines has at least one professional society, annual meeting, textbook, and journal. Each has boundaries, and each has links to other subdisciplines.

Using easily accessible archival sources, a historian could trace the appearance of new courses, departments, associations, and journals. University archives contain documents justifying the establishment of new programs; new associations have charters; new journals have statements of purpose. In many cases, the pioneers in these fields have written about their founding, and many people who participated in early developments are alive and available for interviewing. Publishers' archives contain correspondence about the founding of journals and about decisions to enter a field with a textbook; they also contain data about numbers of subscriptions and about textbook sales. It would not be difficult to establish chronology, motivation, successes, and failures.

An economist or political scientist could look at the funding activity of private foundations and government agencies. When do scientists who describe themselves as working in a new subdiscipline begin to attract grants? When does a new discipline appear in official lists of eligible funding areas? When do separate grant programs, with separate review panels, appear? What motivates these changes? Do new professional associations lobby for them? Do scientists on review panels and the staffs of the agencies that work with them recognize the need for change and achieve it through bureaucratic channels? Such information could be extracted from government records and interviews.

A sociologist might use surveys to determine the status and quality attributed to a subfield by its members and by outsiders. Measures of success, value, acceptance, institutionalization, and other qualities difficult to quantify could be established. Relationships among subfields could be mapped by looking at association memberships and leadership, at editorial boards, and at disciplines and affiliations of journal contributors.

What would we learn from such work? For each twigged discipline studied, we would learn who founded it, when, where, how, and why. With several such studies in hand, we could begin to generalize about the process of becoming a discipline in the late twentieth century, about the reasons for establishing new areas of study, and about what validates a field.

Grafting would have to be looked at quite differently, however, because it seems to be an ineffective way to establish a discipline. Neither of the subdisciplines of history that I mentioned, it seems to me, has established itself; rather the techniques they have appropriated have been put to use in the service of the parent discipline. Thus, biographers (one of the most traditional groups of narrative historians) now freely use psychological techniques, and social historians (one of the most innovative groups) use statistical methods. The mainline discipline has coopted the techniques, leaving the would-be subdisciplines with little to do. This is merely an impression based on observation. I hope that someone will take the time to look at the history of these attempts—the published arguments over legitimacy, the establishment of journals and societies, the nature of the early work in the field, its evolution, and its incorporation into the mainstream of the discipline.

Some of the questions relevant to publishing studies would relate to the role of journals—a subject that recurs in looking at the birth of all new disciplines—but some are unique to these fields. For example, to what extent did the off-putting nature of tables and other statistical materials (off-putting at least to the traditional audience for history) contribute to the very modest interest of book publishers in quantitative history? And to what extent did this lack of interest stunt the field's development? Has the introduction of statistics courses into the history curriculum changed the receptivity of readers and publishers? Psycho-history was well received by publishers and readers, yet it did not thrive. Are publishing interest and success irrelevant to a field's development, or are we looking at a more complex phenomenon?

Discovering the origins of an entirely new field, and tracing its development or failure, will be more difficult, in part because the likely candidates for study are closely tied to contemporaneous social and cultural movements, which are themselves not fully understood. In other cases, such as artificial intelligence, they are linked to new technologies that are changing so rapidly that study would be premature. Most new fields are also interdisciplinary or multidisciplinary rather than subdisciplinary, which complicates matters further. And in many cases they experience severe internal strains arising from ideological or methodological differences. Nevertheless, better understanding than we now have is possible.

Applying the same archival and interviewing research methods that might illuminate twigging, historians could study the introduction of new courses; the establishment of centers, interdisciplinary majors, certificate and degree programs, and departments; the introduction and development of new journals; the appearance of writing in the new field in mainstream journals; and the first appearance of books, book series, and even publishers dedicated to the field. They could look at the rise of conflicting ideologies or methodologies.

Political scientists could study the relationship between the women's movement and the development of women's studies as a discipline, or between the civil rights movement and the development of African-American studies. How do the political, intellectual, and academic movements interact? How does politicization affect the internal dynamics of a discipline and its acceptance within the academy?[6] Communications experts might look at the media coverage of emerging, controversial disciplines and at the impact of publicity on the academy. Those interested in language could study the changes in names and descriptive terms used in the literature.

Sociologists and historians might also look at the impact of these new fields on the disciplines from which they emerged. The vocabularies, methodologies, ideologies, and concerns of these new specialties have entered the thought and works of scholars at some disciplinary remove. For example, very little work can now be done in intellectual, social, political, or economic history that does not take into account gender, race, and ethnicity. Feminist studies have even had an impact on the more "objective" hard sciences, where we are learning that, for example, cardiology research conducted on populations of white men yields results not necessarily valid for white women or black people of either sex.

The Role of Publishing Studies

The answers to many of these questions will come from studies of publishing. Horowitz points to three functions that publishing can serve in this connection. First, a publisher can be

> a filtering agent—an independent, autonomous factor, able to permeate the university or scholarly environment as a whole, to sift through opinions and evaluations until he perceives a degree off agreement about what work is important. Publishing gives scholars and researchers a way to move beyond parochialism and organizational constraints.

Second, publishing "is a broker of innovation. It cannot stimulate innovation; it can only respond. But without the broker, it would be difficult to verify scientific innovation or intellectual imagination." Third, in an electronic environment, publishers can use marketing tools such as subscription lists to facilitate scholarly interaction, by creating networks, for example (Horowitz, 1991:34–35). Keeping these functions in mind can help us to understand the rise and dissemination of intellectual innovation.

When, how, and why are journals founded in a new field? Does the peer review system prevent the entry of new approaches into mainstream journals? Do university presses shy away from nontraditional books? Did feminist publishers establish themselves in reaction to rejection by the mainstream or for independent reasons? Do academic publishers follow academic trends, lead them, or fight them? Why does one publisher innovate and another hold back? Are for-profit publishers more receptive to new ideas than university presses? Horowitz has suggested, for example, that for-profit publishers are more likely to be receptive to innovation than are learned societies, which rely on collegiality and consensus for their survival: "Intellectual high-risk areas are best served by commercial publishers or independent academic presses. In addition, subjects that are of interest across disciplines can best be exploited by commercial publishers who already have established relationships in more than one discipline" (Horowitz, 1991:34).

Do trade publishing successes such as *The Feminine Mystique* and *The Female Eunuch* encourage or discourage interest among academic publishers? How, when, and why do new academic disciplines find their way into textbooks? For example, do college text publishers decide to include women's history in their books because faculty have demanded it, because they foresee an as yet unexpressed demand, because authors insist on it, or for some other reason? Can we untangle the chicken-and-egg relationship between the availability of textbooks and the offering of courses?

Recalling Horowitz's warning against "editorialist bias," we must also examine not only whether publishers decide to publish in new fields but how they publish innovative works: cautiously and quietly, or bravely and with a flourish? For, as Horowitz has noted, "the extent of the resources a publishing house commits to marketing a publication says something about how important it thinks the work is and what kind of financial return it expects the publication to yield. Users perceive this fact, and respond accordingly" (Horowitz, 1991:35).

Although the research required to answer these questions would involve a great deal of routine slogging, the answers are far from trivial. In fact they would tell us how the academy and the government respond to social change cloaked in academic gowns. They would tell us who determines what information and opinions about gender roles (or race or ethnicity) will be made available to college students and the reading public. And they will tell us a great deal about how new ways of looking at the world become academically respectable and socially acceptable.

The study of declining disciplines could be equally informative. Did home economics disappear because of a decline in academic respectability? student interest? social utility? To what extent did the changing mission and self-image of American universities contribute to reduced support? What disappears first: books? journals? departments?

Whatever the answers prove to be for home economics, they will undoubtedly be different from those we unearth when examining the decline of geography. The change in women's status and their educational expectations undoubtedly played an important role in the disappearance of cooking from the curriculum, but there is no obvious extra-academic reason for the wane of geography. The relationship between publishing and the fate of geography is likely to be anomalous but fascinating. Although geographers write books and articles, the public associates them mostly with maps. Indeed, with the exception of music, there is probably no other field with a publishing genre to call its own. In addition, geography is declining as an academic field at the very moment when new technology is enhancing its possibilities and glamour. Finally, geographers are fighting back, and the tale of decline may have a surprise happy ending. A successful resuscitation would be important to understand.

Academe and Society

Irving Horowitz would, I suspect, be the first to remind us that academic disciplines do not rise and fall in a vacuum: the nature of the society influences the direction of academic work, and academic studies affect social development. As examples of these phenomena we might note Horowitz's descriptions of the rise of the social sciences in Britain and in the United States:

> The linkage between the British political and educational systems may have delayed the evolution of an independent social science curriculum at the more traditional places of learning; but when the penetration did take place (by economics in the eighteenth century, administration in the nineteenth century, and political science in the present century), the situation was ready-made for the close cooperation between social science and social policy. And with the defeat of ideological Toryism (based as it was on "classical studies") by the close of the Second World War, the last shreds of opposition to social science vanished. The impulses of British social science to welfare projects dovetailed neatly with the welfare projects outlined by the political apparatus. And the mutual suspicions of scientists and policy makers characteristic of an earlier epoch in British history dissolved into mutual reinforcement and even joint celebration. (Horowitz, 1967:343–44)

In the United States, too, the social sciences have influenced policy:

> First, a strong social reform tendency developed early in opposition to general theories of change and revolution. American social science has been consciously,

almost self-consciously, dedicated to issues of practical reform. This has led major foundations and philanthropic agencies to lose interest in the direct alleviation of social problems through charity and to invest heavily in indirect means of alleviation: social science programs.

Second, development of a pluralistic educational system made room for many and diverse social scientific activities....

Third, an entrepreneurial spirit developed in American social science to accommodate growing government needs. (Horowitz, 1967:344-45)

Studies of all of these topics relating to disciplinary change and maturation, if they kept Horowitz's properly broad (if daunting) view in mind, would contribute to an overall effort to understand how the media of scholarly communication interact with the messages and the messengers. Publishers and editors are not passive conduits. Whether as gatekeepers, filters, or brokers, they evaluate scholarship, encourage it, discourage it, reward it, and shape it. They help to determine what we know and when we know it.

The influence of publishers is not always recognized, even by publishers themselves, but it is real and viewed with great ambivalence. Scholarly publishers are regularly accused of conservatism, of fearing to risk their capital and reputations on innovative work. When they do venture into new fields, they are frequently charged with giving way to trendiness, of pandering to popular tastes, of allowing political motives to enter into publishing decisions, and so forth. Whatever role publishers may have played in the development of academic disciplines, it surely is not that of innocent bystander.

Maturity and Public Acceptance

Since World War II, public and private investment in research has increased dramatically, flooding scholars, libraries, and the general public with information, ideas, theories, interpretations, and artistic creations. Dissemination technology has spread the deluge over an enormous area. Information no longer reaches only those who read; it is broadcast to those who watch television and listen to the radio. Those who seek information no longer rely on the card catalog of the local library; they have an enormous variety of databases, bibliographies, news services, and specialized information services (legal, financial, etc.) beneath their fingertips at a computer keyboard. Anyone with a computer, a modem, and the money to subscribe to such services can gather more data, more quickly, than anyone even dreamed of having twenty-five years ago. And, of course, we also have the ability to manipulate those data in ways that were impossible, or at least extremely time-consuming, then.

But if communicating information has become an instant electronic process, communicating ideas remains a mystery. How does a scholar's newfound understanding reach peers, educated generalists, and eventually the public? Why do some ideas attract broad interest quickly, while others lie dormant or even perish? And what role do publishers play in all of this?

As Irving Horowitz has noted, an academic discipline can be judged to have "arrived" only when it reaches a broader audience:

> The dissemination of sociological findings has become a serious and full-scale matter in the United States. The fact that a huge audience exists for such books as William H. Whyte's *The Organization Man;* David Riesman's *The Lonely Crowd;* Michael Harrington's *The Other America;* C. Wright Mills' *The Power Elite;* and E. Franklin Frazier's *Black Bourgeoisie* (among others) is an indication that sociology has come of age as a public source of legitimacy. We determine biology's coming of age, not only with the findings of Charles Darwin, but with the ability of a wide audience to absorb the generalizations of T. H. Huxley; and physics' coming of age not so much with the ability of Einstein to introduce a new concept of space, but rather with the capacity of Gamow and Giedeon to translate this fourth dimensionality into a style of art and architecture, and a style of life generally. (Horowitz, 1968:134-35)

Most scholars think about questions of dissemination in narrow, practical ways: How should I write up my research? To what journal should I send it? Is it time to write a book? Who would be the best publisher? Will I get on the "Today" show this time?

Subconsciously, most scholars subscribe to what we might call a "trickle-down" model of the transmission of knowledge. A scholar makes a discovery, offers it to peers at a meeting, incorporates their suggestions, and has it published in a journal. The original researcher and his peers use this discovery and others to make new discoveries, which are similarly disseminated among themselves. Some knowledge remains at that level. Some, however, becomes part of a broader area of knowledge accessible to other well-educated readers through publication in more general journals, through books, or, as Horowitz has noted, through reviews and popular articles (Horowitz, 1991:105). Eventually, such knowledge is incorporated into textbooks and becomes part of the understanding of all college-educated people. Some finds its way into lower-level texts. Some enters general consciousness through the popular media.

As Horowitz has pointed out, this process operates because the publishing industry includes different kinds of publishers who issue different kinds of publications for different audiences and market them on different terms in different ways (Horowitz, 1991:97–114). At each level of communication, the audience increases. For example, Horowitz has estimated the "core social-science market in the United States" at roughly a quarter of a million people and "the secondary market for popular science" at about ten times that number. He attributes the interest of this larger audience to the "therapeutic potential" of social science writing, which supports the self-help variety of the literature (Horowitz, 1991:200–201).

This "trickle-down" model is undoubtedly valid for some kinds of knowledge, at some times. But it is extremely limited. First of all, it is print-bound. It makes little allowance for dissemination through popular electronic media such as television. Horowitz offers an example illustrating the impact of such transmission: an article in the scholarly journal *Society* was picked up by CBS, and the twenty minutes of coverage they provided reached roughly 25 million people (Horowitz, 1991:202). This is too important a phenomenon to neglect.

The model also makes little allowance for the transforming potential of newer media such as electronic networks. More important, it fails to discriminate among various kinds of knowledge that intuition and experience tell us are communicated differently. For example, studies that have immediate practical application—such as clinical trials in medicine—reach both practitioners and the general public very quickly. Discoveries with little impact on daily life—such as an advance in physical chemistry—may take much longer to reach the public and in fact may never reach them at all in their original, unapplied form. A genuine understanding of how new knowledge is transmitted will require detailed study of specific instances of successful and failed communication. Although the transmission of knowledge in the life and physical sciences is of course important, I will limit my discussion here to the social sciences.

To select subjects for study, we must have some notion of the variables that affect the style, media, and speed of communication. I have mentioned one of the more obvious variables: practical applicability.

We can see intuitively that the immediate usefulness of a discovery will make it likely to reach a broad public quickly. But usefulness, I would argue, is part of a far larger complex of variables that affect the transmission of a discovery. First, the urgency and seriousness of the problem that the discovery purports to solve will be important. A second consideration that will affect the method and speed of transmission is the economic impact of the discovery: Social science research that would have an impact on government spending for prisons or health care, for example, would be more likely to be broadly disseminated than research that did not save money.

To examine these variables, we need to discover who the actors are and how they work together. Does the person who makes the initial discovery control its dissemination? How important are the academic gatekeepers—the editors and peer reviewers of the professional journals? Are they more eager to accept and promote ideas that are likely to reach the public, or is this not a concern? Are applicability, urgency, and economic impact concerns that motivate academic gatekeepers? To what extent do the criteria of the academic gatekeepers overlap those of the popular gatekeepers—the editors of newspapers, popular magazines, and television news shows? On what basis do these popular gatekeepers make decisions about newsworthiness? What are the roles of public officials and popular activists in the case of discoveries with policy implications?

Also important, of course, are the authors. Most academic authors give little thought to popularizing their work. There is little reward for the hard work of synthesizing the research of an entire field, which is frequently necessary for popularization. And, as Horowitz notes, interest in ideas may not translate into interest in the books in which they are expressed, the

> confusion of specific interest in the ideas, findings, or conclusions in the research with general interest in reading the book.
>
> Sometimes an outright translation of the research into terms that a general audience finds appealing is undertaken by a professional writer.... If a professional-book publisher elects to persuade an author to accept publication of the work as a trade book, that publisher has a major undertaking. (Horowitz, 1991:105)

Intuition suggests that, in determining whether and how knowledge reaches the general public, one crucial variable will be the comprehensibility of the knowledge. Is a discovery that is easy to understand more likely to receive public attention than one that requires a great deal of prior understanding and information, or that is clearly beyond the comprehension of much of the population? Well, maybe.

Some of the scientific discoveries that attract the most public attention are those that are most difficult to understand. The success of Carl Sagan's exposition of the cosmos and of Stephen Hawking's theory of the origins of the universe are good examples. Their books were bestsellers. Sagan's television series attracted a huge audience, and a movie has been made about Hawking.

A good case can be made, however, that although Sagan and Hawking have entered the public imagination, their ideas have not fully entered the public understanding. Few people make it past chapter 4 of Hawking's book; few people understand relativity; few people comprehend the cosmos. (A quick and revealing study might be done to compare the number of people who purchased *A Brief History of Time* with the number who actually read it. A true/false quiz might be added to see how many understood it.) Complexity may be a bar to understanding without being a bar to interest. What piques public interest in subjects that strike fear into the hearts of college students and that few of us can hope to master?

One possibility lies in the personality of the discoverers, and their ability to convey their enthusiasm as well as their knowledge. Sagan and Hawking are fascinating people as well as superb writers. Another possibility is that their publishers promoted them effectively. Another possibility is institutional: Most major newspapers, magazines, and wire services have science editors who are trained to explain the complexities of astronomy, chemistry, and physics to the rest of us. How many newspapers have social science or humanities editors? Perhaps scientific societies are more effective at promoting their disciplines than associations of humanistic scholars, so that even though the humanities are easier to understand, they receive less attention. Certainly NASA invests more in promoting its activities than does the National Endowment for the Humanities.

Social Acceptance of New Knowledge

The last variable I propose to examine is one that I believe strongly affects the transmission of knowledge about society and humanity: the compatibility of new knowledge with existing worldviews, political views, and religious beliefs. This is similar to the issue of congruence with existing scientific theories, but its impact, I believe is quite different. Theories that challenge the scientific establishment fascinate the public; theories that challenge treasured views of society and religion seem rather to create fear and hostility.

We have known all of this at least since Galileo, but of course much has changed. Religious leadership is less powerful and more diverse; society is more pluralistic and more tolerant (or at least more secular); change and innovation are viewed positively—at least within limits. Equally important, the ways new ideas are communicated have changed. Far more of us are literate, and few of us submit readily to a single authority. Most literate people consider themselves able to judge new ideas without an interpreter or arbiter, whether religious or secular. This makes resistance to change more interesting, but more difficult to analyze.

For example, we might turn to theories in the humanities that have taken decades to reach public consciousness in contrast to medical and scientific discoveries that have traveled more quickly. Here, the trickle-down process may indeed be at work, but the mechanics remain unknown.

The discipline of history has changed dramatically in the past thirty years. One of the major changes can be characterized as a shift to the study of ordinary people—those who were not leaders. This shift has required changes in methodology, in the sorts of texts consulted, and in the kinds of questions asked. Intuitively, one would expect this approach to have immediate popular appeal, especially when contrasted to traditional history, which is frequently characterized as "one damn [thing, date, battle, president, king] after another." Yet only now are these approaches beginning to compete effectively outside the academy with traditional views.

Some of the reasons for this lag have to do with the nature of the sources and methods of the new social science history. Because ordinary people left few written accounts of their lives, historians have had to use official records and statistical methods to get at the reality of their world. Occasionally such research turns up stories of immense dramatic appeal—Natalie Davis's discovery of Martin Guerre is an obvious example. But in the aggregate it is undramatic, and most of it was written up with little concern for narrative quality. I suspect, however, that this was only one source of the lag.

For nonhistorians, history is about conclusive events and great men (I use the term nongenerically). The great men may be glorified or debunked, but they are always central. Similarly, the events may be glorious victories or ignominious defeats, but something must always happen. Great men control events; what goes on outside that focus is peripheral and the parts of ordinary people are played by extras.

If this view were restricted to the past, it would not be so tenacious. For many people, however, this view extends to the present. Only in times of extreme social tension (the 1960s, for example) do the actions of ordinary people seem to matter, and in such times popular action provokes strong reaction. Research on the fate of the "new" history might well reveal that its acceptance has paralleled social acceptance of a "new" society, that interest in ordinary dead people in history can arise only when we accept the importance of ordinary living people in society.

For historians, learning about ordinary people has meant learning about not just hard-working yeoman farmers and skilled urban artisans but also about hard-working prostitutes and skilled urban criminals. It has meant extending our understanding and portrayal of southern plantations into the slave quarters. For U.S. historians it has meant studying the lives of American Indians, African-Americans, Latinos, and Asian Americans as well as the lives of European immigrants. In short, the new history requires us to view our society as pluralistic and to acknowledge the importance of experiences that threaten our traditional view of the United States, past and present. In a broader context, it challenges our view of European cultural dominance.

What has publishing to do with all of this? Like other scholars, historians share information and ideas through scholarly journals and books. By tracing the appearance of new historical studies in established journals, the establishment of new journals, and the publication of monographs by scholarly publishers, we can learn about its acceptance within the profession. But because history books are regularly read by nonacademics, and because the discipline is basic to elementary and high school curriculums, we can learn a great deal more.

History books regularly appear on best-seller lists and win major literary prizes. The History Book Club is an established institution. It would not be at all difficult to see whether and how the sorts of history books that appear on best-seller lists, win prizes, and are selected for book clubs have changed over time. Do new history subjects and methods appear in these popular arenas? If so, when? If they appear much later in popular circulation than in academic circles, why does that happen? Because no one was writing new history for the general reader? Because trade publishers were not receptive? If publishers ignored change in the discipline, was it because of their own dislike (or lack of interest)? because of perceptions of the market? Or did a few publishers experiment with such books and lose money?

What kinds of reviews did the new history receive in the major review media? When did the reviews begin? In September 1992, the *New York Times Book Review* ran a review essay on the "new Western history." By then, most academic Western historians had regarded the approach taken in such books as standard for years. What took the *New York Times* so long to catch up? The "new Western history" has evoked a great deal of hostility, mainly because it demythologizes the West and deromanticizes the frontier. The Lone Ranger dies hard, as do many other myths, and not only in he West. Is it this quality that slows absorption into the American bloodstream?

If new ideas about history do trickle down from scholarly media to popular books and to textbooks, we should find them showing up at last in textbooks for college and elementary and high school courses. College textbooks are theoretically problematic: Although they affect students' understanding, they are chosen by faculty members. Thus, the appearance of new ideas in college texts is simply further evidence of academic acceptance. Elementary and high school textbooks are far more interesting for our purposes. Because they are selected by committees of school administrators, teachers, and sometimes community members, they tell us about acceptance outside the academy.

In 1991, the first elementary-high school social studies series to absorb the new history appeared, with much fanfare and much controversy. The Houghton Mifflin series accepts the diversity and pluralism of the United States as a positive fact about American life. It features ordinary people and families. In including minority groups, it goes beyond the occasional biography of a great black man or token photographs. Designed to meet California criteria, it has been adopted in other states as well. If it succeeds, and if other publishers follow suit, the new history will begin to change Americans' consciousness of ourselves and our nation. Some scholars have already begun to study the California-Houghton Mifflin story, and it will be well documented.[7] As in all such cases, the controversy over the books, the protests, and the adoption failures will be as revealing as the series' successes.

Democracy relies upon a well-informed public, and the areas in which the American public needs information and knowledge have increased in number and grown in technical difficulty. It is vital for us to understand more about how what scholars learn becomes what everyone knows—and about how that communication sometimes fails.

And here, I think, we return to the central message of Irving Horowitz's work on publishing: that it cannot be studied in isolation, that its internal workings are important only insofar as they relate to its external mission, that it is part of a political and economic as well as an intellectual culture. Because publishing studies are in their infancy, much of our effort will necessarily be devoted to micro-level studies. But if we keep Horowitz's larger frame in mind, we can do a better job of selecting what to study, asking the right questions, and understanding the answers.

Conclusion

Just as scholars have generally neglected publishing as a field of study, publishers have been surprisingly incurious about themselves. They have been ready to defend the freedom of the press, but they have not looked much beyond that in understanding their role in developing popular understanding of new ideas or appreciation of new writing. Even in accepting the role of "gatekeeper," publishers have viewed themselves simply as making choices among existing ideas, generally claiming to make those choices on the basis of what the reading public wants.

As publisher, scholar, and endlessly curious human being, Irving Horowitz has helped to change both society's view of publishing and publishers' view of their place in society. Because of his unusual position in the world of publishing, he has been able, at least on occasion, to provoke publishers into removing the blinders they wear about their roles. In both his writings (which he has deliberately placed in journals that publishers read, such as *Publishers Weekly* and *The Bookseller*) and his participation in publishers' associations, he has encouraged and even demanded debate where consensus and complacency reigned. In his work with groups like the Association of American Publishers and the Society for Scholarly Publishing, he has organized discussions and convention sessions that bring people from outside the world of publishing at least briefly to the inside.

We have a long way to travel before we can claim truly to understand how publishing and scholarship, publishing and teaching, and publishing and learning have interacted to create our existing knowledge system, let alone understand how that system can be enhanced. But we might never have set out on the road at all if Irving Horowitz had not pointed the way. Equally important, we might have spent years wandering blinkered along the road, ignoring its intersections with the major thoroughfares of our society and polity. Instead, we can now travel a route that is perhaps less direct than we might have wished but that is nevertheless headed for a worthwhile destination.

Arizona State University
Department of History

Notes

1. A recent monograph that beautifully combines the study of editorial, design, and marketing considerations is Thomas Bonn's *Heavy Traffic and High Culture: New American Library as Literary Gatekeeper in the Paperback Revolution* (Carbondale: Southern Illinois University Press, 1989). For the most recent, and complete, study of distribution and transportation in the United States, see Ronald J. Zboray, *A Fictive People: Antebellum Economic Development and the American Reading Public* (New York: Oxford University Press, 1993).
2. James L. W. West III does a superb job of using textual studies as a basis for publishing studies in his *American Authors and the Literary Marketplace since 1900* (Philadelphia: University of Pennsylvania Press, 1988).
3. For European analyses, see, for example, Elizabeth Eisenstein, *The Printing Press as an Agent of Change,* 2 vols. (Cambridge: Cambridge University Press, 1979); Lucien Febvre and Henri-Jean Martin, *The Coming of the Book: The Impact of Printing 1450–1800,* trans. David Gerard, ed. Geoffrey Nowell-Smith and David Wootton (1976; reprinted in London, 1984); Roger Chartier, *Cultural History: Between Practices and Representations,* trans. Lydia G. Cochrane (Ithaca, NY: Cornell University Press, 1988), and *The Culture of Print: Power and the Uses of Print in Early Modern Europe,* trans. Lydia G. Cochrane (Cambridge: Polity Press, 1989); and Gary Marker, *Publishing, Printing, and the Origins of Intellectual Life in Russia, 1700–1800* (Princeton, NJ: Princeton University Press, 1985).
4. See, for example, the collection of articles in *Book Research Quarterly* 5, no. 2 (Summer 1989) on basal readers and in *Publishing Research Quarterly* 8, no. 4 (Winter 1992–93) on social studies texts, as well as *Textbooks and Schooling in the United States,* the 89th yearbook of the National Society for the Study of Education, edited by David L. Elliott and Arthur Woodward, 1990 (distributed by the University of Chicago Press).

5. The classic sociological study of editorial decision making remains Lewis A. Coser, Charles Kadushin, and Walter W. Powell, *Books: The Culture and Commerce of Publishing* (New York: Basic Books, 1982). A more recent entry is Paul Parsons, *Getting Published: The Acquisitions Process at University Presses* (Knoxville: University of Tennessee Press, 1989). The literature on peer review, especially in the life sciences, is enormous. For a recent compilation see *Peer Review in Scientific Publishing, Papers from the First International Congress on Peer Review in Biomedical Publication* (Chicago: Council of Biology Editors, 1991).
6. Such studies would benefit from examinations of these movements such as *The Knowledge Factory* (Chicago: Aldine, 1970), the study of 1960s student rebellion that Horowitz undertook with William H. Friedland, which includes discussions of student influences on curriculum.
7. See Gilbert T. Sewall, "Social Studies Textbooks in the 1990s," and David L. Elliott, "Reforming Social Studies: Implications for Curriculum and Textbooks," *Publishing Research Quarterly* 8, no. 4 (Winter 1992-93): 6-11, 71-80.

References

Horowitz, Irving Louis. *Philosophy, Science and the Sociology of Knowledge.* Springfield, IL: Charles C Thomas, 1961 (reprint ed., Westport, CT: Greenwood, 1976).
———, ed. *The Rise and Fall of Project Camelot: Studies in the Relationship between Social Research and Practical Politics.* Cambridge: The Massachusetts Institute of Technology Press, 1967.
———. "On Learning and Teaching Sociology." In *Professing Sociology.* Chicago: Aldine, 1968.
———. *Communicating Ideas,* 2d ed. New Brunswick, NJ: Transaction Publishers, 1991.

26

Scholarly Productivity:
A Compulsive Quantifier's Appreciation

Nathaniel J. Pallone

That Irving Louis Horowitz defies categorization into those neat and mutually exclusive pigeon-holes that are used to compartmentalize even highly visible and highly productive people virtually goes without saying. Indeed, among those who know him well enough to intuit that he would appreciate the humor in the statement, it might be added that he even defies description. Yet, during a long and industrious career that has witnessed both the production and the application of scholarship even through the unusual stratagem of creating new vehicles and instrumentalities for its dissemination (a stratagem similar to that pursued, on rather a smaller scale, by John Dewey), there has been one constant: Horowitz has chosen to function within the academy, which has been his home base.

However others may categorize or describe one, how one describes oneself provides the quintessential index to the self-definition that is closest to the core, and for Horowitz that self-definition is, and has been through a very long and very productive career, crystal clear. Routinely, he has identified himself in every published work first through his academic title (for nearly two decades, as the Hannah Arendt Distinguished Professor of Sociology and Political Science at Rutgers—The State University of New Jersey). Only very occasionally (and when appropriate to a particular audience, as in *Communicating Ideas: The Crisis of Publishing in a Post-Industrial Society,* a work on the future of academic publishing, but not in *An American Utopian,* his remarkable intellectual biography of C. Wright Mills) does he add the title editor-in-chief, *Transaction/Society,* or the presidency of Transaction Publishers.

Others might define themselves as editors, or publishers, or Renaissance-style intellectuals, or even Socratic gadflies (and Horowitz could well find either temporary lodging or a permanent residence in each of those compartments) who also happen hold academic appointments; this is not so with Horowitz, for whom being a scholar has always taken first priority . To the extent that self-description defines for each of us our primary reference group, that in which we are proudest to claim membership and that by whose standards of accomplishment we freely acknowledge we wish to be judged, there seems little doubt that Horowitz sees himself first and foremost as an academic man.

Doubtless, there have been many, many opportunities for him to shift moorings, whether into the world of publishing or political activism, but Horowitz has chosen to remain identified as an academic, through the early years in a small (and not overly distinguished) college in upstate New York to the years in Buenos Aires and St. Louis, and, for nearly a quarter century, at Rutgers. Other contributors to this volume have undertaken to appraise and assess Irving Louis Horowitz (ILH to those who work with him) through the prism of his stature as scholar, creator, author, substantive contributor to the knowledge base in an array of disciplines and cross—disciplines, seminal thinker about the fabric and dynamisms of the good society in a complex world, insistent avower of the rights and responsibilities of the person of knowledge, builder of a publishing empire now in the fullness of its maturity firmly ensconced as a world leader in the social sciences. I am privileged to write in appreciation of Irving Louis Horowitz as a colleague in the academy and role model for a generation of younger scholars.

The Essential Functions of the Academy

Though controversy remains over the relative priority to be accorded to each, general consensus has been reached that the *generation* and the *dissemination* of knowledge, inside and beyond the classroom, constitute the essential, interrelated functions of American universities in the second half of the twentieth century. Upon these twin functions pivot every other academic function: empirical and conceptual research, historical analysis, dissemination through instruction and publication, public service.

Rather too simplistically, those pivotal functions have often been equated with "research" and "teaching," yielding a quasi-dichotomy that quite falsely portrays the life of the mind, the stimulation of which is the raison d'etre of the academy. Indeed, that false dichotomy not infrequently yields to all manner of indecorous suspicion that the academic who devotes the major portion of his or her energy to research and publication is, on the face of it, likely negligent in his/her instructional obligations. Not only is it my own conviction, based on thirty-three years as an academic (half of which were spent as a senior university officer concerned with just such issues as stimulating, facilitating, and operationalizing the measurement of faculty scholarly productivity), but there is also burgeoning empirical evidence that nothing could be further from the truth.

As merely a hint of the direction of the evidence: In a well-known study at Southern Illinois University in the mid-1970s, the correlates of student evaluations of instructional effectiveness were investigated. In a situation in which there was not the slightest indication that the students who evaluated classroom effectiveness had any systematic knowledge of the productivity of the faculty member being evaluated, it was nonetheless the case that the number of articles published in peer-reviewed journals by the faculty member under evaluation emerged as the strongest single predictor of such evaluations. What is remarkable is that one variable (assessment of instructional effectiveness) is clearly an attribute of students, not of the faculty member, while the other (scholarly productivity) is clearly an attribute of the faculty member, not of students. Nor do those familiar with life in the academy find such an empirical datum particularly surprising: Ought we not expect that it is the faculty member sufficiently energized about extending the frontiers of knowledge in his/her discipline through research and publication who will communicate enthusiasm and intellectual curiosity to his or her students?

Whatever the partisan straw men periodically and rhetorically constructed by the "teaching primacy" or the "research primacy" camps in order to fuel whatever controversy remains, however, there remains little serious disagreement that the contemporary academic undertakes both the obligation to generate and the obligation to disseminate knowledge, inside and beyond the classroom. In the leading universities of the continent, moreover, there is agreement that it is the conjunctive "and" rather than the disjunctive "or" that properly links those obligations—that is, that the twin functions of generation and dissemination of knowledge should be closely woven into a single, seamless garment. It is such a single, seamless garment that Horowitz has worn throughout his long and illustrious academic career.

Horowitz's Prodigious Scholarly Productivity

The first academic publication to bear Irving Horowitz's byline appeared in 1951; as 1992 ended, his career output had topped 630 entries, without replication—that is, without "double indemnity" for those works that have been reprinted, translated, or republished in other sources. For those interested in such statistics, that level of productivity averages to fifteen in-print publications per year, or one every three and a half weeks. At a time when the mean level of postdoctoral publication among social scientists hovers at something approximating 1.6 publications per decade, "prodigious" may be too tame a descriptor.

Were translations (into such languages as German, French, Italian, Polish, Norwegian, Swedish, Spanish, Portuguese, Czechoslovakian, Arabic, Japanese) and reprints to be independently enumerated, the cumulative list would easily top 1000 entries. (His study of Project Camelot, originally published in 1965, had by 1992 been reprinted no fewer than thirty times in diverse anthologies, compendia, and collections in this country and abroad; *Cuban Communism* is now in its eighth edition; and a 1971 paper on popular culture even found its way into two different anthologies intended for college freshmen enrolled in English composition courses, as an exemplar of the discursive essay.)

A Compulsive Quantifier's Approach to Analysis

Aggregate numbers, of course, tell only part of the story. Even a rudimentary analysis should divide scholarly products into categories generally accepted within the academy. More thorough approaches might even calculate "impact factors" (indices invented by scholars in the communications disciplines to reflect the frequency with which a particular journal, article, book, or author is cited by other journals, articles, books, or authors) and/or "titular colonicity" ratios (an index that reflects the frequency with which titles with colons occur as a fraction of an author's total output, presumably and largely tacitly reflective of whether the author's level of conceptualization properly corresponds to the Aristotelian distinction between the universal and the particular). While your correspondent has never outgrown the compulsion to quantify instilled during his early training in empirical psychology (likely, as an abreaction to even earlier training in scholastic philosophy, with its conscious abhorrence for quantification), I cannot quite bring myself to contemplate calculating Horowitz's titular colonicity ratio—and might even suggest that such a task is analogous to the risk one takes in being a member of the defensive line on a Big 10 gridiron . Thus, let us be content with what is typically termed a *gross* rather than *discriminate* approach to analysis.

Our first task is to array (try as we might, we can't shake off the compulsion to compartmentalize) Horowitz's publications into categories that are in standard use in the academy. These include three widely accepted compartments: those publications that have appeared in peer-reviewed scholarly journals, indeed increasingly under conditions of "blind" review; scholarly books; books intended not primarily for scholarly audiences (as, for example, when the late B. F. Skinner undertook to depict a world organized according to the principles of operant conditioning, in his 1948 novel *Walden II*).

A final compartment has traditionally been reserved for "other" works—principally those that have appeared in journals and magazines that circulate primarily outside the scholarly community, though their contents may depend to some large extent on the scholarly expertise of their contributors. This final category has often proved problematic. An article appearing in a Sunday magazine supplement of a local newspaper by an economist analyzing the impact of an urban redevelopment plan proposed for the region, for example, would certainly fit into this fourth category, and it would be quite clear that the published work drew upon its author's scholarly expertise. On the other hand, an article in the same source by an agronomist whose hobby is stamp collecting would also find lodging within this compartment, but in this case it is not quite so clear that scholarly expertise has been tapped.

In a 1973 analysis of the first decade of *Transaction/Society* in the *International Social Science Journal,* Horowitz himself attempted a further clarification of this fourth category by coining the term *social science journalism* to denote those publications that strive less to generate new knowledge within the discipline of the author but rather to apply current knowledge from his/her discipline to emerging issues in public or social policy. The term was repeated by Howard Becker in his 1984 essay "The Three Lives of Irving Louis Horowitz." Despite an illustrious parentage and benison, the term seems less than accurate when applied to *Transaction/Society*, which has built a strong reputation as a leading voice in the social science analysis of public policy; and that is quite a different matter, in an altogether different arena, than the mere reportage of events in the social sciences, as was the prevailing ethos in such publications as *Behavior Today, Psychology Today, Sociology Today*. If, for example, as a psychologist concerned with criminal sanctions, I undertake an analysis of the deterrent effect of the death penalty from the perspective of what is known about the psychology of reinforcement and extinction (a sanction that is conceptually and legislatively, but rarely, in fact, linked to a particular behavior has little effect on changing or shaping behavior), am I not better advised to seek its publication in a journal specializing in the analysis of public policy than, for example, in a journal specializing in studies in learning? No novel contribution will be made by the work just described to the psychology of learning and extinction, but application of knowledge from that subdiscipline to a matter of grave public concern may constitute a novel contribution to public policy clarification. Thus, one man's social science journalism may be another's primary scholarly productivity.

In 1974, also in the *International Social Science Journal*, Horowitz essayed a further refinement, identifying *Transaction/Society* as a "mediating journal" that endeavors to "reach out to an [audience] beyond the scientific community." In many ways, that view presaged his perception of the emerging cross-disciplinary, problem-focused character of the contemporary social and behavioral sciences. Despite such ambiguity, it may prove pointless to attempt to improve on a term coined by Horowitz and blessed by Becker; we might simply adopt it to categorize those publications by Horowitz that do not properly fall within one of the first three categories.

To operationalize this category in Horowitz's case, however, is somewhat trickier than it might be were he not also editor-in-chief of *Transaction/Society*, which he himself insisted upon categorizing in his 1973 paper as "social science journalism." There seems little question that *Commonweal, The Nation, Atlantic Monthly, Public Opinion, Science, The Chronicle of Higher Education, Change, Sociology Today*, and *Psychology Today* (to enumerate some of those not-primarily-scholarly and/or "mediating" journals in which Horowitz has published) are indeed properly regarded as circulating primarily outside the scholarly community. It is not at all clear that *Transaction/Society* should be so categorized; certainly, every young scholar I know (along with his/her department chairperson) regards *Transaction/Society* as the equivalent of the major scholarly journal in his/her own discipline. In general, with a circulation among social scientists, interdisciplinary researchers, and well-educated but nonspecialist readers that is substantially in excess of professional journals, this reputation is firmly in place.

There is the additional issue that some of Horowitz's work in *Transaction/Society* has clearly been substantive analysis (one thinks of the 1983 "National Interests and Professional Ethics: Struggling for the Soul of a Discipline" or the 1987 "Disenthralling Sociology," both critical analyses of the present and future state of the discipline), while other contributions have been in the nature of editorial or introductory commentary to symposia or theme-centered issues. Nonetheless, because Horowitz serves as editor-in-chief, there is the implicit expectation that his contributions thereto do not undergo quite the same peer-review process as papers that are contributed by other authors. Still, since Horowitz often recycles his papers for book publication, one can argue that the review process for himself is quite stringent.

We are now ready for a first pass at analyzing in gross terms Horowitz's overall scholarly productivity. Figure 26.1 is a simple pie chart that arrays Horowitz's publications between 1951 and 1990 into the three generally accepted compartments or the "new" Horowitz-Becker-denominated compartment, with the caveats and misgivings earlier noted about the latter category. Figure 26.2 divides those publications into five-year intervals and arrays them into three categories, with the "nonscholarly books" compartment (accounting for only two entries over the total forty-year period, *Communicating Ideas* and his award-winning autobiography *Daydreams and Nightmares*) not represented.

Quite clearly, Horowitz's publications fall overwhelmingly into the "scholarly" arena, with articles, essays, and reviews in scholarly journals accounting for 67 percent of his productivity over this period and some sixty scholarly books accounting for another 10 percent (figure 26.1). Even at the risk of possible misclassification of some entries in this category, "social science journalism" accounts for only a modest fraction of his total oeuvre. His two "not primarily for scholars" books

FIGURE 1: Four decades of ILH's published scholarly productivity, 1951–90, arrayed by publication source and target audience.

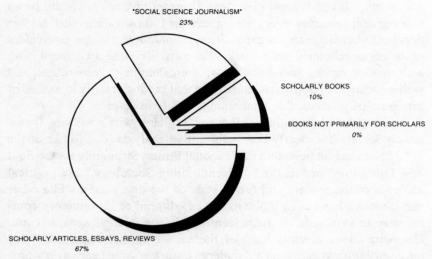

"SOCIAL SCIENCE JOURNALISM"
23%

SCHOLARLY BOOKS
10%

BOOKS NOT PRIMARILY FOR SCHOLARS
0%

SCHOLARLY ARTICLES, ESSAYS, REVIEWS
67%

FIGURE 2: Four decades of ILH's published scholarly productivity, arrayed by publication type for eight 5-year time intervals.

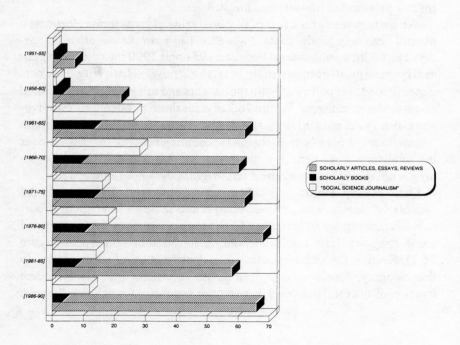

[1951-55]

[1956-60]

[1961-65]

[1966-70]

[1971-75]

[1976-80]

[1981-85]

[1986-90]

SCHOLARLY ARTICLES, ESSAYS, REVIEWS
SCHOLARLY BOOKS
"SOCIAL SCIENCE JOURNALISM"

0   10   20   30   40   50   60   70

account for only .3 percent of his total productivity. Were we to collapse categories, scholarly publications constitute 77 percent of the total.

In figure 26.2, we have a depiction of Horowitz's publications arrayed by type at five-year intervals. Given what figure 26.1 has told us, it is not surprising that scholarly publications lead at each interval. But it may be worth observing that "social science journalism" publications tended to peak nearly three decades ago, indeed at the very point at which *Transaction/Society* was in its infancy, and have diminished since, both in terms of absolute incidence and as a proportion of the total in any time interval. To this observer, there seems at least one profound truth embedded in these data—namely, that, unless he who plans to contribute to "social science" or "mediating" journalism also and simultaneously contributes to the generation of new knowledge in his discipline; he ceases to be an academic, but instead becomes a journalist. Or, to put the matter differently: It is the continuing contribution to expansion of knowledge in his/her discipline that yields that level of credibility that renders an academic a likely candidate to contribute meaningfully to "social science" or "mediating" journalism.

In figure 26.3, we return again to the aggregate, in this case in an attempt to categorize the totality of Horowitz's productivity according to the focal topic or topics each publication addresses, or the domain to which each speaks. Some of the categories reflected are admittedly somewhat speculative and arbitrary. Three—social theory, social policy and social analysis, and political theory—are relatively straight-forward and, to that extent, would likely remain stable across observers called upon to "sort" the Horowitz oeuvre independently. By far the largest category, "public policy," includes books, articles, and essays which bring the theoretical and methodological perspectives of sociology and political science to bear on a vast array of policy issues, including war, genocide, education, and family structure. Other observers might well segregate some of the publications represented in this category into "standard" sociology or political science. Publications dealing specifically with human rights issues are accorded a separate category, though another observer might collapse this category into the "public policy" arena. Similarly, publications categorized under "popular culture" include works on music and art, to be sure, but also on information exchange, intellectual property, technology transfer, and academic publishing; another observer might wish also to collapse this category into the "public policy"

FIGURE 3: ILH's aggregate scholarly productivity, 1951–90 arrayed by focal topic.

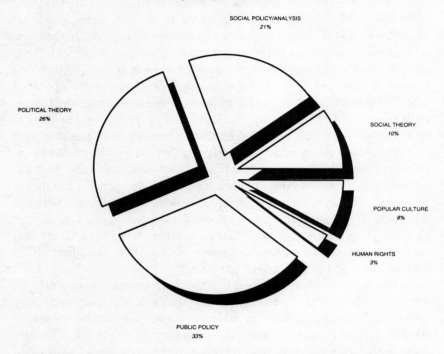

SOCIAL POLICY/ANALYSIS
21%

POLITICAL THEORY
26%

SOCIAL THEORY
10%

POPULAR CULTURE
8%

HUMAN RIGHTS
3%

PUBLIC POLICY
33%

arena. On its own terms, however, figure 26.3 suggests that Horowitz's publications have been divided not disproportionately between sociology, political science, and public policy.

Toward an Empirical Definition of Irving Louis Horowitz

In his masterful book on *The Quest for Identity,* Allen Wheelis suggests that the indispensable test for the accuracy of one's self-definition lies in "the accrued confidence that one's meaning for oneself is matched by one's meaning for others." Suppose one knew no more of Irving Horowitz than is represented in the data reviewed in this document; how might one go about constructing an *inferential* and empirically based definition of Irving Louis Horowitz? First, if one accepts that it is the obligation of the academic to generate and to disseminate knowledge, the data clearly identify him as an academic fulfilling precisely those roles. Moreover, since his scholarly productivity over the forty-year period reviewed here has exceeded the norm for postdoctoral American social scientists by no less than 10,000 percent, one might conclude that Irving Horowitz is an academic of some very great distinction. Second, if one reviews the focal areas in which he has published, it is clear that he is an academic whose specialties are social theory, social policy, political theory, and public policy. If, finally, one aggregates these *empirically derived* predicates, they constitute a description that does not vary by much from the quintessential self-description Irving Louis Horowitz provides—the Hannah Arendt Distinguished Professor of Sociology and Political Science. If any emendation is required, it seems clear enough that the term *public policy* might well be added.

Rutgers, The State University of New Jersey
Department of Criminal Justice and Clinical Psychology

27

Daydreams and Nightmares as
Sociological Autobiography

William N. Dunn

The standard festschrift frequently begins with a surface account of the honoree's life and times, briskly proceeding to predictably appreciative essays extolling his contributions to the stock of knowledge. This approach is regrettably antibiographic in spirit and consequence; it decontextualizes scholarship and thereby conceals from celebrants and readers alike the concrete circumstances that have shaped an exceptional scholar.

The antibiography is particularly inappropriate in the case of our colleague and friend, Irving Louis Horowitz. The products and processes of his scholarly development are plainly inseparable from the context of his Harlem childhood, a context in which rare acts of empathy, caring, and love were eclipsed by terror, deception, and agonizing uncertainty. Horowitz's autobiography, *Daydreams and Nightmares: Reflections of a Harlem Childhood,*[1] is the memoir of one who not only survived enormous personal adversity, but prevailed. Yet it is also a rich sociological narrative that reveals a dialectic of ethnic vilification and human dignity, social segregation and self-reliance, urban squalor and cultural pride, that has continued to characterize urban underclasses of all colors and ethnic origins since Horowitz's childhood in the Harlem of the 1930s.

Autobiography in the Sociology of Knowledge is my first concern. Horowitz's early life and subsequent scholarly development supply compelling evidence that the productions of social scientists do not speak for themselves. Intellectual productions in sociology and other disciplines never originate in a neutral stance toward class, status, power, privilege, and other objects of scientific reasoning. Sociological observations are theory dependent; sociological theories are expressed in a directive rather than neutral observational language; and the language of sociology is a product of personal and social constructions of reality that affect and are affected by objects of sociological reasoning. The contextual innocence of the social sciences is a thing that never was.

An intelligent understanding of the development of sociology and other social sciences, no less than that of its major producers, requires that we probe the contexts in which knowledge claims are formed. One method for probing these contexts is the sociological biography, a methodological vehicle that seeks to uncover and understand common as well as exceptional intellectual productions by investigating the personal, social, and historical conditions that have affected the creation of knowledge.[2]

The sociological autobiography is likewise probative in intent, although it has peculiar limitations and strengths as a method of discovery. On one hand, the value of sociological autobiography is limited by the ever-present danger of auto-critique in the hands of self-indulgent or deluded autobiographers. The distinct advantage of the sociological autobiography, however, is that it is a relatively direct means for probing the personal, social, and historical contexts in which ideas are generated, as these contexts are understood by autobiographers themselves. Thus, the sociological autobiography is both an interpretive personal memoir and a sociological datum.

The central questions of sociological autobiography are essentially epistemological: What procedures are employed by autobiographers to explain the origins of their knowledge claims? Are these claims the products of professional socialization into the beliefs, values, and norms of sociology? Do they also originate in professionally unmediated beliefs that conflict with the publicly announced culture, or conventional wisdom, of the discipline? What is the relation between the specialized knowledge of the discipline and ordinary knowledge acquired prior to or apart from professional socialization? What are the results of combining diverse sources of so-called ordinary and specialized knowledge, as evidenced by the character of an author's work? Can contributions to the theory, methodology, and substantive findings of the discipline be attributed to unique properties of the social, personal, and historical contexts in which the autobiographer lived and worked?

The thesis of this chapter is that Horowitz's *Daydreams and Nightmares: Reflections of a Harlem Childhood* belongs to a rare genre of starkly honest autobiography that not only lays bare otherwise hidden contradictions within and between specialized and ordinary knowledge, but uses these contradictions as a dialectical vehicle for enlarging our understanding of sociological and ordinary knowledge alike. The understanding of these interdependent forms of knowledge offered by *Daydreams and Nightmares* is conveyed through the lenses of a unique sociological frame of reference formed by the intersection of the multiple cultures of pre-1945 Harlem. The sociological understanding generated at the nexus of these cultures is profoundly different from that of most social scientists, who are linked to urban underclasses as reluctant spectators.[3]

The Dialectical Confinement

In *Daydreams and Nightmares* we find that young Horowitz's move from Harlem to Brooklyn at the age of thirteen was experienced as an escape from prison: "One escapes Harlem the way one leaves a prison: hoping never to return. But the stripes of the prisoner and the Harlemite remain. A spiritual osmosis takes place when the stripes of a confined life are woven into the fabric of the mind."[4] Yet *Daydreams and Nightmares* also reveals that this is a partial truth; it was not a single set of stripes, but three, which can be visualized as a complex fabric of intersecting stripes of different sizes and consequences, cross-woven in a complex pattern that represents the culture of the black Harlem underclass, the embedded culture of pre-Soviet Jewish immigrants, and the culture of pediatric medicine in local hospitals. Later, this pattern is cross-woven once more by the professional culture of philosophical and sociological pragmatism.

The sociological concept of "marginality" hardly does justice to the complexity of this cultural intersection, which is more akin to the multiplex or block model of social network analysis than a relatively well-formed seam marking the intersection of ways of life. This intersection has little in common with a cultural "free space," if indeed the idea of freedom has any meaning at all in this context. The intersection was rather a dialectical nexus of different forms of confinement; and escape required the creative synthesis of aspects of previously opposed ways of life. The sociological frame of reference that evolved from the conflict-ridden transition from Harlem to Brooklyn, and later to the high culture of world-class intellectual discourse, is best viewed as a cultural multiplex, which is a dialectical product of the clash of four cultures: the culture of a permanent struggle for survival in black Harlem, the subculture of impoverished Jewish immigrants nested (or interred) within the dominant black culture, the empathic culture of medical care experienced by physically handicapped or chronically ill children at Sydenham Hospital, and the culture of intellectual abstraction characteristic of university life at City College and Columbia University. The mental template formed by the nexus of these four cultures affected subsequent scholarly achievements.

If we were able to create programs in the social sciences that would adequately prepare nascent social scientists for the complexity, equivocality, and uncertainty of urban America and the world political economy in the period since 1945, we probably could do no better than to supply students with aspects of the preprofessional as well as professional "socialization" experienced by Irving Louis Horowitz. To be sure, Horowitz's experiences were acquired with great pain and immense personal costs. For this reason, compelling as it is from a human standpoint, it is tempting to see Horowitz's life as a stunning victory over adversity—and it is that. Yet Horowitz does not see it just this way, which is as much a tribute to his unpretentious honesty as it is testimony to his courage, sensitivity, and depth of multicultural understanding.

The Unity of Cultural Contradictions

In contrast to the public presentation of self by most successful professionals, who choose to veneer their past or simply conceal it, *Daydreams and Nightmares* is profoundly informative precisely because of its unimpeachable honesty. Subtle but significant is the book's subtitle, *Reflections of a Harlem Childhood,* which affirms the continuity of Harlem and the present. *Daydreams and Nightmares,* to paraphrase Horowitz's commentary on H. L. Mencken's own autobiography, is an uncompromisingly honest self-analysis, an unusual auto-critique that has no traces of self-recrimination or self-indulgent celebration of triumphs over a "disadvantaged" youth that come so easily to less forthright autobiographers. Indeed, Horowitz the dialectician adopts the stance that his personal and professional history is what it is *because* of these early experiences, not *despite* them: "[T]he drama is still being lived."[5]

The four cultures that intersect to form Horowitz's frame of reference as social scientist, a kind of sociological *Alexandria Quartet,* are well suited to the demands of probing the obscene inequalities, ethnic and religious prejudice, and everyday terrors that continue to disfigure urban America and, following the end of the cold war, societies caught in a newly emerging and unanticipated fall into accelerating impoverishment, social dislocation, and political fragmentation. Quite apart from the formal methodological desiderata advanced to justify multiple triangulation as a strategy of validity-enhancing research practice,[6] Horowitz's multicultural frame of reference permits and even compels a form of dialectical inquiry in which rival interpretations of the same data are integral to the research act. Like an ethnographic factorial experiment lived through, he has reflexively applied to the multiple cultures, of which he remains a member, the multiple conflicting perspectives developed in Harlem and the superordinate, geographically unbounded world of professional sociology and academic publishing.

In contrast to sociologists who draw primarily or solely on the intellectual resources supplied through professional socialization, Horowitz has been able to complement social science theories and methods with perspectives, insights, and criticisms that originate in a naturally acquired dialectical epistemology. This naturalistic epistemology, a kind of ethnographic grid, has helped shape his distinctive contributions to scholarship in at least four pressing areas addressed elsewhere in this volume: scholarly communication and knowledge utilization, the violence of state-sponsored genocide and the struggle for peace in war economies, the continued exploitation of working-class America, the cruel choices surrounding the adoption of normative models of development, and the conditions of progress in sociology as a policy science.

The norms of survival in Harlem placed no premium on the acquisition of knowledge as a cultural prize. Hustling baseball tickets at the Polo Grounds, or serving as bag boy, or the runner for numbers runners, required considerable knowledge. But the knowledge is what academics call usable knowledge: "The unwritten code was clear: intelligence was measured by what one could observe and translate into action, and not by the transmission of spoken words."[7] This perspective of the relation between knowledge and action is plainly unacceptable to many "basic" social scientists afflicted with the false consciousness of physics envy. New York sociologists, in contrast to sociologists and political scientists in Chicago, placed a low value on Harlem as a "laboratory" for research. This was among the reasons that Horowitz's transit to the professional culture of sociology was experienced as a mighty, autodidactic struggle.

In contrast to the profession's explicit or latent philosophic intellectualism—where the aim of sociology and other social sciences is confined to the generation and testing of true propositions, which are those conforming to the norms of science as we define them—Horowitz acquired a natural attitude of epistemological pragmatism early in life. At the age of 10, already an independent child of the streets, he proved to himself and others that he had sufficient knowledge not only to successfully negotiate the constant physical dangers of the streets, but also to competently exploit periodic opportunities for financial gain by hustling tickets or serving as bag boy for numbers runners, both enterprises operated as joint ventures with the New York police. This naturalistic pragmatism was later "decriminalized," reconstructed, and made philosophically whole by studying pragmatic philosophy and pragmatic sociology with Edel and Mills. Significantly, the dominant professional cultures of philosophy and sociology were largely unsympathetic to the work of both mentors.[8]

Medicine and the Moral Order

In the Harlem period, rare acts of generosity, empathy, and love, while uncharacteristic of the Horowitz family as a whole, were provided by sister, mother, and father, in rapidly declining order of magnitude. Any regular experience of generosity and empathy, however, came from multiple hospitalizations for reconstructive surgery on a cleft palate and hare lip. The culture of pediatric medical care in Sydenham Hospital involved, in addition to other medical staff, surgeons who were part of a second wave of Jewish immigrants. In contrast to the first wave, the second post-Nazi wave was composed of numerous professionals who were neither poor nor uneducated; they were knowledgeable, competent, and well-established—economically, socially, and professionally. Professional medicine, at least in the domain of pediatric care, was now often supplied by those who had fled Nazism, thus making Horowitz a dialectical beneficiary of fascism in his first contact with European intellectuals.

The children's ward at Sydenham embodied much of the culture of a caring family; it was a sanctuary from the dangers of the external world, and, in Harlem, these were not the usual dangers. They were everyday terrors. The hospital culture stood in sharp contrast to that of family, school, and the streets; through his own suffering he developed "a keen appreciation for the suffering of others. There was a feeling of shared battle, which was constantly reinforced by doctors, parents, and other patients as well."[9] The material and physical culture of the hospital, however, was one of pain and aching expectation of the next surgery.

What counted was not only the primacy of actions over words, actions that for their time constituted some of the most efficacious surgical treatment available. Equally important was that actions were motivated by empathy and caring, affections that were absent on the streets and in school and rare in the family. In effect, the hospital was both a surrogate family and, later, a normative ideal for the ethics of professional practice, in sociology and other social sciences. Whereas many young people make their first step into adulthood and independence through religious ritual, and increasingly through the feeble ritual challenge of operating an automobile, neither were open to Horowitz. His bar mitzvah was an indifferent ritual organized in part to conceal from others a physical deformity, thereby participating in a process of stigmatization, rather than a rite of passage into adulthood.

The first transitional step into adulthood was made by leaving the surrogate family of the hospital. Here, he decided by himself and for himself that he had experienced enough pain from surgery, delaying the final corrective treatment for many years. The decision to leave Sydenham involved the determination that "however I looked was how I was going to look, and that however I spoke at that point was how I was going to speak."[10] This conscious choice also required leaving the most empathetic and caring way of life he had known, one that provided a sanctuary from the streets and from, very likely, an early death. The experience with this surrogate family, which had no ulterior motives, is closely related to the professional ethic of empathy for and active service to the ostensible beneficiaries of a profession, in this case sociology, and not the mere well-intentioned words of those for whom theorizing is paramount. The establishment of *Transaction/Society,* a journal designed to reach beyond the narrow group of academics and create a basis for transforming words into deeds, is one notable product of this ethic. Professionals should empathize with those who experience the problems that are objects of social science research. Social scientists have an obligation to contribute to the moral order.

Sociology as Combat

A naturalistic epistemology of pragmatism acquired on the Harlem streets, along with a combative style of communication appropriate for early childhood survival, were also transformed into a disputatious posture toward the uses of the social sciences for policy-making and practice improvements. The social sciences are not simply about the creation of knowledge; the problem is to put knowledge to good use in the field of action. The frontal attack on deceptive or morally corrupt social science—deceptive because it is dishonest with presumed beneficiaries and morally corrupt because it does not improve the human condition—is evident in *The Rise and Fall of Project Camelot* as well as *The Use and Abuse of Social Science*. The social sciences, like the streets of Harlem, require an activist theory of knowledge that has been justified by pragmatism, as well as Marxism, while university-based research on public policy should not resemble a spectator sport or a game played at the Polo Grounds, or a musical performance in Central Park or at the Apollo. The social sciences should serve practical improvements, even as social scientists must be vigilant to identify and expose abuses that have their counterpart in Harlem street scams, the self-serving deceptions of Russian or Soviet autocrats, or the self-delusions of authoritarian fathers who confuse morally righteous discipline and child abuse. The social sciences are a human trust, not a game of performance, and combative public debate is an essential check on their performance.

Dispassionate intellectual discourse had no standing in the culture of Harlem or that of the Horowitz family, deeply disappointed immigrants who had escaped czarist persecution in the Ukraine only to find that they constituted an underclass-within-an-underclass in the new world. The combative passion needed to survive Harlem and cope at home, essential in the period before Horowitz's move to Brooklyn, was inconsistent with the accepted style of classroom communication prevalent in the new environment of Brooklyn's P.S. 193, where something akin to naturalistic ethnomethodological "breaches" forced the counterintuitive discovery that words mattered more than fists. The transfer of this same combative passion to intellectual discourse, which later became one of the marks of Horowitz the scholar, occurred first in the classrooms of

P.S. 193. In what was perceived as a courageous act by classmates, Horowitz challenged the one-sided adulation of the Soviet political system by the teacher. The inheritor of socialist ideology from a father who was nevertheless ambivalent about communism, young Horowitz dared to openly challenge his teacher and her account, widely shared in the wartime America of the early 1940s, of the unequivocal virtues of the Soviet Union: "I spoke with passion, if not with eloquence—the same sort of combative passion that marked my growing up. And it worked! The spirit of combat also existed in the intellectual realm."[11]

This combative passion, a product of the intersection of two cultures, is inconsistent with the implicit code of scholarly discourse followed by many social scientists. It is a source of anxiety or plain fear to those who fail to see, as did John Stuart Mill in *On Liberty,* that passionate and even thundering intellectual debate by those who actually believe in their ideas is a necessary condition of the truth-approximating process of science. This same thundering debate can be seen in objectivated form in the books and periodicals published by Transaction Publishers and Transaction Periodicals Consortium, which represent opposing beliefs that range from radical political economy to modern conservative thought.

Daydreams and Nightmares sets a high standard for the sociological autobiography, for it does supply a rich and starkly honest narrative that reveals the personal, social, and historical contexts that have shaped an exceptional scholar. The narrative is much more than an evolutionary account, however, since it is punctuated by a succession of passionate and sometimes combative dialogues between Horowitz the child, boy, man, and mature scholar. And it is these dialectical moments that enable us to see the present in the past.

Reprise

Conflicting cultures conjoin to form and transform structures of knowledge and action representing developmental episodes: the innocent child detached from a troubled and emotionally unresponsive immigrant family; the white street child negotiating the terrors and pleasures of black Harlem; the physically handicapped and stigmatized youth for whom the hospital was at once a sanctuary and surrogate family; the juvenile delinquent establishing personal efficacy through stealth and street combat; the developing adolescent turning unapproved behaviors into those valued by peers; the sophomoric abstractor escaping the concreteness of a brutal past; the auto-didactic sociologist struggling to synthesize conflicting cultures; and the world-class social scientist with a combative passion for ideas, a distrust of political authority and sensitivity to intellectual and political deception, an openness to rival points of view born of a high ratio of doubt to trust, an impatience for knowledge that is not translated into action, and a commitment to a professional ethic which insists that we shape the moral order by empathizing with and attempting to better the human condition. All are necessary conditions for doing social science in a world in which empathy, generosity, and love are rare and terror, deception, and agonizing uncertainty commonplace.

University of Pittsburgh
Graduate School of Public and International Affairs

Notes

1. Irving Louis Horowitz, *Daydreams and Nightmares: Reflections of a Harlem Childhood* (Jackson: University Press of Mississippi, 1990).
2. See Irving Louis Horowitz, *C. Wright Mills: An American Utopian* (New York: The Free Press, 1983).
3. The existence of such differences does not entail a commitment to the solipsistic proposition that an impermeable boundary separates "insiders" and "outsiders." Horowitz's life provides ample evidence that this proposition is plainly false. The classic critique of the proposition is Robert K. Merton, "Insiders and Outsiders: A Chapter in the Sociology of Knowledge," in *Varieties of Political Expression in Sociology* (Chicago: The University of Chicago Press, 1972), 9–47.
4. Horowitz, *Daydreams and Nightmares*, 90.
5. Ibid., vii.
6. For example, Norman Denzin, *The Research Act* (New York: The Free Press, 1970); and Donald T. Campbell, *Methodology and Epistemology for Social Science: Selected Papers*, ed. E. Sam Overman (Chicago: University of Chicago Press, 1988).
7. Horowitz, *Daydreams and Nightmares*, 41.
8. For systematic treatments of the works of both mentors see *Ethics, Science, and Democracy: The Philosophy of Abraham Edel*, ed. Irving Louis Horowitz and Horace S. Thayer (New Brunswick, NJ: Transaction Publishers, 1987); and C. Wright Mills, *Sociology and Pragmatism*, ed. Irving Louis Horowitz (New York: Oxford University Press, 1966). The latter work was Mills's dissertation at the University of Wisconsin, while the former is a festschrift for Abraham Edel.
9. Horowitz, *Daydreams and Nightmares*, 14.
10. Ibid., 16.
11. Ibid., 96. At his sister's insistence, Horowitz frequently attended meetings of the Young Communist League. The death of her boyfriend in the defense of Republican Madrid, followed by the 1939 Ribbentrop-Molotov Pact, led to her withdrawal from politics.

28

Irving Louis Horowitz:
A Brief Career Summary

Prepared by Deborah A. Stanley

The books by social scientist, editor, publisher, and writer, Irving Louis Horowitz have analyzed the political implications of forces as diverse as communism in Cuba, the changing shape of publishing technology, religious figure Sun Myung Moon of the Unification church, and the work of American sociologist C. Wright Mills. In *Who's Who* he has described himself as "having one mission in three parts: the writing, publishing and teaching of social science." Described as both a "neo-conservative" and a "left academic" by Jeff Greenfield in *The New York Times Book Review,* the Harlem-born Horowitz began his teaching career at the University of Buenos Aires and continued his international role in social theory through posts in Venezuela, Mexico, India, and Tokyo. He received a special citation from the Carnegie Foundation for International Peace in 1957 for his book, *The Idea of War and Peace in Contemporary Philosophy.*

Francine du Plessix Gray in the *New York Review of Books* noted that the Horowitz edited volume *Science, Sin, and Scholarship* warned of Moon's growing influence on American politics and scholarship. Gray described the book as "a carefully edited" work "documenting the persistence with which Moon has infiltrated powerful groups in America from the federal government to the universities." Upon its appearance, the work received a two-page spread by Allen Lacy in the pages of *The Chronicle of Higher Education.*

Published in the same year was *Dialogues on American Politics,* a debate between coauthors Horowitz and Seymour Martin Lipset on polity, equality, presidency, and development. Faulting it for its "narrowly construed boundaries" and its tendency toward simplification, Jean Bethke Elshtain, writing in *The Nation,* nevertheless found in it the "occasional insight or interesting tidbit." Jeff Greenfield described the discussions of policy and equity as "provocative" in *The New York Times Book Review,* while taking exception to the description of "post-Watergate Democratic Congressmen as adherents of the 'new politics.'"

In *The New York Times Book Review,* Steven Lukes lauded *C. Wright Mills: An American Utopian* as an "excellent book" for its illumination of the "complex interplay between man and image, creation and reception." Some argument surrounded Horowitz's portrayal of Mills, however, a portrayal that Dan Wakefield, writing in *The Nation,* characterized as having "shifted dramatically" from the author's earlier assertion that Mills was "'the greatest sociologist the United States has ever produced.'" Although Robert Westbrook wished for a fuller biographical portrayal of Mills, he wrote in *The New Republic* that Horowitz did "effectively debunk the Mills myth."

In 1986, Horowitz's *Communicating Ideas: The Crisis of Publishing in a Post-Industrial Society* explored the future of publishing in an era of rapid technological advancement, raising issues both practical and ideological, including the consequences of the easy reproduction of documents and the potential political influence of a wider communication of knowledge. While Robert T. Golembiewski, writing in *The Times Literary Supplement,* questioned some of the book's underlying premises, he applauded Horowitz for failing to "pander to his audience with facile anti-technology talk." The sociologist, Joseph Gusfield, described *Communicating Ideas* as an "intelligent book" in *The Los Angeles Times Book Review,* finding Horowitz "alive to the possibilities and barriers for academics to reach wider audiences and for lay persons to utilize scholarship."

In 1991, *Daydreams and Nightmares: Memories of a Harlem Childhood* received the National Jewish Book Award in biography and autobiography. It was widely reviewed. John W. Bowling in *The University Bookman* called the book "a little gem of an autobiography" adding that "Horowitz evokes the sensations and emotions of a childhood bordering on the fantastic." Carlos Alberto Montaner, writing in *The Miami Herald* hypothesizes that "Horowitz had to write the book to frighten off his very own ghosts, to deal with old offenses. The book is all the more moving because of this," adding that "the prose touches home." William

Helmreich, a leading authority on the holocaust and its survivors in America, wrote in *The Jerusalem Post* that the book is "written in a beautifully sparse, yet richly evocative style.... This superb and emotionally powerful account is an inspiration."

Horowitz's most recent effort, *The Decomposition of Sociology,* continues a tradition of vigorous discourse as to the nature of social science, what Nathan Glazer in *The Atlantic* refers to as a "swashbuckling style." While claiming to "detect a subtext...from the left wing to probably what is today considered the right of American sociology," Glazer concludes by agreeing that while "Horowitz does not have the whole story— who has?—he gives a good number of pieces of the explanation." Paul Gottfried, on the other hand, in his review of the book in *Chronicles,* links the effort to a struggle for openness in publishing, arguing that Horowitz "keeps open the research questions that politically correct universities are working to push down the memory hole...reminding his fellow social scientists what they should be about."

References

America (4 May 1974); (16 April 1977).

American Journal of Sociology (September 1974); (September 1975).

American Political Science Review (June 1974).

Atlantic (April 1994): 20–25.

Choice (January 1973); (September 1974); (June 1977).

Christian Century (20 March 1974).

Chronicle of Higher Education (16 October 1978): 10–11.

Chronicles (January 1994): 28–29.

Comparative Literature Studies (December 1973).

Jerusalem Post (4 March 1991): 7.

Los Angeles Times Book Review (14 December 1986): 4.

Miami Herald (24 September 1991): 13.

Motive (February 1968).

Nation (3 March 1969); (24 March 1979): 310–12; (15 September 1984): 212–13.

New Leader (28 April 1969).

New Republic (26 March 1984): 40–42.

New York Review of Books (25 October 1979): 8.

New York Times Book Review (25 February 1979): 18; (13 November 1983): 11.

Political Science Quarterly (Summer 1977).
Progressive (April 1974).
Saturday Review (7 June 1969).
Time (5 January 1970).
Times Literary Supplement (3 August 1967); (24 June 1977); (12 June 1987): 646.
University Bookman 31, no. 2 (1993): 29–31.
Virginia Quarterly Review (Spring 1977).

Biographical Information

Personal. He was born on 25 September 1929, in New York City, New York; son of Louis Horowitz and Esther (Tepper) Horowitz; married Ruth Lenore Narowlansky, 1950 (divorced, 1963); married Mary Ellen Curtis, 1979. He has two children from the first marriage: Carl Frederick and David Dennis. His early years were detailed in *Daydreams and Nightmares: Reflections of a Harlem Childhood,* which won the National Jewish Book Award in biography and autobiography for 1991. He was educated at James Madison High School in Brooklyn, and when his parents moved after World War II he went to DeWitt Clinton High School in the Bronx, from which he graduated in 1947. His higher education began at the College of the City of New York (now City College of the City University of New York), B.S.S., 1951; Columbia University, M.A., 1952; University of Buenos Aires, Ph.D., 1957; Brandeis University, postdoctoral fellow, 1958–59.

Addresses. He resides at Blawenburg-Rocky Hill Road, 1247 State Road, Route 206, Princeton, New Jersey 08540, where he and Mary have lived since 1974. His offices are at Rutgers University: professional—Department of Sociology, Lucy Stone Hall, Post Office Box 5072; publishing—Transaction Publishers, Building 4051; New Brunswick, New Jersey 08903.

Career. His first teaching assignment was as a graduate assistant at the City College of New York in 1952. He next served as assistant professor of social theory at the University of Buenos Aires, 1956–58. Upon his return to the United States he became assistant professor of sociology at Bard College, Annandale-on-Hudson, New York, 1959–60; Hobart and William Smith Colleges, Geneva, New York, assistant professor of sociology and chairman of Department of Sociology and Anthropology,

1960-63; Washington University, St. Louis, Missouri, associate professor, 1963-65, professor of sociology, 1965-69; Rutgers University, New Brunswick, New Jersey, graduate professor of sociology and chairman of Department of Sociology at Livingston College; from 1975-85 he served as chairman of the sociology section for all Rutgers campuses. In 1979 he was appointed by the Rutgers board of governors as Hannah Arendt Professor of Sociology and Political Science.

Visiting Appointments. Horowitz served as visiting professor or visiting lecturer at the Central University of Venezuela in Caracas, 1957; University of Buenos Aires, 1961 and 1963; State University of New York at Buffalo, 1960; Syracuse University, 1961; University of Rochester, 1962; London School of Economics and Political Science, 1962; University of California at Davis, 1966; University of Wisconsin at Madison, 1967; Stanford University, 1968-69; University of Calgary, 1970; American University, 1972; Queen's University in Canada, 1973; Princeton University, 1976; University of Mexico (UNAM), 1978; Tokyo and Hosei Universities, 1980.

He served as Fulbright-Hays senior lecturer on three separate occasions: in Argentina in 1961, in Israel in 1969, and in India in 1977. He was advisory staff member, Latin American Research Center, 1964-67; consultant to the International Educational Division, Ford Foundation, 1958-60; member of the advisory board, Institute for Scientific Information, Inc., 1969-73; consulting editor, Oxford University Press, 1964-69; and Aldine-Atherton Publishers, 1969-72. He is the founding president of Transaction/Society, which incorporated in 1968, five years after its founding. Since its establishment, he has served as an external board member of Radio Martí and Television Martí programs of the United States Information Agency, 1985 to the present. He was also an external board member of the methodology section of the research division of the General Accounting Office of the United States. He has given expert testimony at least twenty times to various congressional committees and subcommittees—ranging in subject from proposals to establish a National Social Science Foundation in 1965 to the Free and Independent Cuba Assistance Act of 1993.

Organizations. Horowitz is a founding editorial board member of *Academic Questions* of the National Association of Scholars 1988- ; past chairman of the board of the Hubert Humphrey Center of Ben Gurion University, 1990-92; board member of *North-South Maga-*

zine of the North-South Center of the University of Miami, 1994– ; editorial board member of *Orbis* of the Foreign Policy Research Institute, 1988– ; past fellow of the American Association for the Advancement of Science, 1983–87; member of the Council of Foreign Relations, 1977– ; member of the Carnegie Council, 1988– ; member of American Association of Publishers, 1969-92; 1993– ; member of the American Political Science Association, 1966– ; past president of the New York State Sociology Society, 1961–62; past member of the American Sociological Association; Society for the Study of Social Problems, and Society for International Development; Latin American Studies Association.

Awards. Special citation by Carnegie Endowment for International Peace, 1957, for *Idea of War and Peace in Contemporary Philosophy;* Man of the Year in Behavioral Science, *Time,* 1970; Centennial Medallion, Saint Peters College, 1971, for outstanding contribution to a humanistic social science; presidential outstanding achievement award, Rutgers University, 1985; Jewish Book Council, National Jewish Book Award, 1991.

Works Authored

The Renaissance Philosophy of Giordano Bruno, Coleman-Ross, 1952 [thesis].

Claude Helvetius: Philosopher of Democracy and Enlightenment, Paine-Whitman, 1955.

Idea of War and Peace in Contemporary Philosophy, Paine-Whitman, 1957; second edition, Humanities Publishers, 1973.

Sociologia Cientifica/Sociologia del Conocimiento, Libreria Hachette, Coleccion el Mirador, 1958 [dissertation].

Philosophy, Science and the Sociology of Knowledge, Charles C. Thomas, 1960; second edition, Greenwood, 1978.

Radicalism and the Revolt against Reason: The Social Theories of Georges Sorel, Routledge & Kegan Paul, 1961; Humanities, 1961; revised edition, Southern Illinois University Press, 1968.

The War Game: Studies of the New Civilian Militarists, Ballantine/Random House, 1963.

Historia y Elementos de la Sociología del Conocimiento, University of Buenos Aires Press, 1963.

Revolution in Brazil: Politics and Society in a Developing Nation, E.P. Dutton Publishers, 1964.

Three Worlds of Development: The Theory and Practice of International Stratification, Oxford University Press, 1966, second revised edition, 1972.

Professing Sociology: The Life Cycle of a Social Science, Aldine, 1968, revised edition, Southern Illinois University Press, 1972.

The Struggle is the Message: The Organization and Ideology of the Anti-War Movement, Glendessary, 1970.

The Knowledge Factory: Student Activism and American Crisis, (with William H. Friedland), Aldine, 1970, revised edition, Southern Illinois University Press, 1974.

Foundations of Political Sociology, Harper & Row, 1972.

Israeli Ecstasies/Jewish Agonies, Oxford University Press, 1974.

Social Science and Public Policy in the United States (with James Everett Katz), Praeger/Harcourt Brace, 1975.

Ideology and Utopia in the United States, 1956–1976, Oxford University Press, 1977.

Dialogues on American Politics (with Seymour Martin Lipset), Oxford University Press, 1978.

Taking Lives: Genocide and State Power, Transaction Publishers, 1976, revised third edition, 1980.

Beyond Empire and Revolution: Militarization and Consolidation in the Third World, Oxford University Press, 1982.

C. Wright Mills: An American Utopian, The Free Press/Macmillan, 1983.

Winners and Losers: Social and Political Polarities in America, Duke University Press, 1984.

Communicating Ideas: The Crisis of Publishing in a Post Industrial Society, Oxford University Press, 1986; second expanded edition, Transaction Publishers, 1991.

Persuasions and Prejudices: An Informal Compendium of Modern Social Science, 1953-1988, Transaction Publishers, 1989.

Daydreams and Nightmares: Reflections of a Harlem Childhood, University Press of Mississippi, 1990.

The Conscience of Worms and the Cowardice of Lions: The Cuban-American Experience, 1959–1992 North-South Center of the University of Miami, 1993.

The Decomposition of Sociology, Oxford University Press, 1993.

Works Edited

Conference on Conflict, Consensus and Cooperation, Hobart & William Smith Colleges, 1962.

Power, Politics and People: The Collected Papers of C. Wright Mills, Oxford University Press, 1963.

The New Sociology: Essays in Social Science and Social Values in Honor of C. Wright Mills, Oxford University Press, 1964.

The Anarchists, Dell, 1964.

The Rise and Fall of Project Camelot, Massachusetts Institute of Technology Press, 1967; second revised edition, 1974.

Latin American Radicalism: A Documentary Report on Left and Nationalist Movements (with John Gerassi and Josue deCastro), Random House, 1969.

Sociological Self-Images: A Collective Portrait, Pergamon, 1969.

Cuban Communism, Aldine, 1970; eighth edition, Transaction Publishers, forthcoming, 1994.

Masses in Latin America, Oxford University Press, 1970.

Sociological Realities: A Guide to the Study of Sociology (with others) Harper & Row, 1971; second revised edition, Van Nostrand, 1975.

The Troubled Conscience, Center for the Study of Democratic Institutions, 1971.

The Use and Abuse of Social Science, E.P. Dutton, 1971; second revised edition, 1975.

Equity, Income, and Policy: Comparative Studies in Three Worlds of Development, Praeger/Harcourt Brace, 1977.

Science, Sin and Scholarship: The Politics of Reverend Moon and the Unification Church, Massachusetts Institute of Technology Press, 1978.

The American Working Class: Prospects for the 1980s (with John C. Leggett and Martin Oppenheimer), Transaction Publishers, 1979.

Constructing Policy: Dialogues with Social Scientists in the National Political Arena, Praeger/Harcourt Brace, 1980.

Ethics, Science and Democracy (with H. S. Thayer), Transaction Publishers, 1987.

Editorial Board Service

Sociological Abstracts, 1962–73
Transaction/Society, 1963 to the present
Studies in Comparative International Development, 1964–79
International Studies Quarterly, 1966–70
Indian Journal of Sociology, 1971–75
Journal of Jazz Studies, 1973–82
Social Indicators, 1973–79
Social Praxis, 1973–77
Policy Studies Review Annual, 1976–85
Third World Review, 1976–83
Civil Liberties Review, 1976–79
Journal of Conflict Resolution, 1966–72
Journal of Political and Military Sociology, 1973–89
Journal of Contemporary Jewry, 1976–81
Indian Sociological Bulletin, 1963–69
Social Theory and Practice, 1970–75
Journal of Symbolic Interaction, 1977–80
Journal of Interamerican Studies & World Affairs, 1980 to the present
Orbis, 1985 to the present
Academic Questions, 1988 to the present
North-South, 1993 to the present

Doctoral Dissertations
Supervised at Washington University and at Rutgers University

Aguiar-Walker, Neuma (1967) *Modernization and Mobilization in the Brazilian Labor Movement*

Carlson, Josephine (1974) *The Politics of Powerlessness: George Wallace and His Movement, 1964–1972.*

Clairmont, Donald H. (1969) *An Historical and Experimental Study of Utility* (co-chaired with Robert H, Hamblin).

Crowley, John Gifford (1984) *Social and Economic Determinants of Urban Fertility Differentials in Mexico and Brazil.*

Edgar, Richard Eugene (1967) *Patterns of Influence in the Organization of Welfare Agencies in St. Louis.*

Fidel, Kenneth (1968) *Social Structure and Military Intervention: The 1960 Turkish Revolution.*

Greil, Arthur L. (1981) *Georges Sorel and the Sociology of Virtue* (co chaired with Michael Curtis).

Humphreys, Laud (1970) *Tea Room Trade: Impersonal Sex in Public Places* (co-chaired with Lee Rainwater).

Karch, Cecilia A. (1977) *The Tourist Industry, Modernization and the Development of the Caribbean Region.*

Katz, James Everett (1972) *Presidential Politics and Scientific Research, 1961–1972: Science Policy Under Kennedy, Johnson and Nixon.*

Kelley, Robert T. (1977) *A Factor Analysis of Assistance to Families with Dependent Children in Select Districts of New Jersey.*

Kim, Byoung 'Philo' (1991) *Two Koreas in Development: A Comparative Study of Principles and Strategies of Capitalist and Communist Third World Development.*

Levine, Judith G. (1976) *Rock Music, Political Deviance and Marginal Life Styles.*

Machado, Antonio Silva (1977) *Cooptation of Marginal Groups: Urban Labor Markets in Brazil.*

Mutchler, David M. (1970) *Organizational Conflict within Latin American Catholicism.*

Odetola, Theophilus Tunde (1973) *The Nigerian Military and Nation-Building in Post Colonial Nigeria.*

Pitts, Ruth Ann (1968) *DeGaulle and the Political Parties: A Study in the Legitimacy of the French Republic.*

Romalis, Coleman (1969) *Barbados and St. Lucia: A Study in Differential Socioeconomic Development in Two British West Indian Islands.*

Ramos, Aaron Gamaliel (1985) *The Structure of Political Parties in Puerto Rico; with a Special Emphasis on the Question of Statehood.*

Saxe-Fernandez, John (1971) *Hemispheric Militarism and the Concept of Pax Americana.*

Simon, David (1975) *United States War Deserters in Canada: A Test of the Lonely Crowd Hypothesis.*

Sprehe, John Timothy (1968) *Values and Belief Systems of Sociologists* (co-chaired with Alvin W. Gouldner)

Varnis, Steven L. (1990) *Reluctant Aid or Aiding the Reluctant: United States Food Policy and Ethiopian Famine Relief.*

West, Maragrita P. (1974) *Twin-Track Coalitions: A Study of the National Welfare Rights Organization.*

Zimmerman, Michael (1983) *Old Age Poverty in Pre-Industrial America.*

Gale Publishers
Detroit, Michigan

[partial listing]

Section Eight

Closing Remarks

Critical Responses to Friendly Critics

Irving Louis Horowitz

James E. Katz

It must be said at the outset that any comparison over career lines between myself and Max Weber is in itself an inestimable compliment. Weber is the towering figure of sociology in the twentieth century—which is to say, the towering figure in the discipline period. He is that because he never permitted himself to be locked into categories or disciplinary boundaries. Weber could write, with equal fluency, newspaper columns on contemporary Weimar politics, or fundamental monographs on ancient religions, or economic history of the Western world.

What is too easily overlooked in Weber is the degree to which he started from the present and looked backward for sources of knowledge and inspiration. By that I mean he worked hard at understanding ancient religions, medieval agrarian systems, traditional economies, and so forth. His impulse was thus fixed on how the past informs the present. I am simply no match for Weber in such historical terms. And in that sense, I must admit to being a lesser figure. Indeed, it boggles the mind to think just who, among contemporary social scientists, can match Weber as a student of economic, political, and religious history. The work load in these areas have become so parceled and subdivided that we may never quite see a figure equal to Weber in scope and stature. My own candidates, in an American context at least, would be Harold Lasswell and Peter Berger. In Europe, the Weberian tradition persisted through thick and thin through the efforts of such towering figures as Ferdinand Toennies and René Koenig.

However, it is interesting to note how few of these people (with the exception of Lasswell for a brief spell at least) thought in policy terms.

And here one is essentially looking ahead to events not yet transpired rather than presumably to what once was. One might argue that policy is, or at least should be, rooted in history. But this is not uniformly the case, since one fashions policy in terms of normative no less than historical considerations. In that sense, my differences with Weber are slightly different from those posited by Dr. Katz. They are rooted less in a difference of perspectives than in different images of the tasks of social research. Where I share an absolute common ground with Weber is the belief that not everything in life is subject to meliorative reform. On the other hand, I admit to a belief that not everything in life is subject to historical laws or quasi-historical correlations.

Indeed, I must make a bow to Georg Simmel, who stands next to Weber on the pantheon of sociological greats. For as we shut down the century it becomes clear that the intimate concerns are on a par with the worldly claims. It is Simmel who understands the underbelly, the subjective side of social life. Whether it is the meaning of money to persons, the role of the stranger in community affairs, or a variety of considerations best explained by the private realm in the public space, Simmel spoke to those concerns over the future of the person in a technological age that haunts us at night, and occupies policy analysts like Jim Katz by day. I would go further and declare that Mills's critique of American life as a place that elevates private troubles over public issues is downright fatuous, resting on the false notion that what is big is necessarily what is significant. Nothing could be further from the truth. For the protection of the person, the enhancement of the individual is the bedrock of the democratic spirit.

Still, I count myself a Weberian with pride. He uniquely was able, with equal fluency, to endow his work with two principles: a firm grip on empirical events coupled with a remarkable talent for infusing such events with relevant theory. Katz is correct to note that Weber was cautious about fatuous levels of generalities, and gratuitous praise (either given or received). In this, he was remarkably marginal to the fashions of his times—and it is evident that he who could hardly care less for the praise of those weak of mind and thin on principles. And I suspect for these very reasons Weber remains easily accessible to the contemporary reader.

We all must learn from Weber the truth of social science: It is a modest undertaking aimed at helping us understand our world. Furthermore,

it must not be viewed as an open sesame to guarantee success in changing that world. His savage critique of German society and culture, his
cautious response to doctrines of egalitarianism, his intrinsic spirit of
democratic life as the best hope of human beings, and the last hope of
Germany to stave off the bureaucratic nightmare—which indeed did
follow—makes one, myself, proud of the identification with Weber. I
shall wear Katz's analysis as a badge of honor, even where I must take
issue with specific points in his analysis.

Before we leave Weber as such, it is important to restore color to him.
American commentators on him from William Buxton to S. M. Miller
have managed to bleach him, to deprive him of the fierce devotion to
political democracy that characterized his work. Whether Weber's
Economy and Society constitutes a "system" as such, or whether he was
a socialist in hiding, all manages to avoid what we know profoundly
characterizes him—and which his essays on science and politics continually reaffirm: a clear-eyed spirit of antitotalitarianism. He saw the
iron cage of fascism and feared it might work. He saw the communist
start-up and already saw in its fanatic impulse to factionalism signs of
disintegration. Thus, to be a "Weberian" without at the same time being
a democrat is to be an oxymoron, a believer in form over substance.

The work of Weber appears often in this volume, and I am not trying
to burden Katz's essay on this score. But his raising Weber in such sharp
colors enables me to respond in a way I had always hoped to do, but had
not in the past. My writings on Weber have been contextual rather than
addressing contents. The one exception is my work on party charisma in
the 1960s. In that effort, I tried to show that the movement from charismatic to rational authority often takes a long intermediate form. Weber
recognized as much in dealing with the papacy. It is from his observations on the charisma of the chair, that I began to see how a similar
phenomenon exists in the world of military rule generally.

Nonetheless, such efforts fully factored into account, it always seemed to
be gratuitous, and still does, to attempt to appropriate for oneself the label
Weberian. In his very democratic soul, in his critical historical reviews, in
his disdain for perfect systems over imperfect realities, Weber himself cautioned against would-be followers. Weber knew politics, but was himself no
politician. One could do worse than heed such an approach.

Before taking my departure of Jim's essay, I should like to respond to
the issues he raises on the relation of planning, prediction, and technol-

ogy—especially computer technology. I have not thought of my views as overly optimistic, but perhaps I have stated them in so casual a fashion as to invite such a line of criticism. In my view, technology is directly linked to science and industry. Hence, it should not be viewed either as panacea or Pandemonium. The values embedded in technology relate to discovery at one end and modernity at the other. A tool is not a good or an evil, neither is the collectivity of tools or products that permit us to operationalize the scientific world in which we live.

Once it is understood that technology exists as a direct line from science to industry, its relationship to everyday life and valuational theory becomes far simpler to assess. In that sense, the study of the future is itself neither a sign of optimism or pessimism, just a normal extension of efforts at prediction and explanation utilizing whatever machines and mechanisms are at our disposal. I have never envisioned myself as a new technocrat or a member of a cyberocracy. Indeed, I shall address the concerns expressed by Dr. Katz. Indeed, I have often raised with him my deep feelings that one of the master themes of the fin de siècle is that of privacy and publicity and that the risks to private life are far more extensive, far more Orwellian, than we might have earlier imagined. This is one reason why I have always felt that a strong dose of Weber must always be tempered by a solid dash of Simmel. We need to know more about the private person behind the public square—and nowhere more so than in advanced technological settings, which are widely perceived as anomie.

If I may offer a concrete illustration of the above theorem: It is no longer doubted that within the next decade, perhaps even by the close of the century, the use of cellular phones will be at the 200–300 million level. And there is also little doubt that the information available at our fingertips through instant global communication is also a matter of a few years. At the same time, such rapid technical changes have only highlighted inherited problems of the relationship of government snooping versus individual secrecy. Codes to protect the person are broken so that they can offer information to federal agencies. Cryptographers are far more advanced than those who broke enemy codes during the Second World War, but the same sort of ethical issues remain to be dealt with. It is the heart and soul of social science research to examine the connections between the technological and the valuational. Personal assessments of how optimistic or pessimistic one ought to be are matters of distant, even remote, significance.

Katz himself introduces the enormous positive side of technology in modern society: its ability to galvanize the Russian people against totalitarian plotters, and the ability of the Chinese students to alert the outside world of events in ways that were formerly bottled up by those who rule with an iron fist. In short, while the chapter draws attention to my interest in technology, society, and value theory, it does not quite do justice to a view of the situation that distinguishes mechanical objects created by human beings from human beings manipulating mechanical objects with specific ends in view. That there are unresolved issues with such a relativistic position is doubtless correct. But a resolution in any complete sense is virtually impossible given the dynamic state of affairs that obtains in the world of science and technology. To stop the world at a certain point and create a system is, in my own judgment, a mistake— a piece of hubris driven by ego and going up in smoke at the very point of creation. If we must rest content with pushing forward a social science of value theory, so too must we work harder to create a technology for the advancement of social science. These interactions, these emerging linkages, rather than systematic outcomes, attract my attention— and I daresay, the same is true for Jim Katz.

Howard G. Schneiderman

I must first register a deep appreciation to Howard Schneiderman. His effort at understanding my notions of democracy, liberality, power, and authority in a historical rather than ideological context is extremely helpful to me and, hopefully, insightful to others. The emphasis on *Radicalism and the Revolt against Reason* is properly placed. It is one of my more important efforts, and it is a landmark in my personal evolution.

The work itself was published by Routledge and Kegan Paul. It took a long while because it had a tough group of readers. After publication, Norman Franklin told me that the readers were Isaiah Berlin, Herbert Read, and Stuart Hampshire: Berlin for his knowledge of Sorel and fin de siècle Europe, Read for his allegiance to anarchist ideas, and Hampshire for general moral and philosophical grounding. Having such a group makes one work doubly hard.

To accommodate such divergent scholars means to be level-headed and, yes, liberal, in the best sense of that word. I mention this for I cannot take credit for arriving at a critique of left and right simply by cogitations about the world. The help of a reading committee was never more apparent—and the old Routledge exemplified that tradition of scholarly publishing we can all envy and seek to emulate. The process of scholarship is itself, at its highest level, an expression of the liberal democratic spirit. If nothing else, fanaticisms cancel out, while fine-tuning chimes in.

The question of liberalism and its relationship to democracy has been debated for centuries, and certainly goes back to Adam Smith and John Locke in our own Anglo-American frame of reference. My own sentiment is that liberalism is—like radicalism and conservatism—an ideology and not a science. Nor for that matter is it the same as democracy. To be sure, when liberalism stood for a common starting point, and a belief in equity as the ground of and for a social contract, then its proximity to democracy was very close.

The dilemma arose for liberalism as an ideology when it veered away from starting point to terminal point considerations—that is to say, when it became in the vernacular of horse racing a search for equitable outcomes through handicaps for fast horses and entitlements for slow horses. For at that point, liberalism encouraged resentments of all sorts: It made people "aware" of historical differences in past treatments and it made others aware that they were to be punished for the sins of their forebears. As a result, neoliberalism, instead of serving as a healing doctrine, a consensual arrangement of the political commonweal, became itself a huge source of friction and potential antidemocratic sentiments.

One sees this in the rise of demands for curbs on free speech or free expression in the name of combating sexism, racism, or the other "mantras" to which Howard alludes. It is also found in the idea of class resentments—the rich against the poor for the welfare system, and the poor against the rich for monopolizing so much power and money. In effect, when liberalism turns statistical instead of normative, it becomes a measurement for how far we must still travel to find the perfect system and is no longer a device for an appreciation of how far we have come as a nation or as a system. While this approach avoids the problem of celebrationism, it darn near invites the opposite problem of social chaos. In its very demands for a more perfect order it turns on democracy itself; liberalism becomes an impatient vehicle, a veritable drum beat, arguing against policy-making as a give and take, as a system of fine-tuning differences of opinions and groups.

When *Radicalism and the Revolt against Reason* was being produced, nearly thirty-five years ago, the process of this liberal disintegration was still nascent. It was far simpler to see radicalism as irrational and conservatism as traditional, with liberalism somewhere in the middle serving as a linchpin of the democratic order. It is for this reason that I am deeply pleased at Howard Schneiderman's remarks on consistency and inconsistency in my thought over time. I stand guilty of the charge of rejecting neoliberalism as an ideological voice, not because of normative concerns, but rather as a consequence of its sharp departure from democratic theory. This "ism" wants to end in the same place, whereas classical liberalism aims at a shared starting point. The ancient Greeks were wise to understand that times and things change rapidly, while norms and values change slowly. And in the realm of politics, norms and values still rule supreme.

Sociology as a discipline tends to emphasize change and change agents because its constituency model, based upon the presumed needs of the have-nots, so dictates. But in the fear of being labeled conservative or worse, the field has ignored a sense of permanence in things. While the field has had many reactionary as well as revolutionary diversions, it has blundered badly in seeing that the needs of ordinary people are precisely for a stake in society. It is only when such a stake is denied to them, that they may turn to extremes.

The attraction of sociology for such extremes derives from an impatience with things as they are. But such impatience does not always stem from sociological experience as much as ideological sentiment. It is not liberalism or even neoliberalism that preserves a social science discipline from decomposition or disgrace. It is its continued adherence to the canons of science as such. That such canons may prove porous, even feeble at times, is no argument for its abandonment, only its improvement. I do not think that Howard and I disagree one jot on this belief. But perhaps I have a lesser faith that any single ideology holds a greater number of truths than do all others. This is not a matter of apriori judgment. It is a matter of testing and retesting our beliefs in the crafty world in which we live.

That the world conspires while we hire is key. The collapse of classical liberalism, and its replacement by a liberalism in which ends rather than means become supreme, does indeed make the task of social science harder. A consensus over instruments to pursue truths is far closer to social science and public policy concerns than an ideology in which all fundamental issues of distinction—class, race, gender, ethnic, national—are taken for granted, and we are left with the deadly chore of realizing what others declare to be universal goals. The problems of liberalism are real enough, and heavy enough. But the problem of social science is compounded by the new liberalism by converting the scientific into the heuristic. For this reason it bears constant repetition that social research is not attached to any particular ideology, since one of its missions, as Mannheim knew perfectly well, is a critique of all ideologies. That was the aim of *Radicalism and the Revolt against Reason* thirty-five years ago. It remains our shared mission today.

Jeanne Guillemin

My work on *Taking Lives* benefited greatly at the time of publication from the wisdom and support of Anselm Strauss, who wrote the foreword to the book; and now, it benefits no less from the contextual as well as content analysis rendered by Jeanne Guillemin. One of the more humbling aspects of this volume is the frequent comparison to Max Weber. But I have already addressed this elsewhere. The comparison of my work on genocide and state power with the monumental efforts of Hannah Arendt to understand the nature of modern totalitarianism also pays me an undeserved compliment.

Wearing Hannah Arendt's name as the special chair I have held at Rutgers University since 1979 has always struck me as a grave responsibility—no pun intended—one that imposes a deep responsibility to discharge with honor as well as intellect. For Arendt understood that in the world of human affairs, the moral basis of action involves judgments and doctrines that go far beyond intellect as such. Whether this is a plus or minus is hard to say. Certainly, a Peircian would cite this disjunction as evidence for the frailty of the human condition. I suspect that as a neo-Kantian, Arendt would simply accept the disjunction as fact or as datum, and proceed from there to explain why it should be so. We also owe to her a deeper understanding of the disastrous consequences of the pervasive separation of the intellectual from the ethical.

It is true that if in social theory we are all the children of Weber, then in political theory we should be the children of Arendt! That does not imply a slavish imitation of her efforts or even agreement with many of her admittedly controversial propositions about the polis. It does signify an awareness that, uniquely, she helped to set the tone of the twentieth-century debates on the nature of human freedom and the place of arbitrary power in curbing such freedom. Of course, she was not alone in this task. Aleksandr Solzhenitsyn in Russia, Raymond Aron in France, Isaiah Berlin in England, Jean Francois Revel, and Jacob Talmon in Israel are a few of the people who come quickly and readily to mind. Together, they gave renewed meaning to the European political tradition.

So the first thing I would do to amend Guillemin's essay is to note that Arendt herself was part of a democratic upsurge in search of a theory. While she was indeed European in origins and orientation, her love affair with America should not be minimized. Guillemin does well to recall Arendt's illuminating comparisons of the French and American revolutions precisely in terms that favored the latter. The French made a revolution based upon passion, and as a result, it soon led to bloodshed and revenge rather than the much desired freedom, liberty, and equality. The American founders made a revolution based on compassion, a rich blend of British tradition and Greek theory, which enabled the revolution not only to survive, but to do so with a minimum of bloodshed or indeed without taking lives and making victims out of losers.

Guillemin is quite probing in seeing such a vision as essentially based on the individual rather than the social system, and aimed at erasing disciplinary boundaries rather than necessarily enriching one at the expense of another. Indeed, although Arendt held a post in the faculty of political science, she mentioned to me that she never so much as took a course in the subject, much less felt at home teaching it! I do not believe that such a starting point in the person is necessarily conservative, any more than a starting point in the social structure is necessarily radical. Rather, Arendt and I share the same suspicion of a starting point that places systems maintenance above human life. To hold the former dearly and the latter cheaply is neither conservative nor radical. It is just plain dangerous for the care and feeding of people. Guillemin knows this well, and for that I am appreciative.

Problems arise less in general propositions and more in specific propositions. For example, the issue of the uniqueness of the Holocaust versus the generality of genocide is an important issue. It is fought over by people on the same side—the democratic side—of the academic barricades. But it nonetheless is a complex and divisive issue. I am not certain that Guillemin appreciates the distinction between the total, 100 percent destruction, or attempt at destruction, of the Jewish people, and say, the partial, 10 percent destruction of the Polish people. It is a terrible fact of Nazi rule that millions of Polish people as well as Jewish people perished during the Second World War. But it is an even more terrible fact that these numbers represent different phenomenon in qualitative, sociological terms.

I do not think that *Eichmann in Jerusalem* got it quite right. The behavior of one man in the dock may have been "banal" but this was intellectual hubris. Arendt mistook talk for action. This psychologizing of the victimizer caused her to lose her usually sound political judgment. For, in fact, nothing was ordinary about the Holocaust. It represented a fundamental shift in Nazi war aims: from any possible victory over the Allied powers to a decimation of a captive people. Raul Hilberg, Lucy Dawidowicz, and R. J. Rummel, among others, have documented how this shift occurred, and with what terrible and special consequences for the Jewish people. The Nazis sought, and achieved, a victory of sorts out of the ashes of its pending defeat. They succeeded in the destruction of an entire people, even as their empire crumbled. One witnessed the anomaly of German troop trains to the Russian front being held up so that human beings could be led to the slaughter houses of Eastern Europe along the same tracks.

In this, people like Talmon and Berlin better understood the nature of totalitarianism than Arendt. It is perfectly sound to say that subject peoples have a way of surviving—that natality rather than mortality may be the optimistic side of the coin when it comes to evaluating the situation of the Jewish people fifty years after the Holocaust. But one needs to be careful in distinguishing the Shoah from genocides against other peoples. Guillemin asks a rhetorical question: "If the Holocaust pertains only to Jews, and can be understood and interpreted only by them, who else should care?" If I may dare offer a response: The Holocaust does pertain uniquely to Jews. For even if other genocides take as many or nearly as many lives— whether in Armenia in the past or Cambodia in the recent present— the effort to totally destroy a people is different than the effort to partially destroy and thereby render helpless a people.

As for the second part, of course, any person of sound mind and good will can interpret the Holocaust. This has never been in question. The real problem has been in the rhetorical third part of that sentence: "who else should care?" The answer is that precious few did actually care! The consciousness of the Holocaust has become generally diffused among the populations of the Western democracies far more recently than the acts of barbarism as such. Indeed, one might argue that had more people cared, and in operational terms that would have meant at the least establishing an early warning system worldwide, the consequences of the Holocaust might have been mitigated if not entirely averted.

In my writings I have often called attention to the microscopic details of the Holocaust. By that I mean the everyday occurrences. A decade separates the coming to power of the Nazis from the most hideous wholesale period of slaughter. Indeed, five years separates Kristallnacht from the round-the-clock burnings and gassings of human beings at Auschwitz. The key to understanding totalitarianism—well known by Arendt, Aron, and Talmon alike—is the evolution of political evil. The extermination of a people does not take place on the day power is seized. But it is the outcome of a lengthy process. All is not lost on day one of the new dictatorship. All is lost when nothing is done on day two to reverse the process.

I say this not as criticism of Guillemin's overall position, which I entirely share, but as a response to the idea that we can relativize death completely. The need for a genocide convention is real. The need to defend the interests of the Armenian people or specific Indian tribes under assault are genuine. But we need to understand the clinical nature of the assault on Jews as an effort to destroy a theology no less than a people, a classical culture no less than its human carriers. It is the totality of the Nazi effort that was so unique. In that, not even Stalinism rivaled Hitlerism—even though in overall raw figures, the number of lives taken by the communists may, and by a two to one margin did in fact, actually exceed those taken by the Nazis.

For the rest, I find myself in deep sympathy with Guillemin's paper. It is a finely rendered account of my work against Arendt's backdrop. It is a matter of pride to receive such comparative analysis. Indeed, I probably owe more to Arendt than I was able to acknowledge in my 1964 review of her work *On Revolution.* For example, I am not quite as certain of the "populist" strain as Guillemin indicates was the case for Arendt in 1972. Her book after all is a sharp reminder that popular theories of democracy can quickly turn into popular moods of antidemocratic practices. In this, she was at one with Talmon's masterpiece on totalitarianism. She may have been a "revolutionary conservative" as I noted, but, unlike Georges Sorel, she was not a conservative revolutionary! And the distinction here is vital and certainly favors Arendt over the French anarcho-syndicalist.

But in the great pull of time, these neat distinctions are intimate discourses among friends. The larger issues, the central frames of reference, are so well reasoned and understood by Guillemin, that I can only utter or mutter a sense of gratitude for her effort in adding her voice to a still small chorus of social scientists who see the issues of birth no less than those of death, the giving of life no less than taking lives as central considerations for any twenty-first century social science that claims to be morally worthy and empirically viable.

Abraham Edel

It is a great privilege to comment on Abe Edel's reflections on my past work, since his role in my intellectual formation surely ranks so high as to be nonquantifiable. He not only was a master teacher of ethics, he also permitted, nay compelled one to reflect on one's own inherited beliefs. Edel gives meaning to the concept of teacher as role model: instilling a love of the dialectic of learning, civility in the conduct of discourse, and intelligence in the study of self and others. And like all great teachers, Edel was something of a paradox, even in the late 1940s: gentle of manner but tough to the point of dogmatism in belief, a relativist in the study of the world but a moralist in the process of behavior. I suspect that this combination of personal affability and unbending scholarship is what made him so special in my eyes and to my mind.

Thank God for the City College of New York (CCNY). For whatever else was wrong with that school—and even in the mythical 1940s, it was not just a blessed place for the poor—one could hardly go through its education system without questioning every inherited premise. Neither the method of authority nor the faith in tradition were enough, only the emphasis on evidence and experience. Indeed, this was a university based as much on the work of Charles Sanders Peirce as upon that of Morris Raphael Cohen. And if this were true for the school as a whole, it was doubly so for the philosophy department to which I was attached and belonged. This was a department that fiercely fought out the battles of the society more keenly than most. The people Morris Cohen chose to teach in that department reflected that spirit of open debate and Socratic dialogue that infected all of the students.

To reflect on the professors in that department was itself an exercise in reverence as well as recall. I had Mortimer Kadish, who went on to Case Western Reserve, as my first teacher in basic philosophy. And now, a half century later, I find myself publisher of his major works. I had Arthur Pap in formal and symbolic logic. Pap was at CCNY only for a short while. But to have him as a teacher was to experience Wittgenstein, and not just to learn truth tables. He brought a touch of Europe with its conceits and cultivation to our Harlem campus. If a better grounding was possible in the logic of social science, I have not heard it. It should be a mandatory starting point for all those who go into empirical research or theoretical exegesis; only in this way can the young learn not to reinvent the wheel, to presume an act of discovery what may well have been known to the pre-Socratics. One learns how to think, and one also learns that others long before us have thought.

My professor of political theory was the very fine Henry M. Magid. I recollect him saying one day: "How strange it is that the empirical world moves with such startling rapidity, while the moral world drags its feet so slowly." We hardly give a backward glance to Euclid, but we still read Plato with the same sense of curiosity and wonder that must have been true for members of Plato's own academy. This dichotomy of an empirical world of change and a moral world of structure has been very much part of the way I have thought of social life since my undergraduate days. Indeed, if I were to summarize the entire twentieth century it is one that exhibits miracles of electronics, flight, and medicine at one end and the horrors of the Holocaust and repeated acts of genocide across the globe at the other. I fear that Magid, which is Hebrew for a wise man, was terribly much on target. He was a sad man who died prematurely and left too little by way of a literary output. I have always suspected this duality of vision haunted him, and explains much about the collectivity as a whole.

The City College Department of Philosophy of the 1940s was the center of gravity of the social science honors program. This curiosity was more a function of a group of men (for indeed, they were all men at the time) for whom worldly events played so important a role in personal development. Yervant Krikorian was not just an epistemologist, but a strong figure in worldly Armenian efforts to develop an intellectual posture. Daniel Bronstein was not just a logician but a powerful critic of communism in all its forms. Phillip P. Weiner not only was an expert in American pragmatism but a veteran of the Spanish Civil War. Henry Magid was not just a student of utilitarianism, but a forceful advocate of Jewish causes. Edel was not simply an ethical theorist, but a leader in faculty efforts at unionization.

All of these people had rich lives, too rich to be encumbered by a pure theory of logical empiricism. As a result, the department became a vestige of past efforts to broaden the vision of philosophy to include the word "social" and a harbinger of future efforts to become political. Relevance was not so much a goal, but an everyday experience. As a result, the social science honors program was spearheaded by this group. One could hardly expect otherwise; for these were the children, the intellectual offspring of Morris Raphael Cohen. This was Cohen's department and these were Cohen's children. And the cohort that gathered about this clan were the grandchildren of Cohen. And is this not what the process of teaching and learning is all about—the maintenance and extension of our culture?

The great fault line was less philosophical than ideological. For, in retrospect, it was the broad commitment to naturalism that united the City College people. To be sure, it was a naturalism tinged with an excessive faith in scientism. But a certain optimism also infused the spirit of M. R. Cohen. CCNY, unlike Chicago, had a philosophy department more at home with Aristotle than with Plato among the ancients, and certainly more at ease with John Dewey than with Josiah Royce among the American classical figures in philosophy. Perhaps in this instance, the impact of Columbia was equal to that of Cohen! But the professorate differed fully and bitterly over questions of ideology, of political rather than metaphysical belief—in Marxism with or without Leninism-Stalinism, or in socialism with or without Marxism. Here stood a bunch of happy atheists ready to die for the faith in one or another variety of socialism!

The impulse to move from philosophy as linguistic analysis to sociology as political analysis was thus very strong. Add to this volatile mixture an intellectual environment in which everyone from Friedrich Engels to Ludwig Wittgenstein were preaching the same message—the death of classical metaphysics and epistemology, and the birth of positive social science—and some sense of what the City College environment contributed to my development becomes somewhat clearer. And in this process Edel loomed largest for me. His broad knowledge in the history of social thought, coupled with a piercing sense of how ethical issues are framed and formed in specific anthropological and sociological contexts, seemed the very perfection of learning, and for me the height of the educational experience.

Some of that comes through in the first part of the chapter that Edel contributes to this volume. And I will forego any specific reply, since it stands as a working paper in the communitarian tradition, one in which the play of words like community and communication are part of a larger picture of efforts to create social integration at higher levels. So I would rather confine my remarks to Edel's specific categorizations of my work—both intellectually and operationally, with respect to Transaction. Indeed, since I will be commenting at some length on other papers that take up my work with respect to Transaction, I can further narrow my reply down to the final few pages, in which Edel sees my work as falling into three periods.

It is indeed proper to note that my early work was connected to social philosophy, and that I moved over to the study of the sociology of knowledge, and, by the late 1960s, took up questions of Latin America. But like life as such, such divisions are far too neat and tidy. I have continued to write on questions of war and peace as I did all my life. I continue to be fascinated by how sometimes lesser (I will not call them minor) figures such as Giordano Bruno, Claude Helvetius, and George Sorel illumine major themes. And I remain deeply interested in Latin American affairs, although the foci has shifted from Argentina and Brazil to Cuba and the Caribbean.

These are simply illustrative of long-standing interests in conflict and consensus, development and change, and the history of social and political thought as such. These are not periods, so much as dots along the way to giving shape to substance. We all divide up our worlds into manageable chunks: for some, the divisions are between epistemology, ethics, and ontology; for others, between sociology, psychology, and politics; and for me, between how people interact, when interactions yield results, and why the actions of some count for so much, while those of others hardly matter at all. In this sense, I probably am more indebted to the work of Harold Lasswell, whom I happily got to know later in life, than to my formal academic mentors.

Carving up the world implies a concern with putting it back together again. And this is where the early training in philosophy has proven to be of inestimable value. For the rage for syntheses even more than the concern for analysis characterized the work of the City College group I was fortunate enough to work with. And this group, through the social science-integrated program, included outstanding people in psychology, history, and political science. They all seemed to share in the ethos of the college. The metaphysical question: "what does it mean?" pre-empted the epistemological question: "is it true or false?" This is not to in any way imply that the group was cloudy, or lacked a commitment for precision. Rather, the passion was reserved for levels of generalization that seem, in retrospect, less characteristic of other times and places in my life.

In that process, in that search for the synthetic, mistakes were made. Some of them were serious: the terrible overestimation of the positive value of the Soviet contribution to civilization, and even more, the terrible underestimation of the costs in human life to forms of society that promised so much and delivered so little by way of economic development. Edel was not exempt from such mistakes. That they were made in the name of the good old cause, in the name of equity and decency, helps assuage a sense of guilt, but only marginally. The fact is that the absolutism practiced was different from the relativism preached. It was not until the extraordinary work of Arendt, Lasky, Solzhenitsyn, Popper, Aron, and Hook—the Europeans and Europeanized Americans who saw the communist future and knew it was not working—that we were bailed out of an intellectual impasse, worse a quagmire.

The City College group prepared us, or at least myself, to deal with the master themes of modernity with honesty and compelling directness. The debt to people like Edel can thus never be overestimated. But they themselves could not get beyond the quarrels of the day, or, for that matter, the disputations among themselves, into the larger and fuller picture needed to make sense of the world. In this, we were at least prepared by the City College experience to cope with the "greats" of the century as they were known in the first half of the century; we were "turned on" to Keynes, Toynbee, Mannheim, Weber, Dewey, Freud. We read their texts, not snippets in anthologies. We studied them as if they were an extension of Talmud. We argued about Trotsky, Stalin, Kautsky, and Liebnecht, but we did so "armed" with the practice of high theory. For this, among many other things, I remain eternally grateful to Edel's role in this process of discovery and growth.

Aaron Wildavsky

Aaron's contribution goes to the heart of the matter of democracy directly and unambiguously: to what extent is the notion lodged in economic, political, and cultural considerations. It is clear that for Aaron, democracy is, in its origins and practice, a cultural formation. Indeed, in other writings he makes it clear that the great difficulty in installing democratic regimes overnight or even over decades is a matter of culture, not politics, and still less economics. The Russians are quite capable of reading books on parliamentary procedure. And they have shown a remarkable ability to adapt to the ways and wiles of the marketplace in theory. They are less able to assure such practices at an everyday level. Overthrowing totalitarian regimes is a precondition for democratic rule. But it is not a sufficient reason for democratic regimes. We have all learned this disjunction painfully in the rise of rampant nationalisms that have replaced rigid communisms in Eastern Europe and the former Soviet Union. And Aaron's work on a wide variety of subjects—from public budgeting to environmental risk—have constantly emphasized the big gulf between getting rid of miserable governments and installing worthwhile cultures.

It is for this reason that his approach to democracy rests on a presumably simple homily: "the willingness to leave office when defeated at the polls." The key to this resides in the word "willingness." For inherent in Wildavsky's theory of democracy is the concept of choice to be sure, but no less the concept of culture that makes choice acceptable as a mode of political behavior. It all sounds simple, until one looks at a Freedom House map of open and closed societies in the world. There is simply no automatic correlation between open economies and open societies. On the other hand, there is a quite high correlation of closed economies and closed societies. And that is why the key to the puzzle of democracy takes a cultural form.

My own thinking on this subject, and several others as well, is so close to Wildavsky's that there is small point in simply repeating what he said better over the years. Perhaps the one area in which we had a slight difference of emphasis is on the role of the private person in a democratic order. True to the political science tradition, especially the one so brilliantly crafted at Yale University over the years, Aaron dealt with democracy as a process of participation. I have always felt, and do so even more keenly now, that the subject of democracy must also include as a vital element, nonparticipation. That is to say, a culture of consensus cannot be formed through coercing people into taking public action. While public participation is desirable, and even necessary to maintain a sense of public desires, there are a wide variety of issues and attitudes that are not shared, but not opposed either. Hence, the democratic system must allow for the private spirit; and that signifies a whole range of behavior that may include the idiosyncratic no less than the nonparticipatory.

Let me clarify this by immediately adding that by "private" I do not mean solipsism, but social. People have a sense of importance and a scale of values: space and time to oneself; commitment to friends and family over and above differences in belief systems; decisions that are not harmful to the public good, but not necessarily advantageous to the commonweal either. A democratic society cannot endure simply in terms of what leaders accomplish or how they rotate into or out of power. Those who possess power need a mandate to rule. But such a mandate may derive from the silent contentment of an electorate, and not only their participation or empowerment. I realize that such a position is not exactly part of the common vernacular, and that it raises serious questions about the extent to which such a high level of sanctioned privatization may itself contribute to an erosion of democracy. But as in so many other areas, this sociological sensibility about democracy is a risk that the political system must admit to if the cultural formation underwriting democracy is to persist. People will know when and how to participate "when the time comes." That is, after all, an article of democratic faith. At the same time, those who adhere to such a faith must accept the rights of citizens not to participate in every celebration or engage their minds and bodies for every crisis.

The discussions that Aaron and I had on the question of democracy touched on many of these points. But such discussions are necessarily and painfully ended by Aaron's untimely passing. The death of a scholar of Wildavsky's magnitude compels one to reflect on the public character of the contemporary state of social science in America, no less than on the personal characteristics of the deceased individual. Aaron was so much a mover and a shaker of national policy that his passing can only be considered a national tragedy. That I can write this in this festschrift without the slightest trace of hyperbole or embarrassment is itself testimonial to his stature.

Like any major figure, he may have been rooted in a specific discipline—in his case, political science—but he was not circumscribed by it. He wrote with equal fluency on subjects ranging from presidential policy-making, environmental politics, public budgeting and finance, biblical exegesis, planning in comparative international perspective, and the organization of scholarship and style of research. Whatever the theme or topic, Aaron created his own intellectual center of gravity. Like listening to Mozart, reading a work by Aaron was always both recognizable and distinctive, variations on the theme of authenticity. His opinions were always so sharply etched that, were they not deeply rooted in the best of social research, he could easily be jeered, or worse, dismissed by "specialists." As it was, Aaron's work has the wonderful capacity to be—nearly instantly—part of the master dialogue of the field on which he was writing.

Our personal relationship dated back thirty years. Indeed, it was about then that his famous essay "The Two Presidencies" appeared in the pages of *Transaction/Society*. In it Aaron outlined the duality of domestic and foreign policy functions inherent in the postmodern presidency. I would have to say that it is probably one of the top five articles reprinted in other places and in foreign languages. Aaron's work is so sharply etched and clearly stated that he was cited with unusual frequency; that such references were not always positive or flattering meant little to him, since for Aaron the soul of social science is in the dialogue itself.

Being comparable in age and background made our relationship special, or so I would like to believe. But it is probably the case that a person of quality always has the capacity to make one feel special. Aaron's family came from Poltava, next-door neighbors to mine, who came from Slavuta. We both grew up with strong Yiddish (rather than Hebrew) linguistic roots. Aaron was from Brooklyn, and I from Manhattan; the experience of being cement poor impacted us both. But comparisons shift into contrasts as well, since his family life was warm and supportive; his sense of family life is well reflected in his *Society* autobiographical article "The Boy from Poltava."

Aaron was of sturdy moral fiber. Like the prophets of whom he wrote, this characteristic is not always appreciated or understood. What at times came across as opinionated was in fact carefully rendered judgments on the implications of ideas no less than behavior. Indeed, he saw the two as inextricably linked. This gave his political science a peculiarly antipolitical cast. For unlike so many who dream the dreams of power, or at least of occupying a basement room in the White House, Aaron cared not one whit for personal aggrandizement of political power. He well understood that the demands of truth seeking pre-empted such blind ambitions. That is why *Speaking Truth to Power* was meant by Aaron to be taken as a theme, no less than a title, of one of his more famous works.

With the death of Aaron, our generation of scholarship has lost a maximum leader. His works, especially briefer essays collected in such volumes as *Speaking Truth to Power,* offer a quintessential, Montaigne-like insight into the proper use of the essay form as a social science vehicle for presenting moral dilemmas in a clear-eyed fashion. The chapter in this volume is clearly in that tradition. Whether the rising generation of scholarship can give us figures of equal or greater worth is purely speculative, hardly a fit subject for a brief digression on the passing of a dear friend, but that is the task, the challenge to be faced. For if a social science agenda in rigorous pursuit of both truth and meaning is to be maintained, and I think that it will be, then the work of Aaron Wildavsky will be a beacon directing our attention and energy. The transmission of a public culture is after all the ultimate purpose of a personal career. It is what Aaron would want from us. It is what we owe to his living memory.

I realize that this statement is less a response to what Aaron's paper is about than an encomium. However, to sit and take pot shots at a recently deceased colleague strikes me as singularly inappropriate. We both went through the long intellectual trek only to find that the victory belongs neither to political science and theories of power nor to sociology and doctrines of institutions. Instead, it turns out that culture in its purest anthropological sense is more determinant and less determined than our generation of researchers were ever willing to allow. It is a matter of chance that a festschrift does honor to me. But it is a matter of choice for me to pay homage to Aaron—one so close in spirit and in substance to my own interests.

Peter F. Drucker

I shall reverse the causal sequence in responding to Peter Drucker, by risking a commentary on rather than a response to his remarks. For I feel that our relationship has occasioned something special: a coming to terms with the risks of dictatorship in relation to entrepreneurship. Now I do not wish to imply that Peter has been silent on the need for democracy, or even the repugnant nature of totalitarian regimes. Rather, in an exchange stimulated by an essay of mine on "Hitler," Historians and the Holocaust" in *The Jewish Quarterly,* and now amplified in these remarks, "Politics in the West: Totalitarian and Democratic," Peter has turned his attention to Stalinism.

For Drucker is quite on target to see that this is the second time in a half century that political correctness has infected academic life; but even more, the web of totalitarian thought is unified by its premises—even when there are ostensible differences in ideologies. In a curious way, Drucker's chapter is the essential counterpart to the book written by Stephen Koch entitled *Double Lives,* a study of the covert Soviet propaganda network, in that both clearly understand that the bone in the throat of Bolshevism was the American tradition of liberalism in politics and free enterprise in economics.

Drucker notes that the first wave of Stalinism was directed at the American blacks—and when this failed, the American communist movement was given the assignment to penetrate the trade union movement. And when in turn this failed, then the academy in particular and intellectual life in general became a target of Stalinism. While these were overlapping projects, what is both true and disturbing, is Drucker's reminder that the totalitarian temptation, as Jean Francois Revel calls it, was held at bay not by the academy as such, but by a few brave administrative figures. The rise of McCarthyism became a vehicle for the dismantling of the academic apparatus precisely because the universities were so inept to engage in discourse or capable of debate with its own communists.

I would add, and elsewhere discuss, that the academic struggles at the City College of the City University of New York were launched, indicating that some struggles were indeed mounted. But these resistances were sporadic. Drucker makes an interesting distinction between the first and second waves of political correctness: The Stalinists aimed at capturing the liberal arts, professors in the disciplines. But now, the essential path to political correctness is the administrative apparatus, those who control budgets and appointments within the bureaucracy as such. In a strange way, the new extremists are far more adroit at the politics of economics than were the old Marxists, despite their claims to being in possession of a science of society.

The understanding that Drucker brings to the issue is the need for the democratic persuasion to be fought for with an uncompromising passion, in his words, with commitment, relevance, and values. Most disturbing is the thought that Drucker puts forth that political correctness may make the university a place of the higher irrelevancies, not that it will succeed in shaping the minds and hearts of the young. In the absence of victories in the "real world" we face the prospect of extremist victories in the "academic world." What makes this so risky is not only the absurdity of this dichotomy, but in accepting such a dualism, we ignore the very real fact that the structure of academic lives and communities are much rooted in the real world.

I am grateful for Drucker's gracious words about my own role in the struggle against Stalinism and its aftermath. Indeed, the purpose of putting out a collection of my briefer pieces entitled *Persuasions and Prejudices* was to show that my thought over time has indeed shown a political consistency. But by that I do not mean political rigidity. Rather, it was and remains an urgent requirement to bring to bear social scientific criteria for measuring the worth or truth content of political statements. The old formulas about liberalism and social science do not work because liberalism itself has become something quite different than a New Deal struggle for decency in the workplace and equity in treatment. Liberalism has frequently become the ideology of affirmative action, of political correctness, of a multiculturalism in which there exist satrapies but no center. As such it can no longer be entreatied to serve a useful academic or scientific role.

If a third wave of political correctness is not to be an agenda item, and still more serious, a second wave of McCarthyism—defined by MacKinnonism—is to be avoided, then the capacity of social science to act as a "cause" for itself and in itself will need to be considered. The easy alliances of social science in the past with the liberal persuasion of British constitutional tradition, or the conservative faith in German statist beliefs must give way to something superior, and that something is the appreciation of how social science is to society what physical science is to nature: a modest map and guide to the world being studied and managed.

Throughout the century, social science has come up short with respect to a critique of the political process. Our inner history is stamped by colleagues serving as cruel masters of Nazism by designing "demographic studies" isolating the areas of concentration of Jews in Berlin or Vienna. Others have subverted the science of physiological psychology by converting Pavlov's work into rubbish about the "creation of a new man." Others still have confused the study of society with the art of revolution making. Too many well-intentioned liberated sociologists have proffered "revolutions of the mind" predicated on the use of drugs and sex as recreation, all the while playing Russian roulette with risks of injury through overdose and death through communicable disease. It is to Drucker's credit that he understands well that McCarthyism is no answer to Stalinism, and that reaction is of little use in the struggle against racialism.

It is interesting how, in my own work, I have drawn such deep inspiration from George Orwell, Aleksandr Solzhenitsyn, Raymond Aron, Albert Camus, and such "marginalized" figures as Robert Nisbet, Sidney Hook, Lewis Feuer, and Lezek Kolakowski—and not a few of the senior figures represented in this work. But in the main, the social scientific community has retained a cool and correct silence when it comes to the former Soviet Union and its satellites. Too many have taken to the spurious argument that communism is dead, long live socialism, as if Marxism were a new Thomism, in which the historic church (or party) sins, but never the idea of perfection embodied in the church (or party) triumphant. Such figures save their hostile rhetoric precisely for the Druckers of the world, for those who seek to show the empirical and the ethical correlates of political democracy to a business civilization. But this is struggle that must be fought. Moreover, it is struggle that must be won if the United States is to prevail intact. From Milton Friedman to Michael Novak this is understood. But from too many other mainline figures such basic approaches are neither understood, nor when understood, appreciated.

This is not a pretty picture, but then again, the world that Drucker has observed and painted in his autobiographical memoirs of Europe and America are not especially inviting. In this shared struggle for a university in which the free exchange of ideas is not corrupted by dogmatism or polluted by deracination, we find further justification for the title *The Democratic Imagination*. But for now, winning the cold war off campus should be viewed as an opportunity for victory on campus. Should this eventuality not come to pass, then the role of social research in relation to both domestic and foreign policy will change dramatically.

My own surmise is that we already see some broad structural changes of near irreversible proportions, with basic social research taking place in places like the Abt Associates, RAND Corporation, the American Enterprise Institute, and within government at agencies such as the General Accounting Office and the Bureau of Management and Budget. The universities threaten to become emptied of meaningful social content. This would be a catastrophe on the way to a new round of totalitarianism. And the students of the next generation would be left to hang out to dry in a closed world of open minds. The decomposition of sociology need not be celebrated by others with snickers of delight, for such terminal cancers await all those who substitute ideological purity for scientific research.

Such a negative scenario is hardly inevitable, nor is it uniform—even for sociology. But we have the examples of Nazi Germany and Soviet Russia to indicate that the life of learning cannot only be menaced, but even castrated in the service of totalitarian regimes. Drucker is not asking that we believe in some abstract history, only in his own concrete experience. It sounds like history by virtue of his years of eloquent service. But for the young it should be viewed as little else than an early warning signal that all is not well in the democratic culture.

Walter Laqueur

I have had the opportunity to express my overall appreciation for the work of Walter Laqueur in the festschrift that appeared in his honor several years ago. So if I pass over the encomiums to the substance of his essay, I hope that he appreciates the fact that his towering contributions to the scholarship of twentieth-century life is factored into every word of this response. Social scientists frequently bemoan the fact that their ideas do not "travel well," do not "cross borders" despite shared methodologies. This has certainly not been a problem for Walter, whose works are as well read in Moscow, Berlin, London, and Jerusalem as in Washington D.C. Dare one speculate that the fault in the lack of social scientific universalism inheres not in the discipline but in the topics and treatments?

This chapter on anti-Americanism engages Walter as social investigator no less than historian, and it compels a consideration of basic issues that extend beyond those of Germany: the contradictions between elites and masses, media mavens and actual public opinion, youth and age, and moods and actions. Indeed, the last may be the most innovative part of the essay, since the measurement of phenomenon-like "anti-Americanism" involves what George Homans liked to call sentiments rather than acts.

My own statement on anti-Americanism in the Third World focused on Latin America. And it may well be that my findings disappointed those who work with the category of anti-Americanism as a central phenomenon of our times, or at least of the cold war times. I was struck by how little anti-Americanism figured into "classical" Marxist figures in South America. Indeed, many of the old timers I had gotten to know in Argentina in the late 1950s were exceptionally fond of the United States, and felt a special kinship for the English language. If anything, they felt that the advanced stage of American industry would make the transition from capitalism to socialism simpler and far less painful than it was in the Soviet Union. They also had a healthy regard for democratic processes and legal safeguards of individual rights. In other words, the sources of animosity toward the United States were not embedded in Marxist ideology as such.

So then, where is one to find anti-Americanism? And here we have a set of answers ranging from national xenophobia, to generational conflict, to political rivalry. Indeed, Laqueur continually draws our attention to the confused and contradictory elements in survey research data on a wide range of issues involving the United States, from troop withdrawal to cultural penetration of the media. He brilliantly summarizes the situation by saying that "the problem of the young generation in Germany is not the existence of a strong anti-American movement, but the absence of a party of freedom, or to put it differently, the inability of Western democracy to imbue our own children with its own values."

One is tempted to say that this is no less a problem within American shores as well. After all, the struggle about multiculturalism and political correctness has to do precisely with the issue of what it means to be an American. Having defined Americanism as a series of etchings by the late Norman Rockwell, it becomes a short step for the politics of sentiment to blame every ailment currently extant on the wealthiest nation on earth. The reason that anti-American cuts right and left is that the assault on plutocracy (especially mendacious in national socialist propaganda) is a staple of the politics of discontent as such. And discontent is obviously higher in the young than the old. For it is the young who feel far less obligated to conform to the social order.

I am somewhat skeptical of the notion of anti-Americanism as an explanatory variable. There are just too many contradictions to make it work. Every nation is assigned unpleasant characteristics, which may be more or less accurate. Every culture defends itself by a assaulting others that may be threatening its supremacy—in that the French are probably far more hostile to the United States than the Germans! And every generation sees power as such as a risk and danger, and cries to be left alone. In this, the big power is the parental authority writ large. But the skips and jumps from mass youth sentiments to the precise forms of ideological animosity exhibited by Frankfurt critical theory are simply too much to contain the concept of anti-Americanism as a viable concept or even a heuristic tool of analysis.

Laqueur himself appreciates the dilemma in the concept, since he concludes that adopting American modes of dress and fast food eating does not necessarily translate into support for NATO. And he allows for the fact that the spirit of "anti" is part of being young, whatever the object of assault. What I asked in *The Knowledge Factory* still troubles me: To what extent is the youth question one of social class? In an age in which large categories of industrial life have collapsed or atrophied, we must seek to explain new forms of organization to explain political action and social movements. The great strength of the young is their energy and courage to act. The great weakness is that such characteristics are transitory in nature. Being young is after all more than a matter of style or belief, it is a fact of biology. And biology is a more potent category than sociology in explaining behavior!

My own feeling is that anti-Americanism is a footnote to traditionalism, or, put negatively, the revolt against modernity. The United States has, for much of the century, exemplified modernity no less than democracy. And it was with the rise of the Third World that one began to see the rise in anti-Americanism. Hence, clericalism, traditionalism, and plain old-fashioned totalitarianism are better guides to the anti-American spirit than the attitudes of rival great powers, or segments thereof. In this, I suspect that we can expect to see anti-Americanism come into play within the United States precisely by those sectors and groups for whom the values of modernization and a commercial civilization itself become anathema, or at least subject to challenge. And in the absence of a communist rival power, such sentiments can be given free play with a minimum amount of risk.

Ultimately, the analysis of ideology and belief must be anchored to the studies of class, race, nation, ethnicity, gender, religiosity, and so forth. These are the basic social scientific variables that serve to explain and predict behavior. Otherwise, anti-Americanism becomes an appellation attached to survey research data, and becomes further an ephemeral framework bound to lose its potency. Laqueur well notes that ideological trashing does not mean an unwillingess to perform basic obligations—either for Germans or other youths. And hence, we must examine more deeply how the subjects of nationalism and generations become the stuff of rivalry between nations and generations. To do otherwise is to get wrapped up in a defense of America or so-called Americanism, and thus to lose the very objectivity we need in approaching ideological sentiments and political biases.

If I may conclude this note on Laqueur's essay by referring to his opening remarks: I do not believe that it is correct to speak of anti-Americanisnm as something "to be found among the left as on the right." Quite the contrary, the appellation deserves to be confined to the left, because the right has uniformly seen itself as a guardian of Americanism as an ideology. For better or worse, within a domestic context, it is the left that carries the force of anti-Americanism. The anomaly is that in Europe the reverse seems to be the case: It is the extreme right that has spoken with full force and animus on the American civilization. This is one reason why contexts must always be specified, not for pedantic but for analytic reasons.

There are limits to antinationalism as well as to nationalism. The study of German youth may benefit from such a concept, but the study of American youth may not yield such fruitful results. For that reason, historians and social scientists need to work in closer concert with each other, not to amuse one another with theories, but to refine each other's sensibilities in areas where the study of ideological formations intersect with critical factors in stratification, such as youth and age, and wealth and poverty. This is not so much a criticism of Laqueur, as a plea to a professional world in which social scientists meet historians only at the plane of political analysis, ignoring the equally critical study of national structures and economic systems.

Martha Crenshaw

As Martha Crenshaw well knows, my interest in questions of political terrorism derive from larger theoretical concerns with the anarchist and revolutionary traditions as such. And at a yet higher level of abstraction, my concern is how rulers and ruled alike must balance order and change, systemic survival with systematic innovation. It is this intellectual mooring that prevented me from converting a tactic—which is what terrorism is, an effort to force-feed change—into a theory, or worse, a journal! My work in the early 1960s on the *fin de siècle*, antirationalist radical movements, and anarchism as such, made me aware of the extent to which the problem of terror can best be seen as part of the process of revolution.

At the same time, and at the risk of sounding like a political idealist, much of the impulse for terrorism derives from a powerful imagery of the state as a handmaiden of repressive, exploitative social classes. For the symbolism of "smashing state power" or "seizing state power" only makes sense if in fact the state functions in this cruel "antisocial" fashion. In every case I know, the ideology of the terrorist is linked to the metaphor of a heartless state. Terrorism needs victimizers as well as victims, for otherwise the terrible cost in human life often extracted, or at least demanded, cannot be justified.

The other side of my own thinking is linked to the tradition of Montesquieu in France and John Stuart Mill in England—and that might be called, and variously has, the meliorative or constitutional model of the state—in such a doctrine of checks and balances the state is not the armed praetorian guard of the bourgeoisie (or any other class), but the relatively autonomous, and at times, benign, guardian of the rights of the poor, or at least the adjudicator of all people. Liberal and conservative politicians alike share in this constitutional framework. Again, this very coupling permits the terrorist to see the enemy as larger than life, or at least, larger than any single ideological opponent.

This latter constitutional model invites fine-tuning through the policy process, not the smashing of state machinery. The collapse of the communist empire did not necessarily signify the end of the antiterrorist model. Indeed, the Marxian and communist tradition was terribly worried about terrorism in its own right; from Stalin to Gorbachev, terrorism as a prime method has been ridiculed, more out of fear than any animosity of the terrorists.

The state turns out to the enemy of the terrorists, whether it be the proletarian or bourgeois state. For the terrorist, it is, of course, authority as such that defines the enemy within. For terrorism, whatever else, again as Martha Crenshaw so nicely articulates, is a tactic dedicated to the reduction and ultimate elimination of legitimacy from existing political authority. Indeed, one problem of the terrorists is any sort of success, as in the Paris Uprisings of 1968, since the vacuum created does not easily translate into new forms of authority and law, but just more and different types of terrorism. This is also the Robespierre problem writ large.

So the deep structure of violence and terror is not related to the silly relativist formula of one man's terrorism is another man's revolution. but rather goes to the mental set of a post-Hegelian world in which the state fails to command universal affection and respect, and the reverse generates animus and hatred. This mental set of the person of violence is key. Those who believe in the meliorative potentials of a political order are hardly likely to see mechanisms of change beyond or outside the extant system. But those who deny any meliorative potential to the existing order, who see themselves as having no stake in the social order, offer fertile grounds for recruitment to acts of terror.

Martha's summary of the current status of research and knowledge on terrorism is pellucid, and her evaluation of my own contribution to the area is more than fair. Indeed, this is an area that has benefited greatly from cross-disciplinary work, with political scientists like Ted Gurr, Harold Lasswell, Thomas Schelling, Alex Schmid, and Paul Wilkinson taking the lead. This is an international group, and hence an international effort at analysis. So one might well ask, why is it that sociologists and psychologists have lagged so badly in the study of terrorism? Why indeed have those who might have been expected to pioneer in the research area, or in the actual study of those defined and detailed as terrorists, been studied so loosely and randomly. For we are in an area, which Martha herself well appreciates, where there is as much fascination with the examiners as the examined.

My answer ex cathedra for the sociological neglect is the incredible commitment to a pair of contrasting ideologies that have proven barren. First, there are those who think of the social system as an equilibrium, something like a clock, which "functions" well when it runs properly and on time. This confusion of Calvinism with scientism has led an older generation of scholars to either neglect terrorism, or perceive of it as an aberration as part of a larger disparagement of conflict models of behavior. To be sure, the "conflict theorists" have hardly helped matters by seeing themselves as involved in a holy war with "consensus theorists."

The plain fact that conflict and a variety of strategies for gaining ends that are outside the social equilibrium are as natural as consensus, and that their sense of a stake in the social order is a natural condition of society, is repugnant to those who think that war has anything to do with peace, that they are each other's mirror image at the level of the human psyche no less than the political system. The academic class simply finds abhorrent the Hobbesian idea of war and conflict as a natural state. We prefer to inject our moral preferences for tranquility into the historical realities of intranquilities.

As a result, we find the notion of terrorism as a strategy for what the French call making a rupture simply disgraceful. But we also then turn about and claim that certain acts of physical violence are simply matters of civil disobedience and are moral, while similar acts that are marked as unpleasant are best seen as terrorist in character, unworthy of statement of moral probity in the perpetrators as a guiding purpose.

This is not a plea for a return to a pure theory of relativism; again, as Martha well enunciates, we are not dealing with a simplistic model of "one man's terrorist is another's freedom fighter." That formulation is simple-minded. Rather, it is that forms of violence as strategies sometime involve acts of mayhem and murder, and even entail the punishment of third persons, or innocent parties. This may be viewed as a morally repugnant and legal reprehensible way of seeking social or political change. And one may argue for stringent judicial and political measures to combat such forms of seeking change outside of democratic norms, but this strikes me as a different line of argument than either pure relativism or pure morality.

The struggle for democracy is precisely rooted in the procedural basis for seeking and gaining change. Terrorism is universally a tact and strategy for seeking changes, whatever their character, outside of such democratic procedures. Clearly, in situations in which democracy or democratic options are not available, terrorism outside the state differs from state terrorism in volume and style. The mass execution of people in Nazi Germany, or in Idi Amin's Uganda, or dozens of other places described by R. J. Rummel in his massive and unique works work on the subject cannot be defended against the terrors of the defenders of the

Warsaw Ghetto, unless one has a Hegelian-like passion for law as order, and order as passivity.

The challenge of terrorism, as is customarily understood, is to test the norms of democracy, to remain open to the private lives of persons while resisting the capacity of a few people to destroy the system of the many; again the sense of stake is important, as is the fact that terrorism produces antibodies, stimulating enormous resistance to changes in the social order that are unwanted and unsanctioned.

The study of terrorism compels us to treat the impulse to war as close to the surface as those sentiments compelling to peace. We know from Hobbes that the Behemoth is strong and worthy of awe if not support. We know from Sorel that the anarch is equally compelling, and worthy of awe, if not support. Terrorism is the collective equivalent of manslaughter, of taking matters into one's own hands. For the most part, individuals perform acts of violence in disregard of politics. The terrorist is a person who performs similar deeds with the added scaffolding of an ideology. This may be nothing more than rationalization, or it may be a genuine cry of the heart. But whenever we study terrorism we are in the realm of the edges of human passion, the world of extremities; Lasswell was such a great figure because he understood this, and sought in a variety of ways to integrate not just pathology and politics but the violent nature of supposedly ordinary politics. We tend to celebrate those who take their own lives in a noble cause, the Buddhist monk who sets himself on fire as a way of calling attention to the condition of suppression in his part of the world. But we tend to denigrate those who set fire to others for the same purpose.

What we end up learning about terrorism is the tenuous and shaky nature of social orders as such. We also end up with a deeper sense of the democratic, that democracy is a process, a procedure, for adjudicating differences that can avoid life and death issues—whether of the suicidal or homicidal character—no less than a way of determining the more pedestrian issues of who rules or for how long. This is a distance from Martha's fine exposition, and, I must add, appreciation of my role in the study of terrorism. But it brings me full circle to where I started in 1956.

In an early work on *The Idea of War and Peace in Contemporary Philosophy* I looked at the great social and political figures to see what they had to say on the subject. I still find myself looking and reading the works of Russell, Whitehead, Einstein, James, and others—but with a heightened awareness that through the analysis of terror we are in a realm of the personal no less than the political, the moral no less than the military, the rational no less than the passionate. And if I may paraphrase and alter Alfred North Whitehead's judgment: In the realm of terror everything is a footnote to Aristotle's *Politics*—and not Plato's *Republic*!

Anselm Strauss

The key to understanding my view of policy-making is to appreciate the fact that whatever that phrase turns out to be in practice—a form of directing social change to certain predetermined outcomes by executive decree, legislative relief, or judicial review—it is not social science. The belief in policies is a faith in remedies. At times, such a faith is warranted, while at other times (and places) such a faith is not warranted. One might also add that the longer the time frame for policy-making the less likely the chances of measurable success.

The easy slippage from one to another is part and parcel of the decomposition of sociology, of a belief that action follows theory and hence policy follows social research. It is to presume that the truths discovered are somehow capable of being translated into specific programmatics for the relief of those who are said to need help. Again, it would be pleasant to believe that policy-making provides an open sesame for solving the ailments that afflict us all. But the social sciences are not easily captive of pleasantries, nor should they be. We examine policy, from initial design to final implementation, experientially. That is, we look at the consequences of actions no less than the sentiments that start us on the slippery slope to cure-alls.

While I like to think that social science can inform public policy, it cannot ever be the same. For social science must always retain a critical component, and that means a critique of each and every remedy proposed. It is not that social research is inherently obstructionist, it is that social research is inherently driven by a need to explore weaknesses as well as strengths in all sorts of proposals for change. And as a myth-breaking tool, social science should never be part of a myth-making device—whether it is called policy, planning, futurology, or any other sort of oracular device.

I sense from Anselm's paper that he is of two minds on this subject. While in his tougher moments he shares this distinction between social science and public policy, his belief that social science is somehow always and everywhere an ally to change and progress fudges matters badly. Indeed, I do not share the view that social research always comes up with a vision favorable to a particular ideology. Whether it is William Graham Sumner's stark defense of the role of tradition in the establishment of the normative grounds of society, or James Coleman's vision of public choice as flight from cities to suburbs rather than reconstruction of the inner cities, there is an element in social science that has always cautioned against facile solutions, especially when such remedies are from the top down.

True enough, the burden, more than the benefit, of sociology in recent years has been along the axis of Anselm's thinking. In part this is due to the fact that sociology uniquely seeks to service the down and out, the poor, the needy, those who require a public voice. Sociology historically, in the United States at least, has been a voice of the alienated, the outsiders. Anselm's work reflects the best of how this sentiment is translated into reality. But in the world of political science, a place in which elites of all sorts form interest groups and exercise power bloc relations, these same dynamics do not operate. Hence, it has always been the case that advocacy of policies differ between and among the social sciences, no less than between those who benefit from continuity vis-à-vis those who are advantaged by change. In other words, the social sciences themselves have such differentiated constituencies, that it is difficult to speak with assurance, much less with one voice, for a singular policy on any given issue.

This is not to argue against the role of sociology as a handmaiden to public policies that assist the poor and minorities. It is plainly the case, however, that this is a function of the social position of sociology, not of the intrinsic merits of the argument for a sociology of public policy. My own work has sought, from start to finish, although perhaps not with the clarity warranted, to make a distinction between science and policy in general, and social science and public policy in particular. This is not a negotiable premise, since for me, that which is scientific in our work, that which is subject to the laws of nature and society, and demands evidence for belief, cannot simply be a function of policy requirements, however pleasant or even popular at the moment.

My essay on the AIDS epidemic pointed to how difficult it is to establish policy guidelines in a world in which some people view AIDS as divine retribution for sinful behavior, while others view it as a manifestation of keeping homosexuality bottled up in unsanitary conditions and mindless rhetoric. To expect policy-making from social science, say on the size of the budget the government should allocate to AIDS research vis-à-vis cancer or heart disease research, is to hope for miracles. Worse, it is to enlist social science to a cause that may or may not be reflective of larger pathologies rather than growing or expanding liberations. A "partisan" theory of sociology may lead to support of certain policies, but it hardly verifies the scientific basis of such theory, and that is the Achilles heel of all roads to heaven marked social science.

Social scientists do a lot of talking about policy-making, but do precious little more. That is because they too often come with a set of data indicating some inquiry or another, and implicitly declare: "do something about this." They are more impatient with legislative "grid-lock" than most political zealots. And while in part this is understandable, it is also part of a culture that fails to take seriously the political nature of society itself, or, more specifically, that a system based on checks and balances is intended precisely to move slowly, cautiously, into uncharted seas. In that sense, the political process supervenes, or checkmates, the policy process. I am not sure that Anselm does not too readily fall into this trap of self-righteousness, of moving from an injustice into a demand for a remedy, without always considering prospects for remedies being worse than the disease.

In that sense, one must return to first principles: Social science is not the same as social policy or even social change. It also has a commitment to understand moral traditions and political obligations. These are not words that easily come to the lips of a sociologist, but they are at the core of an interactionist position based upon democratic principles. For the "generalized other" of Mead turns out to be none other than people who hold different views from our own, and who stubbornly insist on laying bare the dangers of new policies to displace existing inequities. Not every policy is good because it is new, and not every tradition is bad because it endures. My good friend, the late Harold Lasswell, never forgot this, but I fear that my even better living friend, Anselm Strauss, sometimes falls into this trap. The best of intentions may sometimes be the worst of policies. The twentieth century is a testament to the high risks in the overidentification of social policy with social science. The clearer the lines of distinction, the better will be the fate of both advocates and critics.

Howard S. Becker

Having Howard Becker go "on record" with respect to C. Wright Mills will certainly be viewed as a blessing to his colleagues. Indeed, it represents Becker's continuing effort to establish the foundations of his own richly textured view of symbolic interactionism. I certainly appreciate his reading of my own work in the prism of Mills, and, in particular, my biography of him. The affection Becker shows for Mills is certainly warranted, albeit a trifle belated. As I tried to show early on in *Mills: An American Utopian,* he may have been educated in Texas, but his mentors had more in common with Chicago sociology than with anything else taking place in the field of sociology during the 1930s, the period of his intellectual formation. Alas, Mills learned more from the Chicago School as a set of methods for doing field work than as a deep-seated respect for the smarts as well as rights of all human beings.

Rather than contest what Becker writes of Mills, or even the judgments he makes of his colleagues and critics, I should like to confine these remarks to why I see myself in quite different tones other than that of disciple or follower. Indeed, I never had a strong subjective attachment to Mills. I suspect, curious fellow that he was, that my objectivity is a determining reason for his confidence in me. He relished his public acclaim, but in private life trusted his critics more than his celebrators. It should be remembered that when Mills was producing *The Causes of World War Three* and *Listen Yankee,* I had already written *Radicalism and the Revolt against Reason*—a book Mills read and cited in his final effort on the Marxists. But he felt distinctly uncomfortable with my effort. I suspect he saw himself as one of the radical irrationalists, at the end at least. I should like to expand upon this sense of mutual discomfort, hopefully without denigration, denial, or respect.

Ultimately, whether in a permanent pique with his Wisconsin mentor, Hans H. Gerth, or a direct reexamination of Weber as such, Mills rejected the ethical grounds of Weber's theory in favor of a "polycentric" neo-Marxism. He wanted to believe that the European left embraced the best (if not the only) serious thinking of the decade. In the great struggle between politics as a vocation, and sociology as a calling, he chose the former. And in his choice of grand themes, Mills chose—with devastating consequences—the study of power over the grounds of authority. For Wright the decision was easy: he went with the pamphleteering tradition of Marx and the muckrakers against the waffling tradition of Weber and the sociological obscurantists. This was his way of talking and thinking, not mine.

While it is true that at an earlier period, I couched this difference in mechanical terms, as the difference between professionalism and occupationalism, by the time of Mills's death in 1962 I had already cast my lot with the "wafflers" and against the "muckrakers." The increasing stridency of the American political process in the 1960s only confirmed this decision. By 1964 I was writing on the Stalinization of Castro's Cuba, and distinguishing between clear opposition to the war in Vietnam—and in this opposition the record will show my firm and unambiguous resolve—and any support for the repressive regime of Ho Chi Minh in North Vietnam.

In a nutshell, Mills chose politics—not as a vocation but as an ideology—over sociology as a science, or some clumsy effort at it. I chose the latter with the expected consequences Jim Katz noted in his paper: a marginalization in a field, which, as a whole and as an organizational effort, came to share the Millsian course of action. There is a certain irony to all of this. But at the end of the day, Mills went from a twenty-four hour a day sociologist to a twenty-four hour a day political crusader. As my C. Wright Mills: An American Utopian tried to make clear, this passage in time led to what Irving Howe once referred to as a bludgeon against sophisticated reasoning. This was not a path I could follow.

This is not the place to dissect the relationship of Mills and his colleagues at Columbia or at Chicago. Even the best of his friends, like Daniel Bell, were at odds with Wright by the twilight and close of his career. Edward A. Shils could never be described as a friend of Mills. On the other hand, I am not sure that "vicious" quite does justice to the seriousness of the debate over The Sociological Imagination. Rather, Shils viewed himself as an embattled defender of the Weberian tradition (perhaps with more zeal than was called for), and saw in Mills a veritable Gustav Schmoller. And it will be remembered that Weber too was hardly kindly disposed to those who defined sociology by the touchstone of ideology.

My book on Mills was more than twenty years in the making. Indeed, it is already more than ten years behind me. I am pleased that Howie liked my effort—I have sufficient correspondence on hand to show that Shils did not! In retrospect, I do not think I would change much in the appraisal. But I would certainly have sharpened the conclusion to note that the utopian tradition, in its longing after earthly paradise, while it may have some noble aspects, finally ends in a surrender and abandonment of science as a vocation. In this I see Mills's career as one of tragedy rather than triumph. His great early writings on the sociology of knowledge and the social psychology of careers, followed by the equally grand trilogy on social stratification in the United States, slowly unraveled.

Opposition to war hardened into a categorical animosity for America; faith in social change led him to a desperate embrace of pragmatic varieties of totalitarian communism. These were not sociological decisions but ideological ones. And these were not bastions nor decisions that I could share then, and even less so now. Having died thirty-two years ago, what Mills would say about specific events and places must remain moot, nor is this the place for such speculation. I will say that the sociological imagination can yield to totalitarian temptations—and has for some. It can also enrich the democratic imagination, and become a part of that great daily struggle for a decent world. In that sense, I hope to have been true to the best instinct of Millsian intellectual pursuits, if not his singular political causes.

William A. Donohue

I am somewhat taken aback and yet appreciative at the number of commentators who have traced my sociological roots to Max Weber. To say that it is an honor to be in such company is to put my sense of debt mildly. And it is certainly the case that Bill Donohue is accurate in seeing my work as a quest for policy-making in the context of an autonomous social science.

This is a tricky and complex effort. After all, at some level, policy-making implies the meliorative potentials of a social system. It is also implies that the future somehow can be made better than the present as a result of human intervention. Finally, policy entails some sort of partisanship, however couched in minimalist terms. Calling attention to concerns of the poor is, after all, not by definition, an objective scientific standard of measurement.

As a result, there is a creative tension involved in some epistemic faith in objectivity coupled with a strong commitment to changing things, which must always involve a degree of subjectivity. It is for that reason that the sociological tradition of Weber—and perhaps one should add only slightly lesser lights like Mannheim, Toennies, Michels, and Durkheim—what can be called the continental tradition, needs to be augmented by the British or better, constitutional tradition extending from Locke to Mill. For without an appreciation of the distinctly political limits as well as prospects of government, the linkage of policy to objectivity itself becomes distorted.

While I had given occasional congressional testimony on various issues prior to the Project Camelot affair, it is probably true that this is, as Bill Donohue claims, the first big involvement I had with policy. But in truth, it probably should be seen as an involvement in antipolicy rather than policy, since the aim of my work was essentially whistle-blowing—calling attention to everything that can go wrong (and did) in a single project involving potentials for overseas civil action in a counterinsurgency environment. A quite famous sociologist at the time of my initial essay on Project Camelot warned me that its issuance would cost me dearly in professional circles. That prognosis was plain wrong. Objective circumstances were aligned with subjective sentiments in revealing the dark side of the involvement of social science with the policy process.

Donohue understands well that the concerns I had were not to void policy-making by government agencies, but rather to infuse such an activity with the best of social science. And that meant overt rather than covert intelligence wherever possible, civilian rather than military pre-eminence in operations research, methodologies appropriate to goals sought, and appreciation of the limits of research.

I am in Donohue's debt for discussing my views on policy in a forth-right, decade by decade manner. Indeed, he is probably less severe with me than I am with myself. For it took me a while to appreciate the wonderful possibilities of not having a policy recommendation for every season. Indeed, were we not to have a policy on prospects for counterinsurgency in Latin America, and a stronger effort at supporting civilian regimes of a democratic sort, the United States would have better served its own national interests as well.

The key role of social science research in the *Brown v. Board of Education* decision indicated that the three branches of government are not windowless monads. The profound research performed by Gunnar Myrdal and Arnold Rose in the modern era, and by Robert E. Park and Booker T. Washington in an earlier period, was the empirical ground on which judicial reform was feasible. *Plessy v. Ferguson* and all doctrines of separate but equal—from railroad carriages to classrooms—were not overthrown by the logical foundations of law, but by the need to prevent the nation from breaking apart on the race issue.

It is not without irony that separate but equal becomes something of a rallying cry only forty years after the *Brown v. Board of Education* decision. Indeed, the mayor of New York felt called upon to say that a white man should be excluded from consideration for a post as chairman of the board of New York City Education simply on the basis of his race! What all this points to is the need for a sociology of policy. For it is only in this way that the objectivity portion with which we start can be recaptured at the end of the rainbow.

I appreciate Bill Donohue's declaration that there is no late or early Horowitz. I like to think he is quite correct in this. Indeed, I published a collection of my reviews and review essays under the rubric *Persuasions and Prejudices* just to disabuse those who claim to have spotted a fundamental shift in my thinking. In these shorter pieces, and they extend from 1953 to 1988 , I tried to exhibit those traits of analysis that would reveal a pattern of intellectual consistency.

To be sure, the problem is that general principles do not always translate into common grounds when it comes to policy-making. Individuals, even the best intentioned ones, can have shared democratic and humane values and find themselves locked in battle on specific issues. Sometimes these can be quite acrimonious. Thus, good people found themselves on opposite sides with respect to the conduct of the Vietnam War and now, a quarter century later, doves on the question can be found beating the drums madly for the bombing of Bosnia and other hawk-like actions.

And that is why the constitutional tradition is so critical. For it is that element in American life that preserves us from fanaticism. Without Locke, Montesquieu, and Mill, again prototypes among others, we run the risk of reducing democracy to interest group demands. Speaking of the American Civil Liberties Union—and Bill speaks often on that subject—I am reminded of an observation I made some years back that the first amendment is not an absolute truth. Yet, we need an organization that acts as if it were, in order to maintain the dialogue that goes on constantly on issues relating to privacy versus the right to know, personal choice versus public obligations, free expression versus social constructs, political expression versus symbolic unity. For this reason, the ACLU remains a much needed organization.

Innovation is to social policy what tradition is to system maintenance. Policy is neither superior nor inferior to tradition. The nature of law is procedural: to guarantee a level playing field of ideas and interests. In this sense the democratic society is not a series of do's and do not's but one in which the "game of democracy" as such is programmed for continuance. Bill Donohue understands this better than ever, given his sensitive role in the prevention of defamatory statements aimed at the Catholic faith and its peoples.

Michael Oakeshott had it right: The rational society is essentially one in which debates rage and disagreements are profound, yet individuals remove themselves from the field of battle or the field of policy and manage to engage in civil discourse over a warm meal together. W. E. B. DuBois long ago struck the same chord when he noted that the essential tragedy in black-white relations was not simply one of law and policy, but the inability of people of the two races to sit and have a cup of tea together. This all seems so simple and straightforward in the telling at least. Clearly, it is far less so in the performance of everyday life.

A central reason why the quest for an autonomous social science remains central to our times is to remind the policymakers and their collective apparatus that the assumptions behind policy involve the potentials for meliorative reform. And not every situation is subject to remedial performance. It is easy enough to assert the role of social research as a handmaiden to policy formation. It is a far more difficult task to assert that remedies are not available either in specific areas or as a general guide. That is when the fate of the social research becomes more dicey or subject to the whims of the policymaker.

The objectivity of which Donohue speaks cuts in opposite directions: as a struggle against the sort of historicism and biologism that leads to totalitarian denial that remedies are ever possible, and against the sort of positivism that leads to liberal assertions that remedies are always available. I take this to be an amplification of Donohue's remarks on my work rather than an argument with the author of these kind remarks.

John D. Martz

The broad and deep understanding exhibited by John Martz on the theoretical implications of my work are much appreciated. It is indeed the case that I have always maintained that "thirdness" in gross national product or life-style levels do not imply a transitional phenomenon to either a pure free market doctrine of modernization of the sort advocated by Walt W. Rostow, and certainly not the sort of dependency theories advocated by Andre Gunder Frank and Immanuel Wallerstein among others.

Martz's essay allows me an opportunity to succinctly update this struggle of and for the developmental model as a reality unto itself. The great difficulty I have with the modernization model, and one curiously confirmed by the recent post-Maoist China experience, is that the tremendous emphasis on creature comforts and commodities in general serves only to exaggerate the differences in social classes. In so many Third World settings, modernization is a highly stratified phenomenon, one that does indeed provide succor to some, while pointing up the absence of shared wealth to many.

As a result, the pure theory of the market comes to rest not on democracy, but, as we have seen with Pinochet in Chile and Deng in China to cite two ready at hand examples, on dictatorship, on rule from above in the name of the marketplace. The hidden hand of Adam Smith, in the absence of political democracy, is too easily converted into the nailed boot of classical totalitarians. There is no automatic correlation of free markets and free minds. Indeed, in the absence of classical liberal and constitutional modalities, the free market becomes a playground for inequality and corruption. Just how many more examples of this we need before the lesson is clear is hard to say. It is a tribute to John Martz that he has learned this lesson very well indeed.

At the other end, with the debacle in Eastern Europe and Russia, and the near total collapse of communist systems in that part of the world, holding up the Second World as a model of development has lost most, if not all, of its shimmer. The disguised Leninism that underwrites dependency theories was weaker than the original version. For Lenin at least carefully studied conditions with which he was faced as a party leader and policymaker. So much stuff that passes for dependency is an excuse to focus upon Washington, and analyze the world as if it was a simple cause effect response to decision making in the United States or in the Western capitalist democracies in general.

What took place was a tragedy for developmental studies—a conversion of a social science into a political ideology. Dependency became a simple-minded code word and code book for presumptively radical visions and utopian hopes, foisted on others with a heavy dosage of anti-Americanism. It must be said frankly that such work took the study of development away from concrete national circumstances and into the realm of intellectual rubbish. All sorts of academic contortions were introduced to "save" dependency theory from itself: the notion that centers other than Washington needed to be explored, such as Tokyo and even Moscow; the theory that there were semiperipheries as well as peripheries. It took on the ghastly trappings of a pre-Copernican theory of epicycles and cycles, anything to preserve the idea that the sun and all its planets revolve about the earth.

The present moment has a danger of its own, one I admit to having underestimated. In its thirst for intellectual respectability along with practical autonomy, many elements in the Third World have disaggregated development from democracy. Thus, we have situations in which military abuses of electoral norms from Haiti to Nigeria are explained away, in which the right to development and the right to debt relief are heralded as universal laws in order to disguise outrageous and corrupt political domination and bureaucratic practices. In this artless way, economic considerations are held primary while political concerns are held to be off-limits to the student of development.

We have a situation in which basic civil rights as outlined in the United Nations Universal Declaration of Human Rights are not part of the new Third World agenda. There are too few avowals of the rights of free expression, freedom of worship, or freedom to assemble without punishment. On this, one finds a common front extending from Cuba to China to Iraq and North Korea. Thus, in the very collapse of communism, from its ashes as it were, comes a new variety of totalitarians— one which fixes blame and responsibility for all economic woes on Western capitalism, while carefully denying the autonomous realm of the political process. Such a condition as exists in the mid-1990s has dramatically changed what we were confronted with in the mid-1950s, but not necessarily for the better.

We have labored under a false delusionary belief that democracy is the wave of the Third World future. We have reached that plateau of mindlessness by assuming that in the absence of overt military rule we were all on the road to democracy. This clearly is a profound error in judgment and analysis. The forms of dictatorship are as varied as those called democratic. Whether we are reviewing civil or military authority we need to do so in terms of the specifics of behavior of leadership, and eschew generalities based on premises outmoded and outdated. I would only emphasize that this is not intended as a critique, but instead a support for the sort of analysis which Professor Martz has provided in his paper.

Finally, I think it important to note that I titled my work *Three Worlds of Development* and not *The Third World* precisely because of my sense of the dynamism and fluidity in world relations. I also wanted to emphasize that mine was a work that dealt with constructs that could be used in the study of the United States no less than the Third World. Alas, this aspect, this search for theory, has tended be obscured in any number of evaluations of this work.

For example, one might take the military paradigm in the book and see how, between 1790 and 1890, the United States embarked on a course of national consolidation and integration; then from 1890 through 1960 this sense of mission became globalized, and the United States sought an international consolidation commensurate with its power following two world wars. Finally, with Korea, Vietnam, and the mini-wars of the 1980s and 1990s, the United States has become the linchpin of efforts to link its national interests with democratic aspirations—even if these entail modest, short-lived military engagements.

We forget that analysis of the United States in such terms is of recent vintage. That the sort of analysis developed in *Three Worlds* although obviously not restricted to that text, or any other for that matter, helped us to move beyond a parochialism characteristic of writings that were predicated exclusively on doctrines of the national interest. The inclusion of the Second World, of the communist world, even in its present state of disarray, also permits a dynamic sort of theory construction that places U.S. interests and activities in global context. Hopefully, the sort of analysis provided by John Martz will serve to extend just such efforts on the part of others.

Simon M. Fass

Simon understands well the choice of frameworks in developmental theory—a set of options having to do with dependency, modernization, or developmentalism taken on its own terms. It has always been Simon's immense strength to be in possession of the anthropological understanding that to study means to get to know. Thus, whether he is working on Haiti or the Sudan, he has the benefit of firsthand experience. A key element is Simon's immersion in French language and culture. It is hardly an accident that we have probably ten students of anglophonic Africa and of francophonic Africa. Americans tend to be linguistic idiots and the study of areas in which other colonial cultures dominated, such as the French, are left to others, sometimes with tragic consequences.

But the ferocious sense of justice that Simon possesses is not a function of language. After all, it is hardly self-evident that French colonialists were kinder to their subjects than were British colonialists! Rather, it is a sense that the view from below, or better, from inside the whale, produces something less than a rosy picture of the developmental process. I suspect that the Haitian experience convinced Simon that exploitation and corruption are systemic and not simply imported properties of foreigners. Indeed, one might argue that the input in Haiti of a national liberation struggle headed by Toussaint L'Ouverture did not prevent an outcome quite similar, perhaps worse, than what one found and still finds in other parts of the Caribbean. In that sense, the classical model of Marx is a far superior tool than the neocolonialist model of Lenin, in explaining everyday exploitations.

Of course, this still continues within the very soul of Africa for a sense of mission and meaning. What is one to do with Hastings Banda and his Malawi? Where embedded in rural impoverishment is a special school system in which imported English headmasters instruct a black elite in British colonial history, Latin verses, and Xenophon's account in classic Greek of the fall of Athens? It would be easy to deride and dismiss such efforts. I rather suspect that in the soul of Africa a struggle is going on precisely between the universal and the particular. Simon's work helps us to understand as much. For United Nations educational programs do more to equip the researchers than the natives with both types of information.

Schools and schooling are rooted in societies and schisms. Again, Simon well understands the struggles between Muslim and Christian, Eurocentric and Afrocentric, and, to use the vernacular of the moment, democracy and autocracy. The empirical evidence suggests that theory is a mold to be broken rather than a blueprint to be followed. And in his keen sense of the world of the outsider—the native peoples, the younger generations, the rural persuasions—he is able to overcome the arrogance of the ruler and the rules set forth by those who study the ruled. What we get is a devastating account of policies forged in universalist terms, that all children should go to school, that should a crop of particularist circumstances arise, family solidarity comes first.

But the challenges Simon speaks of, the challenge of the basics of life support as such, extend far beyond prescriptions. He is wise to note that participating democracy is very much a part of such life supports. The ultimate heresy of course is the recognition that formal modes of education may themselves be part of the problem no less than the solution. It might be asked whether in a world of global technification, and instant information dissemination and retrieval, the study of Latin and Greek originals does more than prolong and internalize the struggle over administrative domination. It might also be asked if a purely technical approach does not also contribute to the same team of administrative-bureaucratic rule.

The question of democracy in Africa is clumsy and awkward, but it is an agenda item. As the work of Claude Welch and others have indicated, the impulse to democracy is alive and well in a variety of sick societies extending from South Africa to Nigeria to Egypt. The old colonialists fared so well in Africa because they could enlist the tacit and active support of those local elites who feared losses greater than gains from independence. But when independence did come, they often became the sources of developmental impulses—and in military tunics, the sources of national integration.

In *Three Worlds* I tried to indicate that Africa was quite different from Asian and Latin America in that development was statist and bureaucratic rather than entrepreneurial, whereas the military were often glorified constabularies modeled on the older colonial impulse to harness the subjects rather than liberate the people. As a result, the postcolonial world remained predemocratic in its soul. The armed forces sometimes imposed a national will and other times reflected ethnic separations and abrasions. The administrative cadres reflected dominant tribal formations rather than national standards of merit. It has to be said with some frankness that Haiti in this sense reflects some of the African trends more than typical patterns of Latin American development. Whether this is a function of French Bonapartist tradition or an artificial transposition of ethnic and trivial loyalties or combinations and permeations of religion that veered sharply to mystification rather than rationalization—all this needs to be studied and understood, not for the sake of pure knowledge, but the sake of getting beyond the very morass of which Simon speaks.

The radical viewpoint, one that Simon comes close to admitting rather than announcing, is that education itself is a derivative concept, and worse, it is at times even destructive of positive values and inherited biases. The Western modernizing emphasis on education is often a disguised emphasis on civility not democracy, on accommodation rather than resolution of problems. My problem with modernization theory is not an argument with the contemporary work, as is the case with the rise of antimodernization (especially as a Muslim fundamentalistic revolt), but rather with its ability to create comfort zones in the Third World about which Western politicians and intellectuals can prattle all things native. That is to say, modernization has been a partial success and in this very partiality has created forms of stratification that threaten rather than secure the equilibrium of the Third World. Worse, this sort of modernism, based on goods for one self rather than services for others, postpones the day of democracy for those who are not participants. It also raises some terrible questions as to whether democracy, in order to grow, must itself become a form of the revolt against the modern. Simon's fieldwork helps us penetrate such questions. UNESCO's Parisian headquarters, with its smug emphasis on the educational vista as an end unto itself, only disguises such questions. Thus, the issues raised in his paper belong to the sociology of knowledge as well as the sociology of development.

Tunde Olatunde Odetola

I have had few students who better understood, or applied with greater creativity, my approach to the theory and practice of internationalist stratification. For the subtitle of my approach to development is critical in distinguishing my approach from either the modernization theories of Lipset, Apter, and Wiener or the dependency theories of people like Gunder Frank, Wallerstein, and their varied and several followers. For the social foundations of developmental theory cannot become too far removed from stratification without losing its rotundness in reality.

With respect to the question of nationalism, the gentle reminder offered by Professor Olatunde is entirely appropriate. I did indeed tend to cluster nations in larger supranational structures, and not study with sufficient care what was taking place at the nation-state levels. On the other hand, this was not an entirely unconscious decision. I felt, and still feel, that unless we develop some deeper understanding on multinational corporations, international organizations, and regional trade and military blocs, we shall miss the forest for the tree. Too much writing on nations presumes rather than explains exceptional circumstances. Hence, it becomes virtually impossible to achieve a grasp of world societies without becoming either oracular at one end or trivial at the other. In an effort to correct this imbalance, *Beyond Empire and Revolution* attempted to adjust the theoretical underpinnings of *Three Worlds of Development* so that the realities of global struggle could be retained, but not at the expense of nationalism.

It should be noted that even what we often refer to as national is supranational in character. For example, both the Muslim and Catholic religions—spearheads of national revivals in places as remote from each other as Poland and Iran—are hardly purely national in character. More pointedly, they survived the battering of modernization and communization intact, and hence were cultural and organizational repositories that could accommodate the new situation faced by the collapse of both forces.

For what took place between 1965 and 1982 (the publication dates of *Three Worlds* and *Beyond Empire* respectively) was the start of a cataclysmic reconsideration of what constitutes development as such. For neither Muslim nor Catholic faiths repudiated development or economic advance. They rather called attention to inquiries in the distribution of the goods of present-day societies, both in international terms, as Tunde notes, but also in national structures . The moral force of religion in this counterreformation derives from attempts to address stratification questions. And for that reason, the emphasis in my work on this subject remains a centerpiece to present analytic concerns as well.

I would argue that the shared values of modernization held by capitalism and communism—with the latter drearily and unsuccessfully claiming to keep abreast of the former, without managing to do so—gave tremendous impetus to this profound upheaval stretching from one end of Europe to another and throughout the Middle East. The trouble is that the price extracted in terms of political democracy in the Middle East and to political legitimacy in Europe continues to be extremely high. And if we are to take a keen on-site look, both elements are at work in such African nations as Nigeria.

The collapse of communism is curiously not the same as the collapse of the Second World. In China, Cuba, Vietnam, North Korea, and all sorts of nondescript places, the Second World continues its efforts. Indeed, at the risk of waving a red cape, it might be argued that the end of totalitarian communism has strengthened the movement of democratic socialism in such places as Sweden, Norway, and Finland. Still, the balance of world forces has obviously shifted, so that even if the model remains essentially usable, the weight of the elements within the model have changed. The relationship of the First to the Third World is different, and to be sure, the Third World itself has changed along a variety of economic axis that requires careful and constant reexamination.

Clearly, such detailed study is beyond this examination of Tunde's chapter. But in his conclusion, he raises a number of issues that require study. For example, it has been assumed, and I think improperly, that more democracy means less militarism. I suspect that this is wishful thinking. Budgets go up for military hardware even among newly formed democracies. Indeed, even those nations that loudly proclaim adhesion to democratic values employ the armed forces as a measure of sovereignty. In that sense, my idea of the military as a critical variable in the study of international stratification seems to be no less valid (alas, I say this without a boast) than in the past.

As Tunde demonstrated in his own work, from the moment of Nigerian sovereignty the strain, the tension, has been between democratic systems of rule inherited from the West and military systems of power inherited from the East. For my work on development is essentially to take four elements: economy, polity, society, and military and evaluate each almost as a Heisenberg indeterminacy principle. It may fudge matters to try rolling all into one ball of wax. It is better, we are better, for being able to disaggregate and carry these elements of international stratification as a package, weighing each of the four elements in discrete form. In doing this with *Cuban Communism* I may have missed a grand synthesis, but at least I was able to account for the major elements—and that is no small achievement in a world without a clear compass.

I have cautioned many people that, along with my notion of three worlds of development and four elements in international stratification, we still need to look at each of the two hundred nations in the world in precise and exacting form. It is ludicrous, as the dependency people would have matters, to find a "key" in the behavior of Washington or American imperialism, and derive all truths about a nation from such far away analysis. The very people who decried armchair sociology have been most guilty of precisely such analysis through cloudy telescopes. In that sense I view my approach as more methodological than theoretical It provides a set of guidelines for looking at a particular nation in a global context without losing the focus on the national structure being examined. Tunde has understood this well, and for that I am most grateful.

But in turn, Tunde needs to appreciate the extent to which a nation is not a world. Nigeria is not Africa. It is however part of the growing trends within Africa, and tensions with the Third World, to factor in authoritarianism within free market environment. Nigeria has not done this well. It is subject to terrible fits of corruption, authoritarian despotisms, and uneven development that makes what took place in Eastern Europe pale in comparison. Nigeria is now one of nine new African countries that Freedom House entered into its 1993 dishonor roll of states moving from free to "not free" status. Tunde is beginning to examine the African continent in such terms. It joins such new entrants as Burundi, Eritrea, Ethiopia, Guinea, Ivory Coast, Kenya, Mozambique, Swaziland, and Tanzania. That Nigeria shows patterns of development that are moving counter to what one finds in Latin America and Southeast Asia is unnerving.

We must all begin to examine the extent to which the Third World is breaking up—along a democratic totalitarian axis—with unforeseen consequences to the economy and the society as a whole. This breakup was only fragmentarily understood by myself, because I underestimated the nation-state and the potentials of multiethnic politics and religious fanaticism to void basic civil rights, even within the Third World. There is such a thing as thinking too big as well as too small. When one is forced to examine places like Nigeria, Haiti, and Korea—as my colleagues here have done—one must also begin to come to terms with the limits of paradigms in the face of the unlimited potential for mischief of politics.

Byoung-Lo Philo Kim

One of the important lessons of social research is that the size of the field of investigation does not uniquely determine its worth. I have often been asked how one can study three worlds when it is hard enough to understand three people interacting! To be sure, this would appear as a daunting question, save for the fact that it is arguably easier to examine three worlds or four nations than three or four individuals.

The reason this is so has to do with something that Weber hit upon in his own studies on ancient religions and modern economies: rationalization. Essentially, collective behavior washes out idiosyncrasies, or at least cancels them. It is not that personality does not matter in politics— nothing could be further from the truth. Rather, the checks on irrationalities and eccentricities are far higher as one goes up the scale of power, size, and abstraction.

Given this as an axiom, or perhaps a phase rule that is not universally the case by any means, we can study leadership as a function of national policy, identity, ambition at a horizontal axis, and the interaction of global systems and strategies at a vertical axis. The work of Professor Kim takes on significance at this level, since he examined in perhaps greater detail and with more acumen than anyone else how, in the context of the "two Koreas," many of the concepts that I developed in *Three Worlds of Development* played out on a national canvas.

Indeed, Korea is a unique "case study," as was Germany prior to its recent reunification. One can "control" for such variables as common language, territorial contiguity, and shared cultural uniformities, and then examine how it is that over a stipulated length of time, in the case of Korea from 1945 to 1990, political systems provide the ground for such profoundly different results. What makes this even more startling is that Korea between 1945 and 1960 witnessed greater economic growth in the communist North than in the free market South. Why such a dramatic shift over the recent thirty-plus year time frame becomes a matter of enormous concern as well as interest.

My own work with respect to the Third World portion of the three worlds centered on Latin America, and assuredly, my interest in the Second World centered on the former Soviet Union. Thus, Kim's work takes on great significance in terms of theory construction: That is to say, to what extent do such notions as I developed hold up in different geographical locations? For the answers have great meaning in measuring the relative importance of economic and political variables, say, with respect to geographical and cultural factors.

Philo's work does me great credit. In utilizing both *Three Worlds* and *Beyond Empire and Revolution* in an Asian context, far removed from the culture, language, and traditions of Latin America, the worth of such broad strokes as I have provided in earlier efforts can be tested in the specific settings in which development as a function of military, economy, polity, and society can be examined. Philo decisively answers the importance of development with respect to a free market and social planning context. Indeed, this answer has been repeatedly provided the world over in the rejection of the communist structures of Eastern Europe and Russia.

But that is hardly the end of the story. We still must explore the issue of development as a function of various types of market mechanisms— ranging from the centralized authority of state planning commissions of a sort prevalent in Japan, to a high tax-based social welfare-regulated private sector as in Sweden, and the more traditional capitalist systems that, for the first time, must face the state not as its protector or benefactor, but as downright adversary. In this sense, the extent to which the polity and the economy do not simply coexist in functional disharmony, but come to a parting of the ways is far more evident in the 1990s than in the 1960s, when my own work in this area was done.

The struggle between capitalism and communism that takes place in Korea does have several elements of a Manichean struggle between good and evil. But that would quite miss the point. Korea is more like a place in which competing varieties of developmental strategies coexist, neither of which can claim much of a moral high ground. Philo is keen to show that both North and South Korea reveal elements of Third World behavior inside the belly of the struggle between capitalism and communism. This is generally important to highlight the uneven nature of development even in systemic no less than political terms.

But there is a more disturbing element to this narrative: the perseverance of corruption, deception, political chicanery. Favoritism has a pervasive aspect in a nation like South Korea. And while those more sanguine might say that this is the "price" or "cost" of development, there is a limit to such bland amoral theorizing. For, in fact, a point of dysfunctionality is reached rather quickly. A nation can absorb perhaps a 10 percent level of bribery and corruption and still maintain growth and stability. What is less clear is the capacity of such newly emerging societies to do likewise in the presence of a 20 percent level of corruption, presuming one can quantify development patterns in this way.

The work of Kim on Korea, Odetola on Nigeria, and Fass on Haiti compel some appreciation of the thin-skinned character of newly formed capitalist systems—whether in Asia, Africa, or Latin America. It should occasion less than joy to note that these societies are becoming more democratic and less authoritarian. Perhaps. We have seen reversals of developmental fortune in places like Iran, and one can only say that the hammer of totalitarian rule still has the potential for reemerging should the benefits of democracy fail to materialize; and in the absence of a culture of democracy, in the absence of a civic content beyond the formal rules of governance, such prospects for reversal remain terribly alive and intact.

Thus, while it may be appropriate to note that the balance of forces have shifted from planned economies to free markets, or that militarism seems to pose less of a threat to Third World stability than it did thirty years ago, it is well to note that we have hardly reached an age or a stage of new harmony in places like Korea. An old journalistic gag line has it that two of the world's ten worst run nations are located in Korea. This sort of skepticism may yet prove a more serviceable way of looking at the developmental process than a position that starts with allies and enemies. While it may be true that only the stars are neutral, it is no less the case that it take a fool to believe that only the adversaries of democracy are partisan—or worse, always empirically correct and morally refined.

Ernesto F. Betancourt

The name Betancourt in Latin America is such an honorable estate unto itself that the need to reciprocate encomiums hardly exists. Whether we are dealing with the late Romulo of Venezuela or the current Ernesto of Cuba we have paragons of democratic politics and free intellects. I learned much from Ernesto. Indeed, our meetings, formal or informal, were uniformly learning experiences. In some measure it is because he is one of those rare people who have been wedded to partisan causes— and be assured that the freedom from tyranny in Cuba is a partisan cause—and yet has been able to see the larger picture in both global and intellectual terms.

As I have explained in the seventh edition of *Cuban Communism,* the evolution of my thinking on Cuba was aided by a firsthand knowledge of Argentina. Having seen what a catastrophe Perón was for the people of that great nation, it was with genuine unease that I watched the ushering in of Castro from the belly of the whale as it were—a post-Perónist Argentina reeling from inflation and class warfare that veered left and right like a rudderless ship on the high seas. Still, for the first five years I remained a rather passive supporter of the revolution, perhaps not unlike the democrats within the 26th of July movement who felt the winds of change and were exhilarated by future prospects while remaining apprehensive about current developments.

Ernesto is correct to note that my first break with the Castro regime became transparent in the debates with Carlos Fuentes. I felt then and continue to believe that the military coup d'état in Brazil during March 1964 was precipitated by a broad acceptance by Jango Goulart to the Cuban revolution. The visit by Ernesto "Che" Guevara was clearly a signal of the internationalization of the Brazilian political process. It was one that could not be prevented from drifting into communist hands without some action, whether it be internal or external. That the Brazilian military were toughened during the Vargas years was plain enough, and even with their strong affiliations with American foreign policy, they were involved in a national drama they could neither prevent nor ultimately control.

For saying this rather obvious statement, I was denounced by the *World Marxist Review* in loud and certain terms. Being called a defeatist, a pessimist, and a counterrevolutionary were among the obvious epithets. But what troubled me was the total euphoria of otherwise intelligent left critics and commentators. It was as if they were enthralled by anti-Americanism to the point where the obvious movement of Castro and his movement to a hard and fast military/party state was viewed as the necessary price one had to pay for ridding the hemisphere of the United States. And this is where I came in! Every movement of the Soviet Union to dictatorship was prefaced and justified by the need to cleanse the state, the party, the community, and ultimately millions of innocent individuals of the curse of revisionism, bourgeois tendencies, and a myriad of curses which seem to afflict anyone connected with the democratic virus.

The publication of "The Stalinization of Castro" was a calculated personal decision. Having been crowned, quite against my wish or will, as the "heir apparent" to the Millsian legacy, the publication of this statement—even though it took place in a left socialist publication, *New Politics,* edited by a courageous pair of plainspoken socialists, Julius and Phyllis Jacobson—did not save me from the hardest sort of critiques. These have also been alluded to by Carmelo Mesa Lago, so there is no purpose to repeating ancient history, even if that history refuses to die as long as Castro remains what must euphemistically be called, "in power." Having thus burned my bridges to a movement that claimed Mills as a spiritual heir, often without a shred of reason for doing so, I at least was liberated from being heir to anything other than what I wanted to be heir to! I lost some friends and colleagues, but then again, I kept faith in myself. Friends can be acquired, a soul is a little harder item to come by.

Betancourt covers many of the points I raise in my work, and does so from a different vantage point than Carmelo Mesa-Lago. Indeed, he sees the series of events stretching from Chile, Uruguay, Peru, Jamaica, Nicaragua, and Grenada as being directed by the Castristas, and ultimately he is unable to distinguish a national revolutionary posture from a knee-jerk anti-Americanism. It was astonishing that social scientists were so captive and enamored of the Castro regime that they were nearly uniform in overlooking the risks in the Sovietization of Fidel and emphasizing the potential for the institutionalization of the revolution. By that point, only those whose hopes far exceeded their analysis could maintain the idea of institutionalization or more, a Cuba that would perform vanguard services for Latin America in true Leninist fashion, the way Stalin had for Eastern Europe.

Ernesto's summary of the evolution of my thought on Cuba is so complete and fair-minded that I am in the awkward position of having to supply a sense of self-criticism that he is kind enough to gloss over. The most serious weakness stemmed from an overestimation of Cuban dependency on the Soviet Union for its survival, and a corresponding underestimation of the natural barriers to democratic rule. For here we are (at least as of this writing) five years after the end of the Soviet system, and a solid decade after the Gorbachev era began, and we have Castro still in power. True enough, we have had all sorts of dangerous presumptions that the end is at hand, but these sorts of apocalyptic visions, often taken up by business and legal interests smacking their lips awaiting the great recovery of nonexistent fortunes and existing but run-down properties, have thus far proven less than forceful as measures of prediction.

We learn from the Cuban experience, or even from its demise: the power of out migration as a safety valve letting off the steam of resentment by the simple act of exile; the value to dictatorship in shutting off

debate by the simple act of sealing off the island from the rest of hemisphere not to mention the rest of the world; and the potentials for devo-
lution as well as evolution, backwardness as well as development under
conditions of total control. Cuba does not need to imprison dissenters, it
is an island which in effect has become a prison of the whole; the nation
is the prison, the Cuban people are the prisoners. And rebellion is no
easy matter under such circumstances. Ernesto in passing remarked that
Fidel's singular opening to the exiles in 1976 created the base for the
Mariel boat life of 1980. I believe this is an accurate reading of past
events. It also helps us explain why Fidel has not made a similar "mistake" for the past several decades.

What do we carry away from this thirty-five year dictatorial nightmare? What is it that social science can learn from the Castro experience? We will eschew what it can teach, since the answer thus far is
shameful in its results and consequences. But we can learn even in adversity. At the risk of trying Ernesto's patience, I would summarize my
findings thus:

First, have trust in people, not leaders. Have regard for their survival
not the utopian meandering and promissory notes that are never ful-
filled. Second, have trust in events not ideologies. Anyone looking at
Cuba for the past thirty-five years—and "looking" may mean little more
than examining hard data and soft press reports—would have been driven
the same conclusions that I had. But it was this bizarre notion that the
Cuban model was invincible and triumphant that led to the ultimate sin
in seeing it also as a good. Third, history is a guide not a model. The
most terrible part of the Castro revolution is the idea that it could be
replicated everywhere and anywhere. From Regis Debray to Ernesto
Che Guevara, the conversion of a singular event based on one hundred
years of national Cuban history was converted into a clandestine
groupthink. The incredible defeats of the Castristas from Venezuela to
Bolivia should have cautioned social scientists as to the limits of model
building carried to actions. That no such cautionary note was struck,
that social sciences joined in the claque of the ideological crowd, results
not only in needless defeats but senseless loss of human lives.

Political events have a double life: They impact the larger communities from whence they emanate, and they impact in a special way the
professions that give meaning to such political events. The search for
democracy is a requirement of the human race. The absence of democ-

racy is a disaster for the social scientists. We have a tradition of being all too ready to follow, nay celebrate, cranks, crooks, and even downright creeps, in the name of the remaking of society or worse, the unraveling of society. We are too often fueled by political hatreds at the very movement we are announcing political loves. And once and for all it is time to get beyond love or hate as an analytic tool. Not everything we like comes to fruition, not everything we loathe is beaten. And dare one add, not everything we deem worthwhile deserves a positive fate, while not everything we criticize deserves a quick dismissal.

We march under our own banner—that of honest social research and decent analysis, subject to modification, revision, correction, and if necessary abandonment. The banners of national chauvinism and global restoration are not for us to carry. The nightmare of watching close friends and colleagues fall prey to the blandishments of petty tyrants only reinforces this sense that there is something beyond social science, and that is common—in dealing with one another, and in reflecting on our own infirmities and weaknesses. Only by getting beyond the culture of labeling will we be able to get on with the task of restoring the dignity of ordinary life and the life of ordinary people to dignity. But this means we cannot take ourselves too seriously. We need the grace of humor such as Ernesto Betancourt has in abundance.

Social science is not simply the next best thing after providence. We are not simply politicians in waiting, individuals ready to serve a tyrant in his policy searches mindlessly and unreservedly. We must not confuse opposition to shortcomings in our own house with a blind support for tyranny in the houses of others. Opposition to colonialism does not imply a defense of Third World dictatorships. Conversely, just criticism of a democracy does not, should not, imply support for solutions based on tyranny. This I have learned slowly, haltingly, and with the help of people like Betancourt, through the thirty-five years of the Castro regime. With all due apologies for the avuncular tone of these comments, I pass them along to my colleagues as the alpha and omega of a life in developmental studies.

Carmelo Mesa-Lago

The chapter by Carmelo Mesa-Lago on my writings on Castro's Cuba are so fair-minded at the expository level that he leaves little to add except a deep appreciation. To have such a level-headed colleague in an area known for its explosiveness and damaging allegations at personal levels is no small statement of the worth of scholarship—or for that matter, just how the democratic imagination works at its highest levels. Our differences however remain real.

Such differences start with the very title of his piece: I categorically deny that the phrase "socialist Cuba" is an exact reflection of the system that has been put in place by Castro for the last thirty-five years. In this matter, Ernesto Betancourt's views are far closer to my own; we are dealing with a traditional caudillo type who builds a cacique system, and then enshrines this travesty with the rhetoric of socialism. In addition, he draws inspiration from the worst totalitarian features of Soviet dictators to give his regime a muscle and a staying power that could only be the envy and joy of Latin American dictators who came before him.

Carmelo is the veritable *decano* of Cuban studies. He sees it as part of the corpus of social scientific, especially economic, examinations of the Castro regime from its inception to the present. Indeed, he epitomizes the extraordinary ability of émigré Cuban scholars to use social research in ways that illustrate the potency of honest work on a dangerous subject, and to do so without rancor or bitterness. Against the shouts and screams of ideologists, Carmelo has always upheld the honor of science by simply demanding that truth must preempt passion in the conduct of our affairs. Indeed, it is such a search that distinguished the life of the mind to begin with.

It is fair to add that Carmelo from the outset operated within a university context far removed from the bastions of Cuban émigré geographical strength, and, as a result, faced a good deal more wrath than those who criticized him for being less than thundering. Raised fists may work in Miami, but it takes a good deal more persuasive tools to work in Pittsburgh. I might add a personal appreciation that Carmelo never treats Cuba as a professional vocation unto itself. He has studied Eastern Europe in great depth, as well as other parts of Latin America. It is the nature of command and market economies and how they impact the social fabric that is at the heart of his work—and I would add, at the soul of his commitment to democratic values.

So there is little need to dwell further on the huge areas in which our thought overlaps. Let me rather address candidly those frames of refer-

ence in which we do not share a consensus. At the core of our differences, such as they are, are three areas: first, a difference in emphasis of
economic and political factors in the malaise of Castro; second, a different reading of historical and causal sequences; and finally, a different
view of Castroism as an ideology. Rather than labor those areas on which
we have a strong agreement, I would like to emphasize, admittedly in
far too brief a span, those areas that divide us on the meaning of this
long-lived tyranny.

Carmelo is of the opinion that the economic malaise in Cuba, caused
most recently by the collapse of the Soviet Union and the special role
that nation played in the survival of Castro's Cuba, is at the root of the
increased political repression within the island. Indeed, it is hard to deny
that the end of Soviet aid, and the relative isolation of Castro in economic terms, has been a big factor in the sickness of its economy. Nor
can one deny that hardships have increased in the recent years. But I
maintain that Carmelo has his sequencing wrong. The political repression predates the economic malaise by several decades!

The fact that I could write an essay for *New Politics* entitled "The
Stalinization of Cuba" as early as 1964 indicates how far advanced the
machinery of repression became independent of economic hard times.
Indeed, one might well argue that Castro's incredible megalomania was
fueled by early economic successes, that he saw the prospects for further economic development through political consolidation. After all,
Fidel was under the influence of the Stalinists—especially the sort of
thinking put forth by Paul Baran and Leo Huberman in those early halcyon days. Carmelo still waffles on the issue of Stalinization. It serves
no serious end to say that we stand together on the major points of my
analysis, and then claim that the objections to my theses have merit on
the minor points.

This is no small matter, since the idea put forth by Carmelo in his
recent work *Cuba After the Cold War* (1993) would indicate that economic troubles caused political repression. I would say that the regime
from the outset was repressive. This was understood first subjectively,
by the flight of hundreds of thousands of refugees, especially from the
professional and commerce, and only later appreciated by the scholars.
The former were interested in new lives and careers, only the latter were
interested in squaring old ideologies with new realities.

The underestimation of the totalitarian nature of the Castro regime
was partially a consequence of the overestimation of the socialist char-

acter of the economy. Carmelo did not fully factor in the traditional *cacique* elements in Fidel. The labels were different, but the bottle contained similar equations: a strong military faction, rule by political decree, constant major decision making by the leadership—in short, whether we are looking at rightist or leftist regimes, we see precisely the absence of democracy that would have eased Cuba's burdens, or that could have led to a normalization of relationships with the rest of the world once the communist bloc disintegrated.

It was this inversion of the economic and the political that led to a series of blunders even among stalwart opponents of tyranny. The attempt to establish bilateral relationships between the University of Pittsburgh and the University of Havana—which Carmelo after all championed, signing the formal documents establishing this special relationship—was performed in hothouse isolation of larger political realities. The effort at normalization even at micro-levels, while well intentioned, only exposed the political impotence of the oppositional forces in Havana. It was this misreading of the nature of Stalinization that informed Carmelo's faith in some sort of rapprochement long after many others writing on the subject felt it appropriate to do so.

I raise this not to blow bubbles at Carmelo. His motives in seeking some sort of normalization were pure of mind and heart. Alas, he did not have a signal from Fidel along the same lines. And this was not a function of economic malaise, but of political rigidities of the Cuban Stalinists. They could not back away from their ideological commitments, and yet could not sustain them in the face of post-cold war environment. As a result, Castro is part of a series of terrible contradictions: to build an infrastructure of hotels for foreigners while keeping these off limits to Cubans, establishing supermarkets where only hard currency could be spent, and thus encouraging the very black market and collapse of the native currency he desperately sought to avoid, permitting the resurgence of gambling and prostitution and deviance among the youth, while maintaining strict adhesion to a puritanical version of Marxism-Leninism.

In short, the unraveling of the regime was not primarily a function of the collapse of Soviet and East European communism, but of a series of policy decisions by Castro driven by ideological commitment and cultural closure. Even the hint of private sector, free-market solutions sent Fidel into a frenzy. For that matter, overtures toward rapprochement with the rest of Latin America or the United States were always based on ridiculous premises that the rest of the hemisphere must make concessions to him. This one-way traffic across a bridge that had little to offer on the other side is what doomed Castroism—and not the economy.

But this is jumping the gun, as it were, moving to a contemporary framework. I admit that Castro attempted to play a world role long after the failed adventures in other parts of Latin America. Surely the Angolan adventure demonstrates as much. But this proved to be such a dreary flop, and so short-lived, that agreements involving settlement in Angola that took place in London did not even involve Fidel. Indeed, my point that Fidel was a Stalinist who mistook Cuba for Russia stands. And the events of the last five years confirm as much. I appreciate Carmelo's point that Castro at times acted independent of his Soviet sponsor, even in contradiction to its wishes. But this was because, according to Fidel, it was Soviet "revisionism" that failed to seize proper military and political initiatives. That is to say, the Stalin-Lenin line was carried forth by Fidel, not Gorbachev.

I am not certain what Carmelo's disagreement is with my work on the militarization issue. Indeed, every ounce of data he adduces relates to the exponential growth of the armed forces in recent years, all of which tends to confirm the Stalinization hypotheses. But I suspect that his faith in socialism is far greater than mine—certainly when it comes to Cuba, whether we are talking of past or present decades, this charade must be stripped away as a necessary prelude to serious analysis. It is not a matter of whether Carmelo and I agree or disagree on a specific point, but rather what is to be the overall characterization of the regime. It is this I miss in Carmelo's own work, no less than his critique of my formulations.

Carmelo's problems are magnified by again drawing attention to the notion of regime institutionalization. My argument was predicated not necessarily on the charismatic nature of Castro, but the inability of a regime such as this to achieve even nondemocratic institutionalization. In part the point is moot. But one would have to believe in tooth fairies to assume that a post-Castro epoch would simply maintain the "socialist" character of the Cuban regime intact. And yet, again I find him taking the Soviet post-Stalinist model as viable, much less typical.

I would claim that the collapse of the Soviet empire indicates precisely a failure of nondemocratic regimes to institutionalize. To speak of institutionalization a la Soviet Union between 1971 and 1985 may save a theory, but it does little for reality. Why, for example, does this process cease in 1986? Why is the rectification process introduced precisely at a time when institutionalization should have been enhanced? Why does Fidel retake control of the economy? Certainly not out of fear of a decimated bureaucracy or administrative apparatus. Could it be, my friend, that he never relinquished personal authority to start with?!

In discussing political issues, one notices that Carmelo shifts dates so that the keys become 1970–75 and then 1975–89. In short, Castro's global strategies seems to reveal little correlation with his economic policies. If he were to take less seriously the words of Fidel, and more the deeds, at least some of the differences between us could be better resolved. And we could get beyond a laundry list of agreements and disagreements into a fundamental characterization of the regime. Again, this is absent in Carmelo's analysis—a balanced appraisal of an unbalanced regime is no solution.

It is true that my attitude toward normalization changes over time. The United States lives in a world of different social systems, even now, and cannot demand adhesion of social systems as the price of diplomatic recognition. Certainly, I felt that the Bay of Pigs invasion was a disaster, and the potential for rapprochement set back as a result. However, the changes duly noted in my position are not a function of whimsy, but of changing approaches by Castro. Military intervention by Cuba in all parts of the world made normalization virtually impossible. My reading of events was not a function of a growing exile community in Miami, but a growing desperation in Havana.

It is not my stand against normalization, it is the Castro government's inability to accept any sort of reality check on its potencies that compelled me to take a harder stand on normalization of diplomatic relations. Indeed, the fact that Castro's position was repeatedly denounced within the last stages of the Soviet Union as adventurist and dangerous, indicates that the changes were not in analysis, but in the policies of the Cuban government.

We are now in the final stage of Castro's regime. As I have indicated elsewhere, the first part of the discrediting of Castro has already taken place. He simply is no longer feared by his people, and no longer the archangel of Marxism-Leninism. But in the absence of opposition, or better the vacuum created by the decimation of the civil administration bodies and the military forces alike, we are left with a huge political black hole waiting to be filled. All of this, Carmelo knows well—probably better than I. No one wants to see needless suffering, certainly not of the Cuban people. The issue becomes how best to curb such sufferings by massive aid to the Castro regime, or a continuation of the present policies intended to force him from power and permit something better to take its place.

In summary, I find the "balance sheet" approach to my work on Cuba to be only partially successful. One could just as well make the same sort of bookkeeping set of trial balances on Carmelo's work. Indeed, he does this to himself, and in this very essay—shifting moods as well as assessments paragraph by paragraph. The key remains structural analysis. My friend, from the opening sentence to the very last sentence of his chapter, speaks of "Cuban socialism." I speak, and have spoken, of "Castro's Stalinism." These may overlap in certain areas. But from this distinction flows considerable differences in analysis and opinion. But from such dialectical exercises we may arrive at greater truths about the agonies of the past thirty-five years. We may even end up with ways to avoid such quagmires to begin with. And on this Carmelo and I stand shoulder to shoulder.

Jaime Suchlicki

I am moved by Professor Suchlicki's words not simply for the honor which he bestows on me as a person, but because we have worked together for so many years on a shared antitotalitarian cause: the downfall of the dictatorship of Castro in Cuba. We share in common a love of Argentina and Carlos Gardel, family roots that were replanted in Buenos Aires from Eastern European Jewish *shtels,* and a deep and abiding affection for the best traditions of the two Americas. Suchlicki is a scholar with a no-nonsense approach to ideas and events. He is utterly without pretense, and, at the same time, aware that ideas do matter—especially ideas held in the deepest recesses of the collective conscience of ordinary souls.

To be sure, we both appreciate that such commitments are beyond the realm of social science or history for that matter. But they matter to both in that honest social science and decent history writing are much harder to accomplish in totalitarian than in democratic systems. It seems obvious, even trite, to point out this distinction. But as long as social scientists still continue to believe that they represent a "vanguard," then the rest of us who bring up the "rearguard" are well advised not to fall asleep at the intellectual wheel.

It was through Jaime's efforts that *The Conscience of Worms and the Cowardice of Lions* was made possible. He worked tirelessly to make it possible for me to deliver the Bacardi Lectures in 1992, and, better yet, to create an environment at the North-South Center that deepened my sense of the situation in Cuban-American circles. The deep background of those lectures was not to emulate or imitate what others are better able to write about, but rather to treat the Cuban exile community in the same way that we dealt with the great migration of German and Russian intellectuals in the earlier portions of the century. That is to say, the victims of Hitlerism and Stalinism had much in common with the victims of Castroism. That deserved to be dealt with in detail.

In some special way, this little book is a companion piece to *The Decomposition of Sociology,* albeit on a far more modest scale. But it too addressed the outrageous assault on everyday knowledge that typified the "Kremlinologist." For the "Castrologists" were simply a weaker subspecies of that strange totalitarian type—one that could never discard the idea that the dictator knows best, or that "armed with the weapon of theory" (or one might substitute history) the maximum leader can in his person determine the course of events and fashion the will of people. Indeed, not a few of the most offending types were found to be supporters of both European and Cuban totalitarianism. And why not? They fed off each other at the same troth. These were North American scholars, usually social scientists (for journalists were far wiser and closer to the action).

I have worked with Jaime on a great many practical and intellectual tasks; moreover, I have been the beneficiary of his boundless personal kindnesses. He is at home in just about every circumstance; and he knows Mexico and Argentina as well as Cuba. But the key to his work is the old Max Lerner phrase: ideas are weapons. And all of his own work is so infused. The brevity of my response should not be taken as dismissive. Quite the contrary, as with the case of brothers, silence speaks to knowing things shared.

William B. Helmreich

Professor Helmreich's chapter on my writings on the Jewish condition (I prefer the word "condition" to "question" since the former connotes permanence and durability, whilst the latter has an eerie ring of transience with a strong implication that Jews are not just a question but somebody else's problem) is most welcome. Since my concerns have for the most part been scattered, and not yet systematized, I have a sense of profound indebtedness for the synthetic skills that Willi has brought to this task.

At some point in the future, when and if the Almighty gives me the joys of lolling about Miami with my Jewish and Cuban friends—and hopefully a few others who know something about pain and pleasure—I want to prepare a book on Jewish marginality. For, in addition to the themes that are more customary in the literature, and these range from the terrible Holocaust to the extraordinary rebirth of Israel, I have been struck by the special place in Western culture of the nondevout, or at least nonpracticing Jew. In literature, the sciences, and social research we are witness to the amazing cross-fertilization of secular values and Jewish tradition.

To be sure, the internalization of the experience of European high culture and American mass culture has a price as well as a benefit. For the other side, or better non-Christian side of anti-Semitism and philo-Semitism, are Jewish responses to modernity. And while a few others have written on the subject, I confess to remain dissatisfied with the state of this area of work. Indeed, Willi has made tremendous contributions in this area of study in works ranging from Jewish survivors of the concentration camps to the special tensions of orthodox Yeshiva life in America.

I sort of stumbled into this theme of Jewish marginality, as Helmreich indicates, in writing opening essays for books reintroducing works of such major figures as Daniel Bell, Morris Raphael Cohen, Yaacov Talmon, and Issac Deutscher, to name several of these. Indeed, even the sociology department that Willi lauds and that I was part of for seven years—Washington University—provided a special display of marginality as a Jewish intellectual fate. Jules Henry, Alvin Gouldner, and Joseph A. Kahl, among others, wrestled with their Jewish demons in private. But in public their interests ranged from African tribes and ghetto miseducation in Jules's case, to the impact of ancient Greek philosophy on modern sociology and bureaucracy in Alvin's case, to social stratification and Mexican development in Joe's case.

Were it not for the minimalist definition of being a Jew provided by Abba Eban—to maintain contact with a Jewish community and to support the highest aspirations of Jews for a national homeland—I probably would be compelled to rank myself in this category. But as it turns out, Abba Eban is a shrewd old fellow. Living up to this minimalist credo turns out to be more complex and vexing than one is led to believe in simply listening to this remarkable blend of British civility and Jewish resolve. One is tempted to add a spin on the old Shavian cliche of "my looks and your brains" by adding, with a sigh of relief, it could have been worse: Jewish civility and British resolve.

Willi teases out a position I have on black-Jewish relations, for which I am deeply grateful. As he knows, I have not written to any degree on the black condition in America. And the reasons are also made apparent by him: the experience of Harlem was, and perhaps remains, too close rather than too removed. Anyhow, I am not much for alliances and pronouncements at this level. For me, as a nonspecialist in this field, my task is to publish the best work being done in the area, and personally, to treat people for their intrinsic merit and take joy in the things that bind. And for me this has to do with playing basketball every Saturday at the YMCA. The bonds that I have forged with my fellow players, many of whom are black—and who range in their professional lives from sales person at Xerox to prison guard at a state hospital to accountant at a branch of Minnesota Mining—are the ground floor of racial reformation. At this stage, others will have to take the elevators to resolve larger issues.

Since I will be commenting at length on *Daydreams and Nightmares* in my response to Professor Dunn's essay, let me simply acknowledge its centrality in my thinking on Jewish marginality, if I may be permitted such a tortured phrase. That others viewed the book similarly is indicated by the National Jewish Book Council award that was given to the book in 1991. The commingling of Jews and blacks makes the American experience unique. In Europe, the Jew could be readily isolated as the villain. And while there are black fascists willing to engage in a similar rhetoric, the fact remains that this is a terribly tiny segment of black life, and even this must come gift-wrapped as part of a special black Muslim faith. To be sure, the black people are too busy defending their hard gained rights and struggling against continuing forms of racism to worry much about the Jewish condition.

In my own experience, the black sense of Jewishness as something apart from whiteness as such remains weak. In this, the Jews may be said to suffer from a double sense of alienation: being different from the dominant currents of the white Protestant culture, and assuredly distinct from their fellow sufferers in stigma, the black culture. It may turn out that the various linkages and couplings between peoples—Jews who are white, blacks who are Christian—may yet soften the edges of animosity and permit the American nation to move forward in concert. Indeed, the enormous gains registered over the course of the twentieth century by both Jewish and black people augur well in this regard. The sociological problem, the policy problem, is that in this forward mark, too many blacks have been left out of the loop. The sharpness of distinction between black wealth and success and black poverty and failure remains far too sharp and far too dangerous.

In this, the Jewish tradition could be helpful. For it is not that Jews are always kind to each other. Indeed, there have been Jewish landlords tormenting Jewish tenants, Jewish factory owners exploiting Jewish garment workers, and yes, Jewish kapos supervising the deaths of Jewish inmates. These are terrible episodes in Jewish history. But they are episodes, never norms. For in the overwhelming cases, Jewish life recognizes the centrality of the individual as a sacred creature of God. There is not the sort of frightening and terrible Hobbesian war of all against all that characterizes much of black ghetto life. I suspect that the power of the Muslim faith among the black poor is precisely an attempt to restore some sense of communion through individual rights. That Willi has spent a lifetime trying to unravel these issues is a grand argument for having students. For, as Weber once noted: that which we fail to do, others will. And in the case of Willi, we know it will be done well.

I would only take slight—very slight—umbrage at one formulation. I do not see myself as an eclectic liberal; nor do I see this position as the ideological equivalent of the democratic imagination. Rather, I see myself as a social commentator paid to do social science. One might invert this and say that I am a social scientist doing social commentary! In any event, this is different than either eclecticism or liberalism. There are some things to which I cling as near and dear, with scarcely a hint of wide-ranging embrace. Put another way, one can be wide-ranging in a choice of stratagems and tactics in order to reach set goals. But even this path is abetted and aided by game theory and public choice analysis derived from the social sciences.

Similarly, liberalism as a cast of mind, that is, liberality of vision and decency to opponents with differing views, is far different than a liberal-

ism with a preset agenda aimed at insuring that all people end up at the
same finish line at the same time. To do that is to impose the sort of
weights and measures of the great god of government on an unsuspecting people. My "liberalism" derives from the premise that we all have a
right to a starting gate position; my "conservatism" stems from an equally
strong view that we have an obligation to run as fast as we can and reach
the finish line before others if we can. But again, I take this as the
wisdom of social science writ large, and not the special divination of a
genial ideology. We march under the banner of political democracy as a
protective cover for our actions as social scientists, not as a slogan that
we must impart to the unsuspecting. We all need to retain a lively sense
of the Jamesian premise that les intellectuelles are a class for themselves and in themselves. Otherwise we will be stoned as false prophets
time and again, and never quite figure out who or what hit us!

Michael Curtis

The theme that Michael Curtis deals with is indeed near and dear to me.
Just prior to framing a response to his probing statement, I had the pleasant
task of reviewing *Tropical Diaspora* by Robert M. Levine. In my mind at
least, this brought together concerns I have for Cuba and Israel at the national level and religion and ethnicity at the political level. An Armenian
colleague, Gerard Libaridian, has reminded me that my interests in nations
have tended to the small places: Cuba, Israel, and Armenia.

And this is true. I have tried to account for this "small power" chauvinism in the privacy of my mind, and find that there are multiple sources
for such concerns: some obvious, others less so. Certainly, being Jewish, and growing up in a world at war where there was no Israel made it
quite plain that the need for a national homeland was an absolute necessity for the survival of the Jewish people. It is one thing to celebrate the
"Jewish idea" apart from land, but such spirituality is, alas, not shared
by the world at large—for whom real estate, living room, turf, call it
what one will, is a dominant coin of the realm.

My interests in Cuba are well known and need no elaboration in this
particular segment at least. The years overseas in Argentina sharpened
my sense of Cuba, and being ensconced in Buenos Aires at the time of
the Castro revolution only served to further sharpen that sense of something important taking place throughout the Latin and Brazilian cultures.

But as several less than kind critics, especially the one for foreign affairs, pointed out, even my Bacardi Lectures at Miami were saturated with a concern for the Jewish people and the peculiar contradictions within American Jewish intellectual life in their collective responses to the theory and practice of Castroism.

And even my interests in the Armenian genocide were sparked by the Holocaust. My work on *Taking Lives: Genocide and State Power,* of necessity, raised all sorts of questions of the common thread or uniqueness of the Holocaust, and beyond that, the search for twentieth-century examples of mass murder at the hands of the state. While we now have the work of the mighty R. J. Rummel, of whom not enough good things can possibly be said, at the time of my writings on this subject—essentially the mid-1970s—an explanation not just of the Holocaust, but of the utterly cavalier treatment of the subject of life and death by sociologists, needed my attention, or so I thought.

And if I may segue into Michael Curtis's essay by means of a political science framework, it was an insight of Robert Dahl, enunciated in what can be called a big little book on the subject of states and democracies, that contributed to my concern for small states. Dahl pointed out that democracy, certainly in its origins if less so in its execution, requires a sense of stake and participation—and this is achieved far better in small sovereignties than in omnibus nation-states. Quite beyond Dahl's more famous writings on power diffusion in small towns, I find this the most prescient and valuable part of his contribution. It is at any rate the one that links for me my concerns for these three small states—each imperiled, each subject to tremendous pressures from big powers, and each serving as a beacon to a diaspora of worth and substance.

Thus, while in general, conversation about center and periphery in Jewish life relates Israel to the United States, in my own evolution this has not been the case. Michael raises disturbing issues about differences between Israeli and American images of Jewish existence. The data reveals enormous support for Israel, far more modest support for Zionism, and hardly any wish to migrate to Israel—at least for the overwhelming portion of Jewish Americans. These realities are termed harsh by Michael; I suspect that they reflect a different sense of what it means to "strengthen Jewishness." I suspect that an element that is critical, and yet hardly discussed in the literature, is that Israel, for all of its merits, is not an ideal society. From

Ben Gurion to the present, one senses that Israelis may hold the United States as first among equals in terms of a democratic tradition, but its Jews as second to Israel in terms of a Jewish tradition.

In part, the problem still inheres in the title *Israeli Ecstasies/Jewish Agonies*. But over time, this has been somewhat neutralized by the evolution of a condition that can be termed *Israeli Agonies/Jewish Ecstasies*. For in the more than two decades since that book appeared, Israel has witnessed another regional war, a war in which it had to sit with its hands tied while the United States and its allies took out the Iraqi war machine, a period in which the feared and loathed PLO became a partner in the land of Eretz Israel, and, generally, a period in which Israel had to adjust its sights to becoming a small regional power, rather than the spiritual leader of world Jewry. In the meanwhile, the Jewish condition in the United States and Western Europe certainly did not deteriorate, and in basic measures of economic power and political influence has in all likelihood increased, affirmative action and multiethnic rhetoric notwithstanding.

Curtis casually but nonetheless realistically calls attention to the Trinitarianism of Jewish life: ethnicity, religiosity, and nationality. But this is a view from the diaspora—a pluralism that holds the separation of temple and state to be as vital as the distinction of church and state; Curtis is correct to call attention to the benefits to Israel of this situation. He is still more on target in indicating that the differences between U.S. and Israeli notions of democratic culture are quite appealing to American Jews, and unnerving to Israeli Jews. It is still too early to assess the benefits or damages caused by Israeli recognition of the Palestinians and the goal of statehood. It is too much to ask of Yitzhak Rabin to factor in American Jewish sensibilities in the conduct of Israeli foreign policy. At the same time, it is also too much to ask of American Jews to simply rubber stamp Israeli turns and twists of policy.

There is a sort of sad optimism in Michael Curtis's final statement about a search for peace. It is not at all clear that Israel is any nearer that goal with respect to a formal agreement and timetable with the Palestinians than it was without such an agreement. Indeed, I suspect that as Israel pursues a proper goal of nationhood, sovereignty and secure borders, that its spiritual mission as the center of world Jewry will diminish. The paradox might well be that as Israel achieves its primary national objectives, the religious unity of the Jews will be somehow more rather than less tenuous, and the cultural formations of Israelis and American Jews will sharply diverge.

The American democratic tradition is fueled by elements that are remote in Israeli life: I have in mind the Greek notion of the demos as such, not to mention the civilities that this tradition imposes on its citizens, and the British tradition of constitutionalism coupled with empiricism. These are very difficult elements in a national culture to identify, and one runs the risk of moving from typology to stereotype. That as it may be, as the century wears on and we approach the half century mark in the history of modern Israel, we see elements that make for a pulling part of the early magnetism between Israelis and American Jews. This may be bemoaned and regretted, but it is hardly contestable.

What we are also witnessing is a weakening of the bonds of religiosity as such in America. While there is a general adhesion to the Judeo-Christian tradition, actual practices tend to become spongier, more private, and less affiliating. Jews may be lost to secularism, but so too are Christians. An overall faith in divine guidance and providential support remains. But in truth, Israelis seem to be undergoing their own crisis of faith, their own participation in a world culture defined less by religious tradition than cultural artifact. What we find is that while Judaism remains important, its centrality diminishes. While Israel remains critical, its specific policies become marginal.

In that sense, we perhaps are moving to a condition in which the very concept of centrality and marginality diminish. And even if these tendencies are not greeted with much enthusiasm in the Jewish world of America or Israel, they are the stuff of reality that remain on the agenda of living history. The theocratic ideal, however benign, is at loggerheads with democratic practice. I suspect that Judaism will adapt to this digression by accepting the notion of itself as having three branches: orthodox, reform, conservative; two roots: Ashkenazic and Sephardic; two sexes: male and female; as many forms of worship as there are languages in the world; and many epicenters: New York, Paris, London, Buenos Aires, and Jerusalem.

If such a Judaism will be wrenching and distinct from what we have known in the past, it will nonetheless choose such a course unhesitatingly, rather than pass slowly and quietly in the night. It should not be forgotten that the People of the Book are also a people of many books. It is the Jewish people as a committee of the whole, rather than the Israeli state, that serves as a beacon unto all nations. We surround sacred text with commentary, and over the centuries, such response itself becomes sacral in character. Having been born in a context of Yiddishkeit, grown up in a world of Israelis that rejected this tradition with a certain contempt, and now witnessed a third generation of Jews—in Tel Aviv and Los Angeles for whom Yiddish is again a living language (for both secularists playing Klezmer music and clericalists studying Talmud I might add)—I am quite uncertain as to what the forms of Jewish life will be in the years ahead. But I am nonetheless convinced that a people who have endured so much in the world and given so much to that world will survive to recreate a Jewish tradition that will mock our doubts and overcome our fanaticisms. Clearly, such assertions are in the realm of moral sentiments rather than empirical generalizations. But after all, is this not what the Jewish tradition is all about?

Raymond Horricks

I am grateful to Ray Horricks for his remarks on my writings on cultural themes. Indeed, if I have one big regret as a sociologist it is that I have done far too little in this area. For in our epoch, who is to say what is more important, the conduct of a war or its representation on celluloid? The act of a sexual assault or the assertion on radio and television that such assaults are a commonplace? The fears of the sociologists of culture writing immediately after World War II have proven utterly gratuitous and groundless.

Contrary to the expectations of the so-called Frankfurt School, high culture has not vanished in a sea of capitalist vulgarities. And just as dubious were the claims of the day, by people like Dwight MacDonald, for example, that the peoples of Western culture would simply become creatures of a disastrous middle culture, or mid-cult. It is apparent, in retrospect, that these social scientists were promoting their own agendas as to what constitutes a fit and proper culture for the rest of humanity.

A colleague of mine from Israel bitterly opposed the expansion of the private sector into television and radio, fearing that it would doom the "mission of culture to educate." In that high-cult expression of contempt for ordinary people this liberal and otherwise urbane scholar showed a deep suspicion for the democratic spirit, which at some level has to do with the right of free choice, without which the marketplace of ideas would remain barren .

As it is, most of my writings on cultural themes and persons are connected to the politics of the times. The review essay on Solzhenitsyn's *Gulag Archipelago* done in the mid-1970s was provoked by a realization that the entire communist nation was a prison house, and not simply an identifiable string of work and labor camps scattered throughout the northern perimeter of the late and unlamented Soviet Union. The essay on Orwell was stimulated by Steiner's essay on the corruption of the German language under nationalist socialism. Indeed, this is a minor motif struck by Solzhenitsyn as well. It seemed to me at the time that Orwell understood, better than anyone else I know, the relationship of a culture to a language. Moreover, when language itself becomes debased either through slogans, sloppiness, or oversimplification, we end up with a dictatorship, with tyranny. Hence, defense of a culture is the first line of defense of democracy itself.

The two film reviews on Bunuel's *Discreet Charm of the Bourgoisie* and Cimino's *The Deer Hunter* are in a somewhat different category. I had the pleasure of meeting Bunuel in Mexico City in 1964, and simply wanted to repay an intellectual debt. While I was not entirely in sympathy with this film, it struck me as a farce with a terrible bite. I still cannot figure out whether Bunuel was the revolutionary or the conservative. His bourgeoisie is, after all, filled with mannerisms born of cowardice, and avarice that was a consequence of converting affluence into opulence with disastrous social consequences. And anyone familiar with the bourgeois manners and mores of Mexico City or Buenos Aires knows how close to the marrow Bunuel was, the ideological angle of vision of his classic work.

The Deer Hunter was, and in my opinion remains, the most important film on the Vietnam War. For while pointing up the horrors of war as such, this was a film that also emphasized what everyone already knew to be the truth: that this was a distinctly working-class war, from which ordinary youngsters working in the mills of Pittsburgh received few so-called educational deferments. Such legislation effectively made this war the exclusive "possession" of the 50 percent of youngsters who did not go to college, while it was the other half left to protest the horrors they never experienced. This was also a film in which American values, including those of a transplanted Russian orthodox church culture, were at the bedrock of those who fought. And above all, this was a film of a defense of a free culture that never confused opposition to war with defense of tyranny. I share with Ray Horricks the firm belief that *The Deer Hunter* was that epic novel on film that rivals *The Best Years of Our Lives* for its capacity to capture war as a domestic national experience even more than a ton of history books.

I share with Ray a love of jazz music. Indeed, I think that Ray is one of those handful of critics whose respect for the music includes its treatment with the same integrity and sobriety that writers on classical music have long exhibited. As readers of *Daydreams and Nightmares* will appreciate, growing up in Harlem a few blocks from Minton's Playhouse and the Apollo Theater made a love of jazz virtually inevitable. My four or five essays on the subject have, however, been interested in a specifically sociological theme: the relationship and interpenetration of audience and artist, the context of music and its impact on its content. Some day, if I can live to that day, I want to do a book on American music history in just these terms.

The Europeans have spent so much time examining the "nature" of "high culture" that they have forgotten to look at the milieu in which music and art are created. On the other hand, some Americans have committed the opposite sin, seeing culture as defined exclusively by the marketplace, who buys and who sells. As a result, the analysis of the art object as such gets drowned in a sea of sillinesses. It might be true to claim, as some in the subjectivist tradition do, that one cannot be defined as a poet if another does not purchase his or her book of poems. But that hardly begins to address, much less exhaust matters. For we are still left with the task of distinguishing the durable from the perishable, the worthwhile from the worthless, the innovative from the derivative. The intellectual trick is to combine both the pragmatic and the theoretical in the same schema.

It is precisely in such a linkage of pragmatic and theoretical considerations that the social scientific transition can move beyond or at least contribute to the advanced study of a culture. For otherwise, we may as well describe the aesthetic realm as an extension of business and be left with a *Forbes* write up of an actor's millions, or as a branch of the history of ideas, in which we go hopping about from one Impressionist painter to another as if France never existed except as a backdrop to a new style of putting paint on a canvas.

In music the cardinal sin is hero worship and static analysis, as if musicians simply appear on the scene, do their stuff, take their drugs, and die heroic deaths in cheap run-down Parisian hostels. Hopefully, with a new generation of articulate musicians like Gunther Schuller and Wynton Marsalis, the jazz criticism of the past will be dead and buried, to be followed by the sort of serious analysis this great American art form truly deserves. We finally seem to have transcended the Maileresque "White Hipster" phenomenon, in which the culture of drugs and sexuality replaced the actual study of what jazz artists create.

It turns out, at least from what I have discovered in my own limited efforts, that the problems of music, its organization, performance, and innovation, are quite similar across the spectrum of styles. Perhaps that is why "cross-over" types of musicians have increasingly come to dominate the jazz and popular music world, and, indeed, moved in the opposite direction, with classical artists performing in jazz ensembles and opera sopranos putting out Christmas albums. When we reach a point in which a music critic examines the music being performed, rather than being segregated in the commentary on one specific type of music, we will then achieve a level of creativity equal to if not greater than what was achieved in past centuries.

Quite apart from this sense of programmatics, there is a special pleasure in writing objectively about that which one enjoys subjectively. I know that Ray has this special sense, and I daresay that others who deal with cultural themes feel similarly. That is why for so many of the cultural critics, the review of films, television, music, dance, novels, or what have you is a special add-on to more vocationally centered activities. Indeed, the risk of dilettantism must always be countered by a sober sense of professional capacities and limits. But, for the present epoch, at least within the social sciences, where any display of interest in art and culture is viewed with suspicion, such concerns must be considered minor and livable.

Arthur Asa Berger

Arthur Asa Berger's contribution to the festschrift represents an important development in his own thought—a seriousness that comes through many years of struggle with the relationship of culture and communication. The questions he asks are important. I share with Arthur a belief that the notion of a public culture avoids many of the problems connected to high culture at one end and popular or mass culture at the other. The concern on such matters derives almost exclusively from the advocates of a high culture. Scarcely any "defenses" of mass culture are written, because its advocates are so busy in the process of its creation.

I feel that the issue—the sociological issue at least—is less centered on culture, high, middle, or low, than on control. That is to say, those who feel that BBC is the only proper television outlet in the United Kingdom are really saying that the arbiters of a culture belong to a small subset of a ruling class. They differ only in rhetoric from the totalitarians who at least have the decency not to coat their ideology with notions of high culture. The same situation exists in professional life. There are those who believe that only one organization can truly dispense the findings or the largesse of one science. This is equally a matter of power, not science.

I do not know whether my writings on culture can be viewed as either pre- or postdeconstructionist; and I confess not much to care. In truth, the sort of polarities that Berger finds in my writings on culture derive in part from a dialectical tradition—in which, thinking in polarities helps me understand the full range of prospects in any given idea—and also from the history of ideas tradition—in which one examines the variety of meanings and assumptions that attach to critical words like "beauty," "health," or "class." This is a tradition that extends from Aristotle in antiquity to Arthur O. Lovejoy in our century. I have no monopoly on these approaches. But yes, they are under utilized in social sciences, preempted by quantitative and building-block approach to acquiring knowledge.

Let me nonetheless address some of the concerns and shortcomings that Arthur raises in my approach to specific themes—whether critical remarks on film or on music. Some of these I have dealt with in responding to Raymond Horricks. I love the motion pictures. And I have a personal library of some five hundred films. Perhaps some day I shall be able to put some of this "accumulated wealth" to good use. For now, let me address how difficult is the business of prediction in culture. With respect to rock and roll, I am not sure whether my predictions were premature or just plain wrong. Indeed, there are times we learn as much from mistakes honestly arrived at, as correct prognosis impurely framed. I will say that rock has moved from big markets to small clubs, the big mega-watt stations to smaller FM stations, and finally, that its role as an organizer of social thought has been taken over by rap music in the black world, and country music in the white world. That one can speak in such stratification terms indicates the potential for a sociology of culture, but it does not quite come to terms with Arthur's critical vision of my type of thinking. So let me turn to the more exacting task at hand: a defense of my vision of culture.

It would be hard to be Horowitz and not have an interest in music! Let it be said that my concerns are much less distinctions between forms of music than the qualities of musical content. It is the sad differentiation between "classical," "jazz," and "rock" that needs to be broken down. Those who write that classical music is somehow far richer in emotional range than jazz music are revealing a terrible lack of knowledge of the music as such. At the other end, the jazz artists who write of the classical tradition as a series of "moldy figs" or worse reveal an abysmal ignorance of just what riches exist in the European inheritance. But again, as we have seen in area after area of culture, the issues are really about power and its imposition, and not the construction or deconstruction of a culture.

My essay "On Seeing and Hearing Music" is a first effort at a sociological theory on the subject as a whole. I am not sure with whom Berger is arguing, but my point is rather his. Namely, if it is the case that the compact disk provides a very fine musical experience as such, along the lines outlined by Glenn Gould—whom I confess to greatly admire— then why do people continue going to the concert hall or the jazz club? One can argue that rock and rap remain essentially dance forms, and hence intrinsically sociable in character. But this is not the situation whether one can hold constant sitting in a seat listening to a piece of music "live" or staying at home or a sealed room listening in private. The point is not the quality of recorded performance versus that of live performance, although I would argue that the experience of listening to a Glenn Gould recording—without coughs from an audience of thousands—is quite a good deal less "alienating" than glowering at such people in concert halls!

Essentially, I am claiming that Gould may be correct at the technical, recording level, but misses the point of concert going—as embodied in nine or perhaps eleven points, including having a good old time of it. As a result, the burden of my remarks is to show that the process of making music is inherently a social act. I remain unsure what is so weak in this line of analysis as to require alteration or outright abandonment. Predicting trends in culture is a risky business, but at some level, prediction is the business we are in! For otherwise, we are reduced to historians looking at the past or statisticians summarizing the present. But prediction involves explanation, and the papers I have written on music are centered on just this aspect of prediction.

My critique of Keith Jarrett is of a different, and lesser, order of magnitude. For my concern is how the new technology, which threatens to permit huge collections of materials in one small package offer not just unlimited opportunity but also unlimited boredom! Jarrett is a fine jazz innovator. His Köln concert provided stunning and early evidence of how variations on themes can be extended to jazz motifs, and yet stretch back to incorporate the work of Mozart and Haydn and Bach and their own sense of room for the musicians to improvise. But the new technology also permits a certain egotism to unfold. Solos become ends unto themselves, variations are performed, but no theme is detectable. Every single piece of art has a beginning, a middle, and an end, just as art as such is boundless and endless. It is my opinion that Jarrett has confused a single piece or performance with musical culture as such. Just why this is evidence that I can accept innovation in one art form and not another remains unclear to me.

There is a straw-man element to Berger's critique. For on one hand he fastens me with a label of deconstructionist that I have never accepted, or certainly never enunciated, and then goes on to note that the trouble with deconstructionism (and presumably myself) is that if texts have no intrinsic meanings beyond their readings, how can one have extra-textual or extra-musical analysis? Indeed, I would have the same concerns. The analysis of culture is a concept that moves far beyond the artifact of language as such. If I read Bunuel properly, it is the entrapment in immediacy, as evidenced by the conclusion to eat oneself into oblivion even as the rest of the world blows apart, that characterizes his sense of the bourgeoisie. In other words, is the social class of parasites, if I may use such a rhetoric, that invites Bunuel's ridicule—and ours as well.

Berger offers six interpretations of a single, dare one say, singular "joke." But he is not content with a Rashomon Effect, that is, a choice among five distinct ideological frames of reference. And he is right to reject such a pure relativism. Instead, he opts for multidisciplinary or interdisciplinary analysis. But this, it seems to me, is to move a considerable distance beyond deconstructionism. However, perhaps Arthur needs to recapture his sense of humor when it comes to others! I have in mind his start and finish with the statement by the late Melvin Tumin, who I presume is a stand-in for the sociological method as such, that popular culture is worth about a half-hour in his seminars. Knowing Mel as colleague and neighbor in Princeton I know that he was simply pulling Arthur's leg! There is scarcely a sociologist from my generation better versed in the arts and musics of our time or one for whom the issue of culture is more paramount!

What this indicates is that culture is more than constructions and options of analysis, it is what people feel and may not articulate in words at all. That is why, or rather that is one good reason, for taking the person and his or her society as an analytic frame of reference unto itself. If we read a script we learn some things about a play or a film. But if we see a variety of actors perform and read these words, then our response is different—not only positive or negative, but impacted by shadings of meaning. The new book by John Gross on *Shylock: A Legend and Its Legacy* in tells us that this character from *The Merchant of Venice* can be played negatively and positively, with empathy or as an antipathetic character. But he also tells us, when stripped away, Shakespeare wrote an anti-Semitic play, albeit a brilliant one. That I submit is what the analysis of culture is about—multileveled rather than multicultured.

Cultural analysis is always about words and more than words, about performance and more than performance, about personalities and ideologies. I suspect that Arthur, in moments when he is less given over to the enthrallment of current academic vocabularies, knows this full well—or at least as well as I. For now, I will try in my own proximate work to address the issues he raises with a seriousness it deserves and that he brings to the subject in his own comedic works.

Until we stop treating the areas of culture as a footnote to literature, or worse, the "superstructure" that sits upon an economic "base," we will never arrive at a sociology of culture worth much. We need to get back to the great tradition of Karl Mannheim, Paul Honigsheim, and Florian Znaniecki, and move away from fashions set by hagiographers of cultural figures and denigrators of cultural traditions. In an area such as music criticism we have been blessed with such major figures as

Samuel Lipman, Joseph Horowitz, and Richard Taruskin. Thus far, we have few equivalents in the study of jazz and popular music. To be sure, the pioneering work of Ron Serge Denisoff indicates what can be done in this vast wasteland. Too often, necrology substitutes for biography, and mindless verbiage about "the genius of [fill in the name of the moment]" replace the sort of scalpel-like precision one finds in the culture as such. The study of the social sources of cultural forms requires neither deconstruction, nor for that matter, construction. It does require the same intensity, dedication, and knowledge base with which we address institutions and persons in other spheres of social life.

R. Serge Denisoff with George Plasketes

The great strength of the Millsian analysis of culture was his ability and willingness to treat this subject seriously—as part of the mosaic of social life, and not as some sort of footnote to "real issues." Moreover, he was smart enough to get beyond the metaphysical rubbish of culture as some sort of "superstructural" reflection of economic wealth. It is not that such relationships are unknown, it is that their relative importance is precisely what sociology must determine—empirically, not in an apriorist manner.

Since Denisoff and Plasketes were kind enough to cite my reflections of thirty years ago on this Millsian legacy, it is best that I simply focus on my own thinking, or better, where Mills stops and the world of culture continues. For Mills shares an American sociological trait of knowing much about culture writ large and saying little about actual cultural figures. This is in the tradition of pragmatism, since what seemingly matters is the context of culture, that is, the "marketplace" in which art, music, and novels are bought and sold.

What is left out of the reckoning is the content of culture, that is to say, the specific meanings that are attached to specific works. In this, we owe much to the work of the European tradition, to Siegfried Krakauer on film, Leo Lowenthal on the novel, and Arnold Hauser on classical painting, who appreciated that the starting point of culture is genuine stuff, real materials of creation, but the terminal point is some sense of quality in culture. And for that one needs a combination, a linkage of content with context. Indeed, what marks the work of Ron Denisoff apart from others is precisely this innate capacity, this instinct to focus on the popular culture as both an object of enjoyment and a subject worth studying.

Again, since this chapter points to the role of Transaction in the promotion and publication of works in the sociology—and I would add the anthropology—of culture, I would like to speak briefly about my personal efforts in this regard. It should already be clear that I have not been at peace with either those who see the task of a sociology of culture to define the economic marketplace or those who work hard to establish criteria of greatness in art apart from changing societal requirements and contexts. In this, I suspect I am closer to people in philosophy ranging in epistemological difference from John Dewey to Jacques Maritain, both of whom wrote brilliant and lasting contributions to the subject, than to most sociological efforts, which strike me as feeble and puerile in comparison.

Hopefully, I will be remembered, if at all, in this area not for making the sociology of culture "respectable." It is too damned respectable without my intervention. Rather, my aim has been to link art, audience, and artist. This triadic relationship is one I have believed in on theoretical grounds. Growing up in Harlem at a time when the most significant clubs playing jazz were therein located, I began to appreciate the centrality of music in black life, the social roots in human joys no less than blues, and the wider intellectual meanings of the work of Ellington, Waller, and Basie, and later, Gillespie, Monk, and Miles. This was not a clinical activity, but part of my own growing experience. I tried to deal with this theme in one chapter of *Daydreams and Nightmares,* but in later life did so in intellective terms.

Indeed, it always struck me that when the Europeans wrote of culture it had a distinctly European flavor, which is understandable; but that when Americans addressed similar themes, they too did so in terms of our European inheritance. I am equally at home in these European works, and those who know me realize what a powerful value music as such has had in my life. But I came to all this through jazz—so that it was through an effort to understand Charlie Parker that I listened to Igor Stravinsky. Only in later life, when I became personally acquainted with Lalo Schifrin, did I appreciate the fact that I was scarcely the only one to grow a culture in this manner.

So the materials of my essays on culture have almost uniformly been drawn from the American contribution to popular music. Indeed, that may well be why I was so pleased to sponsor Ron's major works through the auspices of Transaction. Be that as it may , the theme of the "three A's"—art, artist, and audience—strikes me as a good way to learn about the three B's of Beethoven, Bach, and Brahms, or, for that matter, the three G's of Gershwin, Goodman, and Getz! But before professional journals of sociology can publish usefully in this field, practitioners must become alive to the wonders of the subject.

Within sociology we have had a group of people quite dedicated to jazz, for example. Perhaps this is a function of higher sensibilities to the black contribution to our civilization, or simply a way to translate a regard for the subject of deviance into something more profound. Yet, with the exception of Howard Becker, and perhaps a few others from the "Chicago School" influenced by his special form of ethnography, this interest in jazz is little more than trotting out the clarinet for a few blues bars at an annual convention. And with the passing of the "moldy figs," even this embarrassing sop to a musical culture has dissolved.

The task before us—and if I have life after this festschrift, before myself as well—is to link the tradition of contextual analysis with the study of cultural contents, and to do so with the banalities of the former and the ostentations of the latter. The work of journals such as *Popular Music* and *Society* certainly is a crucial starting point, and gatherings of social scientists for whom cultural themes are central are also important. The importance of a field is not measured by requesting admission to the halls of the graven images or officialist journals, but by the penetration of a field into the common, shared culture.

My guess, and it is only such, is that the sociology of culture will find a ready professional home in the future in the structure of communications research. It is this area that has best appreciated the place of culture in social life. And it is this field that provides some new and exciting prospect for linking technical issues of cultural languages with the direction of aesthetic creativity as such. All sorts of permutations and combinations are taking place in the larger culture . And as one would suspect this is also the case for new forms of aesthetic expression.

The linkage of the social sciences and cultural formations thus offers opportunities hitherto unimagined, or at least unwritten. I would like to see my own terribly limited efforts in this area as part of a wider movement. This will provide a healthy skepticism for the communications researchers of the period ahead, and a healthy appreciation by the people working in communications and information of the powerful instruments offered in such applications as advertisement, marketing, and promotions, no less than film, television, and museums.

The question of popular culture and the academy raised by Denisoff and Plasketes ceases to be polite when issues such as rap lyrics and dirty pictures and coarse graffiti enter the scene. It is easy enough for universities to integrate the lyrics of Peter, Paul, and Mary, something else again when we need to factor in the hard pornography of a Sister Souljah. When the *New York Times* leads the pack in chastising popular musical forms for overt sexuality, maleness, or racism, then the issue of university integration becomes difficult.

I am not sure that either Wright Mills or Charles Reich could envision forms of protest that have such a harsh tone as we hear today. Indeed, the new music often juxtaposes movements that we like to think of as sharing a common base in multiculturalism and rainbow coalitions. But these pleasantries fall apart in a rap culture in which men against women and black against white becomes normatively insinuated. We want our cultural cake but are not easily persuaded that it is worth eating. This raises several issues: (1) the quality of a musical or artistic culture apart from a message; and (2) the character of messages that get out of hand, that we do not want to hear. For so long we have easily identified youth with radicalism that when we hear a young culture that is apparently identified with reaction or counterculture, the radicals of yesteryear become unnerved, if not unhinged at the prospect.

In that sense, the need of a sociology of culture is much like a sociology of policy: to recognize the organic relationship of these aspects of reality, but not to become entrapped by them. Partisanship will always be tested by a generation waiting to be heard. Sociology needs to investigate how this insinuates itself in social life, for example, how the rage for country and western dancing is an installation of decency and civility in a largely white world that cuts across age and class, but not race. We need to study how outrage as well as direct rage are part of being young and alienated, and in this way, how rap music and African art may also instate themselves in social life. The sociologist needs to get out the scalpel and critically examine such developments, and all the while maintain a sense of aesthetic representation of what is good in cultural terms no less than what is true in political terms.

We already have under our belts some fine work in this new world of crossovers. In this, the work started by people like Bernard Rosenberg and David Manning White and David Riesman, which seemingly was aborted, has in fact become part of a larger picture of society—one in which culture is neither footnote nor reflex, but simply an expression of the mosaic of social life, sometimes more important, other times less so, sometimes discussing great works, other times explaining or explaining away inferior works. My, what a glorious era the twenty-first century beckons to become in these terms!

Mary E. Curtis

The key, if one may speak metaphorically, to my efforts in the publishing world are simple enough to understand. They are difficult only in the execution. To start with the simple: I have never thought of myself as a publisher, despite spending more than forty hours weekly for the past forty years on this "avocation". Instead, I think of my social science activities as having had three essential components: teaching, writing, and publishing. Each of them involve the written as well as the spoken word. Nathaniel Pallone captures this spirit in his own contribution.

Transaction is a "mission" publisher—no more and no less than a religious publisher is a firm with a mission. Our ulterior purpose is to "convert" people to the ways and wiles of the social sciences. To be sure, it is a trifle disquieting to speak of social science in these terms; but in operational terms, Transaction, and before that, Paine-Whitman, represent an effort to transmit a culture, a frame of reference, and ultimately a way of seeing. It is not that others have not published social research before, during, and doubtless after Transaction bites the intellectual dust. Rather, it is that the firm provided, and happily still does, to use a monstrous word, "niche publishing" in social science.

The age of system building came to a crashing halt in philosophy with Kant and Hegel. It took another fifty years for the same face of recognition to register in the social sciences. We had great system builders of our own: Talcott Parsons in sociology and David Easton in political science to mention but two. But it is now recognized that systems, even the best of them, come crashing down, as soon as the world is confronted by a new set of facts. The system builder, in his very attempt to hold firm, begins to look and his disciples act, like Ptolemy in the face of the Copernican Revolution—hold firm to the theory, damn the reality, and make whatever tortured adjustments are necessary on an ad hoc basis to preserve the system. In this way, even the best of the system builders turn reactionary with a vengeance. They are not so much for-gotten as become curious objects of study in how not to do science.

In the face of this profound shift in social science from theories de-rived from systems and theories that reflect realities, it also becomes evident (or at least should) that the role of the individual "great" or "ge-nius" cannot be established by founding yet another new system. In-stead, the second half of the twentieth century in particular, and in all areas, has shown the profound importance of cooperation of many tal-ents toward a common end. Those who work in and under laboratory conditions know this instinctively. Those who work with literally thou-sands of authors learn this same truth of our times slowly.

Social science is the work of many people. This volume, this festschrift, isolates some of my efforts, and does so with great intel-ligence and warmth. Yet, it is a fact—one that must be understood—that the greatest contribution I have ever made is not to a grand synthesis, pleasant as that may be to contemplate in one's hallucina-tory moments, but to organizing social science as a publishing frame of reference—one that stands outside any one discipline, and beyond any one organizational control unit, and with the notion that social science thrives in shared circumstances.

Social science is also a community of friendly users no less than ad-miring or disapproving colleagues. For without that life blood of con-nection between science and policy, the connection of social research to relevant audience would also be shattered. Transaction has, for more than thirty years, stood for this principle. In this we helped to define the century in ways that my own individual efforts pale against.

I am hardly the first to have understood this. Denis Diderot in fash-ioning the *Encyclopedie, ou dictionnaire raisonne des sciences, des arts et des metiers,* brought together the best minds of his age and his nation. The very act of creation of this huge set of volumes was a demonstration of democracy, of the fact that enlightenment meant a shared achieve-ment of the many, and not just the insight of the few. The *Encyclopedie* broke the hold of the past not by forging a system of antireligion. In-deed, that aspect of the French enlightenment is more an embarrassment and a liability than anything else. Rather it made knowledge public, not secret. It gave exact information a theoretical standing that required no metaphysical excuses.

With all his looking backward to feudal times, William Morris, and his Kenescott Press performed the same service in England. The Socialist League of Hammersmith was simply an umbrella under which Morris and his colleagues defined the very culture of England. It gave new meaning to Chaucer. And if Morris failed to give "new meaning" to socialism, in the very effort to show that the culture of a nation is embedded in the typescript of a book, a revolution swept the world that converted this dedicated medievalist to a modernist in the best sense of the word, to show the future to the present.

Nor has sociology been lacking in this vision. Emile Durkheim in particular understood the collective nature of the collective conscience. His *Sociologie Annees* may not have given the world a system, or even a new sense of purpose, but it did provide an integrating framework of people who commented upon and reviewed what was taking place in the world of social research in every major language, and in drawing together the various strands of sociology, so that its full impact could be realized.

I find it interesting that Durkheim himself, while writing on everything from the division of labor in society, to suicide, to the forms of religious experience, was careful to avoid the pitfalls of system building. He understood better than most that theory construction and system building were quite distinct activities. And I suspect that his daily involvement in the world of social science publishing helped him in this understanding.

This may appear a windy prologue to Mary's chapter "The Scholar as Publisher," but I think a necessary one, since for me, scholarship and publishing have been so intertwined that I have come to believe that the very relationship is itself an expression of social research in our times. I am deeply grateful to Mary for her chapter. She knows me on an everyday basis: as my wife, my partner at Transaction, and as a person who, in her own right and her own way, has been a central force in social science publishing. Her efforts at Praeger as director of social science publishing and at John Wiley as vice president in charge of scientific journals gave her a base of operation as well as understanding. So I am deeply appreciative that someone so close can yet speak so positively—no easy chore in the best of circumstances and the most ideal of marriages.

Still, it is a fact that Mary grew to maturity in a specific culture of publishing. Her experiences at CBS, after it purchased Praeger, helped shape many of her ideas. And these were further enriched by her tenure at Wiley. So it is as if a medievalist (myself) in this case must explain to a modernist (Mary) the "thick text" that characterizes a passage from individual scholarly activity to shared professional publishing. It is not that I abjure or dismiss the market economy in which we live. Indeed, I take great pride in having navigated Transaction through many perilous times and waters.

What I do take exception to is the idea that one can learn the skills of a social class, or subset of a class, and "plug" those skills into any activity from show making to book publishing. I am not accusing Mary of doing this, and certainly not of adopting the Harvard Business School model in which one learns a method and a style and then goes into the world and "applies" these to specific businesses. But there is a sense in which the driving force, the motor if you will, of my publishing approach is perhaps passed over too lightly in favor of explaining my publishing activities.

Publishing has become large enough to suffer divisions of labor of its own, sometimes dangerously narrow divisions. I have long felt, and continue to feel, the pedagogy of the oppressed students notwithstanding, that notions of textbook, trade, and professional publishing are essentially artificial. They may make useful marketing tools, and then again, they may not. Ultimately, I have fashioned Transaction to reflect what my dear colleague at Oxford University Press, and my own editor of a dozen books, once said to me: "Never mind text or trade. Worry about whether a book is good or bad." In a sense, this is an extension of the E. B. White dictum: Be sure to avoid publishing bad books, and the rest will take care of itself.

Well all of this is easier said than done, especially in a world of social science in which literary manners are poor, and the sense of style all too frequently nonexistent. To be sure, the challenge I confronted is not only to show that social science is a commodity, and hence subject to the laws of the marketplace, onerous as those may be at times, but also to provide a place in which good writing is required and regarded. This is all second nature to people in the humanities and fine arts. But this all had to be learned from scratch in the social sciences.

Indeed, the more recent social sciences, at the time we started Transaction, developed a cult of bad writing, as if to prove that the distinction between the esoteric and the exoteric was identical with the differences between professionals and amateurs. Treading a fine line between communicating to wider audiences and doing so without compromising the social science was a learned habit—a painfully learned one. Not every new publication aimed at a popular market achieved that goal. And for the most part, such efforts have failed miserably as publications as well. So the task I faced was not simply economic, but also pedagogical and the hardest people to teach are one's fellow colleagues.

And what we must all learn is that the new environment is a hard one for social science publishing no less than social science as such. We are faced with monopolization as a function of retail book outlets, as a function of mergers and acquisitions, and as a consequence of a drying up of certain old fields and the emergence of new fields. When chains like Barnes & Noble and Dalton's and Walden Books account for more than 50 percent of retail market share, when social science firms like Basic Books and The Free Press are swallowed whole by HarperCollins and Macmillan, respectively, and these in turn become footnotes to the News Corporation and Viacom, and when certain disciplines become ideological fortresses of the nineteenth century against the coming into being of the twenty-first century, then we have problems far greater than those attacked by the Copyright Clearance Center.

There are no magic solutions or formulas. But I suspect that in the next century, whether information is delivered in CD-ROM form or traditional hard copy, the editorial decision making will come together in a unique way. Academics will draw closer to publishing, and publishing will come to depend heavily on the talent produced by the academies. Forms of association will evolve; new mixes in the relationship of universities to publishing will emerge. The old university press will seek profits, and the new publishers will seek status. This is less a matter of prophecy than recognition of changing circumstances that we face in common.

If much writing on scholarly publishing has become spongy recently, it is because defining the exact parameters in this world have become hard to establish. The confluence of issues in which technical, legal, and moral considerations crisscross with publishing as such have become virtually impossible for a single person to penetrate. It will be left for people like Mary, who combine in their person the search for a science of society with the craft of publishing, to provide such rich textures of analysis. For my part, I am content to have been given the joy and grace of taking part in a small bit of the future of scholarly publishing, and show that indeed, it does work—albeit imperfectly and haltingly. Now that we can speak with confidence of a sociology of communication and information, we can perhaps break the current logjam of issues in search of theories.

In point of fact the chapter written by Mary is so thoroughgoing and careful that one is tempted to say "thank you my dear wife and colleague" and let it go at that. But she raises such important issues that they merit amplification, if not response. It is correct to note that the bulk of my writings on publication predate the 1990s. This is for a variety of reasons: good people started working harder in the theory and practice of publishing; and my activities on behalf of various professional organizations were sharply reduced as a result of a feeling that other scholarly work merited greater attention. Indeed, with people like Mary Curtis and Scott Bramson sharing the load at Transaction, we had the sort of talent that is the envy of firms substantially larger than our own.

Having said this, I would not want it thought that my interest in basic issues about publishing have diminished over time. Rather they have become melded with other, larger considerations. Everything from piracy to freedom to read were seen, or better are now seen by myself, as simply an extension and special case of issues about publicity and privacy on one hand, and the contours of a free society on the other. Publishing has for too long been parochial in linking its interests with the larger parameters of American democracy. This may seem surprising, but alas, it is true. Organizational constraints tend to dim an interest in the big picture. And for me, the unique element in publishing is precisely its ability at systemic linkages of concerns that appear on the surface as disparate and remote. The need to escape parochialism is particularly important, especially in a field not exactly noted for solid analysis.

Still, even in this period, along with Mary, I have written a statement on scholarly publishing for the *Encyclopaedia of Publishing* and a variety of briefer statements on law, technology, and publishing in the present publishing era. I would also note that a number of the papers in the second edition of *Communicating Ideas* derive from the late 1980s, which is again indicative of trying to keep up with trends and, at the least, not resting on my oars. It might well be that with a changing of the guard at Transaction, I will have somewhat more time to address the sort of consensus that Mary speaks of and that indeed she has taken the lead on within the publishing community.

Beth Luey

The title of Beth Luey's contribution is "Planning Expeditions into Uncharted Territory." While I deeply appreciate the sentiment behind the title, I rather look upon my publishing role as more akin to unplanned expeditions into charted territory. That is to say, it was more a matter of trial and error that led me to appreciate that I was part of an industry called publishing, or at least its subset known as scholarly publishing. Beyond that, Transaction had to figure out what it was not as well as what it was. Indeed, I think this is probably a useful exercise for any publisher, given the changing nature of academic disciplines at one end and the volatility of professional publishing at the other.

There were a variety of conceptual sightings that permitted Transaction to evolve the way it did: First, a recognition that social science is a field of publication unto itself. That took place early on, since *Transaction,* later rechristened as *Society* was a single publication to start with. Second came an awareness that we were in the world of ideas, not restricted or constructed formats, that delivering the "product" called social science could be done in a variety of ways: from a quasi-popular magazine to scholarly journals to academic books. This was a wrenching decision, since it entailed placing resources in a variety of formats and shrinking *Society* to a core audience along the way. Third came a decision to treat social science publishing as an end unto itself, a "mission" publisher much like religious publishers define themselves. Again, this was no easy conclusion to draw, given the heavy biases against business and religion one finds in academic life.

I confess to being less enamored of the distinction of public or private ownership than I was at the outset of this adventure some thirty-two years ago. Just as universities as such are involved in a variety of economic "mixes" so too are publishers. For example, despite the name, I suspect that Oxford University Press is far more of a business than Transaction can ever hope to be! We are, for all our private sector structure, linked to a university. And this is no mere formality. I shall be ever grateful to Rutgers and its various presidents from Mason Gross, to Edward Bloustein, to Francis Lawrence—the three leaders under whom I have served and who in turn stood by the press through thick and thin—and there have been many thick walls and thin ice situations we have faced over the years.

And in this, I can only loudly second Beth Luey's words that "academic disciplines do not rise and fall in a vacuum."

If I have a concern it is with continuing overemphasis on gatekeeper functions of publishing. The gates are broken, the filters are changed, the intellectual brokers come and go. The publisher is responsible more for the quality of what gets published than the ideology or policy of who gets published. And this reflects a modest sense of publisher roles. Very often, the trends are set by newspapers and news weeklies, by issues that are dealt with as urgent by society at large. It is true that there is a trickle-down as well as a percolating up effect. Beth is so wise in the ways of publishing that she knows these movements are equally real and valid. The mediating function of Transaction derives from living in two worlds: one of public policy, the other of social science research. Beth's illustrations of difficult concepts translated into scholarly works and then filtered into the popular media are entirely valid. At the same time, she wisely points to the special nature of individuals who bring ideas to life with literary grace and open-hearted decency for an audience of nonspecialists.

Whether the work of scholarly and professional publishing instills fear and hostility rather than joyful acceptance is hard to say. We have to keep in mind how little consensus there is within professional communities. And if that is the case, to expect open-hearted acceptance of every new idea by the larger public is simply more than we, as professionals, have a right to anticipate. As a result, the publishing community, certainly in social science and the humanities, must be open to new ideas, but not prematurely dismissive of old values. The sense of balance is critical. Transaction has a Library of Conservative Ideas, but we also have an equally strong series on the Library of Liberal Ideas. The smart publisher, at least one who wants to hang around a while, would be well advised not only to worry about who to keep out, but also worry about who to bring in!

Speaking of mediating roles, Beth raises Natalie Davis's *Martin Guerre* volume. But if we are frank, it is clear that it was the French film with Gerard Depardieu that made the book a popular item. The market is big and ubiquitous. We published a title called *The Politics of the ACLU* in 1985—a good book, but not exactly a best-seller. But once the ACLU became a campaign item in the 1988 presidential elections, it became an "important book," that is, a book with a large public impact.

I confess not to share Beth's pessimistic belief that "only in times of extreme social tension do the actions of ordinary people seem to matter." The "actions" of ordinary people may take different forms in the mid-1990s than the mid-1960s—but in a democracy, such actions matter, and a lot. It is not the task of publishers to advocate a "new" society, it is their responsibility to provide options—old and new, the not tried and the discarded.

Historians and moralists alike have to take up the question of the differences or similarities of hard-working farmers and equally hard-working prostitutes. After all, the weight does not necessarily fall on the energies expended at work so much as the quality and character of such work. Much of Beth's commentaries on this subject pertain to textbooks rather than scholarly books. And texts, as Merton has pointed out are essentially summaries of existing knowledge, not breakthroughs into new knowledge. And a publisher like Transaction, who may on occasion publish a text, is essentially living on the edge of research. Sometimes we fall off the cliff, other times we take off and fly away.

Beth is right to note that a part of my intellectual energies have been dedicated to the education of fellow publishers. They have lived too long with a Harvard Business School model, in which one can be an executive in a shoe company one day and in publishing the next. I do not believe this for a minute. The parameters of marketing, advertising, and promotion are different in such cases. The warehousing, shipping, and inventory volumes are also quite different. And above all, the sense of need for shoes vis-à-vis books are radically different. As a result, we need to constantly participate as publishers in the schooling of those of our colleagues who do not believe in their products, but view them as a simple means to an end—profit making or bottom-line thinking.

Indeed, we are traveling a route that is circuitous, and it may also involve going backward in order to move forward. For example, in the earlier period, scholars and publishers were much closer to each other. In European and Latin American publishing, such linkages still are far stronger than in the United States. Perhaps that is why they reveal a stronger market share in the scholarly areas than in the United States. One can only look in amazement at the sort of technical works featured in window displays in Paris, Hamburg, Buenos Aires, or Tokyo. One is also impressed by the sense of scholar as hero one finds in scholarly catalogues that emanate from Europe. Perhaps this is little but the last hurrah of feudal rather than instrumental relations. I think not. My own belief is that the worthwhile destination of which Beth speaks can be reached more effectively and more rapidly by a sense of the author no less than an appreciation of a single work.

In every field of endeavor there are big people who set the agenda of a discipline, indirectly for a larger set of communities. Those people are critical to a social science list no less than other lists. To be sure this "conspiracy of excellence" theme may smack of elitism, but then again, what is the so-called gatekeeper function if not an assignment of priorities to certain works and hence their elevation to a special status. In the words of logical positivism, we say of such titles what we say of values: "Here then is an idea embodied in a book. It is important. I say so. Do likewise." Should such pronouncements prove inaccurate, then the market will answer with a resounding thud: "I have read this book. I say it is not important. I shall not follow your edicts in the future."

Clearly, the line of relationships is far from being so direct. In real publishing world terms, we receive and review inventory reports of sales, and they tell us not whether a book is good or bad, but whether it has sold or not. The scholarly publisher must navigate treacherous waters and decide the extent to defy or respond to the signals of the marketplace. Ultimately the issue is not one of gatekeeping but one of judgment, not that of the publisher (except to start with) but of the readership. This is a harsh lesson in democracy, but all successful publishers learn it sooner or later—and if too much later, then by ex-publishers.

Beth is right to note how important the process of publishing is to my overall activities in social research. But that process is often sideways rather than top-down or bottom-up. And it is also one in which we must learn from as well as teach to our readers . There is a fine line between tendentiousness and teaching, one that has be learned and relearned by everyone connected with the academic world and its surroundings. I like to think that in this special sense, there has been a cross-fertilization in my own work between personal scholarship and professional publishing. Beyond the twig is the branch. Beyond the branch is the trunk. Beyond the trunk are the roots. And the deeper we sink these roots the stronger will be the tree of social knowledge as such.

Nathaniel J. Pallone

While it is nice to be charted and diagramed, and learn that contrary to intuitive, personal beliefs, levels of productivity do not necessarily go on a downward spiral with age—all the things that my dear colleague Nat Pallone did in his chapter—such data must also be taken with a grain of salt. But the same salts must be applied in reverse, with respect to Jim Katz's indication that the citation index on me is gratifyingly high.

The problem with citation indices are manifest at two ends. There are very talented people who have written more than me by a factor of five times, as Walter Laqueur, and by a ratio of at least three-to-one as is the case with Seymour Martin Lipset. But these esteemed colleagues categorically excluded, I can also think of a few idiot savants who have also outproduced me by a substantial extent! So ultimately, the quantification of quality, must be taken with several heavy rocks, as well as several grains of salt.

Quantification also has a problem with a "pie" that indicates less than 4 percent of my output is concerned with human rights. Here I must note that much of my work is concerned with such moral concerns. The problem is that "human rights" has been, by the magic of academic course offerings and political finessing, turned into a "field" of study and or policy. This is a dangerous and misanthropic development. I do not think phrases like human rights and ethical judgments must be trumpeted about in titles to warrant being a part of one's intellectual considerations.

For my part, the study of human rights is inextricably linked to the study of human abuse—and the ultimate abuse is the taking of lives arbitrarily, capriciously, and willfully by organs of power. Taking lives or counting bodies may not be an "area of academic concentration" but it surely is the alpha and omega of why social science stands outside of and beyond the level of policy work. We can wag a finger, raise a voice, file a report, all for the purpose of extending life.

The abuse of human rights begins with the person and ends with the state. But rights imposes responsibilities. They cannot be understood apart from each other, as if we are dealing with political slogans of the Bolshevik era. In that sense, the ultimate human right is a recognition of the fallibility of human judgment as such. The ability to internalize a recognition of fallibility, that humans are error-prone creatures, makes possible a respect for others. Of course, Professor Pallone understands this no less than I. But to formulate areas of interest in terms of percentages is a risky business. I seriously doubt that Nat and I are even remotely at odds on such a formulation. But I did want to make plain a belief that the amount of work I have done will count for little unless it is somehow found useful in the work of others.

All divisions of social scientific work are ultimately conventions. The universe is not divided into physics, chemistry, biology, or sociology— our universe of discourse is so divided. When asked what I teach, I often answer with a quip: "Horowitz 101 in the fall semester followed by Horowitz 102 in the spring semester." This does not signify giving vent to pure egoism, although lord knows, it may do just that at times. It does mean that a life is one, a person is one, and a cluster of writings are also a unity. It is the uniqueness of the person that gives a special quality to the diversity of subject matter covered. Without the unity of the person, one has eclecticism or worse: words bought and paid for hire.

I have such great respect, indeed affection, for Nat Pallone that I feel badly having to recall first principles in an essay that attempts to demarcate my areas of interests. But it has become something of an academic curse to speak of a field of interest. For what is too often entailed is its opposite: a set of boundary maintenances, outside of which the academic dare not tread. I suspect that Nat knows this as well as I do.

We need to reconsider the degree to which specialization has become a function of professionalization, and in turn, determine whether this syndrome has positive or negative consequences for the pursuit of learning. I confess not to know the answer to my own question. But it certainly requires study lest we all take for granted the very essence of what we are bound to study: the nature of social systems, and the place of the human being within those variegated and complex systems.

William N. Dunn

Bill Dunn has written a very sharp, probing statement on *Daydreams and Nightmares*. I have in the past tried to dismiss efforts at converting my memoir of a childhood in Harlem as a sociological treatise. But Bill is more probing, and not easily put off. He is also, painfully correct in his observations. It will not be the first time that a memoir is better understood by its reader than by the author. Bill's probing essay helps me to understand why in all these long years, I have assiduously avoided writing on the theme of black America—it was all too close, too painful. Returning to Harlem has always seemed implausible—like the psychiatrist who wanted to practice without engaging in self-analyses. In that sense, the book enables me to speak freely on the subject that always seemed beyond my reach: race relations in America.

I have always been unnerved by white sociologists mouthing the phrases of black militants, as if this is in expatiation of sin. It does no such thing. Mouthings simply are recognized as fraudulent redundancies. I have come to believe that it is variables performing in tandem that makes for volatile behavior. Thus, it is the connection of race and poverty in Harlem that triggered such huge resentments and struggles. It is ethnicity and religion that may perform a similar role in Israel or Ireland. And in Harlem, for the most part, race was a given, a fact of culture. Being black did not create violence unto itself; it was always the dangerous combinations, the one-two punch of race and religion, or race and gender, or race and economy that turned the society nasty, brutish, and ultimately ungovernable. It also turned personal relations sour, ticklish, and ultimately untenable.

Let me illustrate this by a personal note, an extension of *Daydreams and Nightmares* if you will. Bill's powerful statement deserves more than easy literary mannerisms. When I was seventeen years old and worked as a busboy in a mountain resort, I had what is euphemistically known as a May-September romance—it was better understood as a sexual encounter with a young woman a few years older, working in the resorts (but at another site). She was pretty, smart, and tough. Her favorite book was *The Fountainhead,* which had recently been published and was something of the rage. I took what was the standard left-liberal line (and I guess still is) asserting that the book was neofascist in its implications of individualism and heroism. She was more bemused than amused by my heavy-handed assault.

The whole scene was weird: Here I was a smart-assed Jewish kid rebuking a black women five years my senior for taking to heart a book that was supposedly unauthorized reading from a liberal perspective. I had the gall of a teenager and part-time lover to instruct her on the quality of her reading habits. In truth, I was unnerved, and recognized in her someone with whom I was far overmatched. Indeed, were this not the case, we would never have had an affair to begin with! The heat may have been with me, but the play was with her. Without bothering to reply to my criticisms of a book I had barely understood much less digested, she simply cut to the chase and asked if I would dare carry on this same relationship back in New York City that we were conducting in a remote part of Peekskill. She needed no answer; it was clear on my face that this would go no further.

But I knew then that *Daydreams and Nightmares* was part of a hidden life of growing up, that it could not be recreated after I left the scene and source of my discontent. Native sons, even white ones, can't simply go native like anthropologists, and study people as if they were remote tribes with exotic customs. That young girl, she was as filled with rage as I was, as capable in English language as I was, as filled with the need to love as I was. But there was a difference: Ayn Rand made it possible for her to be with me on the streets of the city or in the mountains of the state. Karl Marx did not make this same set of options possible for me. There are limits to being clever. I learned as much that hot August when I was seventeen. I also learned that without courage there can be no comment. Above all, I learned that ideological correctness is far less worthy a guide than an intelligent novel.

But I would like to close my response to Bill Dunn by an appreciation that my work was not intended as an extension of sociological analysis. It may have had such a serendipitous outcome, but the input was less abstract, less pedagogic as it were. *Daydreams and Nightmares* was written as a child envisions a world, and not as an adult effort at interpreting that world. By that I mean, it was part of an effort to view things as episodes, as chapters, and not with the sort of causal inference and reasoning attributed (not infrequently in error) to adults. What a strange world we inhabit when a child of the lower depths is described as having "combative passion" and in possession of "thundering intellectual debate," whereas the modern academic culture is defined in terms of noblesse oblige and intellectual quietude.

It was, as Bill Dunn knows well, once the case that discourse and passion went together. The arguments of medieval schoolmen, the break away of people like Nicholas von Cusa, Siger of Brabant, Giordano Bruno, the new scientists of astronomy such as Galileo and Copernicus, all were stamped with heroism—sometimes gentle other times thundering—but courage was their mark. But here we are at the end of the twentieth century, and veterans of the Harlem brigade are viewed as the final repository of courage and integrity.

Bill Dunn's sensitive and intimate portrait of *Daydreams and Nightmares* is written with a passion to match my own narrative. And it would be a churlish, not to say, foolish, author who would spurn such a strong endorsement. Indeed, of all the works I have written, none has been as gratifying in results and as apprehensive in origins. It is not a convention in social science writing to speak with candor about oneself. This is a consequence of many things: an absence of an autobiographical tradition, a fear of the academic consequences of self-revelation (look at what happened to Veblen and W. I. Thomas, for example), and a socialized state of affairs in which autobiography is akin to tooting one's horn. Bill Dunn understands all of its elements, working at cross-purposes, so very well.

I have received something in the neighborhood of three hundred personal letters on this slender effort; nearly all have one similar characteristic: They identify with one or several facets of the life of the child—of growing up in the midst of betrayal, misunderstanding, personal travail, and intense feelings of loneliness. And all children feel those special moments of awkwardness that were compounded by my cleft palate and hare lip. So it is that whether it is disquiet at gift giving and receiving, dog rearing, special places of the heart like a stadium, or small thefts to make ends meet, I have been greeted with the sort of warm response that has filled me with relief at doing the book, no less than pleasure, or relieve pain at seeing others take pleasure in the anecdotes.

But is it a new genre, is it sociological biography, or better, is it a different kind of writing from that done by others? And here, despite Dunn's strong endorsement, I probably come down, with regrets, on the negative response side. It is true, and deeply insightful of my colleague to link this work with my professional interests in marginality, socialization, urban affairs, and political issues of the time. Indeed, Professor Dunn probably has seen more deeply than I such intertwined relationships, and for this I am grateful.

But the work was written, almost intentionally, as a way to get beyond profession jargon, to see if I could write a childhood memoir—not a childish one—in the tradition of H. L. Mencken, George Orwell, and Graham Greene. For they were my mentors in this enterprise. It is to the English literary tradition that I turned to seek out a model of frankness, and yet avoid sentimentality and maudlin self-indulgence. It is this tradition that avoided too the sort of ridiculous self-congratulatory modes all too typical of the few social scientific autobiographies that have been written. I realized too that the interesting formative period did not involve formal schooling, but, for the most part, the inner life of the family. A sort of Eugene O'Neill's *Long Day's Journey into Night.*

But of course, Bill would have every right to say that such grand figures of our English language are enduring precisely because they produced inadvertent sociological masterpieces. Then again, one might say that the relationship between a work in sociology and in literature is inevitable, since after all the former is a species of language, or at least ought to be. What this points to, what one of the linchpins of my work suggests is that the act of creation and the art of writing are so close, that when we look at true masterpieces of the social sciences, we are drawn to the inevitable conclusion that the poetic twist is an essential component. I recollect Philip Rieff once saying in *Freud: The Mind of the Moralist* that Freud introduced all sorts of literary devices to heighten the sense of drama and even melodrama in deciding his "cases"—a sense of mystery became part of solving psychiatric puzzles. In that very specific sense, I will accept as a given the sociological interpretation of *Daydreams and Nightmares.*

The idea put forth by Dunn of a naturalistic epistemology is one I find most appealing. It links up with the broader notion of ethnomethodology. The trouble I find in the general decline of doing ethnographic fieldwork is directly related to a deep fear of self-revelation. The risks of being ostracized, of saying something—anything—that can be construed as politically incorrect or morally outrageous, is now so great that the very foundation of ethnography is menaced. There was a time when fieldwork was a vibrant tradition. This is no longer the case. The legal consequences of W. I. Thomas studying the unadjusted girl to Laud Humphreys examining homosexual behavior in public places have become so great that sociologists prefer the false options of mindless method and factious ideologies to taking risks. Thus, the risk taking involved in *Daydreams and Nightmares* was well worthwhile, if it moves a discipline back on track with respect to observing first and judging later.

To be sure, I tried not to judge period. In an age that Richard Ofshe properly calls "making monsters," creating false memory traces of childhood abuse, it is far more important to understand those conditions that make for hard life and times. Violence, fear, even torture, of one person by another, one parent of another, do not come about as abstractions, but as consequences of circumstances that are bad and values that never existed. All children suffer the tremors of having been betrayed, of not getting what they want or felt they deserved, or harsh treatment at the hands of other children.

All of these elements are at work in each generation. Indeed our parents suffered likewise at the hands of their parents. It is important for all of us to appreciate that notions of child abuse must be tempered by differing standards of what constitute proper upbringing and/or punishment, that memories of parental mistreatment may be terribly in error, distorted by the prism and angle of vision through which children incorporate experiences of the world. Innocent acts become statements of guilt. Efforts to instill moral codes may be interpreted as illustrations of terrible moral lapses. Ultimately a child grows up, and growing up means accepting responsibility for the sorrows of life and the mistakes we make, not just those which others may have inflicted or visited upon us.

The private realm deserves its privacy. The rush to make public our sentiments and feelings, in acts of self-justification, do nothing but feed a resentment that serves to infantilize us. I held out no didactic lessons in doing *Daydreams and Nightmares*. But in retrospect, and to amplify Dunn's remarks, I see the little autobiography to address in a clinical, but never derisive manner, the trials of growing up absurd, as Paul Goodman called childhood. There is no sequel because childhood is a unique phase of life. There is no sequel, because the tremors and terrors of childhood are also a unique phase. A life is led. We celebrate not the life as such, but the triumphs that come in the face of adversity, and the recognition that those who come after us as those who came before are part of a great chain of being that we call culture. Autobiographies are statements of one life; they are also comments on what is to be avoided as well as what is to be pursued in the conduct of that culture. Perhaps that is why they are so endlessly fascinating. The autobiography is a capsulated statement of the human condition. It can be seen as big or small, major or minor, eloquent or banal—it carries our hopes to others across time and space. This may or may be part of the sociological condition. It certainly is the core of our moral concerns.

In Lieu of a Conclusion

There is always a danger that a festschrift is viewed as a summing up, rather than an ongoing dialogue, a conclusion fixed in cemetery stone.

One way of overcoming such contributory predilections and reader expectations is by simply not having a conclusion! After all, if one can get through such a mass of ideas and opinions and still have the need for more, then something is wrong somewhere. But there are professional as well as personal reasons for not becoming ensnared in satisfying the instinct for closure. Let me outline them, and be done with the matter.

First and foremost, the life of democratic theory is that being wrong is not a crime against society or science. Nor therefore should such error be punished as such. Intellectuals as the first victims of the tyranny of absolutist regimes should be the last to champion linkages of personal punishment with scientific error. Theory is as much concerned with sensibility as structure, with feelings as much as form. How we respond to error, the civility of discourse itself, is critical to my approach. The battlefield of ideas are strewn with system builders. For individuals who are convinced that they have a special divination never before seen on the earth, only grandiose theorizing will suffice. To them, Whitehead had the answer: all philosophy is a series of footnotes to Plato. For my part, I would add that all social theory is a series of footnotes to Aristotle.

Second, the need to keep pace with changes in ordinary affairs requires that we start with facts and truths and end with ideas and beliefs. To reverse this process, to start with general theory, is but to insure fanaticism. The last temptation of the theorist is to fit reality into his or her model of social life. Once the researcher yields to that temptation, all is lost. Vanity replaces modesty, and the need of the scholar becomes the preservation of "face" rather than the recognition of our fallibility and finitude. In this, we can learn much from the Western tradition in which we are as much defined by weakness as strengths, or if the religious variant be preferred, sin as well as science.

Third, and here I am reminded of an event in my life in which I introduced the late Harold Lasswell to a Rutgers University audience. I touched on major highlights of his career, listing his achievements in what I thought to be a thoroughgoing way. When I completed the task, leaving the podium with a certain air of self-satisfaction, Harold got up and began his lecture with an appreciation of my words, but adding a caveat: "Irving, you must not confuse the task of introducing a speaker with that of providing a funeral oration for the living dead." Alas, Harold had a stroke not long thereafter—but not before he delivered the final manuscript of a work on architecture and power, one that went substantially beyond his already enormous intellectual efforts. I now remind my readers that these contributions to understanding my work are just that. Indeed, my replies are incomplete because I would hope to make them part of the process of my own further growth.

Finally, if I am right in assuming that the dialogue is itself the key to the intellectual game, then a total summing up must itself appear as some sort of anomaly. It is to fall into a trap in which death itself is announced as some variety of grand theory. At the same time, dialogue prevents trivialization, serves to avoid a narrow empiricism in which one provides answers so trivial as to have little impact beyond a small circle of devoted admirers. And here we come full circle to the original point I make about the modesty of democratic theory and the high risks of grand systems.

To those left dissatisfied, or worse, displeased, with such an approach, go my sincere apologies. To have made such a long trek in order to receive a meager meal is indeed frustrating. But I take comfort in the Weberian notion that what I have failed to clarify, others will. I also take joy that along the way I may have earned the respect of supporters and opponents alike. The book is complete, but my life, I am pleased to note at last report, is not. And so it is with nature and society as such. What tentative conclusion could bring about greater joy or more absolute satisfaction!

Name Index